CW00693302

ISBN 978-0-656-10832-9
PIBN 10653755

THE MONIST

A QUARTERLY MAGAZINE

DEVOTED TO THE PHILOSOPHY OF SCIENCE

VOLUME XXV

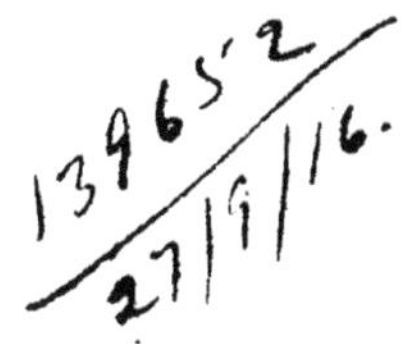

CONTENTS OF VOLUME XXV.

ARTICLES AND AUTHORS.

BOOK REVIEWS AND NOTES.

VOL. XXV. JANUARY, 1915 NO. 1

THE MONIST

ST. THOMAS IN INDIA.[1]

IN determining how much the religions of India owe to Christianity, our first task must be to examine the earliest possibilities of the extension of Christianity into India and to test the oldest records of this extension.

We ought first to observe that the assumption of the introduction of Christian ideas into India *by way of Alexandria* is very improbable. This has been proved conclusively by J. Kennedy.[2] The commercial intercourse by way of Alexandria between the Roman empire and southern India, which is abundantly attested for the first two Christian centuries by the discovery in southern India of Roman coins (from Augustus down), had ceased by the beginning of the third century. At this time commerce took its way to the farther Orient partly across the Persian Gulf and partly over the Ethiopian Adulis in the Red Sea. This was due to Caracalla's massacre in Alexandria in 215 A. D. which destroyed the significance of Alexandria in the commerce of the world. It also put an end to the colony of Indian merchants in Alexandria, of which Dio Chrysostom in Trajan's reign gives an account (*Orat.* XXXII), and with it to the direct commercial intercourse between Alexandria and India, for the Roman coins found in southern India stop abruptly with Caracalla.

[1] Translated by Lydia G. Robinson from the first chapter of Part II of the author's work, *Indien und das Christentum* (Tübingen, 1914). In the bibliographical references the following abbreviations will be observed: ERE, *Encyclopædia of Religion and Ethics*; IA, *Indian Antiquary*; JAOS, *Journal of the American Oriental Society*; JRAS, *Journal of the Royal Asiatic Society*; ZDMG, *Zeitschrift der Morgenländischen Gesellschaft.*

[2] JRAS, 1907, pp. 478-479, 953-955.

But might not the Indian colony in Alexandria have brought about the transmission of Christian influences to India *before* 215 A. D.? Just here lies the great improbability which we have intimated above. These Indian merchants, presumably Indians of Dravidian race, were ignorant people, according to the testimony of Dio Chrysostom (*Orat.*, XXXV). They would have taken no more interest in religious questions than did the Greek traders of their time. The absolute indifference of the author of the Periplus of the Red Sea towards religious matters has been mentioned elsewhere (See *Open Court,* July, 1914).

Moreover the Indians in Alexandria could hardly have heard anything of Christianity in the time of Antoninus, since the Alexandrian Christians at that time were mainly Greeks and were compelled to hold their meetings secretly because Christianity was forbidden. It would therefore have been much easier for Christians to have received information about the Buddhist religion from Indian Buddhists who chanced to live in Alexandria than the reverse, since the Indians were not compelled to keep their religion secret.

Isolated references of a later date to Indians at Alexandria prove nothing with regard to the possibility of a transmission of Christian doctrines. Such a reference is the one to the visit of the Brahman who "related incredible things" in the house of the former consul Severus in Alexandria about 500 A.D., as we learn from Damascius,[3] or the acquaintance of a few Indian scholars with the astronomy and astrology of Alexandria in the fifth and sixth centuries—a knowledge, moreover, which need not in the least have come directly from Alexandria, but might equally well have been transmitted through the famous school of Edessa which later moved to Nisibis. A popular religion is not affected by the forms of a strange faith as suddenly as the conver-

[3] In *Photii Bibliotheca,* ed. Bekker, II, p. 340, in J. Kennedy, *op. cit.*, p. 956.

sion of single individuals often takes place in consequence of the appealing and convincing talk of missionaries; but influences of this kind presuppose a gradual infiltration of foreign ideas during a somewhat long and close contact between two religious communities. Hence we must here take a very different standpoint from that involved in the discussion of the relation of Buddhist and Gospel narratives to each other. Strange stories travel from mouth to mouth and from people to people and finally become clothed in the garb of another religion; but dogmas and forms of worship are adopted by the followers of a different religion only in case of direct, lasting and intimate intercourse, when the ground for the adoption of such foreign elements is prepared by similarity in religious disposition or mental inclination.

Accordingly if Alexandria is not to be taken into consideration for the transmission of Christian ideas into India, the next question is, what value has the tradition that the apostle Thomas preached Christianity in India?

In the *Acta S. Thomae apostoli*, the original Syrian text of which was written in the first half of the third century, it is reported that Christ sold his slave Thomas into India to build a palace for Gondophares (Gundaphorus), the king of the Indians, who had sent to Jerusalem for a skilled architect. Thomas journeyed by water to northern India and received great sums from the king with which to do the building, but he spent all of it upon the poor for benevolent purposes. When Thomas was about to be punished with death for this by the enraged king, he was saved by the statement that he had built a palace in heaven for the king with these treasures. The king saw this palace in his dream, whereupon Thomas succeeded in converting the king and his brother Gad to Christianity. But later, after numerous miracles and conversions in the neighboring kingdom, whither he had betaken himself at the request of the general Siforus, he was executed by lance thrusts at the command of King Mazdai (Misdeus) and buried on the scene of his martyrdom.

This place is not named in any version of the Acts of St. Thomas. Beginning with the seventh century it is called Καλαμίνη in Greek and *Calamina* in Latin sources. According to ecclesiastical tradition the bones of St. Thomas were later taken from this place to Edessa and in 394 were transferred from a little old church into a large basilica.

A tradition differing from this Thomas legend exists among the native Christians in southern India on the coasts of Malabar and Coromandel who regard the apostle Thomas as the founder of their church and call themselves Thomas Christians even to-day. According to their tradition St. Thomas is said to have come from the island Sokotara to Malabar in the year 52. They also shift Calamina, the place of his martyrdom and burial, to Mailapur near Madras. However the earliest evidence for this localization is found in Marco Polo at the end of the 13th century.[4]

Those who believe in such stories can only reconcile the contradiction existing between these two traditions by assuming that St. Thomas made two different missionary journeys to India.

The tradition of the Thomas Christians in southern India has not found credence in scholarly circles in recent years, except in isolated cases. Thus R. Collins has expressed his conviction that St. Thomas was the apostle of Edessa as well as of Malabar.[5] W. Germann[6] regards as historical the evangelization by St. Thomas of southern India and

[4] To-day the place is called "St. Thomé" as the Portuguese named it upon their arrival in India on the basis of the legend found there among the Nestorians.

[5] IA, IV, p. 155.

[6] *Die Kirche der Thomaschristen.* Gütersloh, 1877.

the Indo-Iranian borderlands and also believes that the apostle died at Mailapur near Madras and that his body was removed from there to Edessa. We can understand this of a man who has the standpoint that "without the greatest miracle (the resurrection of Christ) the Christian faith would be vain" (p. 32). A. E. Medlycott, Bishop of Tricomia,[7] shares Germann's conviction in all points without, however, being able to prove it by the mass of his material which, though scholarly, has little importance for the question of historicity. Lately a young investigator, Karl Heck, has followed in the footsteps of these men with an investigation[8] which bears witness of scientific seriousness and comprehensive knowledge, but of course cannot prove the impossible. Heck substantiates the identification of Mailapur with Calamina by explaining that Calamina is only a "city of the kingdom of Kola" on the coast of Coromandel (pp. 34, 42). In Mazdai he recognizes Mahâdeva, a king of southern India (p. 19). These things are purely imaginary and we will see later on that a very different conclusion has been drawn from the names Calamina and Mazdai. Heck's expositions in the first part of his essay on the dispersion of the Jews in the time of Christ are interesting. In his opinion the Jewish communities in the Orient were the objective points for St. Thomas and the stages of his alleged journeys (pp. 13, 38, 40). We must acknowledge also that on page 39 Heck at least assumes the land route by way of Edessa, Nisibis and Seleucia for the apostle's missionary journey to the kingdom of Gondophares, and not the ocean route as does the narrative in the Acts of St. Thomas.

On the whole the view has long prevailed in scientific circles that not only the tradition of the Thomas Christians in southern India but also the legend in the Acts of

[7] *India and the Apostle Thomas.* London, 1905.

[8] Karl Heck (Professor in Radolfzell), *Hat der heilige Apostel Thomas in Indien das Evangelium gepredigt? Eine historische Untersuchung.* 1911.

St. Thomas lacks any historical foundation. But in recent decades, especially in France, England and America, there has been a reaction, since the discovery of coins and the inscription of Takht-î-Bahî have shown that a king Guduphara (= Gondophares) reigned over Parthia and the Indo-Iranian borderland in the first half of the first century after Christ, and hence that the Indian king who appears in the first part of the Acts of St. Thomas is historically attested for the place and time of the alleged apostolate of Thomas. This fact has made a strong impression, and in a number of prominent scholars has produced the conviction that a trustworthy recollection is the basis of that part of the Thomas legend in which the apostle carries on his work in Parthia and northwestern India. This conviction found further support in considerations regarding the international commercial intercourse of those times.

The first to raise the question as to whether contemporary relations actually existed between the apostle Thomas and the king Gondophares who has been proved historical by the discovery of coins, was Reinaud, in the year 1849. But the first to express himself in this sense with any attempt at a scientific basis is the eminent French Indianist Sylvain Lévi;[9] nevertheless in the last sentence of his article (p. 42) the journey of the apostle Thomas to India is characterized in an apposition as *réel ou imaginaire.* Those who have declared themselves to be completely, or almost completely, convinced of the historical character of this journey are E. Washburn Hopkins,[10] W. R. Phillips,[11] J. F. Fleet,[12] W. W. Hunter,[13] Vincent A. Smith,[14] G. Grierson,[15] and of German investigators mainly

[9] *Journal Asiatique,* 1897, I, pp. 27f.
[10] *India Old and New,* p. 141.
[11] IA, XXXII, pp. 1f, 145f.
[12] JRAS, 1905, pp. 223f.
[13] *The Indian Empire,* 3d ed., p. 286.
[14] *The Early History of India,* 2d ed., pp. 218-221.
[15] JRAS, 1907, p. 312; similarly ERE, II, p. 548*b*.

the Jesuit Joseph Dahlmann, with whose book on the subject[16] we must occupy ourselves more closely.

The English and American scholars just mentioned have not perceived that they have become victims of a fallacy. From the fact that the king of the Thomas legend is historical they have forthwith drawn the conclusion that the apostolate of Thomas in the domain of this king is also historical, and have overlooked the fact that some well-known personage from history, and particularly a king, happens to appear with extraordinary frequency in legends behind which no one would suspect an historical event. This observation does not apply to Dahlmann, for he has kept before him the possibility "that into the fabric of a legend some actually historical features may be woven, and yet if this were proved little would be gained for the question of the authenticity or unauthenticity of the legendary tradition. For particular geographical and historical features may be woven into the legend—the names of historical personages, circumstances whose reality is beyond question, citations of locality which correspond to the truth—and yet the tradition as such may lack intrinsic authenticity."[17] But I can not find that Dahlmann has allowed himself to be guided in his investigation by the critical spirit which speaks in these words.

Further, Dahlmann says on page 6: "In a dark and suspicious corner of early Christian literature where we push step by step up the luxuriant lattice of free discovery we see we are lost when we take the Apocrypha for guide. Poetic fancy there carries on so capricious a play that it seems impossible to draw the line between truth and invention, historical tradition and arbitrary adornment. The

[16] *Die Thomas-Legende und die ältesten historischen Beziehungen des Christentums zum fernen Osten im Lichte der indischen Altertumskunde* (Number 107, a sequel to the *Stimmen aus Maria-Laach.* Freiburg i. Br., 1912).

[17] *Op. cit.*, pp. 12-13.

story of the apostle's journey to India is no exception to this rule." These remarks are perfectly correct; but instead of applying them practically Dahlmann utilizes the Acts of St. Thomas as a *historical source* of the greatest significance, although it "betrays not the slightest knowledge of Indian relations, customs and usages or even of Indian geography."[18]

By drawing upon what we know with regard to the ocean traffic and commercial relations of the first century A. D. and with regard to the art of the Gandhâra country (i. e., the Kabul valley and surrounding territory) and all other material which bears upon the question, Dahlmann with his usual eloquence has tried to prove what it is his heart's desire to believe, but what nevertheless can not be proved. He finds himself here, as in several previous works, in the deplorable position of fighting with great scholarship, energy and enthusiasm for an untenable position. What an eminent Catholic Indianist once said about an older work of Dahlmann is true also in this case:[19] "Unintentional self-deception indeed seems in our author to go hand in hand with an unmistakable purpose and to play him an evil trick."

The historicity of the kernel of the Thomas legend lies particularly close to Dahlmann's heart for the following reason. Some years previously[20] he tried to prove that the Mahâyâna school of Buddhism which arose in the extreme northwestern part of India at the beginning of our era owes its most valuable ideas to Christian influences and that it is only as a result of this enrichment that northern Buddhism has attained its enormous expansion. But this thesis is absolutely untenable.

When we see what Dahlmann's purpose is we can understand how much it meant to him to furnish a proof

[18] Winternitz in *Deutsche Lit. Ztg.*, 1913, col. 1755.

[19] Edmund Hardy in *Lit. Zentralbl.*, 1898, col. 1194.

[20] In his *Indische Fahrten*, Freiburg i. Br., 1908, 2 vols. Chapters 25-27.

that Christianity had penetrated into the Indian borderland by the middle of the first century. For this it was positively necessary that the apostolate of Thomas in that locality be historical. To the reasons which his predecessors had brought forward for this, Dahlmann added a new one in his *Indische Fahrten*, namely the combination of apostleship and artistic handiwork in the person of Thomas. Dahlmann believed that he could explain the alleged Christian influence in the art of Gandhâra by the activity of the apostle Thomas in the Indian borderlands. In his new work Dahlmann takes a somewhat different standpoint. He grants[21] that the general similarities which exist between early Christian art and the art of Gandhâra can be explained by the fact that the artists of both groups have drawn from one and the same source, namely from the classical art of the Roman empire; and further he says (p. 100): "That the Buddha-type of Gandhâra should have arisen in connection with the Christ-type, as Fergusson and Smith are inclined to assume, is nŏt merely improbable but absolutely impossible." But he lays the greatest weight upon the fact, "that the Parthian-Indian field of labor ascribed to the apostle in the legend is connected by special commercial and artistic relations with the Roman province (Syria) from which Christianity proceeded" (p. 108).

I would like to answer the argument for the legendary artistic occupation of the apostle by the pertinent observation of O. Wecker,[22] that in the legend of St. Thomas the Christian apostle is not brought into relation with the kind of artistic activity which most clearly betrays connection between Gandhâra and the west, that is to say with sculpture, but with the work of an architect and carpenter

[21] *Thomas-Legende*, pp. 96f.

[22] *Tübinger Theol. Quartal-Schrift*, XCII, p. 561. Wecker refutes Dahlmann's demonstration in a happy manner but does not come out against belief in the historical character of the Thomas legend with as great decision as might be desired. For him the possibility still exists that Thomas may really have been in India. *Ibid.*, pp. 559-560.

which may probably be accounted for by the imagery of the construction of church or temple current in Christian modes of speech.

On the other hand Winternitz, who in other particulars takes throughout the standpoint which I represent, asserts[23] that in the Syrian text of the Acts of St. Thomas the apostle says to the merchant Habbân who brings him from Jerusalem: "In wood I have learned to make plows and yokes and ox-goads and rudders for boats and masts for ships; and in stone, gravestones and monuments and palaces for kings." Winternitz thinks that we can regard the gravestones and monuments as well as the decorations of the palaces as referring certainly to the Gandhâra sculptures. I would like to contradict this; for according to the legend Thomas is brought merely for the purpose of building a palace for King Gondophares, and in the Greek version of the Acts of St. Thomas in the corresponding passage he only declares that he understands how to make "(tomb-) pillars and temples and royal palaces out of stone." Probably this is the way the Syrian text also is to be understood. But what Winternitz goes on to say is very true: "Though the dependence of the Gandhâra art upon the west is certainly historical, yet it is not exactly probable that Grecian artists would have been sought in the streets of Jerusalem."

Moreover, it should be pointed out that according to the legend the apostle Thomas did not build at all in the realm of Gondophares and that he is said to have come to this kingdom not by the land route through Syria but by the ocean. Accordingly in Dahlmann's sense the artistic activity of the apostle and the artistic relations between the Parthian-Indian realm and Syria have nothing to do with the case in hand, and it is a simple fallacy when he says on pages 109-110: "The historical elements which

[23] *Deutsche Lit. Ztg.*, 1913, col. 1752.

are woven into the legend may be referred to two fundamental data: to the association of the apostle's name with the name of a Parthian-Indian king and to the latter's relations with western art. From this double connection the conclusion may be drawn that the kernel of the tradition, i. e., the knowledge of a missionary journey which brought the apostle Thomas into contact with a Parthian-Indian kingdom, can not be invented but must rest upon a *historical foundation*."

The way in which Dahlmann makes the second part of the legend of St. Thomas, dealing with the martyrdom and burial of the apostle in the realm of King Mazdai, serve his purpose is characteristic. He adopts Sylvain Lévi's very doubtful identification of King Mazdai with the Indo-Scythian king Vâsudeva (epigraphically BAZOΔEO) in which Sylvain Lévi thinks he has found a contemporary of Gondophares. But Vâsudeva lived considerably later than Gondophares, in all probability not until the end of the second or beginning of the third century, so that Dahlmann is obliged to explain the apostle's martyrdom in the realm of King Mazdai as an invention of poetic fancy. Nevertheless Dahlmann finds a historical kernal even in this part of the Thomas legend. To him Mazdai is an actual king who governed the realm, which is said to have formed the field of the apostle's activity, at the time when the latter's relics were alleged to have been brought from India to Syria. "The anachronism which transforms a prince who lived one hundred and fifty years later into a contemporary of the apostle was caused by the report that the relics came from the realm of King Mazdai" (p. 147). A very arbitrary assumption! That Dahlmann believes also in the tradition of the transference of the bones of St. Thomas to Edessa was to be expected from the whole drift of his expositions.

The other names of the second part of the Acts of St.

Thomas Dahlmann knows also how to interpret historically and geographically. General Siforus is the Parthian satrap Sîtapharna; the place of martyrdom Calamina is Kalyâna in the vicinity of Bombay; the mountain Gazus where St. Thomas met his death after his passion denotes the Ghats mountains (pp. 153, 156-157). Dahlmann is a master at imaginary combinations. Even in the tradition of the Thomas Christians in southern India, which he regards as unauthentic, he finds valuable evidence for the historical character of the traditions of northern India, as is shown in the last chapter of his book.

In reality the whole Thomas legend is as much invented as, in Dahlmann's opinion, is the apostle's martyrdom in the kingdom of Mazdai. This became clear in 1864 by the critique to which Alfred von Gutschmid subjected the Thomas legend in his famous essay, "Die Königsnamen in den apokryphen Apostelgeschichten."[24] Gutschmid justly emphasizes the great intrinsic improbability that Christianity should have spread so early into so remote a region before it had obtained a firm footing anywhere in western Iran; for the natural way from Syria to India would have been by land. Gutschmid furnishes a further proof, which for the most part still holds to-day, that the first part of the Thoms legend is a transformation of a *Buddhist* missionary tale.[25] White India or Arachosia (hence the special kingdom of Gondophares) was converted to Buddhism in exactly the period in which the Thomas legend is set. Accordingly we have here a very similar case to that of the legend of St. Bartholomew which was originally a story of Jewish conversion with the scene laid in Armenia or Media but later was given a Christian setting and significance and transferred to India.[26] Ernst Kuhn in a personal letter plausibly identifies the Indian king Polymius in

[24] *Kleine Schriften*, edited by Franz Rühl, II, pp. 332f.

[25] Rejected by Winternitz, *Deutsche Lit. Ztg.*, 1913, col. 1754.

[26] Wecker, *Tüb. Theol. Quart.-Schr.*, XCII, p. 556.

the *Passio Bartholomaei* with Pulumâyi. I assume that of the three Andhra kings of this name, Pulumâyi I (26-58) and not Pulumâyi II (138-170) or Pulumâyi III (229-236) is meant.[27] We would then have in the legend of Bartholomew exactly the same case as in the Thomas legend, namely that a known Indian king from the middle of the first century has been interwoven into the apocryphal story of the apostle.

Ernst Kuhn has likewise most kindly called my attention to the fact that the palace which Thomas claimed he had erected in heaven for King Gondophares corresponds to the Buddhist Vimânas from which the Vimânavatthu received its name. This work is a description of the celestial abodes and their delights with a list of the good works for which the inhabitants of these heavenly worlds will be rewarded by the enjoyment of such bliss.[28]

The recasting of the Buddhist original into the Thomas legend hardly took place before the beginning of the third century. Gutschmid has expressed the very probable view that the Christians became acquainted with the supposed story of Buddhist conversion through the Syrian Gnostic Bardesanes who was well informed on Buddhist and Indian conditions in general.

At any rate there were no Christians within Indian boundaries before the third century. The wider extension of Christianity in general, of course, began in the middle of the second. The earliest account of the presence of

[27] The pe iods of these reigns are given according to the approximate calculation of Vincent A. Smith, *The Early History of India*, 2d ed., in the chronological table following page 202.

[28] This combination is opposed by Winternitz (*op. cit.*, col. 1754) on what in my opinion is an insufficient ground. Perhaps Winternitz will abandon his opposition when he learns of Kuhn's further observation that the description of the visit to hell of Gad, the brother of Gondophares,—at least in the Syrian poem of Jacob of Sarug—exactly resembles the story of Revati in the Vimânavatthu (Chap. 52). Cf. S. R. Schröter, "Gedicht des Jacob von Sarug uber den Palast, den der Apostel Thomas in Indien baute," ZDMG, XXV, pp. 360f; and L. Scherman, *Materialien zur Geschichte der indischen Visionslitteratur*, pp. 56f.

Christians in Parthia and northwestern India in Origen—hence in the first half of the third century—is an indirect one.[29] The statement of Bardesanes, who speaks of the existence of Christian communities in Parthia, Media, Persia and among the Bactrians and Geles, would lead us[30] to a somewhat earlier period, that is to say, to the *beginning* of the third century. But now since later research has shown that the Syrian original "On Fate" in which this statement originates was not written by Bardesanes himself but by one of his disciples, the note is probably later than that of Origen. If this disciple of Bardesanes had known of any Christians within Indian boundaries he certainly would not have kept silent about them in his enumeration. It therefore still remains doubtful whether the first entrance of Christianity into the land of the Indus took place as early as the first half of the third century.

Historically we know absolutely nothing about St. Thomas except that he was one of the twelve apostles, and these Wellhausen regards as a council instituted after the death of Jesus. I may here introduce a few sentences containing information that seems to me serviceable from a letter that Th. Nöldeke wrote me on this question January 6, 1910: "The introduction of Thomas in the Gospel of John is as arbitrary as a number of similar references to persons and places in the Fourth Gospel. The statement that the body of Thomas was removed to Edessa (the earlier sources leave out the 'from India') is probably only an adjustment of two traditions, one saying that he was buried in Edessa where his tomb is shown, and the other in the legend [of his burial in India]. Neither of course is historical."

All investigators who are inclined to regard as histor-

[29] Harnack, *Mission und Ausbreitung des Christentums in den ersten drei Jahrhunderten*, 2d ed., II, p. 126.

[30] In Eusebius, *Praep. Evangel.*, VI, 10.

ical[31] the basis of the Thomas legend, i. e., his apostolate in Indo-Iranian countries, are in my judgment driven to it by an apologetic impulse though perhaps unconsciously. They do not, however, observe at the same time how greatly they would increase the "Buddhist peril" for the New Testament if they were right. For if there had been Christians in one of the many Buddhist countries as early as the middle of the first century, hence before the Gospels were written, then the natural connection of these Christians with Syria and Palestine would cause the contested transmission of Buddhist elements into the Gospel—especially into the two that bear the names of Luke and John—to appear in a much clearer light than is the case without the historical basis of the Thomas legend.

* * *

The absolute unreliability of the Thomas legend must be established before we can proceed in a scientific manner to the questions as to how early the so-called Thomas Christians had settled along the coast of southern India and where they had come from. Unfortunately the preliminary question as to how the name "Thomas Christians" originated can not be answered with certainty. Various possibilities present themselves by way of explanation. Travelers of the early Middle Ages may have called the Christians whom they found in southern India "Christians of St. Thomas" on the basis of the familiar Thomas legend, and the native Christians may have adopted and retained this designation—this is Burnell's view.[32] Or else the

[31] G. Faber has recently joined their ranks and in his work *Buddhistische und neutestamentliche Erzählungen*, p. 24, declares that the authenticity of the apocryphal Acts of St. Thomas "according to the recently published extremely keen and comprehensive treatment of Joseph Dahlmann can in his opinion no longer be questioned." This sentence and his further expositions on the subject (p. 26-27) Faber would probably not have written if he had read my review of Dahlmann's book in the *Ostasiatische Zeitschrift*, I, pp. 360f, or Winternitz's later criticism in the *Deutsche Lit. Ztg.*, 1913, col. 1750f. At any rate Faber will not find any of the German Indianists to agree with him.

[32] IA, III, p. 309.

name may have originated, according to a probability frequently expressed, by a confusion of St. Thomas with Thomas of Cana (also called Thomas Kama or some similar form, and Mar Thomas) under whose leadership a large number of Christians, alleged to be from Bagdad, Nineveh and Jerusalem, immigrated to Malabar in the year 745 and strengthened the Christian communities already there upon whom this reinforcement must have made a strong impression. This Thomas founded for the new Christian immigrants the city of Mahâdevapattana in the neighborhood of Cranganore, erected many churches in that locality, established seminaries for the education of the clergy and acquired important privileges for the Thomas Christians from the rulers of the country.[33]

There are still other possibilities of confusion, for in those days there was a large number of prominent men by the name of Thomas.[34]

W. W. Hunter[35] represents a view which differs from both of the possibilities mentioned. He proceeds from the idea that the Persian church had appropriated the name of "Thomas Christians" in the seventh century and that in time this designation spread to all branches of that church, hence also to Malabar; that the old legend of the

[33] G. M. Rae, *The Syrian Church in India*, pp. 162-163; Lassen, *Indische Altertumskunde*, 2d. ed., II, p. 1121; Karl Heck, *Hat der heilige Apostel Thomas in Indien das Evangelium gepredigt?* pp. 21-22. The accounts of this "Thomas Cananaeus" are very contradictory; his home is assigned both to Jerusalem and to Armenia. At any rate he was an influential and very well-to-do merchant who was bishop of the Christians of southern India at the time of his death. K. Kessler in Herzog's *Realencyklopädie*, 3d ed., XIII, p. 735, placed him in the beginning of the ninth century; Germann (*Die Kirche der Thomaschristen*, p. 92), and others (see V. A. Smith, *The Early History of India*, 2d ed., p. 222, note 1), even as early as the year 345. The coincidence in the two last figures of the dates 745 and 345 makes it probable that in the date 345 we may have an old error of the pen or print for 745, which has been handed on. Ad. Lipsius, *Die apokryphen Apostelgeschichten*, I, 1883, pp. 283f., has accepted Germann's statements about the confused traditions with regard to this man without taking exception to the double number 345/745. Lassen (*op. cit.*) suggests the year 435. Here again we have the three figures of the year 345 in another arrangement.

[34] Germann, pp. 99-201.

[35] *The Indian Empire*, 3d ed., p. 287.

Manichaean Thomas of the third century, and the later activity of the above-mentioned Thomas of Cana, the reviver of the church of Malabar, had by the eighth century increased the respect for that name among the Christians of southern India. Thus far his assumptions seem to consist of conjectures without foundation. But afterwards his expositions amount to the old and very probable confusion theory when he adds the remark that perhaps in their comparative isolation and ignorance the Christians of southern India had mixed up the three names and had concentrated the legends of the three Thomases upon the person of the apostle, and that before the expiration of the fourteenth century this process had ended in the conviction of those Christians that their St. Thomas and Christ were one and the same person. The last remark of Hunter arises from an erroneous conception; for Thomas, the "twin brother of the Lord," has elsewhere also often been confused with Christ, especially by the Syrian Christians. Hence the identification is not the work of the isolated Thomas Christians in Malabar, but originates in the home of Nestorianism.

How long the Thomas Christians have been in southern India is not easy to determine. In his treatment of the subject—unfortunately very short—Harnack[36] is right in saying: "That the 'Thomas Christians' who were again discovered in India in the sixteenth century[37] extend back

[36] *Mission und Ausbreitung des Christentums,* 2d ed., II, pp. 126-127. H Achelis, *Das Christentum in den ersten drei Jahrhunderten* (2 vols., Leipsic, 1912) does not touch at all upon the question of the extension of Christianity into India.

[37] Harnack has overlooked the fact that Marco Polo had already rediscovered them at the end of the thirteenth century, and that several other witnesses from the fourteenth and fifteenth centuries follow him. A. Burnell says (IA, III, p. 311, note): "The most important historical notices of Nestorians and Syrians in India which I can find are: (1) by Friar Odoricus, who about the beginning of the fourteenth century was in southern India and mentions fifteen houses of Nestorians at St. Thomas's shrine; (2) by Nicolo Conti who traveled in India in the fifteenth century. Speaking of Malepur (St. Thomé) he says: 'Here the body of St. Thomas lies honorably buried in a very large and beautiful church; it is worshiped by heretics who are called Nestorians and inhabit this city to the number of a thousand. These Nestorians are

to the third century can not be proved." In France, England and America, there is a different opinion. In these countries scholars seem inspired with the desire to prove the authenticity of apocryphal legends, and to attribute a greater antiquity to the expansion of Christianity than strict historical critique can concede. We may here recall the judgment of those scholars on the Thomas legend. Hopkins[38] states without any qualification, "that Pantaenus was expressly sent to teach the Brahmans in India, and found a Christian church already established there in 190 A. D." This belief is shared by W. W. Hunter[39] and J. Kennedy[40] whereas in Germany it is the universal and well-justified assumption that southern Arabia is to be understood by the India to which Pantaenus (according to Eusebius, *Hist. eccl.*, V, 10) went as missionary from Alexandria.[41] All of southern Asia was called India in those days; and when Eusebius reports that Pantaenus had already found a Christian community in India possessing the Gospel of Matthew in the Hebrew language, we can, in fact, only think of a less remote country, that is, of southern Arabia, where the Jews were living in great numbers at the time.

Directly before the above mentioned note on Pantaenus Hopkins says without mentioning his source: "We know also that a great colony of Jews emigrated from Palestine —ten thousand in all—and settled on the Malabar coast in A. D. 68." Now this remark is by no means consistent with the essay, "Christ in India"; for the Jews would certainly not have made the extension of Christian-

scattered over all India.' (*India in the Fifteenth Century* published by the Hakluyt Society, p. 7.)" The traveler Giovanni de' Marignolli in the fourteenth century also told about the place and the Thomas legend that clung to it. Colonel Yule, *Cathay and the Way Thither* (Hakluyt Society, 1866), II, p. 375; Rae, *The Syrian Church in India*, pp. 124-125; *Encyclopædia Britannica*, s. v. "Marignolli."

[38] *India Old and New* in the essay "Christ in India," p. 141.

[39] *The Indian Empire*, 3d ed., p. 285.

[40] JRAS, 1907, pp. 479, 955-956.

[41] Harnack, *op. cit.*, p. 126; G. Krüger in Herzog's *Realencyklopädie*, 3d ed., XIV, p. 627, *s. v.* "Pantaenus"; *Die Religion in Geschichte und Gegen-*

ity into India any business of theirs. But the incredibility of the statement in itself is obvious and is increased by the consideration that even in our own time, according to the census of 1911, there are only 18,000 Jews in all India. My inquiries for the source of the fantastic information of Hopkins have been without success. I have only found the following note by W. W. Hunter:[42] "Whether these Jews emigrated to India at the time of the dispersion, or at a later period, local tradition assigns to their settlements an origin anterior to the second century of our era." Th. Nöldeke wrote me January 20, 1910, on the subject as follows: "Whence Hopkins gets his information about the 10,000 Jewish emigrants to India in 68 A. D. I can not imagine. At any rate it is nonsense (so he says 'we know!'). Your assumption that southern Arabia, [or rather, Abyssinia (Αἰθιοπία in the broader sense)] is here called India is certainly correct, but even then the account is unhistorical. Of course the Jews have carried on propaganda in both places, especially in Abyssinia, with great success; but we have no *historical* account of the origin of these undertakings nor even about Jews, or Arabs converted to Judaism, in northern Arabia."

In fact the oldest evidence for the existence of Christian communities on the western coast of southern India is found in the account of Kosmas Indikopleustes, which is based upon observations during the years 525-530. Kosmas, an Egyptian merchant who in his younger years had made several business journeys to India and had later become a monk, is the author of a startling work on "Christian Topography," in which with great garrulity he opposes scientific geography and especially the great geog-

wart, edited by Schiele and Zscharnack, III, p. 468. Rae, *The Syrian Church in India,* pp. 67f, regards the India of Alexander the Great, i. e., the valley of the Indus, as the scene of the operations of Pantaenus. Edmunds agrees with him, *Buddhist and Christian Gospels,* 4th ed., I, pp. 145-146.

[42] *The Indian Empire,* 3d ed., p. 284.

rapher Ptolemy. Kosmas denies that the earth is round and declares that it is an elongated disk surrounded by high walls upon which the firmament rests like a roof. The change from day to night is caused by the sun revolving around a monstrous mountain in the extreme north. This monkish folly to be sure does not arouse any predisposition in favor of Kosmas's account of his journeys, and his trustworthiness is not exactly increased by the fact that he saw the tracks in the Red Sea made by the wheels of Pharaoh's chariot when pursuing the children of Israel. But the way in which Kosmas in the midst of his stupid description of the earth tells what he had seen previously as a merchant in India, gives the impression of actual observation. W. Vincent[43] finds no echo to his statement that Kosmas was never in India. It is disproved by reference to the correct Indian names and words which Kosmas introduces (καστοῦρι, "Moshustier" in Book XI is, by the way, the earliest record of the Sanskrit *kastûrî*). Evidently the west coasts of India and Ceylon were well known to Kosmas. From what he tells us about these localities the following is of interest to us:[44] "On the island Taprobane (Ceylon)....there is also a Christian church and clergy and believers,....likewise also in Μαλέ (= Skt. *Malaya*, 'Malabar') where pepper grows; and in the city which they call Καλλιάνα there is also a bishop who is appointed in Persia." And in the section "On the island Taprobane" in Book XI Kosmas completes the above account with the words:[45] "This island also possesses a church for the Persian Christians living there, and a presbyter appointed in Persia and a deacon, and the whole ecclesiastical service; but the natives and the king belong to another people and have many shrines on this island." With the

[43] *The Voyage of Nearchus* (1797) in the French Version of Billecoq, pp. 363n, 544n.

[44] Kosmas, ed. Winstedt, III, p. 119.

[45] Page 322.

last words Kosmas indicates that the natives in Ceylon profess another religion, namely, Buddhism.

By "Male where pepper grows," we are without any doubt, according to Burnell, to understand the seaport Travancore. As far as the city Kalliana (Sanskrit *Kalyâna*) is concerned, we may hesitate between two ports of this name on the western coast. One of these, thirty-three miles northeast of Bombay, the Kalyân of to-day on the Ulhas river, is known as an ancient provincial capital; the other lies about thirty-two miles north of Mangalore. This second place, which to-day is an unimportant village, Burnell regards as the city referred to by Kosmas; for, as he says, Kosmas names as the chief articles of export from Kalliana χαλκός (by which only steel could be understood) and cotton cloth; and that steel seems to have been produced only in the southern part of the Dekkan, in Maisur and Salem.[46] This argument is easily refuted, for χαλκός does not mean steel or hardened iron. It means of course what it has always meant except when it has denoted bronze, namely copper, for which the Greek language has no other term. All probability then is in favor of the idea that the account of Kosmas refers to the famous old city, Kalyâna (or Kalyânî), in the vicinity of Bombay.

Kosmas's particulars about the bishop of Kalliana ordained in Persia and about the exclusively Persian Christian community in Ceylon leave no doubt as to the descent of the Christian in Southern India and the error of their own tradition. When Burnell says: "All the trustworthy facts up to the tenth century.... go to show that the earliest Christian settlements in India were Persian,"[47] he is certainly as much in the right as he is mistaken in his assumption that the earliest colonists in southern India were Manichaean immigrants. This latter asumption, and

[46] Burnell, IA, III, p. 310.

[47] *Op. cit.*, p. 311. Cf. also J. Kennedy, JRAS, 1907, p. 956; O. Wecker, *Tüb. Theol. Quart. Schr.*, XCII, 1910, p. 541.

the basis upon which it rests, was rejected by Collins[48] and since then has not found any supporters.

The Persian descent of the Christians in southern India is likewise attested by the Pahlavi inscriptions found in that locality which have been discussed by Burnell in the essay already frequently cited.[49] The earliest of these inscriptions do not date back farther than the seventh or eighth century.[50]

When we inquire into the occasion that brought the earliest colonies of Persian Christians to southern India, next to the commercial interests the Persian persecutions of the Christians in the years 343 and 414 suggest themselves. Fugitives might have been driven by these persecutions to India, just as at a later time the Pârsîs who were oppressed by Islam found a new home in this tolerant land which first learned religious intolerance from its Mohammedan conquerors. Since there was no authentic witness for the presence of Christians along the southwestern coast of India *before* Kosmas, as we have seen, we may assume that the first Christian colonies in Malabar were founded by persecuted Persian Christians in the middle of the fourth century.

J. Kennedy has repeatedly asserted[51] that even at this time there was a monastery of Persian monks in the interior of Ceylon. Now no one who is acquainted with the fact that the earliest conventual communities were established then for the first time in Egypt and Syria, the very cradle of Christian monasticism, will consider it possible that at that early date the Christian custom of founding monasteries could have penetrated as far as remote Ceylon. At first I thought that Kennedy had confused a Buddhist

[48] IA, IV, pp. 153f.

[49] IA, III, pp. 311f.

[50] Hardly to the fifth. Cf. the bibliography in Wecker, *op. cit.*

[51] JRAS, 1907, pp. 480, 957, note 3, following Labourt, *Le Christianisme dans l'Empire Perse*, p. 306. (In Kennedy the reference is wrongly given as p. 606.)

with a Christian monastery, but then I considered it necessary nevertheless to investigate his source and found to my surprise that it consisted merely of this legendary note in Labourt: "S'il faut en croire l'hagiographe Zâdoê, prêtre et solitaire, chef du monastère de Saint-Thomas dans le pays de l'Inde, dont le siège est fixé sous les pays de Qatrayê, à Ceylan, l'île noire...." Qatrayê, as my colleague Seybold informs me, is one name for eastern Arabia.

As a proof of the early entrance of Christianity into India Grierson cites[52] that "Chrysostom (fourth century) tells us of Christian treatises translated into Indian languages." Here he doubtless means the often quoted passage in Johannes Chrysostomus, *Hom.* on John ii. 2:[53]

ἀλλὰ καὶ Σύροι καὶ Αἰγύπτιοι καὶ 'Ινδοὶ καὶ Πέρσαι καὶ Αἰθίοπες καὶ μύρια ἕτερα ἔθνη εἰς τὴν αὐτῶν μεταβαλόντες γλῶτταν τὰ παρὰ τούτου δόγματα εἰσαχθέντα ἔμαθον ἄνθρωποι βάρβαροι φιλοσοφεῖν.

But this witness, especially in consideration of the ambiguity between 'Ινδός and 'Ινδία existing at that time, is absolutely worthless. Even the added phrase καὶ μύδια ἕτεα ἔδνη shows what we must think of the conglomeration of national names in this pathetic homiletic passage. Since there is no other trace of a translation of the New Testament or of any other Christian document into Indian languages from so early a time nor even from any of the following centuries up to the beginning of modern times, we must not see a historiacl witness in the words of Chysostum, but merely a thoughtless rhetorical expression.[54]

The date when the Christians in southern India became subordinate to the Nestorians, can be determined with practical certainty. Burnell's view[55] that this did not occur

[52] JRAS, 1907, p. 498. Edmunds, in *Buddhist and Christian Gospels,* 4th ed., I, p. 146, also regards this evidence as authentic.

[53] Migne edition, *Patrol.,* LIX, 32.

[54] Tiele, *Theologisch Tijdschrift,* 1877, p. 71, in Carl Clemen, *Religionsgeschichtliche Erklärung des Neuen Testaments,* p. 28, note.

[55] IA, III, p. 311.

before the eleventh or twelfth century because we find first mention of Syrians living in India in travelers' reports in the Middle Ages requires no refutation. Nor is W. Koch's[56] statement correct, that the Nestorians became connected with the Thomas Christians in India proper in the seventh century, because we have evidence of a connection between the Thomas Christians in southern India and Persian Nestorianism as early as the beginning of the sixth century. Kosmas's statement that the bishop of Kalliana and the presbyter at Ceylon had been appointed from Persia shows the dependence of the parishes there on the Nestorian patriarchate. In the beginning of the sixth century the only ecclesiastical head in Persia was the Nestorian catholikos of Seleucia-Ctesiphon, because in the second half of the fifth century King Pêrôz (Pheroses) declared in an edict that Nestorianism was to be the only permitted form of Christianity in his kingdom, which led to the cruel extermination of the Persian Christians adhering to the orthodox church,[57] and because in the year 498 the bishop of Seleucia formally renounced his allegiance to Antioch and by so doing founded the dissenting church of Persian Nestorians.

When M. Haug[58] tried to place the date of the Nestorian church in India back in the fifth century, he was certainly under the influence of Catholic tradition, according to which Nestorianism spread about 486 to Malabar from Babylon, i. e., probably from the district between the Euphrates and Tigris.[59] The authenticity of this tradition is contradicted by the intrinsic improbability that Nestorian influence could have expanded in a foreign country at a time of severe internal conflict. We may assume that this did not take place until the beginning of the sixth century,

[56] In the article "Nestorianismus" in Michael Buchberger's *Kirchliches Handlexikon*, II, p. 1104.

[57] Rae, *The Syrian Church in India*, p. 107.

[58] In Germann, *Die Kirche der Thomaschristen*, p. 301.

[59] Hunter, *The Indian Empire*, 3d ed., p. 279.

after the consolidation of the Persian dissenting church. This is also the opinion of Rae[60] who, to be sure, bases it only on the Persians' growing fondness for ocean travel and for the increase of commerce.

The Christian parishes on the west coast of India at that time combined with those scattered through Arabia to form a diocese under the control of the metropolitan of Persia. We must not, however, overestimate the spread of Christianity on the coast of western India in those days. When Kessler[61] says that the entire western coast of India must still have been Christian at the beginning of the seventh century this is merely a conjecture. The words "must have been" alone prove the weakness of the position. Nor is there evidence to show that in the preceding sixth century the entire west coast of India had been Christian.

Further expositions of Kessler in the same place teach that the union of the Christian parishes in India with the Nestorian patriarchate had become greatly relaxed by the middle of the seventh century and after a temporary strengthening broke off entirely in the ninth century. I here quote the most important sentences: "Shortly after Kosmas, about 570, the presbyter Bôdh had to inspect the churches of India as periodeutes;....but Jesujahb of Adiabene (*Patr.* 659-660) complains in his writings that through the fault of Simeon, the metropolitan of Persia, and that of his predecessor the churches of India had become quite orphaned....The 'Thomas Christians' in India were assigned a metropolitan for the first time under the patriarch Timotheus (778-820)....This union with the Nestorian patriarchate seems to have been discontinued soon afterwards."[62]

[60] *The Syrian Church in India*, pp. 116, 118.

[61] In the article "Nestorianer" in Herzog's *Realencyklopädie*, 3d ed, XIII, p. 728.

[62] *Ibid.*, pp. 728, 735.

The time when the Thomas Christians made themselves ecclesiastically independent coincides with their political independence, for in the eighth and ninth centuries the Christians in Malabar obtained from the native princes the right of self-government and such important privileges that for the time being they formed an independent state with kings of their own.[63] In their seclusion the Thomas Christians did not in the least preserve their religion uncorrupted, and in the fourteenth century they even abandoned baptism. However, up to the time of their persecution by the Jesuits they occupied a very respected position in southern India on account of their high moral tone.[64]

To-day the small communities of Thomas Christians in southern India, together with the Nestorian parishes in the Kurd mountains and on the Lake of Urmia comprise the scanty remnant that is left of the Nestorian church which once was so strong in central and upper Asia.[65]

The result of my discussions for our subsequent inquiry I can summarize thus: The small Christian communities in southern India known by the name of Thomas Christians consisted first (in the fourth and beginning of the fifth centuries) of Persian immigrants; these were joined later by Jews and native Indian members of the Dravidian race.

Christian influence upon Indian religions could not have been felt from these communities before the Neo-Brahmanism of the twelfth century; for previous to that the centers of religious life lay in *northern* India. Therefore for this earlier time we can only consider the Christians *in the northwestern borderland* as possible mediums of Christian thought. There, as we have seen above, there may possibly have been Christians in the first half of the third century, but the evidence is not sufficient for us to

[63] *Ibid.*, p. 735; Rae, *The Syrian Church in India*, pp. 154f.
[64] Weber, *Krishnajanmâshtamî*, p. 322.
[65] Kessler, *op. cit.*, p. 733.

make this assertion definitely. There are no Nestorian Christians farther in the interior of northern India before the seventh century.

We may expect *a priori* to find Christian influences in Buddhist Sanskrit literature before we do in the Brahman because the Indian borderland was entirely Buddhistic in the first centuries of our era, and moreover foreign elements of a homogeneous character would be able to enter more easily into cosmopolitan Buddhism than into nationalistic Brahmanism. It will be well to keep this fact before our eyes, especially in judging early Krishnaism.

RICHARD GARBE.

TÜBINGEN, GERMANY.

SENSATION AND IMAGINATION.

Of all the direct two-term relations which can subsist between subjects and other entities, of the kind with which theory of knowledge is concerned, *acquaintance* is the most comprehensive. I do not mean that this is *a priori* necessary, but that, so far as can be seen by observation, it is in fact true. If an instance to the contrary could be established, no prejudice ought to prevent us from admitting the instance; in the absence of such an instance, however, I shall assume that all direct two-term relations of a subject to other entities, in so far as such relations can be directly experienced by the subject in question, imply acquaintance with those other entities. There are various words, such as sensation, imagination, conception, immediate memory, which denote two-term relations of subject and object, and we have to inquire whether these are distinguished by the nature of the relation or only by the nature of the object. Differences in the object (except when the object is mental) do not directly concern theory of knowledge, at any rate in its analytical portion; but differences in the *relation* to the object do directly concern the analytical portion of theory of knowledge. In the present article, we have to consider whether the difference between sensation and imagination is a difference in the object or in the relation.

The epistemological importance and difficulty of this inquiry have not, I think, been sufficiently appreciated by any writer except Hume; and even Hume, though aware of the problem, offers a quite unduly simple solution. What is required is to find a tenable interpretation of the feeling that objects of sense are "real" while objects of imagination are "imaginary" or "unreal." In accordance with the maxim explained in our last article, it is not open to us to say that the objects of imagination are "unreal"; the whole conception of "reality" or "unreality," "existence" or "non-existence," as applied to particulars, is a result of logical confusion between names and descriptions. A color visualized, or a sound heard in imagination, must be just on the same level as regards "reality" as a color seen or a sound heard in sensation: it must be equally one of the particulars which would have to be enumerated in an inventory of the universe. Nevertheless, there is undoubtedly *some* important difference between sense-data and imagination-data, which is confusedly indicated by calling the former "real" and the latter "unreal." One outcome of this difference is that sense-data, but not imagination-data, are relevant to physics, being in fact that part of the material world which is immediately given. It is therefore of the utmost importance to epistemology to decide both how imagination and sense are distinguished, and what is the basis for the difference which we feel as regards their power of giving information about the material world.

In the first half of this inquiry, the following criterion will be useful. If we can find a case where the object is the same in two experiences which yet differ intrinsically, then the two experiences must involve different relations to the object. Thus if an object O can be given either in sensation or in imagination, and if the two experiences can be seen to be different by mere inspection, without taking account of their relations to other experiences, then we must conclude that sensation is a different relation from imagination. For two complexes which involve the same related terms can only differ if the relations differ in the two complexes. If, on the other hand, it should appear that, whenever the object is given, sensation and imagination become intrinsically indistinguishable, we shall conclude that the relation involved is the same in both. If, lastly, we find that the object of sensation is never identical with the object of imagination, then our criterion fails; but in this case we at least know that the difference in their objects is quite enough to account for the fact that sensation and imagination are distinguished, and that there is no logical necessity to suppose the relations different.

The use of the above criterion may be made clearer by considering the difference between belief and doubt on the one hand, and the difference between true and false belief on the other hand. If I first doubt a given proposition, and then believe it, the two experiences are quite different intrinsically, and therefore the relation involved must be different in the two cases. In the case of true and false belief, on the contrary, the objects must be different when the belief is true and when it is false; moreover inspection shows no other intrinsic difference between true and false beliefs except the difference of their objects. Hence we may conclude that belief is one relation to objects, which is the same in the case of true beliefs as in the case of false beliefs. We cannot, by the nature of the case, find a true belief and a false belief which have the same objects in the same order, and therefore the more stringent form of our test is inapplicable; but it is sufficiently nearly applicable to make it practically certain that true and false beliefs differ only as regards their objects.

In the case of sensation and imagination, I believe that sometimes, though rarely, their objects may be identical, and that then they are still intrinsically distinguishable. I conclude that different relations to objects are involved in the two cases, although the distinction is facilitated partly by differences in their usual objects, and partly also by means of their external relations to other things. This is the proposition which I wish to establish in the present article.

Before we can advance, it is necessary to have a definition of sensation and imagination respectively. In this, the usual psychological accounts are not of much use to us, because, in the first place, they do not regard either sensation or imagination as involving a relation of subject and object, and in the second place, they assume, as a rule, a knowledge of physiology which, as explained in the preceding article, we must at our present stage do our best to ignore.

Thus Stout says:[1] "One characteristic mark of what we agree in calling sensation is its mode of production. It is caused by what we call a *stimulus*. A stimulus is always some condition, external to the nervous system itself and operating upon it." He proceeds to explain the importance of distinguishing the stimulus from the object of sense-perception. Thus the stimulus and its causal connection with the sensation are only known by means of a body of knowledge not derivable without much inference. The connection with a stimulus will not appear necessarily in any intrinsic quality of a sensation; and so far as I can discover, no intrinsic quality distinguishing sensations from other experiences is given by Stout.

What James says about sensation comes much nearer to giving us what we require. He says:

"Its [sensation's] function is that of mere *acquaintance* with a fact. Perception's function, on the other hand, is knowledge *about* a fact." (*Psychology,* II, p. 2.) Again: "As we can only think or talk about the relations of objects with which we have *acquaintance* already, we are forced to postulate a function in our thought whereby we first

[1] *Manual of Psychology,* p. 127.

become aware of the *bare immediate natures* by which our several objects are distinguished. This function is sensation" (*ibid.*, p. 3).

He does not discuss "acquaintance," and it would be unfair to assume that he means by it what we mean. Nevertheless, if we take him to mean what we mean, his statement is one which we can in a great measure accept, and which at least has the merit of giving an *intrinsic* character of sensation. But although sensation has the characteristic which he mentions, it would seem that other experiences also have this characteristic; for he identifies sensation with acquaintance, and we are in fact acquainted with objects logically similar to those of sensation in imagination and immediate memory, and with objects of another kind in conception and abstract thought. Thus some further characteristic is required to distinguish sensation from other kinds of acquaintance.

One obvious characteristic, which distinguishes sensation from conception and abstract thought, is that its objects are *particulars*. A particular is defined as an entity which can only enter into complexes as the subject of a predicate or as one of the terms of a relation, never as itself a predicate or a relation. This definition is purely logical, and introduces nothing belonging to theory of knowledge. Thus we may say that sensations are always cases of acquaintance with particulars. But this is still not a definition, since it fails to exclude imagination and immediate memory.

In the analysis of memory there are special difficulties, which make it doubtful how far it is to be included under acquaintance. But assuming that there is a kind of memory which involves acquaintance with its object, such memory may be distinguished from sensation and imagination by the fact that its object is given as in the past: there is a temporal relation of subject and object which is involved in the actual experience of memory. Being in the past is not an intrinsic property of the object, but a relation to the subject; thus memory will have to be distinguished from sense and imagination as a different relation to objects, not as the same relation to different objects. This topic will be resumed in the next article; for the present, it is enough to observe that memory is excluded if we say that the acquaintance we are concerned with must not be with an object given as past.

Sensation and imagination together, therefore, may be defined as "acquaintance with particulars not given as earlier than the subject." What is meant by "given as earlier" is a question requiring discussion; for the present, we may say that we mean "having an immediately experienced relation to the subject of that kind which underlies our knowledge of the past." The further definition of this relation must be reserved for the next article.

Since no acquaintance with particulars given as future occurs, it might be thought that "particulars not given as earlier than the subject" might be identified with "particulars given as simultaneous with the subject." But such identification presupposes, what must not be assumed without discussion, that an experienced particular must be given as in some temporal relation with the subject. If this can be denied, we may find here an intrinsic difference between sense and imagination. It may be that in sense the object is given as "now," i. e., as simultaneous with the subject, whereas in imagination the object is given without any temporal relation to the subject, i. e., to the present time. It is difficult even to discuss this question without an analysis of our perception of time, but let us make the attempt.

The theory I wish to examine will maintain that, whatever time-relation may in fact subsist between the subject and an object which is imagined, no time-relation is implied by the mere fact that the imagining occurs. I do not know whether this theory is tenable or not, but I think there is more to be said in its favor than might be thought at first sight. I propose, therefore, to do what I can to make the theory seem *possible,* without coming to a decision as to its truth or falsehod.

It may be said that, while we are imagining, the object imagined may undergo processes of change—for example when we imagine a tune or when we mentally recite a poem. This of course is true, and might be thought to imply that the object must be contemporaneous with the imagining subject. But such an inference would be erroneous, as may be seen by the analogy of abstract thought. I may reflect that twice two are four, and then that twice three are six, and so on throughout the multiplication-table. In this case, I have different objects before my mind at different times, but none of the objects are themselves in time at all. In like manner, I may at one time imagine one object, at another time another object, or even at a continuous series of times a continuous series of objects—for example, the sound of a violin-string running down—while yet the objects imagined may be destitute of temporal position, or may have a temporal position which cannot be inferred from the fact that they are now imagined. An object imagined at one moment but not at another need not itself undergo any intrinsic change during the time between the two moments: it may merely cease to have that relation to the subject which consists in its being imagined. But such cessation may easily produce the belief that the object itself was at the time when it was imagined, though, as is clear in the case of abstract objects, this is in no way implied by the change that has occurred.

Consider, again, the kind of imagination which is connected with memory. In remembering, say, my breakfast this morning, I shall normally use images which are called up at will and are said to be "of" my breakfast. It might be thought that in this case the object is in the past. But this would involve confusing the image with true memory. The image is not *identical* with the past sense-datum which it helps me to remember; and it is only when there is such identity that the object is in the past. I think in the case of *immediate* memory there is such identity, but in this case the object is not an image. When we use images as an aid in remembering, we judge that the images have a resemblance, of a certain sort, to certain past sense-data, enabling us to have knowledge by description concerning those sense-data, through acquaintance with the corresponding images together with a knowledge of the correspondence. The knowledge of the correspondence is obviously only possible through some knowledge, concerning the past, which is not dependent upon the images we now call up. This, however, belongs to the analysis of memory, which is not our present problem; for the present, all that is necessary to observe is that the images which are said to be "of" past sensible objects are not themselves in the past, and therefore form no objection to the hypothesis that images are not given in such a way as to enable us to assign a date to them.

One merit of the above theory is that it accounts, in a manner consistent with logic, for what is called the "unreality" of things merely imagined. This "unreality" will consist in their absence of date, which will also explain fully their irrelevance to physics.

(If the above hypothesis is adopted, we can lay down the following definitions:)

"Imagination" is acquaintance with particulars which are not given as having any temporal relation to the subject.

"Sensation" is acquaintance with particulars given as simultaneous with the subject.

It is to be observed that, in the above definition, it is not asserted that an object imagined has in actual fact no temporal relation to the subject, but merely that this temporal relation, if it exists, forms no part of the experience of imagining. The question whether this is the case or not must be capable of being decided by introspection, but introspection is difficult, and I cannot myself arrive at any certain conclusion in this way. We may observe, however, that "imagining" must not be held to include after-images, which, from our present point of view, belong rather to sensation; from the physiological point of view, also, they differ wholly from imagination, since they depend upon the recent stimulation of the sense-organ.

Leaving, for the present, this possible method of distinguishing sensation and imagination, let us consider other alleged differences. namely:

1. the physiological difference, in relation to stimulus,
2. the different relation to the will,
3. the less degree of vividness in images,
4. the different relation to belief and "physical reality."

We will consider these alleged differences successively.

1. The difference in causal relation to stimulus, as already pointed out, is one which is not relevant at our present stage; that is to say, if this were the only difference between sense and imagination, we should have to construct our theory of the knowledge of external reality before distinguishing between sense and imagination, since a knowledge of external reality is presupposed in the recognition of a different relation to stimulus. Now theories of our knowledge of external reality generally rely on sensation to the exclusion of imagination; hence unless we can invent a theory which uses both equally, we must not rest content with the proposed method of distinguishing between them. For this reason, it is important to examine other proposed distinctions.

2. It may be said that images are capable of being called up at will, in a way in which objects of sense are not. This, if true at all, is only true when stated with very careful limitations. We have at most times considerable choice as to what we shall see or touch, though of course we are limited to what is visible or palpable from where we are. As to what we shall imagine, we are limited by our imaginative powers, and though the field of choice is different, it is just as truly limited as in the case of sense. It is true that we can, more or less at will, call up images of past events, whereas in sense we are confined to what is at the present time. But this is a difference in the area of choice, not in the relation to the will. Moreover images may appear with just as little cooperation of the will as in the case of sensations. Stout, after explaining the sudden shock of a flash of lightning or a steam-whistle, says "no mere image ever does strike the mind in this manner" (*Manual,* p. 417). Macbeth speaks of

> "that suggestion
> Whose horrid image doth unfix my hair
> And make my seated heart knock at my ribs
> Against the use of nature."

The whistle of a railway engine could hardly have a stronger effect than this; and in morbid and insane states of mind images must frequently have the violence of sensations, with the same independence of the will. This distinction, therefore, cannot be accepted as adequate.

3. The view that images can be distinguished from objects of sense by their smaller degree of vividness has already been partly answered by anticipation under our previous heading. Stout sums up as follows:

"Our conclusion is that at bottom the distinction between image and percept, as respecting faint and vivid states, is based on a difference of quality. The percept has an aggressiveness which does not belong to the image.

It strikes the mind with varying degrees of force or liveliness according to the varying intensity of the stimulus. This degree of force or liveliness is part of what we ordinarily mean by the intensity of a sensation. But this constituent of the intensity of sensations is absent in mental imagery" (*Manual,* p. 419).

I believe this, however true as a general rule, to be liable to exceptions which make it quite useless as a test. A very strong emotion will often bring with it—especially where some future action or some undecided issue is involved—powerful, compelling images which may determine the whole course of life, sweeping aside all contrary solicitations to the will by their capacity for exclusively possessing the mind. And in all cases where images, originally recognized as such, gradually pass into hallucinations, there must be just that "force or liveliness" which is supposed to be always absent in imagination.

4. We may attempt to distinguish sensations from images by the belief in their "reality," in their power of giving knowledge of the "external world." This difference is hard to analyze or to state correctly, but in some sense it has plainly a large element of truth. Images are "imaginary"; in *some* sense, they are "unreal." They cannot be employed to give knowledge of physics. They are destitute of causal efficacy, they are not impenetrable, and altogether they fail to compel respect. But however true it may be that images differ from objects of sense in these respects, it is impossible that these differences should be the ultimate source of the difference between imagination and sense. The "unreality" of images requires interpretation: it cannot mean what we should express by "there's no such thing," for this phrase is only applicable to a thing described, not to a thing immediately given. The word "unreal," as applied to something immediately given, has always some rather complicated meaning. A visual object,

such as Macbeth's dagger or a reflection in a looking-glass, is "unreal" if it is not correlated with the usual tactile sensations; and the "unreality" of images might consist only in their not obeying the laws of motion and in their being generally unconventional in their behavior. But in any case, "unreality," as applied to objects of acquaintance, is some complicated conception, always derivative from some other difference between the objects so condemned and the objects recognized as "real." The difference, therefore, which undoubtedly exists between images and objects of sensation, in respect of our belief in their "reality," must be derivative from some other and simpler difference. If it be the case, as was suggested earlier, that images are not given as simultaneous or in any other time-relation with the subject, then an image need not exist at the moment when it is imagined, nor indeed at any other moment; such a difference as this, between images and objects of sense, would, it seems to me, amply account for the feeling that images are "unreal." This feeling, therefore, on examination, is found to afford a confirmation of our theory.

The case of dreams demands discussion: is dreaming sensation or imagination? The four differences which we have considered leave the matter doubtful. (1) Physiologically, in relation to stimulus, dreams cannot count as sensations, except in certain cases, e. g., where a door banging makes us dream of some noisy event such as a naval battle. In this case, the noise in the dream may be considered sensation, while the rest of the dream is taken as imagination together with false interpretation. But as a rule, for example with all the objects we see in dreams while our eyes are shut, the relation to stimulus which is supposed to be characteristic of sensation is absent. Thus as regards this criterion, the greater part of the objects in dreams would count as images. (2) As regards the relation to the will, dreams belong rather with sensation. The procession of objects in a dream is received by us passively, in the same sense and to the same degree as the objects of waking sensation are received passively. But this difference between sense and imagination, we found, is by no means absolute: some images seem to come in just the way in which sensations come. Thus although, under this head, it would be more natural to put dreams with sensations, yet we cannot lay very much stress on this fact. (3) As regards the less degree of vividness of images, it would seem that dreams on the whole belong with images rather than with objects of sense. People, for example, whose visual images are not brightly colored, but are all of some dim shade of gray, are likely to see a similarly colorless world in their dreams, though often the power of visualizing in dreams will be more nearly that which the dreamer possessed in youth than that which he possesses now. Most people, I think, would say that the world of dreams has the fragmentary indistinctness of the world of images: it is fairly finished in the parts that specially interest the dreamer, but creation has been scamped elsewhere and it remains very much in the rough. It may be doubted, however, whether this is not equally true of the world of sense, and only seems untrue because we always pass away from sense to "physical reality" by an unconscious inference. What we see out of the corners of our eyes is very dim, but we do not feel it so, because as soon as we look at it straight we find it is distinct. Nevertheless, it must be admitted, I think, that as a general rule sensations have a vividness and distinctness which is lacking in imagination, and that in this respect dreams resemble imagination rather than sense. (4) What makes dreams really puzzling is their relation to belief and "physical reality." While they last, their relation to belief appears to be precisely that of sensation: they never seem, at the moment, to be our own invention. Yet, when we wake, they are dismissed from belief on the ground that they do not fit in with our constructions of "physical reality." There is thus a conflict between belief (while we are dreaming) and "physical reality" (after we wake). As regards the belief, dreams belong with sense, while as regards the "physical reality" they belong with imagination. In this, dreams resemble hallucinations; they also resemble what we are told of the imagination of children, who sometimes, as Galton states,[2] "seem to spend years of difficulty distinguishing between the subjective and objective world."

The conclusion which is *suggested* by these considerations is that dreams belong mainly, but not wholly, to imagination, but are mistakenly supposed by the subject to belong to sensation even in their imagined parts. I do not mean that the subject, as a rule, definitely *judges* that they belong to sensation, but that his feelings towards them, while he is dreaming, are such as he would usually only have towards objects of sense, and such as he would cease to have if he recognized that the objects in question were mere images. In order that this theory may be tenable, it is not necessary to suppose that there is no intrinsic difference between imagining and sensating, but only that the difference is one which sometimes remains unfelt. If it is the case, as it seem to be, that a great majority of imagined objects differ in recognizable ways from sensible objects—by greater dimness, vagueness, subjection to our will, etc.—then it would be surprising if, when an imagined object fails to differ in these ways from an object of sense, the subject is mistakenly led to regard it as an object of sense, overlooking the less easily detected difference of relation which, if we are right, constitutes the true *differentia* of imagination. The way in which hallucinations

[2] Quoted by James, *Psychology*, II, p. 55.

and delusions often begin as mere vivid images, recognized as such, and only gradually acquire a hold on belief, suggests that, to the end, they remain different from sensations. Dreams will then be, in the main, identical in nature with hallucinations, and will be accounted for by the fact that in sleep our imagination is unusually active and our critical faculties unusually slight. All such experiences, which, if accompanied by belief, are recognized as sources of error, will be classed with imagination. With this conclusion, a great simplification will be introduced, at a later stage, into the problem of our knowledge of the external world.

If the hypothesis that images are not given in any time-relation to the subject is rejected, as perhaps it may have to be, it will be necessary to find some other way of explaining what is meant when images are said to be "unreal." We must in any case, I think, allow that imagination and sensation are different relations to objects, since, in spite of the differences usually to be found between images and sense-data, the difference between the two experiences of imagining and sensating seems too clear and profound to be accounted for by such differences alone. It seems evident that, if images have any given time-relation to the subject, it must be that of simultaneity; hence in this respect they will be indistinguishable from sense-data. We cannot hope, therefore, in this case, to explain the "unreality" of images by the nature of the relation of imagining; and I do not think that there is anything in the *intrinsic* character of images by which we can explain it. We must, therefore, if we allow images to be simultaneous with the subject, define their "unreality" by means of their behavior and relations.

The "unreality" of images may, on our present hypothesis, be defined as consisting merely in their failure to fulfil the correlations which are fulfilled by sense-data. An imagined visual object cannot be touched, that is to say, if we perform those movements which, in the case of a visual sense-datum, would procure a sensation of touch, we shall not have a sensation of touch, nor, as a rule, an image of touch. Again, images change in ways which are wholly contrary to the laws of physics; the laws of their changes seem, in fact, to be psychological rather than physical, involving reference to such matters as the subject's thoughts and desires. This would, I think, sufficiently explain what is meant by the "unreality" of images. I do not, therefore, know how to decide between our present and our former hypothesis as to the nature of imagination.

We may now sum up the above discussion. In spite of certain differences usually to be found between images and sense-data, we decided that there is also a difference, usually recognizable introspectively, between the relation of imagining and the relation of sensating. We failed to find any way of deciding between the view that an image is given as simultaneous with the subject and the view that it is not given as in any time-relation to the subject. If it is given as simultaneous with the subject, its "unreality" must consist merely in its failure to obey the laws of correlation and change which are obeyed by sense-data and which form the empirical basis of physics. If, on the other hand, imagination involves no time-relation of subject and object, then it is a simpler relation than sensation, being, in fact, merely *acquaintance with particulars.* The object imagined may, on this view, have any position in time or none, so far as the mere fact of its being imagined is concerned. *Sensation*, on the other hand, is a relation to a particular which involves simultaneity between subject and object. Sensation *implies* acquaintance with the object, but is not identical with acquaintance. It is not a definition of sensation to say that it is acquaintance with an object which is in fact simultaneous with the subject: the simultaneity must be not merely a fact, but must be deducible from the nature of the experience involved in sensation. We might take sensation as indefinable, and define simultaneity by its means; but whether this is really feasible is a question which must be postponed until we come to consider our experience of time-relations. The "unreality" of images, which cannot be taken in a strict sense, may, we found, on this theory, be interpreted as expressing the fact that they are not given with any definite position in time. Dreams and hallucinations, we found, are to be classed, mainly, though not wholly, with images, and the mistaken view that they are sensations, which is normally held by the experiencing subject, may be accounted for by the fact that their objects have characteristics generally associated with objects of sense.

The next problem which must occupy us is a problem raised by our definition of sensation, and involved in any theory of memory, namely the problem of our acquaintance with time-relations. This problem will occupy us in the next article.

BERTRAND RUSSELL.

CAMBRIDGE, ENGLAND.

ORTHODOX AND LIBERAL CHRISTIANITY.

A VIA MEDIA.

THE Christian church—using that term in its most comprehensive sense — is to-day divided into two great parties. It may, perhaps, be difficult to get a name for each that will satisfy both parties. Those I mean by "orthodox" perhaps would object to the word as misleading and would describe by it what is known in church history as the great movement in the seventeenth century known as orthodoxy. Liberalism does not so much oppose this as ignore it as almost beneath notice. This old traditional orthodoxy is, therefore, dead and need not be here considered. Those who inherit the orthodox tradition call themselves the Positive School, and stand opposed to the Liberal School. This is the real antithesis in Germany, and more or less in this country as well. The outstanding differences between the two schools are not difficult to trace. According to the Positive school, which inherits the orthodox tradition, Christianity is a great cosmic scheme of redemption, the fundamental presupposition of which is the fall of man, and the fundamental fact of which is that Jesus Christ is a Saviour or Redeemer. According to the second, Christianity is an ethical system of teaching or precept, and Jesus Christ is the supreme teacher and moral and spiritual guide. According to the first the important thing about Jesus Christ is what he did; according to the second what he taught. To the one Jesus Christ is supreme because of the act of atonement accomplished once and once for all on the cross of Calvary; to the other, because of what he revealed in his teachings as to the character of God and the nature of man. To the one the apostle Paul is the expositor *par excellence* of what Christianity is because he sets it forth as a great redemptive scheme; to the other the synoptic Gospels are the supreme authority because they contain, it is presumed, the ethical and spiritual teaching man needs for his guidance. The one believes that Christianity stands or falls with the supremacy of the apostle Paul, the other believes that we have really outgrown the speculations of the apostle Paul, and that we must fall back upon the teaching of Jesus in the first three Gospels.

It is obvious that orthodox or positive Christianity has practically the whole Christian church on its side, past and present. This does not of course settle the question, for in many things the Christian church has been mistaken. But it is well that we should be aware what a radical change is involved in the transfer from the one position to the other. If it were possible to ask any one of the great fathers of the church the question, what is Christianity? the answer would not be doubtful. They would have said, Christianity is the religion of redemption, and what is most vital in it is contained in whatever is essential and permanent in the doctrine of the incarnation and atonement of the superpersonal Son of God. As we know it, and as the church has known it, Christianity is the religion of St. Paul. Such certainly would have been the answer of St. Athanasius, the father who gave shape to the first great creed of the church,—the Nicene, which was formulated in the first ecumenical council assembled at Nicæa in 325 A. D., at the command of Constantine, the first Christian emperor. He would not have understood any Christianity that had not its fundamental starting point in the incarnation of the Son of God and did not culminate in his death. The essence of Christianity, according to the Nicene conception of it, does not consist in any ethical teaching about God or man, but in God becoming man in Christ in order that man might become God. The same idea would have been given by St. Augustine, the greatest of the fathers of the west, whose teachings made possible the western or Latin church, and whose theology was embodied four centuries later in the Athanasian creed. He would not, perhaps, have put the matter in exactly the same form as did St. Athanasius, but in so far forth as emphasis on the redemptive character of Christianity is concerned the two fathers would have been at one. In the same line of teaching would have been St. Thomas Aquinas, Duns Scotus, and indeed all the great theologians of the middle ages. And when we come across the line that separates the ancient from the modern world, and enter the churches of the Reformation, we find essentially the same teaching, that Christianity is a redemptive system having its vital center in the death of the Son of God. Luther, Calvin, Knox, Cranmer, all the heroes of the Reformation, were at one with the pre-Reformation church in so regarding Christianity, however much they may have differed from it in matters not so vital. None of them would have recognized or understood a Christianity whose essence consisted in the precepts of the Serman on the Mount, and not in the death of the Son of God on the cross.

It is only in comparatively recent times that the attempt has been made to conceive Christianity as a body of ethical and spiritual teaching, it originated with liberal Christianity which began its course by repudiating the Christ of the church in the interest of the Jesus of the synoptic Gospels, whom it conceived as historical. Its cry was "Back to Jesus." Let us be done with the doctrines of the church;

the Christianity we want and which the world needs is the Christianity which Jesus himself taught in the Galilean villages, and which has come down to us in his parables and precepts. Comparisons were drawn between the creeds of the pre-Reformation and Reformation churches and the teaching of the Master, always to the disparagement of the former in favor of the latter, and the promise was sometimes held out that the ultimate form of Christianity would be what was called the "simple teaching of Jesus." The most important duty was thought to be the return to primitive Christianity, and the wiping out of all the creeds of the intervening centuries as so much useless speculation. And inasmuch as the apostle Paul was the first and arch-offender, in that it was he who led the infant church away from the teaching of Jesus into dependence upon the death of Christ, the first duty was to repudiate the apostle Paul.

Paul's Epistles have thus been the *bête noire* of liberal theologians, and his fundamental blunder was the fall of man. This was put forth in the interest of optimism, and as being in harmony with the doctrine of evolution. It was not seen that it was essentially pessimistic and ran counter to the evolutionary theory, in that it invited us to see as the Christian centuries evolved the progressive obscuration of Christianity by Greek philosophy, and by the other products of secular culture, and not the progressive rational development and ever richer unfolding of the essential truth at the heart of the faith. It is not that the church has not attached importance to the teaching of Jesus, in which is set forth the nature of the kingdom of God, the transformation of the inner life of man which is necessary for entrance into that kingdom, the duty of self-denial, of self-sacrifice, of purity, of forgiveness. All this the church has held and taught was a vital part of Christianity, and must enter into the religion of the future as an integral part of it; but at the same time all branches of the church have maintained that the moral and spiritual teachings of Jesus are not so essential to mature Christianity as the doctrine of the death of Christ on the cross. It would seem as if some sure and vital instinct has held the heart of the church true to this central fact; no heresy has been deemed so deadly as a denial of the efficacy of the death of Christ for human salvation. The late Dr. Dale of Birmingham held that the essential Christian gospel is not found in the ethical teachings of the synoptic Gospels; that we must go to the Epistles to find it, for the reason that the essential gospel was something which God had done for man, and not simply moral and spiritual teaching, however pure it might be, which men were to follow and obey. The essential gospel of Christianity is involved in something God has done for man, and not in something said by Jesus to man. And what God has done for man has its culmination in what Jesus did on the cross of Calvary; and hence with a sure instinct the church has followed the apostle Paul rather than the synoptic Gospels. And yet it is not necessary to put the apostle Paul and the teaching of Jesus in opposition and contrast as has so often been done; it is only necessary to see that in the light of the death of Jesus alone can his teaching be seen in its most genuine significance.

When the Gospels are properly read they culminate in the death of their central figure. It is not the Epistles of Paul alone that emphasize the death of Jesus. From the very first he has his face set toward Jerusalem where he is to die. The cross is the center of the Gospels no less than of the Epistles. It is therefore a false contrast which liberal Christianity constantly draws between Paul and Jesus. It was a true instinct that enabled the artist to see the "shadow of the cross" in the carpenter's shop at Nazareth. For the whole evangelic story has both its meaning and culmination in the cross. Especially is this seen when the non-Markan source of Matthew and Luke, which the critics call "Q" is separated from the rest of the Gospels. Evidently this is a part of the Gospels of which neither Matthew nor Luke is the author. It is common to them both; they have each of them adapted it to their purposes; it existed before they touched it substantially as it exists now. There are slight variations in the way in which each evangelist quotes this non-Markan source, but they are so slight that there is no doubt that it was the same document from which the two borrowed. Matthew best preserves the language and Luke the order of the original source. It contains no history, has nothing about the death or resurrection of Jesus. It has no record of any miracle wrought by him. It is almost wholly impersonal and ethical. It is the latest form of the *"irreducible minimum"* to which research has driven the higher criticism of the New Testament in its search for the origin of Christianity in the teaching of Jesus. A very high value is attached to it by the liberal critics because of the witness the fragment is supposed to bear to the reality of the life and teaching of Jesus. It is, so the critics tell us, the oldest fragment in the Gospels. It can be separated from the rest of the Gospels of Matthew and Luke. For long the critics have been convinced that the Gospel of Mark was the earliest source of our knowledge of Jesus, but now they are as convinced that "Q" antedates anything we have in the Gospels. The great value of this document consists in the fact that it tells us what were the teachings of Jesus. Says Dr. C. H. Gilbert, an American liberal critic, in a recent issue of the *Hibbert Journal,* "Of this teaching the earliest, the most various, and complete collection is that which is designated by the letter 'Q.'" "It is the most authoritative document," he tells us, "on the nature and scope of Christianity" just because it is supposed to be a collection of the words of Jesus. "No part of the New Testament is of the same weight as the words of Jesus, him out of the fulness of whose spiritual forces the Christian movement sprang." When this non-Markan source is removed from the Gospels of Matthew and Luke, what is left behind bears almost as much testimony to the death of Jesus as do the Epistles of Paul. It is dominated by the Pauline point of view, and contains many Pauline elements. The Gospel of Mark is decidedly Pauline, and the Gospel of Mark is the substratum of those of Matthew and Luke. They follow Mark in so far as they relate historical facts, with the exception of the nativity stories which are not in Mark. They vary the story as they tell it, but the substance is Markan. The attempt, therefore, of the liberal critics to put Paul in opposition to Jesus breaks down, for Mark, Matthew and Luke all alike point to the death of Jesus as that on which all rests.

The attempt to find in "Q" the *fons et origo* of Christianity has a long history behind it, and it can be understood only in the light of that history. It is really a part of the controversy between the Roman church and Protestantism that arose with the Reformation, and has been raging ever since. Where is the norm of true Christianity to be found by which to test the various forms of it that arise in the course of its history? The Roman church answers this question by its doctrine of development. There is no fixed norm; it exists in the church itself which was established by Jesus Christ; and the church has the power of declaring from time to time what the true Christianity is. There is at the heart of this claim of the Roman church a profound truth which no branch of Protestantism has yet accepted in its fulness. It is the truth that the church is a living organism,—a growing organization. Every Protestant church is based on the idea that somewhere the norm is to be found—and one sect differs from another according to its answer to the question where? All the conflicts of the Protestant sects with one another have been around this one question. Those who claim to stand nearest to the Roman church— the Anglicans—agree with that church in so far as to say that the norm is not to be found in the New Testament, but in the subsequent centuries. A few years ago an influential party of the Church of England presented a petition to the Primate, praying that the variation in doctrine and ritual allowable in the Church of England should be confined to those which have the sanction of the first six centuries. The motive in the movement was to check the Romeward or papal tendencies in the church. The signatories believed that if a law was passed to the effect that no doctrine or ritual be allowed in the church except it had the sanction of the great fathers of the first six centuries, an end would be put to the doctrines and practices of the extreme ritualists, which had their origin in the middle ages. The signatories to this petition expressed special loyalty to the Nicene creed, which was framed in the fourth century. The more liberal clergymen and members of the Church of England delight to call themselves "Nicene men," and there is an idea in many minds outside of that church that the liberal theology of the present day is a revival of the Greek theology embodied in the Nicene symbol. The watch-word of the Broad Church party for many years has been "Back to Nicæa." Frederick Denison Maurice gave the start to this tendency many years ago now, in urging the desirability of a fuller study of the early theologians of Alexandria. The advice was followed, and liberal churchmen have found many resemblances between the theological renaissance of the present day and the views of the great fathers of the early Greek church. Certainly there is a freshness and breadth in the writings of Clement, Origin, and Athanasius not to be found in those of Augustine and the Doctors of the middle ages. But that does not prove that we can return to Alexandrian Christianity and accept the Nicene Creed as our own, any more than we can go back to the ninth century and accept the Athanasian Creed as our own. The attempt to bind the church which is a living organism to any past age is an impossible task.

The non-sacerdotal or non-episcopal churches of the Reformation have sought for the norm of Christianity in the New Testament. Not at once indeed was this position taken. The Confession of Augsburg, the creed of the Lutheran church, which was drawn up by the Reformers themselves, fixed the limit beyond which genuine Christianity was not to be found at the fourth century. But all forms of Presbyterianism and Congregationalism have planted themselves on the New Testament. This is final, they said. To this law and testimony all must conform. The theology which alone can be a foundation of the church must be a Biblical theology. At first, all of the New Testament was supposed to be binding on the church; but it was soon discovered that the Epistles of Paul contained the germ of the errors into which the church had fallen, and therefore if the church was to be founded on pure doctrine it must find its basis in the Gospels only. Persecuted in this city those in search of the true norm of Christianity found that they must flee into another,—they must go still farther back. The higher criticism was born and introduced a new element into the problem. The Gospel of John was found not to be above suspicion. It was clearly seen not to be a biography of Jesus, and what was demanded by this party was a Christianity which Jesus himself preached, and certainly that was not found in the Gospel of John, which was manifestly a theological treatise based on the theology of Alexandria. The cry was "Back to Jesus," just as the cry of the Anglicans had been "Back to Nicæa." The real Jesus was to be found in the synoptics, and most diligently have the synoptics been searched for the purpose of discovering this "real" Jesus. For a while the idea that the synoptics were the final resting-place of the church seemed to satisfy all parties, but soon it was discovered that the search could no more stop there than in the Nicene creed. The chief agent in making the discovery has been, of course, the higher criticism, as soon as it was applied to the solution of the synoptic problem.

It was some time before Christian scholars could bring themselves to apply the same methods of criticism which have proved so fruitful in the case of the Old Testament to the New. The feeling has been that the New Testament is a different kind of book from the Old, and consequently must be treated differently. The reason for that feeling doubtless was that the central figure of the New Testament is wholly different from any of the characters of the Old,—that they were human, and he divine,—and therefore the literature that deals with him must not be treated in the same way as the literature that deals with them. Very slowly has the conviction worked itself into the heart of Christian scholars that so far as methods of criticism are concerned there is really no difference between the Testaments, that not even a blank leaf separates them, and that the younger scripture is comprehended in the scope of the literature of the Hebrew people, that it is a natural product of the human mind, just as truly as the Old Testament is, carrying to their legitimate conclusions the ideas of the elder scripture. Not designedly indeed, but really though unconsciously, the purpose of the criticism of the New Testament, especially in Germany, has been to undermine the doctrine of the divinity of its central figure and to discover a human Jesus. The presupposition of the study has been that a thick accretion of tradition and superstition has gathered around his name, and the object of the criticism has been to peel this off and to get at the realistic human figure. The triumph of the study would have been the denuding from the supernatural Christ of the church of all miraculous elements, and the reconstruction of the earthly history of the man Jesus. The supernatural features with which the Gospels clothe the figure the critics were convinced were not historical. One by one they were set aside—not only the manner in which he entered the world and left it, but all the deeds attributed to him that proved his divinity. The critic has been in search of a purely human Jesus and in "Q" he professes to have found him; for here is only impersonal and ethical teaching with no death on the cross and no resurrection from the dead.

But the Christ of the church is not such a Jesus. The important question is whether the Christian church can make the great change of belief which the acceptance of such a Jesus would involve and remain the Christian church. If the critic's evidence for his thesis is so overwhelming that it must be accepted—well, then it must; but it is important that the churches of Christendom should realize the kind of Jesus the critics are presenting them with, and the vast revolution in belief which it involves. It has often been remarked that all of Christianity was involved in the controversy between Athanasius and Arius, and that the victory gained at Nicæa was a victory for Christianity itself. But here would seem to be even a greater issue. Christianity from the beginning has been conceived as a redemptive scheme, the good news of a divine being coming down from heaven to rescue fallen man, the Christ or Saviour not being a member of the fallen race, but apart from it and superior to it. To make the Christ or Saviour a member of the race, no matter how specially endowed with moral and spiritual qualities, is to alter the whole conception and to tear out the heart of the evangelic story. The Christian church has never yet consented to put its Christ into the same category as the prophets of the Old Testament or the philosophers of Greece, but this is just what will have to be done if the Jesus of the critics is to be accepted as the Christ. Here are the words of the critic already quoted: "They [the hundred verses more or less that make up the document called 'Q'] present Jesus as a great spiritual prophet, as one who was in the line of Isaiah and Jeremiah." It is true that Dr. Gilbert adds that Jesus is presented as the master of Isaiah and Jeremiah, but he is superior to them in the same way as Aristotle is superior to all others in the realm of philosophy. As the Stagirite is "master of them who know in the realm of philosophy, then he who spoke the words of 'Q' is master of all who know in the realm of ethics and religion." No one doubts that Aristotle was a man, strictly within the human range, as much so as any of those with whom he is compared, and no one doubts that Isaiah and Jeremiah were human beings. The root idea of "Q" as Dr. Gilbert reads it is that Jesus was a teacher, not a Redeemer or Saviour as the Christian church has all along conceived him. As a teacher he spoke "winged words" indeed, but he does nothing as a Redeemer or Saviour. No words of "Q" lead up to anything "generically different from the conception of a prophet, or beyond that of the supreme and final prophet." Nor is Dr. Gilbert alone in this. Says a brother critic, Prof. S. J. Case, "The Jesus of liberal theology is not a supernatural person, at least not in any real sense of that term as understood by the traditional Christology" (*The Historicity of Jesus,* p. 151). "Jesus can best and most truly be known as a man among men. The religion which has Jesus for its object is to be sharply distinguished from the personal religion of Jesus." It is now believed by the liberals that he did not set himself forward as an object of worship and reverence, but that his primary concern was to point men directly to God, the God whom he himself worshiped. The author quotes Harnack, the leader of the liberals. "He desired no further belief in his person and no other attachment to it than is contained in the keeping of his commandments. . . . This feeling, praying, working, struggling, and suffering individual is a man who in the face of his God also associates himself with other men." (*What is Christianity*, p. 125.) The method in which the liberal critics defend the historicity of Jesus involves the same thing. It is significant that theologians of strict orthodoxy stand aloof from the discussion of this question as though it does not concern them. The old controversy was between liberal and orthodox, and it may be said that the latter is not altogether displeased to see his old enemy attacked. It had been gaining a victory all through the last century, and doubtless was beginning to think that it was master of the field. But the triumph is really a defeat, for it means the destruction of Christianity as Christianity has been known in all ages of its history. Professor von Soden, for example, in his pamphlet *Hat Jesus gelebt?* maintains that we are as little justified in asking whether Jesus lived as we would be in putting the same question with regard to Socrates or Alexander, and easily shows how absurd it would be to entertain any such doubt or to ask any such question. The Jesus whom Dr. Gilbert and Professors von Soden and Harnack and the critics generally would commend to us is not the Christ the Christian church has all along believed in, and it is not the Christ it believes in today. If Jesus was a man as Socrates, Alexander, Isaiah, and Jeremiah were men, then the whole Christian world has been under a delusion. The discovery that Jesus was a man merely as those named were men, would be regarded as destructive of Christianity just as would be the discovery that Jesus never lived at all. It would be the destruction of Christianity as Christianity has been understood by the great saints and theologians of the past, and as it is understood today by the Greek Church, by the Lutheran Church, by the Congregational churches of all lands, and by all branches of the Presbyterian Church.

The evidence is lacking that "Q" is the utterance of an individual Jesus. The greatest part of it is made up of ethical teaching which might have come from a Hebrew prophet. It is Hebrew ethics at their best. There is nothing that might not have come from a Hebrew prophet, and there is no personal claim put forth by the speaker. There is nothing against the supposition that the teaching was put into the mouth of Jesus by those who worshiped him as a God. Suppose that the story of a historical Jesus did not arise until after the destruction of Jerusalem in the year 70 A. D. Then there would be need of something to take the place of the old Jewish hierarchy in the new religion. The new faith would have to speak with the voice of authority, just as there would have to be something in it which would take the place of the stories of the suffering and dying gods of the East which had flooded the whole Greco-Roman world. To put teaching into the mouth of some hero or prophet or Messiah of the past was the universal custom of the time, and was not considered reprehensible as we would consider it today. The whole Old Testament is the evidence of this fact, for almost all of it is pseudepigraphic. It is not our business either to approve or condemn the literary practice of the first or second century, but simply to understand it; this in any case was what the evangelists Matthew and Luke did with the document the critics call "Q"; what they put into their Gospels was borrowed from somewhere. Dr. Gerald Friedländer in his *Jewish Sources of the Sermon on the Mount,* shows that the precepts of the sermon and the petitions of the Lord's prayer are derived from the Old Testament. Professor Pfleiderer shows that Matt. xi. 25ff, on which the liberal critics depend for proof of the personal note which is absent from all the rest of "Q", is part of a Christological hymn which betrays its ecclesiastical origin in its artistic metrical form. "The artistic arrangement of strophes in something like a sonnet-like form points to the moulding hand of the church." And the contents of the passage show that it was derived from earlier utterances from Paul, Cor. i. 19, "For it is written, I will destroy the wisdom of the wise, and will bring to nothing the understanding of the prudent." And Paul's thought was a familiar one in all the mystery institutions of antiquity, that it is only to specially endowed persons or specially prepared persons, initiated ones, that the higher truths were revealed. "It is just this specifically Pauline thought—that the true knowledge of God and of Christ is hidden from the natural man and only revealed to the mind of man by the Spirit of God, who is the Spirit of the Son of God—which the Evangelist makes (verse 22) Jesus himself express in words which are so strongly distinguished by their dogmatic character from Jesus's usual manner of speaking in the synoptic Gospels, and have such a remarkable affinity with the Pauline and Johannine theology (John i. 18; x. 5; xii. 3; xvii. 10) that one can hardly avoid the impression that we have here, not so much a saying of Jesus himself, as a Christological confession of the apostolic community in the form of a solemn liturgical hymn." (*Primitive Christianity,* II, p. 144). As elsewhere in the New Testament the critics fail to find the *fons et origo* of Christianity in "Q." If there is no death and resurrection of Jesus in "Q" there is no Christianity in it as Christianity has been understood in all the ages of its history, there is only Jewish ethics.

The one fallacy that runs through the whole liberal criticism of orthodox Christianity is the supposition that nothing can be true that is not historically true. The presupposition of the Pauline conception of redemption is the fall of man; but science has proved that man never fell, and besides, it is said, there is no mention of a fall in the teaching of Jesus. But is the fall of man something that can be taught by science? What an immense assumption it is that it was a fact of science which the Spirit of Truth was wishful to teach in the story of the Garden of Eden! Suppose that there is much more in the old dogmas of the church than even the devoted believers in them imagine? Suppose that Paul, when he said "All have sinned and come short of the glory of God," did not refer to anything that took place on the plane of history? Suppose that he knew quite as well as the modern tyro in science that man was not created perfect in body and mind? Suppose that the old story of the fall did not mean what the seventeenth century divines imagined? Suppose that it is an allegory or symbol having a spiritual or esoteric meaning, that the sphere with which it deals is the super-historical sphere—a very real sphere to the apostle Paul—that the fall denotes, therefore, a fact in the spiritual life of man, not only of the first man, but of every man. The inference drawn by many in our day that the ancient writers who told the story of the fall were either fools for giving such idle tales, or men who did not know what they were talking about, because, forsooth, they were ignorant of the story of physical science—was too hasty. Perhaps these men were wiser than our modern theologian or man of science. Perhaps the story enshrines some deep-seated reality which is borne witness to by human experience. This would seem likely, because the story has satisfied the needs of multitudes of men and women, and these not the weakest of the race, but some of the strongest both intellectually and spiritually. These men and women have believed the story, not because in going back into the centuries they have come upon a perfect man, but because looking within they have come upon certain facts of spiritual experience which the old story seemed to explain. Perhaps the ancient authors had not the remotest intention of teaching anything about man's first condition on the planet. Be that as it may, these facts of inner spiritual experience are as open to us as they were to him, and we should read the old story in the light of them and not in the light of any facts of physical science.

Every man feels within himself that he has fallen below the standard which he has set up for himself; he has not been the man he ought to have been. Theologians have called this fact of universal experience the sense of sin, and nothing is so wide spread as this sense of sin. It is not confined to Christian lands, therefore it cannot be the product of Christian theology. It must be something innate, something that belongs to man as man, as an inhabitant of this planet. It does seem that man could be better and greater than he is now, that his ideal is higher than his real. Wherever man is found he seems discontented with himself, as though he had fallen from some high estate. His reach always exceeds his grasp; he is always attempting more than he can accomplish, beginning tasks he cannot end. The soul of man is never satisfied with any achievements; it always aims at more than it can perform, always imagines more than it can accomplish, as though it had come from a higher realm and was greater than it seems. If we look deeply into the soul of any earnest man we shall find this in proportion to his earnestness. The apostle Paul found a contradiction in his nature,—while he was obedient to the law of God after the inward man there was another law in his members that brought him into captivity to the law of sin and death. The apostle of science, Thomas Henry Huxley, found the same thing—the course of cosmic evolution setting in one direction and man setting himself against it in another direction. What is the explanation of the fact that man is in incessant conflict with himself? It would be explained were it true that the soul, the real man within, is not the product of cosmic evolution, but has come from a higher world into this lower one, that man is really a spiritual being or immortal essence tabernacling in mortal flesh.

Suppose that it were true what religious faith in every age and land has affirmed, that the soul of man has come from afar, from God who is its true home, and that here it has no abiding dwelling place, and is moving about, as Wordsworth expresses it, in worlds not realized? That would explain all these spiritual experiences just mentioned. How would it be possible to express such a truth otherwise than by saying that man has fallen from some higher world, that this world in which he is now is not his true home, and that here he is not living his true life? That is exactly what the apostle Paul means by "death," that man's condition in this world is a state of separation from the divine consciousness in a higher world. He means that man fell from that high estate when he came into this world of matter and form. The soul came from this upper realm, and this upper realm is the true home of the soul for which it yearns. The essence of the fall of man was the awakening within man of a desire for a separate life. How shall we speak of the soul in its own celestial home before it became incarnate in mortal guise? If we do speak at all of it it must be in the language of symbol and parable, for on such a theme the literal truth will not be possible for us. And what better symbol or parable could be found than that of Eden, if only we remember that no garden of earth is meant, no condition of physical perfection, but the soul's home in God. Its consciousness was one with the divine consciousness; it had no will separate from the will of God. What a confirmation of the Pauline doctrine of the fall is the one fact that comes out of every scripture and every mythology the world over,—that the man that is, is a degeneration of the man that was. In Plato we have allegory upon allegory describing the soul of man before the fall in its heavenly home, and its condition in this lower world. The soul here is like a dweller in an underground den, with chains on legs and arms and neck, sitting with back to the light, seeing nothing but the shadows of things passing before it on a wall in front. Or it is, as it were, living at the bottom of the sea. And the great master tries to describe what a wondrous world would meet the eye could the soul come to the surface as fish sometimes come to the surface of the sea.—"A world whose mountains, stones, our emeralds, and sardonyxes, and jaspers, being but chips from them—a sun ever shining, never dimmed,

> "All that is most beauteous imagined there,
> In happier beauty, more pellucid streams,
> An ampler ether, a diviner air,
> And fields invested with purpureal gleams,
> Climes which the sun who sheds the brightest ray
> Earth knows is all unworthy to survey."

The world, in fine, of the unfallen soul where, as Plato expresses it, are "Temples and sacred places in which the gods really dwell, and the denizens of this radiant world hear the voices of the gods, and receive their answers, and are conscious of them and hold converse with them;" and they see, continues Plato, "the sun, moon, and stars, as they really are, and their other blessedness is of a piece with this" (Churton Collins, *Poetry and Criticism,* pp. 268-9).

We have an echo of this Platonic doctrine in Paul's declaration, "For you died, and your life is hid with Christ in God" (Col. iii. 3). The "dead" of Paul were those who had fallen from the plane of true being, this higher realm of which Plato speaks, into the realm of matter and form. This is the natural condition of man in this world. There is indeed no historic fall—science has set that aside—but Paul's doctrine still stands as the fundamental presupposition of the doctrine of redemption of which the New Testament is full.

Now what is true of the doctrine of the fall is true of the orthodox system as a whole. That system in its entirety constitutes one of the most complete and impressive products of the human mind. Hebrew prophetism, Greek philosophy and Oriental mysticism furnished the materials for it. Its central feature is the story of the deliverer who is to undo the ruin of the fall. A promise was given close upon that catastrophe by God himself that a deliverer would come in his own good time, who would redeem at least some of the children of Adam, and restore them to their original condition. There was a long preparation for his coming, and a long expectation on the part of the people. Finally the long looked-for era dawned, and an angel was sent to announce the advent. Strange stars were seen in the east heralding the approach of the wondrous child, and a heavenly choir sang anthems when he was born. His birth was of course supernatural as was fitting the work he had to do, and in his boyhood he showed marvelous wisdom. First of all he set himself to conquer the evil power of the universe for himself, to gain self-mastery and self-conquest. Then he set out in the plenitude of his strength, mighty in the kingship of his own nature, to conquer the evil of the world. No need to linger over the well-known story; it is known to all. The Christ at last is put to death as a sacrifice for the sin of the race. He is not a mere martyr to his convictions. He is the propitiation for the sins of the whole world. And this is witnessed by his resurrection from the dead, and by his ascent to heaven and taking his place at the right hand of God. And the stupendous drama was to close by his second advent to earth at the end of the age, when he would reign over a renovated earth in a perfect kingdom of God.

Now it is easy to marshal proofs to show that this story is not historical. Of course it is not. The critic has no difficulty in showing that all the supernatural features of the story are hundreds even thousands of years older than our era, which proves that we are not dealing with literal facts, but are in the presence of a story which the world has repeated to itself over and over again. It differs from many other myths in being "circumstantial enough and sober enough in tone to pass for an account of facts, and yet loaded with enough miracle, poetry, and submerged wisdom to take the place of a moral philosophy and present what seemed at the time an adequate ideal to the heart" (Professor Santayana). What heart can remain unmoved when it contemplates the millions that have found refuge in it, guidance in a perplexing world, strength and courage in days of weakness, solace in affliction and comfort in death. And it is true, though not historically true. Religious truth if it is to be taught at all must be taught by means of symbols. The history of these symbols is the history of the soul of man. The enlightenment which has made the discovery that the system is not historically true is not half enlightened enough. Indeed it takes little enlightenment to see that it is incompatible with the facts of science and history; it takes more enlightenment to grasp the moral facts of man's life from which it sprang, its ideal or true meaning, and its proper function in the world. It brings us face to face with the mystery and pathos of the life of man on earth. Far better than to point out the incompatibility of the scheme with the world as science and history disclose it, is to honor the unconscious piety that produced it, and to understand the deep religious needs it embodies and meets.

All this should warn us not to be too hasty in throwing

aside the stories of the virgin birth and physical resurrection, because they are not historical. One of the reasons why orthodox Christianity has been under the shadow within recent years and why liberal Christianity has flourished is the fact that the stories of the supernatural birth and miraculous resurrection have been discredited. They have been discovered to be legends or myths; and the effect of that discovery has been the reducing of Christianity from the religion of redemption to an ethical system. The doctrines of incarnation and atonement have been supposed to rest upon these stories, and when the foundation is taken away the building falls. But if Paul's doctrine of the fall still stands in spite of the triumph of the doctrine of evolution, his doctrine of redemption may also stand in spite of the fact that no educated person can any longer believe in the virgin birth and physical resurrection as historical facts. All the liberal critics are agreed that these two stories are not historical. If nothing can be vital in Christianity but what is left historical by the critics, then we are indeed in a parlous state, for it is very little they do leave us as historical. All that has made Christianity the religion of redemption they have surrendered. Is nothing real but what is historical? There is a type of mind that seems unable to understand that any story can be true, or of any value to the world, unless it be literally and historically true. But surely this is a shallow way of thinking which does not understand the working of the human mind, and does not look deeply into the nature of the myth which has enshrined some of the greatest truths of the world. The great master of myth was Plato, and when he wished to deal with the transcendent realities of life and religion—God, the soul, the good—transcendent because they cannot be realized adequately in experience, overleaping as they do, the limits of all possible experience —he used the myth, and not the language and method of science. That is because these truths are ideals of the reason and not of the logical understanding (to use the language of Kant) and cannot find their satisfaction in the details of actual life, as the latter can, but which are really aspirations and efforts after the ultimate reality. Myth, therefore, is the only method in which religion can teach its great truths, for the reason that these truths can never find either scientific proof or full embodiment. Man must however live and act as though they had both, otherwise his life and action have no basis and no stimulus. In reality, the ideas of the reason,—the concept of the soul, of God, of a God who is wise and good, of a universe that is intelligible,—never can have any concrete embodiment; it is the function of the myth to represent them as having concrete form. These representations are not true in the sense that the light they give

> "Never was on sea or land,"

yet they are

> "The fountain light of all our day,
> A master light of all our seeing."

They'

> "Uphold us, cherish, and have power to make
> Our noisy years seem moments in the being
> Of the eternal silence."

They are

> "truths that wake
> To perish never...."

Let me use the words of the accomplished author of *The Myths of Plato,* Prof. J. A. Stewart, to make my meaning clear: "When a man asks himself, as he must, for the reason of the hope in which he struggles on in the ways prescribed by his faculties, he is fain to answer, 'Because I am an immortal soul, created with these faculties by a wise and good God, under whose government I live in a universe which is his finished work.' This answer, according to Plato, as I read him, is the natural and legitimate expression of the 'sweet hope which guides the wayward thought of mortal men,' and the expression reacts on—gives strength and steadiness to—that which it expresses. It is a 'true answer' in the sense that man's life would come to naught if he did not act and think as if it were true. But soul, cosmos as completed system of the good, and God are not particular objects presented, along with other particular objects, in sensible experience. This the scientific understanding fails to grasp. When it tries to deal with them,—and it is ready enough to make the venture—it must needs envisage them, *more suo,* as though they were particular objects which could be brought under its categories in sensible experience. Then the question arises, Where are they? And the answer comes sooner or later, They are nowhere to be found. Thus science 'chills the sweet hope in which man lives,' by bringing the natural expression into discredit" (*Myths of Plato,* pp. 49-50). Because the ideas of reason which are the presuppositions of religion are aims, aspirations, ideals, and never can be embodied adequately in historical experience, Professor Santayana is justified in thus expressing himself: "Religious doctrines would do well to withdraw their pretension to be dealing with matters of fact. That pretension is not only the source of the conflicts of religion with science and of the vain and bitter conflicts of sects; it is also the cause of the impurity and incoherence of religion in the soul, when it seeks its sanctions in the sphere of reality, and forgets that its proper function is to express the ideal. For the dignity of religion, like that of poetry and of every moral ideal, lies precisely in its ideal adequacy, in its fit rendering of the meanings and values of life, in its anticipation of perfection; so that the excellence of religion is due to an idealization of experience which, while making religion noble if treated as poetry, makes it necessarily false if treated as science. Its function is rather to draw from reality materials for an image of that ideal to which reality ought to conform, and to make us citizens, by anticipation, in the world we crave." (*Poetry and Religion*, pp. 5-6.) What is vital in Christianity, just because it is the religion of redemption, is not found in any historical facts. It is transcendent, that is to say, it overleaps the limits of all possible experience, and can find adequate expression only by means of myth and legend such as the critics tell us the stories of the virgin birth and physical resurrection are. These myths or legends, however, are not the foundation of the doctrines of incarnation and atonement which constitute the essence of the faith; they are, on the contrary, their product, and they can and will live when these stories are everywhere admitted to be legends or myths. To cast them away as valueless because they are myths or legends is to empty the most precious parts of the New Testament into the sea.

We have seen that the story of the fall cannot be historical. It is the symbol of a timeless fact in the history of man, taking place in every soul of the race—all the more true because not historically true. Its meaning is cosmic rather than historic. The story is not the foundation of the truth; the truth is the foundation of the story. Many other stories in other religions symbolize the same truth, but the truth is independent of them all and would stand were they all proved legends or myths. The presupposition of the Pauline doctrine of redemption, therefore, is not set aside with the discovery that there never was a historic Adam. We cannot tell whether Paul attached strict historicity to the Genesis story, but one thing is clear, such historicity is not necessary to the interpretation he gave it. By "Adam" Paul meant the man of flesh as distinguished from the man of spirit whom he symbolized by "Christ." The question of the historicity of either Adam or Christ is a comparatively unimportant one; what is important is that he regarded both as factors in a cosmic process of development. Paul's great interest, all admit, was not the historic Jesus, but the heavenly Christ. He regarded the career of the historic Jesus as a mere episode in a life that was cosmic or universal, lived on a plane above the historical. The "Jesus Christ" of Paul has little resemblance to the partly historicized figure of the synoptic Gospels. He is a mystic being who was revealed within the soul of the apostle and who dwelt there as an abiding presence. He was a being who could be formed within the soul of the members of the church or community. It is difficult to believe that the churches or communities to whom Paul preached his view of a spiritual Christ revealed to him by his own ecstatic experiences and visions were derived from the church of Jerusalem of which Peter and James and John were the founders, and which were organized around the story of an historic Jesus. Paul was at open variance with these apostles and spoke of them as "pillar apostles" not in a very complimentary way. In the letters of Paul we are introduced to communities or churches entirely different from those which took the synoptic Gospels as their inspiration and guides. Paul does not follow the synoptic tradition. He follows a Christ of his own and speaks of his own gospel. To Paul the views of the "pillar apostles" seemed materialistic.

It is difficult to believe that there were any such record of the life and teaching of Jesus in existence as the synoptic Gospels contain in the possession of the church at Jerusalem; for with an authority such a record would imply, how could Paul have had any chance of successfully withstanding the "pillar apostles," or of persuading the communities or churches formed by them to leave them and follow him? Paul's Epistles bear witness to churches or communities which had been long in existence when he visited them. He has no affinity with churches or communities that were based upon the tradition of a historical Jesus such as we have in the synoptic Gospels; but he has a very close affinity with those other churches or communities which believed in a mystic Christ, and whose technical terms were all derived from the Gnosticism which recent research has shown to be pre-Christian. Paul was not converted to a belief in a historical Jesus; he was changed from being an official persecutor of the messianic sects to a preacher of a mystic Christ or spiritual messiahship, which he did not derive from man. The Christ he preached was born of his own immediate experience and revelations. He did not go through the cities of the Mediterranean, Corinth, Ephesus, Colosse, and the province of Galatia, proclaiming that a great teacher had appeared in Palestine, and quoting from his teachings. His Epistles being witness, Paul lived in a different world from the Evangelists, and dealt with different subjects. The "Jesus Christ" with whom Paul deals in his Epistles is one who never did anything, never wrought a miracle, never performed a deed of mercy, and never uttered a word of teaching, but simply died and rose from the dead. That is to say, the Christ of the Pauline letters is not the Jesus of the Gospel story. The incidents of the Gospels are not the mental and spiritual background of his words and phrases, and give no clue to his meaning. What emerges clear as daylight from Paul's Epistles is that the churches or communities he established as well as those he found already established when going on his missionary journeys, were not communities organized around a historical Jesus; they were of a mystic nature resembling the Therapeutae of whom Philo speaks, or the Essenes, people devoted to the cultivation of the life of contemplation and of union with

God. It is not an unlikely assumption that it was with one of those communities that Paul spent his time after his conversion, and that it was the light and inspiration he received from that source which emboldened him to be the apostle he afterwards became. What we have in the synoptic Gospels is, in parts, teaching inferior, that is, lower in spiritual tone and insight than that current in the mystic sects to which Paul belonged and ministered. They believed in a Saviour who was a heavenly being; belief in the Logos was a fundamental part of their creed.

Paul's real background is the teachers of Greece and not the synoptic Gospels—the teachers of Greece as modified by the wisdom of Egypt. No one can read his Epistles with any degree of attention without seeing that Paul was a Jew who was greatly influenced by the mystical sects that had come in like a flood from the east and spread all over the Greco-Roman world in the first century of our era and before, and had profoundly modified the philosophy that had come from Greece. This amalgam, made up of Hellenism, Judaism, and Oriental mysticism, has received the name of Gnosticism. It was a very wide-spread tendency in the centuries preceding the beginning of our era, and assumed many different forms, so much so that it is difficult sometimes to see the common resemblance. Paul's language which was not derived from the synoptic tradition bears a close resemblance to the terms used in these various Gnostic sects scattered all over the East. Their teachings were termed "mysteries," and Paul speaks of "the mystery which was hid from ages and generations being now made manifest to the saints," of "the wisdom of God in a mystery, even the hidden mystery which God ordained before the world unto our glory." Instead of the letters of Paul being moulded upon the Gospel story, containing quotation and reference to miracle and parable and precept, they are saturated with the language of Gnosticism, and repeat on almost every page the terms in common use in the mystery sects of his time. Especially is there a close resemblance between Paul's language and that of the literature of Hermes the Thrice Greatest, which is the key to the wisdom of Egypt, and which takes us back to the best in the mystery traditions of antiquity. The theme of all the treatises of that body of literature is the man-doctrine, the man-mystery, or man-myth. Briefly put it is the story of the descent of man from his heavenly home, and then his return to that state of glory after having mastered the powers of evil. There is nothing so ancient as this man-doctrine; it is lost in the mists of antiquity, and in the centuries immediately preceding our era it was a well developed doctrine in the whole Greco-Roman world. It was the jealously guarded secret of every mystery institution of the ancient world. It is a great hindrance to the understanding of the New Testament, especially the Epistles of Paul, that this man-doctrine of the ancient mystery institutions of antiquity as it is taught in the Sermons of the Thrice Greatest Hermes, is so little known. Perhaps this is not to be wondered at when we remember how recent is the discovery of the writings, and what a prejudice has been raised against them on account of their resemblance to the New Testament, as though they were worthless imitations of it. Professor Flinders Petrie in his *Personal Religion in Egypt Before Christianity* rightly says that as the treatises of Thrice Greatest Hermes are clearly earlier than the apostolic age, they are among the most needful for the understanding of the modes of thought of that time. The apostle Paul cannot be understood without an acquaintance with the sermons of Thrice Greatest Hermes. Here are found the terms which the apostle is constantly using. Paul has been a writer difficult to understand because he does not define his terms. But why should he define them when he was using the terms of his predecessors and contemporaries well known to those to whom he wrote? In his Epistles we have echoes of what was taught in Egypt and Greece two or three hundred years before, which has come down to us in this body of literature. The apostle and the author of these treatises, are evidently, as Charlotte E. Woods rightly says in *The Gospel of Righteousness,* treating of the same deep mysteries and are anxious to make known the same spiritual truths.

When two writers use the same terms it is evident that they are dealing with the same theme. And the theme of both is the spiritual story of man—the eternal process or progress of man toward divinity. This is redemption; and redemption, no one needs to be told, is the theme of Paul. The goal of this process or progress is Christhood. In the literature of Hermes is set forth with Oriental imagery and symbol which often obscure by their abundance and splendor, the story of man which in the New Testament is the story of the Christ. It was the claim of the second century Gnostics that Christianity was none other than the consummation of the inner doctrine of the mystery institutions of all the nations. The end of them all was the revelation of the mystery of man which was hid, as Paul says, from ages and generations. And it is the same story that is taught in the Gospel records by means of a symbolic life. In the history and person of Christ we are to see a living prophetic picture of the final development of man. In Christ every man, therefore, possesses both the guarantee and the representation of his own destined perfection. In the Gospel story we are to see the birth of this inner man or Christ, his growth, his conflict with the lower nature, his gradual mastery of all lower forces, and his final triumph and glorification.

There was not, therefore, such a sudden break as has been supposed between paganism and Christianity; the latter did not come upon the world suddenly and miraculously like the rise of the sun at midnight; the two blended into each other with almost insensible gradations. There was, in this sense, a Christianity before Jesus, and all the characteristic ideas and terms such as we find in the pages of Paul and John,—Logos, Saviour, only-begotten, second birth, resurrection, mystery, etc., were in use in the pre-Christian Hermetic literature of Egypt. Plato taught that there were original patterns or models of all natural objects, existing in the divine mind prior to their creation. Especially was there an archetypal man. In one of the Hermetic books we have this text: "All-Father Mind, being life and light, did bring forth man co-equal to himself" (*Corpus Hermeticum,* I, li). This is essentially Platonic, for this "man" is not any actual man, but the archetypal or prototypal man, "the spiritual prototype of humanity and of every individual man." This archetypal man is very real though unhistorical. The idea or plan or model of an organ, a house, a steam-engine, is prior to its existence as a material fact, and is the real cause of its existence as a material fact. As there is an ideal leaf according to which the actual leaf is formed, so there is an ideal or archetypal man according to which every man is formed. Physical science emphasizes this fact in its doctrine of conformity to type. It is the ideal of the animal or plant that determines the direction of the particles that make and build up the animal or plant. The potential or archetypal oak within the acorn causes the entire growth of the tree. This enables us to understand the immanence of Christ as Paul conceived of it. Philo wrote with no knowledge of Christianity, "The first Son of God is the divine image or model of all else, the original species, the archetypal idea, the first measure of the universe, the heavenly man." The Kabbala teaches that the first account of the creation in Genesis refers, not to the creation of the actual world, but to the perfect ideal world and to the ideal man. It was in the atmosphere of this ancient teaching that Paul lived. This is the key to his Christology. It is the missing link between him and his spiritual progenitors. Christ is the image and likeness of God, the divine pattern or archetype after which man's nature was fashioned. It is God's life in man, so that God not only dwells in man, but is the very basis and ideal of his being. When Paul said, "Other foundation can no man lay than that is laid which is Jesus Christ," he was not pointing to a historical Jesus, but to Christ, the archetypal man, who evolves within man.

The first great process in the manifestation of the divine life is that of involution. Spirit, the active principle, descends into matter, the receptive principle, and endows it with the qualities which we observe it is now possessed of. This endowment or descent is symbolized in the New Testament by the death of Christ. After his death his body according to the ancient symbolism is dismembered or scattered. "Now," says Paul, "ye are the body of Christ, and members in particular," which means that Christ dies and comes to life again in the souls of men. The fullest truth about human life is that it is the evolution of the archetypal man. The deepest mystery of creation is that it is the sacrifice of God himself, the Calvary of Deity. The cross did not mean to Paul merely or solely the death by crucifixion of the man Jesus. In the ancient world there was no symbol so wide spread as the symbol of the cross. It is obvious that it could not mean the death of Jesus which was a local happening; it meant the sacrifice of God in creation, the world-passion, Deity laying down his life in the universe of matter and form. And to Paul the cross was the symbol of this heart-moving conception. It was the power of God and the wisdom of God. The interpretation of Paul's determination not to know anything among men save Jesus Christ and him crucified which makes him mean only that he would know nothing but the historical fact of the death of Jesus upon the cross of Golgotha eviscerates his message of all real content. The cross is the ground plan of the universe. To know the cross from this higher standpoint is to know all there is to know; there is nothing beyond it. This was the mystery hid from ages and generations but now made manifest. The divine sufferer was not a Jewish teacher merely, who by his revolutionary opinions proclaimed in the teeth of the authorities of his country and time had brought upon himself the death penalty. All this was but the symbol of a profound mystery which opened up the heart of Deity himself to the gaze of the world. The divine sufferer was God himself who in creating the universe sacrificed himself for it. The cross, therefore, represents the greatest of all sacrifices, not something that happened once, and once for all, but something that is eternal and timeless, the sacrifice of God in his own creation that could not be unless he poured his own life into it, and restricted himself within its forms and substance. Great is the mystery of the cross, unthinkable in its magnitude is this sacrifice, for it means nothing less than the identification of the infinite with the finite in its lowest forms. Here is the profoundest mystery open to human contemplation, to speak or think of which is possible only in forms of symbol and parable. The literal truth is too vast, too mysterious, too sublime to be made known to human comprehension. It is the mystery before which we are told the angels veil their faces; and to gain a single glimpse into it one may well surrender all other knowledge and determine, as Paul did, to know nothing else. Creation is nothing other than God's primal and continual self-revelation; it is the great Father coming down and voluntarily incarnating himself for us and for our salvation. The cross of Jesus is the parable of this infinitely larger truth. It testifies to the perpetual sacrifice of Deity himself within his own universe. It is the Lamb slain from the foundation of the world, that is to say, prior to human history, the emblem of divine body and blood voluntarily sacrificed in outward physical nature and entombed deep in the lower consciousness of man destined one day to rise from the dead in power and great glory.

K. C. ANDERSON.

DUNDEE, SCOTLAND.

NEWTON'S HYPOTHESES OF ETHER AND OF GRAVITATION FROM 1672 TO 1679.

IN preceding articles we have considered at some length the nature and growth of Newton's conception of mass. We have now to trace the fortunes of Newton's views on ether and on the connected question as to whether or no gravitation is an essential property of matter. Writers on mechanics have often unduly neglected the theories of the ether given in Newton's optical papers, and writers on optics have often overlooked the mechanical significance —which was continually emphasized by Newton himself —of theories of the ether. Many of the books referred to are the same as in my former articles on Newton in this magazine.

I.

The first well-known author to abandon the ancient emission theory of light was Descartes.[1] Three kinds of matter have, according to him, separated, in the course of the evolution of the universe, out of the homogeneous, boundless and continuous substance which constitutes space; and the sensation of light is caused by the transmission of pressure by the small spheres of the second kind of matter. Colors are caused by different velocities of rotation of these particles which they have in virtue of oblique pressure; the most rapid rotation giving rise to the sensa-

[1] Rosenberger, *op. cit.*, pp. 21-22; cf. E. T. Whittaker, *A History of the Theories of Aether and Electricity from the Age of Descartes to the Close of the Nineteenth Century.* Dublin and London, 1910, pp. 4-9.

tion of red, a slower one to that of yellow, and slower ones still to those of green and blue. The order of the colors was taken from the order of colors in the rainbow.

In contrast to the view of Descartes, Hooke's fundamental supposition was, according to Newton,[2] that "the parts of bodies when briskly agitated excite vibrations in the ether which are propagated every way from those bodies in straight lines, and cause a sensation of light by beating and dashing against the bottom of the eye; something after the manner that vibrations in the air cause a sensation of sound by beating against the organs of hearing." Again, to quote some later words of Newton, Hooke "changed Descartes's pressing or progressive motion of the medium to a vibrating one; the rotation of the globuli to the obliquation of the pulses, and the accelerating their rotation on the one hand, and retarding it on the other, by the quiescent medium to produce colors, to the like action of the medium on the two ends of his pulses for the same end."[3]

In fact, Hooke maintained that light is an actual motion and not, as Descartes did, a tendency to motion, and began the development of the undulatory theory. His hypothesis of colors (1667) was "that blue is an impression on the retina of an oblique and confused pulse of light, whose weakest part precedes and whose strongest follows."

Apart from these hypothetical considerations, it[4] had long been known to every writer on optics and to every practical optician that lenses with spherical surfaces do not give distinct images of objects. This indistinctness

[2] Letter to Oldenburg of July 11, 1672; Horsley's edition of Newton's *Opera*, Vol. IV, pp. 325-326. Cf. § III below.

[3] This view of Descartes's theory and of Hooke's opinions was given by Newton in his letter to Oldenburg dated December 21, 1675; *General Dict.*, Vol. VII. p. 783; *Macclesfield Correspondence*, Vol. II, p. 378. Cf. Brewster, *op. cit.*, Vol. I, pp. 88-89, and the end of § IV below. A very full account of that part of Hooke's work on physical optics which antedates Newton's first optical memoir was given by Rosenberger, *op. cit.*, pp. 35-42. Cf. also Whittaker, *op. cit.*, pp. 10-15.

[4] Brewster, *op. cit.*, Vol. I, pp. 37-39.

was believed to arise solely from their spherical figure, in consequence of which the rays which passed through the marginal or outer parts of the lens were refracted to a focus nearer the lens than those which passed through its central parts. The distance between these foci was called the "spherical aberration" of the lens, and various methods were suggested for diminishing or removing this source of imperfection. Descartes had shown that hyperbolic lenses refracted the rays of light to a single focus, and accordingly we find the early volumes of the *Philosophical Transactions* filled with schemes for grinding and polishing lenses of this form. Newton had made the same attempt, but finding that a change of form produced very little change in the indistinctness of the image, he thought that the defect of lenses, and the consequent imperfection of telescopes, might arise from some other cause than the imperfect convergence of the incident rays to a single point. This conjecture was speedily confirmed by the brilliant discovery of the different refrangibilities of the rays of light. With regard to the views of the predecessors[5] of Newton respecting the nature and origin of colors, Descartes held the opinion we have already mentioned; Grimaldi, Dechales, and others regarded them as arising from different degrees of rarefaction and condensation of light; and Gregory (1663) defined color to be the hue (*tinctura*) of igneous corpuscles emerging from radiant matter. When recounting the opinions of preceding writers, Newton alleged that in all of them the color is supposed not to be innate in light, but to be produced by the action of the bodies which reflect or refract it. This, however, said Brewster,[6] is not strictly true. Isaac Voss, in a dissertation of 1662 which Newton probably never saw, distinctly maintained that all

[5] An account of the theories of light and colors of Aristotle, Kepler, De Dominis, Marci, Descartes, Voss, Grimaldi, Hooke, Boyle, Barrow, and others was given by Rosenberger, *op. cit.*, pp. 11-45, 51-52.

[6] Cf. Rosenberger's criticism, *ibid.*, pp. 25-26.

the colors exist in light itself, or, to use another of his expressions, that all light carries its colors along with it. This conjecture cannot however be regarded as in any way anticipating the great discovery of Newton, "that the modification of light from which colors take their origin is innate in light itself, and arises neither from reflection nor refraction, nor from the qualities or any other conditions of bodies whatever, and that it cannot be destroyed or in any way changed by them."

II.

Newton, in a letter of January 18, 1672, to Oldenburg, the secretary of the Royal Society, announced that he proposed to send, for the consideration of the Royal Society, an account of the discovery which led him to concentrate his attention on the making of reflecting[7]—and not refracting—telescopes, and which was, said he, "in my judgment the oddest, if not the most considerable, detection which hath hitherto been made in the operations of nature."[8]

Newton's letter of February 6 to Oldenburg, which contained an account of his theory of light and colors, was read on February 8 and printed in the *Philosophical Transactions*[9] for February 19, both for the purpose of "having it well considered by philosophers," and for "securing the considerable notices thereof to the author against the arrogations of others." At the same time a committee, con-

[7] Newton's constructions and exhibitions of, and controversies about, his reflecting telescopes were dealt with by Brewster, *op. cit.*, Vol. I, pp. 37-53, and Rosenberger, *op. cit.*, pp. 52-59.

[8] *Isaaci Newtoni Opera quae exstant omnia*, ed. Samuel Horsley, Vol. IV, London, 1782, p. 274 (this will be referred to as *Horsley*); Thomas Birch, *The History of the Royal Society of London,*.. Vol. III, London, 1757, p. 5; Brewster, *op. cit.*, Vol. I, pp. 71-72.

[9] No. 80, February 19, 1672, pp. 3075 sqq.; *Phil. Trans., abr.*, Vol. I, pp. 134 sqq.; notice in Birch, *op. cit.*, p. 9; and Rosenberger, *op. cit.*, pp. 59-69. The letter was printed at length in *Horsley*, Vol. IV, pp. 295-308. Cf. Brewster, *op. cit.*, Vol. I, pp. 72-77; Rosenberger, *op. cit.*, pp. 59-69; Whittaker, *op. cit.*, pp. 15-16.

sisting of Seth Ward (Bishop of Salisbury), Boyle and Hooke, was appointed to peruse and consider it, and to give a report upon it to the Society.

Newton had, in the beginning of 1666, obtained a triangular prism, "to try therewith the celebrated phenomena of colors." For this purpose, "having darkened," as he expressed himself, "my chamber and made a small hole in my window-shuts to let in a convenient quantity of the sun's light, I placed my prism at his entrance, that it might be thereby refracted to the opposite wall. It was at first a very pleasing divertisement to view the vivid and intense colors produced thereby; but after a while applying myself to consider them more circumspectly, I became surprised to see them in an oblong form, which, according to the received laws of refractions, I expected should have been circular." The length of the colored spectrum was in fact about five times as great as its breadth. After more experiments, Newton found the explanation to be that ordinary white light is really a mixture of rays of every variety of color, and that the elongation of the spectrum is due to the differences in the refractive power of the glass for these different rays.

"Amidst these thoughts," said Newton,[10] "I was forced from Cambridge by the intervening plague." This was in 1666,[11] and his memoir on the subject was not presented to the Royal Society until more than five years later. In it he propounded a theory of colors directly opposed to that of Hooke. "Colors," he said,[12] "are not qualifications of light, derived from refractions or reflections of natural bodies (as is generally believed), but original and connate properties, which in divers rays are divers. Some rays are disposed to exhibit a red color and no other, some a yellow and no other, some a green and no other, and so of

[10] *Horsley,* Vol. IV, p. 300.
[11] Cf. my article in *The Monist* for April, 1914.
[12] *Horsley,* Vol. IV, pp. 301-302.

the rest. Nor are there only rays proper and particular to the more eminent colors, but even to all their intermediate gradations. To the same degree of refrangibility ever belongs the same color, and to the same color ever belongs the same degree of refrangibility...The species of color and degree of refrangibility proper to any particular sort of rays is not mutable by refraction nor by reflection from natural bodies, nor by any other cause that I could yet observe. When any one sort of rays hath been well parted from those of other kinds, it hath afterwards obstinately retained its color, notwithstanding my utmost endeavors to change it."

Not very far from the beginning of his experiments, Newton, in his own words,[13] "began to suspect whether the rays, after their trajection through the prism, did not move in curve lines, and, according to their more or less curvity, tend to divers parts of the wall. And it increased my suspicion, when I remembered that I had often seen a tennis-ball, struck with an oblique racket, describe such a curve line. For, a circular as well as a progressive motion being communicated to it by that stroke, its parts, on that side where the motions conspire, must press and beat the contiguous air more violently than on the other, and there excite a reluctancy and reaction of the air proportionably greater. And for the same reason, if the rays of light should possibly be globular bodies, and by their oblique passage out of one medium into another acquire a circulating motion; they ought to feel the greater resistance from the ambient ether on that side where the motions conspire, and thence be continually bowed to the other." But he could not observe any such "curvity."

III.

The publication of Newton's memoir gave rise to an

[13] *Horsley,* Vol. IV, pp. 297-298. Cf. Rosenberger, *op. cit.*, pp. 62-63.

acute controversy,[14] and Hooke was among the foremost of Newton's adversaries. Indeed he was the only one who seems to have had an effect on Newton's views on the ether. It seems that this unpleasant controversy had much to do with the reluctance to publish his results which Newton ever afterwards showed. Hooke viewed Newton's discoveries through the medium of his own theory, and, when he sent in his report on February 15, 1672, he was thanked "for the pains he had taken in bringing in such ingenious reflections," but it was not "thought fit to print the two papers together, lest Mr. Newton should look upon it as a disrespect in printing so sudden a refutation of a discourse of his which had met with so much applause at the Society but a few days before."

In Hooke's report[15] on Newton's communication, criticism was directed solely at the hypothetical part. He expressed his ready agreement with Newton's experiments and thought his hypothesis "very subtle and ingenious," but could not "think it to be the only hypothesis, nor so certain as mathematical demonstration." In the course of the report Hooke said: "But grant his first supposition, that light is a body and that as many colors as degrees thereof as there may be, so many sorts of bodies there may be, all which compounded together would make white, ...";[16] thus indicating that Hooke considered Newton's corpuscular hypothesis to be of some importance in Newton's doctrine of light and colors.

Newton replied to Hooke's criticism in a letter[17] addressed to Oldenburg and dated July 11, 1672. As to the supposition attributed to him by Hooke, he replied:[18] "It is

[14] Cf. Brewster, *op. cit.*, Vol. I, pp. 77-86, 89-96; Rosenberger, *op. cit.*, pp. 73-101.

[15] Birch, *op. cit.*, Vol. III, pp. 10-15; Rosenberger, *op. cit.*, pp. 73-75.

[16] Birch, *op. cit.*, Vol. III, p. 14; Rosenberger, *op. cit.*, p. 74.

[17] *Horsley*, Vol. IV, pp. 322-342; Rosenberger, *op. cit.*, pp. 75-82. Cf. Brewster, *op. cit.*, Vol. I, pp. 90-91.

[18] *Horsley*, Vol. IV, pp. 324-326.

true that from my theory I argue the corporeity of light, but I do it without any absolute positiveness, as the word *perhaps* intimates, and make it at most but a very plausible consequence of the doctrine, and not a fundamental supposition, nor so much as any part of it, which was wholly comprehended in the precedent propositions. And I wonder how Mr. Hooke could imagine that, when I had asserted the theory with the greatest rigor, I should be so forgetful as afterwards to assert the fundamental supposition itself with no more than a *perhaps*. Had I intended any such hypothesis, I should somewhere have explained it. But I knew that the properties which I declared of light were in some measure capable of being explicated not only by that, but by many other mechanical hypotheses; and therefore I chose to decline them all, and speak of light in general terms, considering it abstractedly as something or other propagated every way in straight lines from luminous bodies, without determining what that thing is; whether a confused mixture of difform qualities, or modes or bodies, or of bodies themselves, or of any virtues, powers, or beings whatsoever. And for the same reason I choose to speak of colors according to the information of [our] senses, as if they were qualities of light without us. Whereas, by that hypothesis, I must have considered them rather as modes of sensation, excited in the mind by various motions, figures, or sizes of the corpuscles of the light, making various mechanical impressions on the organs of sense, as I expressed it in that place where I spoke of the corporeity of light.

"But supposing I had propounded this hypothesis, I understand not why Mr. Hooke should so much endeavor to oppose it. For certainly it has a much greater affinity with his own hypothesis than he seems to be aware of; the vibrations of ether being as useful and necessary in this as in his own. For, assuming the rays of light to be small bodies, emitted every way from shining substances, those, when they impinge on any refracting or reflecting superficies, must as necessarily excite vibrations in the ether as stones do in water when thrown into it. And supposing these vibrations to be of several depths or thicknesses, accordingly as they are excited by the said corpuscular rays of various sizes and velocities,—of what use they will be for explicating the manner of reflection and refraction, the production of heat by the sun's beams, the emission of light from burning, putrefying, or other substances whose parts are vehemently agitated, the phenomena of thin transparent plates and bubbles and of all natural bodies, the manner of vision, and the difference of colors, as also their harmony and discord,—I shall leave to the consideration of those who may think it worth their endeavor to apply this hypothesis to the solution of phenomena.

"In the second place, I told you that Mr. Hooke's hypothesis, as to the fundamental part of it, is not against me. The fundamental supposition is that the parts of bodies, when briskly agitated, excite vibrations in the ether, which are propagated every way from those bodies in straight lines, and cause a sensation of light, by beating and dashing against the bottom of the eye, something after the manner that vibrations in the air cause a sensation of sound by beating against the organs of hearing. Now the most free and natural application of this hypothesis to the solution of phenomena I take to be this: that the agitated parts of bodies, according to their several sizes, figures, and motions, excite vibrations in the ether of various depths or bignesses, and which, being promiscuously propagated through that medium to our eyes, effect in us a sensation of light of a white color: but if by any means those of unequal bignesses be separated from one another, the largest, a sensation of red color; the least, or shortest, of a deep violet; and the intermediate ones; of intermediate colors."

In this reply to Hooke, Newton pointed out the character of experimental science, the duties of scientific men, and the unquestionableness of experiment and observation. But it is not necessary to quote this part of the reply. I have quoted at length the parts referring to the ether and to the connected question of hypotheses as to the nature of light, and in what follows I shall continue to do this for Newton's other memoirs. The connection of the ether with the principle of gravitation will gradually appear; at present the most noticeable thing is that in 1672 Newton granted as a matter of course the existence of an ether.

"It may be," said Rosenberger,[19] "that Newton, in his first memoir only adopted the emission-theory of light because it was the simplest and most convenient, and did not make a further study of other theories. But before his reply to Hooke's report, he certainly examined the undulatory hypothesis very carefully, and the supporters of this hypothesis were greatly indebted to him, for without question he was the first to show how it was possible to arrive, starting from the undulatory hypothesis, at a definition of colors and at an explanation of the dispersion of light on refraction."

IV.

At the end[20] of a letter written by Newton to Oldenburg on November 13, 1675,[21] Newton wrote: "I had some thoughts of writing a further discourse about colors to be read at one of your assemblies; but find it yet against the grain to put pen to paper any more on that subject. But, however, I have one discourse by me on that subject, writ-

[19] *Op. cit.*, p. 82.

[20] *Horsley*, Vol. IV, p. 355; Brewster, *op. cit.*, Vol. I, p. 132; Rosenberger, *op. cit.*, p. 101.

[21] The date was not given by Horsley.

ten when I sent my first letters to you about colors, and of which I then gave you notice. This you may command, when you think it will be convenient, if the custom of reading weekly discourses still continue."

Newton again wrote to Oldenburg on November 30, 1675,[22] that he intended to have sent the papers that week, but that upon reviewing them it came into his mind to write another "little scribble" to accompany them. This "little scribble" was his "hypothesis" to which we shall presently refer. The whole discourse was produced in manuscript on December 9, 1675, with the title of: "A Theory of Light and Colours, containing partly an Hypothesis to explain the properties of light discoursed of by me in my former papers, partly the principal phenomena of the various colours exhibited by thin plates or bubbles, esteemed to be of a more difficult consideration, yet to depend also on the said properties of light."[23] The "scribble" in particular, was entitled "An Hypothesis explaining the Properties of light discoursed of in my several Papers," and was stated by Brewster[24] to have been contained in a letter to Oldenburg dated January 25, 1676,—a date which seems to be a mistaken one.

In the letter[25] to Oldenburg which accompanied the papers forming his "discourse," Newton wrote: "I had formerly purposed never to write any hypothesis of light and colors, fearing it might be a means to engage me in

[22] Brewster, *op. cit.*, Vol. I, p. 132; Rosenberger, *op. cit.*, pp. 101-102.

[23] This has been referred to in § IX of my paper on "The Principles of Mechanics with Newton from 1666 to 1679" in *The Monist* for April, 1914.

[24] *Op. cit.*, Vol. I, p. 390.

[25] Birch, *op. cit.*, Vol. III, pp. 247-248; Brewster, *op. cit.*, Vol. I, pp. 132-134; Rosenberger, *op. cit.*, pp. 101-102. This letter, and the "Hypothesis" introduced by it were read to the Royal Society, and the "Hypothesis" was printed in Birch, *op. cit.*, pp. 248-260, 261-269, and Brewster, *op. cit.*, Vol. I, pp. 390-409 (cf. Rosenberger, *op. cit.*, pp. 102-111), but not in Horsley's edition of Newton's works. The experimental part of the paper (Birch, *op. cit.*, pp. 272-305) was included without alteration in the first and second parts of the second book, and the first eight propositions of the third part of that book, of the *Opticks* of 1704. On the "Hypothesis" the conclusions from it which Newton drew, and the controversy with Hooke to which it gave rise, see also Brewster, *op. cit.*, Vol. I, pp. 136-145, 151-161.

vain disputes; but I hope a declared resolution to answer nothing that looks like a controversy, unless possibly at my own time upon some by-occasion, may defend me from that fear. And therefore, considering that such a hypothesis would much illustrate the papers I promised to send you, and having a little time this last week to spare. I have not scrupled to describe one, so far as I could on a sudden recollect my thoughts about it; not concerning myself whether it should be thought probable or improbable, so it do but render the paper I send you and others sent formerly more intelligible. You may see by the scratching and interlining it was done in haste; and I have not had time to get it transcribed, which makes me say I reserve a liberty of adding to it, and desire that you would return these and the other papers when you have done with them. I doubt there is too much to be read at one time, but you will soon see how to order that. At the end of the hypothesis you will see a paragraph to be inserted as is there directed. I should have added another or two, but I had not time, and such as it is I hope you will accept it."

In his reply to Hooke of July 11, 1672, Newton had stated that what he called the fundamental supposition in Hooke's hypothesis—namely, that the waves or vibrations of the ether could, like the rays of light, be propagated in straight lines without a very extravagant spreading and bending every way into the quiescent medium by which they are bounded—seemed impossible, and added: "I am mistaken if there be not both experiment and demonstration to the contrary." However, Newton at once suggested a modification of Hooke's hypothesis, so that it could better account for the phenomena, as we have seen towards the end of § III above.[26] But it is certain that Newton did not regard either this hypothesis or that of 1675 as expressing his

[26] Cf. *Phil. Trans.*, 1672, No. 88, p. 5088. Cf. also Brewster, *op. cit.*, Vol. I, pp. 135-136, 390.

own convictions, or as of having any more than an illustrative value. "Because I have observed," he said, "the heads of some great virtuosos to run much upon hypotheses, as if my discourses wanted a hypothesis to explain them by, and found that some, when I could not make them take my meaning when I spoke of the nature of light and colors abstractly, have readily apprehended it when I illustrated my discourse by a hypothesis; for this reason I have here thought fit to send you a description of the circumstances of this hypothesis, as much tending to the illustration of the papers I herewith send you." And he added that he would not assume either this or any other hypothesis; yet that he would, while describing this hypothesis, "sometimes, to avoid circumlocution, and to represent it more conveniently," speak of it as if he assumed it and propounded it to be believed. "This," he said, "I thought fit to express, that no man may confound this with my other discourses, or measure the certainty of one by the other, or think me obliged to answer objections against this script; for I desire to decline being involved in such troublesome, insignificant disputes."[27] Newton, however, confessed that he did not see how the colors of thin transparent plates could be well explained without having recourse to ethereal pulses;[28] and shortly afterwards remarked: "Were I to assume an hypothesis, it should be this [that mentioned in § III above], if propounded more generally so as not to determine what light is, further than that it is something or other capable of exciting vibrations in the ether."[29]

Newton then proceeded to describe the hypothesis. "(1) It is to be supposed therein that there is an ethereal medium, much of the same constitution with air, but far rarer, subtler, and more strongly elastic. Of the existence of this

[27] Brewster, *op. cit.*, Vol. I, pp. 136, 391-392.
[28] *Ibid.*, p. 391.
[29] Ibid.

medium the motion of a pendulum in a glass exhausted of air almost as quickly as in the open air is no inconsiderable argument. But it is not to be supposed that this medium is one uniform matter, but [that it is] composed partly of the main phlegmatic body of ether, partly of other various ethereal spirits, much after the manner that air is compounded of the phlegmatic body of air intermixed with various vapors and exhalations. For the electric and magnetic effluvia and the gravitating principle seem to argue such variety. Perhaps the whole frame of nature may be nothing but various contextures of some certain ethereal spirits or vapors, condensed as it were by precipitation, much after the manner that vapors are condensed into water, or exhalations into grosser substances, though not so easily condensable; and after condensation wrought into various forms, at first by the immediate hand of the Creator, and ever since by the power of nature, which, by virtue of the command, increase and multiply, became a complete imitator of the copy set her by the Protoplast. Thus perhaps may all things be originated from ether.

"At least the electric effluvia seem to instruct us that there is something of an ethereal nature condensed in bodies. I have sometimes laid upon a table a round piece of glass about two inches broad, set in a brass ring, so that the glass might be about one-eighth or one sixth of an inch from the table and the air between them enclosed on all sides by the ring, after the manner as if I had whelmed a little sieve upon the table. And then rubbing a pretty while the glass briskly with some rough and raking stuff, till some very little fragments of very thin paper laid on the table under the glass began to be attracted and move nimbly to and fro; after I had done rubbing the glass, the papers would continue a pretty while in various motions, sometimes leaping up to the glass and resting there a while, then leaping down and resting there, then leaping up, and perhaps down and up again, and this sometimes in lines seeming perpendicular to the table, sometimes in oblique ones; sometimes also they would leap up in one arc and down in another divers times together, without sensible resting between; sometimes skip in a bow from one part of the glass to another without touching the table, and sometimes hang by a corner and turn often about very nimbly, as if they had been carried about in the midst of a whirlwind, and be otherwise variously moved,—every paper with a divers motion. And upon sliding my finger on the upper side of the glass, though neither the glass nor the enclosed air below were moved thereby, yet would the papers as they hung under the glass receive some new motion, inclining this way or that way, accordingly as I moved my finger. Now whence all these irregular motions should spring I cannot imagine, unless from some kind of subtle matter lying condensed in the glass, and rarefied by rubbing, as water is rarefied into vapor by heat, and in that rarefaction diffused through the space round the glass to a great distance, and made to move and circulate variously, and accordingly to actuate the papers, till it returns into the glass again, and be recondensed there. And as this condensed matter by rarefaction into an ethereal wind (for by its easy penetrating and circulating through glass I esteem it ethereal) may cause these odd motions, and by condensing again may cause electrical attraction with its returning to the glass to succeed in the place of what is there continually recondensed; so may the gravitating attraction of the earth be caused by the continual condensation of some other such like ethereal spirit, not of the main body of phlegmatic ether, but of something very thinly and subtly diffused through it, perhaps of an unctuous or gummy tenacious and springy nature, and bearing much the same relation to ether which the vital aëreal spirit requisite for the conservation of flame and vital motions does to air. For if such an ethereal spirit may be condensed in fermenting or burning bodies, or otherwise coagulating in the pores of the earth and water into some kind of humid active matter for the continual uses of nature, (adhering to the sides of those pores after the manner that vapors condense on the sides of a vessel,) the vast body of the earth, which may be everywhere to the very center in perpetual working, may continually condense so much of this spirit as to cause it from above to descend with great celerity for a supply. In this descent it may bear down with it the bodies it pervades, with force proportional to the superficies of all their parts it acts upon, nature making a circulation by the slow ascent of as much matter out of the bowels of the earth in an aëreal form, which for a time constitutes the atmosphere, but being continually buoyed up by the new air, exhalations, and vapors rising underneath, at length (some part of the vapors which return in rain excepted) vanishes again into the ethereal spaces, and there perhaps in time relents and is attenuated into its first principle. For nature is a perpetual circulatory worker, generating fluids out of solids, and solids out of fluids, fixed things out of volatile, and volatile out of fixed, subtle out of gross, and gross out of subtle, some things to ascend and make the upper terrestrial juices, rivers, and the atmosphere, and by consequence others to descend for a requital to the former. And as the earth, so perhaps may the sun imbibe this spirit copiously, to conserve his shining, and keep the planets from receding further from him: and they that will may also suppose that this spirit affords or carries with it thither the solary fuel and material principle of light, and that the vast ethereal spaces between us and the stars are for a sufficient repository for this food of the sun and planets. But this of the constitution of ethereal natures by the bye.

"In the second place, it is to be supposed that the ether

is a vibrating medium like air, only the vibrations far more swift and minute; those of air made by a man's ordinary voice succeeding one another at more than half a foot or a foot distance, but those of ether at a less distance than the hundred-thousandth part of an inch. And as in air the vibrations are some larger than others, but yet all equally swift, (for in a ring of bells the sound of every tone is heard at two or three miles' distance in the same order that the bells are struck,) so I suppose the ethereal vibrations differ in bigness, but not in swiftness. Now these vibrations, besides their use in reflection and refraction, may be supposed the chief means by which the parts of fermenting or putrefying substances, fluid liquors, or melted, burning, or other hot bodies, continue in motion, are shaken asunder like a ship by waves, and dissipated into vapors, exhalations, or smoke, and light loosed or excited in those bodies, and consequently by which a body becomes a burning coal, and smoke flame; and I suppose flame is nothing but the particles of smoke turned by the access of light and heat to burning coals, little and innumerable.

"Thirdly, the air can pervade the bores of small glass pipes, but yet not so easily as if they were wider, and therefore stands at a greater degree of rarity than in the free aëreal spaces, and at so much greater a degree of rarity as the pipe is smaller, as is known by the rising of water in such pipes to a much greater height than the surface of the stagnating water into which they are dipped. So I suppose ether, though it pervades the pores of crystal, glass, water, and other natural bodies, yet it stands at a greater degree of rarity in those pores than in the free ethereal spaces, and at so much a greater degree of rarity as the pores of the body are smaller. Whence it may be that spirit of wine, for instance, though a lighter body, yet having subtler parts, and consequently smaller pores than water, is the more strongly refracting liquor. This also may be the principal cause of the cohesion of the parts of solids and fluids, of the springiness of glass and other bodies whose parts slide not one upon another in bending, and of the standing of the mercury in the Torricellian experiment, sometimes to the top of the glass, though a much greater height than twenty-nine inches. For the denser ether which surrounds these bodies must crowd and press their parts together, much after the manner that air surrounding two marbles presses them together if there be little or no air between them. Yea, and that puzzling problem *by what means the muscles are contracted and dilated to cause animal motion, may receive greater light from hence than from any other means men have hitherto been thinking on.* For if there be any power in man to condense and dilate at will the ether that pervades the muscle, that condensation or dilatation must vary the compression of the muscle made by the ambient ether, and cause it to swell or shrink, accordingly. For though common water will scarce shrink by compression and swell by relaxation, yet (so far as my observation reaches) spirit of wine and oil will; and Mr. Boyle's experiment of a tadpole shrinking very much by hard compressing the water in which it swam, is an argument that animal juices do the same: and as for their various pression by the ambient ether, it is plain that that must be more or less, accordingly as there is more or less ether within to sustain and counterpoise the pressure of that without. If both ethers were equally dense, the muscle would be at liberty as if pressed by neither: if there were no ether within, the ambient would compress it with the whole force of its spring. If the ether within were twice as much dilated as that without, so as to have but half as much springiness, the ambient would have half the force of its springiness counterpoised thereby, and exercise but the other half upon the muscle; and so in all other cases the ambient compresses the muscle by the excess of the force of its springiness above that of the springiness of the included. To vary the compression of the muscle therefore, and so to swell and shrink it, there needs nothing but to change the consistence of the included ether; and a very little change may suffice, if the spring of ether be supposed very strong, as I take it to be many degrees stronger than that of air.

"Now for the changing the consistence of the ether, some may be ready to grant that the soul may have an immediate power over the whole ether in any part of the body, to swell or shrink it at will; but then how depends the muscular motion on the nerves? Others therefore may be more apt to think it done by some certain ethereal spirit included within the *dura mater,* which the soul may have power to contract or dilate at will in any muscle, and so cause it to flow thither through the nerves; but still there is a difficulty why this force of the soul upon it does not take off the power of springiness, whereby it should sustain more or less the force of the outward ether. A third supposition may be that the soul has a power to inspire any muscle with this spirit by impelling it thither through the nerves; but this too has its difficulties, for it requires a forcible intruding the spring of the ether in the muscles by pressure exerted from the parts of the brain; and it is hard to conceive how so great force can be exercised amidst so tender matter as the brain is; and besides, why does not this ethereal spirit, being subtle enough, and urged with so great force, go away through the *dura mater* and skins of the muscle, or at least so much of the other ether go out to make way for this which is crowded in? To take away these difficulties is a digression, but seeing the subject is a deserving one, I shall not stick to tell you how I think it may be done.

"First, then, I suppose there *is* such a spirit; that is,

that the animal spirits are neither like the liquor, vapor, or gas, or spirits of wine; but of an ethereal nature, subtle enough to pervade the animal juices as freely as the electric, or perhaps magnetic, effluvia do glass. And to know how the coats of the brain, nerves, and muscles, may become a convenient vessel to hold so subtle a spirit, you may consider how liquors and spirits are disposed to pervade, or not pervade, things on other accounts than their subtlety; water and oil pervade wood and stone, which quicksilver does not; and quicksilver, metals, which water and oil do not; water and acid spirits pervade salts, which oil and spirit of wine to not; and oil and spirit of wine pervade sulphur, which water and acid spirits do not; so some fluids, (as oil and water,) though their parts are in freedom enough to mix with one another, yet by some secret principle of *unsociableness* they keep asunder; and some that are *sociable* may become *unsociable* by adding a third thing to one of them, as water to spirit of wine by dissolving salt of tartar in it. The like *unsociableness* may be in ethereal natures, as perhaps between the ethers in the vortices of the sun and planets; and the reason why air stands rarer in the bores of small glass pipes, and ether in the pores of bodies may be, not want of subtlety, but *sociableness*; and on this ground, if the ethereal vital spirit in a man be very *sociable* to the marrow and juices, and *unsociable* to the coats of the brain, nerves, and muscles, or to any thing lodged in the pores of those coats, it may be contained thereby, notwithstanding its subtlety; especially if we suppose no great violence done to it to squeeze it out, and that it may not be altogether so subtle as the main body of ether, though subtle enough to pervade readily the animal juices, and that as any of it is spent, it is continually supplied by new spirit from the heart.

"In the next place, for knowing how this spirit may be used for animal motion, you may consider how some things unsociable are made sociable by the mediation of a third. Water, which will not dissolve copper, will do it if the copper be melted with sulphur. *Aquafortis,* which will not pervade gold, will do it by addition of a little sal-ammoniac or spirit of salt. Lead will not mix in melting with copper; but if a little tin, or antimony, be added, they mix readily, and part again of their own accord, if the antimony be wasted by throwing saltpetre, or otherwise. And so lead melted with silver quickly pervades and liquefies the silver in a much less heat than is required to melt the silver alone; but if they be kept in the test till that little substance that reconciled them be wasted or altered, they part again of their own accord. And in like manner the ethereal animal spirit in a man may be a mediator between the common ether and the muscular juices to make them mix more freely, and so by sending a little of this spirit into any muscle, though so little as to cause no sensible tension of the muscle by its own force, yet by rendering the juices more sociable to the common external ether, it may cause that ether to pervade the muscle of its own accord in a moment more freely and more copiously than it would otherwise do, and to recede again as freely, so soon as this mediator of sociableness is retracted; whence, according to what I said above, will proceed the swelling or shrinking of the muscle, and consequently the animal motion depending thereon.

"Thus may therefore the soul, by determining this ethereal animal spirit or wind into this or that nerve, perhaps with as much ease as air is moved in open spaces, cause all the motions we see in animals; for the making which motions strong, it is not necessary that we should suppose the ether within the muscle very much condensed, or rarefied, by this means, but only that its spring is so very great that a little alteration of its density shall cause a great alteration in the pressure. And what is said of muscular motion may be applied to the motion of the heart, only with this difference: that the spirit is not sent thither as into other muscles, but continually generated there by the fermentation of the juices with which its flesh is replenished, and as it is generated, let out by starts into the brain, through some convenient *ductus,* to perform those motions in other muscles by inspiration, which it did in the heart by its generation. For I see not why the ferment in the heart may not raise as subtle a spirit out of its juices, to cause those motions, as rubbing does out of a glass to cause electric attraction, or burning out of fuel to penetrate glass, as Mr. Boyle has shown, and calcine by corrosion metals melted therein.[30]

"Hitherto I have been contemplating the nature of ether and ethereal substances by their effects and uses, and now I come to join therewith the consideration of light.

"In the fourth place, therefore, I suppose light is neither ether, nor its vibrating motion, but something of a different kind propagated from lucid bodies. They that will may suppose it an aggregate of various peripatetic qualities. Others may suppose it multitudes of unimaginable small and swift corpuscles of various sizes springing from shining bodies at great distances one after another, but yet without any sensible interval of time, and continually urged forward by a principle of motion, which in the beginning accelerates them, till the resistance of the ethereal medium equal the force of that principle, much after the manner that bodies let fall in water are accelerated till the resistance of the water equal the force of gravity. God, who gave animals motion beyond our understanding, is, without doubt, able to implant other principles of motion in bodies which we may understand as little. Some would readily

[30] Boyle's *Essays of the strange subtlety, etc. of effluviums, etc., together with a discovery of the perviousness of glass to ponderable parts of flame.*—Note of Newton.

grant this may be a spiritual one; yet a mechanical one might be shown, did not I think it better to pass it by.[31] But they that like not this may suppose light any other corporeal emanation, or an impulse or motion of any other medium or ethereal spirit diffused through the main body of ether, or what else they imagine proper for this purpose. To avoid dispute, and make this hypothesis general, let every man here take his fancy; only, whatever light be, I would suppose it consists of successive rays differing from one another in contingent circumstances, as bigness, force, or vigor, like as the sands on the shore, the waves of the sea, the faces of men, and all other natural things of the same kind differ, it being almost impossible for any sort of things to be found without some contingent variety. And further, I would suppose it diverse from the vibrations of the ether, because, (besides that were it those vibrations, it ought always to verge copiously in crooked lines into the dark or quiescent medium, destroying all shadows, and to comply readily with any crooked pores or passages as sounds do,) I see not how any superficies, (as the side of a glass prism on which the rays within are incident at an angle of about forty degrees,) can be totally opake. For the vibrations beating against the refracting confine of the rarer and denser ether must needs make that pliant superficies undulate, and those undulations will stir up and propagate vibrations on the other side. And further, how light, incident on very thin skins or plates of any transparent body, should for many successive thicknesses of the plate in arithmetical progression, be alternately reflected and transmitted, as I find it is, puzzles me as much. For though the arithmetical progression of those thicknesses, which reflect and transmit the rays alternately, argues that it depends upon the number of vibrations between the two superficies of the plate whether the ray shall be reflected or trans-

[31] Rosenberger (*op. cit.*, p. 106) remarked that this is the basis on which, later, gravitation was maintained to be a primitive force of matter.

mitted, yet I cannot see how the number should vary the case, be it greater or less, whole or broken, unless light be supposed something else than these vibrations. Something indeed I could fancy towards helping the two last difficulties, but nothing which I see not insufficient.

"Fifthly, it is to be supposed that light and ether mutually act upon one another, ether in refracting light, and light in warming ether, and that the densest ether acts most strongly. When a ray therefore moves through ether of uneven density, I suppose it most pressed, urged, or acted upon by the medium on that side towards the denser ether, and receives a continual impulse or ply from that side to recede towards the rarer, and so is accelerated if it move that way, or retarded if the contrary. On this ground, if a ray move obliquely through such an unevenly dense medium, (that is, obliquely to those imaginary superficies which run through the equally dense parts of the medium, and may be called the refracting superficies,) it must be incurved, as it is found to be by observation in water,[32] whose lower parts were made gradually more salt, and so more dense than the upper. And this may be the ground of all refraction and reflection. For as the rarer air within a small glass pipe, and the denser without, are not distinguished by a mere mathematical superficies, but have air between them at the orifice of the pipe running through all intermediate degrees of density, so I suppose the refracting superficies of ether between unequally dense mediums to be not a mathematical one, but of some breadth, the ether therein at the orifices of the pores of the solid body being of all intermediate degrees of density between the rarer and denser ethereal mediums; and the refraction I conceive to proceed from the continual incurvation of the ray all the while it is passing the physical superficies. Now if the motion of the ray be supposed in this passage to

[32] Mr. Hooke's *Micrographia* where he speaks of the inflection of rays.—Note of Newton.

be increased or diminished in a certain proportion, according to the difference of the densities of the ethereal mediums, and the addition or detraction of the motion be reckoned in the perpendicular from the refracting superficies, as it ought to be, the sines of incidence and refraction will be proportional according to what Descartes has demonstrated."

After some further discussion of refraction and reflection on this hypothesis, and the causes of transparency, opacity, and color, the "scribble" concluded with an application of the hypothesis to the colors of thin plates, to the inflection of light, and to the colors of natural bodies.

After the reading of the first part of this discourse on December 9, Hooke[33] said that the main part of it was contained in his *Micrographia,* and that Newton had only carried what that work taught farther in some particulars. When this remark was communicated to Newton, he seems to have been greatly offended, and on December 21 he wrote a letter[34] to Oldenburg, pointing out the difference between his hypothesis and that of Hooke. Although he was "not much concerned at the liberty of Mr. Hooke's insinuation," yet he wished to "avoid the savor of having done anything unjustifiable or unhandsome" to him. He therefore separated out the part of the hypothesis that belongs to Descartes and others. This part was as follows: "That there is an ethereal medium; that light is the action of this medium; that this medium is less implicated in the parts of solid bodies, and so moves more freely in them, and transmits light more readily through them; and that after such a manner as to accelerate the rays in a certain proportion; that refraction arises from this acceleration, and has sines proportional; that light is at first uniform; that colors are some disturbance or modification of its rays

[33] Brewster, *op. cit.,* Vol. I, pp. 138-139.

[34] *Horsley,* Vol. IV, pp. 379-381; Birch, *op. cit.,* Vol. III, p. 278; Rosenberger, *op. cit.,* pp. 111-114.

by refraction or reflection; that the colors of a prism are made by means of the quiescent medium accelerating some motion of the rays on one side where red appears, and retarding it on the other side where blue appears; that there are but these two original colors or color making modifications of light, which by their various degrees, or, as Mr. Hooke calls it, dilutinga, produce all intermediate ones."

When we have put this on one side, continued Newton, we find that:

"The remainder of his hypothesis is, that he has changed Descartes's pressing or progressive motion of the medium to a vibrating one; the rotation of the globuli to the obliquation of the pulses; and the accelerating their rotation on the one hand, and retarding it on the other, by the quiescent medium, to produce colors, to the like action of the medium on the two ends of his pulses for the same end. And having thus far modified his by the Cartesian hypothesis, he has extended it farther to explicate the phenomena of thin plates; and added another explication of the colors of natural bodies fluid and solid.

"This, I think, is in short the sum of his hypothesis. And in all this, I have nothing common with him but the supposition that ether is a medium susceptible of vibrations. Of which supposition I make a very different use; he supposing it light itself; which I suppose it is not. This is as great a difference, as is between him and Descartes. But besides this, the manner of refraction and reflection, and the nature and production of colors in all cases, which take up the body of my discourse, I explain very differently from him; and even in the colors of thin transparent substances, I explain everything after a way so different from him that the experiments on which I ground my discourse destroy all he has said about them. And the two main experiments, without which the manner of the production of those colors is not to be found out, were not only unknown to him when he wrote his *Micrographia* but even last spring, as I understood in mentioning them to him. This therefore is the sum of what is common to us: that ether may vibrate. And so if he thinks fit to use that notion of colors arising from the various bignesses of pulses, without which his hypothesis will do nothing, his will borrow as much from my answer to his objections as that I send you does from his *Micrographia.*

"But it may be that I have made use of his observations. And of some I did: as that of the inflection of rays, for which I quoted him: that of opacity arising from the interstices of the parts of bodies, which I insist not on; and that of plated bodies exhibiting colors; a phenomenon for the notice of which I thank him. But he left me to find out and make such experiments about it as might inform me of the manner of the production of those colors to ground a hypothesis on: he having given no farther insight into it than this, that the color depended on some certain thickness of the plate. Though what that thickness was at every color, he confesses in his *Micrographia* he had attempted in vain to learn. And therefore seeing I was left to measure it myself, I suppose he will allow me to make use of what I took the pains to find out. And this I hope may vindicate me from what Mr. Hooke has been pleased to charge me with."[35]

The friendly letters which passed between Newton and Hooke shortly after this, and which were discovered by Brewster,[36] seem to show that both Hooke and Newton disliked controversy and held those just views on the proper attitude of one's mind to "natural philosophy" which are not very difficult to put into noble language,

[35] A paper entitled "Observations" accompanied this letter but was not printed. In it, according to Brewster (*op. cit.*, Vol. I, p. 139), Newton said that Hooke in his *Micrographia* had "delivered many very excellent things concerning the colors of thin plates and other natural objects," of which he had not scrupled to make use in so far as they were relevant to his purpose.

[36] *Op. cit.*, Vol. I, pp. 139-145.

but which are not so easy to express with such good feeling as these letters show.

After the publication of the "Hypothesis," Newton seems[37] to have conversed with Robert Boyle on the subject of its application of chemistry, and in 1679 wrote him a long letter which we must next examine.

PHILIP E. B. JOURDAIN.

CAMBRIDGE, ENGLAND.

[37] *Ibid.*, p. 145.

SOME MEDIEVAL CONCEPTIONS OF MAGIC.*

MAGIC is attracting attention to-day. Students of folk-lore and of the history of religon cannot afford to neglect it. Anthropologists have found that it colors much of the life of primitive man, and sociologists have begun to deal with it as an important social manifestation. It occupies no small part of the written remains of Assyria and Babylonia and of the Greek papyri; in fact, its traces are evident throughout the literatures of Hellas and of Rome. The middle ages too, although they have as yet received little attention from serious modern students of magic, were a time when there was a great deal of magic and no little talk about it.

It may help us in forming a satisfactory definition and theory of magic for our own use, if we note some previous definitions of it by men who actually lived in the midst of it and believed in it. In the case of the savage we apply our term "magic" to certain of his practices, but medieval men used the very same word "magic" as we, and on the whole the extant writers of the twelfth and thirteenth centuries discuss magic more fully and directly than those even of the days of the elder Pliny and Apuleius. The present article will set forth a number of discussions of magic or significant allusions thereto in books and writers of the twelfth and thirteenth centuries. Space will not permit me to give even an idea of the vast collection of

* The author has not seen proofs of this article, owing to his absence abroad.

medieval beliefs and practices which one might classify as magic. We must limit ourselves to a few authors who define magic and omit the many who illustrate the thing without designating it by that name.

THE "POLYCRATICUS" OF JOHN OF SALISBURY.

We turn first to *Polycraticus,*[1] written about 1159 by John of Salisbury, who studied and taught in various schools of western Europe, then was long employed in official church business, and finally became bishop of Chartres in 1176. The *Polycraticus* seems designed as somewhat light reading for the cultured public, and treats such "trifles" (*nugae*) as gambling, hunting, the theater and music. John confesses that the book is little more than a patchwork of others' opinions without acknowledgment of authorities; what he probably prides himself on most is the Latin style and the numerous quotations from classical and Christian authors. In short, it is a conservative work, repeating traditional attitudes in an attractive, dilletante literary form and with such rational criticism as some study of the classics may be supposed to produce when qualified by scrupulous adherence to medieval Christian dogma.

John's discussion of magic is what one might expect from these premises. He gives, except for slight changes in arrangement and wording and the introduction of a few new items of information, a stock definition prevalent among Christian writers at least since the time of Isidore of Seville. In his *Etymologies* (VIII, 9) Isidore put together from such sources as Pliny the Elder, Jerome, and Augustine an account of the history and character of the magic arts which would fill about five ordinary pages. This passage, somewhat altered by omitting poetical quotations or inserting transitional sentences, was otherwise copied

[1] Johannes de Saresberia, "Polycraticus sive De nugis curialium et vestigiis philosophorum," Migne's *Patrologia Latina*, Vol. 199.

word for word by Rabanus Maurus in his *De consanguineorum nuptiis et de magorum praestigiis falsisque divinationibus tractatus,* and by Burchard of Worms and Ive of Chartres in their respective *Decreta,* while Hinemar of Rheims in his *De Divortio Lotharii et Tetbergae* copied it with more omissions.[2] It was also in substance retained in the *Decretum* of Gratian, whose epoch-making work in canon law appeared in the twelfth century.

This stereotyped theological definition of magic regards it not as one of many superstitions or occult arts, but as a generic term covering various superstitions and occult sciences. Very sweeping are the powers attributed to magicians. "The magicians, so-called on account of the magnitude of their evil deeds, are those who by divine permission agitate the elements, strip objects of their forms, often predict the future, disturb men's minds, despatch dreams, and slay by mere force of incantation." Magic thus includes prediction of the future as well as transformation of nature and bewitching of human beings. It subdivides into *praestigia* or illusions; *maleficia* or sorcery, literally "evil deeds"; and "various species of evil *mathematica,*" a word used here in the sense of divination. Varro, "most curious of philosophers," distinguished four kinds of divination from the four elements, namely, pyromancy, aeromancy, hydromancy, and geomancy. Under these four heads, John asserts, are to be classed many subvarieties. His list, however, includes some arts which might better be put under *praestigia* or *maleficia* than under divination. He names necromancers, enchanters, *vultivoli* (sorcerers employing human effigies of wax or

[2] Migne, *Patrologia Latina,* Vol. 199, cols. 406-409; 110: 1007-1110; 140: 839ff; 161: 760ff; and 125: 716-729. Moreover, Burchard continues to follow Rabanus word for word for some ten columns after the conclusion of their mutual excerpt from Isidore, while Ivo is identical with Burchard for 15 more columns. I think that I am the first to point out the identity of these five accounts. Professor Burr, in a note to his paper on "The Literature of Witchcraft" (*American Hist. Assoc. Papers,* IV, 241, 1890) has described the accounts of Rabanus and Hinemar but without explicitly noting their close resemblance, although he characterizes Rabanus's article as "mainly compiled."

clay), *pythii* or *pythonici, imaginarii* (who try to control spirits by use of images), *specularii* (who predict by looking into polished basins, glistening swords and mirrors), interpreters of dreams, chiromancers, *arioli, aruspices,* astrologers of various sorts, and so on.

We have already heard John speak of the evil deeds of the magicians. In a subsequent discussion in the second book of the *Polycraticus,*[3] where he treats more fully and perhaps with more originality the various species of magic, his attitude continues to be one of unvarying, though not always very vehement, condemnation. He occasionally makes criminal charges against magic, such as exposing children to vampires or cutting them up and devouring them,[4] and exclaims, "What shall I say of the necromancers....except that those deserve death who try to obtain knowledge from death?"[5] He occasionally asserts that an occult art is irrational, as when he remarks that the error of chiromancy, "since it is not based on reason, need not be opposed with arguments,"[6] or when he sneers with Cicero and Augustine at divination from sneezes and "inane incantations and .... superstitious ligatures,"[7] or when he affirms that the reputed nocturnal gatherings of witches are a delusion and that "what they suffer in spirit they most erroneously and wretchedly believe to happen in the flesh."[8] But his chief reason for condemning the magic arts is the traditional Christian view, as old as Origen and Augustine, that they are due entirely to the influence of demons.* Scripture forbids them and God does not see fit to grant men such divining or transforming powers which he reserves for himself in signs and miracles. Indeed John's charges that magic is criminal and

[3] *Polycrat.,* Liber I, Prologus, and Caps. 1-23; Migne, 199: 415-475.

[4] *Polycrat.,* II, 17. [5] *Ibid.,* II, 27. [6] *Idem.* [7] *Ibid.,* II, 1.

[8] *Ibid.,* II, 17. See too the Canon, *Ut episcopi* in Burchard's *Decreta,* Lib. X, Cap. 1.

* See my article on "The Attitude of Origen and Augustine Toward Magic," in *The Monist,* January, 1908.

irrational are but corollaries of his main thesis. These arts must be evil if demons are behind them, while their incredible pretensions can be explained only by the hypothesis of demon aid.

Although John repeats a stale definition, he indicates that the magic arts are still alive. Many varieties of ancient divination he says are now defunct;[9] but books on oneiromancy are current.[10] A priest, who taught John psalms as a boy, used to dabble in magic,[11] and John even gently chides Thomas à Becket, then chancellor of England and to whom he dedicates his book, for having recently consulted both an aruspex and a chiromancer.[12] At the same time John is anxious to know what "those triflers" had to say, and it must be admitted that his condemnation of some varieties of divination is a bit perfunctory and that he dwells rather fondly upon omens from classical history and upon the interpretation of dreams.

HUGO OF SAINT VICTOR.

Hugo of Saint Victor, another clerical writer of the twelfth century, gives in his *Didascalicon* a brief description of magic which differs in form but agrees substantially with John's.[13] After the usual meagre historical account of its origin, in the course of which he twice identifies magic with *maleficia*, he says:

"Magic is not included in philosophy but is a distinct subject, false in its professions, mistress of all iniquity and malice, deceiving concerning the truth and truly doing

[9] *Ibid.*, II, 27.

[10] *Ibid.*, II, 17. Gratian seems to condemn the same book in his *Decretum*, Secunda pars, Causa XXVI, Quæst. vii. Cap. 16. Four such dream books by Daniel are to be found in the British museum, and all were printed before the close of the fifteenth century.

[11] *Polycrat.*, II, 28.

[12] *Ibid.*, II, 27; and see Ramsay, *Angevin Empire*, 119-120.

[13] Printed in Migne, Vol. 176 as "Eruditionis didascalicae libri septem," but Haureau rejects the seventh book (*Les Œuvres de Hugues de Saint-Victor*, Paris, 1886). Magic is discussed in Book VI, Ch. 15 (Migne, cols. 810-812).

harm; it seduces souls from divine religion, promotes the worship of demons, engenders corruption of morals, and impels its followers' minds to every crime and abomination."

He thus makes four points against magic: It is not a part of philosophy, in other words, it is unscientific; it is hostile to true religion; it is improper, immoral, and criminal; it is false and deceptive. These four points may be reduced to two: (1) since law, religion, and learning all condemn it, it is unsocial in every respect; and (2) it is more or less untrue and unreal. At the same time it is clear that to Hugo's mind magic is a broad field more or less coordinate with those of religion and philosophy. He subdivides it, as did John of Salisbury, into *praestigia, maleficia,* and *mathematica,* but also into *sortilegia* and *mantice.* These last two, however, refer, like *mathematica,* to arts of divination. *Sortilegia* is divination by lots; *mathematica* covers the activities of *aruspices,* augurs, and readers of horoscopes; while under *mantice* are included geomancy, hydromancy, aeromancy, pyromancy, and necromancy.

GUNDISSALINUS.

Gundissalinus, an archdeacon of Toledo who made translations from the Arabic about the middle of the twelfth century, in a classification which he borrows from Alfarabi, makes "nigromancy according to physics" the fourth of eight subdivisions of "natural science," instead of a department of magic; but admits that he as yet has no detailed acquaintance with it.[14] Yet he has given us a hint of the influence that the transmission of Arabian culture is likely to have upon the attitude toward magic in the Christian West, and in the succeeding century we note a considerable change.

[14] Gundissalinus, *De divisione philosophiae* (ed. by Ludwig Baur, Münster, 1903), pp. 20 and 38.

THOMAS AQUINAS.

In the thirteenth century Thomas Aquinas, who makes a number of allusions to magic in the course of his works,[15] adheres to the essential features of the theological definition, condemning magic as evil and as the work of demons.[16] In the case of the three *magi* of the Gospel story, however, he explains that, while in common speech *magi* are called enchanters (*incantatores*), in the Persian language the word designates philosophers and sages.[17]

Aquinas carefully distinguishes magic from miracle.[18] A miracle is contrary to the order of all created nature and can be performed by God alone. Many things that seem to us marvelous or occult are not, strictly speaking, miraculous. Such are the occult virtues of physical bodies "for which a reason cannot be assigned by man."[19] Such are the marvels worked in our lower world by the influence of the consellations. Even more exceeding human comprehension are the doings of demons, who, Aquinas is convinced, can not only deceive the senses and affect the human imagination but also truly transform bodies. Yet even their feats are not true miracles in violation of natural order; they simply add to the marvelous virtues of physical objects and the potent influences of the stars something of their own peculiar powers. After all, their feats can be explained, they operate by means of art; God alone is a cause absolutely hidden from every man.

As for magicians, in their feats they make use of herbs and other physical bodies; of words, usually in the form of "invocations, supplications, and adjurations"; they also

[15] I have used the complete edition of Aquinas's works in 34 volumes, edited by Fretté and P. Maré, Paris, 1871-1880.

[16] *De potentia,* VI, 10; *Contra Gentiles,* III, 104-106; *Quodlibet,* IV, 16 Aquinas makes considerable use of Porphyry's *Letter to Anebo.*

[17] Commentary on Matthew, Cap. 2.

[18] *Summa,* Prima pars, Quaest. 110, Art. 4 and Quaest. 111, Art. 3; *Contra Gentiles,* III, 101-103; *De potentia,* VI, 5; *Sententiae,* II, Dist. 7, Quaest. 2-3

[19] *Summa,* Secundae secunda, Quaest. 96, Art. 2.

employ figures and characters, sacrifices and prostrations, images and rites, carefully observed times, constellations, and other astrological considerations.[20] As a result hidden treasure is found, the future is revealed, closed doors open, men become invisible, inanimate bodies move and speak, apparitions of rational beings are summoned and answer questions. In such feats of magic Thomas firmly believes, but he will not admit that the magician and his materials and procedure are a sufficient cause. Demons really perform the magic. Words, figures, spells are mere signs to them; the poor magician is their dupe. It looks, Thomas admits, as if spirits came only when invoked, and as if they often came unwillingly, and sometimes performed at the magician's bidding good deeds which must be very distasteful to them as evil beings. But in all this they are simply deceiving mankind. "It is not true then that the magic arts are sciences, but rather that they are certain fallacies of the demons."[21]

Aquinas further charges that the practitioners of magic are generally criminals, perpetrating illicit deeds, adulteries, thefts, and homicides; and that at best magic does not aid man in science or virtue but in trivial matters like the discovery of stolen goods. In discussing the "motory art," which professes to acquire knowledge by fasting, prayers to God, figures, and strange words, he declares that demons cannot illuminate the intellect, although they may express in words some smattering of the sciences.[22]

But in thus denying that the magic arts are sciences, Aquinas indicates that many thought them so, and that magicians believed themselves able by personal endowments, by subtle use of occult natural properties, by rites and ceremonies, and by the art of astrology, either to

[20] *Contra Gentiles,* III, 101-105; *De potentia,* VI, 10; *Summa,* Prima pars, Quaest. 115, Art. 5.

[21] *Quodlibet,* IV, 16.

[22] *Summa,* Secundae secunda, Quaest. 96, Art. 1.

work wonders directly and immediately or to coerce demons to work wonders for them. He thus gives us a glimpse of a different conception of magic from the old theological one.

Moreover, his own conception is scarcely that of John and Hugo. For one thing, he does not explicitly subordinate as many arts to magic as they do. Superstition is perhaps more in favor with him as a generic term than magic. He defines superstition as "a vice opposed to religion by its excess, not that it does more toward a divine cult than true religion, but that it introduces a divine cult either to what it ought not or in a way that it ought not."[23] But the chief difference between Aquinas and John and Hugo is that Aquinas justifies as scientific and moral matters which they classed under magic, and which would to-day be regarded as unscientific. He discusses the casting of lots, various forms of divination, "the occult works of nature," and the art of astrology in a manner not entirely hostile to their respective pretensions.[24] Thus while still holding that most arts of divination are the work of evil spirits, he believes that some kinds of divination have a natural basis and are not magic. He believes that bodies can be transformed by the occult virtues of natural things as well as by demons in magic. He recognizes much of astrology as a science, not as magic, although rejecting the extreme pretensions of astrologers. But into his interesting opinions on such points we have no time to go further here.

ALBERTUS MAGNUS.

Albertus Magnus was a contemporary of Aquinas and, like him, a great theologian and commentator upon Aris-

[23] *Ibid.*, Quaest. 92.

[24] *Summa,* Secundae secunda, Quaest. 95, Arts. 5-7; and the two brief treatises, *De sortibus* and *De occultis operibus, naturae.* His opinions concerning astrology are scattered through a dozen works.

totle. In his *Summa* and *Sententiae*, both theological works,[25] Albert, like Aquinas, more or less adheres to the traditional Christian attitude toward magic. He affirms that to employ "magic virtues" is evil and apostasy from the faith, whether one openly resorts to "invocations, conjurations, sacrifices, suffumigations, and adorations" or to some simpler and apparently innocent operation which none the less requires demon aid for its performance. Even of "mathematical virtues" (i. e., of astrological forces) one must beware, especially "in images, rings, mirrors, and characters," lest the practice of idolatry be introduced. Like Aquinas, he believes in the potency of magic. Though in one phase of magic, *praestigia* or illusions, things are made to appear to exist which have no reality, magic can also actually transform objects.

Again, like Aquinas, Albert insists that the feats of magic do not compare with miracles. They do not even happen as instantaneously, although they occur much more rapidly than the ordinary processes of nature. But except for this difference in speed they can usually be explained as the product of natural forces, and by the fact that demons are aided in their operations by the influence of the stars. To change rods into snakes, for instance, as Pharaoh's magicians did, is merely hastening the process by which worms generate in putrefying trees. Indeed, Albert is inclined to believe that the demons "produce no permanent substantial form that would not easily be produced by putrefaction." Even the magic power of fascinating human beings is, after all, only analogous to that of the sapphire to cure ulcers and of the emerald to restrain sexual passion. Thus even in his theological writings Albert attributes magic more to natural forces and to the stars, and less to demons than Aquinas did, or perhaps

[25] *Summa*, Secunda pars, Quaest. 30; *Sententiae*, II, Dist. 7 (Albertus Magnus, *Opera omnia*, ed. Borgnet, Paris, 1890-1899, 38 vols.)

we should say that he more closely connects the demons with forces of nature.

Moreover, a much more favorable opinion of magic may be found in Albert's biblical commentaries in his explanation of the *magi* who came to Bethlehem. Now he asserts that "the *magi* are not *malefici* as some wrongly think," and that they also differ from *mathematici,* enchanters, necromancers, *arioli, aruspices,* and diviners. Etymologically the *magus* is a great man (*magnus*), "who, having knowledge of all necessities and inferring from the effects of nature, sometimes predicts and produces the marvels of nature....And this is laudable."[26] Again in his commentary on Daniel he quotes Jerome's description of the *magi* as "masters who philosophize about the universe; moreover, *magi* are more particularly called astronomers who search the future in the stars."[27] Thus we have magic almost identified with astrology and with natural science, and distinguished from a number of occult arts which the traditional definition identified with it.

In Albert's scientific writings we find yet a third conception of magic suggested by a number of scattered passages in which he refers to magic as if it were a distinct and definite branch of knowledge in his day, of which, though he himself does not treat, he does not seem to disapprove. In one place he refers to writings by Avicenna on magic and alchemy;[28] in other passages he mentions magic together with astronomy and necromancy. The "prodigious and marvelous" power of stones and of images and seals in stones, he twice assures us, cannot be really understood without a knowledge of "these three sciences."[29] He therefore will not discuss the subject in a treatise on minerals as fully as he might, "since those

[26] In Evang. Matth., II, 1. It is interesting to note that to-day the *Catholic Encyclopedia* still insists concerning the three wise men, "Neither were they magicians: the good meaning of μάγοι though found nowhere else in the Bible is demanded by the context of the second chapter of St. Matthew."

[27] I, 20. [28] Borgnet, *Opera,* Vol. V, p. 26. [29] *Ibid.,* pp. 48 and 55.

powers cannot be proved by physical laws (*principiis physicis*), but require a knowledge of astronomy and magic and the necromantic sciences, which would be considered in other treatises. Albert's friends (*socii*), however, are curious to know the doctrine of images even if it is necromancy, and Albert does not hesitate to assure them that it is a good doctrine in any case. Yet in his theological works he declared the art of images evil "because it inclines to idolatry.... and....is employed for idle or evil ends."

Albert also counts the interpretation of dreams among "magical sciences" and speaks of the interpreters as wise men (*sapientes*).[30] Visions, however, which occur "when one is awake....but the senses diverted....are most employed by magicians, who indeed make a specialty of such diversions of the senses and such apparitions and of certain potions which close and stupefy the senses, and through the apparitions then made they conjecture the future."[31] In one passage Albert remarks that whether fascination is a fact or not is for magic to determine; in another place he classifies fascination as a department of magic.[32] In his treatise on the vegetable kingdom he declares that the consideration of "the divine effects" of certain plants is the especial concern of those interested in magic, and he also mentions "those who practise incantations" and necromancers as employing herbs for their marvelous properties.[33] In his treatise on animals he says that enchanters value highly the brain, tongue, and heart of the bird hoopee, and adds, "We shall not consider this matter at this time, for the investigation of it belongs to another science," —presumably magic.[34] On the other hand, in his work on minerals, although he quotes Socrates as having said that an incantation may be performed by suspending or

[30] *De somno et vigilia*, III, i, 10. [31] *Ibid.*, III, i. 3.

[32] *Ibid.*, III, i, 6; and Borgnet, *Opera*, V, 24.

[33] *De vegetabilibus*, V, ii, 3 and 6.

[34] *De animalibus*, XXIII, 111.

attaching objects as well as by prayers, adjurations, characters, and images, he proceeds to discuss suspensions and ligatures, especially the wonderful effects produced by wearing certain gems suspended from the neck, on the ground that they operate more naturally, and more properly belong to physical science than to magic.[35] In another treatise, mentioning "astronomers, augurs, magicians, interpreters of dreams and of visions, and every such diviner," he admits that almost all men of this class delight in deception and have little education, but he insists that "the defect is not in the science but in those who abuse it."[36]

These brief allusions to magic indicate that Albert regards it as distinct from the natural sciences except "astronomy," with which he connects it rather closely, but astronomy of course for Albert includes astrology and is a science of superior bodies and stands above the sciences of inferior creation. He says that it is a fundamental principle in the science of the *magi* that all things made by art or nature are moved by celestial virtues.[37] But of demons in connection with magic he says nothing in his scientific writings.

In the *Speculum astronomiae* ("Mirror of Astronomy")[38] which also seems to be from Albert's pen, a different attitude appears. Instead of nonchalantly correlating magic, astronomy, and necromancy, as was done in the treatise on minerals, the author says nothing of magic and is concerned to distinguish between "astronomy" and necromancy, and in particular between astrological and necromantic images. His aim now is, while admitting the harmful character of necromancy as dealing with demons

[35] *Mineral*, II, iii, 6. [36] *De somno et vigilia*, III, ii, 5. [37] *Mineral.*, II, iii, 3.

[38] Contained in volume X of Borgnet's edition. Franz Cumont (*Catalogus codicum astrologorum Graecorum*, V, i, 85) says that Borgnet's text of the *Speculum* is full of errors, and gives a partial new version from manuscripts. Mandonnet, "Roger Bacon et le 'Speculum astronomiae,'" *Revue Neo-Scolastique*, Vol. XVII (1900), argues that Bacon was the author, but his argument is based in large measure on false premises.

and contrary to the Catholic faith, to defend astrology from any such imputations, and to draw up separate lists of books which are bad and necromantic and of those which are "astronomical" and of value. Some of the books now condemned as necromantic are, however, the very ones which in the treatise on minerals[39] Albert cited concerning the science of the *magi* and which in his theological *Summa*[40] he cited as authorities on necromancy. It therefore becomes evident that the *Speculum astronomiae* is a piece of special pleading, written in reply to a contemporary attack upon necromantic and astrological literature. In fact the author cannot restrain himself from advising that the necromantic books be preserved rather than destroyed.

Albert spoke in his scientific writings as if he might sometime write some separate treatises on magic. Two little works have come down to us which somewhat answer that description. They have been regarded as spurious, but were certainly influential, since there seem to be about as many printed editions of them alone as of all Albert's other numerous works. Their titles are *Liber aggregationis, or The Secrets of the Virtues of Herbs, Stones and Animals,* and *The Wonders of the World* (*De mirabilibus mundi*).[41] The former seems to be professedly a book of magic since it opens with the assertion that "magical science is not evil, since through knowledge of it evil can be avoided and good attained." The author then plunges at once into the subject of the occult virtues of herbs, stones, and animals. By these, combined with varied ceremonies and due observance of astrological considerations, such marvels can be worked as to alter the attitude of others toward oneself, reveal hidden crimes, deprive men

[39] II, iii, 3. [40] II, ii, 30.

[41] I have used an edition printed in Amsterdam in 1740 in which these two treatises are bound together with the *De secretis mulierum*, and with the *Physiognomy* of Michael Scot, mentioned below in note 46.

of sleep or force confidences from them when asleep, quiet barking dogs or make cows dry, free prisoners, become invisible, acquire knowledge or a good intellect, tell if one's wife be true, incite sadness or joy or love, freeze boiling water, produce an inextinguishable fire, make the sun bloody or a rainbow to appear, feel no pain under painful circumstances, drink to excess and not get drunk, conquer enemies, escape perils, overcome wild beasts, interpret all sorts of dreams, read others' thoughts, and predict the future. As in Albert's allusions to magic in his scientific writings, so here nothing is said of employing demons to produce these results, and so marvelousness rather than employment of spirits appears as the chief feature of magic.

In the *De mirabilibus mundi* "marvels" rather than "magic" are the theme, but the author has read "the books of necromancy and the books of images and magic books,"[42] and most of the marvels which he instructs how to produce would probably be pretty generally regarded as magic by his contemporaries. Such are to make men seem headless or with the heads of animals or three heads or the face of a dog, or to make men appear in any form even as angels, or to make the entire house seem full of serpents or elephants. The author regards the human soul and its desires as the greatest force in effecting marvels, though he also recognizes the potency of occult virtues in natural objects, of heat and cold, of the influences of the stars, of procedure fitting the end sought, of suffumigations, and of demons.[43] Little, however, is said of demons except in connection with "the science of necromancy in which are manifested the immaterial substances which direct and assist man."[44] Despite his faith in marvels the author recognizes that "it is the wise man's task to make marvels cease" by adequate explanation of them.[45]

[42] P. 159. [43] Pp. 158, 166, 170. [44] Pp. 168-169. [45] P. 158.

MICHAEL SCOT.

We come next to writings which emphasize more the participation of demons in magic and which illustrate in detail the relations between magic, "astronomy," and necromancy which Albertus Magnus suggested. These writings are as follows: (1) An elaborate treatise of the early thirteenth century on astrology, astronomy, and various related fields such as music and geography, dedicated to his patron the emperor Frederick II by Michael Scot,[46] who was no mere court astrologer but the introducer to medieval Christendom of many of the works of Aristotle and a translator of other writings from the Arabic; (2) A commentary of the early fourteenth century upon that brief but standard medieval astronomical treatise, *The Sphere* of Sacrobosco, by Cecco d'Ascoli,[47] who after being professor of astrology at the university of Bologna and court astrologer to the duke of Florence was condemned to the stake by the Inquisition in 1327; (3) A book of magic called *Picatrix*,[48] translated from Arabic into Spanish by order of the learned Alphonse X of Castile who reigned 1252-1284 and who is notable for his astronomical tables and mild law concerning magic.[49]

Michael Scot combines traces of the patristic definition

[46] Scot's work divides into four parts; a general preface, a *Liber introductorius*, a *Liber particularis*, and a *Liber physionomiae*. Of these the first two exist in the Bodleian MS. 266 (saec. XV, 218 fols., long double columns, text greatly abbreviated, and in many different hands illustrated); and at Munich, Staatsbibliothek, Cod. Lat. 10268 (saec. XIV, 146 fols.). The *Liber particularis* is found only at the Bodleian in MS. Canon Misc. 555, where it occupies fols. 1-59, and the *Liber physionomiae*, fols. 59-88. The last, however, has been separately printed. (See note 41.)

[47] I used two editions of 1499 and 1518 at the British Museum.

[48] The work is extant in Latin translations in MSS. XX, 20, and XX, 21 of the National Library at Florence. Both manuscripts have the same colophon, dated in 1536 and the pontificate of Paul III, but their contents are not always identical although they roughly correspond. Symphorien Champier, writing in 1514, refers to Picatrix in his edition of the *Conciliator* of Peter of Abano.

[49] *Los Codigos Españoles concordados y anotados*: *Codigo de las siete partidas*, 2d ed., Madrid, 1872, Vol. IV. La setena partida: Titulo XXIII: Ley 1-3. Divination of the future by the stars is sanctioned in the case of persons properly trained in astronomy, although other varieties of divination

of magic with the attitude of an astrologer and with citations from Arabian sources and from books of necromancy and of the notory art. Thus he condemns magic and necromancy, but lists as "arts which are in a certain measure palliated under the name of astronomy," geomancy, hydromancy, aeromancy, pyromancy, nigromancy, augury, physiognomy, praestigiomancy, the notory art, lot-casting, and alchemy.[50] He represents magicians as acquainted with secrets of nature and as employing herbs as well as characters and incantations.[51] He states that alchemists, nigromancers, and workers in the notory art owe more to astrology than they admit,[52] and informs us that by astronomical images very wise demons can be conjured to give responses.[53] He also mentions "the virtues who rule the circles of the planets," "the legion of damned spirits" who exist in the winds,[54] and the evil spirits in the moon who are wise in all sciences and may be invoked by conjurations.[55] He states that since demons are by nature fond of blood, and especially of human blood, nigromancers or magicians in performing their experiments often mix water with real blood or use wine that has been been exorcised to make it bloody, "and they sacrifice with flesh of a living human being, such as a bit of their own flesh or of a corpse, and not with the flesh of brutes, knowing that the consecration of a spirit in a ring or a bottle cannot be achieved except by the performance of many sacrifices."[56] Scot also lists the names by which spirits may be invoked.[57] Thus he shows more interest in necromancy than is consistent with his formal condemnation of it and magic.

are forbidden; and while those who conjure evil spirits or who make waxen, metallic or other images with the aim to harm their fellows are to be punished by death, those who employ incantations with good intentions and good results are pronounced deserving of reward rather than penalty.

[50] Bodleian MS, 266, fol. 22. [51] *Ibid.*, fol. 23. [52] *Ibid.*, fols. 2 and 20.
[53] *Ibid.*, fol. 21. [54] *Ibid.*, fols. 28-29. [55] Canon misc., fol. 17.
[56] Bodl. MS. 266, fol. 22. [57] *Ibid.*, fol. 172.

CECCO D'ASCOLI.

The attitude of Cecco d'Ascoli is very similar.[58] He gives a classification of the magic arts almost identical with that by Hugo of St. Victor, but states that he derives it from the *Liber de vinculo spiritus* of Hipparchus. He of course does not regard astrology as a part of magic, and declares that while one can learn something of the future through magic, the science of the stars is "a more excellent way." Magic is, he says, "emphatically censured by holy mother church."[59] This fact, however, does not restrain him from frequently citing magic books such as Apollonius's *Liber artis magicae,* nor from telling his students—his commentary is evidently a set of classroom lectures—all the necromancy that he happens to know. Thus when Sacrobosco describes the *coluri,* or circles whose function is to distinguish the solstice and equinox, Cecco comments that Hipparchus in the *Liber de hierarchiis spirituum* tells of incubi and succubi who inhabit these circles and by whose virtue in a greater conjunction divine men are born such as Merlin was and Antichrist will be.[60] When Sacrobosco mentions the four cardinal points, Cecco is reminded of Hipparchus's statement in the *Liber de ordine intelligentiarum* that certain princes of the demons "hold the four parts beneath the sky. For expelled from heaven they occupy the air and the four elements."[61] When Sacrobosco speaks of the zenith or poles in a purely astronomical way, Cecco quotes Hipparchus again as saying, "O wonderful zenith and godlike nature, etc.," after the manner of an invocation, or Solomon in the *Liber de umbris idearum* as exclaiming, "O arctic *manes*, O antarctics

[58] The fololwing references to Gecco's Commentary apply to the edition of 1518 in which it occupies the first 23 leaves of a collection of commentaries upon Sacrobosco and of other astronomical treatises.

[59] Fol. 3: *a sancta matre ecclesia vituperabiliter improbata.*

[60] Fol. 14.

[61] Fol. 15.

propelled by divinity."[62] When Sacrobosco treats of climates, Cecco remarks that the word may be understood in two ways, astronomically or necromantically. It is in the latter sense that Zoroaster, "the first inventor of the magic art," uses the word when he says, "For those climates are to be marveled at, which with flesh of corpses and human blood give responses the more trustworthily." "By this," continues Cecco, "you should understand those four spirits of great virtue who stand *in cruciatis locis*, that is, in east, west, north and south, whose names are these, Oriens, Amaymon, Paymon and Egim, spirits who are of the major hierarchy and who have under them twenty-five legions of spirits apiece. Therefore because of their noble nature these seek sacrifice from human blood and from the flesh likewise of a dead man or cat. But this Zoroastrian art cannot be carried on without great peril, fastings, prayers, and all things which are contrary to our faith."[63]

Such a belated and somewhat perfunctory warning that these things are contrary to the Christian religion is characteristic of Cecco. Elsewhere he calls these spirits demons and diabolical[64] and states with Augustine that "spirits who are outside the order of grace" cannot truly transmute bodies nor raise the dead, nor do any marvels and feats of magic except those which can be accounted for by the occult virtues of nature.[65] He also asserts that a "Floron," mentioned by Salomon in the *Liber de umbris idearum,* was of the hierarchy of cherubim and was confined in a mirror by a major invocation, and that this Floron knew many secrets of nature and deceived King Manfred and others by ambiguous oracles. "So beware of these demons because their ultimate intention is to deceive Christians to the discredit of our Lord Jesus Christ."[66]

[62] Fols. 20 and 17. [63] Fol. 21. [64] Fols. 17 and 22.
[65] Fol. 16. [66] Fol. 17.

Yet on the next page we find Cecco saying that if any one wishes to make an image in order to obtain responses from a spirit, he ought to observe the instructions which follow; while five pages later he cites a response of this same Floron as to the time when demons are least liable to deceive one and when as a consequence it is best to consult them. In short Cecco's work is less a commentary on Sacrobosco's *Sphere* than a manual of astrological necromancy.

PICATRIX.

Picatrix is a confused compilation of extracts from occult writings and a hodgepodge of innumerable magical and astrological recipes. The author states that he "has compiled this book," that he intends to set forth "in simple language" what past sages have concealed in cryptic words, and that he has spent some six years in reading 224 books by "ancient sages."[67] Whenever modern compilers of the notions of folklore and the magical customs of aborigines shall have exhausted their resources, a rich mine will still await them in this book of magic.

For *Picatrix* is openly and professedly a book of magic. At the close of the first of its four books we are told that its contents are "the roots of the magic art" and that "without them one cannot become perfect in such arts."[68] Throughout all four books "magic works," "magic effects," "magical sciences," and "the operator of magic" are mentioned, and books of magic by Abrarem (Abraham?), Geber, and Plato are cited.[69] It is true that the term necromancy is also employed frequently and a chapter devoted to its definition,[70] and that astrological images and

[67] MS. XX, 20, fols. 1 *verso* and 53 *recto*.

[68] *Ibid.*, 15*v*.

[69] *Ibid.*, 7*v*., 44*r*., 44*v*., 22*v*., 23*r*., 28*r*., 40*r*., 50*r*., 51*r*., 99*r*.,; MS. XX, 21, fols. 78*r*. and 79*v*.

[70] Liber I, Cap. 2. This chapter is much briefer in MS. XX, 21 than in MS. XX, 20.

invocations of demons are the subjects most discussed. But it is said on the supposed authority of Aristotle that the first man to work with such images and to whom spirits appeared was Caraphrebim, the inventor of the magic art.[71] It is also affirmed that the science of the stars is the root of magic, that the forms of planets or astronomical images "have power and marvelous effects in magic operations," while after announcing his intention of listing "the secrets of the ancient sages in the magic art" the first thing that our author divulges is that the influence of Saturn exceeds the influence of the moon.[72]

On the whole then, while magic is not defined at length in *Picatrix,* it seems justifiable to apply it as a general term covering the contents of the book and to regard astronomical images and invocations of demons as two of magic's leading characteristics. *Picatrix* regards magic as a science, as a superior branch of learning, to excel in which many other studies must first be mastered; and he believes that the greatest philosophers of antiquity, like Plato and Aristotle, have written works of magic.

Much use of natural objects is made in the various recipes of *Picatrix.* Here is one brief instance: Adam the prophet says that if you take 14 grains of the fruit of the laurel tree, dry them well and pulverize them and put the powder in a very clean dish in vinegar, and beat it with a twig from a fig tree, you can make any one you wish possessed of demons by giving him this powder to drink.[73] One chapter is especially devoted to "the virtues of certain substances produced from their own peculiar natures," and the author further explains that "in this section we shall state the marvelous properties of simple things as well of trees as of animals and of minerals."[74] In actual procedure, however, the use of several things combined is

[71] MS. XX, 20; fol. 55*v.* [72] *Ibid.,* 32*v.* and 28*r.* [73] MS. XX, 21, fol. 79*v.*
[74] Lib. IV, Cap. 8. MS. XX, 20, fol. 108*v*; *MS.* XX, 21, fol. 86*r.*

usually recommended, as a suffumigation of 14 dead bats and 24 mice, to give a comparatively simple example.[75]

On the supposed authority of Aristotle in a book written to Alexander, detailed instructions are given how to make four "stones" of great virtue and of elaborate composition by procedure more or less alchemistic.[76] Indeed, there are listed all sorts of "confections," compounds, and messes, either, to burn or sacrifice or eat or drink or smell of or anoint oneself with, in order to bring various wonders to pass. The ingredients employed include different oils and drugs, butter, honey, wine, sugar, incense, aloes, pepper, mandragora, twigs, branches, adamant, lead, sulphur, gold, the brains of a hare, the blood of a wolf, the urine of an ass, the filth of a leopard, and various portions of such animals as apes, cats, bears and pigs.

Hermes is quoted as saying that there are many marvels for necromancy in the human body,[77] various parts of which are often employed. Thus in making a magic mirror one is bidden to employ a suffumigation of seven products of the human body, namely, tears, blood, ear-wax, spittle, *sperma, stercus, urina.*[78] Vile and obscene substances seem in great demand for purposes of magic throughout the book. Besides ingredients, all sorts of receptacles and material paraphernalia are listed: vessels, jars, vases, braziers, crosses, candles, crowns, etc. *Picatrix*, like the *De Mirabilibus,* considers heat an important force in magic and mentions both elemental and natural heat, the former referring to the use of the element fire in sacrifice, suffumigation and the preparation of magic compounds, the latter designating the heat of digestion when recipes must be eaten to take effect.[79]

Much is said of the magician himself as well as of the materials which he employs. He should have faith in his

[75] MS. XX, 20, fol. 70*r*.

[76] Lib. III, Cap. 10. MS. XX, 20, fol. 73*v*. MS. XX, 21, fol. 53*r*.

[77] MS. XX, 21, fol. 60*v*.

[78] *Ibid.*, 22*v*.

[79] Lib. I, Cap. 2.

procedure, put himself into an expectant and receptive mood, be diligent and solicitous.[80] Often chastity is requisite, sometimes fasting or dieting, sometimes the wearing of certain garments.[81] He must have studied a long list of other sciences before he can attempt necromancy, but then to succeed in magic he must drop all other studies and devote himself to it exclusively.[82] A little knowledge of necromancy is a dangerous thing, and the ignorant meddler therein is liable to be violently slain by indignant demons.[83] Much depends also upon the magician's personality and natural fitness. No one can succeed in the science of images unless his own nature is inclined thereto by the stars. Some men are more subtle and spiritual, less gross and corporeal than others, and hence more succesful in magic.[84] The ancients, when they wished to employ a boy in magic, used to test his fitness by fire as well as to make sure that he was physically sound.[85]

It has already been implied that great stress is laid upon procedure. Images of persons or things concerned are extensively employed. Thus to catch fish one makes an image of a fish, and to bewitch a girl one makes a waxen image of her and dresses it in clothes like hers. In both cases, however, there is additional ceremony to be observed. The head of a fish should be fashioned first; the image is to be poised on a slender rod of silver, and this is to stand erect in a vessel which is to be filled with water, sealed tightly with wax, and dropped to the bottom of the stream where one is to fish.[86] In the bewitching of the girl, which is told as an actual occurrence, the object was to make her come to a certain man. Hence another image was made of him out of a pulverized stone mixed with gum, and the two images were placed facing each other in a vase where seven twigs of certain trees had been ar-

[80] I, 4. [81] II, 12; III, 5 and 7 and 12, etc. [82] IV, 5.
[83] MS. XX, 20, fol. 12*r*. and MS. XX, 21, fol. 75*v*.
[84] Lib. III, 6 and IV, 1 [85] MS. XX, 21, fol. 47*v*. [86] MS. XX, 20, fol. 10.

ranged crosswise. The vase was then buried under the hearth where there was a moderate fire and a piece of ice. When the ice had melted the vase was unearthed and the girl was immediately seen approaching the house. In the reverse process to free her from the spell a candle was lit on the hearth, the two images were taken out and rudely torn apart and an incantation uttered.[87]

To make a spring that is going dry flow more freely a small and comely virgin should walk up and down beating a drum for three hours, and then another small and good-looking girl should join in with a tambourine for six hours more. To ward off hail storms a company of people should go out in the fields, half of them tossing handfuls of silk toward the sky and the other half clapping their hands and shouting as rustics do to frighten away birds.[88] Tying seven knots and saying an incantation over each is another specimen of the ceremonial in *Picatrix*.

Ritual also plays an important part in the invocation of spirits. If one wishes to invoke the spirit called "Complete Nature" he must enter a spick and span room while the moon is in the first degree of Aries. Various receptacles filled with different foods and combustibles must be arranged in a certain way on a table. Then he must stand facing the east and invoke the spirit by its four names seven times and repeat a prescribed form of prayer for increase of knowledge and of moral strength.[89] To draw down the virtue and power of the moon one crowns oneself in the favorable astrological hour and goes to a green spot beside a stream. There he beheads with a bone—under no circumstances employing iron—a cock with a divided crest. He stands between two braziers filled with live coals on which he casts grains of incense gradually until smoke arises; then, looking toward the moon, he should say, "O

[87] *Ibid.*, fol. 52.
[88] *Ibid.*, 103*v.*; MS. XX, 21, fols. 81*v.*, 82*r.*
[89] III, 6. MS. XX, 20, fols. 54-55; MS. XX, fols. 21, 32-34.

moon, luminous and honored and beautiful, thou who shatterest darkness by thy light, rising in the east and filling the whole horizon with thy light and beauty, I come to thee humbly asking a boon." Having stated his wish, he withdraws ten paces, facing the moon the while and repeating the above formula. Then more incense is burned and a sacrifice performed and characters inscribed on a leaf with the ashes of the sacrifice and a bit of saffron. This leaf is then burned and as its smoke rises the form of a well-dressed man will appear, who will answer the petition.[90]

Throughout *Picatrix* planets and spirits are closely associated. Many instructions are given how to pray to each of the planets and to work magic by their aid, just as if they were demons. It is hard to say whether the spirits are more thought of as forces in nature or the stars as gods. A necromancer who does not know astronomy is helpless, and each planet has a list of personal names associated not only with itself but with its every part and position.[91] Lists are also given of the boons which one may ask from each planet, and of the stones, metals, animals, trees, colors, tinctures, odors, places, suffumigations, and sacrifices appropriate to each planet and sign of the zodiac, in order that one may use the proper materials, eat the right food, and wear the right clothes when petitioning any one of them.[92] Let us remember, too, that the natural qualifications of the magician depend upon his horoscope.

Finally *Picatrix* devotes much space to astronomical images,[93] which, engraved preferably upon gems in accordance with the aspect of the sky at some instant when the constellations are especially favorable, are supposed to receive the celestial influences at their maximum and store them up for future use. That they receive "the force of

[90] IV, 2. MS. XX, 21, fol. 68*v*.
[91] III, 9. MS. XX, 20, fol. 71*r*. MS. XX, 21, fol. 50*r*.
[92] II, 5 and 10; III, 1 and 2.
[93] Liber II, *passim*: also I, 4-5 and IV, 9.

the planets" and do marvelous works, such as the invocation of demons, is, *Picatrix* believes, "proved by nature and by experiment." He lists them for 48 figures made from the fixed stars, for the 28 mansions of the moon, for the signs of the zodiac and the planets. As an example may be given one of the images for Saturn: "A man erect on a dragon holding a sickle in his right hand and a spear in his left hand, and clad in black clothing and a panther skin." This image "has power and marvelous effects in magic works."[94] Characters made up of lines and geometrical figures are also derived from the consellations and are supposed to possess marvelous efficacy.

Some of the results attributed to images and characters are to drive away mice, free captives, throw an army into a town, render buildings safe and stable or impede their erection, acquire wealth for oneself or one's friends, make two persons fall in love, make men loyal to their lord, make the king angry with some one, cure a scorpion's sting, walk on water, assume any animal form, cause rain in dry weather and prevent rain in wet weather, make the stars fall or sun and moon appear to be divided into many parts, ascend into the air and take the form of a falling star, speak with the dead, destroy a city or enemy, traverse great distances in the twinkling of an eye. Similar are the aims of incantations, invocations, and recipes, as has already been indicated in several cases. Ten "confections" are listed that stop evil tongues; eight, that generate discord and enmity; six, that taken in food cure impotency; seven, that induce a sleep like unto death; ten, that induce a sleep from which one never wakes.[95] Others prevent dogs from barking at you, produce green tarantulas or red serpents, remove bothersome frogs from pools, cause water to burn and appear red, enable one to see small objects a

[94] II, 10. MS. XX, 20, fol. 32*v*. MS. XX, 21, fol. 14*v*.
[95] III, 11. MS. XX, 20, fol. 78*v*. MS. XX, 21, fol. 58*v*.

long way off, make the winds and tempests obey you, deprive of memory or sense or speech or sight or hearing, and so on through a long gamut. We note that the aims are now good, now evil, that they are infinitely varied, and that they are very much like the aims of the two works attributed to Albertus Magnus where so little use of demons was made.

THABIT BEN CORRA.

Astronomical images are again associated with magic in a little treatise of fourteen pages by Thabit ben Corra ben Zahrun el Harrani, whom Albertus Magnus, Peter of Abano, Cecco d'Ascoli, and *Picatrix* all cite as an authority on images,[96] and whom Roger Bacon styles "supreme philosopher among all Christians."[97] Hence, although he was born in Mesopotamia in 836 and lived for the most part at Bagdad until his death in 901, we may regard his conceptions as still influential in thirteenth century Europe. His treatise concludes: "And this is what the highest God wishes to show to his servants concerning magic, that his name may be honored and praised and ever exalted through the ages." In the printed edition of Frankfort, 1559, it is entitled *De tribus imaginibus magicis*.[98] Yet no mention is made of demons, and we are told that the material, be it lead or bronze or gold or wax, from which the image is made is unimportant, and that all depends upon the astronomical conditions at the time of construction. However, some sort of non-astronomical ceremony is usually added, such as burying the image, wrapping it in a clean cloth, writing upon it the names of the persons concerned and the end sought, and "naming the image by a

[96] *Mineral.*, II, iii, 3; *Spec. astron.*, Cap. XI; *Conciliator*, Diff. X, fol. 16, GH; *Sphera*, Cap. 3

[97] Bridges, I, 394.

[98] A treatise entitled *Liber prestigiorum Thebidis (Elbidis) secundum Ptolemeum et Hermetem per Adhelardum bathoniensem translatus*, which occupies fols. 70-74 in MS. 328 at Lyons, is possibly the same work.

famous name"—which perhaps has reference to spirits. The objects sought are similar to those in *Picatrix*.

ROGER BACON.

From the picture of magic from the inside and by one favorably disposed toward it which *Picatrix* affords we turn to a last description by one of the most critical and scientific minds of the thirteenth century, Roger Bacon. He mentions magic a number of times in his *Opus maius* and *Opus tertium*, and also wrote a short treatise entitled, "On the Secret Works of Art and Nature and the Nullity of Magic."[99] He uses magic as a generic term and adopts the same fivefold division of it as Hugo and Cecco.[100] Toward it his point of view is that of the Christian man of science rather than of the theologian. He does not sound a religious retreat from magic but a scientific attack upon it. What impresses him most is not its irreligious nor criminal character, although he calls the magicians *maledicti*[101] and is careful to admit the possibility of demons participating in magic, but that magic is fraudulent and futile. He couples the words "false and magical,"[102] speaks of the "figments of the magicians,"[103] and associates magic, not like Albert with necromancy and astronomy, but with necromancy and deception.[104] For him magicians are neither *magni* nor philosophers and astronomers; in half a dozen passages he classes them with old wives and witches.[105]

He represents magic as using sleight-of-hand, ventriloquism, subtle mechanism, darkness, and confederates to simulate results which it is unable to perform.[106] Or by

[99] Roger Bacon, *Opus maius*, ed. J. H. Bridges, Oxford, 1897, 2 vols. and a third published in 1900. Roger Bacon, *Opera inedita* (including the *Opus tertium* and *De secretis*), ed. J. S. Brewer in Vol. XV of *Rerum Britannicarum medii aevi scriptores, London*, 1859.

[100] Bridges, I, 240. [101] *Ibid.*, 395 and 399. [102] Brewer, pp. 47, 95.

[103] *Ibid.*, 532. [104] Bridges, I, 262.

[105] *Ibid.*, 395-6, 398, 399; Brewer, 46-7, 95, 98. [106] Brewer, 523.

use of natural objects it idly flatters itself that it coerces spirits who in reality respond only with evil intent and as God permits. Thus the *mathematici* in particular not only wrongly ascribe fatal necessity to the stars and "invoke demons by conjurations and sacrifices to supplement the influence of the constellations," but they mar their observations of the sky by circles and figures and characters of the vainest sort and by very stupid incantations and senseless prayers in which they put their trust," and they often resort to "confederates, darkness, deceptive mechanisms, sleight-of-hand—methods in which they know there is allusion— and by those methods in which there is no virtue from the sky they perform many feats that seem marvels to the stupid."[107] As for incantations, "the human voice has not the power that magicians imagine"; and when magic words are spoken, "either the magician accomplishes nothing or the devil is the real author of the work."[108] Bacon dismisses the views of magicians concerning fascinations and transformations as "worthless," "stupid," and so on.[109]

But it is clear from Bacon's frequent references to magic that it is a delusion still very much alive. Indeed he expressly asserts not only that magic was prevalent in antiquity, though opposed by philosophy, and that magicians resisted the early church,[110] but also that "every nation is full" of the superstitions sown by demons, witches, and magicians.[111] "Books of the magicians," falsely attributed to Solomon and ancient philosophers and which "assume a grand-sounding style," are in circulation but are really "new inventions" and "ought all to be prohibited by law, since they abound in so many lies that one cannot distinguish the true from the false."[112]

[107] Bridges, I, 241.
[108] Brewer, 531, and 96.
[109] Brewer, 98; Bridges, I, 399.
[110] Brewer, 29; Bridges, I, 29 and 241.
[111] Bridges, I, 395.
[112] Brewer, 526 and 531.

Indeed, Bacon seems to think that magic has taken such a hold upon men that it can be uprooted only by scientific exposition of its tricks and by scientific achievement of even greater marvels than it professes to perform. Perhaps he realizes that religious censure or rationalistic argument is not enough to turn men from these alluring arts, but that science must show unto them yet a more excellent way, and afford scope for that laudable curiosity, that inventive and exploring instinct which magic pretends to gratify. He asserts concerning experimental science: "It alone instructs how to consider all the follies of the magicians, not to confirm them, but to shun them, just as logic deals with sophistry."[113] Bacon also contends that the wonders of nature and the possibilities of applied science far outshine the feats of magicians.[114] Science, in short, not merely attacks magic's front; it can turn its flank and cut it off from its base of supplies.

But Bacon's science is sometimes occult science. Some of his "secret works of art and nature" would be classified as magic by many of our authors. He really goes about as far as Albertus Magnus in credulous acceptance of superstition and marvels, but does not apply the term magic to what Albert admits is magic. Bacon has no intention of classifying as magic all astrology, or all use of incantations, characters, and fascination. He holds that there are two meanings of the word *mathematica,* which may be used to denote either a branch of magic or a part of philosophy, although some theologians ignorantly condemn both alike.[115]

Bacon also complains that the mass of students and professors and many authorities in theology and canon law call all images magical indiscriminately, and that as a consequence "scarcely any one has dared to speak in public"

[113] Bridges, II, 172.
[114] Brewer, 532-537.
[115] Bridges, I, 239 and 247; Brewer, 27.

of the marvels that can be wrought by use of astronomical images, "for such men are immediately called magicians although really they are very wise."[116] Similarly, although haphazard fascination is magic, Bacon holds that just as certain bodily diseases are contagious, so if some malignant soul thinks powerfully of infecting another and desires this ardently and is full of faith in its own power to injure, "there is no doubt that nature will obey thought, as Avicenna shows,....and this much is not magic."[117]

Bacon also does not doubt that the human voice "has great virtue, though not that power which magicians imagine"; and he declares that words are the most appropriate instrument of the soul, as is shown by the fact that almost every miracle from the beginning of the world has been performed by the use of words:[118] "For where the attention, desire, and virtue of the rational soul, which is worthier than the stars, concur with the power of the sky, either a word or some other work must be produced of marvelous power in altering the things of this world, so that not natural objects only but souls will be inclined as the wise operator wishes." Incantations of this sort, "brought forth by the exertion of the rational soul and receiving the virtue of the sky as they are uttered" are philosophical, not magical.[119]

Bacon wants books of magic destroyed, but he states that many writings are reputed to be magic which are nothing of the kind but contain sound learning.[120] He accuses magicians not merely of ascribing falsely various "enormities" to Solomon, but also of interpreting incorrectly and making evil use of "enigmatical writings" which he believes Solomon really did write.[121] After all this we are not surprised at his complaint that men are confusing

[116] Bridges, I, 394. [117] *Ibid.*, 398.
[118] Brewer, 96 and 528-531; Bridges, I, 398.
[119] Bridges, I, 395. [120] Brewer, 532. [121] Bridges, I, 392.

science and philosophy with magic; and that contemporary theologians, Gratian, and "many saints" "have condemned many useful and splendid sciences along with magic."[122] Indeed we strongly suspect that Bacon has made up for himself such a definition of magic that he can condemn it and not be accused of it.

It would be unjustifiable to attempt a final definition of magic on the basis of data from so brief and late a period in its history as the one here considered. But our material seems to offer valuable suggestions toward such a definition. Varying in some respects as are the descriptions of magic which have been here summarized, they seem to be but different views of the same thing. Magic appears on the whole as a great primary division of human thought and activity. Other subjects are subordinated to it, not it to any other field. Where some of our writers draw a line between magic and astrology or between certain other forms of divination and magic, it is apt to be because they approve of the one and feel that they ought to disapprove of the other. Magic appears as a human art or group of arts employing varied materials in varied rites, often fantastic, to work a great variety of marvelous results, which offer man a release from his physical, social, and intellectual limitations, not by the imaginative and sentimental methods of music, melodrama, and romance, nor by religion's spiritual experience, but by operations supposed to be efficacious here in the world of external reality. Some writers lay great stress on resort to spirits in magic, some upon the influences of the heavens, some on both these, and some almost identify the two; but, except as theological dogma insists upon the demoniacal character of magic, it cannot be said that spirits or stars are thought of as always necessary in magic. The *sine qua non* seems to be a human operator, materials, rites, and the aiming

[122] *Ibid.*, 396.

at a result that borders on the impossible, either in itself or because of the means employed.

In our authors it is difficult to account for the occult properties attributed to things and acts, and to discern any one underlying principle, such as sympathy, symbolism, imitation, contagion, resemblance, or association, guiding the selection of materials and rites for magic. This is either because there never was such a principle, or because we deal with a late stage in the development of magic, when the superstitions of different peoples have coalesced, when its peculiar customs have become confused with those of science and religion, after its primitive methods have been artificially over-elaborated, and after many usages have been gradually corrupted and their original meaning forgotten. Whether magic is good or evil, true or false, is with our authors a matter of opinion, in which the majority hold it to be true but evil. Few, however, can avoid a wholesome feeling that there is something false about it somewhere. Finally, our material shows conclusively that the history of magic is bound up with the history of science as well as with folk-lore, primitive culture, and the history of religion.

LYNN THORNDIKE.

WESTERN RESERVE UNIVERSITY, CLEVELAND, OHIO.

CRITICISMS AND DISCUSSIONS.

THE PURELY ORDINAL CONCEPTIONS OF MATHEMATICS AND THEIR SIGNIFICANCE FOR MATHEMATICAL PHYSICS.

As a consequence of the work of Georg Cantor and Bertrand Russell,[1] it has long been recognized that many of the conceptions and theorems familiar to us in the theory of what are called "linear point-aggregates" can be generalized to analogous conceptions and theorems in the theory of simply ordered aggregates. Thus in the theory last mentioned we have the conceptions of Limes, of compactness (*Ueberalldichtsein*), and the continuity of a simply ordered aggregate, and, as I have shown in 1905, that of the continuity of a function and certain theorems on continuous functions. More recently, I have tried to generalize certain fundamental theorems of the theory of point-aggregates.

It should be remarked that the theory of point-aggregates is concerned with the exact investigation of that substratum, so to speak, on which the various parts of mathematics—analysis, geometry, mathematical physics—are built. The "real" numbers of analysis form a "simply ordered aggregate," and we may picture it under the form of a continuous straight line; the "ordinary complex" numbers of analysis form a continuum of two dimensions; and so on.

The purpose of such generalizations of the theorems of ordinary analysis into theorems of the purely ordinal theory of functions—in which the aggregates considered are not assumed to be aggregates of numbers—is what I think is the prime purpose of all generalizations: namely, to extract from often irrelevant detail surrounding a theorem the necessary and sufficient conditions of its validity. Thus in forming an ordinal theory of functions our prime motive is to discover how far the particular properties of the

[1] Cf. *The Monist* for Jan. 1912, Vol. XXII, pp. 149-158.

real (or complex, when we deal with multiply ordered series) number system are essential to the theory of functions.

Thus a theorem known by the names of Heine and Borel has been shown by O. Veblen in 1904 to be equivalent to a process which was often used by Weierstrass (it had been used by Bernhard Bolzano in 1817, and by others), when we deal with the aggregate of real numbers, and confine our attention to ordinary mathematics. But the aspect of things is changed when we proceed to the analogous, but far more general, theory of simply ordered aggregates in general. Here, as I showed in a paper published in 1910,[2] the Heine-Borel process has a distinct methodological advantage over the Bolzano-Weierstrass process, in that it avoids the use of a certain axiom. This it does because the Bolzano-Weierstrass process essentially depends upon the successive division (the successive halving, for example) of the interval of the number-continuum containing the number-aggregate considered, and there is no known way of defining "division" among non-numerical numbers of any ordered aggregate. This statement requires some explanation. We can, of course, define the phrase "a divided by b" to mean anything we like. Thus, if "a" denotes Socrates, "b" Plato, and "divided by" means, say, add together the years (B. C.) of the births of a and b, and divide by some definite number, then "a divided by b" may denote a number which gives the year of birth of, say, Xenophon. But what we want here is a definition which has a meaning when a and b are members of any simply ordered aggregate (as Socrates, Plato, and Xenophon are, if, for example, they are arranged in the order of their times of birth), which meaning reduces to the ordinary arithmetical one when a and b are finite numbers. Now if we are given two transfinite simply ordered aggregates, and a and b are their respective ordinal types (ordinal type is a more general concept than ordinal number[3]), we can, as Cantor has shown, define $a+b$ and $a\ .\ b$ in such a way that, when for a and b we put finite ordinal numbers, $a+b$ and $a\ .\ b$ denote the numbers that these notations denote in ordinary arithmetic. And it would be possible to define $a-b$ and a/b; but when M and N are transfinite, these notations would not denote one and only one number, as they do when a and b are finite, but a whole class of them. Thus $a-a$ may denote 0 or a itself. . . . , and so on. But this would be no use to us in our case. In the

[2] *Quart. Journ. of Math.*, 1910, p. 218.

[3] Cf. *Monist*, Jan. 1910, Vol. XX, pp. 96-98.

Bolzano-Weierstrass process, we are given a simply ordered aggregate of real numbers, and begin by halving it. This process of halving determines one and only one point, and it does this, *not because the aggregate is simply ordered, but because the aggregate is composed of finite, real numbers.* It is because division has been defined as a unique process for the *elements* of the aggregate. Consider the aggregate of real numbers from 0 to 1, including the ends, whose type Cantor has denoted[4] by θ. When halving this interval we do not look for "the" element which terminates an interval extending from 0 and of type $\theta/2$. If there is such an element, there is an infinity of them. What we do is to determine *the one* element of the interval whose coordinate is ½; that is to say, the number got by halving the difference (1–0) of the numbers which are the ends of the interval.

In other words, *it is because the aggregate of real numbers carries with it a scale of measurement,* while a simply ordered aggregate in general does not. Of course, we can give a simply ordered aggregate a scale of measurement which, *suo ipso,* it does not possess, by correlating it with the aggregate of real numbers or with part of that aggregate. Thus, as Mach has pointed out in his *Principien der Wärmelehre,* a thermometer-scale primarily only indicates the hotter and the colder of two given states and does not give us any right to speak of a state A as being, say, "twice as hot" as state B, until we have (as we have now, since Thomson's introduction of the absolute scale) a means of correlating the degrees of expansion of a fluid with the real numbers. Not yet have we an absolute scale of hardness of minerals, so that hardnesses form a simply ordered continuum without any scale of measurement. We may remark, quite by the way, that though there seems to be an analogy between a simply ordered aggregate and the series of integers as defined by Richard Dedekind,[5] and though Schröder in the third volume of his *Vorlesungen über die Algebra der Logik,*[6] which is devoted to the logic of relatives, has pointed out this analogy as a special merit of Dedekind's theory, this analogy on closer inspection seems not to subsist.

The reason why this distinction between the absolute numerical scale and those simply ordered aggregates in which the elements only have relative positions is so important, will appear presently

[4] *Math. Ann.,* Vol. XLVI, 1895, p. 510.

[5] Cf. his *Essays on the Theory of Numbers,* Chicago, 1901.

[6] Leipsic, 1895.

when we come to consider our treatment of space and time in mathematical physics.

But before we go any further we must explain a little the nature of the axiom mentioned above. Suppose that at any stage of a process we have to select an element—it does not matter which one—from a class of two or more. This is the case when we extend the Bolzano-Weierstrass process to simply ordered aggregates in general. If we have to do with real numbers, we may choose the definite point $\frac{1}{2}$ between 0 and 1, the definite point $\frac{3}{4}$ between $\frac{1}{2}$ and 1, the definite point $\frac{5}{8}$ between $\frac{1}{2}$ and $\frac{3}{4}$, and so on; but with a simply ordered transfinite aggregate in general we do not know of any means of finding a *specialized* (*ausgezeichnetes*) element between the ends of the aggregate, and we thus have an arbitrary choice among an infinity of elements between the ends of the aggregate considered. Now a form of the axiom in question is that when there is an infinity of classes of which each contains two or more members, it is possible to carry out for logical purposes—not, of course, *carry out* in the sense that we *"carry* out" the counting of a flock of sheep—the series of acts of arbitrary selection when this series is *infinite*. When the series is *finite* the axiom becomes a provable proposition; but when the series is infinite the method of proof by enumeration fails us.

This axiom, or rather an equivalent form of it, seems to have been first explicitly published by E. Zermelo in 1904,[7] and it has lately been fully discussed in the part entitled "Selections" of the first volume of Whitehead and Russell's *Principia Mathematica.*[8] The chief importance of the axiom lies in its connection with the question as to whether any given aggregate can be well-ordered or not[9]—a question which is outside the range of the subject with which we are at present concerned.

The history of this axiom is sometimes very amusing. Cantor had no doubt about its truth, and avoided using it where he could; Borel felt grave doubts about its validity, and used a form of it without scruple; most mathematicians did not see that it was unproved until Zermelo pointed this out in 1904, and Schoenflies, in the second part (1908) of his *Bericht* on the theory of aggregates, still failed to recognize this axiomatic character. This sort of

[7] Cf. pp. 360-366 of my paper "On the Comparison of Aggregates" in the *Quart. Journ. of Math.* for 1907.

[8] Cambridge, 1910.

[9] Cf. *Monist,* Jan., 1910, Vol. XX, p. 116.

thing is partly due to the neglect by mathematicians of logic and ideography.

Of course, we can only practically measure *relative* positions and motions; but when for scientific purposes we construct a mathematical model of the world, we assume that points of time and space can be represented by real numbers or complexes of real numbers (Cartesian coordinates) or vectors (numbers with two or more units). Now these numbers have, so to speak, an *absolute* position in their scale: each number has its own individuality. Thus, in the sense in which mathematicians speak of an "arithmetical space," in analytical mechanics we necessarily have to do with an absolute "space."

In analytical mechanics our time and space are necessarily aggregates of *numbers* because our description of dynamical events is effected by differential equations, and we cannot define a differential quotient, nor indeed division, for aggregates other than those of numbers. We can define many things usually considered to apply only to aggregates of numbers: thus *limit, continuity* of the independent variable, many of the characteristics—technically known as "closedness," "density in itself," "perfectness" and "compactness"—of aggregates of numbers, the notion of *function* and even of *continuous function* can be defined purely ordinally. But beyond this—into the differential and integral calculus—the purely ordinal theory of functions cannot go. If it could, then it would seem that we should have a means of describing mechanical events in a *relative* space; for a term in a series which can be fully described (for our purpose) by the giving of its ordinal type has, in general (unless, for example, it is the first or the last term), no property distinguishing it from another. To this circumstance is due the fact we observe when we try to transfer certain theorems of ordinary mathematical analysis to the ordinal theory of functions, namely, that whereas in ordinary analysis—owing to the fact that we have a scale of one measurement with the aggregate of numbers and so can determine uniquely a term (say "half-way") between two given ones—certain processes of proof like that of Bolzano and Weierstrass are determined uniquely at every one of an infinity of steps, we require, for the analogous process in the purely ordinal theory, an axiom (known by the name of Zermelo) permitting an infinite series of acts of arbitrary selection.

CAMBRIDGE, ENGLAND. PHILIP E. B. JOURDAIN.

MAGIC STARS.[1]

A five-pointed star being the smallest that can be made, the rules will be first applied to this one.

Choosing for its constant, or summation (S) = 48, then:

$$(5\times 48)/2 = 120 = \text{sum of series.}$$

Divide 120 into two parts, say 80 and 40, although many other divisions will work out equally well. Next find a series of five numbers, the sum of which is one of the above two numbers. Selecting 40, the series 6+7+8+9+10=40 can be used. These numbers must now be written in the central pentagon of the star following the direction of the dotted lines, as shown in Fig. 1.

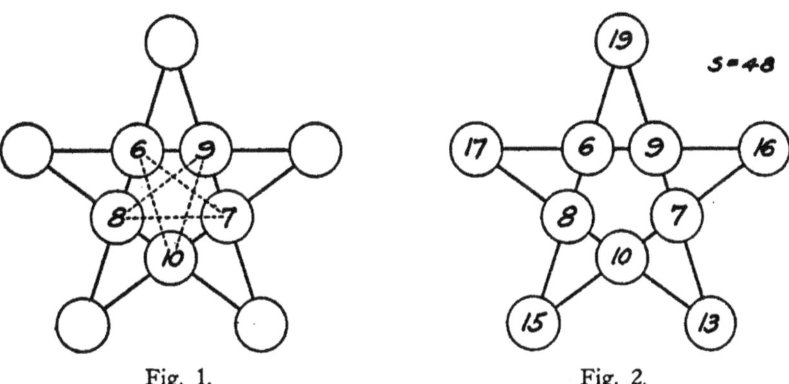

Fig. 1. Fig. 2.

Find the sum of every pair of these numbers around the circle beginning in this case with 6+9=15 and copy the sums in a separate column (A) as shown below:

	(A)
6+ 9=15	17+15+16=48
7+10=17	16+17+15=48
8+ 6=14	15+14+19=48
9+ 7=16	19+16+13=48
10+ 8=18	13+18+17=48

Place on each side of 15, numbers not previously used in the central pentagon, which will make the total of the three numbers = 48 or S. 17 and 16 are here selected. Copy the last number of

[1] We are indebted to Mr. Frederick A. Morton, Newark, N. J., for these plain and simple rules for constructing magic stars of all orders, and to Mr. H. A. Sayles, Schenectady, N. Y., for drawing the diagrams.

the trio (16) under the first number (17) as shown above, and under 16 write the number required to make the sum of the second trio = 48 (in this case 15). Write 15 under 16, and proceed as before to the end. If proper numbers are selected to make the sum of the first trio = 48, it will be found that the first number of the first trio will be the same as the last number of the last trio (in this case 17) and this result will indicate that the star will sum correctly if the numbers in the first column are written in their proper order at the points of the star, as shown in Fig. 2. If the first and last numbers prove different, a simple operation may be used to correct the error. When the last number is *more* than the first number, add half the difference between the two numbers to the first number and proceed as before, but if the last number is *less* than the first number, then *subtract* half the difference from the first number. One or other of these operations will always correct the error.

For example, if 14 and 19 had been chosen instead of 17 and 16, the numbers would then run as follows:

$$14+15+19=48$$
$$19+17+12=48$$
$$12+14+22=48$$
$$22+16+10=48$$
$$10+18+20=48$$

The difference between the first and last numbers is seen to be 6, and 20 being *more* than 14, half of 6 *added* to 14 makes 17 which is the correct starting number. Again, if 21 and 12 had been selected, then:

$$21+15+12=48$$
$$12+17+19=48$$
$$19+14+15=48$$
$$15+16+17=48$$
$$17+18+13=48$$

The difference between the first and last numbers is here 8, and the last number being *less* than the first, half of this difference subtracted from 21 leaves 17 as before.

It is obvious that the constant S of a star of any order may be changed almost indefinitely by adding or subtracting a number selected so as to avoid the introduction of duplicates. Thus, the constant of the star shown in Fig. 2 may be reduced from 48 to

40 by subtracting 4 from each of the five inside numbers, or it may be increased to 56 by adding 4 to each of the five outside numbers, and another variant may then be made by using the five inside numbers of S = 40, and the five outside numbers of S = 56. These three variants are shown respectively in Figs. 3, 4 and 5.

It is also obvious that any pair of five-pointed or other stars may be superposed to form a new star, and by rotating one star over the other, four other variants may be made; but in these and

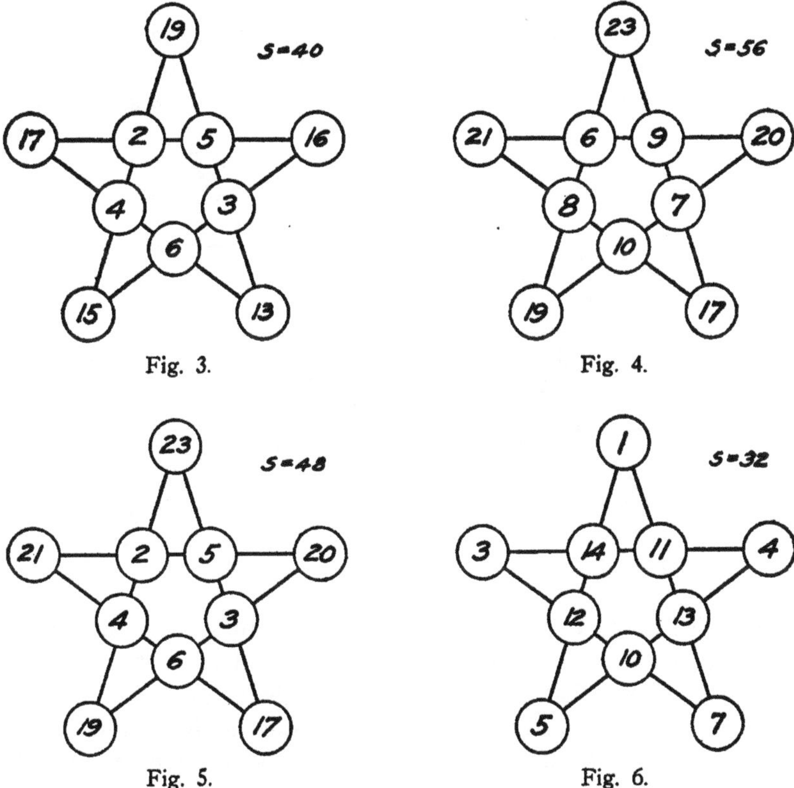

Fig. 3.

Fig. 4.

Fig. 5.

Fig. 6.

similar operations duplicate numbers will frequently occur, which of course will make the variant ineligible although its constant must necessarily remain correct.

Variants may also be made in this and all other orders of magic stars, by changing each number therein to its complement with some other number that is larger than the highest number used in the original star. The highest number in Fig. 2, for example, is 19. Choosing 20 as a number on which to base the desired variant,

19 in Fig. 2 is changed to 1, 17 to 3 and so on throughout, thus making the new-five-pointed star shown in Fig. 6 with S = 32.

The above notes on the construction of variants are given in detail as they apply to *all orders* of magic stars and will not need repetition.

The construction of a six-pointed star may now be considered. Selecting 27 as a constant:

$$(6\times 27)/2 = 81 = \text{sum of the series.}$$

Divide 81 into two parts, say 60 and 21, and let the sum of the six numbers in the inner hexagon = 21, leaving 60 to be divided among the outer points. Select a series of six numbers, the sum

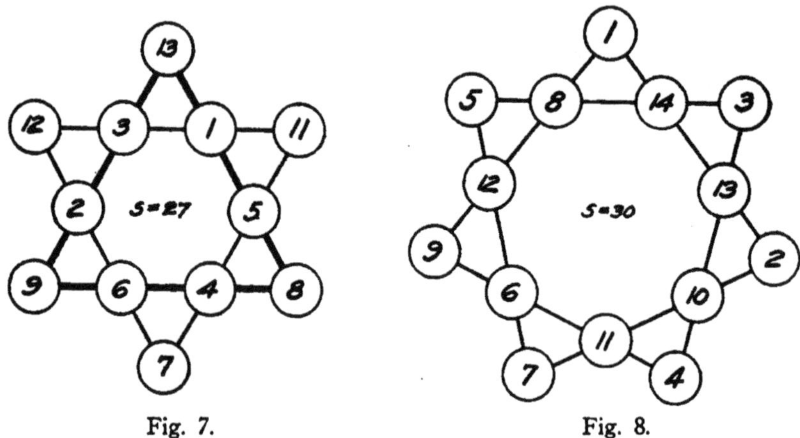

Fig. 7.

Fig. 8.

of which is 21, say 1, 2, 3, 4, 5, 6, and arrange these six numbers in hexagonal form, so that the sum of each pair of opposite numbers = 7. Fig. 7 shows that these six inside numbers form part of two triangles, made respectively with single and double lines. The outside numbers of each of these two triangles must be computed separately according to the method used in connection with the five-pointed star. Beginning with the two upper numbers in the single-lined triangle and adding the couplets together we have:

	(A)
$3+1=4$	$12+4+11=27$
$5+4=9$	$11+9+7=27$
$6+2=8$	$7+8+12=27$

Writing these sums in a separate column (A) and proceeding as before described, the numbers 12, 11, 7 are obtained for the points of the single-lined triangle, and in the same manner 13, 8, 9 are found for the points of the double-lined triangle, thus completing the six-pointed star Fig. 7.

The next larger star has seven points. Selecting 30 for a constant, which is the lowest possible:

$$(7 \times 30)/2 = 105 = \text{sum of the series.}$$

Dividing this sum as before into two parts, say 31 and 74, seven numbers are found to sum 74, say, $6+8+10+11+12+13+14 = 74$, and these numbers are written around the inside heptagon

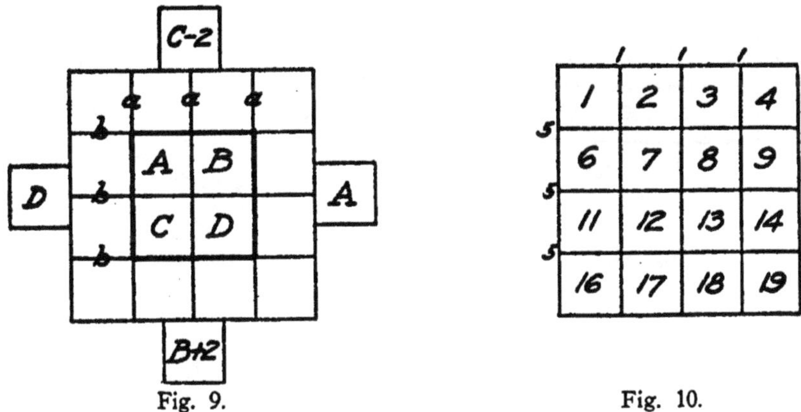

Fig. 9.

Fig. 10.

as shown in Fig. 8. Adding them together in pairs, their sums are written in a column and treated as shown below, thus determining the numbers for the points of Fig. 8.

$14+13=27$	$1+27+2=30$
$10+11=21$	$2+21+7=30$
$6+12=18$	$7+18+5=30$
$8+14=22$	$5+22+3=30$
$13+10=23$	$3+23+4=30$
$11+6=17$	$4+17+9=30$
$12+8=20$	$9+20+1=30$

The next larger star has eight points and it can be made in two different ways, viz., By arranging the numbers in one continuous line throughout as in stars already described having an odd number of points, or by making it of two interlocking squares.

The latter form of this star may be constructed by first making a 4^2 with one extra cell on each of its four sides, as shown in Fig. 9. A series of sixteen numbers is then selected which will meet the conditions shown by italics *a, a, a,* and *b, b, b,* in the figure, i. e., all differences between row numbers must be the same, and also all

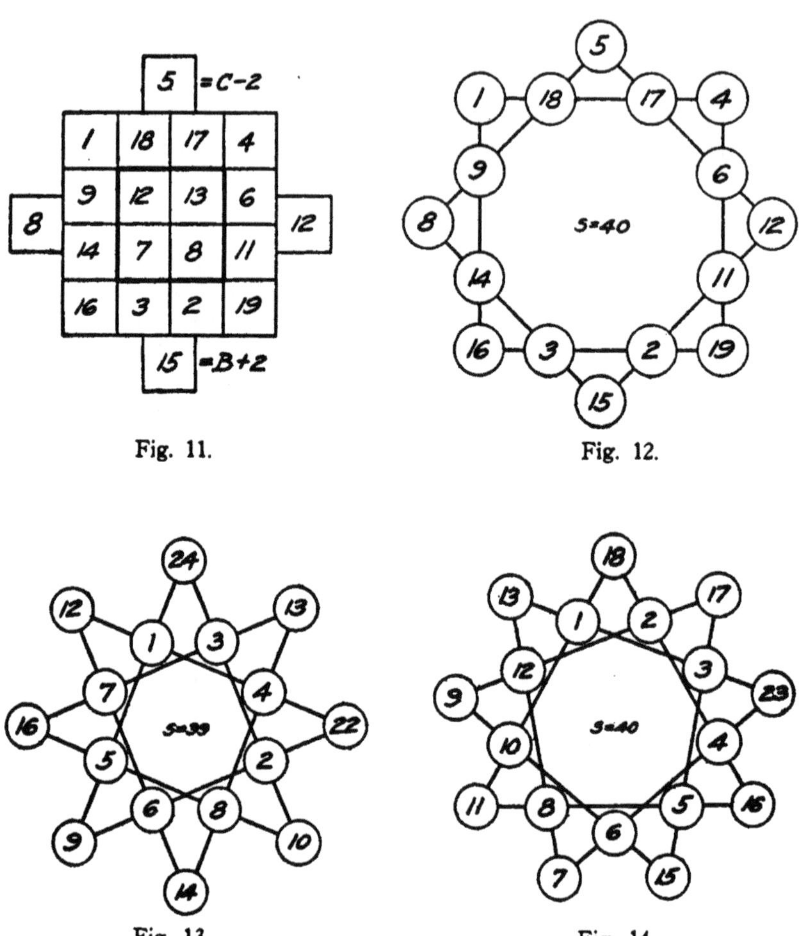

Fig. 11.

Fig. 12.

Fig. 13.

Fig. 14.

differences between column numbers, but the two differences must be unlike. The constant (S) of the series when the latter is arranged as a magic 4^2 must also be some multiple of 4. The series is then put into magic formation by the old and well-known rule for making magic squares of the 4th order. The central 2×2

square is now eliminated and the numbers therein transferred to the four extra outside cells as indicated by the letters A. B. C. D. Finally all numbers are transferred in their order into an eight-pointed star.

A series of numbers meeting the required conditions is shown in Fig 10, and its arrangement according to the above rules is given

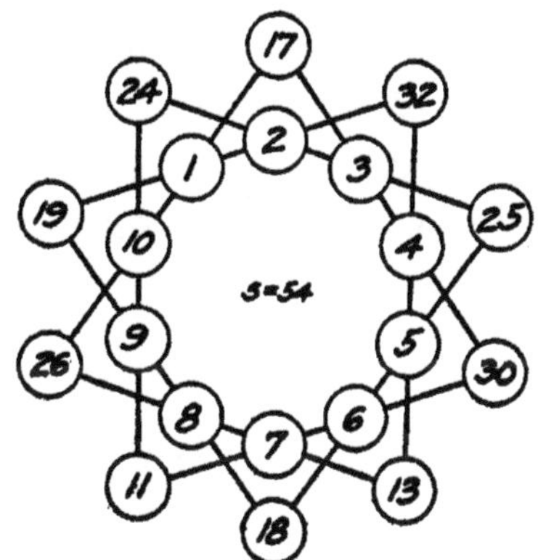

Fig. 15.

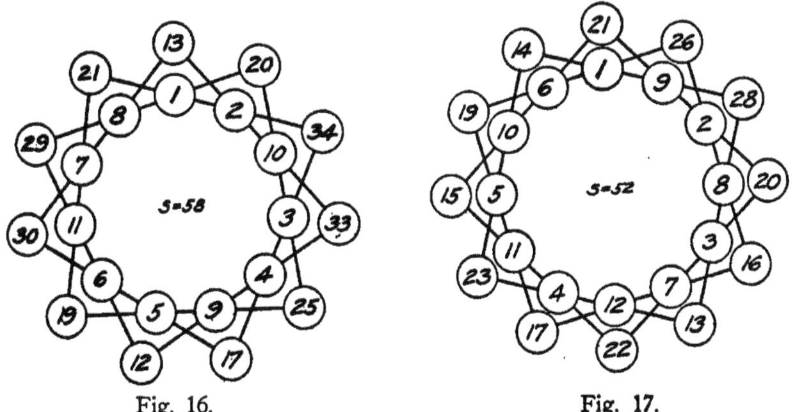

Fig. 16.

Fig. 17.

in Fig. 11, the numbers in which, transferred to an eight-pointed star, being shown in Fig. 12, S=40. The 4^2 magic arrangement of the series must be made in accordance with Fig. 11, for other magic arrangements will often fail to work out, and will never do so in accordance with Fig. 9. The above instructions cover the simplest method of making this form of star but it can be constructed in many other different ways and also with constants which are not evenly divisible by 4.

Turning now to the construction of the eight-pointed star by the continuous line method, inspection of Figs. 12 and 13 will show that although the number of points is the same in each star yet the arrangement of numbers in their relation to one another in the eight quartets is entirely different.

Choosing a constant of 39 for an example:

$$(39 \times 9)/2 = 156 = \text{sum of series.}$$

This sum is now divided into two parts, say 36 and 120. The sum of the first eight digits being 36, they may be placed around the

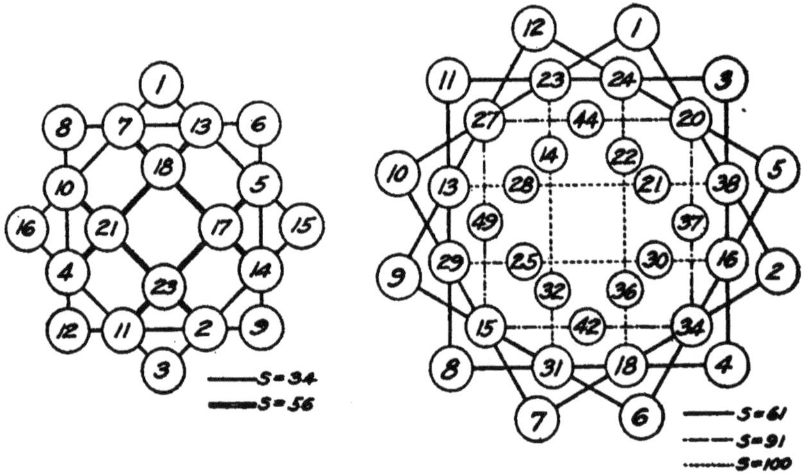

inside octagon so that the sum of each opposite pair of numbers = 9, as shown in Fig. 13. Adding them together in pairs, as indicated by the connecting lines in the figure, their sums are written in a column and treated as before explained, thus giving the correct numbers to be arranged around the points of the star Fig. 13.

These rules for making magic stars of all orders are so simple that further examples are deemed unnecessary. Nine-, ten-, eleven-, and twelve-pointed stars, made by the methods described, are shown respectively in Figs. 14, 15, 16, and 17. Several other diagrams of ingenious and more intricate star patterns made by Mr. Morton are also appended for the interest of the reader.

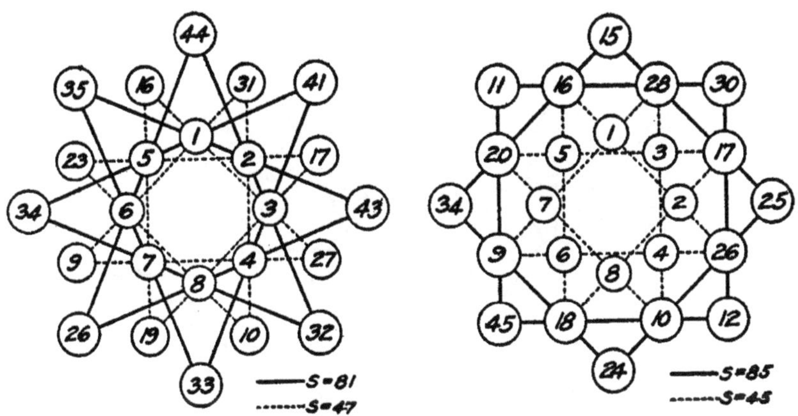
44
35
16
31
41
1
23
5
2
17
34
6
3
43
9
7
4
27
8
26
19
10
32
33
S=81
S=47
15
11
16
28
30
1
20
5
3
17
34
7
2
25
9
6
4
26
8
45
18
10
12
24
S=85
S=45

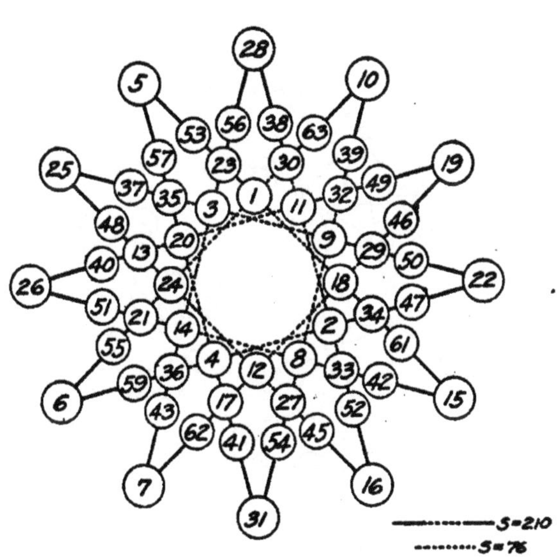
28
5
10
53
56
38
63
57
23
30
39
25
19
37
35
3
1
11
32
49
48
20
9
46
13
29
50
40
24
18
22
26
51
47
21
14
2
34
55
61
36
4
12
8
33
42
6
59
43
17
27
52
15
62
41
54
45
7
16
31
S=210
S=76

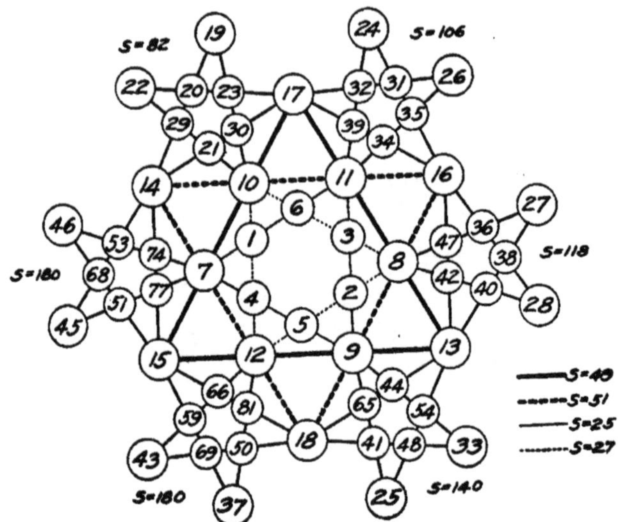
S=82 19 24 S=106
22 20 23 17 32 31 26
29 30 39 35
21 34
14 10 11 16
6 27
46 53 74 1 3 47 36
S=180 68 7 8 38 S=118
77 4 2 42 40
45 51 5 28
15 12 9 13
66 44
81 65 54
59
43 69 50 18 41 48 33
S=180 37 25 S=140
S=48
S=51
S=25
S=27

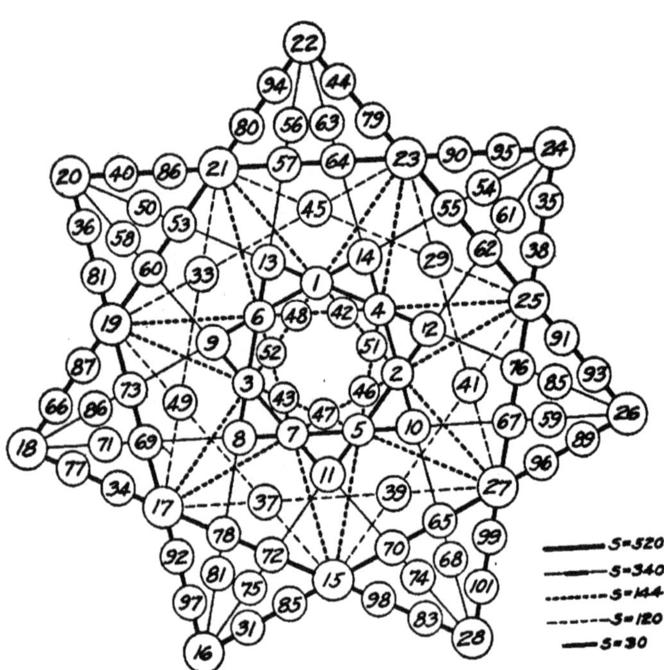
22
94 44
80 56 63 79
20 40 86 21 57 64 23 90 95 24
50 45 54 35
36 58 53 55 61
13 14 29 62 38
81 60 33 1
19 6 48 42 4 25
9 12 91
52 51
87 2 76 93
73 3 41 85
66 86 49 43 46 26
47 67 59
18 71 69 8 7 5 10 89
77 96
34 11 39
17 37 27
65
78 70 99
92 72 68
81 74
75 15 101
97 85 98
31 83
16 28
S=520
S=340
S=144
S=120
S=30

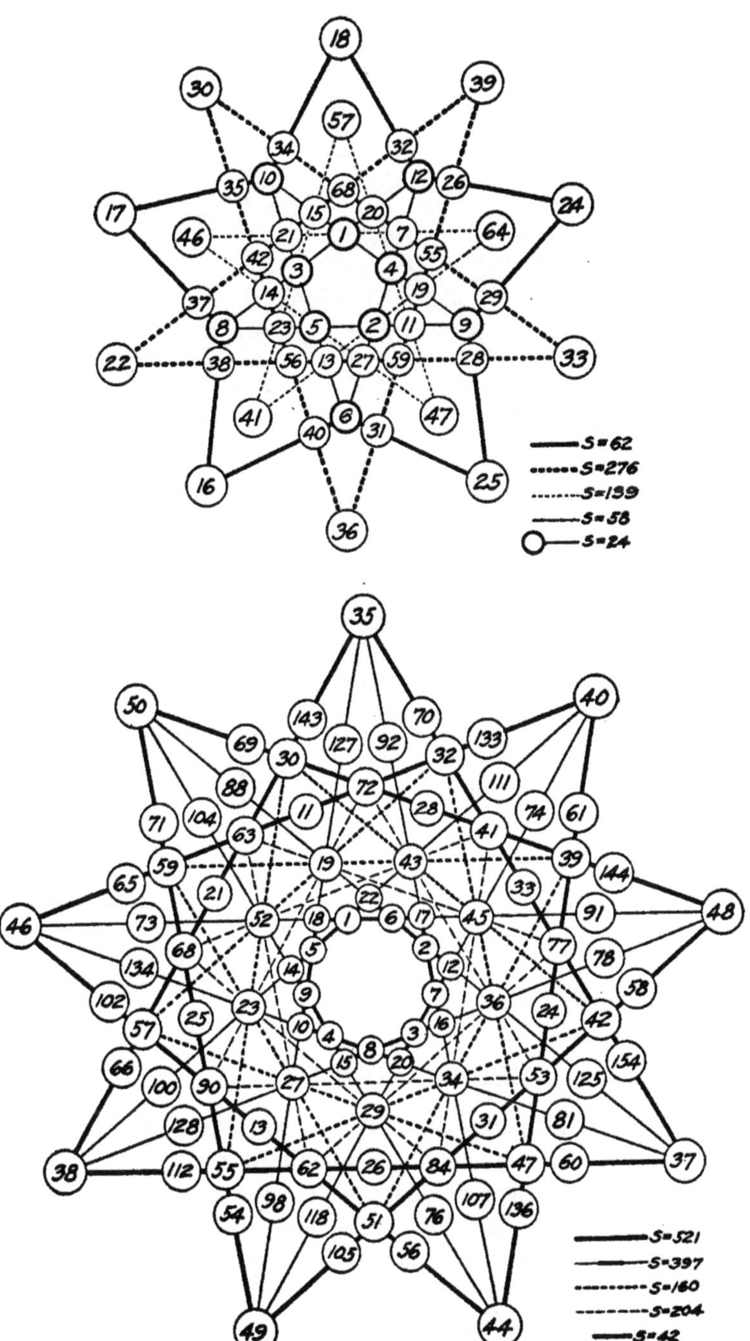
S=62
S=276
S=139
S=58
S=24
S=521
S=397
S=160
S=204
S=42

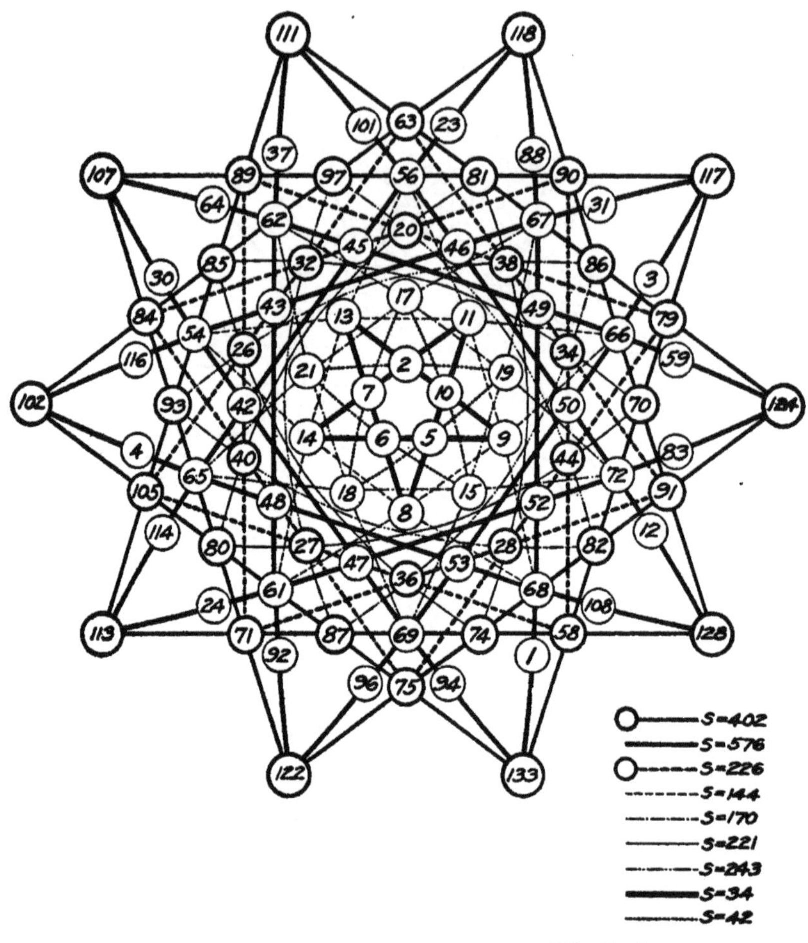

W. S. ANDREWS.

SCHENECTADY, N. Y.

RECENT PERIODICALS.

In *Scientia* (*Rivista di Scienza*) for May, 1914, the first artilcle is by A. Einstein on the principle of relativity. It is only fair, after the criticisms of Marcel Brillouin and Max Abraham, that an article written by one of the chief advocates of the theory should appear in *Scientia*. Einstein distinguishes two theories of relativity: the theory in the "narrow sense" and that in the "wide sense." If we refer a motion to a system of coordinates K, for which the Newtonian equations are valid, any other system of coordinates which is in a uniform motion of translation with respect to K can be substituted for K. The "principle of relativity in the narrow sense" is the hypothesis of the equivalence of all such systems of coordinates for the formulation of the laws of motion and of the general physical laws. Thus, the principle of relativity is as old as mechanics itself, and, from the point of view of experience, its validity could never be doubted. However, the electrodynamics of Maxwell and Lorentz leads to the conclusion that every luminous ray is propagated in the vacuum with a determined velocity c which is independent of the direction of propagation and the state of motion of the luminous source. This deduction seems to be inconsistent with the principle of relativity. But an exact analysis of the content of our spatial and temporal data has proved that this inconsistency is only apparent, since it rests on the following arbitrary hypotheses: (1) The assertion that two events taking place in different places are simultaneous, has a content independent of the choice of the system of reference; (2) The distance between the places where two events simultaneously take place is independent of the choice of the system of reference. If we give up these arbitrary hypotheses, the above principle of the constancy of the velocity of light, which results from the well-attested theory of Maxwell and Lorentz, becomes compatible with the principle of relativity. The theories of gravitation are not all, as Abraham stated, inconsistent with the principle of relativity. The second part of the article is devoted to the "theory of relativity in the wide sense," which has hitherto hardly been confirmed by experience, but to which Einstein has been led from his philosophical standpoint, and which may be regarded as a development, and not an abandonment of the former theory of relativity. Svante Arrhenius discusses the problem of the formation of the milky way. Filippo Bottazzi gives the first article of a study on the fundamental physiological activities, entitled "nervous activity and the elementary processes on which it is founded." J. Arthur Thomson discusses "Sex-characters" and gives a critical review of Kammerer's great work on the collection of experimental data on the origin, evolution and development of sex-characters. A. Meillet has a paper on the problem of the parentage of languages. The difficulty experienced in making all languages enter into the genealogical classification has led certain eminent linguists to take away from the principle of this classification its precision and rigor or to apply it in an inexact manner. This article shows in how far a genealogical classification of languages is possible and useful, and what can be hoped from it. Roberto Michels writes on economy and politics. Aldo Mieli has a critical note on the precursors of Galileo, in which he gives an account of the researches of Pierre Duhem on the origins of Galilean dynamics in the Middle Ages. Jean Buridan, who was rector of the university of Paris from 1327 to 1347, had a very clear idea of what has been called, since Leibniz, *vis viva*. What he called "impetus" he determined by the multiplication of velocity, volume, and density, and explained the cause of the accelerated motion of falling bodies. Buridan also applied to the heavens the dynamics established for earthly motions. "Newton," says Duhem, "had an idea of mass which was not very different from that which Buridan defined." Other people dealt with in this note are Nicole Oresme, who died in 1382, and had anticipated Copernican astronomy and Cartesian geometry, and discovered the Galilean law according to which the space described by a uniformly accelerated body increases with the times; Albert de Saxe, who anticipated a well-known error of Galileo's; and Dominique Soto, who was born in 1494. It is interesting to notice that this work of Duhem's is referred to very fully in the additions to the last German edition of Mach's *Mechanics*. A supplementary volume containing these additions will shorty by issued by the Open Court Publishing Co., so as to make it possible to read these additions in a small volume separate from the English fourth edition, without the expense of buying a large new book. There is also, in *Scientia*, a general review by L. Suali on the history of Indian philosophy. There are various reviews of books and periodicals, a chronicle of recent and forthcoming events and French translations of English, German, and Italian articles.

* * *

In *Mind* for April, 1914, the first article is by C. Lloyd Morgan on "Are Meanings Inherited?", in which the author discusses recent publications by Stout and McDougall. Henry Rutgers Marshall has a short paper on "Psychic Function and Psychic Structure." F. Melian Stawell puts a number of questions about Bertrand Russell's *Problems of Philosophy* (London and New York, 1912). Horace M. Kallen writes on "James, Bergson, and Traditional Metaphysics." C. I. Lewis had, in a paper of 1912, tried to show that "the present calculus of propositions, in the algebra of logic, is to ordinary inference what a non-Euclidean geometry is to our space. In particular, it asserts the presence of implication relations whose existence in our world may be doubted." The purpose of this note is "to outline a 'Euclidean' calculus of propositions—that is, one which will be applicable throughout to our ordinary modes of inference and proof." Charles Mercier, continuing the discussion between various logicians as to whether inversion is a valid inference, decides that it is not, and has some amazing sneers at traditional logic. "For practical purposes," says he, "the syllogism is about as useful as an unreliable apparatus for converting new-laid eggs into stale ones." A sympathetic review, by Miss E. E. C. Jones, of Mercier's *New Logic* (London, Heinemann, 1912; Chicago, The Open Court Publishing Co.), is contained in this number of *Mind.* J. E. Turner makes some critical remarks on Bertrand Russell's treatment of sense-data and knowledge in his *Problems.* Many reviews of books and periodicals and other notes etc., follow.

* * *

In the *Revue de Métaphysique et de Morale* for May, 1914, there is a very thorough study, by D. Rouston of the moral philosophy of Frédéric Rauh. There is a reprodution of Maurice Cauelery's lecture before the Paris School of Advanced Social Studies on the nature of biological laws, in which the author concludes, like O. Bütschli, that we can only grasp that part of vital phenomena which can be explained physico-chemically, and we can say of both vitalism and mechanism: "By their fruits ye shall know them." Emile Bréhier writes on philosophy and myth. Edmond Laskine contributes the second and final part of his critical study of the transformations of law in the nineteenth century. Charles Dunan discusses the practical question of electoral rights. There is the usual supplement containing reviews of new books and periodicals, and other notes.

Φ

BOOK REVIEWS.

ENCYCLOPAEDIA OF THE PHILOSOPHICAL SCIENCES. Vol. I, Logic. By *Arnold Ruge, Wilhelm Windelband* and others. Translated by *B. Ethel Meyer.* London: Macmillan, 1913. Pp. 269. Price $2.00.

This is an English edition of the German encyclopedia of Windelband and Ruge, made under the direction of Sir Henry Jones. The present volume comprises articles from eminent thinkers of Europe and America which are intended to present the determining principle of their thought upon the subject of logic. The views of German logicians are represented by Windelband of Heidelberg, who treats very generally of the phenomenology of knowledge, methodology and the theory of knowledge. The logic of English speaking countries is represented not by Russell or Peirce but by Professor Royce of Harvard who deals particularly with the types of order and with the relation of logic as methodology to logic as the science of order. M. Couturat expresses embarrassment in representing French philosophy, first because he makes no claim to expressing the views of French philosophers on logic, and second because the theories he presents are due to authors of Italy, Germany and England and particularly not of France—though in thus disclaiming for France any part in the logistic movement he is unfair to the significance of his own work in this line. For this new type of logic he prefers the term "logistic" or "algorithmic logic" to the formerly prevalent "symbolic" or "mathematical" logic or the "algebra of logic." From the point of view of this modern logistic he explains the principles and methodology of the logic of propositions, of concepts and of relations, and the relation between logic and language.

Benedetto Croce of Naples, in treating of "The Task of Logic," disregards the claims of the logisticians on the ground that logistic while providing rules for practice cannot be a science, and he considers logic as essentially a science, but a philosophical as distinct from an empirical science. He says: "It is no part of its business to assist thought,—to further the progress of natural science, mathematics or any of the special sciences, to facilitate research or to simplify the art of disputation. It is a theory entirely devoted to the task of inquiring into the nature of thought, as exemplified in science as a whole and in the particular sciences."

Another Italian, Professor Enriques of Bologna, treats the problems of logic in a more representative and eclectic manner as the science of exact thinking. He summarizes logical principles, operations, concepts and relations, discussing also definition and deduction. He then analyzes briefly the validity of logical principles and the relation of logic to metaphysical thought.

In this volume Russia is represented by Nicolaj Losskij who writes on "The Transformation of the Concept of Consciousness in Modern Epistemology and its Bearing on Logic." *p*

VOL. XXV APRIL, 1915 NO. 2

THE MONIST

THE DISCIPLES OF JOHN AND THE ODES OF SOLOMON.

THE purpose of the present study is to prove that the Odes of Solomon were written by one of the Disciples of John at Ephesus, not long before 55 A. D.

The great strength of the movement started by the Baptist is implied by the references to it in Josephus,[1] the Gospels, the Acts and the early Fathers.[2] Some scholars[3] see in the Mandaeans, otherwise known as Sabaeans or "St. John's Christians," a sect on the Persian Gulf which persisted until the nineteenth century, an offspring of the Disciples. The reverence in which they hold John's name, and the emphasis they place upon baptism, support this theory, but if it is correct the sect must have borrowed much from Christianity and other religions.

The doctrines[4] of the community were those of a modified Judaism. There is every reason to suppose that its votaries clung to circumcision and the law, as did the earliest Christians. Their distinctive marks were baptism,[5]

[1] Antiquities, XVIII, 5, 2.

[2] Conveniently collected by W. Bauer, *Das Leben Jesu im Zeitalter der neutestamentlichen Apocryphen*, 1909, pp. 85-7, 101-109.

[3] Neander, *Church History* (English, 1866), I, 376; B. W. Bacon, *The Story of Paul*, 1904, p. 180; *Encyclopædia Britannica, s. v.* "Mandaeans."

[4] It has been asserted that we have in the recently published *Fragments of a Zadokite Work*, a writing of the Disciples. See G. Margoliouth in the *Athenæum*, Nov. 26, 1910 and in the *Expositor*, Dec. 1911 and March 1912. Notwithstanding the dissent of R. H. Charles, I regard this identification as most probable.

[5] Perhaps borrowed from earlier Jewish sects. Josephus, *De Bell. Jud.*, II, 8; and *Test. Levi*, XVI, 3f.

asceticism or "fasting,"[6] including probably abstinence from wine[7] and disapproval of marriage,[8] emphasis on "conversion,"[9] and on the Messianic hope. The asceticism of the sect is brought out by traditions about its founder. Thus Justin[10] writes that he ate *nothing but* locusts and wild honey. Even the insects were offensive to the vegetarian principles of the Ebionites who, by the slight change of ἀκρίς to ἐγκρίς reduced his fare to cakes of honey and oil.[11] Tatian[12] also gave him the Old Testament diet of milk and honey.

The coming of the Messiah is the burden of John's message in the oldest source,[13] and it continued to be very prominent in the teaching of his disciples later. It is certain, however, that neither John nor his disciples recognized this Messiah in Jesus. Our oldest source says nothing of a meeting between John and Jesus, but it does recount that while in prison the Baptist sent to Christ to inquire if he were really the coming one. The answer implies an affirmative, but John's reception of it is not related, and Jesus's subsequent discourse to the multitude proves that Q reckoned John as a good man, indeed, but not within Christ's own circle of disciples, "the kingdom of heaven." Indeed, had the Baptists all recognized Jesus they could not have continued as a separate sect. The pains to deny the

[6] Mark ii. 18-22. [7] Luke i. 15.

[8] Shown by the certification of John's virginity by Tertullian, *De monogamia*, 8 and Pseudo-Clemens, *Virginibus*, I, 6.

[9] This is the best translation of μετάνοια. Cf. W. B. Smith, *Ecce Deus*, 1912, p. 286. Further, the word is used of turning from the false to the true faith in Rev. ix. 20 and xvi. 11, and in the *Martyrdom of Polycarp*, IX, 2 and XI, 1. In Ecclesiasticus xliv. 16, it is used of Enoch's translation, interpreted by Philo as a conversion to a better life, (note in Wace's edition of the Apocrypha, *ad. loc.*). W. W. Jäger has shown that the word was used by the Stoics of ethical conversion (*Umkehrung*), *Göttingische Gelehrten-Anzeigen*, 1913, pp. 590ff.

[10] Dialogue with Trypho, Chap. 88.

[11] Epiphanius, *Haer.*, XXX, 13.

[12] *Fragments of the Commentary of Ephrem Syrus on the Diatessaron*, 1895, pp. 17f.

[13] Q, represented by Matt. iii. 5. 7-12 = Luke iii. 3-9; and Matt. xi. 2-19 = Luke vii. 18-35.

Messianic claims of John, and to make him point to Jesus, in the Third[14] and Fourth Gospels,[15] point, considering the polemic bias of both authors, to the same conclusion. When Paul converted a number of these men at Ephesus he was obliged to inform them of the name of the Messiah whose coming their master announced.[16] Marcion and his fellows, in stating not only that John never recognized Jesus but that he was actually offended at him[17] as at something alien, were probably not giving the results of their Biblical researches but of their observations of the sect. In much later times the Sabaeans — spiritual descendents of the Johannites—represented Jesus as the corrupter of John's baptism.[18] Many scholars,[19] in fact, now recognize that the two movements were distinct, though others still persist in treating the Disciples as merely "imperfectly instructed Christians."[20]

The chief support of this latter view is the verse in Acts, which tells that Apollos, a Disciple of John, "taught accurately the things concerning Jesus."[21] As it stands, this verse is a mistake, due neither to Luke's carelessness[22] nor to his poor source,[23] but to the fact that Apollos's Messianic teaching was so closely similar to that of the Christians that Luke believed that it must refer to the same Christ. The reason for this similarity is not that either sect borrowed from the other, but that both drew on a large

[14] Harnack, *Luke the Physician*, 226.

[15] Baldensperger, *Der Prolog des vierten Evangeliums*, 1898; M. Dibelius, *Johannes der Täufer*, 1911, p. 112; B. W. Bacon, *The Fourth Gospel in Debate and Research*, 1909, p. 290.

[16] Acts xix. 4.

[17] Tertullian, *Against Marcion*, IV, 18; Adamantius, *Dialogue*, I, 26.

[18] Neander, *Church History*, (English, 1866), I, 447.

[19] E. g., McGiffert, *Apostolic Age*, 1897, 291; O. Pfleiderer, *Primitive Christianity*, (English, 1909), II, 255.

[20] R. B. Rackham, *Acts of the Apostles*, 1901, pp. 340f; M. Dibelius, *Johannes der Täufer*, 1911, pp. 90f.

[21] Acts xviii. 25.

[22] B. W. Bacon, *Hibbert Journal*, IX, 748.

[23] Pfleiderer, *loc. cit.*

body of Messianic ideas current in the Jewish writings, particularly the Apocrypha and Pseudepigrapha. Apollos and the evangelists alike based on this source their Messianic doctrine, the only difference being that the Christians applied it all to a definite person, while the Disciples did not.[24]

The best known community of Johannites was that founded by Apollos at Ephesus. Paul came to this great city after being driven out of Corinth, probably in the year 52. Not long after his arrival he made a journey through Antioch, Galatia and Phrygia, thereupon returning and making Ephesus his headquarters for some three years.[25] It is during his absence that Luke places the advent of Apollos and the founding of the Baptist community,[26] but, judging by the strength of the sect and allowing for Luke's scanty sources, it is quite probable that it had been founded some years earlier. Apollos was soon converted to Christianity by Paul's neophytes, Aquila and Priscilla, and the Apostle, on his return, converted twelve other men of the same persuasion. Though Luke rather implies that this was the whole community he is mistaken, for the Fourth Gospel, written at Ephesus half a century later than the period in question, indicates that the Disciples were still strong there.

Paul's First Epistle to the Corinthians, written at Ephesus (xvi. 8, 19), has several allusions to the Disciples of John. The section i. 13-17 is apparently directed against Apollos who laid much emphasis upon baptism. If it were established, as it is asserted by an early writer, that Simon Magus[27] was a Disciple of John, we might see in the phrase "power of God"[28] a catchword borrowed from the Disciples by the Apostle. It is probable that the words "we preach

[24] Reuss, *Les Actes des Apôtres,* 1876, p. 187; W. B. Smith, *Der vorchristliche Jesus,* 2d ed., 1911, Chap. I.

[25] Acts xx. 31.

[26] Acts xviii. 24—xix. 7.

[27] Clementine Homilies, XXIII.

[28] 1 Cor. i. 18; cf. Acts viii. 10.

a Messiah crucified" (verse 23) indicate that Christs of other types had been preached at Corinth, and one of these was not improbably the Messiah of the Baptist. In ii. 10[29] and also in Ephesians v. 14[30] we have quotations from a lost work, the Revelation of Elias. It is remarkable that the only two known quotations from this book should be found in letters either written from or addressed to Ephesus, surely a strong indication that it was early current, if not indigenous, there. Remembering that John was early given the rôle of Elias,[31] and that the author of the Fourth Gospel, with his eye on the Disciples at Ephesus, thought it worth while to contradict this ascription,[32] which, nevertheless, persisted in circles drawing heavily on Ephesian sources,[33] it is surely legitimate to conjecture that this lost Apocalypse was one of the sacred books of the Johannites. As the quotation in Ephesians v. 14 is also very like a verse in the Odes of Solomon, VIII, 3, 4, this surmise is still further corroborated.

The most certain reference to the Disciples in 1 Corinthians is found in the saying that "our fathers. . . .were all baptized unto Moses in the cloud and in the sea."[34] As nothing is known of this in Jewish literature, Paul was either inventing it or drawing on some very recent legend. If the former, his meaning is plain: As the baptism of John prepared for the triumph of Jesus, so the triumph of Joshua (in Greek, "Jesus") was prepared by a baptism in the Red Sea, by Moses. There are two indications, however, that he was following an earlier, Ephesian, source, and, if so, it was surely not unconnected with the Johannites. A somewhat similar thought is found in the Odes of Solo-

[29] According to Origen, Ambrosiaster and Euthalius, *Encyclopædia Britannica*, 11th ed., II, 173.

[30] According to Epiphanius, *ibid.* Of course "the Messiah" here need not refer to Jesus.

[31] Matt. xi. 14.

[32] John i. 21.

[33] In the *Pistis Sophia* which quoted so much from the Odes of Solomon; Bauer, *op. cit.*, 109; also in Justin Martyr's (Ephesian) Dialogue, 49.

[34] 1 Cor. x. 1, 2.

mon,[35] and, far more explicitly, the same comparison of Moses with the Baptist is made by Justin in his Dialogue with Trypho,[36] an Ephesian production.

It is highly probable that 1 Cor. xii. 2 is also an allusion to the yet unconverted Disciples. It is true that any one who did not believe in Jesus might anathematize him, but it is hard to imagine who, save the Johannites, could have done so, claiming to speak by the Spirit. With them emphasis on the Holy Spirit was a cardinal doctrine, dating, according to Q, from the first days. Further evidence of their opposition to Jesus will be given later.

Finally, it may be left undetermined whether baptism for the dead (1 Cor. xv. 29) was one of their customs. Paul does not disapprove of it.

The Epistle to the Ephesians[37] has, apart from many reminiscences of the Odes of Solomon, at least three allusions to the Disciples of John. The expression "sealed with the Holy Spirit of promise"[38] is certainly borrowed from the "baptism with the Holy Ghost" promised by John, as is proved by the statement of Irenaeus (an Ephesian by birth) that "baptism is the seal of eternal life."[39] The second reference is the emphasis on "one baptism";[40] the third is the citation from the Revelation of Elias, mentioned above.

It is sometimes thought that other Pauline epistles were written from Ephesus,[41] and still others addressed

[35] Ode XXXIX, 6. Cf. E. A. Abbott, *Light on the Gospel from an Ancient Poet*, 1912, p. 480.

[36] Chap. 49.

[37] Space will not allow me to go into the much debated question of the authorship and destination of this epistle. I can only say that, after careful study of the subject, I regard the early date of the letter, and its connection with Ephesus, as certain. I think it also probable that it is by Paul and written to a circle of Asiatic churches of which Ephesus was the chief.

[38] Eph. i. 13. Matt. iii. 11.

[39] "Exhibition of the Apostolic Teaching," Chap. 3; *Texte und Untersuchungen*, XXXI, 1907.

[40] Eph. iv. 5.

[41] Galatians and Colossians; cf. Harnack, *Die Entstehung des neuen Testaments*, 1914, pp. 106f.

to persons in that city,[42] but in none of them is there anything pertinent to the present subject.

The next literature bearing directly on the Ephesian Disciples is found in the Johannine writings. The Apocalypse has nothing on them, but the very evident attitude of the Fourth Gospel to them has already been pointed out, its whole treatment of the Baptist, indeed, being conditioned by polemic tendency. A very striking, though I believe hitherto unrecognized, allusion to them is found in 1 John v. 6: "This is he that came by water and the blood, even Jesus Christ; not with water [of baptism] only, but with the water and with the blood [of the eucharist and passion]." The Johannites had, of course, no eucharist, but only baptism, and the words apply better to them than to the Docetists. Another reference is 1 John iv. 1-3 about the spirits which confess not that Jesus Christ has come in the flesh, or that he is of God. This also is usually and quite rightly applied to the Docetists, but did not their doctrines arise naturally from the "Christless Christianity" of the Baptists? The Ignatian epistles have much about these heretics, but nothing else clearly indicating the Disciples. Justin Martyr, at Ephesus, mentions the "Baptists" as a Jewish sect.[43] It is beyond the purpose of the present paper to go into the later literature of Ephesus—the Acts of John, the writings of Ignatius, Papias and the rest.

It remains to be proved that we have, in the "Odes of Solomon," a work written by one of the Disciples. Since their publication, in 1909, by their brilliant discoverer, J. Rendell Harris. they have been the subject of a vast amount of study. Many hypotheses of their origin have been advanced to account for the peculiar phenomena of their dogma. For they present the strangest mixture of Judaism, (supposed) Christianity and heresy hitherto ever

[42] Rom. xvi and parts of 2 Tim.

[43] Dialogue with Trypho, Chap. 80.

met with, and all of it set forth in a style of poetry and exaltation far above the usual level of anything outside the Gospels or Pauline epistles. Full of phrases which strongly suggest the thought of New Testament writers, there is not one indication that the author knew a single book now in our canon. Recognizing the validity of God's law and of worship in the temple at Jerusalem, he is yet broad in his sympathies and highly spiritual in his interpretation of circumcision and sacrifice as of the heart. His great Messianic passages show striking similarities to the story of the Gospels along with divergencies which are difficult to account for. He speaks of the mother of the Messiah now as the Holy Spirit and now as a Virgin; he alludes to his death by crucifixion, and his descent into Hades, but knows nothing of his resurrection. He speaks of Father, Son and Holy Spirit, but never mentions the name of Jesus nor any of his words nor any events in his ministry save the ones just recorded. Full of allusions to baptism, these songs know nothing of the eucharist. Written as the continuation of a Jewish work of the first century before Christ, they narrowly escaped adoption into the New Testament canon. These and many similar puzzles are the conditions for solving the problem of the date and provenance of the newly found work. I believe that they all suggest Ephesus, a date earlier than 1 Corinthians, and an author whose point of view agrees in all respects with what is otherwise known of the Disciples of the Baptist.

First, as to their place of origin. At present they are known only in Syriac,[44] but it is probable that they are a translation from the Greek, for it is certain that they were early read in the Greek, and were inserted in this language in some manuscripts of the New Testament. Harris at

[44] J. R. Harris, *The Odes of Solomon*, 2d ed., 1911, pp. 35ff; Burkitt, "A New MS of the Odes of Solomon," *Journal of Biblical Literature*, XIII, 1912, pp. 372ff. R. H. Connolly in *Journal of Theological Studies*, 1913, pp. 531ff.

first suggested a Syrian, or Syro-Palestinian origin, and this ascription has been accepted by most scholars.[45] F. C. Burkitt,[46] however, thinks that they originated in the Monophysite Syrian colony in Egypt, which produced translations of the Acts of Peter, Paul and Luke. The distinguished Syriac scholar is perhaps right about the provenance of the Syriac translation, but, notwithstanding the fact that the Odes were extensively used in the *Pistis Sophia,* there is slight reason to suppose that they originated in Egypt. Far greater and earlier use of them can be found elsewhere.

The merit of first seeing that the Odes originated at Ephesus belongs to Mrs. Margaret D. Gibson.[47] While editing the Syriac commentary of Ish'odad of Merv (c. 850) on Paul's epistles she found this note to Ephesians v. 14: "It is said to one of the Believers who was at Ephesus; because at that time there were many at Ephesus with different gifts of the Spirit; and they had this also that they could make psalms and hymns like the Blessed David." Again, in Theodore of Mopsuestia (fourth century) she found, in the same connection: "Some say that at that time many graces of the Spirit were given to them, among others that they could make Psalms, as it was given to the Blessed David to do before the advent of Christ." Moreover she found to this verse (otherwise attributed, as we have seen, to the Revelation of Elias)[48] a fairly close parallel in Ode VIII, 3, 4: "To speak with watchfulness by his [the Lord's] light: Rise up and be raised, ye who for a time have been laid low; tell forth, ye who were in silence [i. e., dead]; speak! since your mouth hath been opened." Further she finds that Severianus says that in

[45] *Realencyklopädie für protestantische Theologie und Kirche,* XXIV, 375ff.

[46] *Loc. cit* in note 44.

[47] *Athenæum,* 1914, pp. 530, 559.

[48] This fact causes no difficulty. As we have seen good reason to believe that the Revelation of Elias was an Ephesian production, probably the work of a disciple of John, both the Ode and Paul may have quoted from it.

this verse Paul is referring to a spiritual psalm, and she suggests that the words about "psalms and hymns and spiritual songs" in Ephesians v. 19 apply to the Odes. On conferring with Dr. Mingana she found that he agreed with her, and proposed that the Odes be considered of Ephesian origin and earlier than the Gospels.

Dr. Harris, without definitely committing himself, has spoken favorably of this hypothesis.[49] He points out a further striking parallel between the language of Paul, Ephesians v. 15-18, and that of Odes XI and XXXVIII. "Be not unwise," says the Apostle, "but wise....be not foolish but understand what the will of the Lord is. And be not drunken with wine, wherein is riot, but be filled with the Spirit." With this compare the same thought in Ode XI, 6ff: "Speaking water touched my lips from the fountain of the Lord plenteously: and I drank and was inebriated with the living water that doth not die; and my inebriation was not one without knowledge, for I forsook vanity." Again, in Ode XXXVIII: "They invite many to the banquet and give themselves to drink of the wine of their intoxication, and remove their wisdom and knowledge and make them without intelligence." The same contrast between hurtful and spiritual intoxication is made by Theodore of Mopsuestia.

I shall now proceed to confirm the hypothesis thus started by pointing out the numerous parallels or references to the Odes in other extant Ephesian literature, beginning with some in the middle of the second century, and working backward to the middle of the first.

The Leucian Acts of John have two distinct parallels to the thought of the Odes. The first is that of the "unenvious God,"[50] all the more striking because it is in a way a con-

[49] *Atheneum*, 1914, pp. 760f. His suggestion that Eph. v. 14 comes from the missing second Ode is not necessary. Cf. last note.

[50] Acts of John, 55. Ode III, 7, as translated by Ungnad and Staerk: *Die Oden Salomos*, 1910: "weil es keinen Neid bei dem Herrn gibt."

tradiction to the "jealous God" of the Decalogue. The second is the comparison of Christ to a mirror.[51]

Justin Martyr, who at least spent a good part of his life at Ephesus, speaks of early Christian hymns (First Apology, XIII), and in his Dialogue with Trypho (a debate held at Ephesus) Chap. 22, uses language about the non-observance of the Sabbath closely parallel to that found in Ode XVI, 15.

A resemblance in Irenaeus has been pointed out by Harris to Ode IV, 9. The cup of milk in Ode XIX recalls the language of Irenaeus *Against Heresies,* IV, 38, 1.[52]

Ignatius, who lived in constant intercourse with the Ephesians, seems to have borrowed from the Odes (XI, 6, 7) the phrase about the "living and speaking water" (*ad Romanos,* VII). A far more striking similarity is found in the thought of his Epistle to the Ephesians XIX, that the "three shouting mysteries" of Mary's virginity, and the birth and death of the Lord, "were wrought in the stillness of God," compared with Ode XIX, where it is said that the mixture of God's milk whereby (apparently) the Virgin conceived, was "given to the worlds[53] without their knowing it." The pre-existence of the Messiah is also found in Ode XLI, 14-16 and in Ignatius to the Magnesians, VI, 1.

The parallels between the Odes and the Gospel and Epistles of John[54] are extremely numerous. Harris recognized at once that he was in the atmosphere of Johannine thought,[55] and yet he was unable to point out a single direct quotation of one from the other. Harnack emphasized

[51] Ode XIII, 1; Acts of John, ed. M. R. James in *Texts and Studies,* V, 1, 1897; Bonnet, *Acta Apost. Apoc.,* II, 1, 1898, p. 198.

[52] Conybeare in *Zeitsch. f. nt. Wissenschaft,* 1913, p. 96.

[53] On reading the plural, cf. Newbold in *Journal of Bib. Lit.,* XXX, 189.

[54] The Ephesian origin of this is all but universally recognized. W. Bauer, however, (*Das Johannesevangelium,* in Lietzmann's *Handbuch zum N. T.,* 1912) thinks an Antiochian or Egyptian provenance possible, though not so probable as an Ephesian.

[55] See also P. Wendland, *Die urchristlichen Literaturformen,* 1912, p. 245.

this judgment of Harris; although reference to the name of Jesus, to his earthly life, his word and example fails in the Odes, yet in other respects "even in details the thought of the Fourth Gospel is prepared for it." The Odes are full of φῶς, ἀγάπη, ζωή, γνῶσις, ἀνάπαυσις, ἀφθαρσία—the very staples of Johannine theology. It would be entirely superfluous for me to enumerate in this place all the parallels that can be found. For the greater part of them I refer to the notes of Harris in his second edition. But a few which have either escaped him, or which have particular bearing on my thesis, require to be given.

In Ode III, 11, "he who has pleasure in the Living One will become living," we have a verse that might well find a place in Jesus's sermon on the raising of Lazarus, John xi. 25ff.

Ode IV is a discussion of the theme in the opening words: "No man, O my God, changeth thy holy place; and it is not [possible] that he should change it and put it in another place: because he hath no power over it." The author is arguing that the Jerusalem temple is the only proper place to offer acceptable worship to God, and Harris believes he sees the occasion of the Ode in the closing of the temple at Leontopolis in Egypt, 73 A. D., a place of worship started as a substitute for that at Jerusalem. This hazardous identification is made impossible by considerations of chronology. If (as Harris now seems disposed to recognize) the Odes are quoted in Ephesians, and if (as will be shown below) they are alluded to nine times in 1 Corinthians, their date must be prior to 55 A. D., and they cannot refer to an event twenty years later. And yet I believe we have an important historical fact recorded here, one which also left its mark on the Fourth Gospel. I infer that there was a real discussion of the validity of worship outside of the temple, and that the author took the narrower Jewish view. In time, however, a broader spirit came to prevail, and, as the question continued to be a burning one, the author of the Fourth Gospel devoted to it the important section (chap. iv) in which Jesus discusses it with the woman of Samaria and enunciates the great principle that "God is a spirit and they that worship him must worship him in spirit and in truth," "neither in this mountain, nor in Jerusalem."[56] This procedure is highly characteristic of the method of "John" whose treatment of his subject is entirely from the standpoint of his own day, and who seems to have selected from his sources chiefly that which he thought needed to be corrected.

Verses on the living water in Odes VI, XI and XXX find cognate thoughts in John iv. 14, vi. 35, vii. 37.

The "abundant room in Paradise" (Ode XI, 20) is but another name for the "many mansions" of John xiv. 2. (Also found in Enoch 39, 4 and Secrets of Enoch 61, 2.)

"The dwelling-place of the Word is man: and its truth is love," (Ode XII, 11) was certainly in the mind of him who wrote: "The Word became flesh and dwelt among us ....full of grace and truth" (John i. 14).

The "door" of Ode XVII, 10 is the "way" of John xiv. 5, 6.

Speaking in the person of one greater, our poet calls himself "the shining light, the Son of God."[57] It cannot be without significance that this is precisely the title applied in the Fourth Gospel by the Baptist to Jesus (i. 6ff) and by Jesus to the Baptist (v. 35).

The Apocalypse also has a number of ideas in common with the Odes. One similarity is the use of "Hallelujah" by both. Much space in both writings is given to Paradise and to crowns and rivers and trees of life. The Lord is

[56] I note that the same suggestion has previously been made by Haussleiter in the *Theologisches Literaturblatt*, XXXI, No. 12.

[57] "Wurde ich das glänzende [Licht] der Sohn Gottes genannt." Ungnad-Staerk, Ode, XXXVI, 3.

the sun in Ode XV, 2 and in Revelation xxi. 23. It is not to be doubted that the great dragon with seven heads—namely Rome—in Ode XXII, 5, is the same that appears in Revelation xiii. 3 and xvii. 9.

Similarities in thought or language to the synoptic gospels are almost entirely wanting. I have noted only three, and it is highly significant that two of these certainly, and probably the third also, are to passages about John the Baptist. They will be evaluated below.

There is one parallel to James—the simile of the mirror—but I have noticed none to Hebrews, 2 Peter or Jude. To 1 Peter, on the other hand, there are three, and though two of them happen to have resemblances in Ephesians, they can hardly be explained simply as having been borrowed from this epistle by the author of 1 Peter, for he is closer to the Odes than is Paul. Be it remembered that this writing is a pseudepigraph claiming to originate in Rome but addressed to the churches of Asia and of neighboring provinces. The "sojourners and pilgrims" of ii. 11 remind one of the similar expression in Ode III, 7. In saying that "the Spirit of Christ testified beforehand to the sufferings of Christ" I believe the author had the Odes in mind. (See below.) The remarkable association of the descent into Hades with baptism found in iv. 6ff and in the Odes will also be weighed in its proper place.

Among Paul's letters I have found no parallels to the Odes in Thessalonians, in Galatians, in Philippians, in Philemon or in the Pastoral epistles. There is one parallel in Colossians (also in Ephesians), there are two in 2 Corinthians, four in Romans, nine in 1 Corinthians and nine in Ephesians. This distribution strongly suggests that Ephesus was the home of the Odes, for 1 Corinthians was written from that city, 2 Corinthians and Romans probably soon after leaving it. Taking up the epistles in their inverse chronological order:

Three of the parallels to Ephesians have already been pointed out in quotations from Mrs. Gibson and Dr. Harris. Others are: The use of "the Beloved" as a title of the Christ, Eph. i. 6, Ode III, 5. "I shall be no stranger," Ode III, 7 and Eph. ii. 19. The use made of Psalm lxviii. 18, "leading captivity captive" in Eph. iv. 8 and Ode X, 3. The descent into Hades in Ode XLII and Eph. iv. 10. The comparison of the love of Christ and his people to that of man and wife (also in the Old Testament) in Ode XLII, 9ff and Eph. v. 32. The pleroma of Col. ii. 9, Eph. iii 19, and iv. 13 is probably the "fulness" of Ode XIX, 5. That the reference to baptism as "the seal of the Holy Spirit of promise" is borrowed from the Odes has been proved above (Eph. i. 13).

In Romans xi. 29 the idea that "the gifts and calling of God are without repentance" seems to be dependent on Ode IV, 11. "Redeemed by grace" and "Justified by grace" (Odes IX, 5 and XXIX, 5) are found again in Rom. iii. 24. In Ode X, 4 the idea that the service of God is freedom from sin is given in converse form in Rom. vi. 18. In Ode XXIV, 3 the simile of the abysses crying to the Lord like women in travail strongly suggests the metaphor of the creation groaning and travailing together in Rom. viii. 22.

The association of Father, Son and Holy Spirit, rare in very early Christian literature, is found in Ode XIX and in 2 Cor. xiii. 14. "Subduing the imaginations of the peoples" (Ode XXIX, 8) recalls a similar expression in 2 Cor. x. 5.

In 1 Cor. striving for the crown that cannot wither (ix. 25) is a combination of the ideas brought forward in Ode I and IX, 9. The joining of the believer to God is spoken of in Ode III, 8 and 1 Cor. vi. 17. The assertion that God is zealous to make known to us his gifts is borrowed from Ode VI, 5 by 1 Cor. ii. 12. The metaphor of the mirror (xiii. 12) was certainly suggested by Ode XIII, 1. "I have put on incorruption through his name and have put off corruption by his grace" (XV, 8) is language as close as possible to that of Paul in 1 Cor. xv. 53. The comparison of God and his people to the head and members (Ode XVII, 14) suggested 1 Cor. vi. 5. "Milk for babes" (1 Cor. iii. 2) is a reminiscence of Ode XIX. The parallel between Ode XXXIX, 6ff and 1 Cor. x. 2 has already been discussed.

I believe there is one other local allusion in the Odes, which has also great intrinsic interest. It is in Ode XXIII:

"His [God's] thought was like a letter; his will descended from on high, and it was sent like an arrow which is shot violently from the bow: and many hands rushed to the letter to seize it and to take it and to read it: and it escaped from their fingers and they were affrighted at it and at the seal that was upon it. Because it was not permitted to them to loose its seal: for the power that was over the seal was greater than they. But those who saw it went after the letter that they might know where it would alight, and who should read it and who should hear it. But a wheel received it and came over it: and there was with it the sign of the kingdom and of the government: and everything which tried to move the wheel it mowed and cut down: and it gathered the multitude of adversaries, and bridged the rivers and crossed over and rooted up many forests and made a broad path. The head went down to the feet, for down to the feet ran the wheel, and that which was a sign upon it. The letter was one of command, because all places were assembled together;[58] and there were seen at its[59] [the wheel's] head the head which was revealed, even the Son of Truth from the Most High Father, and he inherited and took possession of everything.

[58] "Weil versammelt waren allzumal alle Orte," Ungnad-Staerk.

[59] As "letter" and "wheel" are both feminine "it" might refer to either.

And the thought of the many was brought to nought, and all the apostates hasted and fled away. And those who persecuted and were enraged became extinct. And the letter was a great tablet, which was wholly written by the finger of God: and the name of the Father was on it, and of the Son and of the Holy Spirit, to rule for ever and ever. Hallelujah."

In explanation of the above Dr. Harris suggests that some book claiming divine authority may have been published, and that this may possibly have been a *"descensus ad inferos,"* but he confesses his inability to penetrate deeper into the enigma here offered. Mr. Newbold[60] has proposed a very elaborate interpretation of this ode, finding in it the gnostic conception of the descent of Christ through different worlds on the wheel of the zodiac; he even thinks that the author cryptically indicates the astronomical times of Christ's conception, birth and baptism. His theory is too complicated and precarious to obtain ready assent.

My own solution of the problem may at first appear startling, and I lay no great stress on it, as all that I wish to prove is amply supported by other evidence. Personally, however, I am convinced that this poem contains a most interesting local allusion. "What man is there that knoweth not that the city of the Ephesians is temple-keeper of the great Artemis, and of [her image] which fell down from heaven?"[61] In this verse the words "her image" have to be supplied, the original having simply διοπέτης. This may have been a meteorite, like the black stone in the Caaba, at some early date roughly hewn into an image. On the girdle and feet of this statue were the far-famed "Ephesian letters," inscriptions in Hebrew characters[62] con-

[60] *Journal of Biblical Literature,* XXXI, 174ff.

[61] Acts xix. 35.

[62] *Realencyclopädie für protestantische Theologie und Kirche,* X, 543; XXI, 619.

sidered magical, and as charms copied and circulated on papyri. These, I believe, constituted the oracular letters written in cypher (such is the significance of the "seal") shot from heaven to earth like an arrow. It will at once be objected that it would be impossible for a Jewish proselyte to see in these objects of a heathen cult a message from his own God. But there is extant direct proof that the early Christian Fathers regarded these charms as, in a sense, holy. Hesychius and Clement of Alexandria[63] quote them, and it is remarkable that of the six words they report, two were interpreted respectively as "light" and "truth,"[64] common factors of the Odes and of the Johannine writings. Everywhere, indeed, the early Christians, to whom the Baptists may safely be compared, were extremely syncretistic. At Ephesus in particular all was grist that came to their mill. The great doctrine of the Logos was first enunciated five hundred years before Christ, by the Ephesian philosopher Heraclitus. The worship of the unmarried mother Artemis was extensively appropriated by the Virgin Mother of Jesus.[65] It was here that, in the teeth of violent opposition from other churches, she was dubbed "Mother of God."[66] The colleges of celibates of both sexes devoted to Artemis[67] were the seed-plots of the later monasteries. The manner of invoking the goddess by a procession was taken over by the local Christians.[68] A certain natural phenomenon, where the earth gushed up and dust was blown out, was at first called the grave of the snoring Icarus, and then

[63] Clemens Alex., *Stromata*, I, 360; V, 415.

[64] κατάσκιον = light; αἴσια = truth. Pauly-Wissowa, *Realencyklopädie für das klassische Altertum, s. v.* "Ephesia grammata."

[65] W. Ramsay, *Expositor*, 1905. See also a letter in the *Nation* (New York), 1906, LXXXIII, 400.

[66] *Realencyklopädie für protestantische Theologie*, XII, 332.

[67] J. G. Frazer, *The Magic Art*, 2d ed., I, 37f; *Adonis Attis Osiris*, 3d ed., I, 269.

[68] On the πομπή of Aphrodite cf. *Archiv für Religionswissenschaft*, 1914, pp. 678f; on the Christian πομπαί cf. Justin Martyr, First Apology, Chap. 13.

was renamed the grave of the sleeping and breathing Apostle John.[69] The feast of Artemis, May 7, was also appropriated to the local tutelary saint.[70] Nay, more, the worship of Christ was prepared for in a high degree. Just four years before Paul's advent the Ephesian senate and people had passed a decree declaring the Emperor "high-priest, god made manifest and common Saviour of human life."[71] All these titles were taken over by the new God-Man, who also appropriated part of the legend and rites of Dionysus, from time immemorial next to Artemis the great deity of Ephesus.[72] In that city, an early authority[73] informs us, the heathen "numbered wine among his mysteries, and taught that, having been torn to pieces, he ascended into heaven."

It will, therefore, be nothing strange if our author sees in a heathen inscription an oracle written by the finger of God. This idea was the natural deduction from the assumption that the image fell from heaven or from Zeus, the supreme deity identified with Jehovah also by the early Christians (Acts xvii. 28). The fact that the characters were Hebrew would be sufficient in the eyes of a Jew to give them a divine authority, but what they said was doubtless pure hocus-pocus, capable of any interpretation whatever. From the extant magic papyri we know that the names of God and even of "Jesus, the god of the Jews"[74] were to be found on the charms in circulation, and there is therefore nothing remarkable in the statement of our author that he read in the letter the names of "the Father, the Son and the Holy Spirit."

All this, however, was sealed from the heathen, who were unable to decipher the cryptogram. The main bur-

[69] C. Erbes in *Zeitschrift für Kirchengeschichte*, XXXIII, 1912, 160f.

[70] *Ibid.*, 161 and 239.

[71] Dittenberger, *Sylloge*, II, 802-4.

[72] Plutarch's Antony.

[73] Justin Martyr, First Apology, LIV.

[74] In the Parisian magic papyrus published by Wessely, quoted by W. B. Smith, *Der vorchristliche Jesus*, 38.

den of the oracle was something else, namely the downfall of the great goddess and the rise of the true God. This explains why the style of the poet, elsewhere so lucid, is here so cryptic. He was unable openly to attack the prevailing religion, just as John of the Apocalypse feared to speak of Rome and Nero save in cypher. The letter lighted on a wheel—in my interpretation the wheel of fortune, the *rota fortunae*[75] which we see in those faithful reflectors of popular beliefs, Cicero's writings. As the wheel of fortune turned, the former head (namely Artemis) ran down to the feet, and a new head came to the top and was revealed, namely "the Son of Truth from the Most High Father, and he inherited and took possession of everything." No words could be more applicable to the fall of one religion and the rise of another. So complete was the triumph that the apostates fled away and the persecutors became extinct.

The wheel had on it "the sign of the kingdom and of the government," namely, of the Roman Empire, regarded at this time by small sects like the Christians as their great protector from the fanaticism of established religions.[76] It had cut down all its adversaries and crossed all rivers, and gathered into one all peoples. It was naturally associated with fortune, for "Fortuna populi Romani" was emblazoned on its banners. Its fall was also expected with the turn of the wheel, i. e., with the decline of heathendom and the rise of the new celestial kingdom.

Having now said all that seems to bear on the provenance of the Odes, we should find it an easy matter to ascertain their date. If they be indeed mentioned by name in Paul's Epistle to the Ephesians, and frequently alluded to in First Corinthians they must necessarily be earlier than the date of that letter, about 55 A. D. There is

[75] W. W. Fowler, *Roman Ideas of the Deity*, 1914, 72ff.

[76] Cf. 2 Thess. ii. 7; the same bias for Rome is seen plainly in Mark, Luke and Acts.

one other reference to them, which also points to their antiquity. We cannot, indeed, quote Josephus[77] in their favor, but there is one pertinent passage preserved by Eusebius.[78] This historian speaks of a certain Antemon[79] who maintained that Jesus was a mere man; he then quotes from an anonymous work written against this heretic, apparently about 230 A. D., in which these words occur: "How many psalms and hymns written by the brethren *from the beginning* celebrate the Christ the Word of God, speaking of him as divine." This is so perfect a description of the Messianic teaching of the Odes that it must needs refer to them, and in so doing testifies to their antiquity. The *terminus a quo* must have been but a few years earlier, not later than the establishment of the community of Disciples of John (or, if they are still considered Christian, of Jesus) at Ephesus. This may have been somewhat earlier than the time given by Luke, but it is not possible that it should have been within some years of the death of the Baptist.

It is now to be proved that the Odes were composed by a disciple of John. This has already been strongly suggested; for, if they were written at Ephesus before Paul had completed his stay there, what other author is so likely? One can read between the lines of Luke's account that the Baptists were the older and, until Paul's arrival, the stronger sect, and it is certain that their influence was felt for many years.

Let it not be objected that if they had been written by a non-Christian author they would not have become generally accepted, and indeed nearly canonized,[80] by the

[77] *Antiquities*, VIII, 2, 5, speaks of "1005 Odes of Solomon"; he also knew John the Baptist, but probably not our Odes.

[78] *Hist. Eccl.*, V, 28, 5.

[79] On him, cf. Harnack, *Dogmengeschichte*, 4th ed., I, 716f.

[80] They are found in MSS of the New Testament and in old canons; cf. Harris, pp. 3ff.

Church. Not only were the Jewish scriptures recognized by the Christians, but there are abundant evidences of late Jewish works being treated as inspired. Thus Paul quotes the Revelation of Elias, and Jude cites the Book of Enoch. The Muratorian Fragment, as is well known, places among the New Testament books "Wisdom written by the friends of Solomon." If the conjectures of Luther and Spitta be correct the Epistle of James is but a Jewish work, twice interpolated with the name of Jesus. Our Apocalypse, too, is possibly based on an earlier purely Jewish work. Q also quotes an unknown "Wisdom of God" (Luke xi. 49).

It is impossible here to examine all the theories put forward as to the origin of these poems. One class of scholars finds in them the product of some Christian heresy, whether Gnostic,[81] or Valentinian,[82] or Docetic,[83] or Montanist,[84] or that of the mystic Bardaisan.[85] It is sufficient to point out that these theories are mutually destructive and that all have been contradicted. A certain number of scholars, indeed, see gnostic elements in the poems,[86] but even the numerous gnostic parallels pointed out by W. Stölten,[87] if examined closely, rather confirm than invalidate my theory. Some of his parallels adduced from Poimander, from Mithraism and from the magic papyri, are perhaps pre-Christian. Many other parallels, notably those in the *Pistis Sophia,* are demonstrably borrowed *from* the Odes, not by them. Others, from the Apocryphal Acts, from the writings of the Mandaeans and from the Gospel of Nicodemus, point in one way or another to Ephesus and the Disciples of John. But yet gnosticism is not the dominant note of the Odes. They are, says Harnack, and Harris agrees with him, only gnostic in the sense that the Fourth Gospel is so.

[81] Gunkel and Gressmann. [82] Preuschen. [83] Battiffol.
[84] Conybeare and Fries. [85] Newbold.
[86] *Dictionary of Religion and Ethics, s. v.* "Gnosticism."
[87] *Zeitschrift für neutestamentliche Wissenschaft,* 1912, 29ff.

A second type of theory, represented by Spitta and Menzies, regards the Odes as purely Jewish. In a sense this is correct and important, but there are many peculiarities of the poet, e. g., his references to baptism and his Messianic dogmas, that imperatively demand further explanation.

A third hypothesis, represented by Harnack, is that the Odes were originally Jewish and have been interpolated by a Christian. Professor Harnack feels called upon to apologize for this intrinsically improbable hypothesis of interpolation, and I think that recent careful research[88] has settled definitely that the Odes are of a single piece. And yet the hypothesis of Harnack and his followers is the logical result of their clear vision that parts of the Odes could have been written by no Jew, and other parts by no type of Christian hitherto known. Harnack confesses, "I know no Christianity like this."

A fourth theory, represented by Harris, Bernard and Abbott, is that the Odes were written by a Christian at a date so early that dogma had not yet become stereotyped. Belief is still inchoate; thought is struggling to the perfect expression not yet attained. This theory, too, accounts for many of the known facts, and yet I think it can be shown that some things in the Odes—failure to speak of Jesus by name, of his word or example, or of the eucharist—are not compatible with it. Practically the only theory left is that here presented, that the Odes are the product of a Messianic movement similar to Christianity in many respects, but not identical with it; and when, in addition, many points of contact with what is otherwise known of the Disciples of John, can be found, a satisfactory answer to the hitherto unsolved problem will at last, it is hoped, have been reached.

[88] G. Kittel, *Die Oden Salomos überarbeitet oder einheitlich?* 1914. R. H. Connolly, *Journal of Theological Studies*, 1912, 298ff.

The author accepts the whole Jewish ceremonial law, just as did pre-Pauline Christians. The temple at Jerusalem is God's only true sanctuary (Ode IV). Circumcision is so highly prized that even the elect archangels are sealed with it.[89] That he insists on circumcision of the heart, is no proof that he rejected that of the body, any more than the same metaphor, Jeremiah iv. 4, is proof that *he* rejected the physical sign. At the same time the author is a missionary to the Gentiles (Ode X), and is perhaps one himself by birth[90] (Ode XLI). We know that even the Jews at this time received proselytes into full fellowship with themselves, on condition of circumcision, and we also note, in our earliest and best source for John the Baptist, that there is especial reason to think that he welcomed Gentiles to his community.[91] Indeed his special note, "conversion," is struck in at least one of the Odes (X, 3). The author is also an observer of the Sabbath; emphasizes the fact that God rested on it, and apologizes for the continued labor of sun and stars on that day "because they know no better."[92] The author is, moreover, deeply versed in the Jewish scriptures.

The high moral tone of the poet is undeniable. He urges men to "pray without ceasing."[93] This is one of the very rare instances in which his language recalls that of a Synoptic gospel (Luke xviii. 1ff). It is noteworthy that the same gospel informs us that John taught his disciples

[89] This is certainly the meaning in Ode IV, 8, proved by comparing it with *Jubilees*, XV, 27.

[90] This interpretation of the words "I am of another race" is far from certain. Just as the Christians were early called "the third race," so the author may have conceived of his own sect as a "chosen people," apart even from the Jews. Bacon, *Expositor*, 1911, I, 330, sees in these words not a reference to the poet's race, but to adoption by the Messiah.

[91] Matt. iii. 9 = Luke iii. 8.

[92] This is my interpretation of Ode XVI. Harris draws from it the opposite conclusion, being unduly influenced by a similarity of language in Justin Martyr, Dialogue XXII. But the two opposite points of view are but illustrations of Romans xiv. 5, where it is said that even of the early Christians, some do, and some do not, esteem one day better than another.

[93] Ode VIII, 23: "ask without ceasing" (Fleming); "ask again and again" (Ungnad-Staerk).

to pray (xi. 1). In noting the same fact Tertullian (*Against Marcion,* IV, 26) is probably not drawing so much on Luke as on his own experience with the Disciples. The asceticism of the author is also plain. Wine is never mentioned save with abhorrence. The spiritual food of believers is "milk and honey"[94]—exactly the fare that we have already seen given by second-century writers to the Baptist and his followers. This food is treated allegorically and mystically, not sacramentally; but it is surely significant that no sacramental use is made of flesh, of bread or of wine. The latter, indeed, is so much detested that its use is said to have been introduced by "a bridegroom who corrupts" and "a bride who is corrupted." Asking who these may be, the poet is told: "This is the deceiver and the error: and they are alike in the beloved and in his bride: and they lead astray and corrupt the whole world: and they invite many to the banquet, and give them to drink of the wine of their intoxication" (Ode XXXVIII, 9-13). Harris is unable to identify these corrupters, but suggests Simon Magus and Helena (p. 66). It is worth while remembering that they were said to be Disciples of John, and that other members of the community were dissatisfied with them. (Clementine Homilies, XXIII).

One also thinks of Cerinthus, an Ephesian, said to have held sensual views of paradise as a place given over to banquets and marriage ceremonies (Eusebius, H. E. VII, 25). His date, however, would be decidedly too late, and a far better identification is suggested by turning to Mark ii. 18-20: "And John's disciples and the Pharisees were fasting: and they come and say unto him, Why do John's disciples and the disciples of the Pharisees fast, but thy disciples fast not? And Jesus said unto them, Can the sons of the bride-chamber fast, while the bridegroom is

[94] Harris, p. 80.

with them?" Here we have the point at issue between the two young sects stated from the opposite side, and with a similarity of phrase that cannot be accidental. Not that the pericope in Mark is an authentic reminiscence of the "historic Jesus." It has on independent grounds been recognized that this is but one of the numerous places in the gospel, in which some controversy or situation of the early church has been referred back to Jesus.[95]

The metaphor of Christ as the "bridegroom" is put into the mouth of the Baptist by the Fourth Gospel (iii. 29), whereas the title "beloved," in the Ode applied to the deceiving bridegroom, is appropriated to Christ in Ephesians i. 6. Still more to the point is that section of our oldest source dealing with John the Baptist, which tells us that Jesus was called a "glutton and a wine-bibber" by those who did not like his "eating and drinking" (Matt. ix. 19). Finally we have already noted that the Sabaeans regarded Jesus as the corrupter of their sect.[96] The "bride" in the Ode is hardly a more definite figure than in the gospels; doubtless the Christian church is vaguely thought of.[97]

One of the most decisive facts in favor of my thesis is that, while the Odes have not the remotest reference to the eucharist,[98] they are full of allusions to baptism.[99] Similarities in phrase between them and the baptismal services and Epiphany hymns of the Eastern Church put beyond doubt the fact that the numerous appearances of living

[95] Wellhausen, *Markuskommentar, ad. loc.* Bousset, *Kyrios Christos,* 1913, p. 48f.

[96] Neander, *Church History* (English, 1866), I, 447.

[97] "Some gnostic society," says Bruston, in *Zeitschrift für neutestamentliche Wissenschaft,* 1912, 111.

[98] Burkitt sees in Ode XXI, 4, "Increasingly helpful to me was the thought of the Lord, and his fellowship in incorruption," some allusion to the eucharist. What can it be? *Journal of Theological Studies,* 1912, 383. F. C. Conybeare thinks that the two cups of milk in Ode XIX, compared with Irenaeus, *Adv. Haer.,* IV, 38, 1, are the two elements of the eucharist. Quite impossible. *Zeitschrift f. nt. Wissenschaft,* 1913, 96. All others are agreed that the Odes have nothing about the eucharist.

[99] G. Diettrich, in *Die Reformation,* May-August, 1910; J. H. Bernard, in *Journal of Theological Studies,* October, 1910, and in his edition of the Odes, 1912; R. A. Aytoun, *Expositor,* 1911, II, 338ff.

and speaking water, of crowns and white robes, of seals and of signs—even though this imagery be in part borrowed from older Jewish sources—allude to the one sacrament of the Johannites. Professor Harris, who once doubted, has now become convinced of this.[100] His earlier objection[101] to the theory of Bernard, who demonstrated the allusions to baptism, namely that "the weak point in his argument lies just here, that the Jewish background of the Odes is too patent to be neglected,"—this answer is the best possible confirmation of our main thesis.

There are also a number of small fingerposts pointing to John the Baptist. The poet, speaking in the person of one greater, says: "I was clothed with the covering of thy Spirit and thou didst remove from me my raiment of skin" (Ode XXV, 8). Dr. Harris's note on this is very learned and very abstruse; I venture to think that a simpler explanation will be found by turning to the early records of the Baptist. John, like his parents (Luke, i. 41, 67) was filled with the Holy Ghost, and he was also clothed in "a leathern girdle and camel's hair," or, as some manuscripts read, "camel's skin"[102] (Mark i. 6). The dove which fluttered over the head of the Messiah (Ode XXIV, 1) is the same dove which came to Jesus after his baptism by John (Mark i. 10). In Ode XXVIII, 3 we read: "My heart is delighted and exults like the babe who leaps in the womb of his mother." The same phraseology is used of John in Luke i. 41. Again the words: "I was called the shining light, the Son of God,"[103] vividly recall the title applied by John to Jesus and by Jesus to John in the Fourth Gospel (i. 6; v. 35). Harris observes that the description of the dove flying above the Messiah, supported as it is by citations from second century writers, points to the use of some lost

[100] *Expositor*, 1912, III, 114ff.

[101] J. R. Harris, *The Odes of Solomon*, 2d ed., 1911, p. 28.

[102] E. Nestle in *Zeitsch. f. nt. Wissensch.*, 1907, p. 238.

[103] Ode XXVI, 3, Ungnad-Staerk.

apocryphal gospel. I agree with him that it, as well as the other passages just enumerated, point to the use of some lost source, only it is not a gospel but some writing about John the Baptist, known and used, either directly or indirectly, by the evangelists. Possibly it was the Revelation of Elias.

I have left until last one class of passages—the Messianic—because of their supreme importance, both for the present question and for the development of Christian dogma. That there is in the Odes a very strong and definite Messianic hope is exactly what we should expect from a Disciple of John. On the other hand we should not expect them to refer to specific facts in the life of Jesus, as, in one or two instances, they have the superficial appearance of doing. This appearance can be accounted for in three ways: (1) The Odes may have been written by a Disciple soon after his conversion to Christianity, when as yet he had heard little of Jesus, and did not accept the sacrament—perhaps Pauline in origin—of the eucharist. (2) Without accepting Jesus as the Messiah it is possible that the ideas of the sect in general, or of this author in particular, may have been colored by contact with Christian Messianic ideas. (3) It is possible that the resemblances between the Odes and passages in the New Testament are due simply to the fact that both drew on common sources for their Messianic dogmas. If there are really allusions to facts in Jesus's life, one of the two former alternatives must be selected; nevertheless I believe that the third one is correct, and that the similarities are due to common sources of inspiration, or possibly to borrowing by the Christians from the Baptists.

In estimating the whole evidence the omissions are as significant as are the parallels. Why does not the name of Jesus occur? It is no retort to ask why the name of John is also passed over in silence, for there is no special occasion to allude to him, but there are numerous passages of a Messianic import, which, did they really refer to Jesus, could hardly have avoided his name. Methodist hymns rarely, if ever, mention John Wesley, but they are full of the name of Jesus. Neither is the answer of Zahn satisfactory, namely that the author is trying to put himself in Solomon's place. All the pseudepigrapha are completely lacking in historical imagination. The name of Jesus was interpolated in prophecies attributed to ancient worthies—e. g. in 2 Esdras vii. 28—even where it was originally wanting.

Secondly, why do all references to Christ's earthly ministry, word and example, fail? Paul's rather surprising indifference to all but the death of the Lord cannot be adduced as a parallel to this, for, however Paul's ideas came to him, whether from other men, or, as he frequently asserts, by direct revelation, he at least states them as historical facts, and applies them to a man Jesus. I see no explanation for the glaring omissions of our poet save that the whole body of evangelic tradition was unknown to him.

Thirdly, why are his statements about the Messiah which agree with Christian doctrines, mixed with others contradicting the New Testament writers? Why, for example, is the Holy Spirit sometimes called the mother of the Messiah (as also in an apocryphal gospel), and why, instead of ascending into heaven, does the Saviour descend into hell? Why are the crucifixion and the sign of the cross alluded to in such extremely vague and dubious terms, suggesting a background not of history but of *a priori* speculation? I am sure there is not one Messianic passage in the Odes not to be more satisfactorily accounted for by turning to earlier Jewish writings, than by recourse to the New Testament.

I need not pause long over such dogmas as that of the

pre-existence of the Messiah, and the use made of the term Logos. The latter conception was a natural offshoot from the speculations of Plato and the Stoa, and both ideas had been adopted and developed by Jewish writings, particularly by the Wisdom of Solomon (*c.* 30 B. C.) and by Philo. At the beginning of the Christian era Wisdom had become a second God, existing from eternity, assisting the Almighty in all his works.[104] It was the creation of this new God, the Logos, which, as Reitzenstein rightly remarks, necessitated the creation of a new religion.[105] The most striking verse in the twelfth Ode, on the subject of the Word, and one surely in the mind of the author of the Fourth Gospel, is (11): "The dwelling-place of the Word is man." This, too, is true to the Stoa, which taught that the Divine Logos dwelt also in human nature.[106] It is more than significant that in the Hermetic writings the favorite words of our poet, ζωή and φῶς, are found as predicates of the Logos, who is also called the Son of God.[107] The pre-existence of the Messiah, and his identification with a Divine Being[108] second only to the Almighty, are dogmas found more than a hundred years before the composition of these Odes, in the Book of Enoch. There (chap. 57) we read: "For from the beginning the Son of Man was hidden and the Most High preserved him in the presence of his might, and revealed him to the elect." It is the very language of the poet: "The Son of the Most High appeared in the perfection of his Father....and he was known before the foundation of the world."[109]

The Holy Spirit, too, was a common pre-Christian con-

[104] W. Schencke, *Die Chokma (Sophia) in der jüdischen Hypostasenspekulation,* 1913. He says that in Proverbs viii. 30, instead of "delight" one should read "assistant."

[105] *Poimandres,* 1904, p. 116.

[106] P. Wendland, *Hellenistisch-römische Kultur,* 1907, p. 16.

[107] P. Wendland, *Die urchristlichen Literaturformen,* 1912, p. 245.

[108] R. H. Charles, *The Book of Enoch,* 2d ed., 1912, p. xxxviii.

[109] Ode XLI, 14, 16. Cf. Ignatius to the Magnesians, VI, 1.

ception. Not only, according to Q, was it an especially prominent feature of the Baptist's preaching, but it is also found in the Psalms of Solomon (*c.* 48 B. C), and was there brought into connection with the Messiah.[110] As the Odes were originally published as a continuation of these Psalms it is hard to see how the author could have avoided mentioning the Holy Spirit. In only one way does he develop the function of this being, in making her the mother[111] of the Son of Man—that ancient synonym for the Messiah. This idea was a natural corollary to the feminine gender of Spirit in the Semitic languages. If the Almighty was the Father of the Messiah, the Spirit inevitably became his Mother.

Now that we have accounted for the Father, the Son and the Holy Spirit, it is not surprising that we should occasionally find them in a close proximity suggesting the later dogma of the Trinity. Thus in Ode XIX, 1, 2: "A cup of milk was offered to me. . . . The Son is the cup, and he who was milked is the Father, and she that milked him is the Holy Spirit."[112] As Paul was familiar with the Odes, it is probable that the first Biblical[113] reference to the Father, Son and Holy Spirit was suggested by this passage. But, indeed, divine families of three were common in oriental religion. "Three in one" was an epithet for Hermes,[114] and there is no doubt that these Odes stand in a close relation to the "Hermetic literature."

Now as to the person of the Messiah himself. No need to pause over the ideas of salvation and a Saviour (Odes V, VII, VIII *et saepe*). The phrase "God my Saviour" is common in Jewish thought, and one eminent scholar has

[110] Psalm Solomon, xvii. 42. The Holy Spirit is also found in the Mithraic liturgy. Reitzenstein, *Die hellenistischen Mysterienreligionen*, 1910, p. 45.

[111] Ode XXXVI, 3. So in the Gospel of the Hebrews, Jerome in Jes. xi. 2.

[112] The reading of Burkitt's new MS of the Odes.

[113] 2 Cor. xiii. 14.

[114] Reitzenstein, *Mysterienreligionen*, p. 14.

already noted that the Saviour of these Odes is not Jesus, but God, or his Servant, or at most the Messiah.[115] The idea of a Saviour God was also common in the heathen world.[116] Most significant of all, the Messianic ideas of Ode XXIV have been found applied to the Mandaean Saviour.[117] These Mandaeans, be it remembered, were probably descendants of the Johannites.

In Ode XIX it is stated in the past tense of prophecy that the Messiah is born of a virgin. In asking whether this idea is dependent on the stories in the First and Third Gospels we must remember that it was written a whole generation before them. It is certain that "the gospel of the infancy" is a graft on the older tradition presented by Mark and Q, and, had we no other evidence in the matter save the Gospels and the Odes, it would be natural to assume that the later in time borrowed from the earlier. The conception, indeed, arose as a perfectly necessary evolution. Once postulated that the Son of God was to appear as a man, how else could he be born? Thus it was with the other saviour gods and heroes of antiquity. Attis, for example, was the son of Nana, a virgin.[118] "The wise Egyptians," says Plutarch,[119] "think it not impossible that a woman can be filled with the spirit of God and thus conceive." This is exactly the idea of Ode XIX; the extraordinary process by which generation is accomplished is doubtless intended to eliminate all thought of carnal intercourse.[120]

It is interesting and pertinent to note that Ephesus was early the seat of a division of opinion on the virgin

[115] B. W. Bacon, in the *Expositor*, 1911, I, 336.

[116] Cf. Ephesian inscription quoted above.

[117] Stölten in *Zeitschrift f. nt. Wissenschaft*, 1912, 29ff.

[118] J. G. Frazer, *Adonis Attis Osiris*, 1906, 163ff.

[119] *Numa*, IV, 62.

[120] I note the emendation to verse 6 proposed by Newbold, *Journal of Bib. Lit.*, XXX, 189, and also those—inspired by an apologetic purpose—suggested by Father Connolly, *Journal of Theological Studies*, 1912, 298ff.

birth. One source for the doctrine was doubtless found in the worship of Artemis. Another source for the gospel story (Matt. i. 23) and also probably for the Odes, is found in Isaiah vii. 14, translated in the LXX "Behold a virgin shall conceive." But, early in the Christian era, Theodotion of Ephesus published another version of the Scriptures, translating the verse correctly, "a young woman shall conceive."[121] It is possibly for this reason[122] that the Fourth Gospel clearly implies that Jesus was born in a natural way. Though this opinion was maintained by the Ebionites, the other prevailed, and the LXX continued to be cited by Ephesian apologists.[123]

There are two apparent allusions to the cross, the first in Ode XXVII: "I stretched out my hands and sanctified my Lord; for the extension of my hands is his sign: and my expansion is the upright tree;" and Ode XLII, 1, 2: "I stretched out my hands and approached my Lord: for the stretching out of my hands is his sign: and my expansion is the outspread tree which was set up on the way of the Righteous One." It is true that it has been proposed[124] to explain this not as an allusion to the cross but to an ordinary tree as in Psalms i. 3, lii. 10, xcii. 13 etc. But this is hardly tenable. Though the imagery is very probably suggested by the Old Testament account of the stretching out of Moses's hands,[125] it is almost certain that the author had in mind a cross. It might be argued that this does not necessarily imply a crucifixion, for the cross was an almost primeval symbol. The *crux ansata* of Egypt was the sign of life and of the resurrection of Osiris.[126] Again,

[121] Eusebius, *Hist. Eccl.*, V, 8, 4.

[122] John was familiar with various versions of the O. T. See W. Dittmar, *Vetus Testamentum in Novo,* Part I, 1899.

[123] Justin Martyr, First Apology, Chap. 33.

[124] F. Spitta in *Zeitsch. f. nt. Wissenschaft,* 1913, 259ff.

[125] According to Justin this was a prophecy of the cross (*Dialogue with Trypho,* Chap. 90).

[126] Frazer, *Adonis Attis Osiris,* 1906, p. 261.

the saying of Plato that God placed the cosmic soul "crosswise [literally, like the letter X] in the universe,"[127] was early seized upon by Ephesian apologists as an anticipation of the cross of Calvary.[128] But as I am satisfied that the dogma of a crucified Messiah was current before our era, I think it probable that the Odes really express it. The Suffering and persecuted Righteous Man first appears clearly as an ideal in the Persian period of Jewish history, in Isaiah liii. 4ff. Psalm xxii is, according to Briggs, "a more vivid description of the sufferings of Christ on the cross than the authors of the Gospels gave."[129] That verse 17, "they pierced my hands and my feet," quoted as a prophecy of Jesus's crucifixion by Irenaeus, Justin Martyr, Augustine, Calvin, Bossuet and a host of others, does really refer to this form of execution, has been demonstrated by Kittel.[130] Commonly practised by the Persians from whom it was borrowed by the Punic peoples and by the Romans, it is elsewhere referred to in the Old Testament (Ezra vi. 11).

The idea of the suffering, and possibly the crucified, Messiah is further developed in Second Zechariah,[131] in a passage early applied to Christ. The Testaments of the Twelve Patriarchs (about 100 B. C.) is of immense importance in the development of Messianic ideas, and contains passages teaching that "a man who reneweth the law in the power of the Most High ye shall call a deceiver; and at last ye shall rush upon him and slay him;"[132] and again that "the Blameless One shall be delivered up for lawless men, and the Sinless One shall die for ungodly men."[133]

[127] Timaeus, 36B.

[128] Justin Martyr, First Apology, LX.

[129] *Commentary on the Psalms*, I, 192.

[130] R. Kittel, *Die Psalmen*, 1914, 84ff, 92.

[131] Zech. xii. 10 to xiii. 7.

[132] Test. Levi, XVI, 3. Although Charles admits that these words may be original he brackets them. As they are found in all versions, including the Armenian, and in both Greek recensions, they must be genuine.

[133] Test. Ben. III, 8. Found in all the versions.

Fourth Maccabees, vi. 28 clearly states the Christian doctrine of the Atonement, and in Wisdom, composed not long before 30 B. C. and of immense influence on the development of the Pauline Christology, we have the most remarkable verses[134] of all:

"The wicked said, For if the Just Man be the Son of God, he will help him and deliver him from the hand of his enemies. Let us examine him with despitefulness and torture that we may know his weakness and prove his patience. Let us condemn him to a shameful death."

Of the Assumption of Moses (7-30 A. D.) R. H. Charles says in his edition (1897): "The author's hero is not one who takes up arms in behalf of Israel, but one who, amid the most bitter persecution that ever befell Israel, was faithful unto death, and, lifting no hand in self-defense, committed his cause unto God."

Three post-Christian works may also be cited as evidence. The Zadokite work complains of those who "justified the Wicked One and condemned the Righteous One" (231). This is certainly not a specific allusion to Jesus's death, even if the author knew of it, but is on an exact par with the verse in James (v. 6): "Ye have condemned, ye have killed the Righteous One; he did not resist you,"—a verse which all scholars from Luther[135] to Bacon[136] refer not to the Passion but to the sufferings of an ideal Just Man. Fourth Ezra, a Jewish apocalypse, also speaks of the death of the Messiah.[137] I think that these citations should make it plain that "through the ages one increasing purpose ran." I trust I have not laid myself open to the accusation, brought by Dr. Conybeare against Mr. J. M.

[134] II, 18ff.

[135] "De passione et resurrectione Christi sagt er [Jacobus] nicht ein Wort," *Luthers Tischreden in der Mathesischen Sammlung,* ed. E. Kroker, 1903, No. 528.

[136] *Encyclopædia Britannica,* 11th ed. *s. v.* "James."

[137] 4 Ezra vii. 29. In verse 28 the word "Jesus," and that word only, is an interpolation, lacking in the oriental versions.

Robertson, of "raking together a thousand irrelevant thrums of mythology, picked up at random from every age, race and clime."[138]

The idea of the Suffering Just Man was so natural that it may also be found in Plato and the later Stoics. As to the more precise conception, that he should be put to death by crucifixion, that also is found in Plato (*Republic*, 362A) as well as in Psalm xxii and possibly in Zechariah. This form of execution being the common one was quite naturally thought of, just as burning at the stake became the typical punishment for heresy in Christendom. That our poet really had Psalm xxii in mind in Ode XXVII on the cross, may be inferred from the fact that he quotes from it twice again in the very next poem.[139] In Justin Martyr's copy of the Bible (at Ephesus) there was also a prophecy, "The Lord hath reigned from the tree," which he accuses the Jews of erasing.[140] "Bearing the cross," however, had become proverbial, and may be read in Cicero, Artemidorus, Bereshith Robba and Plutarch[141] before it found its way into the oldest Christian document,[142] Q. As Q knows nothing of the passion of Jesus,[143] it here furnishes striking testimony to the currency of the idea in proto-Christian circles independently of, and prior to, the crucifixion under Pilate. This evidence is amply supported by other early documents. The saying that Christ suffered "according to the scriptures"[144] clearly indicates that Paul, Mark, Matthew and Luke all found the essential features of his death set forth in the Hebrew Bible. The author

[138] F. C. Conybeare, *The Historical Christ*, 1914, p. 95.

[139] Ode XXVIII, 8 = Ps. xxii. 7; Ode XXVIII, 11 = Ps. xxii. 16.

[140] To Psalm xcvi. First Apology, XLI; Dialogue, Chap. 73.

[141] W. C. Allen, *Commentary on Matthew, ad locum*, X, 16.

[142] Matt. x. 16 = Luke xiv. 27.

[143] This positive statement of Harnack is supported by the latest student of the synoptic problem, W. Haupt: *Worte Jesu und Gemeindeüberlieferung*, 1913. He analyzes Q into several strata, but none of them touch the passion.

[144] 1 Cor. xv. 3; Mark ix. 12; Matt. xxvi. 24; Acts iii. 18.

of 1 Peter only puts it a little more explicitly when he says: "The Spirit of Christ testified beforehand the sufferings of Christ."[145] In saying this it is probable that he had the Odes of Solomon in mind. At any rate I think these poems can be adduced in favor of my present contention. Written, in my judgment, wholly without reference to the "historic Jesus," they yet contain vague allusions to a crucified Messiah. They are, in short, a brilliant example of *das werdende Dogma vom Leben Christi.*

The doctrine of the *descensus ad inferos* found in Ode XLII offers no difficulty. In the first place our earliest witnesses point to an Ephesian origin for this doctrine as applied to Christ. It is found in the Gospel of Peter,[146] in Justin Martyr,[147] in Irenaeus,[148] in 1 Peter[149] and in Ephesians.[150] Secondly, this dogma is founded on a pre-Christian myth of a battle between the powers of Heaven and Hell.[151] It is applied to personified Wisdom, in the Wisdom of Jesus the Son of Sirach.[152] There is therefore no occasion for surprise in finding it in an undeveloped form in the Odes. It was later applied not only to Jesus but to the Mandaean Saviour.[153] This would again indicate some connection of the doctrine with the Johannites, and, as a matter of fact, early legend sent John to Hades[154] as the precursor of Jesus. It is remarkable that the connection already seems to have been made by the author of 1 Peter[155]

[145] 1 Peter i. 11.

[146] On the relation of this gospel to the Ephesian Fourth Gospel, cf. Erbes in *Zeitschrift f. Kirchengesch.*, XXXIII, 234ff.

[147] Dialogue, Chap. 72.

[148] *Adv. Haer.*, IV, 27.

[149] iii. 18ff.

[150] iv. 19.

[151] W. Bousset, *Kyrios Christos*, 1913, p. 38.

[152] In the Latin translation of xxiv. 32. This may be a Christian interpolation, but is not necessarily so, says Bousset, p. 34.

[153] Bousset, 38.

[154] Hippolytus, *Christ and Antichrist*, Chap. 45; Origen, *Hom. IV in Luc.*, ed. Lommatsch, V, 99; *Tract. Orig.*, ed. Batiffol, 155; *Descensus*, II, 2.

[155] iii. 18ff.

who places the *descensus* in close proximity to remarks about baptism:

"Because Christ also suffered for sins once, the righteous for the unrighteous, that he might bring us to God, being put to death in the flesh, but quickened in the spirit; in which also he went and preached unto the spirits in prison which aforetime were disobedient, when the long-suffering of God waited in the days of Noah, while the ark was a preparing, wherein few, that is, eight souls, were saved through water: which also after a true likeness doth now save you, even baptism."

It is plain to me that the author of the lines had in mind some source very like that used by Ode XLII. At any rate the date should decide the question. If the Odes were really written in the middle of the first century they cannot be dependent on legends of the second century, though these may well be dependent on them.

A last word may be devoted to the author's person. The only possible name to suggest is that of Apollos, and we know too little of him to say definitely whether he wrote the Odes or not. His Alexandrian extraction would rather speak in his favor, for his reliance on Philo[156] and Wisdom and the Hermetic literature has already been noted. His career also, as far as we know it, begins and ends at Ephesus, and he is of the right date. It is remarkable that B. W. Bacon has traced his influence in the thought of the Fourth Gospel: "We have no means of proving," says he, "that Apollos ever touched pen to paper; yet it is permissible to say that if any identifiable spirit speaks through the Fourth Gospel besides that of Paul it is such a spirit as that of Apollos.[157] It is just possible that the trope in Paul's phrase "Apollos watered" (ἐπότισε, 1 Cor. iii. 6) was suggested to him by that missionary's

[156] "The Odes and Philo," J. T. Marshall, *Expositor*, 1911, I, 385ff, 519ff.

[157] *The Fourth Gospel in Research and Debate*, 1909, p. 283.

addiction to the said element, but no safe inference as to his authorship can be drawn from that. If Apollos was a Jew by birth, and the author of the Odes a Gentile, they could not have been the same person, but neither of these suppositions is beyond doubt. Perhaps the weightiest argument against Apollos's authorship is that we have no clearer indication in favor of it.

PRESERVED SMITH.

POUGHKEEPSIE, N. Y.

ON THE METHODS OF THEORETICAL PHYSICS.

[A lecture of Boltzmann's on "The Recent Development of Method in Theoretical Physics" was translated in *The Monist* for January, 1901 (Vol. XI, pp. 226-257). But this earlier lecture should be read in connection with it. An exhibition of models, apparatus, and instruments used for the purpose of mathematics and mathematical physics was planned by the German society of mathematicians (*Deutsche Mathematiker-Vereinigung*) for the meeting at Nuremburg in 1892. Such an exhibition had been held—on a larger scale—in London in 1876, and since then the question of models had increased very greatly in practical, theoretical and pedagogical importance. At the last moment the planned exhibition was postponed till September, 1893, when it was held at Munich. Among the eight essays written for and published in the catalogue of this exhibition,[1] issued in 1892, was one by Boltzmann "Ueber die Methoden der theoretischen Physik"[2] which is here translated. An English version was communicated by the Physical Society to the *Philosophical Magazine,*[3] and it is this translation which has served as a basis for the present one. For permission to make use of it I am indebted to the publishers of the *Philosophical Magazine*. The omissions and errors in the translation have been rectified with the help of the original German. I have also verified and completed the references. The additions made in the translation in the *Philosophical Magazine* are given in the Supplementary Note following the essay itself.—P. E. B. Jourdain.]

CALLED upon by the editors of the *Katalog* to deal with this subject, I soon became aware that little that is new could be said, so much and such sterling matter having in recent times been written about it. An almost exaggerated criticism of the methods of scientific investigation is indeed a characteristic of the present day; an intensified "critique of pure reason" we might say, if this expression were not perhaps somewhat too presumptuous. It is not my object again to criticize this criticism. I will only offer a few guiding remarks for those who, without being

[1] *Katalog mathematischer und mathematisch-physikalischer Modelle, Apparate und Instrumente,* edited by Walther Dyck, Munich, 1892; Nachtrag, Munich, 1893. This essay was reprinted in Boltzmann's *Populäre Schriften,* Leipsic, 1905, pp. 1-10.

[2] *Katalog,* 1892, pp. 89-98.

[3] *Phil. Mag.,* 5th series, Vol. XXXVI, 1893, pp. 37-44.

specially occupied with these questions, nevertheless take an interest in them.

In mathematics and geometry, the necessity for economizing labor undoubtedly led at first from purely analytical to constructive methods, and to their illustration by models. Even if this necessity appears to be a purely practical and obvious one, we here find ourselves on ground on which a whole class of modern methodological speculations has grown up, which have been expressed by Mach in the most precise and ingenious manner. He, indeed, directly maintains that the sole object of science is economy of labor.

Seeing that in business affairs the greatest economy is desirable, it might almost with equal justice be maintained that economy is simply the object of the salesroom and of money in general, and in a certain sense this would be true. Yet when we investigate the distances, the motions, the magnitudes, the physical and chemical nature of the fixed stars, when microscopes are invented and we thereby discover the origins of disease, we shall not be very willing to describe this as mere economy.

But what we denote as an object and what are the means for attaining that object are after all matters of definition. What we regard as existing—whether we so regard bodies, or their kinetic energy, or, in general, their properties—depends in fact on our own definition of existence, so that we may perhaps at last define away even our own existence.

But let this pass. The necessity exists for the most complete utilization of our different powers of conception; and since it is by aid of the eye that the greatest mass of facts can be surveyed[1] simultaneously, it becomes desirable to make the results of our calculation perceptible,

[1] We say characteristically enough "*Uebersehen.*" [In English an "*Uebersicht*" would be translated by some such word as "survey." Literally it is "oversight."]

and that not merely by the imagination, but visible to the eye and at the same time palpable to the touch by means of gypsum and cardboard.

How little was done in this direction in my student days! Mathematical instruments were then almost wholly unknown, and physical experiments were often made in such a manner that they could only be seen by the lecturer himself. And as, further, owing to shortness of sight, I was unable to see writing on the blackboard, my imagination was constantly kept on the stretch. I had almost said luckily for me, but this statement would be in opposition to the object of the present catalogue, which can only be to praise the infinite equipment of models in the mathematics of the present day; and it would, moreover, be quite incorrect. For even if my powers of imagination had gained, it could only have been at the expense of the range of my acquired knowledge. At that time the theory of surfaces of the second order was still the summit of geometrical knowledge, and an egg, a napkin ring, or a saddle was sufficient for illustration. What a host of shapes, singularities, and of forms growing organically out of each other, must not the geometrician of the present day impress on his memory! And how greatly is he not helped by plaster casts, models with fixed and movable strings, links, and joints of all kinds!

Not only so, but more and more way is being made by those machines which serve not for mere illustration, but save the trouble of making actual calculations, from the ordinary four rules of arithmetic to the most complicated integrations.

As a matter of course both kinds of apparatus are most extensively used by physicists, who are continually accustomed to the manipulation of all kinds of instruments. All conceivable mechanical models, optical wave-surfaces, thermodynamical surfaces in gypsum, wave-machines of all kinds, apparatus for illustrating the laws of the refraction of light and other laws of nature, are examples of models of the first kind. In the construction of apparatus of the second kind some have even gone so far as to attempt the evaluation of the integrals of differential equations which hold equally for a phenomenon difficult to observe, like the friction of gases, and another which allows of easy measurement, like the distribution of an electric current in a conductor of suitable shape, and then, by observation of the latter, to utilize these values for the determination of the constants of friction. We may also remember the graphical evaluation of the series and integrals occurring in the theory of tides, in electrodynamics and so on, by Lord Kelvin, who in his *Lectures on Molecular Dynamics* even suggests the establishment of a mathematical institution for such calculations.

In theoretical physics, other models are gradually coming into use which I am inclined to class as a third species, for they owe their origin to a peculiar method which is being applied more and more in this branch of science. I believe that this is due rather to practical physical needs than to speculations in the theory of knowledge. The method has, nevertheless, an eminently philosophical stamp, and we must accordingly enter afresh the field of the theory of knowledge.

At the time of the French Revolution and afterwards the great mathematicians of Paris had built up a sharply defined method of theoretical physics on the foundation laid by Galileo and Newton. Mechanical assumptions were made by means of which a group of natural phenomena could be explained, and these principles had attained a kind of geometrical evidence. Men were conscious that the assumptions could not be described as correct with apodeictic certainty, yet up to a certain point it was held to be probable that they were in exact conformity with fact, and accordingly they were called hypotheses. Thus, matter, the luminiferous ether for explaining the phenomena of light, and the two electrical fluids were imagined as sums of mathematical points. Between each pair of such points a force was imagined to act, having its direction in the line joining the two points, and whose intensity was a function, still to be determined, of their distance (Boscovich). A mind knowing all the initial positions and initial velocities of all these material particles, as well as all the forces, and which could integrate all the differential equations arising out of them, would be able to calculate beforehand the whole course of the universe just as the astronomer can predict a solar eclipse (Laplace). There was no hesitation in declaring these forces, which were accepted as originally given and not further explainable, to be the causes of the phenomena, and the calculation of them from the differential equations to be their explanation.

To this was afterwards added the hypothesis that, even in bodies at rest, these particles are themselves in a state of motion, which gives rise to thermal phenomena, and the nature of these particles is very accurately defined especially in the case of gases (Clausius). The theory of gases led to surprising prognoses; thus, for instance, that the coefficient of friction is independent of the pressure, certain relations between friction, diffusion, and conductivity for heat, and so on (Maxwell).

The aggregate of these methods was so productive of results that to explain natural phenomena was defined as the aim of natural science; and what were formerly called the descriptive natural sciences triumphed when Darwin's hypothesis made it possible, not only to describe the various living forms and phenomena, but also to explain them. Strangely enough physics made a turn in the opposite direction at almost exactly the same time.

To Kirchhoff, more especially, it seemed doubtful whether it was justifiable to assign to forces that prominent position to which they were raised by characterizing them as the causes of phenomena. Whether, with Kepler, the form of the orbit of a planet and the velocity at each point is given, or, with Newton, the force at each point, both are really only different methods of describing the facts; and Newton's merit is only the discovery that the description of the motion of the celestial bodies is especially simple if the second differential quotients of their coordinates with respect to the time are given (acceleration, force). In half a page forces were defined away, and physics was made a really descriptive natural science. The structure of mechanics was too firmly fixed for this change in the external aspect to have any essential effect on the inside. The theories of elasticity, which did not involve the conception of molecules, were of older date (Stokes, Lamé, Clebsch). Yet in the development of other branches of physics (electrodynamics, theories of pyro-electricity and of piezo-electricity, and so on) the view gained ground that it could not be the object of theory to penetrate the mechanism of nature, but that this object is, starting merely from the simplest assumptions (that certain magnitudes are linear or other simple functions, and so on), to establish equations as simple as possible which make it possible to calculate the natural phenomena with the closest approximation; as Hertz characteristically says, only to represent nakedly by equations the phenomena directly observed without the variegated garments of hypothesis with which our fancy clothes them.

Several investigators had, before this and from another side, assailed the old system of centers of force and forces at a distance. We might say that this was from the exactly opposite side, because these investigators were particularly fond of the variegated garment of mechanical representation. It might also be said to be from an adjacent side, as they also dispensed with claims to the knowledge of a mechanism behind the phenomena, and, in the mechanisms which they themselves invented, they did not see those of nature, but mere images or analogies.[2] Several men of science, following the lead of Faraday, had established a totally different view of nature. While the older system had held the centers of force to be the only realities, and the forces themselves to be mathematical conceptions, Faraday saw distinctly the continuous working of the forces from point to point in the intermediate space. The potential, which had hitherto been only a formula for lightening the work of calculation, was for him the bond really existing in space, the cause of the action of force. Faraday's ideas were far less lucid than the earlier hypotheses, defined as they were with mathematical precision, and many a mathematician of the old school had but a low opinion of Faraday's theories, without, however, by the light of his own clear conceptions, making such great discoveries.

But soon, and especially in England, it was attempted to get as visible and tangible a representation of the conceptions and ideas which before had played a part in analysis alone. From this endeavor toward visualization arose the graphical representation of the fundamental conceptions of mechanics in Maxwell's *Matter and Motion,* the geometrical representation of the superposition of two sine motions, and all the visualizations due to the theory of quaternions. Thus, the geometrical interpretation of the symbol

[2] Compare the theory of elasticity worked out by Kirchhoff in his *Lectures,* which is of almost ethereal delicacy, clear as crystal but colorless, with that given by Thomson in the third volume of his *Mathematical and Physical Papers,* a sturdy realistic one, not of an ideal elastic body but of steel, india-rubber, or glue, or with Maxwell's language, often almost childlike in its naivety, who, right in the middle of his formulas, casually gives a really good method of removing grease spots.

$$\Delta = \delta^2/\delta x^2 + \delta^2/\delta y^2 + \delta^2/\delta z^2.*$$

There was another matter. The most surprising and far-reaching analogies were seen to exist between natural phenomena which were apparently quite dissimilar. Nature seemed, in a certain sense, to have built up the most diversified things after exactly the same pattern. As the analyst dryly says, the same differential equations hold for the most diversified phenomena.

Thus the conduction of heat, diffusion, and the propagation of electricity in conductors take place according to the same laws. The same equations may be considered as the solution of a problem in hydrodynamics or in the theory of potential. The theory of vortices in fluids as well as that of the friction of gases exhibits the most surprising analogy with that of electromagnetism, and so on.[3]

Maxwell also, when he undertook the mathematical treatment of Faraday's ideas, was from the very outset impelled by their influence into a new path. Thomson[4] had already pointed out a series of analogies between problems in the theory of elasticity and those of electromagnetism. In his first paper on electricity, Maxwell[5] explained that it was not his intention to propound a theory of electricity; that is, that he himself did not believe in the reality of the incompressible fluid and of the resistances which he there assumed, but that he simply intended to give a mechanical example which shows great analogy with electrical phenomena, and he wished to bring the

* Maxwell, *Treatise on Electricity and Magnetism*, Oxford, 1873, Vol. I, art. 29, "Nature of the operator ∇ and ∇^2. This was also afterwards observed by others: Mach, "Ueber Hrn. Guébhard's Darstellung der Aequipotential-Curven," *Wien. Sitzungsberichte*, Vol. LXXXVI, p. 8, 1882. Compare also *Wied. Beiblätter*, Vol. VII, p. 10; *Comptes Rendus*, Vol. XCV, p. 479.

[3] Cf. on this point Maxwell, *Scientific Papers*, Vol. I, p. 156.

[4] *Cambridge and Dublin Math. Journal*, 1847; *Math. and Phys. Papers*, Vol. I.

[5] Maxwell, "On Faraday's Lines of Force," *Cambridge Phil. Trans.*, Vol. X; *Scientific Papers*, Vol. I, p. 157.

electrical phenomena into a form in which the understanding can readily grasp them.[6]

In his second paper[7] he went still farther, and out of liquid vortices and friction wheels working within cells with elastic sides he constructed a wonderful mechanism which serves as a mechanical model for electromagnetism. This mechanism was, of course, mocked at by those who, like Zöllner, regarded it as a hypothesis in the older sense of the word, and who thought that Maxwell ascribed to it a real existence. This Maxwell decidedly repudiated, and only modestly hoped "that by such mechanical fictions any one who understands the provisional and temporary character of this hypothesis will find himself rather helped than hindered by it in his search after the true interpretation of the phenomena." And they were so helped; for by his model Maxwell arrived at those equations whose peculiar and almost magical power Heinrich Hertz, the person most of all qualified to judge, thus vigorously depicted in his lecture of 1890 on the relations between light and electricity: "We cannot study this wonderful theory without at times feeling as if an independent life and a reason of its own dwelt in these mathematical formulas; as if they were wiser than we were, wiser even than their discoverer; as if they gave out more than had been put into them." I should like to add to these words of Hertz's only this: that Maxwell's formulas were merely consequences of his mechanical models, and Hertz's enthusiastic praise is due, in the chiefest place, not to Maxwell's analysis, but to his acuteness in the discovery of mechanical analogies.

It is only in Maxwell's third important paper[8] and in

[6] Maxwell, *Scientific Papers,* Vol. I, p. 157.

[7] "On Physical Lines of Force," *Phil. Mag.* (4), Vol. XXI, 1861, pp. 161, 281, 338, and Vol. XXIII, 1862, pp. 12, 85; *Scientific Papers,* Vol. I, p. 451.

[8] "A Dynamical Theory of the Electro-magnetic Field," *Phil. Trans.,* Vol. CV, 1865, p. 459; *Scientific Papers,* Vol. I, pp. 526.

his textbook[9] that the formulas more and more detach themselves from the model, and this process was completed by Heaviside, Poynting, Rowland, Hertz and Cohn. Maxwell still used the mechanical analogy, or as he said, the "dynamical illustration." But he no longer pursued it into details, but searched for the most general mechanical assumptions calculated to lead to phenomena which are analogous to those of electromagnetism. Thomson was led, by an extension of the ideas which have already been cited, to the quasi-elastic and quasi-labile ether and to its visualization by the gyrostatic-adynamic model.

Maxwell of course applied the same treatment to other branches of theoretical physics. Maxwell's gas-molecules, which repel each other with a force inversely proportional to the fifth power of their distance, may be conceived as mechanical analogies, and at first investigators were not wanting who, not understanding Maxwell's tendency, affirmed that his hypothesis was improbable and absurd.

The new ideas, however, gradually found entrance into all domains of physics. In the theory of heat I need only mention Helmholtz's celebrated memoirs on the mechanical analogies of the second law of thermodynamics. It was seen, indeed, that they correspond better to the spirit of science than the old hypotheses, and were also more convenient for the investigator himself. For the old hypotheses could only be kept up as long as everything just fitted; but now a few failures of agreement did no harm, for it can be no reproach against a mere analogy if it fits rather loosely in some places. Hence the old theories, such as the elastic theory of light, the theory of gases, the schemes of chemists for the benzol rings, and so on, were soon regarded only as mechanical analogies, and philosophy at last generalized Maxwell's ideas to the doctrine

[9] *Treatise on Electricity and Magnetism*, 2 vols., Oxford, 1873; 2d ed., 1881.

that all knowledge is nothing else than the discovery of analogies. With this the older scientific method was defined away, and science now only spoke in parables.

All these mechanical models at first existed indeed only in thought; they were dynamical illustrations in the imagination and could not be carried out in practice in this general form. Yet their great importance was an incitement practically to realize at least their fundamental types.

In the second part of this catalogue is a description of such an attempt made by Maxwell himself, and of one by the author of these lines. Fitzgerald's model is also at present in the exhibition, as well as Bjerknes's model, which owe their origin to similar tendencies. Other models which have to be classed with these have been constructed by Oliver Lodge, Lord Rayleigh, and others.

They all show how the new tendency to relinquish perfect congruence with nature is compensated by the more striking prominence of points of similarity. To this tendency, without any doubt, belongs the immediate future; yet, mistaken as it was to consider the old method as the only correct one, it would be just as one-sided, after all it has accomplished, to consider it as quite played out, and not to cultivate it along with the new one.

MUNICH, August, 1892. LUDWIG BOLTZMANN.

SUPPLEMENTARY NOTE.

[To the translation in the *Philosophical Magazine* are two additions. One is to note 2, and runs:

"The relation of the directions of the old system of centers of force, and of forces at a distance and the purely mechanical one represented by Kirchhoff, to Maxwell's own point of view is expressed by him in the following words: 'The results of this simplification may take the form of a purely mathematical formula (Kirchhoff), or of a physical hypothesis (Poisson). In the first case we entirely lose sight of the phenomena to be explained and, though we may trace out the consequences of given laws, we can never obtain more extended views of the connections of the subject. If, on the other hand, we adopt a physical hypothesis, we see the phenomena only through a medium, and are liable to that blindness to facts and rashness in assumption which a partial explanation encourages. We must therefore discover some method of investigation which allows the mind at every step to lay hold of a clear physical conception without being committed to any theory in physical science from which that conception is borrowed, so that it is neither drawn aside by analytical subtleties, nor carried beyond the truth by a favorite hypothesis.' "

The other addition is a reference, in note 3, to B. Riemann's *Electricität und Magnetismus.*

In the Munich exhibition, Boltzmann's mechanical models were: (1) Apparatus for demonstration of the laws of uniformly accelerated rotation;[1] (2) Machine for the demonstration of the superposition of waves;[2] (3) two pieces of apparatus to show the over-tones of plucked strings;[3] and (4) Apparatus for the mechanical illustration of the behavior of two electric currents.[4]

The exhibition also contained, among the mechanical models of electrodynamical phenomena, G. F. Fitzgerald's model to illustrate certain properties of the ether according to Maxwell's theory;[5] Lodge's two models to illustrate certain electrical phenomena;[6] C. A. Bjerknes's model for the hydrodynamical illustration of electrical and magnetic phenomena;[7] M. Möller and O Günther's models for the representation of electrical vibrations and magnetic lines of force about solenoids;[8] Lodge's model for illustration of dielectric displacement according to Maxwell's view;[9] and H. Ebert's apparatus for the mechanical illustration of electrodynamic induction.[10]

Boltzmann's fourth model referred to above was made independently of, but on the same principle as, one already set up by Maxwell in the Cavendish laboratory at Cambridge. Boltzmann's model is described, with another of Lord Rayleigh's which serves the same purpose, in his *Vorlesungen über Maxwell's Theorie der Electricität und des Lichtes.*[11] Boltzmann also published the following papers on mechanical models of physical phenomena: "Ueber die mechanischen Analogien des zweiten Hauptsatzes der Thermodynamik";[12] Ueber ein Medium, dessen mechanische Eigenschaften auf die von Maxwell für den Elektromagnetismus aufgestellten Gleichungen führen; Teil i";[13] "Mechanisches Modell zur Versinnlichung der Lagrange'schen Bewegungsgleichungen";[14] "Ueber die mechanische Analogie des Wärmegleichgewichtes zweier sich berührender Körper";[15] and the article "Models" in the tenth edition of the *Encyclopædia Britannica.*[16]—P. E. B. J.]

[1] *Katalog*, p. 309. [2] *Ibid.*, p. 360. [3] *Ibid.*, pp. 361-362.

[4] *Ibid.*, pp. 405-408. [5] *Ibid.*, pp. 400-401. [6] *Ibid.*, pp. 401-404.

[7] *Ibid.*, pp. 404-405 (with references to the literature on Bjerknes's investigations).

[8] *Ibid.*, pp. 408-410. [9] *Katalog, Nachtrag*, 1893, p. 116.

[10] *Ibid.*, pp. 116-117; cf. Boltzmann's fourth model referred to above.

[11] Leipsic, 1891, sixth lecture.

[12] *Journ. für Math.*, Vol. C, 1886, pp. 201-212.

[13] *Münch. Ber.*, Vol. XXIIa, 1892, pp. 279-301; *Wiedemann's Annalen*, Vol. XLVIII, 1893, pp. 77-99.

[14] *Jahresber. der Deutsch. Math.-Ver.*, Vol. I, 1892, pp. 53-55.

[15] *Wien. Ber.*, Vol. CIII, 1895, pp. 1125-1134.

[16] Vol. XXX, 1902, pp. 788-791.

ON THE EXPERIENCE OF TIME.*

IN the present article, we shall be concerned with all those immediate experiences upon which our knowledge of time is based. Broadly speaking, two pairs of relations have to be considered, namely, (*a*) sensation and memory, which give time-relations between object and subject, (*b*) simultaneity and succession, which give time-relations among objects. It is of the utmost importance not to confuse time-relations of subject and object with time-relations of object and object; in fact, many of the worst difficulties in the psychology and metaphysics of time have arisen from this confusion. It will be seen that past, present, and future arise from time-relations of subject and object, while earlier and later arise from time-relations of object and object. In a world in which there was no experience there would be no past, present, or future, but there might well be earlier and later. Let us give the name of *mental time* to the time which arises through relations of subject and object, and the name *physical time* to the time which arises through relations of object and object. We have to consider what are the elements in immediate experience which lead to our knowledge of these two sorts of time, or rather of time-relations.

Although, in the finished logical theory of time, physical time is simpler than mental time, yet in the analysis of experience it would seem that mental time must come first. The essence of physical time is succession; but the experience of succession will be very different according as the objects concerned are both remembered, one remembered and one given in sense, or both given in sense. Thus the analysis of sensation and memory must precede the discussion of physical time.

Before entering upon any detail, it may be well to state in summary form the theory which is to be advocated.

1. *Sensation* (including the apprehension of present mental facts by introspection) is a certain relation of subject and object, involving acquaintance, but recognizably different from any other experienced relation of subject and object.

2. Objects of sensation are said to be *present* to their subject in the experience in which they are objects.

3. Simultaneity is a relation among entities, which is given in experience as sometimes holding between objects present to a given subject in a single experience.

4. An entity is said to be *now* if it is simultaneous with what is present to me, i. e., with *this*, where "this" is the proper name of an object of sensation of which I am aware.

5. *The present time* may be defined as a class of all entities that are *now*. [This definition may require modification; it will be discussed later.]

6. *Immediate Memory* is a certain relation of subject and object, involving acquaintance, but recognizably different from any other experienced relation of subject and object.

7. *Succession* is a relation which may hold between two parts of one sensation, for instance between parts of a swift movement which is the object of one sensation; it may then, and perhaps also when one or both objects are objects of immediate memory, be immediately experienced, and extended by inference to cases where one or both of the terms of the relation are not present.

8: When one event is succeeded by another, the first is called *earlier* and the second *later*.

9. An event which is earlier than the whole of the present is called *past,* and an event which is later than the whole of the present is called *future.*

This ends our definitions, but we still need certain propositions constituting and connecting the mental and physical time-series. The chief of these are:

a. Simultaneity and succession both give rise to transitive relations; simultaneity is symmetrical, while succession is asymmetrical, or at least gives rise to an asymmetrical relation defined in terms of it.

b. What is remembered is past.

c. Whenever a change is immediately experienced in sensation, parts of the present are earlier than other parts. (This follows logically from the definitions.)

d. It may happen that A and B form part of one sensation, and likewise B and C, but when C is an object of sensation A is an object of memory. Thus the relation "belonging to the same present" is not transitive, and two presents may overlap without coinciding.

The above definitions and propositions must now be explained and amplified.

1. *Sensation,* from the point of view of psychophysics, will be concerned only with objects not involving introspection. But from the point of view of theory of knowledge, all acquaintance with the present may advantageously be combined under one head, and therefore, if there is introspective knowledge of the present, we will include this with sensation. It is sometimes said that all introspective knowledge is of the nature of memory; we will not now consider this opinion, but will merely say that *if* introspection ever gives acquaintance with present mental entities in the way in which the senses give acquaintance with present physical entities, then such acquaintance with mental entities is, *for our purposes,* to be included under the head of sensation. Sensation, then, is that kind of

acquaintance with particulars which enables us to know that they are at the present time. The object of a sensation we will call a *sense-datum.* Thus to a given subject sense-data are those of its objects which can be known, from the nature of their relation to the subject, to be at the present time.

The question naturally arises: how do we know whether an object is present or past or without position in time? Mere acquaintance, as we decided in considering imagination, does not necessarily involve any given temporal relation to the subject. How, then, is the temporal relation given? Since there can be no *intrinsic* difference between present and past objects, and yet we can distinguish by inspection between objects given as present and those given as past, it follows from the criterion set forth at the beginning of the preceding chapter that the relation of subject to object must be different, and recognizably different, according as the object is present or past. Thus sensation must be a special relation of subject and object, different from any relation which does not show that the object is at the present time. Having come to this result, it is natural to accept "sensation" as an ultimate, and define the present time in terms of it; for otherwise we should have to use some such phrase as "given as at the present time," which would demand further analysis, and would almost inevitably lead us back to the relation of sensation as what is meant by the phrase "given as at the present time." For this reason, we accept sensation as one of the ultimates by means of which time-relations are to be defined.

2. Our theory of time requires a definition, without presupposing time, of what is meant by "one (momentary) total experience." This question has been already considered in a previous article, where we decided that "being experienced together" is an ultimate relation among objects, which is itself sometimes immediately experienced as

holding between two objects. We cannot analyze this into "being experienced by the same subject," because A and B may be experienced together, and likewise B and C, while A and C are not experienced together: this will happen if A and B form part of one "specious present," and likewise B and C, but A is already past when C is experienced. Thus "being experienced together" is best taken as a simple relation. Although this relation is sometimes perceived, it may of course also hold when it is not perceived. Thus "one (momentary) total experience" will be the experience of all that group of objects which are experienced together with a given object. This, however, still contains a difficulty, when viewed as a definition, namely that it assumes that no object is experienced twice, or throughout a longer time than one specious present. This difficulty must be solved before we can proceed.

Two opposite dangers confront any theory on this point. (*a*) If we say that no one object can be experienced twice, or rather, to avoid what would be *obviously* false, that no one object can be twice an object of sense, we have to ask what is meant by "twice." If a time intervenes between the two occasions, we can say that the object is not numerically the same on the two occasions; or, if that is thought false, we can say at least that the experience is not numerically the same on the two occasions. We can then define "one (momentary) total experience" as everything experienced together with "this," where "this" is an experience, not merely the object of an experience. By this means, we shall avoid the difficulty in the case when "twice" means "at two times separated by an interval when the experience in question is absent." But when what seems to be the same experience persists through a longer continuous period than one specious present, the overlapping of successive specious presents introduces a new difficulty. Suppose, to fix our ideas, that I look steadily at a motionless object while I hear a succession of sounds. The sounds A and B, though successive, may be experienced together, and therefore my seeing of the object while I hear these sounds need not be supposed to constitute two different experiences. But the same applies to what I see while I hear the sounds B and C. Thus the experience of seeing the given object will be the same at the time of the sound A and at the time of the sound C, although these two times may well not be parts of one specious present. Thus our definition will show that the hearing of A and the hearing of C from parts of one experience, which is plainly contrary to what we mean by one experience. Suppose, to escape this conclusion, we say that my seeing the object is a different experience while I am hearing A from what it is while I am hearing B. Then we shall be forced to deny that the hearing of A and the hearing of B form parts of one experience. In that case, the perception of change will become inexplicable, and we shall be driven to greater and greater subdivision, owing to the fact that changes are constantly occurring. We shall thus be forced to conclude that one experience cannot last for more than one mathematical instant, which is absurd.

b. Having been thus forced to reject the view that the existence of one experience must be confined within one specious present, we have now to consider how we can define "one (momentary) total experience" on the hypothesis that a numerically identical experience may persist throughout a longer period than one specious present. It is obvious that no one experience will now suffice for definition. All that falls within one (momentary) total experience must belong to one specious present, but what is experienced together with a given experience need not, on our present hypothesis, fall within one specious present. We can, however, avoid all difficulties by defining "one (momentary) total experience" as a group of objects such that *any two* are experienced together, and nothing outside the group is experienced together with all of them. Thus, for example, if A and B, though not simultaneous, are experienced together, and if B and C likewise are experienced together, C will not belong to one experience with A and B unless A and C also are experienced together. And given any larger group of objects, any two of which are experienced together, there is some one (momentary) total experience to which they all belong; but a new object x cannot be pronounced a member of this total experience until it has been found to be experienced together with all the members of the group. A given object will, in general, belong to many different (momentary) total experiences. Suppose, for example, the sounds A, B, C, D, E occur in succession, and three of them can be experienced together. Then C will belong to a total experience containing A, B, C, to one containing B, C, D, and to one containing C, D, E. In this way, in spite of the fact that the specious present lasts for a certain length of time, experience permits us to assign the temporal position of an object much more accurately than merely within one specious present. In the above instance, C is at the end of the specious present of A, B, C, in the middle of that of B, C, D, and at the beginning of that of C, D, E. And by introducing less discrete changes the temporal position of C can be assigned even more accurately.

We may thus make the following definitions:

"One (momentary) total experience," is a group of experiences such that the objects of any two of them are experienced together, and anything experienced together with all members of the group is a member of the group.

The "specious present" of a momentary total experience is the period of time within which an object must lie in order to be a sense-datum in that experience.

This second definition needs some amplification. If an

object has ceased to exist just before a given instant,[1] it may still be an object of sense at that instant. We may suppose that, of all the present objects of sense which have already ceased to exist, there is one which ceased to exist longest ago; at any rate a certain stretch of time is defined from the present instant back through the various moments when present objects of sense ceased to exist. This stretch is the "specious present." It will be observed that this is a complicated notion, involving mathematical time as well as psychological presence. The purely psychological notion which underlies it is the notion of one (momentary) total experience.

Sense-data belonging to one (momentary) total experience are said to be *present* in that experience. This is a merely verbal definition.

The above definitions still involve a certain difficulty, though perhaps not an insuperable one. We have admitted provisionally that a given particular may exist at different times. If it should happen that the whole group of particulars constituting one (momentary) total experience should recur, all our definitions of "the present time" and allied notions would become ambiguous. It is no answer to say that such recurrence is improbable: "the present time" is plainly not ambiguous, and would not be so if such recurrence took place. In order to avoid the difficulty, one of two things is necessary. Either we must show that such complete recurrence is *impossible,* not merely improbable; or we must admit absolute time, i. e., admit that there is an entity called a "moment" (or a "period of time" possibly) which is not a mere relation between events, and is involved in assigning the temporal position of an object. The problem thus raised is serious; but it belongs rather to the physical than to the psychological analysis of time. Within our experience, complete recur-

[1] The word "instant" has a meaning defined later in the present article.

rence does not occur. So long, therefore, as we are considering merely the psychological genesis of our knowledge of time, objections derived from the possibility of recurrence may be temporarily put aside. We shall return to this question at a later stage of this article.

3. *Simultaneity.* This is a relation belonging to "physical" time, i. e., it is a relation between objects primarily, rather than between object and subject. By inference, we may conclude that sense-data are simultaneous with their subjects, i. e., that when an object is present to a subject, it is simultaneous with it. But the relation of simultaneity which is here intended is one which is primarily given in experience only as holding among objects. It does not mean simply "both present together." There are two reasons against such a definition. First, we wish to be able to speak of two entities as simultaneous when they are not both parts of one experience, i. e., when one or both are only known by description; thus we must have a meaning of simultaneity which does not introduce a subject. Secondly, in all cases where there is a change within what is present in one experience, there will be succession, and therefore absence of simultaneity, between two objects which are both present. When two objects form part of one present, they *may* be simultaneous, and their simultaneity *may* be immediately experienced. It is however by no means necessary that they should be simultaneous in this case, nor that, if they are in fact simultaneous, they should form part of what is present in one experience. The only point of connection, so far as knowledge is concerned, between simultaneity and presence, is that simultaneity can only be *experienced* between objects which are both present in one experience.

4. *The definition of "now."* We saw that both "I" and "now" are to be defined in terms of "this," where "this" is the object of attention. In order to define "now," it is

necessary that "this" should be a sense-datum. Then "now" means "simultaneous with this." Since the sense-datum may lie anywhere within the specious present, "now" is to that extent ambiguous; to avoid this ambiguity, we may define "now" as meaning "simultaneous with some part of the specious present." This definition avoids ambiguity, but loses the essential simplicity which makes "now" important. When nothing is said to be contrary, we shall adopt the first definition; thus "now" will mean "simultaneous with this," where "this" is a sense-datum.

5. *The present time* is the time of entities which are present, i. e., of all entities simultaneous with some part of the specious present, i. e., of all entities which are "now" in our second, unambiguous sense. If we adopt a relational theory of time, we may define a time simply as the class of all entities which are commonly said to be at that time, i. e., of all entities simultaneous with a given entity, or with a given set of entities if we do not wish to define a mathematical instant. Thus with a relational theory of time, "the present time" will be simply all entities simultaneous with some part of the specious present. With an absolute theory of time, "the present time" will be the time occupied by the specious present. We shall not at present attempt to decide between the absolute and relative theories of time.

This completes our theory of the knowledge of the present. Although knowledge of *succession* is possible without passing outside the present, because the present is a finite interval of time within which changes can occur, yet knowledge of the *past* is not thus obtainable. For this purpose, we have to consider a new relation to objects, namely *memory*. The analysis of memory is a difficult problem, to which we must now turn our attention.

6. *Immediate memory*. Without, as yet, asserting that there is such a thing as immediate memory, we may define

it as "a two-term relation of subject and object, involving acquaintance, and such as to give rise to the knowledge that the object is in the past." This is not intended as a satisfactory definition, but merely as a means of pointing out what is to be discussed. It is indubitable that we have knowledge of the past, and it would seem, though this is not logically demonstrable, that such knowledge arises from acquaintance with past objects in a way enabling us to know that they are past. The existence, extent, and nature of such immediate knowledge of the past is now to be investigated.

There are two questions to be considered, here as in theory of knowledge generally. First, there is the question: What sort of data would be logically capable of giving rise to the knowledge we possess? And secondly, there is the question: How far does introspection or other observation decide which of the logically possible systems of data is actually realized? We will deal with the first question first.

We certainly know what we mean by saying "such-and-such an event occurred in the past." I do not mean that we know this *analytically,* because that will only be the case with those (if any) who have an adequate philosophy of time; I mean only that we know it in the sense that the phrase expresses a thought recognizably different from other thoughts. Thus we must understand complexes into which "past," or whatever is the essential constituent of "past," enters as a constituent. Again it is obvious that "past" expresses a relation to "present," i. e., a thing is "past" when it has a certain relation to the present, or to a constituent of the present. At first sight, we should naturally say that what is past cannot also be present; but this would be to assume that no particular can exist at two different times, or endure throughout a finite period of time. It would be a mistake to make such an assumption, and therefore we shall not say that what is past cannot also be present. If there is a sense in which this is true, it will emerge later, but ought not to be part of what is originally taken as obvious.

The question now arises whether "past" can be defined by relation to some one constituent of the present, or whether it involves the whole present experience. This question is bound up with another question, namely, can "past" be defined as "earlier than the present"? We have seen that *succession* may occur within the present; and when A is succeeded by B, we say that A is earlier than B. Thus "earlier" can be understood without passing outside the present. We cannot say, however, that the past is whatever is earlier than this or that constituent of the present, because the present has no sharp boundaries, and no constituent of it can be picked out as certainly the earliest. Thus if we choose any one constituent of the present, there may be earlier entities which are present and not past. If, therefore, "past" is to be defined in terms of "earlier," it must be defined as "earlier than the whole of the present." This definition would not be open to any *logical* objection, but I think it cannot represent the epistemological analysis of our knowledge of the past, since it is quite obvious that, in order to know that a given entity is in the past, it is not necessary to review the whole present and find that it is all later than the given entity. This argument seems to show that the past must be definable without explicit reference to the whole present, and must therefore not be defined in terms of "earlier."

Another question, by no means easy to answer, is this: Does our knowledge of the past involve *acquaintance* with past objects, or can it be accounted for on the supposition that only knowledge by description is involved in our knowledge of the past? That is, must our knowledge of the past be derived from such propositions as "*This* is past," where *this* is an object of present acquaintance, or can it be wholly derived from propositions of the form: "An entity with such-and-such characteristics existed in the past"? The latter view might be maintained, for example, by introducing images: it might be said that we have images which we know to be more or less like objects of past experience, but that the simplest knowledge we have concerning such objects is their resemblance to images. In this case, the simplest *cognition* upon which our knowledge of the past is built will be perception of the fact "this-resembles-something-in-the-past," where *this* is an image, and "something" is an "apparent variable." I do not believe that such a view is tenable. No doubt, in cases of remembering something not very recent, we have often only acquaintance with an image, combined with the *judgment* that something like the image occurred in the past. But such memory is liable to error, and therefore does not involve *perception* of a fact of which "past" is a constituent. Since, however, the word "past" has significance for us, there must be perception of facts in which it occurs, and in such cases memory must be not liable to error. I conclude that, though other complications are logically possible, there must, in some cases, be immediate acquaintance with past objects given in a way which enables us to know that they are past, though such acquaintance may be confined to the very recent past.

Coming now to what psychology has to say as to the empirical facts, we find three phenomena which it is important to distinguish. There is first what may be called "physiological" memory, which is simply the persistence of a sensation for a short time after the stimulus is removed. The time during which we see a flash of lightning is longer than the time during which the flash of lightning, as a physical object, exists. This fact is irrelevant to us, since it has nothing to do with anything discoverable by introspection alone. Throughout the period of "physiological memory," the sense-datum is actually *present*; it is only the inferred physical object which has ceased.

Secondly, there is our awareness of the *immediate* past, the short period during which the warmth of sensation gradually dies out of receding objects, as if we saw them under a fading light. The sound we heard a few seconds ago, but are not hearing now, may still be an object of acquaintance, but is given in a different way from that in which it was given when it was a sense-datum. James[2] seems to include what is thus still given in the "specious present," but however we may choose to define the "specious present," it is certain that the object thus given, but not given in sense, is given in the way which makes us call it *past*; and James[3] rightly states that it is this experience which is "the *original* of our experience of pastness, from whence we get the meaning of the term."

Thirdly, there is our knowledge concerning more remote portions of the past. Such knowledge is more difficult to analyze, and is no doubt derivative and complicated, as well as liable to error. It does not, therefore, belong to the elementary constituents of our acquaintance with the world, which are what concern us at present. Or, if it does contain some elementary constituent, it must be one which is not essential to our having a knowledge of time, though it may increase the extent of our knowledge concerning past events.

Thus of the three phenomena which we have been considering, only the second seems directly relevant to our present problem. We will give the name "immediate memory" to the relation which we have to an object which has recently been a sense-datum, but is now felt as past, though still given in acquaintance. It is essential that the object of immediate memory should be, at least in part, identical with the object

[2] Cf., e. g., *Psychology,* Vol. I, p. 630.
[3] *Loc. cit.,* p. 604.

previously given in sense, since otherwise immediate memory would not give acquaintance with what is past, and would not serve to account for our knowledge of the past. Hence, by our usual criterion, since immediate memory is intrinsically distinguishable from sensation, it follows that it is a different relation between subject and object. We shall take it as a primitive constituent of experience. We may define one entity as "past" with respect to another when it has to the other that relation which is experienced, in the consciousness of immediate memory, as existing between object and subject. This relation, of course, will come to be known to hold in a vast number of cases in which it is not experienced; the epistemological need of the immediate experience is to make us know what is meant by "past," and to give us data upon which our subsequent knowledge can be built. It will be observed that in order to know a past object we only need immediate memory, but in order to know what is meant by "past," an immediate remembering must be itself made an object of experience. Thus introspection is necessary in order to understand the meaning of "past," because the only cases in which this relation is immediately given are cases in which one term is the subject. Thus "past," like "present," is a notion derived from psychology, whereas "earlier" and "later" can be known by an experience of non-mental objects.

The extent of immediate memory, important as it is for other problems, need not now concern us; nor is it necessary to discuss what is meant by memory of objects with which we are no longer acquainted. The bare materials for the knowledge that there is a time-series can, I think, be provided without considering any form of memory beyond immediate memory.

7. *Succession* is a relation which is given between objects, and belongs to physical time, where it plays a part analogous to that played by memory in the construction of

mental time. Succession may be immediately experienced between parts of one sense-datum, for example in the case of a swift movement; in this case, the two objects of which one is succeeded by the other are both parts of the present. It would seem that succession may also be immediately experienced between an object of immediate memory and a sense-datum, or between two objects of immediate memory. The extensions of our knowledge of succession by inference need not now concern us.

8. We say that A is *earlier* than B if A is succeeded by B; and in the same case we say B is *later* than A. These are purely verbal definitions. It should be observed that *earlier* and *later* are relations given as between objects, and not in any way implying past and present. There is no logical reason why the relations of earlier and later should not subsist in a world wholly devoid of consciousness.

9. An event is said to be *past* when it is earlier than the whole of the present, and is said to be *future* when it is later than the whole of the present. It is necessary to include the *whole* of the present, since an event may be earlier than *part* of the present and yet be itself present, in cases where there is succession within the present. It is also necessary to define the past by means of *earlier* rather than by means of memory, since there may be things in the past which are neither themselves remembered nor simultaneous with anything remembered. It should be noted that there is no experience of the future. I do not mean that no particulars which are future are or have been experienced, because if a particular recurs or endures it may be experienced at the earlier time. What I mean is that there is no experience of anything *as* future, in the way in which sensation experiences a thing as present and memory experiences it as past. Thus the future is only known by inference, and is only known *descriptively*, as "what succeeds the present."

Having now ended our definitions, we must proceed to the propositions constructing and connecting the physical and mental time-series.

a. Simultaneity and succession both give rise to transitive relations, while simultaneity is symmetrical, and succession asymmetrical, or at least gives rise to an asymmetrical relation defined in terms of it.

This proposition is required for the construction of the physical time-series. At first sight, it might seem to raise no difficulties, but as a matter of fact it raises great difficulties, if we admit the possibility of recurrence. These difficulties are so great that they seem to make either the denial of recurrence of particulars or the admission of absolute time almost unavoidable.

Let us begin with simultaneity. Suppose that I see a given object A continuously while I am hearing two successive sounds B and C. Then B is simultaneous with A and A with C, but B is not simultaneous with C. Thus it would seem to follow that simultaneity, in the sense in which we have been using the word, is not transitive. We might escape this conclusion by denying that any numerically identical particular ever exists at two different instants: thus instead of the one A, we shall have a series of A's, not differing as to predicates, one for each instant during which we had thought that A endures. Such a view would not be logically untenable, but it seems incredible, and almost any other tenable theory would seem preferable.

In the same way as we defined one (momentary) total experience, we may, if we wish to avoid absolute time, define an "instant" as a group of events *any two* of which are simultaneous with each other, and not all of which are simultaneous with anything outside the group. Then an event is "at" an instant when it is a member of the class which is that instant. When a number of events are all at the same instant, they are related in the way which we have in mind when we think that simultaneity is transitive. It must be observed that we do not thus obtain a transitive two-term relation unless the instant is *specified*: "A and B are at the instant *t*" is transitive, but "there is an instant at which A and B are" holds whenever A and B are simultaneous, and is thus not transitive. In spite of this, however, the above definition of an "instant" provides formally what is required, so far as simultaneity is concerned. It is only so far as succession is concerned that this definition will be found inadequate.

Succession, if the time-series is to be constituted, must give rise to an asymmetrical transitive relation. Now if recurrence or persistence is possible, succession itself will have neither of these properties. If A occurs before B, and again after B, we have a case where succession is not asymmetrical. If B occurs both before A and after C, while A occurs before C but never occurs after C, A will succeed B and B will succeed C, but A will not succeed C; thus succession will not be transitive. Let us consider how this is affected if we pass on to "instants" in the sense above defined. We may say that one instant is *posterior* to another, and the other *anterior* to the one, if every member of the one succeeds every member of the other. But now we are faced with the possibility of *repetition,* i. e., of an instant being posterior to itself. If everything in the universe at one instant were to occur again after a certain interval, so as again to constitute an instant, the anterior and posterior instants would be *identical* according to our present definition. This result cannot be avoided by altering the definition of *anterior* and *posterior.* It can only be avoided by finding some set of entities of which we know that they cannot recur. If we took Bergson's view, according to which our mental life at each moment is intrinsically different, owing to memory, from that of a moment preceded by different experiences, then the experience of each moment of life is unique, and can be used to define an instant. In this way, if the whole universe may be taken as one experience, the time-series can be constructed by means of memory. There is no *logical* error in such a procedure, but there is a greater accumulation of questionable metaphysics than is suitable for our purposes. We must, therefore, seek for some other way of constructing the time-series.

It is no answer to our difficulty to reply that the complete recurrence of the whole momentary state of the universe is *improbable*. The point of our difficulty is this: If the whole state of the universe did recur, it is obvious that there would be *something* not numerically identical in the two occurrences, something, in fact, which leads us to speak of "two occurrences." It would be contrary to what is self-evident to say that there was strictly *one* occurrence, which was anterior and posterior to itself. Without taking account of the whole universe, if a thing A exists at one time, then ceases, and then exists again at a later time, it seems obvious that there is *some* numerical diversity involved, even if A is numerically the same. In this case, in fact, where A reappears after an absence, it would seem strained to say that the *same* particular had reappeared: we should more naturally say that a new precisely similar particular had appeared. This is by no means so obvious in the case of a thing which persists unchanged throughout a continuous period. Before going further, we must consider whether there can be any substantial difference between persistence and recurrence.

The view which I wish to advocate is the following. An entity may persist unchanged throughout a continuous portion of time, without any numerical diversity corresponding to the different instants during which it exists; but if an entity ceases to exist, any entity existing at a subsequent time must be numerically diverse from the one that has ceased. The object of this hypothesis is to preserve, if possible, a relational theory of time; therefore the first thing to be done is to re-state it in terms which do not even verbally imply absolute time. For this purpose, we may adopt the following definitions. We shall say that a thing *exists at several times* if it is simultaneous with things which are not simultaneous with each other. We shall say that it *exists throughout a continuous time* when, if it is simultaneous with two things which are not simultaneous with each other, it is also simultaneous with any thing which comes after the earlier and before the later of the two things. The assumption that two things which are separated by an interval of time cannot be numerically identical is presupposed in the above definition. This assumption, in relational language, may be stated as follows: *If A precedes B and is not simultaneous with it, while B precedes C and is not simultaneous with it, then A and C are numerically diverse.*[4] We have to inquire whether a logically tenable theory of the time-series can be constructed on this basis.

The difficulty of possible recurrence of the whole state of the universe, which troubled us before, is now obviated. It is now possible to define an *instant* as a class of entities of which any two are simultaneous with each other and not all are simultaneous with any entity outside the class. It will follow that it is meaningless to suppose the universe to persist unchanged throughout a finite time. This is perhaps an objection; on the other hand, it may be said that, when we suppose that such persistence is possible, we are imagining ourselves as spectators watching the unusual immobility with continually increasing astonishment; and in this case, our own feelings, at least, are in a state of change. Let us, then, suppose that it is logically impossible, as our present theory requires, for the universe

[4] Another form of the same axiom is: *If A both precedes and succeeds B, then A is simultaneous with B.*

to persist unchanged throughout a finite time. Then if two times are different, something must have changed meanwhile; and if this something has changed back so far as its character goes, yet what has reappeared is, in virtue of our assumption, numerically different from what has disappeared. Thus it is impossible that the world should be composed of numerically the same particulars at two different times.

We may now define an *instant* as a class which is identical with all the terms that are simultaneous with every member of itself. We will say that one event "wholly precedes" another when it precedes it without being simultaneous with it; and we will say that one instant is "anterior" to another when there is at least one member of the one instant which wholly precedes at least one member of the other instant. We shall assume that simultaneity is symmetrical, and that every event is simultaneous with itself, so that nothing can wholly precede itself. We will also assume that "wholly preceding" is transitive. These two assumptions together imply our previous assumption, which was that "wholly preceding" is asymmetrical, i. e., that if A wholly precedes B, then B does not wholly precede A. Finally, we will assume that of any two events which are not simultaneous one must wholly precede the other. Then we can prove that "anterior" is a serial relation, so that the instants of time form a series. The only remaining thing that needs to be proved is that there are instants, and that every event belongs to some instant. For this purpose let us call one event an "early part" of another when everything simultaneous with the one is simultaneous with the other, and nothing wholly preceding the one is simultaneous with the other. Let us define the "beginning" of an event as the class of events simultaneous with all its early parts. Then it will be found that, if we assume that any event wholly after something simultaneous with a given event is wholly after some early part of the given event, then the beginning of an event is an instant of which the event in question is a member.[5]

It would seem, therefore, that the physical time-series can be constructed by means of the relations considered in the earlier part of this article. Our few remaining propositions, which are chiefly concerned with mental time, offer less difficulty.

b. What is remembered is past. It should be noted that the past was defined as "what is earlier than the whole of the present," so that it cannot be supposed that whatever is passed is remembered, nor does memory enter into the *definition* of the past.

c. When a change is immediately experienced in sensation, parts of the present are earlier than other parts. This follows, because, since the change, by hypothesis, lies within sensation, it follows that the earlier and the later state of things are both present according to the definition.

d. If A, B, and C succeed each other rapidly, A and B may be parts of one sensation, and likewise B and C, while A and C are not parts of one sensation, but A is remembered when C is present in sensation. In such a case, A and B belong to the same present, and likewise B and C, but not A and C; thus the relation "belonging to the same present" is not transitive. This has nothing to do with the question of persistence or recurrence which we considered under (*a*), but is an independent fact concerned with mental time, and due to the fact that the present is not an instant. It follows that, apart from any question of duration in objects, two presents may overlap without coinciding.

BERTRAND RUSSELL.

CAMBRIDGE, ENGLAND.

[5] In symbols, the above theory, with certain logical simplifications, has been set forth by Dr. Norbert Wiener in his "Contributions to the Theory of Relative Position," *Proc. Camb. Phil. Soc.*, Vol. XVII, Part 5, (1914).

NEWTON'S HYPOTHESES OF ETHER AND OF GRAVITATION FROM 1679 TO 1693.

I.

NEWTON'S letter to Boyle, referred to in the last article in this series, contained an extension of the views described in the "Hypothesis" of 1675, was written on February 28, 1679,[1] and was in fulfilment of a long deferred promise. This promise was, indeed, according to Newton, the chief reason for the communication of notions so "indigested" and unsatisfactory to himself. He added that, as it was only an "explication of qualities" that was desired by Boyle, he set down "his apprehensions in the form of suppositions."

"And first," continued Newton, "I suppose that there is diffused through all places an ethereal substance, capable of contraction and dilatation, strongly elastic, and, in a word, much like air in all respects, but far more subtle.

"2. I suppose this ether pervades all gross bodies, but yet so as to stand rarer in their pores than in free spaces, and so much the rarer as their pores are less; and this I suppose (with others) to be the cause why light incident on those bodies is refracted towards the perpendicular; why two well-polished metals cohere in a receiver exhausted of air; why quick-silver stands sometimes up to the top of a glass pipe, though much higher than thirty inches; and

[1] Reproduced in *Horsley*, Vol. IV, pp. 385-394; and Brewster, *op. cit.*, Vol. I, pp. 409-419; cf. pp. 145-146. Cf. also Birch, *op. cit.*, Vol. III, p. 261; Rosenberger, *op. cit.*, pp. 124-127.

one of the main causes why the parts of all bodies cohere; also the cause of filtration, and of the rising of water in small glass pipes above the surface of the stagnating water they are dipped into; for I suspect the ether may stand rarer, not only in the insensible pores of bodies, but even in the very sensible cavities of those pipes; and the same principle may cause menstruums to pervade with violence the pores of the bodies they dissolve, the surrounding ether as well as the atmosphere pressing them together.

"3. I suppose the rarer ether within bodies and the denser without them not to be terminated in a mathematical superficies, but to grow gradually into one another; the external ether beginning to grow rarer and the internal to grow denser at some little distance from the superficies of the body, and running through all intermediate degrees of density in the intermediate spaces; and this may be the cause why light, in Grimaldi's experiment, passing by the edge of a knife or other opaque body, is turned aside and as it were refracted, and by that refraction makes several colors. Let[2] ABCD be a dense body, whether opaque or transparent, EFGH the outside of the uniform ether which is within it, IKLM the inside of the uniform ether which is without it; and conceive the ether which is between EFGH and IKLM to run through all intermediate degrees of density between that of the two uniform ethers on either side. This being supposed, the [parallel] rays of the sun SB, SK, which pass by the edge of this body between B and K, ought, in their passage through the unequally dense ether there, to receive a ply from the denser ether which is on that side toward K, and that the more by how much they pass nearer to the body, and thereby to be scattered through the space PQRST [PQRST being a line cutting the set of rays from S], as by experience they are found to be. Now the space between the limits EFGH and

[2] The figure to which this refers is quite easily drawn.

IKLM, I shall call 'the space of the ether's graduated rarity.'

"4. When two bodies moving toward one another come near together, I suppose the ether between them to grow rarer than before, and the spaces of its graduated rarity to extend further from the superficies of the bodies toward one another; and this, by reason that the ether cannot move and play up and down so freely in the narrow passage between the bodies, as it could before they came so near together.... I do not think the spaces of graduated ether have precise limits, but rather decay insensibly, and, so decaying, extend to a much greater distance than can easily be believed or need be supposed.

"5. Now, from the fourth supposition it follows that when two bodies approaching one another come so near together as to make the ether between them begin to rarefy, they will begin to have a reluctance from being brought nearer together and an endeavor to recede from one another; which reluctance and endeavor will increase as they come nearer together because thereby they cause the interjacent ether to rarefy more and more. But at length, when they come so near together that the excess of pressure of the external ether which surrounds the bodies above that of the rarefied ether which is between them is so great as to overcome the reluctance which the bodies have from being brought together, then will that excess of pressure drive them with violence together and make them adhere strongly to one another, as was said in the second supposition....[3] Now, hence I conceive it is chiefly that a fly walks on water without wetting her feet, and consequently without touching the water; that two polished pieces of glass are not without pressure brought

[3] "This deduction of molecular attraction and repulsion," said Rosenberger (*op. cit.*, p. 125), "shows clearly how far Newton then was from his system of primitive or elementary forces of all matter, which only differ by the law of their actions."

to contact, no, not though the one be plane and the other a little convex; that the particles of dust cannot by pressing be made to cohere, as they would do if they did but fully touch; that the particles of tingeing substances and salts dissolved in water do not of their own accord concrete and fall to the bottom, but diffuse themselves all over the liquor, and expand still more if you add more liquor to them. Also, that the particles of vapors, exhalations, and air do stand at a distance from one another, and endeavor to recede as far from one another as the pressure of the incumbent atmosphere will let them; for I conceive the confused mass of vapors, air, and exhalations, which we call the atmosphere to be nothing else but the particles of all sorts of bodies of which the earth consists, separated from one another and kept at a distance by the said principle."

By these principles Newton then explained the actions of menstruums upon bodies, the phenomena of effervescence and ebullition, and the transmutation of gross and compact substances into aëreal ones by heat. Lastly, he shortly described a conjecture about the cause of gravity, which is quoted in § IX of the article on "The Principles of Mechanics with Newton from 1666 to 1679" in the number of this magazine for April, 1914.

II.

From Newton's papers of 1672, 1675 and 1679, Thomas Young was led, in 1801, to the view that Newton had abandoned the corpuscular or emission-theory of light for what is nearly the undulatory theory; and Brewster[4] tried to show that Newton's mature views were in favor of the emission-theory, by quoting, in particular, the 27th query to the edition of the *Opticks* published in 1706. This query will be quoted below. Young extracted some passages from Newton's earlier writings which, according to him,

[4] *Op. cit.*, Vol. I, pp. 146-149.

cannot be supposed to militate against his maturer judgment. Brewster[5] also quoted from a letter written by Leibniz to Huygens on April 26, 1694, stating, on the authority of Fatio d'Huillier, that Newton was "more than ever led to believe that light consists of bodies which come actually to us from the sun,...." A very useful summary of the scheme of the world which Newton seems to have favored was given by Whittaker[6] from a comparison of the works of 1672, 1675, 1679, the Scholium at the end of the *Principia* of 1687, and Queries 18, 19, 20, 21, 23, 29 at the end of the *Opticks.* We will next turn our attention to the treatment of ether and the question of the nature of gravitation in the *Principia.*

III.

In the Scholium at the end of the eleventh Section of the first Book of the *Principia,*[7] Newton said:

"I here use the word attraction in general for any endeavor whatever made by bodies to approach each other; whether that endeavor arise from the action of the bodies themselves as tending mutually to, or agitating each other by spirits emitted; or whether it arises from the action of the ether or of the air or of any medium whatever, whether corporeal or incorporeal, any how impelling bodies placed therein toward each other. In the same general sense I use the word impulse, not defining in this treatise the species or physical qualities of forces, but investigating the quantities and mathematical proportions of them; as I observed before in the definitions...."[8]

[5] *Ibid.*, pp. 149-150.

[6] *Op. cit.*, pp. 17-21.

[7] Cf. Rosenberger, *op. cit.*, p. 193.

[8] "Vocem attractionis hic generaliter usurpo pro corporum conatu quocunque accedendi ad invicem, sive conatus iste fiat ab actione corporum vel se mutuo petentium, vel per Spiritus emissos se invicem agitantium, sive is ab actione Aetheris aut Aeris mediive cujuscunque seu corporei seu incorporei oriatur corpora innatantia in se invicem utcunque impellentis. Eodem sensu generali usurpo vocem impulsus, non species virium et qualitates physicas, sed quantitates et proportiones Mathematicas in hoc Tractatu expendens: ut in Definitionibus explicui" (*Principia,* 1687, pp. 191-192).

The fourteenth Section of the first Book deals with the motion of very small bodies attracted by central forces toward the parts of a large body. According to Rosenberger,[9] this Section, "which does not in the least fit into a place in the investigations of the previous Sections, was only inserted to express the altered character of Newton's optical views. In fact, the Section reduces the causes of refraction and diffraction of light to the new notions of attractive forces acting at a distance, and clearly shows that Newton had overcome his tendency toward theories of the ether. In this Section, too, we find the first traces of the idea of the 'fits of easy transmission or reflexion' of light, which were later on so systematically used for the explanation of the colors of thin plates and of the phenomena of diffraction." However, though the analogy of light with streams of corpuscles was indicated, Newton did not commit himself to any theory of light based on this. Indeed, in the *Scholium* to the 96th proposition, which is one of those in this Section, Newton said:

"These attractions bear a great resemblance to the reflections and refractions of light, made in a given ratio of the secants, as was discovered by Snell; and consequently in a given ratio of the sines, as was exhibited by Descartes. For it is now certain from the phenomena of Jupiter's satellites confirmed by the observations of different astronomers, that light is propagated in succession, and requires about seven or eight minutes to travel from the sun to the earth. Moreover the rays of light that are in our air (as lately was discovered by Grimaldi, by the admission of light into a dark room through a small hole, which I have also tried) in their passage near the angles of bodies whether transparent or opaque (such as the circular and rectangular edges of gold, silver and brass coins, or of knives or broken pieces of stone or glass) are bent

[9] *Op. cit.*, p. 197.

or inflected round those bodies as if they were attracted to them; and those rays which in their passage come nearest to the bodies are the most inflected, as if they were most attracted; which thing I myself have also carefully observed. ....Therefore, because of the analogy there is between the propagation of the rays of light and the motion of bodies, I thought it not amiss to add the following propositions for optical uses; not at all considering the nature of the rays of light, or inquiring whether they are bodies or not; but only determining the trajectories of bodies which are extremely like the trajectories of the rays."[10]

"With the second Book of the *Principia*," said Rosenberger,[11] "Newton began a wholly new series of investigations. Up till then he had only treated of the motion of bodies in empty space, without considering any resistance to which these bodies might be subjected. There was hardly any occasion for a conflict with the then dominant physics of Descartes, which started from the hypothesis of a plenum. But when Newton passed over to the determination of the modifications which the motions of bodies experience on the resistance of a medium which fills space, his theorems had either to agree with or contradict the theories of Descartes."

[10] "Harum attractionem haud multum dissimiles sunt Lucis reflexiones et refractiones, factae secundum datam secantium rationem, ut invenit *Snellius*, et per consequens secundum datam Sinum rationem, ut exposuit *Cartesius*. Namque Lucem successive propagari et spatio quasi decem minutorum primorum a Sole ad Terram venire, jam constat per Phaenomena Satellitum *Jovis*, Observationibus diversorum Astronomorum confirmata. Radii autem in aere existentes (ubi dudum *Grimaldus*, luce per foramen in tenebrosum cubiculum admissa, invenit, et ipse quoque expertus sum) in transitu suo prope corporum vel opacorum vel perspicuorum angulos (quales sunt nummorum ex auro, argento et aere cusorum termini rectanguli circulares, et cultrorum, lapidum aut fractorum vitrorum acies) incurvantur circum corpora, quasi attracti in eadem; et ex his radiis, qui in transitu illo propius accedunt ad corpora incurvantur magis, quasi magis attracti, ut ipse etiam diligenter observavi.... Igitur ob analogiam quae est inter propagationem radiorum lucis et progressum corporum, visum est Propositiones sequentes in usus opticos subjungere interea de natura radiorum (utrum sint corpora necne) nihil omnino disputans, sed trajectorias corporum trajectoriis radiorum persimiles solummodo determinans" (*Principia*, 1687, pp. 231-232).

[11] *Op. cit.*, p. 198.

[12] This Scholium was first added in the edition of 1713. The passage in question is: "Denique cum receptissima Philosophorum aetatis hujus opinio

Toward the end of the general Scholium[12] at the end of the sixth section, Newton said:

"Since it is the opinion of some that there is a certain ethereal medium extremely rare and subtle which freely pervades the pores of all bodies, and from such a medium so pervading the pores of bodies some resistance must needs arise, in order to try whether the resistance which we experience in bodies in motion be made upon their outward superficies only, or whether their internal parts meet with any considerable resistance upon their superficies, I thought of the following experiment...."

The eighth Section of the second Book is on motion propagated through fluids. The theory that Newton here developed of periodic vibrations in an elastic medium was in connection with the explanation of sound, but had, of course, a great influence on the formation of the undulatory theory. "The last propositions," said Newton in the Scholium at the end of this Section, "respect the motions of light and sounds. For since light is propagated in right lines, it is certain that it cannot consist in action alone. As to sounds, since they arise from tremulous bodies, they can be nothing else but pulses of the air propagated through it...."[13]

In the first edition of the *Principia*, the third Corollary to the sixth Proposition of the third Book is: "And so there is necessarily a vacuum. For if all spaces were full, the specific gravity of the fluid with which the region of the air is filled, on account of the extreme density of the

sit, Medium quoddam aethereum et longe subtilissimum extare, quod omnes omnium corporum poros et meatus liberrime permeet; a tali autem Medio per corporum poros fluente resistentia oriri debeat: ut tentarem an resistentia, quam in motis corporibus experimur, tota sit in eorem externa superficie, an vero partes etiam internae in superficiebus propriis resistentiam notabilem sentiant, excogitavi experimentum tale...." (*Principia*, 1713, p. 292).

[13] "Spectant Propositiones novissimae ad motum Lucis et Sonorum. Lux enim cum propagetur secundum lineas rectas, in actione sola (per Prop. XLI. et XLII.) consistere nequit. Soni vero propterea quod a corporibus tremulis oriantur, nihil aliud sunt quam aeris pulses propagati, per Prop. XLIII" (*Principia*, 1687, p. 369).

matter, would fall nothing short of the specific gravity of quicksilver or gold or any other very dense body; and therefore neither gold nor any other body could descend in air. For bodies do not descend in fluids unless they are specifically heavier than the fluid."[14]

On the subject of this passage, it seems to be the best thing to depart somewhat from the chronological order, and consider the comments made on this point in the correspondence between Roger Cotes and Newton which took place when, in 1712, Cotes was preparing the second edition of the *Principia*.

In the postscript of his letter of February 16, 1712, to Newton, Cotes said:[15]

"Before I conclude this letter, I will take notice of an objection which may seem to be against the third Corollary of Proposition VI of Book III: *Itaque Vacuum necessario datur etc.* Let us suppose two globes A and B of equal magnitude to be perfectly filled with matter without any interstices of void space; I would ask the question whether it be impossible that God should give different forces of inertia to these globes. I think it cannot be said that they must necessarily have the same or an equal force of inertia. Now, you do all along in your philosophy, and I think very rightly, estimate the quantity of matter by the force of inertia, and particularly in this sixth Proposition, in which no more is strictly proved than that the gravities of all bodies are proportional to their forces of inertia. It is possible, then, that the equal spaces possessed by the globes A and B may be both perfectly filled with matter so that no void interstices may remain and yet that the quantity

[14] "Itaque Vacuum necessario datur. Nam si spatia omnia plena essent, gravitas specifica fluidi quo regio aeris impleretur, ob summam densitatem materiae, nil cederet gravitati specificae argenti vivi, vel auri, vel corporis alterius cujuscunque densissimi; et propterea nec aurum neque aliud quodcunque corpus in aere descendere posset. Nam corpora in fluidis, nisi specifice graviora sint, minime descendunt" (*Principia,* 1687, p. 411).

[15] Edleston, *op. cit.,* pp. 65-66.

of matter in each space shall not be the same. Therefore, when you define or assume the quantity of matter to be proportional to its force of inertia, you must not at the same time define or assume it to be proportional to the space which it may perfectly fill without any void interstices unless you hold it impossible for the two globes A and B to have different forces of inertia. Now, in the third Corollary, I think you do in effect assume both these things at once."

In his reply of February 19, Newton said:[16]

"For obviating the objection you make against the third Corollary of Prop. VI, Book III, you may add to the end of that Corollary these words: 'Hoc ita se habebit si modo materia sit gravitati suae proportionalis et insuper impenetrabilis adeoque ejusdem semper densitatis in spatiis plenis.'"

Cotes replied on February 23 that this addition did not seem to him to come fully up to the objection. After quoting Newton's words, he continued:[17]

"Now, by *materia* you mean the quantity of matter, and this you always estimated by its force of inertia, and therefore it will be supposed that you do in this place so estimate it; but if *materia* be here taken in this sense the objection will not be obviated. Perhaps with some alteration of my words, which you may be pleased to make, the addition may stand thus: 'Hoc ita se habebit si modo magnitudo vel extensio materiae in spatiis plenis, sit semper proportionalis materiae quantitati et vi Inertiae atque adeo vi gravitatis: nam per hanc Propositionem constitit quod vis inertiae et quantitas materiae sit ut ejusdem gravitas.'"

Newton replied on February 26:[18]

"I have reconsidered the third Corollary of the sixth Proposition. And, for preventing the cavils of those who are ready to put two or more sorts of matter, you may

[16] *Ibid.*, pp. 67-68. [17] *Ibid.*, pp. 68-69. [18] *Ibid.*, p. 73.

add these words to the end of the Corollary: 'Vim inertiae proportionalem esse gravitati corporis constitit per experimenta pendulorum. Vis inertiae oritur a quantitate materiae in corpore ideoque est ut ejus massa. Corpus consensatur per contractionem pororum, et poris destitutum (ob impenetrabilitatem materiae) non amplius condensari potest; ideoque in spatiis plenis est ut magnitudo spatii. Et concessis hisce tribus Principiis Corollarium valet.' "

But Cotes again wrote on February 28:[19]

"I have looked over your new addition to the third Corollary of the sixth Proposition, but I am not yet satisfied as to the difficulty, unless you will be pleased to add that it is true upon this concession that the primigenial particles out of which the world may be supposed to have been framed (concerning which you discourse at large in the additions to your *Optice*, p. 343 *et. seqq.*) were all of them created equally dense, that is (as I would rather speak) have all the same force of inertia in respect of their real magnitude or extension in full space. I call this a concession, because I cannot see how it may be certainly proved either *a priori* by bare reasoning from the nature of the thing, or be inferred from experiments. I am not certain whether you do not yourself allow the contrary to be possible. Your words seem to mean so in page 347, line 5, of the *Optice*: 'Forte etiam et diversis densitatibus diversisque viribus.' "

Lastly, Newton replied on March 18:[20]

"I thank you for explaining your objection to the third Corollary of the sixth Proposition. That Corollary and the next may be put in this manner." After that part of the third Corollary which is quoted above, Newton added the words:

"And if the quantity of matter in a given space can, by

[19] *Ibid.*, pp. 75-76.
[20] *Ibid.*, p. 80.

any rarefaction, be diminished, what should hinder a diminution to infinity?

"Cor. 4. If all the solid particles of all bodies are of the same density, nor can be rarefied without pores, a void space or vacuum must be granted. By bodies of the same density I mean those whose forces of inertia are in the proportion of their bulks."

What was the fourth Corollary in the first edition then became the fifth in the second edition. It is:

"The power of gravity is of a different nature from the power of magnetism. For the magnetic attraction is not as the matter attracted. Some bodies are attracted more by the magnet, others less; most bodies not at all. The power of magnetism, in one and the same body, may be increased and diminished; and is sometimes far stronger, for the quantity of matter, than the power of gravity; and in receding from the magnet, decreases not in the duplicate, but almost in the triplicate proportion of the distance, as nearly as I could judge from some rude observations."[21]

This is the form in which these Corollaries are given in the second edition of the *Principia*.[22]

To the last passage Edleston added the note:

"At the meeting of the Royal Society two days afterwards, Newton proposed that Halley and Hauksbee should

[21] "*Corol.* 3. Spatia omnia non sunt aequaliter plena. Nam si spatia omnia aequaliter plena essent, gravitas specifica fluidi quo regio aeris impleretur, ob summam densitatem materiae, nil cederet gravitati specificae argenti vivi, vel auri, vel corporis cujuscunque densissimi, et propterea nec aurum neque aliud quodcunque corpus in aere descendere posset. Nam corpora in fluidis, nisi specifice graviora sint, minime descendent. Quod si quantitas materiae in spatio dato per rarefactionem quamcunque diminui possit, quidni diminui possit in infinitum? *Corol.* 4. Si omnes omnium corporum particulae solidae sint ejusdem densitatis neque absque poris rarefieri possint, Vacuum datur. Ejusdem densitatis esse dico quarum vires inertiae sunt ut magnitudines. *Corol.* 5. Vis gravitatis diversi est generis a vi magnetica. Nam attractio magnetica non est ut materia attracta. Corpora aliqua magis trahuntur, alia minus, plurima non trahuntur. Et vis magnetica in uno et eodem corpore intendi potest et remitti,, estque nonnunquam longe major pro quantitate materiae quam vis gravitatis, et in recessu a Magnete decrescit in ratione distantiae non duplicata, sed fere triplicata, quantum ex crassis quibusdam observationibus animadvertere potui."

[22] P. 368.

make experiments with 'the great loadstone,' in order to find the true law of the decrease, which he believed would be nearer the cubes than the squares. See also *Journal Book,* March 27, April 3, May 15, June 12, 26, *Phil. Trans.,* July-September 1712, June-August 1715. Coulomb's experiments with a torsion balance first established the law to be as the squares."

IV.

The third of "The Rules of Reasoning in Philosophy" (*Regulae philosophandi*) which first appeared in the second edition of the *Principia* and were placed near the beginning of the third Book is that those qualities of bodies which admit neither intension nor remission of degrees and which are found to belong to all bodies within the reach of our experiments are to be reckoned as the universal qualities of all bodies whatever. At the end of this rule, Newton said:

"Lastly, if it universally appears, by experiments and astronomical observations that all bodies about the earth gravitate toward the earth, and that in proportion to the quantity of matter which they severally contain; that the moon likewise, according to the quantity of its matter, gravitates toward the earth; that on the other hand our sea gravitates toward the moon; and all the planets mutually one toward another; and the comets in like manner toward the sun; we must, in consequence of this rule, universally allow that all bodies whatever are endowed with the principle of mutual gravitation. For the argument from the appearances concludes with more force for the universal gravitation of all bodies, than for their impenetrability; of which among those in the celestial regions, we have no experiments, nor any manner of observation."[23]

In the third edition of 1725, Newton added:

[23] "Denique si corpora omnia in circuitu Terrae gravia esse in Terram, idque pro quantitate materiae in singulis, et Lunam gravem esse in Terram

"Not that I affirm gravity to be essential to bodies. By their innate force (*vis insita*) I mean nothing but their force of inertia. This is immutable. Their gravity is diminished as they recede from the earth."[24]

In a general Scholium which first appeared in the second edition and at the end, Newton paid a tribute of some length to the Deity. "This most beautiful system," it began, "of the sun, planets and comets, could only proceed from the counsel and dominion of an intelligent and powerful being." Then Newton went on to say:

"This Being governs all things, not as the soul of the world, but as Lord over all. . . . The true God is a living, intelligent and powerful being; . . . . He is eternal and infinite, omnipotent and omniscient; . . . . He is not Eternity or Infinity, but eternal and infinite; he is not Duration or Space, but he endures and is present. . . . He is omnipresent, not virtually only but also substantially; for virtue cannot subsist without substance. In him are all things contained and moved; yet neither affects the other: God suffers nothing from the motion of bodies; bodies find no resistance from the omnipresence of God. . . ."

Six months after the completion of the second edition of the *Principia,* which was published in 1713 under the editorship of Roger Cotes, Newton sent the following addition to Cotes, which first appeared in the third edition of 1725:

"Blind metaphysical necessity, which is certainly the same always and everywhere, could produce no variety of things. All that diversity of natural things which we find

pro quantitate materiae suae, et vicissim mare nostrum grave esse in Lunam, et Planetas omnes graves esse in se mutuo et Cometarum similem esse gravitatem, per experimenta et observationes Astronomicas universaliter constet: dicendum erit per hanc Regulam quod corpora omnia in se mutuo gravitant. Nam et fortius erit argumentum ex Phaenomenis de gravitate universali, quam de corporum impenetrabilitate: de qua utique in corporibus Coelestibus nullum experimentum, nullam prorsus observationem habemus" (*Principia,* 1713, p. 358).

[24] Cf. Rosenberger, *op. cit., pp.* 212-213.

suited to different times and places could arise from nothing but the ideas and will of a Being necessarily existing."[25]

"This," said Rosenberger, "almost looks as if Newton here wished to state clearly that gravity is a final cause which was directly implanted by God in all matter. But the following sentences contradict this." Then Rosenberger quoted the well-known words from the second edition:

"Hitherto we have explained the phenomena of the heavens and of our sea by the power of gravity, but have not yet assigned the cause of this power. This is certain, that it must proceed from a cause that penetrates to the very centers of the sun and planets without suffering the least diminution of its force; that operates, not according to the quantity of the surfaces of the particles upon which it acts, (as mechanical causes do,) but according to the quantity of the solid matter which they contain, and propagates its virtue on all sides, to immense distances, decreasing always in the duplicate proportion of the distances....But hitherto I have not been able to discover the cause of those properties of gravity from phenomena, and I frame no hypotheses. For whatever is not deduced from the phenomena, is to be called a hypothesis; and hypotheses, whether metaphysical or physical, whether of occult qualities or mechanical, have no place in experimental philosophy. In this philosophy particular propositions are inferred from the phenomena, and afterwards rendered general by induction. Thus it was that the impenetrability, the mobility, and the impulsive force of bodies, and the laws of motion and of gravitation,

[25] "Elegantissima haecce Solis, Planetarum et Cometarum compages non nisi consilio et dominio Entis intelligentis et potentis oriri potuit....Hic omnia regit, non ut Anima mundi, sed ut universorum Dominus;....Et ex dominatione vera sequitur, Deum verum esse vivum, intelligentem et potentem;.... *Aeternus* est et *Infinitus, Omnipotens* et *Omnisciens*,....Non est aeternitas vel infinitas, sed durat et adest....Omnipraesens est non per virtutem solam,

were discovered. And to us it is enough that gravity does really exist, and act according to the laws which we have explained, and abundantly serves to account for all the motions of the celestial bodies and of our sea.

"And now we might add something concerning a certain most subtle spirit, which pervades and lies hid in all gross bodies; by the force and action of which spirit the particles of bodies mutually attract one another at near distances, and cohere if contiguous; and electric bodies operate to greater distances, as well repelling as attracting the neighboring corpuscles; and light is emitted, reflected, refracted, inflected, and heats bodies; and all sensation is excited, and the members of animal bodies move at the command of the will, namely, by the vibrations of this spirit, mutually propagated along the solid filaments of the nerves from the outward organs of sense to the brain, and from the brain into the muscles. But these are things that cannot be explained in few words, nor are we furnished with that sufficiency of experiments which is required to an accurate determination and demonstration of the laws by which this electric and elastic spirit operates."[26]

set etiam per *substantiam*: nam virtus sine substantia subsistere non potest. In ipso continentur et moventur universa, sed absque mutua *passione*. Deus nihil patitur ex corporum motibus: illa nullam sentiunt resistentiam ex omnipraesentia Dei" (*Principia*, 1713, pp. 482-483).

[26] "Hactenus Phaenomena caelorum et maris nostri per Vim gravitatis exposui, sed causam Gravitatis nondum assignavi. Oritur utique haec Vis a causa aliqua quae penetrat ad usque centra Solis et Planetarum, sine virtutis diminutione; quaeque agit non pro quantitate *superficierum* particularum in quas agit, (ut solent causae Mechanicae,) sed pro quantitate materiae *solidae*; et cujus actio in immensas distantias undique extenditur, decrescendo semper in duplicata ratione distantiarum....Rationem vero harum Gravitatis proprietatum ex Phaenomenis nondum potui deducere, et Hypotheses non fingo. Quicquid enim ex Phaenomenis non deducitur, *Hypothesis* vocanda est; et Hypotheses seu Metaphysicae, seu Physicae, seu Qualitatum occultarum, seu Mechanicae, in *Philosophia Experimentali* locum non habent. In hac Philosophia Propositiones deducuntur ex Phaenomenis, et redduntur generales per Inductionem. Sic impenetrabilitas, mobilitas, et impetus corporum et leges motuum et gravitatis innotuerunt. Et satis est quod Gravitas revera existat, et agat secundum leges a nobis expositas, et ad corporum caelestium et maris nostri motus omnes sufficiat.

"Adjicere jam liceret nonnulla de Spiritu quoddam subtilissimo corpora crassa pervadente, et in iisdem latente; cujus vi et actionibus particulae cor-

These extracts, together with extracts from subsequent works which we shall meet later, illustrate the neutral position toward the question as to the nature of gravitation which Newton always tried to maintain in his published work, and emphasized in the second and third editions of the *Principia*. We shall only be concerned with the opinions expressed by Newton's school on this subject when we have finished the examination of all that Newton himself has said on it. As we shall see again in the next section, Newton strongly inclined towards the belief that the attraction of matter was brought about by the intermediary of an ethereal medium, but he seems to have rightly recognized that the question as to whether this attraction is, like hardness or impenetrability, an essential property of matter, or whether a medium is necessary for the action of two bodies on one another, had no bearing on the facts about attraction that were mathematically expressed in the *Principia*: it only concerned physical explanations of this attraction. Besides this, it is probable that Newton knew only too well that, by indulging in speculations which could not be proved or disproved experimentally, he laid himself open to hated controversy. It is true that he had to meet controversies about the experimental truths he had discovered; but in the midst of his very natural irritation, he must have been comforted by the thought that, in this case at any rate, there was really no question of personal opinion involved.

V.

Richard Bentley (1662-1742), who became so famous

porum ad minimas distantias se mutuo attrahunt, et contiguae factae cohaerent; et corpora Electrica agunt ad distantias majores, tam repellendo quam attrahendo corpuscula vicina; et Lux emittitur, reflectitur, refringitur, inflectitur, et corpora calefacit; et Sensatio omnis excitatur, et membra Animalium ad voluntatem moventur, vibrationibus scilicet hujus Spiritus per solida nervorum capillamenta ab externis sensuum organis ad cerebrum et a cerebro in musculos propagatis. Sed haec paucis exponi non possunt; neque adest sufficiens copia Experimentorum, quibus leges actionum hujus Spiritus accurate determinari et monstrari debent" (*Principia,* 1713, pp. 483-484).

as a philologist, was, in 1692, nominated first "Boyle lecturer." In the series of lectures which he accordingly gave,[27] he tried to present the Newtonian physics in a popular form, and to show that it proved the existence of an intelligent Creator. Indeed, it seems true that, as Rosenberger[28] has remarked, England was then the best soil for the growth of the mystical idea of an elementary force directly implanted in matter by God. France and, in part, Germany had adopted the rationalistic philosophy of Descartes, in which all occult forces were banished. Toward the end of the year 1692, Bentley by letter consulted Newton himself, and this was the occasion for the four celebrated replies of Newton, dating from December 10, 1692, to February 25, 1693.[29]

The first of Newton's letters begins: "When I wrote my treatise about our system, I had an eye upon such principles as might work with considering men for a belief in a Deity; and nothing can rejoice me more than to find it useful for that purpose. But if I have done the public any service this way, it is due to nothing but industry and patient thought." The way in which the solar system is constructed is not, in Newton's opinion, "explicable by mere natural causes," but must be ascribed "to the counsel and countenance of a voluntary Agent." Again: "The same power, whether natural or supernatural, which placed the sun in the center of the six primary planets, placed Saturn in the center of the orbs of his five secondary planets;....and therefore, had this cause been a blind one, without contrivance or design, the sun would have been a body....without light or heat. Why there is one

[27] "A confutation of Atheism," *The Works of Richard Bentley* (ed. Alexander Dyce), London, 1836, Vol. III. Cf. Brewster, *op. cit.*, 1855, Vol. II, pp. 124-125; Rosenberger, *op. cit.*, pp. 263-265.

[28] *Op. cit.*, p. 264.

[29] *Horsley*, Vol. IV, pp. 429-442; cf. Rosenberger, *op. cit.*, pp. 265-271. In Brewster's account (*op. cit.*, pp. 125-130) nearly all the points which interest us here are omitted.

body in our system qualified to give light and heat to all the rest, I know no reason but because the author of the system thought it convenient; and why there is but one body of this kind, I know no reason but because one was sufficient to warm and enlighten all the rest..." Further, that cause shows itself to be "very well skilled in mechanics and geometry."

Nearly at the end of the second letter, dated January 17, 1693, Newton[30] remarked: "You sometimes speak of gravity as essential and inherent to matter. Pray do not ascribe that notion to me; for the cause of gravity I do not pretend to know, and therefore would take more time to consider of it." In the fourth letter, he[31] said: "It is inconceivable that inanimate brute matter should, without the mediation of something else which is not material, operate upon and affect other without mutual contact; as it must do if gravitation, in the sense of Epicurus, be essential and inherent in it. And this is one reason why I desired you would not ascribe innate gravity to me. That gravity should be innate, inherent, and essential to matter, so that one body may act upon another at a distance through a vacuum, without the mediation of anything else, by and through which their action and force may be conveyed from one to another, is to me so great an absurdity that I believe no man who has in philosophical matters a competent faculty of thinking can ever fall into it. Gravity must be caused by an agent acting constantly according to certain laws, but whether this agent be material or immaterial I have left to the consideration of my readers."

It may be remarked that, as Newton happened to mention, the words: "It is inconceivable....inherent in it" are very nearly Bentley's own.[32] Bentley wrote: "....

[30] *Horsley*, Vol. IV, p. 437.
[31] *Ibid.*, p. 438.
[32] Brewster, *op. cit.*, Vol. II, p. 466.

should (without a divine impression) operate...." and omitted the phrase: "in the sense of Epicurus."

On this opinion of Newton's, Rosenberger[33] has remarked that a consideration of the context shows that there is only an appearance on Newton's part of a tendency toward a kinetic hypothesis of gravitation; for he added the words "or immaterial," and showed, by his continual emphasis on the necessity there is for an intelligent creator and director of the system of the world, that he, for his part, held that the agent in question was immaterial. Bentley understood Newton's words in this way, and in his lectures laid down without any reserve the proposition that natural actions are brought about by an immaterial agency.[34]

Newton's fourth and last letter was dated by Horsley February 11, 1693, while the third was dated February 25, 1693. Brewster[35] gave February 11 as the date of the third letter, and February 25 as the date of the fourth letter; but what Brewster called (correctly) the third was printed by Horsley as the fourth, and *vice versa*.[36] The only letter of Bentley's on this subject which Brewster found among the Portsmouth Papers, was dated February 19, 1693, and obviously Newton's letter of February 25 is a reply to this. Bentley's long letter was printed by Brewster,[37] and in it gave at some length his own version of Newton's opinions, stated so that Newton might signify his approval or dissent.

It must be remembered that the introduction of a material medium to serve as a vehicle for the actions between bodies is one of the points of Descartes's philosophy, which

[33] *Op. cit.*, pp. 268-269.

[34] Cf. also Whiston's deductions from Bentley's seventh sermon mentioned on page 271 (*ibid.*).

[35] *Op. cit.*, 1855, Vol. II, p. 128.

[36] The numbering was correctly given in Rosenberger's book.

[37] *Op. cit.*, pp. 463-470.

aimed—although the aim was naturally not stated by Descartes at a time when the church was powerful and given to persecution—at the description of the system of nature in rational terms alone, and thus without assuming any intervention of the Deity. Such a scheme would not appeal to the pious Newton, especially as he saw, and expressed in 1687, as we have seen, that an all-pervading fluid of great density—as would seem to be a consequence of its necessary continuity—would offer great difficulties to motion. Indeed, Parmenides, who, in the sixth century before Christ, evolved a primitive cosmology of the same type as that of Descartes, was obliged to put motion in the rank of illusions.[88] As might be expected, common sense nearly always dominated logical ideals in men's minds, and the opposition between logical ideals and common sense was slurred over from the time of Zeno till nearly the twentieth century of our era.

PHILIP E. B. JOURDAIN.

CAMBRIDGE, ENGLAND.

[88] Cf. G. Milhaud, *Leçons sur les origines de la science grecque*, Paris, 1893, pp. 208-209; J. Burnet, *Early Greek Philosophy*, 2d ed., London, 1908, pp. 203-208.

ON THE MEANING OF SOCIAL PSYCHOLOGY.[1]

SOCIAL psychology in its widest sense applies to the social behavior of all animals, but more specifically, and as the term is usually employed, to the social behavior of members of the human race, both individually and collectively.

Behavior is used here in the sense in which it appears in the literature of general psychology, to point to an adjustment on the part of an organism to its environment. But not all adjustments are social, and social behavior implies those interactions or adjustments that occur among men and women and children. They may or may not be accompanied by a social consciousness. It is assumed that the interactions in question were conscious at least in their origins, excepting in cases in which they may have arisen by accident and have been discovered and made use of consciously at a later time; as for example when one discovers that one has already unwittingly adopted a mode of address which elicits favorable response from a neighbor, and therefore deliberately continues to exercise this manner of address, until it once more becomes unconscious. Social behavior, therefore, includes those automatic or relatively automatic adjustments among men—social habits—as well as conscious adjustments. Social psychology, then, is charged with accounting for the development of these so-

[1] The author, Mr. Robert H. Gault, is associate professor of psychology at Northwestern University and managing editor of the *Journal of Criminal Law and Criminology.*

cial automatisms just as general psychology accounts for the growth of automatisms in the life of an organism.

Social psychology implies a social consciousness distinct from consciousness that is not social. By this term we mean here that aspect of human consciousness in which one takes cognizance of one's relations to others and *vice versa*; in which one voluntarily seeks to control another's reactions; in which one anticipates one's reaction to the behavior that may possibly be expressed in the life of another at some future time or the reactions that may occur in the reverse direction; in which one makes adjustment to an ideal that has been developed and expressed by whatever means; finally by social consciousness we mean that aspect of human consciousness in which one responds to what is "in the air," realizing all the while, even though vaguely, that one is doing so because "everybody else is doing it."

Thus we are socially conscious when we stop to consider the possible effect of our actions upon others. The student is socially conscious when in preparation for an intercollegiate debate he works in the quiet of his study week in and week out, arranging and rearranging his material with a view to getting it into such shape that it will elicit signs of approval from the audience and obtain the decision of the judges in response to his effort. The chess player is socially conscious when he anticipates his next move in case his opponent should make a certain play, or *vice versa*; the statesman when he anticipates the needs of the state and provides for them, as well as when, from public expressions, he realizes his error and makes correction. We are socially conscious, furthermore, when we feel constrained to adjust ourselves to an ideal. Whether we associate it with a particular person or not the ideal is personified, and in adjusting to it, or in responding in any way to its appeal, we are indirectly responding to its author. Thus when we are reading a book or looking at a picture we may be socially conscious. Indeed we are so if the book or the picture stimulates the vague or distinct imagery of a recognized ideal. Thus a Millet speaks to us indirectly of the nobility of common labor through an "Angelus"; a Gilbert Stuart of steadfast patriotism through the face of a Washington. When we recognize the symbolic language of the artist we are socially conscious. Finally the youth of '61 was socially conscious when he was entertaining the mental imagery of tens of thousands of other youths like himself all marching eagerly behind the fife and drum on thousands of village greens and feeling his own patriotic impulses swell in response. He is socially conscious when he anticipates that other boys will go out to drill if he will but do so; when he realizes that he is out because his neighbors are also. Reduced to its final terms the social consciousness is the sum total of a certain more or less defined mental imagery. We entertain in our mind's eye either anticipatory or retrospective imagery of responses to behavior, responses that might have been or that actually occurred; and this imagery seems to be aimed at the control of our behavior when we are socially conscious. It comes to fruition in the consciousness of the organism alone. It is an aspect of the total individual consciousness. It excludes the concept of an oversoul and of Urwick's super-consciousness.[2] It is more than the mere consciousness of kind[3] and more than imitative consciousness, though either or both may be a part of it.

When the social consciousness of the organism has been abstracted from the total and we take stock of all that remains we find only those perceptual, ideational, and emotional experiences that come to us uncolored by any sense of their relationship to other selves than our own. The

[2] Urwick, *Philosophy of Social Progress.*

[3] Giddings, *Elements.*

tree on the campus or the chair on the floor may simply mean "something there," changing or unchanging. The moment, however, at which these objects so much as suggest a plan of another intelligence than ours—a plan that arouses even a glimmering reaction of any sort on our part—at that moment the experience becomes social.

As I have already intimated the social aspect of the experience may lapse according to the law of automatization. We may take the picture as a matter of course after a while and be insensitive to the message of the artist. We may develop insensitivity to the appeal of the distressed at our doors. Such a process is within the realm of social psychology just as distinctly as any other process of automatization in the field of educational psychology or elsewhere.

This social consciousness is intensified, to be sure, by the appropriate physical reaction. That is, the social consciousness of the boy of '61 is intensified when he marches with the rest. This is the case, at any rate, until the process of automatization is well on its way.

Social psychology is interested too in the sense of social unity that makes the whole group seem kin. It is this sense, ever present especially to those who live with others of their kind and mingle with them on intimate terms, that makes attractive a proposition that a super-consciousness or a universal sub-consciousness includes the consciousness of each one of us and that it is by dint of this background that we have our sense of social unity. The methods of psychology, however, cannot supply data concerning such a background, if indeed it exists at all.

The psychologist gets a clue to the solution of the problem of the sense of social unity from the basis of his own sense of personal identity. Here his memory and his anticipatory imagery play a large part. As each one of us retrospectively views his behavior and his psychic reactions, one of the most prominent things impressed upon him is that his life thus far has been to a great degree a series of responses to what other people have done and thought in his own immediate vicinity and even in remote regions. With the images that arise in this connection there develop associations with images anticipatory of the responses that we will make to others in imagined situations that may arise in the future; of the responses that others may make to us, and that our neighbors, near or far away, may make among themselves in certain situations. Thus it ministers to my sense of unity with my class to anticipate that a proposal coming either from me or from one of their number for the establishment of an honor system will meet with enthusiastic and honest response. My sense of social unity transcends the immediate present when through the eye of anticipation I confidently see uncounted thousands belonging to future generations modifying the conduct of their thoughts and behavior in response to ideas that are being made extant to-day by myself or by others. The sense of social unity, even the capacity for it, is a question of the mental imagery that we can command.

There are, to be sure, certain limitations upon this command of imagery. We have not met South Sea Islanders in the past and it is with some difficulty that we anticipate their responses. We cannot, therefore, have the sense of unity with them that we have with the people of our town. In other words a consciousness of kind is an essential prerequisite to the development of the sense of social unity. This sense of unity, supported or conditioned by the consciousness of kind, in agreement with the laws of automatization in general, lapses in the course of practice until finally our relations with others of our kind, in wider and wider circles, are taken for granted. Thus if we keep in mind the process of development of social behavior through consciousness to mechanism, we are in accord with DeGreef in his opinion that where people are in close contact with one another there need be no consciousness of social unity. Indeed, in such circumstances one may become so completely identified with one's neighbors as to lose social consciousness as far as one's relations with them are concerned.[4]

This will suggest, therefore, that social psychology, as an account of social behavior, very properly discusses the means—that is, the selection and arrangement of stimuli—by which those interactions that are appropriate to time and place may be brought about; by which, in Professor Ross's phrase, psychic "planes and currents" are established. Finally social psychology is occupied with the means by which old forms of interaction—old psychic planes and currents—are broken up and new ones set on their way. Discovery, invention and criminality are processes that, in this connection, are fraught with meaning for social psychology.

ROBERT H. GAULT.
NORTHWESTERN UNIVERSITY, EVANSTON, ILLINOIS.

[4] The point of view developed above has some points of resemblance to the argument by Prof. A. T. Ormond (*Psy. Rev.*, VIII, 1901, p. 41) that the only way in which social intercourse is possible, or social effects producible, is through the power which each self-conscious individual has of internally representing the consciousness of his fellow.

THE OVERGOD.

> "Was man von Gott gesagt,
> Das g'nüget mir noch nicht:
> Die Ueber-Gottheit ist
> Mein Leben und mein Licht."
> —*Angelus Silesius,* I, 15.

WHEN I was still a child I knew my God.
The mighty ruler of the Universe
Looked down on me and shaped my destiny
With loving fatherly concern. I trusted
In both his wisdom and benevolence,
I felt his presence and kind dispensation
In mine own heartbeat and in every thought
That pulsed through mine own mind, and I would wonder
At all the grandeur of God's great creation.

Such was my faith when I was still a child.
But childhood passed, and I saw more of life;
I saw the bad triumphant o'er the good,
I saw the noble suffer and the vile
Laugh viciously at virtue's sad defeat.
Doubt came to me, but I tenaciously
Would cling to Him, my God! I knew that firmly
I would believe e'en though his non-existence
By every science would be demonstrated.
My faith, heroically militant,
Was strong enough to be invincible.

I saw the law and order in the world:
Should I not bow to Him who made the law?
And where I witnessed merit unrewarded
And wrong triumphant, I would trust that God
Doles out his justice in another world.

A childlike faith in God is beautiful!
It leads through life so well, so easily,
It makes us confident to do the right:
And I was yearning to preserve my faith.
I needed God and thus prayed fervently:
"O God, my God, do not depart from me!
God, leave me not!" E'en then my faith was fading.

Oppressive thoughts came over me! I argued:
"O God, thy laws are mightier than thyself!
Who made the simple rule, 'Twice two is four'?
Who made the laws? Are they not sternly rigid?
Are they not, like arithmetic, results
Which must be as they are? I understand
That other than they are they cannot be.
They are immutable and immanent,
They are for all eternity the same.
Aye, God himself could never change their truth!
O God, my God, the problem is too deep.
Come to my rescue, come to guide my soul
Through this entangling labyrinth of doubt!"

Doubt grew and took possession of my soul:
"Where art thou, God? Give answer unto me.
Oh speak to me and say how I shall find thee;
Oh tell me truly whether thou existest!"

In my anxiety of doubt I waited
In vain for answer. I consoled myself

By saying, "God no longer speaks to men.
He speaks to children in a childlike way,
But not to men, not to the scientists."
And does this mean that God is merely fancy,
A dream of poetry, a fond illusion?
If that be so, well, why not face the truth?
Cease being child and rise to man's estate.

If this our universe is void and drear,
If it is meaningless and has no God,
Dare know the facts hard though they be, and dare
Confront this stolid, soulless, huge machine.
Avoid its cogs and wheels and learn to use
The power which it contains. Boldly set sail
To winds that blow, take helm in hand and steer
Thy ship to reach the other longed for shore.
Be independent, shape thy destiny
With foresight, quit all superstitious awe,
Dismiss false fear of deities and devils.
Yea I myself must be my God and master.
I'll be a man, I'll fight the battle bravely,
I must adapt myself to my surroundings
And also my surroundings to myself.
I'll be no longer slave, I'll take the lead,
And atheism shall the emblem be
Of the dear freedom which my soul has gained.

So we are free, no God rules over us,
No tyrant holds us in subjection! Yea,
The One whom we have feared, whom tremblingly
We loved, revered and worshiped, full of awe,
Has passed away. He died and lives no more.
He is a shadow of his former power,
And we are here to lead our lives ourselves
In liberty, with pride of independence,

And on our own responsibility.
Our boldest self-conceit is justified,
And we have thus attained the highest glory.

And yet, proud man, consider thou hast reached
This eminence by working out thy reason,
By broadening thy knowledge and by gaining
A comprehension of the universe.
Remember, thou hast traced the laws of nature
And thou hast found there is both truth and error,
And men may follow either of the twain.
Wisdom there is, and folly, right and wrong.
Here takest thou thy stand in this wide world
To choose the way in which thou wouldest live,
And blest art thou if noble be thy choice.
Brief is thy span of life; vain are the pleasures
Which would decoy thee to a worthless life.
But by an honest effort mayest thou
Attain the realm of the eternal law.
Thou seest the features that remain the same,
The uniformities that make the world
A well-ordained and regulated cosmos.

These uniformities when understood
Are unavoidable necessities;
They are the same as that "twice two makes four."
And they, so simple, so self-evident,
Furnish the key that will unlock life's problems.
The norm of truth they are, of right and wrong,
And they shall serve thee as thy guide in life.
Yet all these norms, these eternalities,
These many laws of nature, are but one,—
One and the same in different applications,
One and One only, and this One alone,
This one necessity rules all the world,

Our own and other worlds, the known, the unknown,
All real worlds, all that are possible;
All things that are or might be must conform
To absolute consistency, to rules
Described by thought-norms and in number-lore,
To rules mechanical and necessary.

Laws are but uniformities and mean
That sameness of condition brings about
A sameness of result. We state the facts
In formulas and call them laws of nature;
But we must search to find and comprehend them,
To understand their stern consistency,
And universal sway. Never were they
Begotten and they never shall not be.
They are eternal, their validity
Is infinite, and if the world break down,
If nature should flash up and be dissolved,
They still hold good, their rule shall never cease.
They are above all nature, everlasting,
Immutable, and range above all gods.

Yea, if there were a God and he would venture
To build up worlds, he needs must heed these laws:
They are above him, they are higher than
His true or merely fancied sovereign rule.
Though they seem naught, they are omnipotent,
More veritable, more immutable
And more eternal, they are more divine
Than He, the God of our first childhood days:
They are the Overgod, the higher God.

Is it the Overgod for whom I yearned,
Whom I believed that I did comprehend
When once in childhood I believed in God?

Is He perchance the true and only God?
Yea, He alone is verily eternal;
He sways the world with wondrous immanence;
Yet He is truly supernatural,
His thoughts are not like thoughts of mortal beings;
They are not temporal, are not a process
Of coming down from premise to conclusion
In tame successive arguments. His thoughts
Are the eternal glorious laws of nature
Which ever were and ever will remain
To all eternity, world without end,
Parts of Himself, parts of the Overgod
And of the Overgod's divinity.

My God, I now discern thou art not mute,
Thou speakest to thy children. If they ask thee
In the right spirit thou wilt answer give;
If they with due discretion search for truth,
They finally shall find it, and the truth
Alone is God's eternal revelation.
'T is truth in which God speaks, and God's great truth
Speaks clear and constant in the Still Small Voice.

God of my childhood, thou didst fade away,
But I discovered thee again. I found
The God of truth, the Overgod, and now
It dawns on me that thou art He Himself.
There is but one true God—the Overgod;
And thou, God of my childhood, wast a promise,
An image and poetic allegory,
A prophecy and a presentiment,
A child's conception of a greater truth.

Truly the God of law is not a fable;
He is not matter, is not energy,

Nor to the senses is discernible;
But he is more than body, more than power.
He is not individual nor person;
He is much more than things or any beings
Of limitation such as move in space.
He is the factor which creates all things,
Which shapes the world and which begets all order;
He is the lawdom of the universe;
He is the norm of rationality
And thereby He creates the prototype
Of beings that can reason, that can think,
That are responsible for what they do.

He has created personality,
Yet He Himself, the Supernatural,
Is more than personal. The Overgod
Is higher than an individual
And more than any ego. In His image
Egos originate and they reflect
In their minds' mirror His divinity,
The wondrous reason of the cosmic order.
Oh God of law, God of necessity,
Thou cause of evolution and of progress!
Thou buildest up mankind and leadest us
Higher and ever higher. God, my God,
Oh Overgod, thou art the great fulfilment
Of my belief in God. Thou art much higher,
Yet thou art still the same, the selfsame God.
We sink before thee in the dust, and thee,
Great Overgod, we worship on our knees
In deep humility and reverence.

In awe I fell prostrate upon the ground,
But God, the Overgod, spake thus to me:
"Rise up and crawl not wormlike in the dust.

I led thee into freedom and want man
To stand erect before me as my son,
Erect and upright, straight as I have made him,
Not as a slave in cringing attitude.
Tyrants delight in groveling adulation;
So do the gods of savages, not I,
Thy God, the God of truth, the Overgod.

"I live not in the fire, nor in the storm,
But in the still small voice thou findest me.
I want no praise, I dislike supplication,
I hate a bloody sacrifice, and truly
I do despise the unctuous cant of priests.
But I will honor noble freeborn children
Who stand erect and worship me aright.
True worship is not done in flattery
With tongue and lip; acceptable to me
Is homage from the heart and righteous will.
True worship is right thinking and right doing,
Leading a life on earth as son of mine,
Of God thy Father, of the God of Truth."

CRITICISMS AND DISCUSSIONS.

ON THE ORIGIN OF THE HEBREW DEITY-NAME EL SHADDAI.

Some time ago my attention was directed to an article written by M. de Jassy, and printed in *The Monist* for January 1908, wherein the writer sets forth the somewhat novel theory that many of the proper names, as well as other words found in the Hebrew Bible, had their origin in the Sanskrit language. I make no pretensions to a knowledge of Sanskrit, but I take it for granted that M. de Jassy is correct in his showing that certain word-forms are alike or similar in Sanskrit and in Hebrew, though there seems to be little to support his theory that Semitic names may be derived from Sanskrit originals. Rather I should say that where these similarities occur they are both derived from a common source, as the Egyptian, or Akkadian. But be that as it may, I shall for the present endeavor to show that our author is mistaken in his derivation of the Hebrew deity-name El Shaddai. M. de Jassy would derive this from the Hebrew *shadad,* "to destroy," and says that *shad* in Sanskrit also means "to destroy," "subdue," "vanquish," etc. After a careful examination of this and similar words in the Hebrew I find nothing to show that there is any connection between *shad* or *shadad,* "to destroy," "spoil," "conquer," and *shad,* "the female breast," aside from the purely accidental one of similarity in form and sound. It would be just as reasonable to suppose a common original for two words which might happen to be alike in our English, as for instance "hail," frozen vapor, and "hail," to call; or "lay," a song, and "lay," to place in a recumbent position. *The Englishman's Hebrew and Chaldee Concordance* shows that *shad,*[1] "the female breast," occurs about twenty times in our Hebrew Bible, while *shadad,*[2] together with the shorter form[3]

[1] שׁד [2] שׁדד [3] שׁד

(pointed to be pronounced *shōd*), "to spoil," "destroy," "vanquish," is found about eighty times. I think it probable that the root of *Shaddai* is to be found in the Egyptian, whence it passed into Hebrew. It occurs forty-eight times in our Hebrew text, and is always rendered "Almighty" in the English translation. In six instances it is preceded by El, and rendered "God Almighty," though "God the Nourisher" or "Provider" would more nearly represent the sense of the original. In Gen. xvii. 1, El Shaddai tells Abram he will make a covenant with him, and will multiply him exceedingly; in chapter xxviii. 3, Isaac, on the occasion of sending his son Jacob to Padan-aram to find a wife, prays: "El Shaddai bless thee, and make thee fruitful, and multiply thee, that thou mayest be a multitude of people"; in chapter xxxv. 11, we are told that God said to Jacob: "I am El Shaddai, be fruitful and multiply; a company of nations shall be of thee, and kings shall come from thy loins," etc. In Gen. xlviii. 3, Jacob, on his deathbed, repeats this last promise of El Shaddai to his son Joseph, and in chapter xlix. 25, the name of Shaddai is invoked as the giver of blessings from the heavens above, the depths beneath, of the breasts and of the womb. See also Gen. xliii. 14, and Ex. vi. 3. Thus the name of Israel's God as El Shaddai is shown to relate chiefly to the maternal function of nursing, and beyond the idea of strength derived from nourishment, potency or power is foreign to the sense of the original. Gerald Massey, in his voluminous work on ancient Egypt, says (*Book of the Beginnings,* Vol. I, p. 6): "The waters of old Nile are a mirror which yet reflects the earliest imagery made vital to the mind of man, as the symbols of his thought. A plant growing out of the waters is an ideograph of *Sha,* a sign and image of primordial cause....the emblem of rootage in the water and breathing in the air, the two truths of all Egypt's teaching...." The form of the Hebrew letter[4] which has the sound of *sh* proclaims its origin, which is that of plant life, presented in the conventional form so characteristic of early Egyptian art. To further quote Massey (*B. of B.,* Vol. II, p. 161):

"*Sha* in Egyptian denotes all commencement of forms, births, becomings and fertility, the period of the inundation, the substance born of, to make go out, to extract, cease to flow. *Shat* is the "*sow,*" and from the persistence of this type in Israel as the sacred, or the abominable, there can be little doubt that the original symbol of Shaddai, "the suckler," was the *shat,* or *shati,* "the sow," just as

[4] ש

in Britain the sow was a type of the goddess Ked. No picture of the *Dea Multimammae* could more effectively present the feminine nature of Shaddai than the description of this divinity of Israel in Genesis: "Shaddai, who shall bless thee with blessings of the breasts and of the womb."

If it be true that *shad* is of Egyptian origin it was most likely through the Akkado-Assyrian that it came to the Hebrews, as *sidi* or *sedu* was with the former the name for the month Taurus, when that star-group marked the equinox. The bull or ox was named *gud,* and *gud sidi,* "the propitious Bull," was the opening sign of the spring and summer season. "The word *sidi,* 'to prosper,' is, I think, the origin of the divine name *El Sidi*"[5] (Dr. E. G. King, *Akkadian Genesis,* p. 47). When the Aries or Ram cult succeeded that of the Bull, owing to the effects of equinoctial precession, *Gud,* or *Gad,* as type-name of the month, was transferred to that of the Ram, as one of the twelve tribes of Israel, though *sidi,* as Shaddai, continued in the maternal phase to represent *Taurus* and the tribe of Joseph (Ephraim, "the fruitful"). The later Assyrian equivalent of the Akkadian *sidu* is *alap,* hence *Aleph,* "the Ox," and the first letter of the Semitic alphabets, was, some six thousand years ago, under the symbol of the Ox, the opening sign of the year, beginning at the spring equinox. The earliest ideas of divinity seem to have been centered in the female as reproducer, whence the worship was gradually transferred to the male as generator, first in the stellar and lunar, and at last in the solar stage. Then the cast out divinity of one cult became, as frequently occurs in history, the *diabolos* of another, and in Deut. xxxii. 17 we find *shedim* rendered as "devils." "They (*Jeshurun,* meaning Israel) sacrificed unto devils (*shedim*), not unto God (*Eloah*); unto gods (*elohim*) whom they knew not," and in Ps. cvi. 37 we read: "Yea, they (Israel) sacrificed their sons and their daughters unto devils (*shedim*)." This last would seem to indicate that at some former period Israel was not above offering human sacrifices to their imaginary gods. The deity-name El Shaddai always occurs in connection with those of Abraham, Isaac and Jacob, and is said to have been the only name by which he was known to them (Ex. vi. 3), the name JHVH being made known first of all to Moses at a much later date. This would indicate that the feminine principle was recognized as a factor in the nature of the Hebrew deity at that early period, though it was almost eliminated by the later Biblical writers. For,

[5] אל שדי

though *shad* expresses femininity alone, in the form *Shaddai* the masculine principle also is suggested, the *yad*[6] (*i*) being regarded by those versed in Hebrew mysticism as the expressor of the male divinity. To quote Laurence Oliphant (*Scientific Religion*, p. 449): "It is a well-known rule of Semitic philology that similar consonants may be interchanged, one with another, this interchange effecting certain modulations in sense. Thus sibilants may be interchanged with sibilants, dentals with dentals, gutturals with gutturals, etc. Now in the case of *shad* we have a soft sibilant, *sh*,[7] and a soft dental, *d*.[8] Corresponding to *sh*[9] we have two hard sibilants,[10] both equivalent to our English *s*. Corresponding to *d*[11] we have also two hard dentals[12] rendered by the English *t*, (the latter sometimes modified into *th*.[13] These sibilants and dentals may be consequently interchanged with each other, the conversion of the soft consonant into the corresponding hard having just this simple but important effect,—it *inverts* the sense, either partly or wholly, according to whether one only or both the consonants are changed. A remarkable illustration of this rule is afforded by the word *shiddah*,[14] "a virtuous wife," and *sittah*,[15] "a wife who has gone astray."

Thus according to Kabbalistic teachings *Shad* represents the feminine nature in a good or legitimate sense, while *Sat*, or *Set*, becomes the type of the cast out divinity, derived by the Hebrews from Egyptian originals. *Set*, *Seth*, or *Sut* became not merely the opponent of the good Osiris but the incarnation of evil after his expulsion from the Egyptian pantheon, as is shown in the typology of *Sothis*, the Dog-star,—the "dog" which let in the universal "flood" by going to sleep when she should have been on watch. Analogous to these word-forms the opponents of the good Shaddai become, by the inversion of the first syllable only, the partly wicked Siddim, but by the final substitution of *s* and *t* for *sh* and *d*[16] the wholly evil *Set*, amplified at length into *Satan*. As the pure gods of light and life are always depicted as dwelling upon the mountain heights (cf. Jerusalem), so, conversely, the fiends of darkness and evil are consigned to the low, desolate valleys and caverns of the earth. Hence the Hebrew writers represented the barren, rocky region of the Salt Sea, the lowest body of water on the earth, and about the most desolate in its surroundings, situated some twenty miles eastward of Jerusalem, as the abode of the wicked *Siddim*,

6 י 7 שׁ 8 ד 9 שׁ 10 שׂ and ס 11 ד 12 ט and ת 13 ה 14 שִׁדָּה
15 שִׂטָּה 16 That is, the substitution of שׂ and ט for שׁ and ד

and the location of their city of Sodom. Shaddai occurs thirty-one times in the book of Job, and this great poem simply sets forth the conflict between the powers of good and evil, led on one side by Shaddai, and on the other by Satan, chief of the *Siddim.*

"As Shaddai is the maternal giver and preserver of life, so Satan, the antagonist, is the destroyer. Hence through the agency of Satan, the cattle, the asses, the flocks, the servants, and the children of Job are destroyed, and he himself is afflicted with suffering just short of death. The patriarch is wrongly tempted to ascribe to Shaddai the actions of Satan, but he finally emerges victorious, until 'the latter end of Job was more blessed than the beginning'" (Oliphant, *Sci. Rel.*, p. 451).

I shall here consider but one other of M. de Jassy's comparisons between Sanskrit and Hebrew,—that of the name *Mizraim,* for Egypt. Says our author (*Monist,* Jan. 1908, p. 128): "Let us now take an example of less importance, the word *Mizraim,* 'Egypt.' Let us remove the plural ending, or rather the dual form, *aim.* We obtain the word Mizr. Let us now see what *misr* means in Sanskrit. *Misr,* from *misra,* signifies "combined, united, jointed places." *Misr* in Sanskrit means Egypt (the upper and the lower, hence the dual form in Hebrew). It would be idle to continue here."

But I think it a good idea "to continue here," since the author of the above has barely scratched the ground. "*Misr* in Sanskrit means Egypt," but what does it mean *in Egypt,* or rather in the Nile Valley, since Egypt is a comparatively modern name for this perhaps oldest of all civilized lands? In reply I shall mainly follow Gerald Massey, who perhaps went as deeply into Egyptian originals as any man ever has done. To quote from his *Book of the Beginnings,* Vol. I, p. 4:

"The Assyrians call Egypt *Muzr. Muzau* is 'source,' an 'issue of water,' a 'gathering' or 'collecting.' It is the Egyptian *mes,* the 'product of a river.' *Mes* means 'mass,' 'cake,' 'chaos'; it is the product of the waters gathered, engendered, massed. The sign of this mass was the hieroglyphic cake, the Egyptian ideograph for land. This cake of *Mesi* was figured and eaten as their bread of the mass, a seed-cake, too, as the hieroglyphs reveal. And the cake is extant to-day in the wafer still called by the name of the Mass, as it was in Egypt. *Mes,* the 'product of the waters' and the 'cake,' is likewise the name for 'chaos,' the chaos of all mythological beginnings. *Mes* then, the 'mass,' or 'product of the river when caked,' is the primeval land periodically produced from the waters, —the land of *Mesr,* whether of black mud or red. We find a word in Ethiopic similar to *metzr,* meaning the 'earth,' 'land,' 'soil.' *Mazr,* or *mizr,* is an Arabic name for 'red mud.' There is, however, a mystical reason for this 'red' applied to mud as a synonym of 'source' or 'beginning.'.... But the Hebrew name of Egypt, *Mitzraim,* applies to both lands. For this we have to go farther than Lower Egypt, and *mes,* the 'product of a river,' the 'mud' of mythology. 'We may rest assured,' says Brugsch Bey, 'that at the basis of the designations *Muzur* (Assyrian), *Mizr* (Arabic), *Mitzraim* (Hebrew), there lies an original form MRS, all explanations of which have as yet been unsuccessful.' His rendering of the meaning as Mazor, the 'fortified land,' the present writer considers the most unsuccessful of all. *Mest-ru* and *Mest-ur* are the Egyptian equivalents for the Hebrew *Mitzr,* plural *Mitzraim,* and the word enters into the name of the Mestrean princes of the old Egyptian Chronicle. *Mest* is the 'birthplace,' literally the 'lying-in-chamber,' the 'lair of the whelp,' while *ru* is the 'gate,' 'door,' 'mouth' or 'outlet'; *ur* is the 'great,' 'oldest,' 'chief.' *Mest-ru* is the 'outlet from the birth-place.' In this sense the plural *Mitzraim* would denote the 'double land of the outlet from the inland birth-place.'....'It is certain, however,' says Feurst, 'that *mtzr*[17] and *mtzur*[18] meant originally and chiefly "the inhabitants."' It is here that *Mest-ur* has the superiority over *Mest-ru.* The *ru* in *mest-ru* adds little to the birth-place, whereas the compound *mest-ur* expresses both the oldest born and the oldest birth-place. The Hebrew letter *tzaddi*[19] represents a hieroglyphic *Tes,* which deposits a phonetic *T* and *S,* hence the permutation; *mtzr* is equated by *mstr,* and both modify into *misr.* In the same way the Hebrew *Matzebah*[20] renders the Egyptian *Mastebah.* Also *Mitzraim* is written *Mestraim* by Eupolemus..... The Samaritan Pentateuch (in Gen. xxvi. 2) renders *Mitzraim* by the name of *Nephiq*[21] which denotes the 'birth-land' (*ka*), with the sense of 'issuing forth.' In Egyptian *nefika* would indicate the 'inner land of breath,' 'expulsion,' 'going out,' or it might be the 'country of the sailors.' The name 'Egypt,' Greek *Aiguptos,* is found in Egyptian as *Khebt, Khept,* or *Kheft,* meaning the 'lower, or hinder part,' the 'north,' the 'place of emanation,' the 'region of the Great Bear.' The *f, p,* and *b* are still extant in *Kuft,* a town in Upper Egypt; in *Coptos,* that is *Khept-her,* or 'Khept above,' when came the *Caphtorim* of the Hebrew writings

[17] מצר [18] מצור [19] צ [20] מצבה [21] כפיק: cf. Aramaic כפק "to go out."

(Gen. x. 14), enumerated among the sons of *Mitzraim*; and in *Kheb*, 'Lower Egypt.'"

There is much more that might be adduced to show the futility of seeking for the roots of Egyptian words in Asiatic languages, but the subject is too large a one for the limits of a single magazine article. The foregoing examples should help some in dispelling the illusion, however, and I may in the near future add some further testimony, should the editor kindly allow me the space.

F. M. Behymer.

St. Louis, Mo.

THE NATURE AND PERCEPTION OF THINGS.

SOME PRINCIPLES OF THE NEW REALISM.

One of the enduring problems of philosophy is how we perceive physical objects—chairs, houses, men, etc.—and what the nature of these perceived things is. There are two time-honored and familiar explanations of this apparently simple, but really difficult, question. The more ancient and less reflective of these is the doctrine that is known as Common Sense or Naive Realism. This theory maintains, in substantial conformity with the views of the plain man and virtually without analysis, that things exist precisely as they are perceived; that the house that is known as white, square, and as existing at such a point in space *is* white and square, and *does* exist independently of the mind in that portion of space, and that that is all there is of it. It is thus the salient feature of the position that it asserts the identity, at least in cases of true knowledge, of the thing known and the thing existing, and that it regards this identity as a simple and evident fact, requiring little explanation and no defense.

But the slightest reflection shows that the facts of perception are not as simple as this. It is a commonplace, indeed, that things do not always appear as they really are—that, to an observer viewing them under radically different conditions, they present themselves in a rich and confusing variety of garbs. Thus, the house that is white takes on ever deepening shades of gray as night approaches, and appears now in one form, and now in another, according to the angle or distance from which it happens to be viewed. Things as they appear are not one but many, and so cannot easily be identified with existing objects, which are held to be unitary and stable.

It is this discrepancy between things as they are and as they sometimes seem to be that gives rise to the second well-known doctrine of perception, namely, that of Subjective Idealism. This theory meets the difficulty we have been considering by making a sharp distinction, a difference in kind, between appearance and reality. That which appears, so the doctrine runs, is in, or forms a part of, the mind of the observer; it exists, consequently, only when it is known, and varies with the conditions under which it is apprehended. The externally existing thing, on the other hand, is outside the subject's mind altogether, and is not affected by changes in the latter, which modify only ideas. According to this conception, the real object is, of course, unknowable, and to affirm its existence might seem a wholly gratuitous act of thought. But, as a matter of fact, the denial of such trans-experiential realities leads to the solipsistic paradox that minds and their thoughts are the only genuine existences, and it is to avoid this unwelcome position that Subjectivists maintain, in one form or another, the existence of these mysterious entities. The result is that the single and familiar world of Naive Realism is broken into two parts, the realm of private and fleeting thoughts which are all that we immediately know, and the sphere of things-in-themselves which exist objectively, but are beyond human ken.

This theory has the merit of taking account of the well-known fact of error, and is, by so much at least, a reflective account of the problem of perception. The doctrine purchases this degree of intelligibility, however, at a fatal cost, for it turns all known things —"the choir of heaven and the furniture of earth"—into private and unstable phenomena, mere mental states, which exist only when a mind is conscious of them. Save in the wholly impotent sense of hypothetical things-in-themselves, it thus casts all objectivity aside, and with it, the possibility of real explanation. For explanation, in the scientific sense of the word, presupposes reason, truth, and existing things in an over-individual or impersonal sense, and all these Subjectivism denies. The *appearance* of knowledge and reality, and so of a just and comprehensive account of things, remains, it is true. But this is not enough. What we know is only an appearance; we have lost the existence that is common to many observers, and the truth that is the product of genuine intercourse and of common and impersonal methods of verification. In one sense, to be sure, the theory changes nothing, for every known fact finds a place in the private realm which it postulates as real. But in another and truer interpretation it alters everything, for it transforms every fact that it takes account of into a mental state, a private possession, which is dependent for its very being upon my awareness of it. Subjectivism is, in truth, a form of irrationalism. Like supernaturalism, mysticism, and cognate interpretations of the world, it may be internally quite consistent, but it denies the conditions upon which alone reason, in the scientific use of the term, can have any meaning.

If, then, philosophy is to attempt to give an objective and verifiable account of the nature of knowledge and reality—and it can hardly aim to do less—it is clear that it must press on to a more adequate interpretation of the problems which we have before us. The general features which should characterize a new hypothesis of this subject should now be evident from the merits and defects of the positions already mentioned. In common with Naive Realism the new doctrine, to escape irrationalism, must maintain that we know objectively existing things—that known and existing objects are, or may be, one and the same; while, like Subjectivism, it should attempt to give a reasoned account of all this, and to show, in particular, that this identity is not inconsistent with the fact of appearance or error. With the former doctrine, it should agree that there is not two but only one world; with the latter it should attempt to do justice, within this world, to the difference between illusion and reality. An interpretation which seems to unite these different elements better than any other at present known is the New Realism, which, having its roots in the work of Mach, James, Moore, and Russell, has been most vigorously and consistently developed by Perry, Montague, Woodbridge, and other American writers on philosophy.

The New Realism attempts to execute the above program in a twofold manner, partly by a revised theory of knowledge, and partly by a changed conception of existence. The first modification in the doctrine of mind is necessary because it is precisely the traditional or dualistic conception of mind which has led, more directly probably than any other philosophical conception, to the subjective position. By the dualistic hypothesis is here meant the familiar and common sense doctrine that consciousness is a kind of entity or spiritual substance, a second sort of reality over and above matter, and one which, if added to things in one to one fashion, transforms them into psycho-physical beings. Now this view leads inevitably to Berkeleianism, in that, if the conception be taken seriously—if, indeed, it play any useful part in the process of knowing, and do not degenerate into an empty form or activity, a mere name—the mind, in this sense, must shelter within itself some part of the rich and manifold content which we know. Descartes and Locke, together with most modern physicists, hoping to give the mind, thus conceived, some, and yet not too much, work to do, place within it the so-called secondary qualities, leaving the primary ones to the external or material order. But such a division of this world's goods is quite untenable. Reality is one through and through; every part coheres with every other part, and where color, sound, and temperature are, there will extension, figure and motion be also. It is not surprising, therefore, that the latter qualities migrate by degrees into the private and ethereal realm which first sheltered only the secondary qualities. Of worlds, in truth, there can scarcely be two, for one will swallow up the other; and in the present case there can be no doubt that it is the physical, and not the mental, order which is consumed by its rival. It is, therefore, by an impeccable logic that the Subjectivist, starting from a dualistic premise, arrives at the conclusion that we immediately know only the states of our own mind, and that the latter exist only when we attend to them.

It is here, then, that the New Realist must erect his first barrier against the enemy. And he does this, following principally James,[1] by calling in question the whole existence of mind and ideas in the sense just indicated. These alleged realities, he points out, are by no means the directly known, the indubitable facts, that the Subjectivist takes them to be. They are never revealed to us in any impartial survey of knowing, however searching. All that such an inquiry shows as fact or datum, is that we know, and know a certain content, certain qualities, relations, and things. All else—what, for instance, the nature of this process and of this content is —is wholly a matter of interpretation, and cannot be taken for granted just because we know. If, then, "sensations," "ideas," and "minds" be affirmed in the customary manner, they must be supported by definite evidence, and such proof, it is safe to say, has

[1] "Does 'Consciousness' Exist?" *Journal of Philosophy, Psychology and Scientific Methods,* 1904, pp. 477 ff.; also *Essays in Radical Empiricism,* pp. 1 ff. Reid, as is well known, likewise questioned the existence of ideas—called them, in fact, the invention of philosophers (*Inquiry into the Human Mind,* Dedication)—but he did not develop this position to its legitimate end.

never been presented. Their existence seems, indeed, to be a pure assumption, one that has been largely unquestioned because familiar, almost second-nature, interpretation has not been distinguished from naked fact, and so examined on its own account.

And if the question of the nature of knowing be fairly raised, and with due detachment from traditional ideas, the New Realist believes that the usual conception of the subject will be swept aside as a mere fiction, to give place to an interpretation couched in terms of function or relation. According to this theory, which is still in its infancy,[2] knowing is not a spiritual entity or thing; nor does it presuppose any such existence; it is rather just a specialized and highly important function of the physical organism itself. As the latter lives and walks and eats, so, in the case of the human species, it knows, and the last activity implies a supplementary existence as little as do the former. Man is, in truth, as little body and knower as he is body and vital principle, or body and walker, or body and eater. It seems clear that we do not better understand any of these operations by postulating a series of existences whose sole work and content it is to perform them, since the entities thus postulated must, in any case, be explained entirely in functional terms. Essentially the same conception of mind may be expressed in more objective fashion. Knowing, it may be said, is just a particular kind of relation, a constant association, between a nervously endowed and functioning organism, on the one hand, and the selection or apprehension of a real content on the other. According to this theory, the content known is always a part of the objective order, or, at least, of an order which, as we shall show, is essentially homologous with this. "Sensations," "percepts" and "concepts," in the traditional sense, there are none. All that we can properly mean by these abused and treacherous terms is that a datum, which is often independent of the mind, may be sensed, perceived, or conceived; they denote processes and operations always, never the elements or parts of a second kind of existence.

It is not contended that this conception of mind is other than an hypothesis, but the same—though it is seldom admitted—is the case with the opposing or, indeed, with any account of this difficult subject. The claim of the Relationalist is merely that his hypothesis seems to render the elements that enter into knowing less mysteri-

[2] Cf. "A Realistic Theory of Mind," Perry's *Present Philosophical Tendencies,* Chap. XII, and a flood of recent articles by Woodbridge, Montague, Singer, Watson, and others.

ous than does the opposing theory, and that, by so much, it clears the subject of pseudo-problems, and lays it open to fruitful research. It thus bids fair, in his opinion, greatly to simplify the task of psychology,[3] and, in philosophy, along with other advantages, to do away with insidious Subjectivism. Whether or not continued investigation will justify this expectation, only the future can say. For the present we can only show that the new conception contributes to the solution of the problem of perception, and see in the salutary change which it works in this field, signal of its greater usefulness, and so of its truth, in other regions of thought.

The New Realist supplements this interpretation of knowledge by a somewhat novel account of reality.

As, on the theory of mind just outlined, objective existence is a fact of this world, and is not put off into a hypothetical realm supposed to lie behind the latter, it now becomes possible to give an empirical account of existence; and this turns out, like knowledge, to be a describable attribute or relation. For things are said to exist when—to mention only their more important connections—they are spacially, temporally, and causally related to other things. Houses, mountains, and men "exist" in that they are found in definite parts of space, begin at certain instants of time, and vary as other things vary. On the other hand, they are said to appear, or to be known, when they are related to a nervously endowed and functioning organism. Knowledge, then, is the relation of a given content to a subject, existence its relation, principally in the ways specified, to other existences.

This definition of reality, though very rough, is yet sufficient for our purpose, for it tends to show, from a different angle, that known and existing things are, or may be, one. As separate orders of being they necessarily repel one another; they fall apart, the latter from the former, with the result that existence becomes unknowable and merely hypothetical. But, conceived as relations, there is no necessary antagonism between the two. Worlds are mutually exclusive, but a given content can sustain two, or for that matter two thousand, relations at the same time without suffering violence. And this is what we actually find. Objects which are connected spacially, temporarily, and causally with other objects, and which consequently exist, may also be related to a subject, and so be known. By the simple substitution of a dualism,

[3] See especially Watson's article, "Psychology as the Behaviorist Views It," *Psychological Review*, 1913, pp. 158-177.

or more truly a pluralism, of relations for the customary dualism of worlds, our theory renders real existence knowable.

And as these relations are not mutually exclusive, so they are not interdependent. The knowledge relation can be present or absent without affecting the connections which are constitutive of the reality of the object. The latter *exists* the same, all else being constant, whether it is known or not. This may be more generally expressed by saying that knowledge is, as regards reality, an external relation. The familiar doctrine that known existence is dependent upon the subject, even for its existence, is thus definitely set aside for the conception that knowing is constitutive only of knowing, and that reality is otherwise determined.[4] The New Realist insists, in short, that things be distinguished *as known* and *as existing,* and that the permanency of the latter be not confounded with the fluctuations of the former.

It should now be clear how, at least in part, the New Realist establishes his thesis that the object that is known is a permanently existing thing. He does this polemically by showing that the Subjectivist's separation of the two is false—that it is based on the superfluous and confusing assumption of extra-physical entities—and, constructively, by interpreting knowledge as a relation between independent existences, the one a knower, and the other the thing known.

True, the main outlines of this position are not altogether novel. It is well known, indeed, that the hypothesis of direct perception of external reality was advanced with clearness and vigor by Reid, and has since been the common possession of all opponents of Berkeley and his school. But neither Reid nor his successors had a theory which could justify in detail the objective position which they so stoutly maintained. Many of their most important assumptions—as, for instance, the dualistic conception of mind, the doctrine of "mental states," etc.—were precisely those of the rival theory, and, had they been consistently developed, would have ended in it. That they did not, was largely due to the serious concern of these authors for objective facts, and to their comparative neglect, at times, of the internal coherence of their work. There can be little doubt that in the past the principal recourse of Realists, at least at many critical junctures, has been dogmatism. But now all this is changed. Thanks to the efforts of Moore, Perry and

[4] Cf. Perry's "Ego-Centric Predicament," *Journal of Philosophy, Psychology and Scientific Methods,* 1910, pp. 1 ff.

others, a reflective and tolerably consistent doctrine of immediate knowledge and independent existence—whether true or false—has been developed.

To complete our task we should supplement the above discussion by an explanation of the fact of "appearance," in the sense of wrong or "mere" appearance; for it is this phenomenon, as we have seen, which has commonly been regarded as a stumbling block to Realism and as an open door to Subjectivism. We should show, in short, that, as knowledge and existence are conceived by the New Realist, the direct perception of external things does not exclude their erroneous or false appearance. Now it is well known that Naive Realism is unable to account for these facts, and falls an easy prey to Subjectivism because it accepts, in common with the latter doctrine and religious systems generally, the familiar and apparently natural premise that reality is a fixed and unchanging, an ultimate or absolute, order of being. It is thus regarded as a common-place by the exponents of both theories that a table-top which is really square can never appear in any other form. It could not, for instance, be seen as a rhombus, no matter from what angle viewed; nor as brown in color (if "really" yellow) whatever the light which plays upon it. But such appearances are undeniably true. The unsophisticated realist is consequently forced to agree, and the idealist is confirmed in his view, that we do not know real things at all, but only our own ideas, real objects being unknowable. As we hinted a moment ago, the trouble lies in the *a priori* conception that existence is fixed, and necessarily incompatible with false or "mere" appearance. This assumption, when examined in terms of the facts, turns out to be entirely unwarranted. While it is true that, under constant conditions, a given object is stable and determinate, it is equally true that, under other circumstances, it takes on a very different character; and this without losing any of its reality. Nor are the modifications wholly in real things. Alterations in known content quite as frequently occur which, being correlated solely with changes relevant to perception—such as the position of the observer, light, etc.—can have no bearing whatever upon the *existence* of that content, but only upon its *presentation* or *appearance* to a subject. Known content, then, changes as real and as known; and the latter modifications sometimes yield true, and sometimes false, appearances.

We might go on to explain at some length the conditions of valid and erroneous presentation were not such an undertaking aside from our main purpose. Suffice it merely to say, very generally, that whatever is given under "normal" conditions of perception is a true, as that which occurs under "abnormal" circumstances is a false, appearance of the thing known. Thus we correctly perceive the "true" color of an object—the latter being, for the moment, determined by non-perceptual tests—when we see it with normal eyes and in ordinary daylight. Similarly we observe its correct form and size when we view it so that the line of our vision falls perpendicular to the surface inspected, when we see it at a customary distance, and through a medium of uniform and average density. Let any one of these circumstances be changed—let the light grow dim or the angle of vision shift—and we perceive the object, by just that much, not as it "really is," but merely "as it appears to be"—in the present case as gray and not white, as rhomboidal and not square. But what concerns us here is not the precise differentia of true and false appearances but the fact that the latter, as little as the former, and both as little as real things, are subjective existences or states of mind, in the dualistic sense of the term. Real things and appearances, both true and false, are, in fact, all of a piece: they are part and parcel of the same world. Their content, apart from a radical difference of relation, is largely or wholly the same. Between real things and true appearances the identity is, indeed, almost complete; the only difference is that the reference of the first is to other things while that of the second is to a subject. Between real things and true perception, on the one hand, and false appearances, on the other, there is, of course, a disparity of content, which is proportional to the degree of abnormality in the conditions under which the material is apprehended. Fortunately, however, this discrepancy is rarely so great as to make recognition and control difficult, and is never so great as to make it impossible.

Alfred H. Jones.

Brown University, Providence, R. I.

THE JEWS OF MALABAR.

In *The Monist* for January, pages 18 and 19, Professor Garbe denies a reference by Professor Hopkins to an early Jewish settlement on the Malabar coast, and quotes Nöldeke to the effect that it is nonsense.

The authorities for the story are principally German, and I

venture to send a few references, thinking they may be of general interest. They indicate to me the probability of early settlements both Jewish and Christian on that coast, although I should be inclined to doubt whether the number were as large as 10,000. The Indian census shows some 1500 Jews settled in the state of Cochin, and the *Imperial Gazetteer* refers to them as dwelling in a couple of towns only. From a number of friends who have visited that part of the world I have had descriptions of this interesting colony of so-called Black Jews, who seem to have largely lost their racial identity but to have retained their religious tradition, as we note has been the case with other isolated colonies, such as those in Abyssinia and China.

Where a well attested local tradition exists, it does not seem altogether a justifiable argument to laugh it away as nonsense, especially as we know from other sources that there was an extremely active shipping trade between Red Sea ports and the Malabar coast during the first and second centuries and every possibility of migration having occurred to a reasonable extent.

* * *

We read as follows in *Benjamin of Tudela* (Adler's Oxford Edition, 1907, pages 63-65): "Thence it is seven days' journey to Khulam which is the beginning of the country of the sun-worshipers.... And throughout the island, including all the towns there, live several thousand Israelites. The inhabitants are all black, and the Jews also. The latter are good and benevolent. They know the law of Moses and the prophets, and to a small extent the Talmud and Halacha."

"Ritter, in the fifth volume of his Geography, devotes a chapter to the fire-worshipers of the Guebers, who, as Parsees, form an important element at the present day in the population of the Bombay presidency. Another chapter is devoted to the Jewish settlement to which Benjamin refers. See *Die jüdischen Colonien in Indien,* Dr. Gustav Oppert; also *Semitic Studies* (Berlin, 1897), pp. 396-419.

"Under the heading 'Cochin,' the *Jewish Encyclopedia* gives an account of the White and Black Jews of Malabar. By way of supplementing the article, it may be well to refer to a manuscript, No. 4238 of the Merzbacher library, formerly at Munich. It is a document drawn up in reply to eleven questions addressed to Tobias Boas on the 12 Ellul 5527 (=1767) to R. Jeches Kel Rachbi of Malabar. From this manuscript it appears that 10,000 exiled Jews reached Malabar A. D. 68 (i. e., about the time of the destruction of the second temple) and settled at Cranganor, Dschalor, Madri and Plota. An extract from this manuscript is given in Winter and Wünsche's *Jüdische Literatur,* Vol. III, p. 459. Cf. article on the Beni-Israel of India by Samuel B. Samuel in *The Jewish Literary Annual,* 1905."

The Jews of Cochin seem to have settled first at the ancient port of Muziris, the modern Cranganore, the chief port of the Chera kingdom, modern Cochin (Vincent Smith's *Early History of India,* 340-341). Subsequently they were driven out of Cranganore by the Portuguese, who took that place early in the sixteenth century, and landed on the mainland just across the back-waters from that port at Vanji, which was also called Karur or Parur, the Karoura of Ptolemy. The note on this place in my edition of the Periplus was as follows:

"Vanji, according to the *Imperial Gazetteer* (XX, 21), must be placed at the modern Parur or Paravur (10° 10′ N., 76° 16′ E.), where the Periyar River empties into the Cochin back-waters. Parur is still a busy trading center, as well as the headquarters of the district. While now in the district of Travancore, it formerly belonged to Cochin,—that is, to Chera or Kerala. It is said to comprise almost all the Jews in Travancore; and the settlement may date from the end of the first century, when it is known that there was a considerable Jewish migration to southern India."

According to W. Crooke (Vol. I, p. 441) the present Jewish population in India is about 18,000, having increased from 12,000 during the past generation. There is no immigration. There are two well-established colonies; one at Kolaba in Bombay, with a tradition of migration from Yemen in the sixth century, the other in Cochin, who are mostly black and claim an extremely early origin, assigning their arrival in Cochin to the first century. There is no doubt, says Crooke, that they were on the coast in the eighth century.

According to R. Sewell (Vol. II, p. 326) this early colony of Jews on the Malabar coast arrived there as refugees from Jewish persecution in Palestine A. D. 68 approximately. They were a trading colony of considerable importance for a long time. Fleet (Vol. II, p. 58) quotes an ancient Cochin grant, Bhaskara Ravivarman, taken from the *Epigraphia Indica* 3, 66, which establishes the existence of an ancient colony of Jews, certifying the bestowal of a village upon them.

The Black Jews of Malabar are mentioned by most of the medieval travelers. Interesting references are found, particularly in Marco Polo.

The expression "ten thousand" need not be taken too exactly; such expressions are frequently used in the Hebrew scriptures as "round numbers." But as a mere question in anthropology, assuming a migration 1850 years ago, not maintained by fresh accessions, there would be nothing unreasonable in the gradual absorption or reduction of the colony, from an original 10,000 to a present 1500.

WILFRED H. SCHOFF.

PHILADELPHIA.

A NEW ERA IN THE HISTORY OF THE "APOCRYPHA."

During the years 1825-1827 the British and Foreign Bible Society was engaged in a controversy which threatened to put an end to its existence. The bone of contention was the group of fifteen extra-canonical books (or appendixes) belonging to the Old Testament, known in England since the latter part of the sixteenth century as the "Apocrypha." A majority of the directors wished to exclude these books from publication and distribution by the society; the opposing minority clung to the former policy of permitting their circulation in those countries where the branch societies wished to retain them. The whole controversy, it should be borne in mind, concerned only the copies of the scriptures distributed on the continent. In England the apocryphal books, though expressly designated as profane and apparently little read, were still printed in standard editions of the Bible, besides being used to some extent in the church lectionary. As early as 1813 energetic attempts had been made to adopt for the Bible Society a policy definitely opposed to the publication of these "uninspired writings"; but the resulting outcry on the continent, especially in Germany, Austria and Sweden, had restrained the directors from taking the proposed action. At length, in 1825, the Edinburgh branch society sent its ultimatum to London: Either the British and Foreign Bible Society must cease, entirely and finally, from distributing the Apocrypha, or else the Scottish societies must withdraw their support. Apart from other unfortunate consequences of such a secession, the fact that the contribution of the Scotch auxiliaries to the funds of the society had averaged considerably over five thousand pounds a year made the Edinburgh note a very formidable document. The society could not dispense with the support of Scotland; but, on the other hand, how could it afford to take a step which would probably result in lopping off the important continental branches? So the controversy waxed hot, and continued unabated until 1827, when the adherents of the stricter praxis won the day, and the society formally adopted a rule against the circulation of the troublesome group of writings. This action had two chief consequences. In the first place, the most of the branch societies on the continent severed their connection with the parent organization, and thenceforward went their own way. In the second place, the Scotchmen, whose blood was up, now demanded the immediate removal of all those officers of the Bible Society who had stood on the side of the Apocrypha. This demand being refused, they also announced their secession, and an independent Bible Society in Edinburgh was forthwith founded.

The story of this controversy illustrates very well the characteristic attitude in Great Britain toward the extra-canonical books of the Old Testament during the whole history of the English Bible. It is true, of course, that the European churches all through the middle ages had recognized a difference in value and authority between the "canonical" and the "uncanonical" scriptures, and that Luther and his German Bible had added new emphasis to this view. But the Protestant churches on the continent never carried the distinction so far as it was carried in Great Britain, and the "apocryphal" writings which happened to be within reach continued to be more familiar there than in England. The decree of the Council of Trent (1545-1563) which pronounced the most of these writings canonical and authoritative also made much less impression in England than in Protestant Europe.

The Wycliffe Bible (1382) contained only those books of the Old Testament which were included in the Hebrew canon. The translation was made from the Latin (of course), and the preface accompanying it contained a paraphrase of the words of Jerome to the effect that whatever Old Testament writings stood outside this canon were "without authority of belief." Coverdale's Bible (1535) was the first in English to contain the extra-canonical books. Those which he included in the group were the same which have continued to be printed in the successive editions of the English Bible down to the present day. The list was an arbitrary and in some sense accidental one, since it included only those books which were commonly found in Vulgate Latin manuscripts. In the codices themselves, whether Latin or Greek, they were of course scattered about in the places where they seemed to belong, logically or chronologically; it was an innovation to put them by themselves. The first to do this was the German scholar Carlstadt (Wittenberg, 1520). Coverdale printed them in a group at the end of the Old Testament, and styled them "The Apocrypha." Martin Luther, only one year before, had done the same thing, though his list was different from that of Coverdale. In the Articles of the Church of England, as revised in 1553, Article VI (formerly V) took its stand squarely on the sole authority of the Hebrew canon, using generally the long-familiar words of Jerome. There was added a list of the Old Testament books of inferior value, but this named only Third and Fourth Esdras, Judith, Wisdom, Sirach and Second Maccabees. In the revision of 1571, however, the list was increased to include all the books, or parts of books, now included in the Apocrypha of the English Bible. In the Geneva Bible (1560) an innovation was made, in that the translation of the writings of this group was made directly from the Greek instead of from the Latin. In the King James Bible of 1611 we are able for the first time to control the version which lies before us, for we know that it was made chiefly from the Greek of the Complutensian Polyglot. Furthermore, this version of 1611 was not greatly altered in the revision of 1894. The English scholars in charge of the Revised Version of the Bible undertook to do for the Apocrypha what they had done for the Old and New Testaments, confining their efforts, of course, to that list of extra-canonical writings which had formed a part of English sacred scripture ever since Coverdale. The critical apparatus used by them was hardly adequate, and the work was not very thoroughly done; hence the revised English text of these books is perhaps even less satisfactory than that of the canonical scriptures.

In the English Bible, then, the "Apocrypha" has had a remarkably uniform history. The group has been made up of the same writings from the first and has always occupied the same place at the end of the Old Testament. Hardly less uniform has been the neglect of the group, as a whole, by English students of the Bible. It is true that selections from a number of apocryphal books were included in the Book of Common Prayer, so that in this way portions of the uncanonical group became widely familiar; the selections were repeatedly reduced in number, however, beginning in 1604, and their reading restricted to week-day services, until the public use of this semi-sacred scripture was brought down to almost nothing. As a matter of course, in a land where great stress was laid on the authority of the Bible, and where at the same time the apocryphal books were expressly declared to be uninspired and without authority, opposition to any use of these writings which seemed to put them on a par with holy writ was bound to be strong and to increase, both in the Church of England and among the nonconformists. The Puritans objected strenuously to the practice of reading the Apocrypha in church. The Westminster Confession (1647) says of the books that they "are of no authority in the church of God, nor to be any otherwise approved or made use of than other human writings." In a sermon on the unity of scripture, preached in 1643 before the House of Commons by the celebrated scholar Lightfoot, the preacher expressed his disgust at the admission of this inferior matter to a place inside the sacred book: "Thus sweetly and nearly should the two Testaments join together, and thus divinely would kiss each other, but that the wretched Apocrypha doth thrust in between." Between this point of view and that of the Austrian pastor who declared, about 1850, that he would not suffer a Bible without the Apocrypha to remain under his roof[1] there is a wide difference, though hardly as wide as the language used would indicate. But what is of especial importance to the history of Biblical science is this, that in England, more than on the continent, the study of the Apocrypha was, and continued to be, neglected by scholars. Even in this present generation, in the light which historical study has brought, the traditional neglect of the Apocrypha, as uninspired and therefore unimportant, has persisted. Such a comprehensive and thorough work as Driver's *Introduction to the Literature of the Old Testament,* for example, leaves out of consideration this uncanonical Jewish material, most of it contemporaneous and none of it negligible. The lack of a satisfactory English translation has already been mentioned; and to this must be added, that until the present year no commentary on the Apocrypha as a whole, or on any considerable part of the collection, has appeared in English since 1888 (*The Speaker's Commentary,* edited by Henry Wace).

Under these circumstances, the appearance of a comprehensive work by representative English scholars, containing a new and thorough treatment of the Apocrypha, and of all the available extra-canonical Jewish scripture belonging to the same period, is an event of very considerable importance. Such a work has now

[1] W. Canton, *History of the British and Foreign Bible Society,* II, p. 224.

been issued by the Oxford University Press[2] in two bulky volumes prepared under the editorial supervision of Dr. R. H. Charles, well known all over the world as an expert in this field of investigation. The names of most of the twenty-seven other collaborators are already familiar in this country, and the remainder will be familiar from this time on. The size of the two volumes will give some idea of the magnitude of the undertaking, for they are in folio and together contain more than fifteen hundred pages. It is the most complete and valuable collection of this "apocryphal" literature that has ever been made. The nearest approach to it is the similar collection published in 1900 by German scholars under the editorial supervision of the late Professor Kautzsch. The German work, very similar in plan to the English, was also issued in two volumes entitled respectively "Apocrypha" and "Pseudepigrapha." This division, it must be admitted, is not an altogether satisfactory one. Several of the Apocrypha are pseudepigrapha of the most characteristic type; the majority of the so-called Pseudepigrapha are not really such, and some of them have the historic right to be included in the "Apocrypha"—so far as this term can be said to have any definite meaning. It would perhaps have been well to take this opportunity to introduce a new and better terminology. It might, indeed, have seemed desirable to retain the time-honored name so long applied to a portion of the Biblical books. But the term "Apocrypha" has had many meanings, and the group of writings designated by it has been a widely varying quantity. So far as the English Bible is concerned, the fact is at once very noticeable that Volume I of this great Oxford *corpus* breaks through the traditional bounds of the group, changing what had stood unchanged for nearly four hundred years; a new member, 3 Maccabees, is added to the group, while 4 Ezra ("Second Esdras") which had always been a member of it, is transferred to Volume II. We have, in fact, good reason now to say *exit Apocrypha,* with reference to the old English nomenclature; since it is not easy to see why any new edition should ever be issued of the particular fifteen documents which have stood together from the time of Coverdale to that of the Revised Version.

As for the designation Pseudepigrapha, it is undesirable for this large and important collection of writings; first, because it

[2] *The Apocrypha and Pseudepigrapha of the Old Testament* in English with introductions and critical and explanatory notes to the several books, edited in conjunction with many scholars, by R. H. Charles, D. Litt., D.D. Vol. I, Apocrypha; Vol. II, Pseudepigrapha. Oxford, Clarendon Press, 1913.

does not apply at all to the major part of them, and secondly, because even in the case of the remainder it emphasizes unduly—and with a somewhat unpleasant sound—a characteristic which is really of minor importance. It would seem better to make "Apocrypha" cover both volumes, or else to use for both some such title as "Uncanonical Jewish Scriptures."

The collection is intended to include "all the extant non-canonical Jewish books written between 200 B. C. and 100 A. D. with possibly one or two exceptions" (so in the Introduction to Vol. II). It would have been better to say, all of the literature of this class *whose authorship is unknown,* since the two great Jewish writers of the period, Philo and Josephus, are not included. Even with this restriction, the collection contains both less and more than is promised. There are numerous other available monuments of the literature, of the very same kind as these "pseudepigrapha" and perhaps equally deserving to be brought into this *corpus,* which receive no mention here; while on the other hand, the limits 200 B. C. and 100 A. D. are both exceeded by writings in the collection. The student of the Bible, or of ancient literature, who is familiar with the Old Testament Apocrypha, but has not kept track of recent investigations in the allied literature is sure to be much surprised and interested when he looks into the second volume of Dr. Charles's work. He will see not only important progress made in the interpretation of ancient writings already long known, such as the Books of Adam and Eve, the Testaments of the Twelve Patriarchs, the Assumption of Moses, and the Martyrdom of Isaiah, but also a number of titles which until recently were quite unknown, such as the Book of the Secrets of Enoch, the Greek Apocalypse of Baruch, the Story of Ahikar in its oldest form (an Aramaic papyrus of the fifth century B. C., first published in 1911), and the important Fragments of a Zadokite Work, first published in 1910.

The general editor of the work, Dr. Charles, edits no less than seven of the books which it contains, besides contributing more or less to the treatment of several others. This, however, is but a part of his real share in the undertaking. No scholar has done more than he for the study of this literature, not only in his own valuable editions of text and translations—a long list—and in his many special investigations, but also in the extent to which he has succeeded in stirring up other scholars to work with him in his chosen field. It is to him, unquestionably, that we are mainly indebted for the plan and execution of this great task. It is true that his labors as general editor were taken rather lightly by him; the general Introductions to the volumes are hastily written, ill-proportioned, and altogether inadequate; but this is a defect which must be pronounced very small in proportion to what he has achieved. The work of all the contributors is on a high plane of excellence and a credit to English scholarship. There is more unevenness than is desirable in the manner of treatment of the various books: the introductions to Sirach and Tobit are too long, and the annotations in part (the difficult critical apparatus) out of place; Judith has no bibliography; the notes to 2 Maccabees are disproportionately meager. It is unfortunate, too, that the reader should not have been given some definite information as to the nature and origin of the translations which are here placed before him. He is left to find out for himself as best he can whether the English text given is that of the Revised Version, as in 1 Esdras, Judith, Baruch, Epistle of Jeremiah, and one of the two columns in Susanna and Bel and the Dragon; or the Revised Version slightly modified, as in the Wisdom of Solomon; or a new and independent translation, as in most of the remaining books.

But the fact can hardly be too strongly emphasized that the publication of this great body of uncanonical Jewish scriptures, never before brought together in such completeness, marks an epoch. The writings themselves, and the period of history to which they belong, will receive from this time on such attention as they have not received before. The study of both Old Testament and New Testament is now entering a new phase, and the next few decades will certainly see a considerable advance in important respects. Several causes have contributed to make possible a closer examination and a truer appreciation of the history out of which the New Testament grew; and, at the same time, of the background of the latest books of the Old Testament. It seems as though we were at last really approaching a just judgment of the religious impulses which brought into being these great monuments, to say nothing of the dawning consciousness that what we had supposed to be commonplace pamphlets are really products of great literary skill. The Jews had a genius for religion, as has often been said and as Judaism, Christianity and Mohammedanism bear eloquent witness, but their representative writers also had a fine artistic sense and literary taste. In these uncanonical scriptures we have a body of little-used material from the very time when the Jews had outgrown many of the old forms of thought and belief and with the light received from the outside world were trying new modes of expression. We find here all the most characteristic forms of Hebrew literature: edifying narrative of widely differing types constructed with consummate skill, as in Judith, Tobit, and 1 Maccabees; the proverbial philosophy of Palestine (Bar Sira), and some of the more universal literature of this class (Ahikar) which was at least read and studied in the Holy Land; a Jewish-Greek philosophical discourse (4 Maccabees); a magnificent specimen of Alexandrine theology (Book of Wisdom); a belated bit of old Hebrew "prophecy" of the purest type (latter part of Baruch); very clear and definite expressions of the Messianic hope, in poetry of lofty style (Psalms of Solomon); several specimens of that characteristic product of the Semitic imagination called the "apocalypse," such as the Enoch books, 2 Esdras, and others less remarkable; a fine bit of Palestinian "wisdom" composed with a purely literary aim, and without any religious motive (the Story of the Three Youths, in 1 Esdras); and others equally worthy of special mention. One extremely useful service which the great Oxford publication will render is this, that it will show our English and American scholars how very much remains to be done in the investigation of this mass of intra-canonical literature even in the most familiar and best preserved members of the group.

The history of the Apocrypha in the United States has been much the same as in England. The causes which operated in the mother country to open a wide gulf between "canonical" and "apocryphal" scriptures operated in this land also from the first. The American Bible Society, which was founded in 1816 under the influence of its predecessor in London, followed the Apocrypha controversy with keen interest, and was confirmed in its own policy by the result. The Bibles which it issued never contained the objectionable books, and the latter were more and more rarely seen, whether in American or in English editions. So it was not only natural, but a matter of course, that the Biblical scholars of this country in building up their department of science should have confined their attention to those scriptures which recognized authority had declared to be alone of divine origin.

The time for including the apocryphal books in the Bible has doubtless gone by. It was for more than one good reason, indeed, that they were excluded from the sacred canon by the Jews and those who followed their example. It was not merely that the books were known to be of late date; taken as a whole, they stand on a decidedly lower plane than their canonical fellows, viewed from either the religious or the literary standpoint. It was because of their own character, and not through any accident, that they were left at one side. But on the other hand, it is important to bear in mind that it was not the result of mere chance that these particular books were preserved. It was the popular demand, first in the Jewish community and then in the Christian church, that selected them and kept them from perishing. They were not only characteristic products of their own time, but those writings—out of a vast number—which had proved themselves capable of wielding influence far beyond that time. We have, then, good ground for feeling that in studying these books which occupy the lower shelf of sacred scripture we are getting in touch with the common people, the humbler laymen of the two ancient religious communities in which they circulated; since it is to such an extent true that they represent the popular stratum of the religious literature to which they belong, containing not the more abstruse thought, and the outbursts of unusual emotion, produced by men who were unlike their fellows, but rather the feelings and beliefs which were cherished by the multitude. For this reason also, then, seeing that modern historical science tends more and more to find its center of gravity in the life of the common people, it seems certain that these half-forgotten records are destined now to be studied with new interest, not merely by experts in Biblical science and the history of religions, but by all those who have found their way to a truly wide study of literature and life.

Charles C. Torrey.

Yale University.

THE SABIANS.

One of the most important forerunners of Christianity is a sect whose adherents are called in the New Testament the disciples of John, or simply Disciples. They are Jewish separatists closely connected with the Sabians, and according to Neander positively identical with them. They kept the Mosaic law, but had adopted Babylonian and Persian beliefs. In fact we may regard them as a Judaized branch of the Mandæans.

The Mandæans are still found in scanty numbers in the Orient, mainly in Persia and southern Babylonia, but they are gradually disappearing. They are pre-Christian, however, in their origin and have incorporated thoughts from all parts of the world in olden times that were accessible to Babylonia. The term *madda* (= knowledge) appears to be translated into Greek as *gnosis* which gave the name to the sects of the "Gnostics" and has its equivalent in the Buddhist *bodhi* (= enlightenment). It is interesting that at present the Mandæans call themselves *Nasorayya,* i. e., Nazarenes.

The main doctrines of the Mandæans are apparently Babylonian strongly modified by Persian dualism. Their light-god, Mana Rabba, has been identified with his prototype the Babylonian Ea, and his emanation, *Manda de hayye,* with Ea's son Marduk. This *Manda de hayye,* personified as Hibil Ziwa, is the mediator between the light-god and mankind, and his descent to hell has its prototype in Istar's descent to hell, and the same event is attributed to Christ in Christianity.

Other Babylonian ideas, such as the significance of seven and twelve as the numbers of the planets in the seven heavens and the mansions in the zodiac, are traced in Mandæism.

Manicheism, which originated in the latter part of the third century of the Christian era, can be traced do Mandæan sources and emphasizes mainly the Persian dualism.

The word Sabian means "baptizer." It is derived from the Hebrew *tsaba'*[1] and ought to be pronounced *Tsabian,* with a sharp German *z* as initial. Baptism was a prominent rite among the Sabians, and we have good reason to assume that the Christians adopted baptism from them. We read in the Gospels that Jesus himself was baptized by their head, John, who lived as a hermit in the wilderness on the Jordan. Judging from their frequent mention in the New Testament, they must have been very numerous in the dispersion and were mainly distributed all over Asia Minor, having a great congregation at Ephesus.

The mass of the Sabians seem to have turned Christians, but some congregations remained an independent heretical sect which rejected Jesus as "the psychical Christ" while they worshiped a spiritual Christ, supposed to have been higher and nobler than the Christ worshiped by the Christians. In fact the Jesus of the church was sometimes considered as the anti-Christ who was said by these heretics to have falsified the baptism of John. Similar ideas are also found among other heretics, as for instance in the Basilidian sect.

One thing is sure, the Disciples were a sect which preceded

[1] צבע

Christianity. Their religion like the faith of Apollos was very similar to Christianity, but they knew not the historical Jesus, the crucified one, and it is not impossible that they were mentioned in the Gospels solely for the purpose of converting their adherents to Christianity. This assumption renders the statements about St. John the Baptist and his disciples rather dubious, for we may assume that they were purposely made to indicate that St. John was a predecessor of Jesus and not an independent founder of a perfected religion.

Some time ago an interesting book was discovered which bears the title *The Odes of Solomon.* It has been edited and translated by J. Rendel Harris and the problem of its authorship has been much discussed. These odes appear to be pre-Christian, and yet the word "Christ" occurs in them frequently as a translation of "Messiah." They have been written under the inspiration of the Old Testament psalms and show much devotion and religious fervor; nevertheless the life of Jesus is unknown to their author, and they appear to have been written among Jews imbued with a spirit closely allied to Christianity.

It is very interesting that Mr. Preserved Smith points out in his article, "The Disciples of John and the Odes of Solomon," that the origin of these psalms must come from the circle of this remarkable sect, and he believes that their author must have lived and promulgated them in Ephesus, the central seat of the Disciples of John. If Mr. Preserved Smith's view can be maintained it will throw much light not only on the origin of Christianity but also on this its precursor, the sect of St. John.

Considering the undeniable fact that Christianity became the main rival of the Disciples and that large numbers went over from this religious movement into the Christian church, it is natural that those of them that remained became hostile to the new religion. They are the Gnostic sect of the Sabians, who we are told refused to recognize the Jesus as the Messiah. They naturally looked upon him as one who had preserved the true meaning of St. John's baptism.

The story of the Magi was invented to convert Zarathustrians or Mithraists, and we have otherwise no evidence that the Magi ever came to Bethlehem or Nazareth. We shall scarcely be mistaken if we treat the whole incident together with the highly improbable tale of the massacre of the innocents as a legend which found its way into the Gospels from non-Christian sources. We need not add that the tale of the massacre of the innocents is also found in the Indian legends of Buddha and Krishna.

The story of St. John the Baptist seems to have been inserted into the Gospel for a similar reason. We may say, therefore, that we have no positive evidence that John the Baptist ever met Jesus. His existence as the founder or Jewish head of the sect of the Disciples, and the sect itself, must be granted to be historical. It was a powerful movement before Christ and at the time of St. Paul but lost its strength with the appearance of Christianity. It was so similar to Christianity that it was regarded as a heresy, and we can well understand that the last survivors who would not accept St. Paul's doctrine of the crucified Christ explained their own Christ to be spiritual (πνευματικός) and the Christ of the Christians as only psychical (ψυχικός).

We must remember that "spiritual" (πνευματικός) means a religious life on the highest plane, while the term psychical (ψυχικός) denotes the lower soul life. Where St. Paul in 1 Cor. xv. 44 speaks of the psychical and spiritual body our authorized translation renders the word psychical by "natural." Pneumatic or spiritual means calm and intellectual, while psychic or natural implies being passionate and sensuous or even sensual.

According to the same version Jesus was a psychic Christ, but when at the moment of baptism the Holy Ghost descended upon him the spiritual Christ was united with him and he became the true Christ; but this spiritual Christ departed again before the passion and, according to this interpretation, it was the psychic Christ who was crucified. EDITOR.

SIR JOHN HERSCHEL ON HINDU MATHEMATICS.[1]

[The following extract from Herschel's article "Mathematics" in David Brewster's *Edinburgh Encyclopædia* (Philadelphia, 1832) is reprinted because it contains facts little known and arguments too good to be ignored. At the time when the article appeared, Colebrooke's great translation of the standard Hindu works of Algebra was still fresh in the public mind. (London, 1817.)

ALBERT J. EDMUNDS.]

So early as the latter part of the tenth century (A. D. 980) Gerbert, having learned of the Moors in Spain their system of arithmetic, had imparted it to his countrymen the French, whence

[1] Substituting *Hindus* for "Indians," and using the modern spelling of Sanskrit words. I am indebted for a knowledge of this article to the venerable Mary Boole, through my sister, Mrs. F. Eagle.—A. J. E.

it rapidly spread over Europe, and continues in use to the present moment. The Moors and Arabs, by their own unanimous avowal, derived this admirable invention from the Hindus who, there is good reason to believe, were in possession of it at least from the time of Pythagoras. The story of this philosopher's visit to the Brahmins is well known, and a suspicion may be entertained that his time there was better employed than in picking up the ridiculous doctrine of the transmigration of souls. Boetius relates the singular fact of a system of arithmetical characters and numeration employed among the Pythagoreans, which he transcribes, and which bears a striking resemblance, almost amounting to identity, with those now in use, whose origin we know to be Hindu. The discovery (generally so considered) of the property of the right-angled triangle by the same philosopher, is a remarkable coincidence. This was known ten centuries before to the Chinese, if we may credit the respectable testimony of Gaubil. It was well known to the earliest Hindu writers of whom we have any knowledge, and who appear to have derived it from a source of much more remote antiquity. It is scarce conceivable that a *Greek* invention, of such extreme convenience as the decimal arithmetic, should have been treated with such neglect, remaining confined to the knowledge of a few speculative men, till, from being communicated as a mystery, it was at last preserved but as a curiosity; but the aversion of that people to foreign habits will easily account for this, on the supposition of its Hindu origin.

An abstract truth, however, is of no country, and would be received with rapture, from whatever quarter, by men already advanced enough to appreciate its value. We are then strongly inclined to conclude that in the latter as well as in the former instance Pythagoras may have acted only the part of a faithful reporter of foreign knowledge, though the reverse hypothesis, viz., that the first impulse was given to Hindu science at this period by the Greek philosopher, might certainly be maintained.

However this may be, the great question as to the origin of algebra, which has been the cause of so much speculation, seems at length, by the enlightened researches which have of late been made in Hindu literature, nearly decided in favor of that nation. It will be proper to state, as briefly as is consistent with perspicuity, the grounds of this conclusion. The earliest Hindu writer on algebra, of whom any certain or even traditional knowledge has reached us, is the astronomer Aryabhaṭṭa who, from various circumstances, is concluded to have written so early as the fifth century. It is true, the work of Diophantus takes the precedence of this in point of antiquity by about a hundred years, nor is it at all intended to deprive the Greek author of the merit of independent invention. Indeed the comparison of the state of knowledge in the two countries at the periods we speak of, is decidedly favorable to the independence of their views. By what we know of the Hindu author it appears that he was in possession of a general artifice of a very refined description (called in Sanskrit the *kaṭṭaka*, or "pulveriser") for the resolution of all indeterminate problems of the first degree, and also of the method of resolving equations with several unknown quantities. It is very unlikely that these methods should have arisen at once or been the work of one man, especially as they are delivered incidentally in a work on astronomy. Now, of the latter of them we are not sure that Diophantus had any knowledge, as, although he resolves questions with more than one condition, he always contrives, by some ingenious substitution, to avoid this difficulty. Of the former he was certainly ignorant. His arithmetic, indeed, though full of ingenious artifices for treating particular problems, yet lays down no *general methods* whatever, and indicates a state of knowledge so far inferior to that of the Hindu writer that no supposed communication with India about the third or fourth century would at all account for the phenomena. But there is yet stronger evidence. The Brahma-siddhânta, the work of Brahmagupta, a Hindu astronomer at the beginning of the seventh century, contains a general method for the resolution of indeterminate problems of the second degree: an investigation which actually baffled the skill of every modern analyst till the time of La Grange's solution, not excepting the all-inventive Euler himself. This is a matter of a deeper dye.

The Greeks cannot for a moment be thought of as the *authors* of this capital discovery; and centuries of patient thought and many successive efforts of invention must have prepared the way to it in the country where it did originate. It marks the maturity and vigor of mathematical knowledge, while the very work of Brahmagupta, in which it is delivered, contains internal evidence that in his time geometry at least was on the decline. For example, he mentions several properties of quadrilaterals as general which are only true of quadrilaterals inscribed in a circle. The discoverer of these properties (which are of considerable difficulty) could not have been ignorant of this limitation, which enters as an essential element in their demonstration.[2] Brahmagupta, then, in this instance retailed, without fully comprehending, the knowledge of his predecessors. When the stationary character of Hindu intellect is taken into the account, we shall see reason to conclude that all we now possess of Hindu science is but part of a system, perhaps of much greater extent, which existed at a very remote period, even antecedent to the earliest dawn of science among the Greeks, and might authorize as well the visits of sages as the curiosity of conquerors.

TEL

SUGGESTIONS FOR THE FORMATION OF A UNIVERSAL LANGUAGE.

From very early times thinkers have felt the diversity of languages in the different parts of the world to be a great disadvantage and handicap to the progress of the human race.

So have arisen the legends of the "golden age" when all men, and even the animals, had a common speech, and of the loss of this blessing following the loss of innocence.

Although we do not, perhaps, to-day think that if we could give to all nations a common tongue the world would return to a state of primeval blessedness, there are nevertheless many persons in many lands who feel that such a gift would be an inestimable boon to mankind.

That this is the case is evident from the widespread welcome which has of late years been accorded to such notable attempts in this direction as *Volapük, La Langue Bleue* of M. Bollack, *Esperanto,* and its successor *Ido.*

These, despite their simplicity of construction and many other excellent points, either have failed, or probably will fail, to achieve what their inventors hoped for them. And the cause of such failure should most likely be looked for in the fact that their originators have not gone to the root of the matter.

A knowledge of Esperanto or Ido, for instance, is doubtless easily acquired by a European, especially if he has a slight knowl-

[2] This argument has been overlooked by the author of the two able articles on Hindu algebra in the 42d and 57th numbers of the *Edinburgh Review.* It is of particular force in one instance: the elegant property discovered by Ptolemy and annexed at the end of the sixth book of Simson's edition of Euclid. (Note by Herschel.)

edge of Latin and a couple of other European languages besides his own; but it cannot be particularly easy for a Chinaman, a Japanese or a South Sea Islander, owing to the fact that its vocabulary is based upon those of Europe.

Knowing that the inventors of these languages and many other scholars, all far more learned and with far greater opportunities for studying the matter than will ever be his, have given much time and thought to this question, it is naturally with great diffidence that the present writer asks the attention of the public to the scheme which follows, in which, it seems to him, lies the germ of a language framed on scientific principles, a language as easily acquired by the Tartar and the Fijian as by the Englishman and the Italian, a language whose relationship to thought will be analogous to that of phonetic shorthand to speech.

Man as a maker of language must in the beginning have been in the disadvantageous position of not being able to discuss the best way to set about it until he could manage to make himself understood somehow. And by that time the mischief was done.

Now let us for a moment indulge in the extravagant supposition that man in the beginning, though rational and intelligent as now, was dumb. Let us further imagine that he had perfected a code of dumb-show signals by which he could communicate to his fellows every idea which occurred to him. Then let us suppose that all of a sudden the gods—seized by one of these whims which must have made them so difficult to get on with in those times—sent down a messenger with the gift of articulate speech. What would the humans have done? Doubtless, being intelligent as we said, they would have called a solemn assembly of the whole race to decide what was the best use to make of the new possession. They would at once have perceived that sounds would make a much more convenient medium for the expression of thought than sign-making, if once they should agree as to what idea each sound should express. They would first of all carefully try how many distinct and different sounds they could produce. The result of this inquiry would show that there were about sixteen consonant sounds which most of them could enunciate clearly—though certain individuals here and there found some difficulty with two or three of them—and about ten clearly defined vowel sounds. They would then consider whether with this small number of sounds it was possible to express the manifold ideas which from time to time they would need to communicate to each other.

After what would probably be a somewhat lengthy and very animated discussion, the chairman would call upon a noted sign-maker to sum up the result of their deliberations. This gentleman would then address his spectators in their sign language, showing that, as far as he could gather it, the general sense of the meeting was that, with strict economy of the material to be worked on, it would be possible to use speech as a medium for the exchange of ideas; that it was the intention of the conference to appoint a committee to draw up a scheme for this purpose; that before electing the members of that committee and deciding on the date of their next meeting at which the said scheme should be submitted for common approval, it would be as well to summarize broadly the lines on which they wished their committee to work. The chief points to which they would direct the attention of the committeemen were:

1. That to each sound should be allotted a general idea, particular ideas being expressed by the combination of these sounds into words or syllables.

2. That in so far as it was possible to avoid doing so, two different ideas should not be expressed by the same concatenation of sounds.

3. That the grammatical construction of the language should be as simple as it could be made, the necessary rules once decided on being applied consistently and without exceptions.

4. That if it were found possible to give adequate expression to all ideas without making use of such sounds as offered difficulty to this or that portion of the human race, it should be done; that if not, they should be used as sparingly as possible.

We can imagine that the meeting would then break up after having elected the committee and passed a resolution pointing out the evil results which might follow if any one tried to express himself in speech before the date of the next meeting and the final adoption of a scheme.

We can also imagine that at the next "general meeting" of the human race, the signalman of the committee, in the few remarks with which he would introduce the report, would state that, while his fellow committeemen and himself felt that they had succeeded in carrying out the wishes of their electors with regard to recommendations Nos. 1 and 3, they had not been quite so successful in the cases of Nos. 2 and 4.

With regard to No. 2: Owing to the fact that ideas were many and consonants few they had found it necessary to allot to each of this class of sound two meanings, and even to use some of them in a third sense in forming inflexions, and it thus sometimes happened that the same group of sounds did represent two ideas. Thus *it-ar* would be found to stand for "was dark" and *i-tar* for "to darken," and *it* to mean "was" and also "cold," but that he did not feel that any confusion was likely to result from this.

With regard to recommendation No. 4: The committee, owing to this same paucity of consonants, had felt constrained to make use of certain sounds which he feared a large number of his fellow men had a difficulty in enunciating. These were notably *r, s* and *th*. But he would like to point out to his Chinese, Polynesian and French friends that even if these sounds were a little bit hard to say, they were at least quite easy to write, and that communication with distant peoples would largely be written. And here, in a few well-chosen contortions and grimaces, he would explain the method and intention of the art of writing, which he and his fellow committeemen would doubtless have invented and included as an appendix in their report.

Having, he hoped, not unduly trespassed on his spectators' time, he now had great pleasure in submitting to them the result of the committee's deliberations in the form of a rational language to which they had provisionally given the name of *Tēl* (pronounced like "tail") and meaning, as they would shortly be in a position to see for themselves, "The Easily Understood." And the great scheme itself might very well have been in substance that which follows.

Convention I.

Every idea which occurs to us comes through the medium of one of the five senses; and by a happy coincidence five happens to be the number of the clearly differentiated vowel sounds in common use among mankind. Here then we have the basis of the first convention of our rational language.

Let each vowel connote one of the five senses. It does not matter much which vowel stands for which sense, so long as we are all agreed. So we will allot them as follows: *a* to seeing, *e* to hearing, *i* to touch, *o* to taste, *u* to smell.

Our first lesson then, is that whenever the vowel *a* occurs in a syllable its meaning has something to do with seeing; whenever *e* occurs the meaning of the syllable has something to do with hearing, and so on of the other three vowels.

Convention II.

Ideas being many and the sounds which we are capable of uttering but few, we shall have to give each of the consonants two values according to its position in the syllable. This brings us to the second convention: Every word beginning with a consonant other than *n* is a noun, and each consonant standing at the beginning of a word shall have a definite meaning. Here again the allotting of the meanings is arbitrary, but not without considerable thought the following table has been drawn up:

Each word beginning with *b* is the name of a beast,
" " " " *v* " " " " " bird,
" " " " *p* " " " " " fish or reptile,
" " " " *f* " " " " " invertebrate animal,
" " " " *g* " " " " " solid, mineral, etc.
" " " " *r* " " " " " liquid,
" " " " *l* " " " " " gas, vapor,
" " " " *m* " " " " " human being,
" " " " *k* " " " " " plant,
" " " " *s* " " " " " limb, member, part,
" " " " *z* " " " " " manufactured article,
" " " " *d* " " " " " thing,
" " " " *t* " " " " " abstraction,
" " " " *sh* " " " " " shape, space,
" " " " *th* " " " " " time, weather.

Convention III.

The consonants when they occur in the middle or at the end of a word shall have the values given in the table below. These values are adjectival or adverbial as the sense requires. Their meaning also varies slightly according to the vowel with which they are combined.

Thus *b* has the general meaning of "good," "well," and so when combined with the vowel *a* means "good to see," i. e., "beautiful." When combined with the vowel *e*, it means "good to hear," i. e., "musical." When combined with *i* it means "good to feel," i. e., "pleasant." When combined with *o* it means "good to taste," and when with *u* "good to smell," i. e., "sweet-scented."

TABLE SHOWING THE VALUES OF THE CONSONANTS ACCORDING TO THE VOWELS WITH WHICH THEY ARE USED.

	A SIGHT	E HEARING	I TOUCH	O TASTE	U SMELL
B	Kindly Beautiful	Kindly Musical	Kindly Pleasant	Good	Sweet
K	Unkindly Ugly	Unkindly Unmusical	Harmfully Unpleasant	Nasty	Foul
D	Fixedly Motionless	Continuously Deep	Firmly Firm	Strong	Strong
F	Dimly Small	Faintly Faint	Lightly Light	Slightly Insipid	Slightly Faint
G	Keenly Great	Keenly Loud	Heavily Heavy	Keenly Strong	Keenly Strong
L	Graciously Female, Slender	Graciously Treble	Caressingly Soft	Sweet	Soothing
M	Sternly Male	Attentively Bass	Masterfully Hard	Salt	Stimulating
N	Down Low	Murmuring	Aching	Bitter	Rank
P	Lightly Light	Lightly Shrill	Lightly Sharp (pointed)	Lightly Acid	Lightly Sour
R	Frowningly Dark	Rumbling	Roughly Rough	Rich	Musty
S	Swiftly Swift	Swiftly Hissing	With Movement Moving		
T	Coldly Blue	Metallic	Cold	Cold	Etherlike
V	Upwards High	Whistling	Stimulating	Alcoholic	Heady
Z	Warmly Red	Thrilling	Eagerly Hot	Greedily Hot	Greedily Pungent
TH	Straight Level	Flat	Evenly Smooth	Flat	
SH	Yellow	Sharp	Sharply Sharp (edged)		

We are now in the position to form a large number of nouns of one syllable, each consisting of three letters.

For instance let us take the word *bag*. This begins with *b* and is therefore the name of an animal of mammalian order; its vowel is *a* which means "appears"; *g* is the adjective "great." *Bag* is, then, "the animal which looks big." This may be the elephant. It may be objected that it may just as well be the hippopotamus. That is so; but we shall be able presently to add a second syllable which will define it more clearly.

Beg, a reference to the tables will show to be "the loud-voiced animal"; *big,* "the heavy animal"; *bog* is "the strongly-flavored animal," and *bug* "the strongly-smelling animal"—obviously the skunk or the polecat.

At this stage the student will find it an interesting and useful exercise to take any two consonants and put the five vowels in turn between them, and then write down the meaning of the resulting word. In doing so, he must bear in mind that *bag* is the animal which appears great, not the animal which sees greatly, i. e., the keen-sighted animal; that *beg* is the animal which is heard greatly, not the animal with a keen sense of hearing. We shall come to these others by and by.

We may also form a large number of simple adjectives. These begin with a vowel and consist of two letters only. From *k* which means "bad," we get *ak,* "ugly"; *ek,* "unmusical"; *ik,* "unpleasant to the touch"; *ok,* "nasty"; *uk,* "foul-smelling."

The verb "to be" is expressed by the letter *i,* and this vowel as a prefix is the characteristic of all other verbs. By placing it before each of the vowels we get the five verbs: *ia,* "to see"; *ie,* "to hear"; *ii,* "to feel"; *io,* "to taste"; *iu,* "to smell."

From each of these are formed two other verbs with the aid of each of the consonants. In the case where the consonant precedes the sense vowel the latter has an active meaning, and where the consonant follows the sense vowel it has a passive meaning. A few examples will make this clear:

Iga is "to see greatly," i. e., "to gaze"; *iag* is "to appear great," i. e., "to loom." *Ige* is "to have a keen sense of hearing," *ieg* "to sound loud." *Igi* is "to have a keen sense of touch," *iig* "to feel *big,* i. e., "to be heavy, to weigh." *Igo* is "to have a keen sense of taste," *iog* "to be strong-flavored." *Igu* is "to have a keen sense of smell," *iug* "to be strong-scented."

Having got so far, we are enabled to form a new series of nouns by placing consonants before the verbs of the *iga* type, e. g.: *Miga,* "the gazer"; *biga,* "the far-sighted animal, the greyhound"; *viga,* "the hawk"; *sigi,* "the organ which has a keen sense of touch, the finger"; *bigu,* "the hound."

Convention V.

Adverbs are formed by the addition of the letter *u* to adjectives. Thus *ab,* "beautiful," gives *abu,* "beautifully"; *af,* "small," gives *afu,* "little, slightly"; *av,* "high," gives *avu,* "up, upwards."

Convention VI.

The preposition "of" is expressed by the word *o,* and this preposition is used very freely to express obvious relationships, much as it was in old English where it was possible to say, "He was killed of a stone," "They were found of their enemies," "He did it of a Monday morning." By the addition of *o* to adjectives—and in a few cases to other parts of speech as well—prepositions may be formed from them. As these are not quite so obvious in meaning as the words we have up till now considered, a list of the commoner ones is appended.

We have not so far dealt with the combination of two consonants, but it will be as well to say here that *s,* which has movement for its primary meaning, is incorporated in prepositions to give the idea of motion. So from many adjectives we get two useful prepositions of kindred meaning, the one implying rest, the other motion to or from.

From *ab,* "agreeable," we get *abo,* "in accordance with."

From *ak,* "hostile," we get *ako,* "against," and *akso,* "against" (motion).

From *ad,* "fixed," we get *ado,* "at," and *adso,* "to, towards."

From *af,* "small," we get *afo,* "near," and *afso,* "near."

From *ag,* "great," we get *ago,* "far from," and *agso,* "from."

From *an,* "low," we get *ano,* "under," and *anso,* "down, under."

From *ap,* "light," we get *apo,* "outside," and *apso,* "out of."

From *ar,* "dark," we get *aro,* "in," and *arso,* "into."

From *av,* "high," we get *avo,* "upon," and *avso,* "up."

Inflections.

Inflections are, of course, reduced to the smallest number possible.

The noun is inflected for number only, the plural being formed by the addition of *y* to the singular, e. g.:

beg, "dog," *begy,* "dogs"; *sigi,* "finger," *sigiy,* "fingers"; *bagrag,* "whale," *bagragy,* "whales."

It is true that from the word *bigu,* which signifies "dog" generally, we can form the words *biguam,* "a male dog," and *bigual,* "a female dog," but these are compound words rather than inflections in the grammatical sense of the word.

Case is expressed as in English by the position of the word in the sentence, and not by inflection as in Latin. The nominative precedes the verb, the objective follows it, or comes after a preposition.

Maf imi bigu means "The child holds the dog."

Bigu imi maf means "The dog holds the child."

Zer o mamaf i at means "The boy's drum is blue."

The adjective is not inflected either for gender, number, case or degree of comparison. The comparative and superlative are expressed, as in the case of the longer adjectives in English, by putting words equivalent to "more" and "most" before the simple form of the adjective.

The verb is inflected for tense, mood, and voice, but not for person and number. The last two are quite unnecessary when, as in most modern languages, the pronoun is expressed, and in Tēl they are accordingly not found.

The verbal inflections are added immediately to the verbal sign *i,* and precede the letters which contain the meaning of the verb.

The future is shown by the presence of the letter *r*: *ipi,* "to pierce; fut., *me irpi,* "I shall pierce."

A *t* is the sign of the past tense: *me itpi,* "I pierced," "I have pierced," or "I did pierce."

By combining these two we get the future perfect tense: *me irtpi,* "I shall have pierced."

Should any difficulty be experienced in pronouncing the combination thus formed—or indeed at any time in the language Tēl—an atonic *e* is inserted, e. g., *me irt*^{e}*ba,* "I shall have smiled." This *e* is scarcely sounded at all just as in our "the" when said quickly in the middle of a sentence. In writing, this *e* may be omitted altogether, as was always done in the old Egyptian and kindred languages; but it is a good plan for a beginner to put it in, using for the purpose a different form of the letter—say the Greek ε—to distinguish it from the letter which indicates the idea of "hearing." Throughout the remainder of this article a small superior *e* is used to denote this atonic vowel.

The pluperfect is formed by doubling the *t* which signifies the past, inserting the atonic *e* to enable the double sound of the *t* to be heard: *me it*^{e}*tpi,* "I had pierced."

L is the sign of the conditional mood:

Me ilpi, "I should pierce"; *me iltpi,* "I should have pierced."

The infinitive does not differ in form from the indicative:

Mar itga ieb, "The negro wished to sing."

Mamaf ilga itmi vat, "The boy would like to have caught the blue bird."

Zip imta irpi zil, "The needle was seen to be about to pierce the cushion."

The word *imta* in the last example belongs to the passive voice. This is shown by putting the letter *m* immediately after the verbal sign *i,* before the letters indicating mood and tense:

Me ipi, "I pierce"; *Me impi,* "I am pierced." *Me it*^{e}*tpi,* "I had pierced"; *Me im*^{e}*t*^{e}*tpi,* "I had been pierced."

The full conjugation of the verb *imi,* "to hold" or "have," is as follows:

ACTIVE.	PASSIVE.
Pres. *Me imi,* I hold	*Me im*^{e}*mi,* I am held
Fut. *Me irmi,* I shall hold	*Me im*^{e}*rmi,* I shall be held
Past. *Me itmi,* I held, I have held	*Me im*^{e}*tmi,* I was held, I have been held.
Fut-pf. *Me irtmi,* I shall have held	*Me im*^{e}*rtmi,* I shall have been held
Plupf. *Me it*^{e}*tmi,* I had held	*Me imt*^{e}*tmi,* I had been held
Condit. *Me ilmi,* I should hold	*Me im*^{e}*lmi,* Ishould be held
..Past. *Me iltmi,* I should have held	*Me im*^{e}*ltmi,* I should have been held
Inf. pres. *imi,* to hold	*im*^{e}*mi,* to be held
..Fut. *irmi,* to be about to hold	*im*^{e}*rmi,* to be about to be held
..Past, *itmi,* to have held	*im*^{e}*tmi,* to have been held

There is in Tēl no distinction between nouns and pronouns, the latter being expressed by the use of certain nouns.

"I" is *me,* the person heard, the speaker. "Thou" is *ma,* the person seen. For the pronoun of the third person whether "he" or "she," the word *m*^{e} is used which is really simply "the person." If the speaker wishes to emphasize the sex, however, he will use *mam* for "he," and *mal* for "she." In the case of animals *b*^{e}*, v*^{e}*, p*^{e} or *f*^{e} will be employed instead of *m*^{e}*,* according to the class of animal referred to; whilst "it" is *d*^{e}*,* i. e., "thing."

In all cases the plural is formed as in other nouns by adding *y* to the singular. Of course the remarkable custom so prevalent in modern languages, of saying "you" when we mean "thou" will have no place in Tēl, and "you" must always be translated by *ma* when one person only is addressed. The objective case is of the same form as the nominative, and the possessive is expressed by means of the preposition *o*: *Mal* $it^{e}tago$ *me d-imrar o ma,* "She gave me your letter."

The demonstrative pronouns "this" and "that" are respectively *dafo* and *dago,* that is to say, *d,* "thing" compounded with *afo,* "near" and *ago,* "far." The corresponding *mafo* and *mago,* referring to persons, are our "the latter" and " the former."

Mafo (plural, *mafoy*) is also used for all the reflexive pronouns which refer to persons, e. g.: *Me irshi mafo,* "I shall cut myself"; *Mamafy* $it^{e}tki$ *mafoy,* "The boys had hurt themselves." *Dafo, dafoy* are the corresponding "itself, themselves."

We now come to a very important feature of Tēl. This is the use of the "long" vowels. And here it will be as well to say a word as to pronunciation. As Tēl is intended for use as a universal language, it will be best to give to the vowels what are to-day their most widely accepted values, and not those which are peculiar to the English tongue. The following are therefore suggested as the best values to give them:

a has the sound of *a* in "father," *ā* that of *a* in "all."

e has the sound of *e* in "pen," *ē* that of *ai* in "pain."

i has the sound of *i* in "pin," *ī* that of *i* in "machine."

o has the sound of *o* in "not," *ō* that of *o* in "note."

u has the sound of *u* in "put," *ū* that of *oo* in "boot."

The long vowels are used to signify the same sense as the corresponding short ones, but with the meaning transferred to the mental plane.

Thus, long *a* means "appearing to the mind's eye" and "seeing with the mind's eye."

Long *e* means "heard by the mind's ear," "learned"; and "hearing with the mind," "apprehending," "understanding."

Long *i* means "felt by the mind," and "touching with the mind."

Long *o* means "savoring of," etc., and "tasting with the mind."

Long *u* means "having the scent of to the mind," i. e., "suggesting"; also "suspecting," "guessing" etc.

A few examples will show what a wide range of ideas may now be expressed.

Whereas *iab* is "to be well-looking"; i. e., "to flourish," "to be in health"; *iāb* is "to be well-seeming to the mind"; i. e., "to be favorably received," "to be granted," "accepted."

Iba is "to look kindly," "to smile"; *ibā* is "to look kindly on with the mind," "to receive favorably," "to accept."

Iak is "to be ugly," "unbecoming," "in bad condition"; *iāk* is "to seem ugly to the mind," "to be unacceptable," "to displease."

Ika is "to look foully on," "to scowl; *ikā* is "to view hostilely with the mind," i. e., "to refuse," "to reject."

Ab is "beautiful to look at"; *āb* is "beautiful to the mind," "pleasant."

Ief is "to emit a faint sound"; *iēf* is "to be dimly understood."

Ife is "to hear faintly"; *ifē* is "to understand but slightly."

Im is "hard"; *īm*, "difficult."

Imi is "to touch masterfully," i. e., "to grasp," "hold," "have"; *imī*, "to comprehend," "to know."

Ok is "nasty to eat"; *ōk*, "revolting" (to the mind).

Ug is "strong-smelling"; *ūg*, "reminding strongly" (of).

So far we have considered the building of words which comprise not more than three ideas, and these we have found to consist of one, or at most two, syllables. These root words are, however, capable of being combined in a great variety of ways, giving new words of more precise meaning.

In making these compound words it must be borne in mind that the qualifying syllable or letter always follows, never precedes, that which it qualifies.

The qualifying syllable may be originally a noun, an adjective, a verb, or even sometimes a preposition or an adverb.

The word *bag* is "the animal which looks great," and so may stand for any big beast. By adding as a second syllable *rag* which is "the great water," i. e., "the sea," we get *bagrag*, "the whale." If instead of *rag* we add *ris*, "the moving water," i. e., "river," we get *bagris*, "hippopotamus." *Baged* is "the big beast with the deep voice," "elephant." Whilst *bagsiusip*, "big beast nose horn" is "rhinoceros."

Berob, "the grunting animal, good to eat," gives us the "pig." Then from this or any noun we may get a new series of adjectives, e. g.: *A-berob*, "looking like a pig." (It will be as well, by the way, during the earlier stages of our acquaintance with Tēl to separate the elements of the word by hyphens [*a-ber-ob*], or we may be misled into reading the first two letters as *ab*, "beautiful"). *E-ber-ob* is "sounding like a pig," *i-ber-ob* "feeling like a pig," *o-ber-ob* "tasting like pork," *u-ber-ob* "smelling like a pig." From each of these adjectives, again, the corresponding abstract noun can be formed by prefixing *t*: *ta-ber-ob,* "piggishness"; *to-ber-ob,* "a pork-like flavor."

From any noun a verb may be made by the simple expedient of putting the verbal prefix in front of it. Thus from *rar,* "ink," we have *i-rar,* "to write." (Conjugation: *ir*^{e}*-rar, it-rar, irt-rar, it*^{e}*t-rar, il-rar, ilt-rar*; Passive: *im-rar, im*^{e}*r-rar, im*^{e}*rt-rar, imt*^{e}*t-rar,* etc.)

Especially important is the series formed from abstract nouns. These are what are generally called "factitive verbs"; for example, *i-tab,* from *tab,* "beauty," means "to make beautiful," to "beautify." *Tol,* "sweetness," gives *i-tol,* "to sweeten." So we have, *i-tav,* "to raise," *i-tath,* "to level," *i-tif,* "to lighten," *i-tom,* "to salt," *i-tuk,* "to make to stink," and so forth. The only drawback to these is that they are in the present tense of the same form as the past tense of those of the series *iab, ieb,* etc. For instance, *it-ar* is the past tense of the verb *iar,* and so means "was dark," whilst *i-tar* means "darkens." But neither in the spoken nor the written language will this be found to cause any confusion in practice.

A LIST OF THE SIMPLE VERBS FORMED ON THE VOWEL "A" (SIGHT).

iab, thrive; *iāb,* to be correct; *iba,* smile; *ibā,* like; *itab,* beautify; *itāb,* to perfect.

iak, to decay; *iāk,* to look bad; *ika,* to scowl; *ikā,* to dislike; *itak,* to mar; *itāk,* to destroy.

iad, to be still, to sleep; *iād,* to be at rest; *ida,* to gaze; *idā,* to investigate; *itad,* to still; *itād,* to settle.

iaf, to be small; *iāf,* to be unimportant; *ifa,* to see badly; *ifā,* to misunderstand; *itaf,* to diminish; *itāf,* to belittle.

iag, to be great; *iāg,* to matter; *iga,* to see well; *igā,* to long for; *itag,* to enlarge; *itāg,* to extol, praise.

ial, to be feminine; *iāl,* to yield; *ila,* to be coy; *ilā,* to cajole; *ital,* to make effeminate; *itāl,* to subdue.

ian, to be low; *iān,* to be contemptible; *ina,* to look down; *inā,* to despise; *itan,* to lower; *itān,* to lower.

iam, to be masculine; *iām,* to prevail; *ima,* to look sternly; *imā,* to judge; *itam,* to make manly; *itām,* to enforce.

iap, to be light; *iāp,* to be clear; *ipa,* to look sharply; *ipā,* to scrutinize; *itap,* to whiten; *itāp,* to make clear, demonstrate.

iar, to be dark; *iār,* to be hard to understand; *ira,* to frown; *irā,* to puzzle over; *itar,* to darken; *itār,* to involve.

ias, to live; *iās,* to exist in the mind; *isa,* to glance; *isā,* to take in at a glance; *itas,* to create; *itās,* to vivify.

iav, to stand up; *iāv,* to be eminent; *iva,* to look up; *ivā,* to reverence; *itav,* to heighten; *itāv,* to raise (hopes, etc.)

iaz, to be red; *iāz,* to be exciting; *iza,* to look eagerly; *izā,* to regard with enthusiasm; *itaz,* to redden; *itāz,* to excite.

iath, to be level; *iāth,* to be fair, just; *itha,* to look calmly; *ithā,* to consider; *itath,* to level; *itāth,* to adjust.

Two consonants may be used to qualify the same sense vowel. In such a case it does not in the least matter, so far as the sense is concerned, which of them comes first. Thus "green" may be either *at^esh* or *ash^et,* whichever happens to be the easier word to say. You cannot be misunderstood either way.

The numeral adjectives are distinguished by beginning with the letter *y* which, as has been seen, is the sign of the plural in nouns.

The first ten numbers are each formed of a word connected in some way with the number indicated. The others are formed by composition from these.

1 is *ysav* (head)	6 is *ytit* (frost)
2 is *ysia* (eye)	7 is *ydap* (planet)
3 is *ykap* (lily)	8 is *ylis* (wind)
4 is *yset* (hoof)	9 is *yteg* (knowledge)
5 is *ysigi* (finger)	10 is *yāb* (perfect)

The numbers from eleven to nineteen are made by putting "ten" before "one," "two," "three," etc.: 11, *yābsav,* 12, *yābsia,* 13, *yābkap,* and so on.

The multiples of ten have the multiplier in front of the *āb*: 20, *ysiāb*; 30, *ykapāb*; 40, *ysetāb*; 50, *ysigāb,* etc., the words for twenty and fifty being contracted where the two vowels come together. 100 is *yābag,* "great ten."

The ordinals are expressed by, *o shysav,* i. e., "of place one"; *o shysia,* "of place two," *o shykap,* "of place three," etc.

The adverbs "firstly," "secondly," "thirdly"' are made by adding the adverbial sign *u* to the cardinal numbers: *ysavu, ysiau, ykapu,* etc.

Words including the idea of number in a less definite manner are: *y,* "some"; *yag,* "many"; *o thy,* "sometimes"; *o thyag,* "often"; the construction of these should present no difficulty to the student.

Interrogation is expressed by beginning the sentence with the word *que*, or some word beginning with *qu*.

Que siay o mafal i ar?, "Are the girl's eyes dark?"

Interrogative words are: *Quado*, "where"; *quadso*, "whither"; *quasso*, "whence"; *quo*, "why"; *queme*, "who"; *quede*, "*what*"; *quagu*, "how" (to what degree); *quabu*, "how" (in what manner); *quethe*, "when."

The letter *n* as an initial is reserved to express the idea of negation. First we have the simple *ne*, "not." Then we get such adjectives as *nish*, "blunt," from *ish*, "sharp"; and nouns such as *tenish*, "bluntness," corresponding to *tish*, "sharpness." In verbs the *n* comes before the root but after the verbal prefix; e. g., from *iath*, "to be level," we have *inath*, "to be rough," *iltenath*, "would have been rough"; and from *itath*, "to level," *itenath*, "to roughen," with passive pluperfect, *imetet-tenath*, "had been roughened."

One of the most striking features of a language formed on such principles as these is its economy of material, since every combination of sounds carries with it a definite meaning. Whereas all the languages now in use, and probably all the languages which ever have been used, are encumbered with sesquepedalian terms while at the same time they wastefully make no use at all of numbers of the shortest and most easily pronounced combinations.

Thus in our own language we have indeed the words "dig," "dog," and "dug," each compactly and clearly expressing an idea. But we have attached no meaning at all to the equally clear and simple sounds "dag" and "deg."

These simple monosyllables are wasted whilst we take up our time and exhaust our inkpots with such words as "notwithstanding" and "anthropomorphism."

If you take the consonants in pairs and place between them in succession each of the five vowels, you will find, I think, that only in the case of the *b-g* series—*bag, beg, big, bog, bug*—are all the five resulting words made use of in English.

Now in Tēl every such combination would have its meaning and express an idea consisting of three elements. Thus *dag* is "a thing which looks big" and *deg* is "a loud sounding thing."

The foregoing pages do not, of course, claim to contain a perfect language, but only to suggest a principle on which, if a few competent persons were to work together, they might soon evolve a code in which any person who can read and write would be able to express at least his simpler thoughts to any other person equally educated, quite irrespectively of the linguistic affinities of their native tongues.

QUINTIN WADDINGTON.

ASHBURNHAM, DITCHLING, SUSSEX, ENGLAND.

MOTOR RELATIONS OF SPEECH AND IDEA.

Listening to a casual conversation in some foreign tongue gives us an impression in which even the word spacing escapes notice, so that we speak of hearing the "chatter" of Turkish, of Japanese, just as we refer to our perception of the sounds of birds. This paper desires to carry onward some studies in which motor equations are substituted for an understanding of the basis of expression of ideas as sound in words. The expression of signs in words, coming down through the employment of pictures to arbitrary marks is not a parallel study. But it seems interesting to compare, if possible, all languages upon a basis of movements, muscular and osseous. That one movement should be selected and not another is evidently a matter less of chance than convenience. Birds having no teeth will not enunciate dental equivalents. On the other hand, a preference for dental equivalents among a vast majority of languages may indicate a group idea having a basic muscular value.

To eat suggests taste. To eat suggests having within the mouth. So teeth, cheeks, lips, tongue and palate are concerned. But teeth, to a mammal suggest in an especial manner the function of eating. The teeth bite off, as well as chew, so that a word "to eat" without a dental sound might be quite avian, but scarcely mammalian. Eating is not performed in the pharynx, or throat. A guttural letter would scarcely denote the verb "to eat," although in a too hasty swallowing, as "to gulp," we recognize the fitness of the word.

Let us preface a table of the chief consonants:

1. Labial: *p—b—ph* (*f*)—*bh* (*v*).
2. Lingual: *t—d—th—dh.*
3. Guttural: *k—g—kh—gh.*
4. Sibilant: *s—z—sh—zh* (French *j*).
5. Compound: *ts—dz—tsh* (*ch,* in church)—j (English).

The liquids and others:

1. Labial: *m—w.* 2. Lingual: *n—l—y.*

3. Guttural: *ng—r—h*. 4. Sibilant: — — —
5. Compound: *gn* (*gn*, French) [compa*ni*on, English].

In the lingual group we may include palatals and dentals as of common source, although to carry out the most detailed study they would require sub-analysis.

"TO EAT," SEVERALLY STUDIED.

English: *eat*, = *t*. Greek: *esthio* = *sth*.
Italian: *mangiare* = *dzh*. Latin: *edere* = *d*.
French: *manger* = *zh*. Russian: *yest* = *st*.
German: *essen* = *ss* Japanese: *tabe* = *t*.

"TO SWALLOW, TO DRINK, TO GULP."

English: *gulp* = *g*.
Italian: *inghiottire* = *gh* (*g*, hard).
French: *gober* = *g*.
German: *schlucken* = *k* (*ck*).
Greek: *katabrochthizo* ($\sqrt{}$*bronchus*) = *ch*.
Latin: *glutio* = *g* (*gl*).
Russian: *glotokh* and *glonutye* = *g* (*gl*).
Japanese: *nomi-komi* = *k*.

(*Nomi* means "to drink." The *komi* is alliterative modulating the *n*, a lingual, to a *k*, a guttural.)

These lists could be extended. It is evident that onomatopoiesis would not account for simple muscular movements in themselves not vocable.

Following this plan, as in a previous paper[1] suggested, the labials are sounds of approach, of affection, of prehension. The dentals (linguals) are sounds of distinction, of definition, of limitation. The gutturals are sounds of imbibition, of assimilation, of emotion, and are of lower mental status, coarse and less imaginative, less detailed, and less reasoned than the dentals.

To find a sound of past tense, a sound which would limit the verb to a particular time, past, just past, or just passing, we find no better element than a dental (lingual).

PAST PREFIX, SUFFIX, OR FORM.

English: *ed, d, t, en, n*. Latin: *atus, tus*.
French: — — — Greek: *menos, tos*.
German: *te, en, n*. Italian: *ato, ito, uto*.

[1] "Some Curious Psychosensory Relationships," *The Monist*, XVII, 128.

Russian: *l.*
Polish: *l.*
Japanese: *ta.*

PRESENT PARTICIPLE (JUST PASSING), ACTIVE.

English: *ing, ng.*
French: *ant.*
Italian: *ante, ando.*
German: *end.*
Latin: *nt, ns.*
Greek: *ont, n.*
Russian: *ya, shtsh.*
Polish: *ts.*
Japanese: *te.*

From such isolated examples, chosen however among commonplace and colloquial words, no fixed rule could be posited. Nor could any definite rule be asserted. It may, nevertheless, afford the anatomical basis of a relationship between word and idea. Not only in the necessary processes of cerebration, but in the entire nerve-muscle reaction there may occur a definite substratum of necessity in the choice of sounds. This would give us a rational basis for the study of animal sounds in general. A hen's clucking when she calls her little chickens sounds as though her muscles of deglutition were involved in the production of the sound.

The elements of inflection in a language require keener analysis. Chance, or association, may apparently reverse a rule.

Strangely enough, in studying these principles, on reading Japanese, a striking similarity among the words of common usage in that Ural-altaic tongue and German, Italian and Greek roots becomes apparent. This will be seen from the table which is appended to this article, and which could be materially extended. Over one hundred of the common 400 colloquial words in Japanese show a Greco-Latin influence of the consonantal type here outlined. It was the philologist Grimm who said that a similar sound was of more significance than a similar spelling. Müller, too, followed such assonances.

Japanese employs an ending, *tsu,* the *u* being comparable to our French and English *e* silent. This *tzu* has the value of Italian *-zio, -anzio, -angia, -ancio,* etc., and of the French and the English *-ance, -ence.* Here we see the *u* is lost but the *c* equals a *ts.* German and Russian use a *tz* in a similar purpose to close a word. Not only can this be found, but the Japanese *-sa,* used for substantives derived from the adjective ending *shii* (as in Russian, and the *sch* of German) may be no more than a weakened *ts* plus *a.* The use of a *ts* or *s* to denote nouns by derivation is the employment of a final dental which in verbs as *d* or *l* closes action, and in nouns encloses space.

The present linguistic dissector would enjoy extending this communication. He has abundant material in the form of notes from which a future hour may be permitted to draw. Before closing he would like to inquire whether the Turkish suffix of verbal infinitive mode, *-mak, -mek,* can be related to the German *machen,* "to do," "to make."

In view of the pronounced affinity of Rumanian to Italian, can the Ural-altaic Japanese be related across the Caucasus?

The theory of anatomic necessity in vocalization may prove a solid basis of investigation. Modern phonetics classifies more than ever all vocables according to structural enunciation.

COMPARATIVE TABLE OF ROOTS.

ENGLISH	JAP.	GREEK	SANSK.	GERMAN	RUSSIAN	LATIN ROMANIC
generate / grow	*gen*	*gen*	*gen*	*gin*		*gen*
obscure	*ku*	*sko*	*sku*			*scur*
come	*iki*	*heko*		*kommen*		
(go) exit	*iri*					*ire*
here	*achi*					*aqui*
are (to be)	*are*	*histami*		*aron*		
beautiful	*bi*					*bello*
base (bottom)	*batsuza*					*bas*
-logy	*-gaku*	*logos*				*-logia*
healing	*i*	*iatr*				
medicine (sci)	*i gaku*	[*iatrology*]				
boorishness	*burei*					
same (ditto)	*demo* / *do*					*medesimo* / *detto*
dominee (mr)	*don*					*don* / *dominus*
locality	*ho*	*lech*				*locus*
(genit. relation)	*no*	*on*				
(adj.) -an, -ian	*na*	*-anos*			*-a, -ya*	*-anus*

T. H. Evans, M.D.

Brooklyn, N. Y.

BOOK REVIEWS.

A Budget of Paradoxes. By *Augustus De Morgan.* Edited with full bibliographical notes and index by *David Eugene Smith,* Teachers College, Columbia University, New York. Two volumes, pp. 402, 387. Price $7.00. Price for advance order, $5.00.

As booklovers and those who delight to browse in fields that are quaint and curious know, there appeared in the nineteenth century no work that appealed to the tastes of their guild more powerfully than the delightful *Budget of Paradoxes* of Augustus De Morgan. Originally written as a series of articles in *The Athenaeum,* they were collected by Professor De Morgan just before his death and were published posthumously by his talented wife. As a piece of delicious satire upon the efforts of circlers of squares, and their kind, there is nothing else in English literature that is quite so good. Nor should it be thought that the work is technical because it speaks of the arrested mental development of the circle squarers. On the contrary, while it is absolutely scientific in its conclusions, it is written in a popular style which any one can appreciate and which has charmed thousands of readers during the past half century.

The *Budget of Paradoxes* was first written some fifty years ago. Many names which were common property in England at that time were little known abroad, and others have passed into oblivion even in their native land. Incidents which were subjects of general conversation then have long since been forgotten, so that some of the charm of the original edition would be lost on the reader of the present day had the publishers undertaken merely a reprint. The first edition having long since been exhausted but still being in great demand, it was decided to prepare a new one, and to issue it in a form becoming a work of this high rank. Accordingly, it was arranged to leave the original text intact, to introduce such captions and rubrics as should assist the reader in separating the general topics, and to furnish a set of footnotes which should supply him with as complete information as he might need with respect to the names and incidents mentioned in the text.

In preparing this edition the publishers sought for the man whose tastes, experience, and learning would best harmonize with those of Professor De Morgan himself. Accordingly they invited Professor David Eugene Smith, Ph. D., LL. D., to undertake the work. Dr. Smith is known for his *Rara Arithmetica,* which completed the early part of the work undertaken by De Morgan in his arithmetical books; for his *Portfolio of Eminent Mathematicians* and for his part in the *History of Japanese Mathematics* and the translation of Fink's *History of Mathematics,* issued by the Open Court Publishing Company; and for his extensive writings on the history and teaching of mathematics and his contributions to text-book literature. Dr. Smith has worked in De Morgan's library, is thoroughly familiar with all of De Morgan's writings, and has a type of mind which is sympathetic with that of the author of the *Budget.* The publishers have therefore been very fortunate in securing the one man who was best qualified to undertake *con amore* the preparation of this new edition.

Although the original edition of the *Budget* appealed rather to the searcher after the unique and bizarre than to one who wished for information as to men and things, the new edition may properly take its place among the valuable works of reference in our public libraries. The circle-squarers and the angle-trisectors are present everywhere and always, and a popular work that will show them their folly is a thing that every library should welcome. But aside from this, the great care taken by Dr. Smith in his biographical and historical notes renders the work invaluable on a shelf of general reference. His additions have so increased the size of the work that it has been found necessary to issue it in two volumes. σ

The number of *Scientia* (*Rivista di Scienza*) for October, 1914, did not reach England until the end of November. The first article is by T. C. Chamberlin, of the University of Chicago, on "The Planetesimal Hypothesis." He presents evidence that the planets sprang from the sun, not at its birth, but later in the course of its history. "The satellites might easily seem to be the offspring of the planets, and this was the common view in the last century, but there are signs that planets and satellites had a common birth and that the satellites escaped being little planets because their birth-places fell within the spheres of control of their larger sisters to whom they were forced to dance attendance as a first duty, and respond to the common call of the sun incidentally." David Einhorn has an article on archigony and the theory of descent. Camillo Golgi gives the first part of a study of the modern evolution of the doctrines and knowledge about life. This is a lecture given at the beginning of 1914 before the Institute of Sciences and Letters of Lombardy, and this part is on the fundamental bio-physiological problems. Otto Jespersen of Copenhagen writes on the energetics of language, taking as text Humboldt's remark that language is not an *Ergon,* a completed work, but an *Energeia.* Charles Guignebert gives the third and fourth parts of his articles on the dogma of the Trinity; they deal with the Arian crisis, St. Augustine and the symbol of Athanasius, and the immobility, decadence and downfall of the doctrine. R. Maunier has a critical note on the laws of the evolution of art, in which he criticizes a recent work of W. Deonna. S. Magrini gives a general review of work on electrons and magnetons, and W. Oualid gives an annual review of economics. Besides this there are the usual reviews of books and periodicals, and French translations of the English, German and Italian articles.

In *Scientia* (*Rivista di Scienza*) for February of this year, J. Costantin contributes a criticism of Mendelism, discussing the laws of hybridization and the action of the environment. Eugenio Rignano continues his psychological studies on mathematical reasoning. Besides book reviews, a general review by G. Stefanini on the geological history of the Mediterranean, and French translations of the English, German, and Italian articles, the "Inquiry upon the War" is continued. The present number contains articles by a Frenchman, a Briton, and a German: Adolphe Landry writes on the origins, causes and the aftermath of the war; Sir Oliver Lodge writes on "The War from a British Point of View"; and G. von Below writes on militarism and culture in Germany. ϕ

VOL. XXV JULY, 1915 NO. 3

THE MONIST

NUMBERS, VARIABLES AND MR. RUSSELL'S PHILOSOPHY.

PHILOSOPHERS not infrequently take mathematics as a field for the exercise of their fancies. If the starting-point be a really sound philosophy, the result of an excursion into mathematics enures to the benefit of both disciplines. If, however, the start be a metaphysics or a logic that is essentially erroneous, the results attained may be novel or startling, but have no place in the body of our scientific knowledge. To say that the investigations of any particular philosopher comes under this second head seems invidious, yet it is necessary to so stigmatize the false systems if the way is to be kept open for the true. Of all the impediments to the cultivation of mathematical science on a philosophical basis there can be none greater than the putting forth a pseudo-philosophy in the guise of true doctrine. As such an impediment do we esteem the work of Mr. Bertrand Russell, who is a recent writer of some repute, though whether he ought to be classed as philosopher who devotes himself to mathematics or as a mathematician who dips into philosophy is a moot question.

Mr. Russell's labors seem to have as their burden the reorganization of mathematics upon the basis of what he is pleased to term "one of the greatest discoveries of our age"; a discovery, if such it be, largely due to Mr. Russell himself (not to speak of his forerunner, Professor Peano) "that all Mathematics is Symbolic Logic."[1] To encounter such a statement is rather startling to any one who has been accustomed to class mathematics among the deduc-

[1] *Principles of Mathematics,* Cambridge, at the University Press, Vol. I, 1913, p. 5.

tive sciences. Symbolic logic is merely deductive logic treated in a particular way, and deductive logic is not usually understood to take within its scope any special deductive science, but is supposed merely to give an account of the methods of deduction employed in these sciences. The view taken by Mr. Russell is tenable only when mathematics and logic are understood to have scopes different from those usually accepted for them. Indeed the mathematical science developed by the school of Peano and Russell has some radical differences, not merely in scope but also in method, from what is ordinarily expounded under the name of mathematics. These neo-mathematicians hold that mathematics ought not to follow the method of laying down a set of special mathematical axioms and postulates for each branch of the science and deducting therefrom the theorems of that branch. The only principles Mr. Russell would have pure mathematics put forword are "ten principles of deduction and ten other premises of a general logical nature."[2] The natural result is that what Mr. Russell attains are not the theorems of ordinary mathematics. Where ordinary mathematics would deduce from the axioms A, B and C the theorem T, Mr. Russell is satisfied to have mathematics not assert A or B or C at all—much less T—but merely prove and assert the proposition that "A, B and C imply T"; in other words that the theorem T is a logical consequence of A, B and C if these are given as premises.

To replace the ordinary theorems of mathematics by propositions of implication is alone insufficient to bring mathematics into the realm of symbolic logic. Mr. Russell goes still further and so extends the denotations of the mathematical symbols made use of that the propositions of pure mathematics become the merest of shells. A mathematical formula where x and y originally meant quantities

[2] P. 4.

is by Mr. Russell so extended that x and y may have as wide a range of applicability as the X and Y of the canonical logical proposition: "Every X is a Y." Thus if by some far-fetched interpretation of addition, multiplication etc. the formula $(x+y)^2 = x^2 + 2xy + y^2$ can be made to yield a significance when x and y instead of meaning quantities are understood to mean Plato and Socrates respectively, Mr. Russell would bring the formula as thus construed within the mathematical field. Pure mathematics then, with Mr. Russell, is characterized, not by the import of its propositions, but by their form, and its end in each question it takes up is merely to find what form of proposition is implied by a set of propositions of specified forms. It thus becomes identified with symbolic logic provided deductive logic be held to deal, not merely with generalities in the theory of inference, but to have an essential part of its scope the consideration of every possible combination of the types of propositions which it accepts, and to endeavor in each such case to find what form of proposition is to be taken as the type of conclusion inferable from this combination of premises.

We shall not here debate the question of how far this new view of the scope of pure mathematics is worthy of being called a "great discovery." But we must point out that Mr. Russell is not entirely consistent in his adhesion to this view. Under it either pure mathematics must be completely identified with symbolic logic or must be put in the rank of a subdivision of the latter discipline. No other alternative is reconcileable with the statement that "all Mathematics is Symbolic Logic." Mr. Russell however, without seeing the need for first retracting this statement, is led by "respect for tradition" and "desire to adhere to usage" to draw a distinction under which logic "consists of the premises of mathematics" together with certain other propositions not mathematical, while mathematics "consists of all the consequences of the above premises" together with some, but not all, of these premises themselves.[3] Obviously then, mathematics will cover a field that is not included in logic at all, and the mathematics of this field can certainly not be symbolic logic.

Notwithstanding the purely formal rôle that Mr. Russell would assign to pure mathematics, he takes up in his *Principles* various questions that seem to pertain to the matter rather than to the form of mathematical science. After enumerating certain "indefinables of mathematics" he proceeds to the definables, and begins by the discussion of number. The doctrine of number is fundamental in mathematical philosophy; let us see how Mr. Russell handles it.

Numbers, Mr. Russell tells us, are "applicable essentially to classes."[4] This word *class* is a favorite one with Mr. Russell, and he often uses it where another word would be more appropriate. In the present case *group* might well be adopted in preference to class. For ordinarily, when reference is made to a class of objects, what is in mind is something about objects of that class taken individually—not about the objects as constituting a collectivity. Now (except when there is but a single object at hand, a case which gives rise to just as much difficulty when we speak of "class" as when we use the word "group") it is precisely this idea of collectivity, so aptly suggested by *group,* that is in evidence when we speak of number. The number of objects in a group is a number that belongs to the group as a whole, not to any of its objects taken separately.

A number then is something belonging to a group—we replace "applicable to" by "belonging to" without stopping to comment on the impropriety of Mr. Russell's use

[3] P. 9. [4] P. 112.

of the former phraseology—and if we follow Mr. Russell we must regard it as a property of that group. "Numbers," he tells us, "are to be regarded as properties of classes."[5] Presumably Mr. Russell does not use "property" in the sense of the old *proprium,* a name by which certain attributes were distinguished from the essential on the one hand and the accidental on the other; in this sense the statement would not be true, for to have a number is of the very essence of a group. Taking, however, property as a mere synonym of attribute, and substituting group for class, no fault need be found with what Mr. Russell says. A number is truly an attribute of a group of objects. But Mr. Russell too hastily proceeds to inquire "Under what circumstances do two classes have the same number?"[6] when the next question ought in fact to be: Do two groups ever really have the *same* number? In a mere mathematician it is pardonable to be unaware that the question of identity of attributes of distinct objects, or distinct groups of objects, is a debatable one, but surely any writer who aspires to be ranked as a philosopher ought to know that eminent thinkers have been at variance in this matter. Thus, going back only a few years, we find that a brief but very interesting discussion took place between Mill and Spencer as to whether two different objects could be said to have the same attribute.

The point really at issue is this: when one speaks of sameness (or identity) in such a case, is he so using language as to mark all the distinctions that ought to be made, or is he ignoring some of them, is he promoting clearness of thought and speech, or is his phraseology pregnant with obscurity and confusion? This question never seems to have occurred to Mr. Russell, though it arises whether the attributes are qualities belonging to different individuals or are number attributes (quantities) belonging to

[5] P. 113. [6] *Ibid.*

different groups. The primary use of *same* or *identical* in connection with attributes is in the case where an object is viewed continuously for a time by an observer who perceives a certain attribute of that object to undergo no change—to be the *same* at the end as at the beginning of the observation. It is in this primary sense of "same" that we speak of the color of an object *remaining the same.*[7] Quite a different case however is at hand when an observer compares two distinct bodies which are before him and decides that they are exactly alike in color, or compares two distinct groups of objects and decides that they are exactly alike (equal) as to number. Colloquially, it is true, "same" would be used here as well as in the previous case; the two bodies would be said to have the same color, and the two groups to contain the same number of objects, but is this colloquial use of "same" worthy of a philosopher? Is it at all suited to the requirements of an exact science? "Same" in its primary sense is used to express one set of facts concerning attributes; why should it be also used to express facts of entirely different character when there are at hand other words, *like* and *equal,* perfectly adapted to convey this second sense? To use "same" and "identical" in this sense is as absurd and misleading as it would be to call two houses exactly alike the same house.

It would be a great mistake to regard the distinction between identity and equality of numbers as a mere verbal subtlety. True, it is not of any moment so far as computation is concerned; it does not affect the compilation of

[7] Under this first head likewise comes the case in which sameness of attribute is asserted where the asserter has not given continuous attention to the object, having viewed it only at the beginning and at the end of an interval of time, but intends to assert that *if* the observation had been continuous no change would have been noted by the observer. A valid claim to classification under another head may however be granted to the case in which change takes place but the ultimate result is precisely the original state of affairs; where, for instance, a body changes color but finally takes on a color attribute exactly like the one it originally possessed—otherwise put, "returns to the same color."

the logarithmic tables used by the engineer or have any bearing on the numerical calculations by which an astronomer predicts an eclipse. But in the philosophy of mathematics the results of this distinction are far reaching. To begin with, it shows us that 1, 2, 3, etc. are general names like "man" and "animal," and not individual names like "Socrates" and "Plato." Mr. Russell's assertion: "It is plain that we cannot take the number 1 itself twice over, for there is one number one and there are not two instances of it,"[8] is quite untenable. Each of the names 1, 2, 3, etc. is a class name belonging to a class containing many numbers, and we may legitimately speak of a one, a two, a three, etc. instead of adhering to the customary locution which omits the article. In none of these classes, which may most aptly be called *value classes,* is any member identical with another member; thus no three is the same as any other three, though both have the same class name, just as both Socrates and Plato belong to the same class, *man,* and alike have "man" as class name.[9]

Since numerals are general names, it follows that such an equation as $5 = 3 + 2$ is not a singular proposition analogous to "Plato was a contemporary of Socrates," but is a universal proposition analogous to "Every man is an animal." It is an assertion about every five, but should not be read: "Every five is equal to every sum of a three plus a two," for each sum of a three and a two is a five, and though equal to every other five cannot be equal to itself. We must read the equation: "Every five is equal to each sum of a three plus a two unless this sum is itself the five in question," or, better, recognize plainly that the so-called

[8] P. 118.

[9] A vague appreciation of the distinction which ought to be drawn between identity and the belonging to the same class appears in the mathematical use of the word *value.* Mathematicians sometimes speak of two numbers as having the same value; a useful and convenient phraseology if "having the same value" means, not identical, but belonging to the same class, while it is a quite inexcusable circumlocution if what be meant is merely that the "two" numbers are identical—are not two numbers but one and the same number.

"sign of equality" does not concern equality alone but has identity as an alternative possibility, and read our equation as "Every five is equal to or identical with each sum of a three plus a two." That =, as used in mathematics, has commonly two alternatives in view seems to have escaped the eyes of mathematicians. Usually it is read as "equals"; Cayley defines an equation to be "an expression or statement of the equality of two quantities."[10] Schroeder however says that "If a and b are any two names for the same number, we write $a = b$. A proposition of this kind is called an equation."[11] According to this, an equation would always have identity in view, and = would never concern equality at all! Weber is likewise wrong in his definition, telling us that an equation is "a proposition which expresses that a symbol a has the same significance as another symbol b, which we express in mathematical symbolism $a = b$."[12] For, to take the above case of $5 = 3 + 2$, it is not true that 5 has the same significance as $3 + 2$ any more than man has the same significance as mathematician. Every sum of a three plus a two is a five, but not every five has been brought into existence by the addition of a two to a three. Recognition of the true doctrine of number will be found to throw a much-needed light, not only upon the interpretation of equations, but also upon many other matters that mathematics has hitherto left in obscurity. We cannot however stop to dwell on the various ramifications of this doctrine, but must pass on to a further consideration of Mr. Russell's philosophy.

Mr. Russell decides that two groups ("classes") have "the same number" when their members can be correlated in a one-to-one relation, and so defines a one-to-one relation as to enable him to include even the case of groups which comprise nothing at all and give rise to the number zero.

[10] *Collected Mathematical Papers,* Vol. II, Art. "Equation."
[11] *Lehrbuch der Arithmetik und Algebra,* Vol. I, p. 23.
[12] *Encyklopädie der elementaren Algebra und Analyse,* p. 17.

He is not satisfied however to rest here, or with the dictum of "Peano and common sense"[13] that when there subsists such a relation (a relation specified as reflexive, symmetrical and transitive) the two groups have a common property called their number. This definition of numbers "by abstraction" is inadequate, he holds, because nothing is laid down by it which would logically bar there being common to the groups many different properties each answering the description, and thus a number is not by the definition uniquely distinguished among the various properties that groups may have in common. Mr. Russell prefers to give what he calls a nominal definition. Premising first that two groups are to be termed *similar* if they can have their objects put into a one-to-one correspondence, and that a group is to be regarded as similar to itself, he defines the number of a group ("class") as "the class of all classes similar to the given class."[14] This is assuredly the most remarkable definition of a number that has ever been penned. It is as though one would define whiteness as the class of all white objects. Mr. Russell himself, though he characterizes it as "an irreproachable definition of the number of a class in purely logical terms,"[14] admits that his definition appears at first sight to be a wholly indefensible paradox, and his attempt to defend it puts it in no more favorable light. He informs us that "when we remember that a class-concept is not itself a collection, but a property by which a collection is defined, we see that if we define the number as the class-concept, not the class, a number is really defined as a common property of a set of similar classes and of nothing else,"[14] but, even were it true that a number was such a property, this contention would be of no avail to palliate the faults of his definition in which the number *is* defined as the class.[15]

[13] P. 114. [14] P. 115.

[15] On page 131 he tells us that "a class cannot be identified with its class-

What does Mr. Russell really mean? On careful consideration we are impelled to conclude that he is merely indulging in what seems to be his favorite vice—confusion between matters that are in fact quite distinct. As justification of his definition, he tells us that such a word as *couple* "obviously does denote a class of classes." The true facts are that "couple" is a class name, and the class to which it belongs is composed of groups. A couple however is not the class of these groups—it is not the totality of couples. If Mr. Russell wished to define the name *totality of couples* or *all couples* his definition of a number would not be inappropriate. But the totality of couples is not a number.[16] A couple taken alone may be termed a number: a concrete number whose number attribute is an abstract number, a two. Mr. Russell makes however no distinction between concrete numbers and abstract numbers; between a group of objects and the number attribute which belongs to that group (and which for distinctiveness had best be called a *natural number*). He seems on the one hand to think that the definition by abstraction, which defines a number as a property common to certain groups, has reference to precisely the same sort of numbers as a definition framed for such numbers as a couple or a trio, while on the other hand he apparently labors under the delusion that a couple is the same thing as the totality of all couples, a trio the same thing as the totality of all trios, etc. He would not, we presume, contend that a soldier is the same thing as a regiment, but he takes a stand which is just as untenable.

Before going any further into questions that belong to mathematics, properly speaking, we must turn back to

concept." We need hardly say that in describing a class-concept as a *property* Mr. Russell is regarding concepts in a light hitherto unknown to philosophy.

[16] At least it is not such a number (a couple) as Mr. Russell has in view. Of course, if the totality of couples be taken as a group whose members are couples, this group, which will comprise millions of members, has just as much right to be regarded as a concrete number as a group composed of two individual members.

consider Mr. Russell's treatment of certain matters that are purely philosophical. Let us begin with what he calls *terms*. "Whatever may be an object of thought," says Mr. Russell, "or may occur in any true or false proposition, or can be counted as *one*, I call a *term*. This then is the widest word in the philosophical vocabulary. I shall use as synonymous with it the words unit, individual, and entity. The first two emphasize the fact that every term is *one*, while the third is derived from the fact that every term has being, i. e., *is* in some sense. A man, a moment, a class, a relation, a chimera, or any thing else that can be mentioned, is sure to be a term; and to deny that such and such a thing is a term must always be false."[17] This "widest word in the philosophical vocabulary" is not however really the widest, it seems, for only twelve pages later Mr. Russell tells us in an inobtrusive note: "I shall use the word *object* in a wider sense than *term*, to cover both singular and plural, and also cases of ambiguity, such as 'a man.' The fact that a word can be framed with a wider meaning than *term* raises grave logical problems." This retraction of what was first said, coming so soon, does not tend to make us believe that Mr. Russell's original remarks concerning "terms" were based upon long and profound thought. And in fact an examination shows Mr. Russell's view of the matter to be very far from what may be demanded of a philosopher.

To survey the question properly we had best begin with names, or rather with substantive words and phrases, and these for purposes of philosophy we may primarily divide into three classes. First come such as are absolutely meaningless, the word *blictri* being the classical example of nouns of this type. Second come substantives so defined as to connote contradictory attributes; as examples we may cite the phrases "honest thief" and "chaste prostitute."

[17] P. 43.

Such a substantive (unless taken in a non-natural sense) cannot be the name of an object of thought, but it ought not to be regarded as entirely meaningless and might conveniently be spoken of as the name of a chimera. Third come names of objects, substantives having meanings attached to them which do not involve the connoting of contradictory attributes. A conception of an object is, of course, itself an object, and likewise the name of an object is an object which by an exceptional use of language (a *suppositio materialis*) may denote itself instead of the object or objects it ordinarily denotes.[18] There is no such object as a chimera (as we propose to use that word), for to say a substantive is the name of a chimera is to assert that there can be no corresponding object of thought. But the name of a chimera, and even a meaningless substantive, and in general every word or phrase, is an object. One of the first steps in philosophy is to distinguish carefully between a name, a conception corresponding to a name, and an object denoted by a name; the last being in exceptional cases the name itself or another name. In framing a philosophical nomenclature one should do all in his power to enforce these distinctions, but it is not too

[18] The distinction between the primary use of a word or phrase and its use in a *suppositio materialis* is quite ancient, dating back to the medieval logicians. Mr. Russell however seems to be serenely unaware of any such distinction, and by ignoring it he is enabled to put forth an argument that must be characterized as only worthy of a schoolboy. He says (p. 48): "It is plain, to begin with, that the concept which occurs in the verbal noun is the very same as that which occurs as verb. This results from the previous argument, that every constituent of every proposition must, on penalty of self-contradiction, be capable of being made a logical subject. If we say '*kills* does not mean the same as *to kill*,' we have already made *kills* a subject, and we cannot say that the concept expressed by the word *kills* cannot be made a subject." Here Mr. Russell, in attempting to show that a verb such as "kills" and a verbal noun such as "to kill" have precisely the same meaning, seeks support in the absurd contention that both words are alike subjicible. The facts are, of course, that "kills" or any other word or phrase can be made a subject by a *suppositio materialis,* but when we consider the *primary* uses of words and phrases there is a clear demarcation between those which can and those which cannot be made logical subjects. In this use, which is the only one relevant to Mr. Russells' argument, "kills" is not, while "to kill" is, subjicible. And the sentence "*kills* does not mean the same as *to kill*," though making a statement about the primary uses of "kills" and "to kill," is not itself a proposition in which these are given their primary uses, but one in which "kills" and "to kill" each occur in a *suppositio materialis.*

much to say that Mr. Russell, in his nomenclature, gives the impression of being at great pains to obscure them. His use of "term" is a case in point. A philosopher need pay little heed to the colloquial uses of this word, and he may likewise disregard certain authorized applications of it that are not very common. But in logic and mathematics there are well-established uses of "term" which a writer on the philosophy of mathematics should take into account before assigning a new significance to it. In logic a term is simply a class name; thus "man" or "men" is a term, while the phrases "every man" and "some men" are names but not terms. In mathematics a term is sometimes a name; thus a term of a polynomial is an algebraic expression. The word is however also used in connection with series, and here a term is not a name at all, but is a number or other quantity.[19] These meanings of "term" are entirely disregarded in the nomenclature put forward by Mr. Russell. He adopts none of them, but deliberately tears the word from its accepted logical and mathematical uses. Although there is already available for his purpose a suitable name "individual" (or "individual object") he wantonly disregards the law of lexicological economy, and makes "term" synonymous with "individual" and two other words besides. And this is done in a work dealing with logic and mathematics, where there is urgent need for the use of "term" in its proper senses! Mr. Russell makes no attempt to furnish a new word to be used in designating logical terms, nor does he provide us with a specific title for the mathematical terms of either series or polynomials. In all three cases he leaves us in the lurch, and in mathematics, no less than in logic, the adoption of Mr. Russell's terminology would put a great hindrance in the way of precision of thought and speech.

[19] We must warn the reader that we are here not using "quantity" in a sense of which Mr. Russell would approve. He would not call a number a quantity.

We hold, then, that philosophical inquiry has its interests best subserved by using *individual* or *individual object* where Mr. Russell prescribes the use of "term." To use "unit" in Mr. Russell's sense cannot be deemed correct, for an individual is not taken as unit in every discussion in which it enters. The fourth synonym, "entity," is as objectionable as "term," just for the very reason that its use implies every object of thought to have existence "in some sense." Or rather, as Mr. Russell himself would put it, not "existence," but "being," for he draws a distinction between the two. Speaking of any pair of "terms," A and B, he says they "need not exist, but must, like any thing which can be mentioned, have Being. The distinction of Being and existence is important, and is well illustrated by the process of counting. What can be counted must be something and must certainly *be,* though it need by no means be possessed of the further privilege of existence. Thus what we demand of the terms of our collection is merely that each should be an entity."[20] In emblazoning the word "Being" with an initial capital letter, Mr. Russell would seem to imply that this word marked something of great importance. Yet in truth the basis for ascribing Being to "anything which can be mentioned" and to "whatever can be counted" is just one insignificant fact: the fact that the name of anything which can be mentioned is subjicible, forming a sentence when some set of words beginning with "is" or "is not" is put after it; in other words, by conjoining some predicate to this name the object of thought it represents can always be said to be or not to be something. And it surely cannot be held that the mere subjicibility of a name confers, on the object this represents, a mysterious something called "Being."[21] Are

[20] P. 71.

[21] The question of existential import of propositions (which however Mr. Russell does not appear at all to have in view) brings up other considerations. It can be plausibly contended that when we enunciate an affirmative propo-

we to take purely verbal reasons for our ground, and say that the sea-serpent being inexistent, and the author of the *Principles of Mathematics* being existent, both must be put under a common category of objects possessing Being? No advantages attend this course, and there is no reason why we should adopt it. It would substantially be arbitrarily agreeing to use "has Being" in the sense of "can be mentioned." And clearly the statement that "Such and such an object of thought has Being" is utterly futile if it merely means, as it does in Mr. Russell's phraseology, that the object of thought can have a name given to it. If such modes of speech as "has being," "is an entity," etc., are to convey anything worth putting into words we must have a dichotomization of objects of thought into those that have being and those that do not—into entities and non-entities. But apart from the dichotomization marked by the names "existent objects" and "inexistent objects" there seems to be none in connection with which the words "being" and "entity" can be conveniently used. So these words are best made synonymous respectively with "existence" and "existing object." Any object of thought can, of course, be spoken of as having existence in a hypothetical universe, and in talking of that universe we can call the object an entity; but we must not on this account call such an object an entity when there is under discussion any other universe (either the actual one or a new hypothetical universe). The right to be designated as an entity is given, and given only, by existence in the universe under discussion. To take any other view would result in depriving us of a very useful

sition with a certain name as subject we thereby, in certain cases, assert the object to which this name refers to have existence. Indeed the doctrine that affirmative propositions have existential implications, but negative not, is a part of the Aristotelian logic—at least the canons of that logic will not all hold unless this be true of A, E, I and O. Evidently however reservations must be made for such propositions as "So and so is a nonentity," it being denied that the affirmative form here gives an implication of existence, or else propositions of this character must be ruled out of philosophical language entirely.

word, for we could then no longer mark out by the aid of "entity" the existent objects of a specified universe from the non-existent.

In classifying objects as entities and non-entities one has most frequently the actual universe in view. In any event however it is from a cross classification that we obtain the two classes: individual objects and collections of objects. Whether an object is to be regarded as individual or as a collection depends to some extent upon the exigencies of the moment. Thus it is often convenient to take a collection of soldiers collectively as an individual regiment or as an individual army. An object again may be a perception (under which head we would put all states of consciousness) or an object whose existence is founded on a perception or a more or less complicated set of perceptions. Under this second head come sounds (and hence spoken syllables, words and sentences), sights (and hence written letters, words and sentences), etc. Here also come all bodies and the attributes of bodies as well as various other objects which are greater removes from their elemental perceptions. Conceptions are a species of perceptions. A name may denote a conception, and moreover a name which does not do this may have a conception corresponding to it and to the object it denotes. With each type of names that do not denote conceptions there arises a question as to what sort of conceptions, if any, corresponds to names of this type, and the debate over such a problem has not seldom given rise to a discussion classical in philosophical history. For instance, one school of philosophers would say that when a man speaks of any particular triangle he has in his mind a conception corresponding to this triangle and to the individual name that denotes it, and that moreover he may have a conception of a triangle that is "neither oblique nor rectangle, neither equilateral, equicrural nor scalenon, but all and none of these at once" corresponding to the general class name *triangle*. Another school, while admitting the existence of conceptions corresponding to proper individual names (i. e., names put forward as each denoting a single object), even when such a name is the name of a class (a collection which is here taken collectively as an individual), would deny altogether that a general name could have any conception corresponding to it; one might have, they would say, a conception of a particular triangle, or of a collection comprising many triangles, but none of triangles in general. Mr. Russell does not stop to take up any such question, but plunges at once into a classification of individual objects ("terms") which is replete with confusion. "Among terms," says Mr. Russell, "it is possible to distinguish two kinds, which I shall call respectively *things* and *concepts*. The former are the terms indicated by proper names, the latter those indicated by all other words. Here proper names are to be understood in a somewhat wider sense than is usual, and things also are to be understood as embracing all particular points and instants, and many other entities not commonly called things. Among concepts, again, two kinds at least must be distinguished, namely those indicated by adjectives and those indicated by verbs. The former will often be called predicates or class-concepts; the latter are always or almost always relations."[22] Here the name "adjective" would seem to be applied to *words* of certain species, but just two pages previous we find Mr. Russell states: "What we wish to obtain is a classification, not of words, but of ideas; I shall therefore call adjectives or predicates all notions which are capable of being such, even in a form in which grammar would call them substantives." Any comment on the confusion here exhibited between language and what language conveys would be superfluous. Such confusion is

[22] P. 44.

habitual with the author of the *Principles of Mathematics*; indeed we might say it is the corner-stone of his system of "philosophy."

Searching for more light upon what Mr. Russell means by "concept," two remarkable discoveries will be made by the patient reader: first, that concepts *occur in propositions*; second, that concepts *denote*. "A concept *denotes* when, if it occurs in a proposition, the proposition is not about the concept, but about a term connected in a certain peculiar way with the concept. If I say 'I met a man' the proposition is not about *a man*: this is a concept which does not walk the streets, but lives in the shadowy limbo of the logic-books. What I met was a thing, not a concept, an actual man."[23] The old philosophical view was that a concept was a state of consciousness. Mr. Russell's concepts, it seems, are to be found, not in the mind, but in the "shadowy limbo of the logic-books." In the logic-books themselves we can find nothing but words. Since Mr. Russell declares that "a proposition, unless it happens to be linguistic, does not itself contain words: it contains the entities indicated by words,"[24] and as he puts *word* and *concept* in antithesis, saying that we "employ words as symbols for concepts,"[25] he apparently does not regard a concept as a word or set of words. Had we been able to find any "shadowy limbo" in the neighborhood of the logic-books on our shelves we should have bravely ventured into it, and gone through those regions where that dreadful monstrosity, Symbolic Logic, "has its lair,"[26] seeking to encounter Mr. Russell's mysterious concepts, even at the peril of finding them to be Jabberwocks. But the shadowy limbo is not to be found, and filled with disap-

[23] P. 53. On this page *a man*, we are told, is a "concept," but on page 54 Mr. Russell informs us that "*A man*, we shall find, is neither a concept nor a term"! Here he not merely contradicts his statement on the previous page, but puts "concept" and "term" in an antithesis which is assuredly not in accord with his view that concepts are a species of terms.

[24] P. 47. [25] P. 53. [26] P. 66.

pointment we are compelled to abandon the hope of thus ascertaining what Mr. Russell means. At all events a concept, whatever that may be, can "occur in a proposition."

The significance Mr. Russell gives to "proposition" goes hand in hand with his peculiar use of "term." He would base a formal definition of the former word upon the motion of implication: "It may be observed that, although implication is indefinable, *proposition* can be defined. Every proposition implies itself, and whatever is not a proposition implies nothing. Hence to say '*p* is a proposition' is equivalent to saying '*p* implies *p*'; and this equivalence may be used to define propositions."[27] A less technical presentation of Mr. Russell's view is his statement that "A proposition, we may say, is anything that is true or that is false."[28] He also tells us that "propositions are commonly regarded as (1) true or false, (2) mental. Holding as I do that what is true or false is not generally mental, I require a name for the true or false as such, and this name can scarcely be other than *proposition*."[29] Most students of philosophy will be inclined to demur at the remark that propositions are commonly regarded as mental. Rather, they will say, the common practice is to regard a proposition as a written or spoken sentence, corresponding to which there may be a mental *judgment*. Here however this question is of no great importance; we are concerned, not with the practice that is prevalent, but with Mr. Russell's alone. As we have seen, Mr. Russell appears to accept "linguistic propositions" only as an unimportant species of the genus propositions, and when he speaks of propositions not mental he does not seem to have these specifically in view. Given a written or spoken sentence concerning Socrates, Mr. Russell would not ordinarily direct his attention to this sentence in considering what he

[27] P. 66 [28] P. 15. [29] P. ix.

calls the proposition. In the "proposition" which Mr. Russell would ordinarily have in view there occurs, Mr. Russell would say, Socrates himself, and not merely the name of Socrates.[30] *True proposition,* then, in Mr. Russell's sense would seem to mean *fact.* But while one can concede that John Smith may be intelligibly said to occur in the fact or state of affairs described by the sentence, "John Smith is chopping wood," when this sentence is true, it is not easy to see how John Smith (or Socrates) himself can "occur" in anything at all corresponding to a false statement about him. If Mr. Bertrand Russell, by some esoteric method, has discovered that Socrates himself, not merely the name or conception of Socrates, actually occurs in *something* corresponding to each false statement about Socrates, then it is most unfortunate that Mr. Russell's investigations have not enabled him to inform his readers precisely what this something is. And we must record our opinion that Mr. Russell's use of "proposition" is well fitted for only one purpose: the promoting a confusion between a sentence and the fact or fancy with which that sentence is conversant, just as his use of "term" is eminently adapted to create confusion between a name and what that name denotes.

Let us now return to the doctrines expounded by Mr. Russell in matters really mathematical. Part III of his work is devoted to "Quantity." The sense in which he uses this word is somewhat peculiar. He does not take it in what is probably its most suitable use, viz., its use as a generic name applicable at once to concrete numbers, to such denominate numbers as lengths, weights, areas, vol-

[30] We have already cited Mr. Russell's statement that "a proposition, unless it happens to be linguistic, does not itself contain words: it contains the entities indicated by words." On the same page he refers to "the confusion," which he says arises from "the notion that *words* occur in propositions, which in turn is due to the notion that propositions are essentially mental and are to be identified with cognitions." And on page 45 he tells us that "Socrates is a thing, because Socrates can never occur otherwise than as a term in a proposition."

umes, etc., and to the natural numbers and the other abstract quantities analogous to these (e. g., those of such values as o, ½, π, −1, $+\sqrt{-1}$, etc.). On the contrary he puts "number" and "quantity" in antithesis, and speaks of "applying numbers to quantities."[31] He also puts an antithesis between "quantity" and "magnitude." "An actual foot rule," he tells us, "is a quantity; its length is a magnitude....when two quantities are equal they have the *same* magnitude."[32] Here we see again in evidence the blunder of thinking that like attributes are identical; that, for example, two bodies equal in length have the same length. Indeed it is upon this blunder that Mr. Russell founds his criterion for distinguishing between quantities and magnitudes. "A quantity is anything which is capable of quantitative equality to something else." "A magnitude....is to be defined as anything which is greater or less than something else." And there is, Mr. Russell holds, "reason to think....that what can be greater or less than some term can never be equal to any term whatever, and *vice versa.*"

With number attributes, as we have seen, Mr. Russell does not even put the question whether what are colloquially called the same attribute common to different groups ought not more properly to be regarded as like but different attributes. With "magnitudes" however he does give some attention to what he calls "the relative theory" which denies that there is any such thing as "a magnitude shared by equal quantities."[33] His "refutation" of this theory is worthy of note. He lays down eight indemonstrable axioms which he says the theory obliges us to assume, one of these

[31] P. 157. He tells us, page 159, that "In fixing the meaning of such a term as *quantity* or *magnitude,* one is faced with the difficulty that however one may define the word, one must appear to depart from usage." This is one of the many instances in which he slips away from the meaning he nominally gives "term," and uses the word in the customary logical sense.

[32] P. 159. On page 165 he tells us that "all magnitudes are simple concepts."

[33] P. 162.

axioms affirming that, whenever A is a quantity, "A being given, there is always a B [likewise a quantity] which may be identical with A, such that A = B," or, as he also puts it, "If A be a quantity, then A = A." He tells us that "These axioms, it will be observed, lead to the conclusion that, in any proposition asserting equality, excess, or defect, an equal quantity may be substituted anywhere without affecting the truth or falsity of the proposition. Further the proposition A = A is an essential part of the theory. Now the first of these facts strongly suggests that what is relevant in quantitative propositions is not the actual quantity, but some property which it shares with other equal quantities. And this suggestion is almost demonstrated by the second fact A = A. For it may be laid down that the only unanalyzable symmetrical and transitive relation which a term can have to itself is identity, if this indeed be a relation."[34] And Mr. Russell goes on to show—to his own satisfaction, though to us his argument is by no means cogent—that the admission of equality as a symmetrical transitive relation which an individual object ("term") can have to itself leads to a theory of magnitude which is not the "relative theory" at all, but the "absolute theory" that he himself upholds. We shall not here consider whether the first "fact" is really a fact—whether so broad a statement as to the substitution of [symbols of] equals can properly be made in an algebra developed on a philosophical basis. For in any event we are quite unable to see that this "first fact" can give the suggestion which Mr. Russell accredits to it. And as for the "second fact," on which Mr. Russell relies for the definite refutation of the "relative theory": the necessity in that theory for a quantity to be equal to itself, this may really be essential to the theory elaborated by Mr. Russell's fancy as a straw man for him to overthrow. But it cer-

[34] P. 163.

tainly is not the case that an algebra sanctioned by a true philosophy will ever affirm A to equal A. This affirmation is seen not to express a fact at all on making the proper distinction between equality and identity, and recognizing that the mathematical character = does not always concern true equality, but has sometimes reference to identity. It is absurd to say that because mathematicians write A = A and read this "A equals A," a quantity must necessarily be equal to itself. A philosopher ought not to take the customs of mathematical symbolism as foundation for his doctrines.

Another statement of Mr. Russell's bearing on the import of = is of interest enough to cite here. "Among magnitudes, equality...has an absolutely rigid and unique meaning: it applies only to quantities, and means that they have the *same* magnitude.... Among numbers....there is no such thing as equality. There is identity, and there is the relation which is usually expressed by the sign of equality, as in the equation $2 \times 3 = 6$. This relation had puzzled those who endeavored to philosophize about arithmetic, until it was explained by Professor Peano. When one term of the equation is a single number, while the other is an expression composed of two or more numbers, the equation expresses the fact that the class defined by the expression contains only one term, which is the single number on the other side of the equation."[35] As a matter of fact, the explanation which Mr. Russell ascribes to Professor Peano is wholly erroneous. The numeral 6 does not denote a single number: it denotes many numbers; all

[35] P. 341. With his habitual confusion of thought and speech, Mr. Russell here leaves us in doubt as to whether the equation is a sentence written symbolically with numeral expressions as the two members, or whether it is something that the sentence merely serves to express, its "terms" being what the members of the sentence represent. Indeed his words might be fairly construed to imply that the equation is made up of a number (be it noted that he does not say numeral or symbol of a number) on one side and a mere expression on the other, the expression in some strange way being "composed of two or more numbers"!

those comprised in the value class of the sixes. Likewise the expression 2×3 denotes a multitude of numbers, all of which are sixes, but not all sixes are denoted by this expression. For not every six is the result of an operation of multiplying a three by a two, and only the numbers resulting from such operations are entitled to be designated by the expression 2×3. And $2 \times 3 = 6$ means: Every product of a two into a three is equal to or identical with every six (i. e., is equal to every six save that with which it is identical). So here = has reference to both equality and identity.

From quantities[36] we may proceed to the consideration of variables. The conception of a variable is a most important one in mathematics, and can be traced back to the attempts made by Archimedes and other Greek mathematicians at the rectification and the quadrature of circles. In this work it was essential to conceive of a variable and the limit which the latter approached, though it was not until many centuries later that "variable" or any equivalent name was heard of in mathematics. The use of the word does not date back to much before the time of Newton, and the earlier definitions all ascribed to a variable the character of a quantity, quantities being classified as constants and variables. Definitions of this type are by no means obsolete. Thus in a work on differential and integral calculus, published not very many years ago under the auspices of Professor Peano, we are told that "In the questions considered there may appear quantities to which determined and fixed values are supposed to be attributed, and these are called constants, and other quantities supposed to be able to assume diverse values, and these are called variables."[37] An examination however of the vari-

[36] The word "quantity" we shall hereafter use, not in Mr. Russell's sense, but in what we esteem to be the proper one.

[37] *Calcolo Differenziale e principii di Calcolo Integrale* by A. Genocchi, "Publicato con aggiunto dal Dr. Giuseppe Peano."

ables that mathematics takes within its scope shows that such a definition is quite unsuitable. The question as to whether a variable can properly be termed a quantity is closely related to the problem of sameness and similarity of attributes, possessed by different groups or different individuals, which arises in connection with the natural numbers and other quantitative attributes (e. g., lengths, weights, volumes, areas, etc.). We decided in the foregoing pages that two groups alike in number ought not to be said to have the *same* number, but to have different though *equal* numbers, and that two bodies alike in length ought not to be said to have the *same* length, but to have different though *equal* lengths. And so with weights, volumes, areas, etc.

Suppose now that there is only a single body in view, and that a change takes place in reference to one or more attributes. Suppose, for instance, that a bar of metal is heated, and its length changes from 1000 centimeters to 1020 centimeters, while its color changes from black to red. Are the facts well expressed by saying the bar possesses the "same" length and the "same" color as before? If the old definition of variable is to be taken as criterion, we must answer in the affirmative as regards the length at least. For the length of the bar during the change is what would be called a *variable* in mathematics, and the definition in question tells us a variable is a quantity—that is, *one* quantity. And should we take a like ground in reference to color attributes we must say that the manifold colors which appear throughout the change are a color, that is, *one* color. If however we refuse to be bound by an ancient definition, and prefer the only course sanctioned by a sound philosophy—that of so using language as to mark the distinctions to which our senses testify, then we must recognize that such a use of "same," implying identity where there is diversity, is even more repugnant than its application in the sense of equal. And we see that when an object initially possesses a certain attribute and undergoes a change with respect to this attribute, we must then regard as a distinct and separate attribute each stage of the process of change.[38] Such a set of attributes may together constitute a variable, and under this description come most of the variables of physical science. We may have a body with variable velocity—a type of variable which gave frequent opportunity for the exercise of Newton's genius—a body of gas with variable temperature, under variable pressure and with variable volume. We cannot say that any of these variables are quantities unless we wish our language to be an impediment, instead of an aid, to exact thinking.

Even stronger do we find our case when we turn to geometry, and consider the type of variable that first appears in history. Archimedes, in striving to rectify a circle, inscribed in it first an equilateral triangle, then a regular hexagon, then a regular dodecahedron, etc. The perimeters of the inscribed polygons here constituted a variable whose limit was the circumference of the circle, while the areas of the polygons constituted a variable whose limit was the area of the circle. With what show of reason can we say that the perimeter of a triangle is one and the same quantity—one and the same perimeter—as the longer perimeter of a hexagon? How are we justified in saying that the area of a triangle and the area of a much larger ninety-six-sided figure are the same quantity? And yet we must make these assertions if we acknowledge that a

[38] The stages recognized by our naked organs of sense are comparatively few. The various instruments at our disposal for assisting the senses enable us greatly to increase the number of stages that can be deliminated, but this number always remains finite. To assume that a succession of suitable instruments would, if they were at hand, enable us to keep up a continual increase *ad infinitum* in the number of stages detected, and hence to ascribe innumerable stages to the change where we really do not observe so many (which is in effect what is usually done in scientific work) is to adopt a hypothesis, legitimate enough as such, but not to be taken as anything more than a hypothesis.

variable is a quantity. Nor is it only with circles that such difficulties arise. The quadrature (or rectification) of any curvilinear figure by the methods of the modern integral calculus presents similar difficulties. We have a set of rectilinear figures, no two alike, the areas of which (or the lengths of certain lines on which) constitute a variable the limit of which is sought. Surely these considerations are overwhelming against the doctrine which would ascribe to a variable the character of a quantity, and there is no recourse save to abandon that doctrine completely.

A variable, then, is not a quantity, but is constituted by a set of quantities, and the quantities in the set may be natural numbers or other quantities of the same sort, or be concrete quantities, or be such denominate quantities as lengths, areas, etc., It remains for us to ascertain the essential characteristics of such a set, for sets of quantities which do not constitute variables also come under consideration in mathematics. Now the characteristic investigations in which variables appear in mathematics are undoubtedly those where limits are concerned. And it is to be noted that a limit (which is a quantity that may or may not itself belong to the variable) pertains, not to any one quantity in the variable taken separately, but either to the whole set of quantities or to a part of that set so extensive as to comprise innumerable quantities. When it is said that the variable x approaches the limit l, it is not meant that any quantity of x approaches l; such a statement would be utterly meaningless. If, for instance, we have a variable composed of unique representatives of the values 1, 1½, 1¾, 1⅞, etc. arranged in the order here given, then this variable approaches as limit a quantity of value two (a limit which is in this case not in the variable) but it would be absurd to speak of the 1 or of the 1½, or of any other quantity of the variable as approaching a limit.

Again a variable composed of unique representatives of all real abstract values from 1 to 3 arranged in order of value first approaches a limit of value two (which is here in the variable), then attains it, and finally recedes from it, but we cannot say that any separate quantity of the variable approaches or recedes from this or any other limit. A variable may approach a limit throughout its whole extent or throughout only a portion of its range, but in no event can a quantity of the variable be said to approach a limit. And we may lay down that the purpose of taking a set of quantities together as constituting a variable is to investigate matters that concern the mutual relations between quantities of the set, this being the case whether a limit is or is not concerned. Here then is found the essential characteristic of the set of quantities which constitutes a variable: the purpose for which it is formed. There is a sharp contrast in this respect between the sets of quantities comprised in a variable and other sets of quantities which appear in mathematics. Take, for example, the value classes. When we form a value class, and give it a class name, as when we group together all the twos, and provide the class name "two," our purpose is to investigate questions and state propositions concerning every two taken separately or concerning each of some of the twos. When we say $2 + 3 = 5$, we assert that every two plus any three is equal to or identical with every five, an assertion wholly unlike that made in "The variable x approaches the limit l."

On first thought it might appear appropriate to specify, as another distinguishing feature of variables, the taking of diverse values. It seems only natural to say that there must be variation of value in a variable. But to take etymology as decisive in laying down a definition is the method of the pseudo-scientiest, not that of the really scientific investigator. On inquiry into the matter we indeed find that variation is not always at hand. Mathematicians have even coined a specific name, *tratto d'invariabilita* in Italian, *Invariabilitätszug* in German, to designate a portion of a variable (here the dependent variable of a functional relation) in which there is conformity to a single value, and not variation. And moreover there are variables with which variation of value is everywhere lacking. For in analytical geometry the mathematician finds it convenient to regard the abscissas of a line parallel to the y axis (or the ordinates of a line parallel to the x axis) as constituting a variable, though obviously in such a variable all the quantities are of a single value.

While in many mathematical works the ancient definition of variable still lingers on, a new type of definition is beginning to appear in some of the more modern treatises. The innovation is however unobtrusively set down without any word to show that a conception of a variable is being put forth which is different from that embodied in the old definitions. These new definitions describe a variable as a symbol. Thus in that most authoritative of mathematical works, the *Encyklopädie der mathematischen Wissenschaften,* Professor Pringsheim, in his article on the *Grundlagen der allgemeinen Funktionenlehre*, lays down that "By a real variable is to be understood a *symbol,* usually one of the letters of the alphabet, to which is assigned successive different number-values (for example, all possible between two fixed number-values, all rational, all integral)."[39] The only way in which this definition has reference to real variables as opposed to variables in general, is by the use of "number-values" (i. e., real values[40]) instead of simply "values." So in Pringsheim's view a variable would seem to be essentially a symbol to which there are assigned in succession various different

[39] Vol. II, Part I, p. 8.

[40] "Numerical value" would of course not be a correct translation of *Zahlenwerte,* though this is sometimes so translated when used in just the sense taken for it by Pringsheim.

values. To those who are satisfied to accept manipulation of symbols as the Ultima Thule of mathematics, defining a variable as a symbol will doubtless be satisfactory. Such a course produces quite a different impression however upon those who would no more take as the subject matter of mathematics the words and symbols it makes use of than they would rest satisfied with a science of botany which studied such "words" as *coniferae and cruciferae,* and did not investigate the objects these words stand for. Variables in mathematics are not symbols any more than numbers or other quantities are symbols. Variables and quantities are both things represented by symbols. Pringsheim's definition and others of the same type have really reference, not to variables, but to the names or symbols of variables. So construed they seem to mean that when and only when a symbol takes successively a number of different values (that is to say, denotes in succession quantities of these respective values) then that symbol is the symbol of a variable. How very remote this view is from the actual facts in the case is sufficiently obvious from the investigations into the constitution of variables that have been made in the foregoing paragraphs.[41] The most characteristic use of the name or symbol of a variable is, we have seen, not in propositions about the quantities of the variable taken individually, and in the characteristic use (e. g., when we say x approaches a limit) the symbol *does not take any value at all.* It is true that mathematics also sanctions using the symbol of a variable in quite another way—in the equations dealing with functional relations—but this latter use is by no means distinctive of the sym-

[41] One or two mathematicians cursorily define a variable as an *aggregate* of quantities, but go no further into the question of the characteristics of a variable, and say nothing of the distinctive way in which the name of a variable is used. Such a definition is not, on its face, so untenable as the quantity definitions or the symbol definitions, but we cannot regard it as entirely satisfactory. For a discussion of this matter however we must refer the reader to our forthcoming work: *Fundamental Conceptions of Modern Mathematics.*

bols of variables. And before we consider it we shall proceed to see what doctrine Mr. Russell holds as to the nature of variables.

In Mr. Russell's system variables are of prime importance. The reader is introduced to them at the very outset of the *Principles of Mathematics.* "Mathematical propositions," Mr. Russell says, "are not only characterized by the fact that they assert implications, but also by the fact that they contain *variables.*"[42] In his use of the term "variable" Mr. Russell is not content to abide by the ordinary mathematical customs, but seeks to give a much broader field to its application. "It is customary in mathematics to regard our variables as restricted to certain classes: in arithmetic, for instance, they are supposed to stand for numbers. But this only means that *if* they stand for numbers, they satisfy some formula, i. e., the hypothesis that they are numbers implies the formula. This, then, is what is really asserted, and in this proposition it is no longer necessary that our variables should be numbers: the implication holds equally when they are not so. Thus, for example, the proposition 'x and y are numbers implies $(x+y)^2 = x^2 + 2xy + y^2$' holds equally if for x and y we substitute Socrates and Plato. [It is necessary to suppose arithmetical addition and multiplication defined (as may easily be done) so that the above formula remains significant when x and y are not numbers]: both hypothesis and consequence in this case, will be false, but the implication will still be true. Thus in every proposition of pure mathematics, when fully stated, the variables have an absolutely unrestricted field: any conceivable entity may be substituted for any one of the variables without impairing the truth of our proposition."[43]

[42] P. 5.

[43] P. 6. It should be remembered that in Mr. Russell's view "propositions" are not sentences, and that in a proposition "occur," not names, but the things and concepts designated by names. Hence to substitute the entity Socrates

Even in ordinary mathematics Mr. Russell gives variables a rôle much more important than that usually assigned to them: "The variable is, from the formal standpoint, *the* characteristic notion of mathematics. Moreover it is *the* method of stating general theorems.... That the variable characterizes mathematics will be generally admitted, though it is not generally perceived to be present in elementary arithmetic. Elementary arithmetic, as taught to children, is characterized by the fact that the *numbers* occurring in it are constants; the answer to any schoolboy's sum is obtainable without propositions concerning *any* number. But the fact that this is the case can only be proved by the help of propositions about any number, and thus we are led from schoolboy's arithmetic to the arithmetic which uses letters for numbers and proves general theorems.... Now the difference consists simply in this, that our numbers have now become variables instead of being constants. We now prove theorems concerning *n*, not concerning 3 or 4 or any other particular number...Originally, no doubt, the variable was conceived dynamically, as something which changes with the lapse of time, or, as is said, as something which successively assumed all values of a certain class. This view cannot be too soon dismissed. If a theorem is proved concerning *n*, it must not be supposed that *n* is a kind of arithmetical Proteus, which is 1 on Sundays and 2 on Mondays, and so on. Nor must it be supposed that *n* simultaneously assumes all values. If *n* stands for any integer, we cannot say that *n* is 1, nor yet that it is 2, nor yet that it is any other particular number. In fact, *n* just denotes *any* number, and this is sometimes quite distinct from each and all of the numbers. It is not true that 1 is any number, though it is true that whatever holds of any number holds of 1. The variable,

for *x* in a proposition is not, it would seem, to substitute the *name Socrates* for the symbol *x*, but to actually take Socrates out of his grave, and put him, in some incomprehensible way, in the place of the object represented by *x*!

in short, requires the indefinable notion of *any*."[44] This "indefinable notion of *any*" is put by Mr. Russell in sharp contrast to the notions of "all" and of "every." "*All a*'s denotes a numerical conjunction.... The concept *all a*'s is a perfectly definite single concept, which denotes the terms of *a* taken altogether.... *Every a*, on the contrary, though it still denotes all the *a*'s, denotes them in a different way, i. e., severally instead of collectively. *Any a* denotes only one *a*, but it is wholly irrelevant which it denotes, and what is said will be equally true whichever it may be. Moreover *any a* denotes a variable *a*, that is, whatever particular *a* we may fasten upon, it is quite certain that *any a* does not denote that one; and yet of that one any proposition is true which is true of any *a*."[45]

Mr. Russell further tells us: "We may distinguish what may be called the true or formal variable from the restricted variable. *Any term* is a concept denoting the true variable; if *u* be a class not containing all terms, *any u* denotes a restricted variable. The terms included in the object denoted by the defining concept of a variable are called the *values* of the variable: thus every value of a variable is constant."[46]

Finally we are told what a variable is: "Thus *x* the variable is what is denoted by *any term*."[47] "Thus *x* is in some sense the object denoted by *any term*, yet this can hardly be strictly maintained, for different variables may occur in a proposition, yet the object denoted by *any term*, one would suppose, is unique. This however elicits a new point in the theory of denoting, namely that *any term* does not denote, properly speaking, an assemblage of terms, but denotes one term, only not one particular definite term. Thus *any term* denotes different terms in different places."[48] "The notion of the variable.....is exceedingly complicated. The *x* is not simply *any* term, but any term with a certain

[44] P. 90. [45] P. 58. [46] P. 91. [47] P. 6. [48] P. 94.

individuality; for if not, any two variables would be indistinguishable."[49]

Mr. Russell's extension of the word "variable" to cases where what are in question are not quantities is quite in line with his other innovations in terminology. At all of these we are inclined to demur. We shall not however dwell upon such matters here, but will restrict ourselves to inquiring whether Mr. Russell's doctrine, in its application to cases where quantities do happen to be concerned, conforms to the true theory of the variables met with in actual mathematical work. Now it is quite evident, on examining Mr. Russell's remarks, that his idea of a variable has not arisen from a systematic consideration of the variables of mathematics. Mr. Russell's conception of a variable is essentially an etymological one, and what he takes to be variables are not variables at all. We have shown that, with a variable, variation of a value is neither sufficient nor necessary. Mr. Russell however thinks that taking different values is the very essence of a variable. In this view, "If x and y are numbers, $(x+y)^2=x^2+2xy+y^2$" is a typical case of a proposition involving the symbols of variables. And he holds that whenever we formulate a proposition concerning n instead of merely concerning 1 or 2 or 3 or some other particular number then we are dealing with variables. The facts are, to begin with, that a proposition about what Mr. Russell calls a particular number, for example 3 in the equation $3+2=5$, is about a whole species of numbers—the value class of the threes, or rather it is about every number in this species taken individually. And when we go to a general theorem involving such a symbol as n we merely ascend to a genus comprising several (usually innumerable) value classes. When n is used in what Mr. Russell describes as a proposition about any number, it is a class name denoting every number of every

[49] P. 107.

value class whatsoever, and the propositions to which Mr. Russell refers as "about *any* number" may with perfect propriety be said to be about each and every number. Take, for instance, the equation $(n+1)(n-1) = n^2 - 1$. This affirms: *With every number whatsoever the sum of this number plus any one, multiplied into the difference of the same number minus any one, is equal to or identical with the remainder obtained by subtracting any one from the square of the number in question.* It is true that we can read the equation as a proposition in "any number" if we prefer to do so. We can render it: *The sum of any number plus any one, multiplied into the difference of the same number minus any one, is equal to or identical with the remainder obtained by subtracting any one from the square of the number in question.* But there is no diversity of import between this and the rendition first given. The "any" version and the "every" version have precisely the same meaning. The difference is not a philosophical one, but resides merely in the syntactical construction of the one sentence requiring "any" (or "each," which could just as well be used) while the syntax of the other permits the use of "every." In taking the curious view that a general theorem of arithmetic involving such a symbol as n is characterised by being "about *any* number," and in implying, as he does by the opposition in which he puts "any" and "every," that it is not about *every* number, Mr. Russell is propounding a doctrine which is utterly untenable. Between "any" and the n (or other symbol) of a general theorem there is not really the connection imagined by Mr. Russell, and the vague subtleties which fill several pages devoted to "any" in the *Principles of Mathematics* are beside the point. What connection there is lies between the symbol and the whole set of universal syncategorems,[50]

[50] We use "syncategorem" as the title of those words and phrases which are conjoined to class names to indicate the logical quantity. Sometimes "syn-

every, each, any, etc., and does not pertain to any one of the set to the exclusion of the rest. As regards the class to which such a symbol refers the theorem is universal—is a proposition in which the class name of that class is distributed—and if it is to be put into words some universal syncategorem must be conjoined to the class name to indicate the distribution. In the purely symbolic mode of expression sanctioned by mathematics there are however no characters representing syncategorems; these are always taken for granted, mathematics dealing so largely with generalities that whenever a formula occurs the tacit assumption is made that this must be universal with respect to every symbol involved. These symbols are class names to which syncategorems must be conjoined when we pass from formulas to equipollent sentences in which we retain the symbols but none of the signs or other characters of the originals. And thus the *n*, in a proposition about every number ("about *any* number," as Mr. Russell would put it), is a synonym of "number"; it is a class name for numbers of all species. Like other class names, it by itself denotes every member of its class, while when conjoined to a syncategorem every member is or is not denoted, according to whether the syncategorem is or is not universal. In the general theorems of mathematics, since a universal syncategorem is understood though not expressed, every member of the class, that is, every quantity (or every quantity of the type in question, e. g., every number) is denoted, and hence the symbol does simultaneously assume all values (or all values of the type), Mr. Russell to the contrary notwithstanding.

The confusion of such a symbol as Mr. Russell's *n*—a general symbol for quantities of many values—with the symbol of a variable is not peculiar to Mr. Russell, and

categorematic word or phrase" is used in a broader sense in which it applies also to certain words that appear as *parts* of class names, e. g., of, in, at.

seems to be largely due to a one-sided view of the symbol of a variable. There are in mathematics important propositions in which symbols of variables are used in a way which enables them to be construed as here denoting the quantities of variables, just as the class name belonging to a class of quantities denotes the quantities of that class. These propositions are the equations concerned with functional relations between two or more variables. Thus y and x being two variables, there might be a functional relation between these that would in mathematical symbolism be indicated by $y = x^2$, the significance of this equation being that a functional relation[51] subsists under which every quantity in the variable y which has a corresponding quantity in the variable x is equal to or identical with the square of the corresponding quantity in x. And if we choose, we may use the shorter phrase "every y"[52] instead of "every quantity in y," and say "every x" instead of "every quantity in x." With this mode of reading, if one considers only such equations and neglects the more characteristic use of the name or symbol of a variable, it is not surprising that he should confound the names of variables with ordinary class names. There is really an analogy between such a proposition as "Every y having an x corresponding to it is equal to or identical with the square of

[51] We hold that a functional relation between two variables is established whenever there is, first, correspondence between quantities of the two variables and, second, likeness in order of corresponding quantities. It is not essential that *every* quantity in either variable should have a corresponding quantity in the other. For a discussion of this matter we refer to the work already mentioned.

[52] Here y does take values. But the way in which it does so is not by having successive different values assigned to it as Pringsheim wishes us to believe. It does not assume the values represented in the variable *successively*; it takes all of them *simultaneously*. There may be consecution connected with a variable, but it is not a consecution of the times in which a symbol takes different values; it is a consecution in the order of arrangement of the quantities constituting the variable. For the quantities of the variable have commonly an arrangement in order—an arrangement which with some variables is immutable but with others is not. An arrangement under which the quantities are consecutive may, as we have said, occur, but other arrangements are common, and some variables are not even capable of having their quantities arranged in a sequence. So it is certainly not a happy thought to bring succession into the definition of a variable.

the corresponding x," and a proposition in which occurs the class name of a class of quantities formed solely for the study of properties which the quantities of that class possess as individuals. Be it noted however that the closest analogy is not found with those general propositions of mathematics which Mr. Russell takes as typical propositions involving the symbols of variables. Thus consider $a + b = b + a$ which, when put forward as enunciating the commutative law of addition, is a fair example of these general propositions. This should be read: "Every a when any b of the same sort[53] is added to it gives a sum equal to or identical with the sum of the same b as before plus the same a as before." Here we have what might be called an equation of sameness; in reading it we are obliged to specify that the second a taken is the same as the first a, and that the second b is also the same as the first b. Otherwise the proposition would not be true; for a and b are both general class symbols each of which takes all values and denotes every quantity that enters mathematics; and hence if we did not put the specification as to sameness we should be asserting that every sum of two quantities is equal to or identical with every sum of two quantities, whether the quantities entering the second sum were the same as those entering the first or not. Now the equations concerning functional relations do not always carry a stipulation as to sameness; this may be at hand, as in $y = x^3 - x^2$ where the same x must be squared in forming the subtrahend as was cubed to form the minuend, or it may not be needed at all as in $y = x^2$. On the other hand these equations always carry a stipulation totally lacking with $a + b = b + a$: namely a stipulation as to correspondence. For the equality and identity alternative in equations concerning a functional relation

[53] It is necessary to specify that the b taken must be of the same sort as the a. For if it is of a different sort the addition cannot be performed. Thus we cannot add a length to a weight, or add either to a natural number.

between a y-variable and an x-variable holds only of a y and of its *corresponding* x. Stipulations of correspondence, though not at hand in such equations as $a + b = b + a$, can however be found where ordinary class symbols are alone involved. The special equations that arise in connection with certain problems bear such stipulations. Take for example the system of equations $x + y - 10 = 0$, $2xy - 9x - 11y + 54 = 0$, where x and y are symbols of unknown quantities—*quesitive symbols* as we might call them. These equations are satisfied by $x = 7$, $y = 3$, and by $x = 4$, $y = 6$. Here x denotes quantities of two different values, and so does y. We cannot read $x + y = 10$ as "Every sum of an x plus a y is equal to or identical with every ten"; this is not true, for $7 + 6$ is not 10, nor is $4 + 3$. We must say "Every sum of an x plus the corresponding y," and must likewise read the other equation of the system as an equation of correspondence. In quite another way, correspondence is in evidence with the general equations each of which covers a host of special cases. Such an equation is the general equation of the second degree with one quesitive symbol: $ax^2 + bx + c = 0$, which on solution gives $x = (-b \pm \sqrt{b^2 - 4ac})/2a$. This solution, as well as the original equation, is understood to carry stipulations as to correspondence; the equations do not have reference to each set of values that can be formed from the values taken separately by the four literal symbols—if they did the first of the equations would assert such absurdities as $3 = 0$; for x, a, b and c all take the value 1. The equations are understood to hold only for each set of corresponding values; in other words the equality or identity alternative is asserted only of an x, an a, a b and a c which correspond. Mathematicians who deal with the theory of equations not infrequently use the name "variable" in connection with the x of such equations as these, but decline to speak of variables where a, b and c are concerned, thus taking the ground that the symbol of a variable must be quesitive. They ought however to know that in what is usually regarded as the natural habitat of variables—the differential and integral calculus—it is by no means a requisite that the quantities of a variable be unknown. If concerned in a correspondence or taking diverse values or both together be accepted as criterion, then clearly a, b and c in the general equation as well as x ought to be designated as symbols of variables, and so likewise ought x and y in the system of special equations. But the real criterion has nothing to do with variation of value, and nothing to do with correspondence (which does not come into consideration in the constitution of a variable, but only appears on the stage when a functional relation is established between several variables); and none of these symbols are symbols of variables. A set of quantities constituting a variable is characterized, not by the values of its components or by any correspondence into which they enter, but by the purpose for which the set was formed, or, if we wish to be perfectly precise, the purpose which it serves. Take x in the general equation of the second degree: the purpose in view in grouping together the quantities called x's is not to investigate their mutual relations, but merely to facilitate finding the value of the x of each instance that may come to hand as a special case of this general equation, and thus to avoid the trouble of formulating and solving a new equation for each separate case. The x's (and the a's and the b's and the c's) may be made to constitute a variable by carrying out an investigation which does bear on their mutual relations, but when initially grouped together they assuredly do not pertain to a variable at all.

In considering Mr. Russell's doctrine that the ordinary class symbols of mathematics are names of variables, we have. let the reader remember, made due allowance for the fact that he did not well choose the examples he gave of the former, but failed to put forward those most analogous to the latter as used in equations dealing with functional relations. We have gone out of our way to bring to light the cases where the greatest analogy is to be found, thus giving the most favorable aspect to Mr. Russell's contention. And the result of our investigations is assuredly not to sanction the identification of symbols of variables and ordinary class symbols used only to denote the separate members of classes of quantities. Between the symbols of these two types there is, we see, a difference of character which makes Mr. Russell's doctrine utterly untenable. This doctrine, ignoring as it does the really characteristic use of names of variables, must be deemed quite unworthy of a philosopher. What extenuation can be urged in Mr. Russell's behalf? The only one we can conceive as being put forward is the plea that Mr. Russell had a perfect right to use "variable" in a sense peculiar to himself, and to give it, in the discipline he miscalls "mathematics," an application quite different from that which the word has in the mathematics of the mathematicians. Now we willingly concede that deviations from the established meanings of important scientific terms, frequently as Mr. Russell indulges in them, ought not to be looked upon with intolerance. We would not reproach him merely for this: such offenses against current usage are in themselves only venial sins for a philosopher. But, though they are of small moment alone, it is quite a different matter when they have as concomitant a confusion of thought which pervades a whole philosophy and seem to play no small part in bringing about this confusion. And that is precisely what we find with the innovations fathered by Mr. Russell, who, moreover, while admitting that in many cases he apparently departs widely from common usage, does not always seem aware of the extent of his transgressions.[54] Notably with the very word "variable" Mr. Russell is to all appearances serenely unconscious of his flagrant contravention of the terminology sanctioned by scientific use. His application of the name, so far as he uses it in connection with the symbols occurring in ordinary mathematical formulas, he takes as a matter of course, though in fact nothing is more unwarranted than his procedure here. After his initial error we can hardly be surprised at his extension of this application, under which he designates as names of variables the phrases obtained by conjoining "any" to even those general class names that do not pertain to what is ordinarily called mathematics. The extension is a natural result of Mr. Russell's assigning to mathematics the broad field of symbolic logic, and indeed, the misconception of variable is taken as basis for the formal definition of "Pure Mathematics" promulgated in the *Principles*. "Pure Mathematics," Mr. Russell informs us, "is the class of all propositions of the form 'p implies q,' where p and q are propositions containing one or more variables, the same in the two propositions, and neither p nor q contains any constants except logical constants."[55] Elsewhere he tells us, "The variable is, from the formal standpoint, *the* characteristic notion of Mathematics."[56] And he actually says that his definition of Pure Mathematics "professes to be, not an arbitrary decision

[54] Of all the words in a language "not" is one of the few whose meanings are firmly established by a usage uniformly alike in scientific and in colloquial discourse. Will it be believed that Mr. Russell is found making a use of this word utterly opposed to the meaning which has heretofore been universally assigned to it? Speaking of relations (p. 25) he notes that "with some relations, such as identity, diversity, equality, inequality, the converse is the same as the original relation: such relations are called *symmetrical*." And he then proceeds to say: "When the converse is incompatible with the original relation, as in such cases as greater and less, I call the relation *asymmetrical*; in intermediate cases, *not-symmetrical*." Needless to say, in the sense in which "not" had been universally used up to the time Mr. Russell began to write, the asymmetrical and the "not-symmetrical" relations would alike be designated as *not symmetrical*. Yet there is nothing in his remarks to show that Mr. Russell was conscious of how greatly "not" is distorted from its accepted meaning in the nomenclature he devised.

[55] P. 3.

[56] P. 90.

to use a common word in an uncommon significance, but rather a precise analysis of the ideas which, more or less unconsciously, are implied in the ordinary employment of the term."[57] The use of the word "variable" in Mr. Russell's definition may perhaps so impose upon some of his unthinking readers as to make them swallow this contention, but if that word be elided, and a less misleading synonym be put in its place, then Mr. Russell's analysis of the ideas implied in the ordinary employment of the term "Pure Mathematics" will even to the most casual reader appear anything but precise. For what Mr. Russell really means by a variable here is either a *general class name, distributed by the conjunction of a universal categorem or otherwise*, or else the object represented by the distributed class name—the hazy nature of his doctrines makes it difficult to tell which. And it is perfectly ludicrous to say that Pure Mathematics, in the ordinary acceptance of this term, is characterized by such distributed class names or by what they stand for.

We have seen then that in what are perhaps the two questions most fundamental in mathematical philosophy—the doctrine of numbers and the doctrine of variables—Mr. Russell's failure is complete and utter. His delineation of numbers is inadequate, and the definition he puts forward is inadmissible. What he regards as variables are not the variables of mathematics, nor has he penetrated into the nature of what he wrongly takes to be variables. He is to all appearances unaware that "any individual" (which in his view denotes the true variable) and "any *u*" (which he regards as denoting a restricted variable) are nothing more than distributed general class names. He assumes that "any" has always an office radically different from that of "every," and puts forth many would-be subtleties in a laborious attempt to show just how the two syn-

[57] P. 3.

categorems differ.[58] Starting from an erroneous assumption, he succeeds in bringing obscurity over a matter that is on its face perfectly clear, and is after all brought to admit that for "the variable," whose nature is, in Mr. Russell's opinion, inextricably bound up with the question of "any," a satisfactory theory is yet to be found.[59] Rightly or wrongly, after going over Mr. Russell's theories, one feels inclined to ascribe the errors he commits very largely to the curious metaphysics which here and there makes itself manifest. An inkling of Mr. Russell's metaphysics may be gained from what he propounds concerning propositions and concerning objects and terms, things and concepts. In dealing with the latter he puts forward a classification—substantially a doctrine of categories—which appears to be quite original and is likewise preposterous. Had Mr. Russell deferred his work in the field of mathematics until he had elaborated as foundation a sane and coherent doctrine on these points and others of pure philosophy, he might not have so rapidly written a ponderous volume, but assuredly he would have been more likely to have produced a work of real benefit to science. As it is, one can only regret that the author of the *Principles of Mathematics* should have expended so much labor in erecting an imposing edifice upon foundations that are thoroughly unsound.

ROBERT P. RICHARDSON,
PHILADELPHIA, PA. EDWARD H. LANDIS.

[58] In fact, as we have said before, opposition between "any" and "every" is often quite lacking, and, an "any" sentence can in such a case be changed into an "every" sentence with but slight modification. However opposition does sometimes occur, but not in the way Mr. Russell would have us think. Opposition occurs with the potential mood; thus, "Any horse may win the race" is truly opposed to "Every horse may win the race." When we pass to the affirmative indicative and compare, for example, "Every horse is a mare" and "Any horse is a mare," we are no longer able to find opposition; the latter sentence is not of a usual form, but if we grant it any meaning we will naturally accept it as equipollent to the former. With the negative indicative there is however opposition, "Not every horse is a mare" and "Not any horse is a mare" being opposed,. (We need hardly say that we do not use "opposed" in the sense of "incompatible.")

[59] P. 5.

THE DEFINITION OF NUMBER.

"SCIENCE," writes Gaston Milhaud,[1] "in enouncing its ever-increasing series of truths, obviously supplies—whether one reflect upon it or not—the most powerful argument against scepticism. And in this respect mathematics plays a special rôle by reason of the evidence which clothes all its propositions and by reason of the complete satisfaction which its demonstrations give to our thirst for comprehension. There, at least, is a domain where thought in search of clarity, of evidence, and of light, exercises itself in an ideal fashion. Everywhere else, discussion is founded on the right to proclaim as certain an enounced truth, and accord upon the value and legitimacy of each insight comes but slowly: in mathematics this is not so. If, for the choice of axioms, we give ourselves voluntarily to philosophical investigations whose conclusions vary, at bottom there is no one ready to abandon the postulates of ancient geometry, and the question was not even proposed by the Greeks. As to demonstrations, it seems impossible that two minds, however different they may be—granting their disposal, at need, of obvious misunderstandings—will not speedily agree upon the rigor of the reasoning, and consequently upon the rigor of the conclusions. And whether one is aware of it or not, the habit of such a movement of thought creates in us a naive confidence in the puissance of our under-

[1] *Les Philosophes-géomètres de la Grèce*, 1900; pp. 2-3.

standing,—so that it would be a miracle if the philosophical geometer did not somewhere testify to it, did not sometimes under the most penetrating conceptions bear along a disconcerting dogmatism."

We may take this statement, I think, as a fair representation at once of the fascination and the dangers which beset mathematical reasonings. There is no field of human thought, I imagine, which yields so paradoxical a feeling of freedom and of constraint as does mathematics: the freedom springing from the twofold consciousness, first, of our having chosen the postulates from which we proceed, and second, of the endlessness of the possible elaborations of our reasonings; the constraint arising from our sense of the undeniableness, and therefore the necessity, of mathematical demonstrations,—i. e., from their freedom from contradiction. Thus from mathematics we derive the satisfaction which our instinct for law and order always yields in finding itself fulfilled, without at the same time sacrificing our self-gratifying conviction of the importance of the human factor in the operations performed. In the study of physical nature there is always a certain abasement of humanity, due to the passive attitude of scientific observation, accompanied by a feeling of outer and brute constraint; but the mathematician, with an even greater assurance of the necessity of his results, bears with him also a lively consciousness of the significance of his own activity in bringing about these results, and so attains, as it were, a kind of Zeus-like supremacy to the fated ends which, while they bind him, are yet his own enactment.

But is not this doubly reason for caution against mathematical dogmatism? and especially that form of it which rests its denial of our more ordinary intuitions, not upon its eventual translatability, but upon its untranslatability into the forms of our common human experience? Doubtless truth is difficult and obscure; but dare we concede that it is so ineffably obscure as to transcend the discourse of life? Of course I am speaking of the modern science of logistic.[2]

I.

What is the meaning of number? and in what sense are the hairs of our heads and the other phenomena of nature numbered? This is the question.

The old-fashioned view of number found its essence to lie in *discontinuity* coupled with a notion of *series.* "Number is discontinuous," says Clerk-Maxwell;[3] "we pass from one number to the next *per saltum.*" The perception of the discontinuity was regarded as empirical and intuitive. In the language of Aristotle, "We perceive number by the negation of continuity, and also by the special senses, for each sensation is a unity."[4] The perception of the series was usually accredited to the act of counting, though this was often also somewhat confusedly regarded as an act of adding. If I speak of this view in a past tense, it is only because of its long history; not that it is dead.

In the thinking of such men as Hobbes and Locke this conception eventuates in an out-and-out nominalism. "Number," quoth Hobbes,[5] "is exposed either by the exposition of points or of the names of number, *one, two, three, etc.*; and those points must not be contiguous, so as that they cannot be distinguished by notes, but they must be so placed that they may be *discerned* one from another; for from this it is that number is called *discrete quantity,* whereas all quantity which is designed by motion is called *continual quantity.* But that number may be exposed by the names of number it is necessary that they be recited

[2] Which is, by the way, a somewhat unhappy name; for with the Greeks "arithmetic" was the more, "logistic" the less theoretic science.

[3] *Encyc. Brit.,* 9th ed., III, 37.

[4] *De Anima,* 425*a*, 5.

[5] *Concerning Body,* XII, 5.

by heart and in order, as one, two, three, etc.; for by saying one, one, one, and so forward, we know not what number we are at beyond two or three; which also appear to us in this manner not as number, but as figure."

It is always worth while citing Locke in connections of this kind, not because of the analytical value of his expositions, which is usually slight, but because he gives, with a dogmatic perspicuousness that leaves nothing to be desired, the first reflections of ordinary common sense. He says:[6] "By the repeating the idea of an unit and joining it to another unit, we make thereof one collective idea marked by the name two: and whosoever can do this, and proceed on, still adding one more to the last collective idea which he had of any number and gave a name to it, may count, or have ideas for several collections of units distinguished from one another, as far as he hath a series of names for following numbers, and a memory to retain that series with their several names; all numeration being but still the adding of one unit more, and giving to the whole together, as comprehended in one idea, a new or distinct name or sign, whereby to know it from those before and after, and distinguish it from every smaller or greater multitude of units. So that he that can add one to one, and so to two, and so go on with his tale, taking still with him the distinct names belonging to every progression; and so again, by subtracting an unit from each collection, retreat and lessen them; is capable of all the ideas of number within the compass of his language, or for which he hath names, though perhaps not of more."

In this account it is obvious that Locke presupposes: (*a*) the notion of *unity*, which, indeed, he has just previously stated to have "no shadow of variety or composition in it"; (*b*) the notion of a *collection*—his "collective idea"; (*c*) the notion of *serial order*; (*d*) the notion of *quantity*

[6] *Essay*, II, xvi, 5.

—greater and less; (*e*) the notion of a mathematical *operation*—addition, subtraction. Thus the main elements in the concept he is describing are assumed; at the same time there may be a seasoning of hard-headedness in his stout nominalism. For him numbers are names: "Without names or marks we can hardly make use of numbers in reckoning, especially where the combination is made up of any great multitude of units, which, put together without a name or mark to distinguish that precise collection, will hardly be kept from being a heap in confusion." One of the primary issues in the modern discussion of the nature of number is just whether supersensible (or superintuitible) mathematical ideas do not resolve into mere nomenclature and the science itself into a kind of transcendental logomachy.

That the Lockean type of nominalism is by no means extinct is evidenced by the definition of number offered in the *Encyclopaedia Britannica*:[7] "Suppose we fix on a certain sequence of names 'one,' 'two,' 'three,'...., or symbols such as 1, 2, 3,....; this sequence being always the same. If we take a set of concrete objects, and name them in succession 'one,' 'two,' 'three,'.... naming each once and once only, we shall not get beyond a certain name, e. g., 'six.' Then, in saying that the number of objects is six, what we mean is that the name of the last object named is six. We therefore only require a definite law for the formation of the successive names or symbols. The symbols 1, 2,....9, 10,...., for instance, are formed according to a definite law; and in giving 253 as the *number* of a set of objects we mean that if we attach to them the symbols 1, 2, 3,.... in succession, according to this law, the symbol attached to the last object will be 253. If we say that this act of attaching a symbol has been performed 253 times, then 253 is an *abstract* (or *pure*) *number.*

[7] 11th ed., article "Arithmetic."

Underlying this definition," continues the writer, "is a certain assumption, viz., that if we take the objects in a different order, the last symbol attached will still be 253. This, in an elementary treatment of the subject, must be regarded as axiomatic; but it is really a simple case of mathematical induction."

The presupposition of discontinuity and of serial order is as obvious in this last as in the two previously given accounts of the number concept. We set out with our known power of observing differences and naming things —perceptual discrimination and apperceptional unification; but by the time we have accomplished the office of Adam and are taking our earned rest, we discover that the names we have given are vicariously indifferent to the things of "first intention," and in addition that they have won for themselves a wholly novel and stringent interdependence, —the smoke of our experience has transformed itself into a hugely articulate Jinni, and, as by a miracle, number is manifest! Aristotle says,[8] "In general what exists in the essence of number, besides quantity, is quality; for the essence of each number is what it is when taken once, 6 being not what it is when taken twice or thrice, but what it is once, that is, 6." It is very apparent that a succession of qualitative discriminations will not in itself yield quantity; and without an understanding of quantity how can number be defined?

II.

The ideal of the logisticians (though I speak with misgivings) is at once the infallibility and the universal applicability of their reasonings. They would create for us a rational universe entirely freed from the taint of empiricism, mathematical in its certainties, but hypermathematical in its significance,—in short, they would

[8] *Metaph.*, 1020*b*.

achieve what Spinoza so greatly attempted. Because of the annoying miasmas which beset the earth-born speech of men, they would substitute therefor a kind of Esperanto of the soul (*anima intellectiva*) modeled after the discarnate and purified symbolism of mathematics. Clearly the approach to this consummacy of the intellect should be through the concept of number.

First of all, this concept must be relieved of all traces of Lockean empiricism. The simple notion, prevalent among the ordinary, that the idea of number is in some fashion derived from the act of counting is one of which we must be eased. For what is meant by counting? "To this question we usually get only some irrelevant psychological answer, as, that counting consists in successive acts of attention. In order to count 10, I suppose that ten acts of attention are required: certainly a most useful definition of the number 10!"[9] The point is well taken, and we can see that it applies conclusively to the whole British tradition, from Hobbes onward. "We must not, therefore, bring in counting where the definition of numbers is in question."

To be sure, this judgment has not prevailed in the new school *ab initio*. Dedekind states that from examination of what takes place in counting an aggregate of things, we are brought to consider the mind's powers (*a*) of relating things to things, and (*b*) of letting a thing correspond with, or represent, a thing; and that upon these powers as a foundation the whole science of number must be based.[10] *Relation* and *equivalence* are thus fundamental ideas—or, perhaps, operations—which get their meaning from counting, and give its meaning to number; but it may be that the counting here meant is of that purely noetic variety which includes "denumeration" of the in-

[9] Russell, *Principles of Mathematics*, p. 114.
[10] *Was sind und was sollen die Zahlen?*

finite along with "enumeration" of the finite, and which, putatively, owes no dependence to our commoner experience.

But if not counting, then neither is mathematical induction the key to the meaning of number; for mathematical induction, with its dual stress upon *next-to-next* and *recurrence*, is no more than the act of counting transubstantiated by that unity-in-variety which is the root of all perception. "We may define finite numbers as those that can be reached by mathematical induction, starting from 0 and increasing by 1 at each step,"[11] but such a definition does not apply to the vastly greater realm of transfinite numbers,—and it would be obvious waste to devote thought to a definition applicable only to the "little corner," as Poincaré calls it, "where the finite numbers hide themselves."

By what device, then, are we to pry into the mystery of number? What idea — which the mutations of the Wheel of Time have brought back to us freed from the contaminations of a too mortal birth—will give us its eluctant essence? The answer is familiar: A finite cardinal number is a class of equivalent classes; an infinite cardinal number is a class of classes a part of which is equivalent to the whole. It is the idea of *class* which is to resolve for us the riddle of reasoning.

Readily enough our imaginations seize the suggestion. The older, empirical conception of number as somehow directly derived from the act of counting, in reason as in history, is replaced by one in which counting and all other operations flow from an initial insight into a group situation. The point of regard has been reversed, and in place of seeing a perceptual situation built up out of moments, we see the moments emerge from the situation; logical priorism disenthrones empiricism, deduction precedes in-

[11] Russell, *op. cit.*, p. 123.

duction—and, indeed, not unnaturally absorbs the latter, for any induction which may lay a claim to reason is but deduction disguised.[12]

But this might flow from a mere distinction of temperament;[13] for we have long been accustomed to Urania and Pandemos in reason as in love. The matter which calls for a nicer determination is the relation of this term *class* to its content. What does it mean?

It is difficult to be precise in the analysis of terms which are customarily defined only by a set of properties couched in the form of postulates. What one arrives at is a word (*flatus vocis*) with a variety of meanings, but meanings eviscerated of that heart of reality which we feel to be present in our more current, if less critical, living speech. Indeed, all that saves this rarified discourse from the emptiness of nominalism is the requirement of consistency as between the postulates; their freedom from mutual contradiction is their sole claim to a single and central meaning. This (if I understand it) is the only principle of definition recognized in logistic.

What, then, are the properties of a "class"? Clearly, I think, the prime requisite is that it shall constitute a *limit*. I do not mean a limit which conveys a sense of a beyond (if that can be avoided), but a limit which clarifies our sense of the within,—such a limit as, for example, is represented by the cardinal number of the class of finite numbers, or again, such a limit as we ordinarily intend by the word "universe." Without this conscious limitation, which, because we feel it to be a voluntary intellectual retrenchment, a kind of rein upon the imagination, we personify

[12] *Ibid.*, pp. 11*n.*, 441.

[13] This, apparently, is Poincaré's notion of his own divergence from Russell. "M. Russell me dira," he says, "qu'il ne s'agit pas de psychologie, mais de logique et d'épistémologie; et moi, je serai conduit à répondre qu'il n'y a pas de logique et d'épistémologie indépendantes de la psychologie; et cette profession de foi clora probablement la discussion parce qu'elle mettra en évidence une irrémédiable divergence de vues."—*Dernières pensées*, p. 139.

as a "self-limitation," no conception of class could be operant.

Dedekind's solution of the problem of continuity quite consciously rests upon the assumption of *limits,* or limiting values; and what is distinctive of the notion of a "cut" (*Schnitt*) appears to be just that it determines a limit which, so to speak, does not overleap itself, and which consequently gives the base for a self-contained system of values. Every "cut" is, in a sense, a zero, having the particular property that any variable magnitude which approaches the limit loses itself in a value indistinguishable from zero.[14] This, I take it, is also the essential meaning of the *Nul class*—the class of things to which no entity in the (given) universe corresponds; it is essentially a boundary which, because it is empty, cannot be used as a turn or start into continued reasonings.

At least we should suppose that 0-limits could not be so used, but by a kind of transcendental induction just this is attempted. The cardinal number of all finite numbers, which is, of course, infinite, becomes the first transfinite cardinal; and the ordinal ω (ω symbolizes a *progression* modeled on the natural suite $1, 2, 3, \ldots. n; n+1, \ldots.,$ and so may be regarded as the generalization or law of the process of ordering sequentially) becomes the first transfinite ordinal. By applying the conception of a transfinite ordinal to transfinite cardinals, it becomes possible to conceive of, and perhaps create, an infinite series of the latter —transfinites of the order α being followed by those of the order β, and so on. The whole process is reminiscent of Spinoza's assumption of possible infinite attributes, other than thought and extension, of the divine substance, though it seems to want the restraint which left Spinoza content to suggest the possibility, and pass in his philosophizing to the attributive planes with which human experience famil-

[14] *Stetigkeit und irrationale Zahlen,* IV.

iarizes us. By means of such interplays of conception—infinite limiting finite, transfinite limiting infinite—it becomes possible to create whole hierarchies of classes and types, each conclusively including what is below it and conclusively ignoring what is above it. The process is interesting and in its way fruitful, but it is difficult to see how it could be possible except for that self-imposition of limits which distinguish grade from grade and type from type, and it is difficult to see in the imposition any other necessity than the arbitrary will of the thinker. The limits set are limits assumed, and assumed with something of the stark inexplicableness of a primitive tabu—unless we concede that the whole process is a conscious fiction, whose analogue is our empirical concentration of immediate attention on immediate ends.

But besides this external principle of limitation, which makes definable a self-comprehending system, there is another principle of limitation, an internal one, which makes system itself comprehensible. This principle is represented by the idea of *structure* or *form,* without which mathematics and reason alike could not exist. The principle of external limitation might suffice to mark off for us an islet of chaos which we could choose to regard as the universe, but only the acknowledgment of internal limitations could convert this chaotic universe into a cosmos.

Now the relationships of ideas according to this principle of internal limitation assume two general forms: that of *part-to-part* and that of *part-to-whole.* It is obvious[15] that each of these is a relation of *order,* and it is also obvious that each is derivative of the idea of *unity* in the two fundamental senses of unity. For the relation of part-to-whole clearly rests upon the contrasting unities of the element, regarded as an undifferentiated item, and the thing, regarded as an assemblage of elements; and the

[15] "Obvious," not to logistic, but to our linguistic intuitions.

relation of part-to-part, while explicitly concerned only with the relation of item to item, clearly rests upon an implicit whole.[16] Unit and totality, atom and universe, are the two extremes, each of which assumes the mask of unity, and the fact that the atom may be resolved into a universe or the universe contracted into an atom by a simple act of speculative translation does not alter the essential character of these two moments of thought.

The relation of part-to-part would, in the world experientially familiar to us, involve the meaning "next-to-next," or contiguity of consecutive elements. This relation is what makes the experiential world finite and incomplete; it is, therefore, felt as a constraint of the pure reason, mathematical or other. But the logisticians have discovered an escape from this restriction, and like Spinoza have found their freedom *sub specie aeternitatis.* The instrument of emancipation is the notion of the "one-to-one correspondence"; it is through this that the infinite is resolved

[16] For the two types of unity, cf. Bergson, *Données immédiates,* pp. 58f. Of course the logisticians categorically deny that the idea of *class* involves that of "part-to-whole." "Socrates is a man" may mean (1) "Socrates possesses the qualities which mark a human being"—and this is the part-to-whole relationship—or (2) "Socrates is one among men,"—and this is the member-to-class relationship, expressed "x is an a" (symbolically, $x \epsilon a$), where x is a member and a a class. The distinction is true enough, and it is also true that only the part-to-whole relationship is "transitive," i. e., subject to syllogistic treatment. But is it not evident that the distinction is fundamentally the very distinction which a philosophy of number is called upon to explain? Reasoning *qualitatively,* i. e., where your terms are taken "by nature," we get judgments of type 1; reasoning *quantitatively,* i. e., with terms taken "in respect to number," we get those of type 2. In judgments of the member-to-class type number is assumed, not definitely as if counted, but indefinitely as if countable. That is, a plurality, which is a totality or aggregate of some sort (in so far as limited by the reasoning undertaken), is at least hypothetically "taken"; and such a plurality is what is meant by a "class" (except in those shadowy extremes where the class has only one member or none at all). But if there is a plurality or aggregate it must have the configuration of just this (whatever it may turn out to be) aggregate which is being dealt with—just the class in question. Such configuration (which we might call the quality of a quantity) is precisely a whole of which the member is a part,—at least, we use "whole" and "part" in this sense in common speech, and it is certainly significant that the logisticians, in denying that "class" has this meaning, are forced to proclaim the term undefinable except by its use—i. e., it is left in a state of empirical ambiguity. Cf. Russell, *Principles,* Chaps. II, VI; also, Burali-Forti and Padoa in Vol. III of *Bibliothèque du Congrès international de Philosophie.*

into cosmos. The idea is centrally that of the reciprocal uniformity of two groups (classes), such that for every element of the one there is in the other, one, and only one, corresponding element. Two groups or classes so related are said to have the same number, and the infinite is simply a group in which the whole is related to a part of itself in this manner.[17]

Now the notion of a one-to-one correspondence is clearly metempirical. In real life, we cannot make things correspond absolutely except in absolute identification, i. e., in loss of plurality; all other relationships involve some kind of contiguity. Even when we set five fingers against five fingers, what we have empirically is not a one-to-one correspondence of two groups, but right thumb to left thumb, right index to left, and so on; and this holds throughout the empirical universe. The idea of number is, as it were, interposed between the severally adjacent digits, or perhaps I had better say that the groups of five are groups of five because they both (speaking with Plato) "participate" in τὰ μαθηματικά. The correspondence lies between an empirical group which is always finite and incomplete and a metempirical system of numbers (supermundane, if not divine) representing the class of all possible classes. If Spinoza's divine substance, within which all attributes inhere, were to become articulate it would be represented, I conceive, by just such transcendental numbers.

But we are not to think of these numbers as severally interdependent. Their reality rests upon no idea of succession. We must think of decads, duads, monads, triads, tetrads, etc., not of one....two....three....etc. The *order* of the numbers in their own transcendent realm is something superposed upon their cardinal realities,—this

[17] The usual illustration is that of the one-to-one correspondence of all the integers with all the even integers, or of the points on a straight line with the points on a plane.

time by a set of relations which concerns them *inter se.* *Less than, greater than, equal to,* or again *higher* and *lower power,* or again *betweenness* (or "mediacy," since the notion of "between" is significant only when coupled with the idea of transition), are relations of the needed kind. Now each of these sets of conceptions is a variant of the *part-to-whole* relation, of contained and container. This is self-evident in the first-named group. "Less than" and "greater than" obviously rest upon the experiment of mensuration, of reduction to scale, and if the numbers themselves *are* the scale, nevertheless they get their steps or intervals, and hence their *order,* from the experiences whose comparisons they name. A scale may be regarded as made up from the sucessive remainders in a series of approximations, its fineness being determined by the extent to which the approximations are carried,—which, in last resort, must be a matter of industry or of organic structure, in either case empirical. The relation of equality is not so obviously derived from measure, for "equal" may signify not merely identity in step or scale, but also similiformity and equivalence. Nevertheless, when we consider that equivalence is no more than functional identity and that similiformity can be no less than this—that is, that each of these ideas is identity with a reservation—it would seem evident that here too we are dealing with a concept whose final meaning is derived from the part-to-whole relation.

In the case of "higher-lower power" and in the case of "betweenness" the same general relation—part-to-whole—is implicit. Both of these types of expression are derivatives of space-perception; they are geometric in first intention. But as principles of order they have to do not with a static but with a dynamic geometry. The notion of direction or sense is the primary one, but the direction exists not as the expression of an orientation but of a progression; not a set of starting-points or markers but a set of journeys is connoted. Thus we have time as well as space involved in the empirical foundation of numerical order so conceived, the complete idea being the analogue of a movement from any assumed position in any designated direction, the movement being conceived as contained by its determinants. Of course, in the case of "betweenness" this movement may be ideal, and in that case we have merely a case of syllogistic transition, with the "between" represented by the middle term;—but this is simply intellectualizing our journey. Again, the concept of "betweenness" may give rise to right-left, symmetrical-asymmetrical orders; but here, too, we have only special complications of the familiar idea, for right-left are clearly but alternative journeys, a dilemma of roads one or the other of which our action must make real (hence defining the whole);[18] while symmetry and its opposite can hardly be conceived apart from measurement, for indeed the whole notion of proportion is dependent upon some kind of repetition (which again throws us back upon time and space for our analogues).

Thus the logistic conception of number, starting with the assumption of *class* as the essential numerical idea, proceeds in two directions. (*a*) Outwardly, it posits a limit or law within which must fall all the elements which make the class a class, capable of structure. And that this outward limitation is made in good faith as essential to the idea is sufficiently evidenced by the recognized possibility of a class including classes, of a class of classes, and finally of the class of all possible classes,—a veritable hierarchy of types of limitation. (*b*) Inwardly, there are posited two types of structural relation, which may be described as the principles of internal limitation. These are the re-

[18] So also "before-after." Past time is commonly thought as a *retreat* from the present, future time as an *advance*.

lation of part to part and part to whole. From the first is derived that freedom to make comparisons which makes possible—or, *is* the possibility of—the transcendental independence that distinguishes pure number. From the second flows the whole concept of order, and especially the notion of series or progression without which the idea of quantity (i. e., greater-less) could not be.

If we ask what concepts are fundamental in such a construction, three seem to stand predominant: class, element, relation. But the two first, class and element, are surely no other than the two meanings which we commonly ascribe to unity, while relation is quite as clearly *the* function (and therefore the meaning) of plurality. The *one* and the *many* are thus the fundamentals of number,—and already we seem to be within hailing distance of the Hellenic categories; subject and attribute, thing and quality, are recurrently proximate. Has the Wheel of Time indeed completed its circuit? and is philosophy to begin anew? Or were we perhaps right as to the distinction of temperaments, and is logistic but an exercise of the lovers of Uranian reason?

III.

At the beginning of my discussion I quoted from Gaston Milhaud a word of caution in regard to that dogmatism which issues from a too naive confidence in the powers of our understanding, especially when freed, as it is in mathematical logic, to consume its own intentions. I would repeat this caution, having in mind certain developments of this logic based upon the principles already examined.

These developments issue from that abstractive freedom which is the especial pitfall of the Uranian mind. When in a given situation a given form is discovered, the statement of this form is what we call the description of the situation, for it is only forms that we can state. But a form so abstracted—and this is the law of our rational life—is invariably made the measure of new situations. The fact that it can never be applied to a new situation except with some more or less accommodating deformation is a fact which we customarily and conveniently neglect, or if we remember it, it is only for the sake of abstracting from the more comprehensive situation given by the group of deformations a new form of forms which shall serve in its turn for the first of a series of modifications of some super-form of forms, and so on;—i. e., *sf*...*df*...*df′*... *df″*...etc., as it becomes clogged by the impertinencies of fact, is clarified by being transmuted into FS...DF...DF′ ...DF″...etc., and this in turn by εἶδος ... ἐντελέχεια (α′...β′...γ′...), whence, we may presume, the Idea of Ideas breathlessly emerges as we pass above the sphere which bounds our empyrean. If this description be false to the process it has not yet been so demonstrated.

Now there are two modes in which this process is applied in the logistic analysis of number, corresponding to the two types of relation of a class to its limits which we have heretofore stated. These two modes might be described as the modes of external and internal transcendence of unity.

The first of these, the external transcendence, is effected by analogical reasoning the base of which is the so-called "natural" suite of numbers, the succession of positive integers 1, 2, 3,....n, $n+1$,... The number of such integers, which is infinite, is ω; but ω is more than this. It is also *the principle of description which is immanent in the natural numbers naturally arranged*; it is the principle of numerical order as evinced in one-to-one correspondences, and so is the key to the analysis of all denumerable groups. The postulates underlying descriptions of the type ω are (*a*) the postulates of *linear order,* and (*b*) postulates of *sequence*—Dedekind's for example. From the combination of these two ideas issues the conception of a discrete series, though when we consider that the first of these is symbolized merely by the idea of inequality (<, >), i. e., by quantity, and the second by that of *limit*, i. e., by class, it does not appear that "discrete series" spells much more than "whole numbers." Nevertheless, as symbolized in ω, it becomes the beginning of a transfinite hierarchy of orders; for it is the principle (or, shall I say, the analogy) of the suite of finite numbers which sets in order the houses of the infinite,—there the last becomes first, Omega the prior of Alpha, and the unity of the finite integers is transcended by numbers α_ν reaching to the order 2ω, while beyond this we may suspect yet more transcendent orders of hyper-α's.

But this external transcendence of unity is complemented by an internal transcendence; there is not only a metempirical macrocosmos, but a metempirical microcosmos. This is shown forth when in the description of order the notion of sequence is replaced by that of *betweenness* or mediacy, which is to be conceived as a kind of eternal negation of next-to-nextness without loss of plurality. There are two kinds of numerical order exemplifying this internal transcendency. When a series is endlessly linear and yet endlessly median, i. e., when it has no beginning nor middle nor end but only and always a median term between any two terms, it is *dense*. When a series is limitedly linear but has no middle term, it is *continuous*. The endless fractioning of a difference in a process of approximation—as, for example, the endless interstitial fractions required to complete the suite of all rational numbers—is image of the dense series; the clogging of an interval by the sum of its own possibilities is the image of the continuous series—for example, the series $\geqq 0 \ldots\ldots \leqq 1$ is fulfilled by the aggregate of numbers rational and irrational there comprised. Series of each of these types are transfinite; but there is an important difference in structure between them, for only the dense series is denumerable (i. e., figurable by the progression of positive integers), while only the continuum is susceptible of ratio and of measure, for it alone has limit. Of course the dense series is only metempirically countable and the continuous series measurable only metempirically, so that to note that we seem to have here naught but a transcendentalizing of the Aristotelian πλῆθος and συνεχής, plurality and magnitude, is to suggest an empirical meaning for what is by definition beyond experience.

And yet is this suggestion without reason? The transcendentalities of logistic are accomplished in two directions, which might be termed the gross anatomy and the histological analysis of the number-cosmos; and yet, in order that the directions may be meaningful, must we not recognize some proximate and experiential greater-less which is the *here* from which we orient these directions? This seems clearly implied by the important rôle played by the conception of the suite of "natural" numbers, and again by that of the line, in the representation of order. Very likely it is true that finite numbers cannot be satisfactorily defined except in relation to transfinite classes, but can the transfinite be defined without first assuming the finite? As a matter of fact, the transfinite orders seem all to be got by a process of progressive abstraction and recombination of qualities assumed on the analogy of the natural numbers; it is as if, by a cunning complexity of mirrors, the natural suite were made to suffer indefinite distortions, variously deforming its native properties and translating them from plane to plane and from space to space in a succession of *saltus,* as many as one has patience for.[19]

[19] This right of saltation is clearly the foundation of the conception of transfinity. "In recent times there is arisen, in geometry and in particular in the theory of functions, a new type of conception of the infinite; according

The process is legitimate enough if we be not duped by its parlous illusions. That is, we must preserve our sanity (which is nothing less than our common-sense faith in our common-sense intuitions); and for this I can conceive no better rules than are implied in Aristotle's dicta (1) that when we speak with reason we must say something with a communicable meaning, and (2) that "third man" abstractions are wasted breaths.[20] The first of these is a pragmatic statement of the law of contradiction applied to discourse; the second is a caution against the tautology involved in the regress to infinity. If we adhere to the first we cannot shift our perspective (say, from finite to transfinite) without distortion of meaning, i. e., without altering our predication; if we adhere to the second we cannot make abstractions of abstractions without losing reality altogether.

Now it would seem that logistic fearlessly invites both of these perils. In the description of classes, for example, the forms of expression travesty the sense of language. For what can be the common-sense, linguistic meaning of a *Nul-class,* which must be described as that class which contains no element, or of which the universe (of discourse) furnishes no instance? Or again, by what right

to these new notions, in the study of an analytic function of a complex variable magnitude usage calls for the representation, in the plane which represents the complex variable, of a unique point situated in the infinite, that is to say, infinitely distant, but nevertheless determined, and for the examination of the manner in which this function comports itself in the neighborhood of this absolute point as in the neighborhood of any point whatever. It is seen then that the function in the neighborhood of the point infinitely remote acts precisely as it would act in that of every other point located in the finite, so that one is fully authorized in this case to represent the infinite as transported to a point altogether determined. When the infinite is presented in a form thus determined, I call it *infinite properly so-called.*"—G. Cantor, *Acta Mathematica,* 2, p. 382. Poincaré founds his conception of dimension upon the notion of the "cut" (*Dernières pensées,* p. 65; *La valeur de la science,* 97f), which, since it implies a new law in each new location, seems a more legitimate use of the right (or intuitive power, as Poincaré would make it) of overleaping boundaries ideally set. Plato's conception of the cosmos as made up of intervals and limits held together by proportion is not far from this (Timaeus, 35-36, 53-57; cf. Philebus, 14*c*-27*b*).

[20] *Metaph.,* 1006*a.*

of speech may we speak of the class *a* as the "class" which contains only *a*? In the first of these cases we are using the language of plurality about nothing, and in the second about one. And if we go a step further and speak of x' as the sole element of the class whose sole member is x, is this more than a vicious play upon the conception of part and whole?[21] Beyond this there is the x'' which is the sole content of the class whose sole element is x',—and we are fairly launched in the infinite tautologies of the "third man."

Formal refinements of analysis, when freed from the leadings of empirical need, may defeat the very end of analysis. Thought becomes not purified, but anemic; in a world of ideas where not only is language replaced by symbols, but these by symbols of symbols, all linguistically ineffable, it is small wonder that identities and the sense for the law of identity vanish away, so that no longer, in order to reason, do we need to speak significantly as Aristotle would require, nor indeed to speak at all. And with the disappearance of identities from this analytic attrition, it is but to be expected that there will emerge that "liberty of contradiction"[22] which solves infinity by denying sense and confounds truth with paradox. The ultimate reason of the world becomes a relation of relations which, if it could say anything, would say just that the world exists, catholically comprehensive of all contradictions, but which, since it is unutterable, is in so far inferior to the sacred monosyllable *Om*.

I am quite willing to agree that there is a sense in which this world is the best possible world, and indeed a sense in which it is the only possible world, and even a sense in which it is all possible worlds,—but when I have got so far I begin to suspect that I am being duped by my

[21] Perhaps I should mention that Burali-Forti *et al.* make distinction between "is an element of" and "is contained by."

[22] Cf. Poincaré, *Science et méthode*, pp. 195f.

own tongue and I deem it the modesty of reason to conserve my breath. Is there no like nonsensicality in the refutation of the axiom that the whole is greater than the part? And have we made "infinity" a more usable notion (I will not say in logistic, but in reason)[23] because we can juggle a part into a kind of equality with its whole by nominalizing our definitions? Common sense, we may be sure, will be slow to relinquish the intuitions upon which it acts; and will not our humaner reason itself, when it meets contradiction assuming the guise of infallible truth, begin to suspect that the ghosts of Duns and Occam are coruscating behind the scenes?

IV.

The attempts of the logisticians to define number by the unaided agilities of the reason are, in the end, little more satisfying than is the confident empiricism of Locke. No one can question their demonstrations, granted their premises; but no one, in the right mind of common sense, can grant the premises. It is incumbent upon us, then, to ask whether logistic has, after all, quite so efficiently scotched the particular theory whose downfall it proclaims,—I mean the intuitionism especially associated with the name of Kant.

"The pure form of all quantities for the outer sense,"

[23] I seem to discern among the logisticians themselves, when they are speaking the language of philosophy, a tendency to employ the idea of what Cantor terms "the infinite improperly so called" in place of that "properly-called" logistic infinite which could hardly be expected to convey an intelligible idea when severed from its nominalistic illustrations. And speaking of these illustrations, why should we stop with an infinite whose part equals its whole? Suppose we define Chaos as a nul-class ($X=0$), and Cosmos as the class of all ordered classes, infinite in number ($K=\omega$). Then τὸ ὅλον, the Whole, (H), will be equal to a part of itself, a logistic infinity ($X+K=H$, or, $0+\omega=\omega$). But suppose, in addition to infinite K, the Demiurge (since that is his business) determine other ordered classes (K'), as many as he may choose. K' will belong to K, as being ordered classes, but cannot add to the number of K which is infinite, nor to H with which K is already in a complete one-to-one correspondence. Then $K(=K+K') > H(=K+X)$, and the part is greater than the whole. Of course this is a play upon the idea of progression in time; perhaps none the less a fair image of the course of reason,—though "I hold it not honesty to have it thus set down."

says Kant,[24] "is space; the pure form of objects of sense in general is time. But the pure *schema of quantity,* as a concept of the understanding, is *number,* which is a representation conceptually combining the successive addition of unit to like unit. Thus number is nothing other than the unity of the synthesis of the manifold of a homogeneous intuition in general, in that time itself is engendered in the apprehension of the intuition."

Thus for Kant "unity in the apprehension of a manifold" and "time," the empirical image of an *a priori* schema, are the fundamentals of the idea of number. We shall be not far wrong in identifying here the notions of unity, multiplicity, and serial order, which are primitive with Locke and are unevaded by the logisticians. But Kant puts these notions in a somewhat new light: they are no longer *bloss empirisch,* as with Locke, nor are they circuitously inferred from nominalistic definitions; rather, they come into being as elements of that synthetic activity which is the dominant mark of mind. Number is, in this sense, neither empirical nor quite metempirical. The categories of the understanding lie behind the numerical schema, but the schema itself is "only the phenomenon or sensible concept of an object in agreement with the category." Further, this schema—as indeed are schemata in general—is only the *a priori* determination of temporal intuitions, getting its content not through analytic but through esthetic transcendentalities. Indeed, one is tempted to say that Kant, like Plato, puts his mathematical realities in a kind of mid-realm participating at once in νοῦς and αἴσθησις.

The unique position of the number idea appears again in Kant's discussion of the formation of determinate numbers. Judgments of numerical relations, he says, are certainly *a priori* syntheses, but they are not, like the under-

[24] *Kritik der reinen Vernunft,* 182.

lying principles of geometry, universal in character. Accordingly, they are to be termed *number-formulas* (*Zahlformeln*), not axioms, and they are endless in number, i. e., as many as numbers themselves.[25] Kant conceives the formative judgments as synthetic apprehensions of aggregations of units. In their generation we may make use of sensible intuitions, as in computing by aid of the fingers, but the actual realization of a sum would be impossible apart from the *a priori* schema. "The arithmetical judgment is always synthetic, as may the better appear when we consider the larger numbers; for it is then clearly evident that, apply our concepts as we will, without the help of intuition, by mere conceptual division into elements, we can never discover a sum."[26]

Couturat retorts upon Kant that it is practically impossible to have precise and complete intuitions of numbers of the order of millions, and that these could never be calculated exactly if recourse to intuition were necessary. "What is true of the large numbers," he continues, "is true also of the small, and consequently it is not intuition but reason that enables us to say that 2 and 2 make 4."[27] Evidently Couturat overlooks the case of the phenomenal calculator who handles millions as the average mortal handles units, and without being able to analyze the process; or again, the undoubted fact that the average civilized man would be a mathematical prodigy to the average primitive. And again, it is not easy to see that there is a more excessive dogmatism in assuming that our intuitions of the great numbers are in character with our intuitions of the small, than in asserting that because we have no intuitions of the great (supposing this true) we can therefore have none of the small,—which is Couturat's position.

Nevertheless, there is justice in Couturat's criticisms,

[25] K. *d. r. V.*, 205-6.
[26] *Ibid.*, 15-16.
[27] L. Couturat, *Les principes des mathématiques*, p. 256.

especially to the effect that Kant's notion of "numerical formulas," calling as it does for an infinity of irreducible synthetic insights, ill conforms to our notion of rationality, and is, indeed, only a masked intrusion of the old empirical view of number. The difficulty with Kant's view is that the number syntheses reduce to no law, which offends our sense of the reasonable, hyper-conscious as it is when touched on the side of mathematics. Kant's *a priori* synthesis is after all only a designation, and, as Poincaré says, to christen a difficulty is not to solve it.

Poincaré's own view—which may be described as Kantian with a saving salt of empiricism—is an interesting variation. The foundation of the idea of number is mathematical induction, and the essence of mathematical induction is reasoning by recurrence, while reasoning by recurrence has for its proper character just that "it contains, as it were condensed into a single formula, an infinity of syllogisms." Such a rule cannot come to us from experience; experience can show it to hold for a limited portion, but only for a limited portion, of the endless suite of numbers. If it were a matter only of this limited portion the principle of contradiction would suffice, permitting us to develop as many syllogisms as we wish; but when it comes to embracing an infinity in a single formula, when the infinite is in question, then this principle fails, and it is just here too that experience is impotent. The rule of recurrence, "inaccessible alike to analytic demonstration and to experience, is the veritable type of the synthetic judgment *a priori*." [28]

Why, then, Poincaré asks, does such a form of judgment impose itself upon us so irresistibly? "Because it

[28] *La science et l'hypothèse*, Chap. I. Cf. p. 37: "Nous avons la faculté de concevoir qu'une unité peut être ajoutée à une collection d'unités; c'est grâce à l'expérience que nous avons l'occasion d'exercer cette faculté et que nous en prenons conscience: mais, dès ce moment, nous sentons que notre pouvoir n'a pas de limite et que nous pourrions compter indéfiniment, quoique nous n'ayons jamais eu à compter qu'un nombre d'objets."

is only the affirmation of the power of the mind which knows itself capable of conceiving the indefinite repetition of an act once this act is found possible. The mind has a direct intuition of this power; experience can be only an occasion for making use of it and hence of becoming conscious of it."

But there is another and an important feature of reasoning by recurrence which Poincaré emphasizes, and this is the *inventive* character of its judgments. They are not only intuitive, born of the nature of the mind, they are also creative; and indeed it is mathematical induction alone which can apprise us of the new. Each number, then, is to be looked upon as an invention—not due to physical experience, but a self-discovery of the mind. But invention and the self-discovery of the mind do not cease so long as life lasts; and so, says Poincaré in another connection,[29] "when I speak of all the whole numbers, I mean by that all the whole numbers that have been discovered and will one day be discovered.... And it is just this *possibility* of discovery that is the infinite."

The psychological temper of this view is apparent; in so far it is empirical. But the validity of mathematical judgments is independent of the vagaries of experience; it is derived from the structure of the mind rather than from the accidents of a conscious life, and in so far the judgments are *a priori* and metempirical. Whether mathematical truths represent not only the organization of mind but also the organization of nature is an epistemological question for which Poincaré suggests an interesting answer, but it is properly a question, not of mathematics, but of metaphysics.

Analogous to Poincaré's view is that of Bergson, which also must be regarded as Kantian in type. Bergson begins his analysis of the number concept with the categories of

[29] *Dernières pensées*, p. 131.

unity and multiplicity: every individual number is to be regarded as a ratio between the one and the many, unit and totality. "There are two species of unity," writes Bergson,[30] "the one definitive, which will form a number in adding itself to itself; the other provisional, that of this number which, in itself multiple, borrows its unity from the simple act by which the intelligence perceives it. And it is undeniable that when we image to ourselves the unitary components of the number we believe ourselves to be thinking of indivisibles, this belief entering as a considerable factor in the notion that we can conceive number apart from space. In every case, viewing the matter more nearly, we shall see that each unity is that of a simple act of the mind, and that, this act consisting in uniting, it is necessary that some multiplicity serve as its matter."

The two poles of the idea of number, unity and multiplicity, correspond in Bergson's view to the subjective and objective elements of experience,—ultimately and respectively to time and space, use and generation. "You can never draw from an idea which you have constructed more than you have put into it, and if the unity with which you compose your number is the unity of an act and not of an object, no effort of analysis can evoke from it more than unity pure and simple. Without doubt when you equate the number 3 to the sum of $1 + 1 + 1$, nothing prevents you from holding as indivisible the units which compose it, but this is because you do not utilize the multiplicity with which each of these units is big. It is, moreover, probable that the number 3 presents itself to our mind in this simple form, because we are thinking rather of the manner in which we obtained it than of the use we can make of it. But we ought to see that if all multiplication implies the possibility of treating any number soever as a provisional unity which will add itself to itself, in-

[30] *Les données immédiates de la conscience*, pp. 58-65.

versely the units in their turn are veritable numbers as great as one may wish, though one provisionally assumes them to be indecomposable in order to combine them *inter se.* Moreover, by the very fact that the possibility of dividing unity into as many parts as are desired is admitted it is regarded as extended." In fine: "What properly pertains to the mind is the indivisible process by which it fixes its attention successively upon the diverse parts of a given space; but the parts thus isolated are conserved in order to be added to others, and once added among themselves they are open to a new decomposition of whatever sort. They are then parts of space, and space is the matter with which the mind constructs number, the milieu in which the mind places it."

Thus in the Bergsonian view numbers are ratios mediating time and space. The order in which they fall is first of all the order in which achieved experience presents itself, i .e., it is spatial. But space-perceptions are all provisional in character; consequently numbers are all provisional in character. Numerical order is not continuous, but composed *per saltum* (*par sauts brusques*); we form our numbers turn by turn, each assuming the character of a mathematical point separated by an interval of space from the point following, but as we recede in our series from the points first formed these tend to unite into a line, their synthesis being the necessary consequence of our averted attention. But "once formed according to a determinate law, the number is decomposable according to any law whatever"; and here we reach the apparent freedom and apriority of the mathematical reason, a number in course of formation is not the same as a number once formed; it is only the latter that is really divisible.

Doubtless to minds enamored of the eternal, Bergson's view will seem a veritable anarchy; perhaps metaphysically it is so; but it can hardly be denied that it gives a fair description of the manner in which we actually learn and apply our numbers, and it gives also an intelligibility to the old-fashioned notion that number is generated by successive acts of attention which the old-fashioned explanations do not possess. This is due, of course, to the assumption of an intuitive reason, differing from Kant's—as with Poincaré—chiefly in its more direct reliance upon the course of conscious events, upon psychology conceived as mental history.

Nor is it altogether fanciful to see in Bergson's view a striking analogue of Plato's. Like Plato he conceives number as essentially a ratio. Like Plato he conceives the realm of numbers as a median realm, uniting the one and the many, participating in the one direction in the essential unity of thought, in the other expressing itself as the multiplicity of things. Number is the category which unites subjective and objective, ideal and material,—or in Bergsonian terms, time and space.

V.

The types of definition of number which we have been considering raise certain inevitable issues—none more inevitable than the question of the relation of psychology to logic, and of both these sciences to epistemology.

If we contrast the older empirical conception of number with the logistic view, we see at once that the former defines number from the point of departure of number genesis while the latter analyzes its nature irrespective of its origins. From this we may guess both the reason for the dependence of the older conception upon the act of counting, in the definition of number, and the reason for the aversion to counting (for their denials of its significance amounts to this) on the part of the logisticians. For there can be no question that, historically considered, the invention of counting is the beginning of a science of number;

nor again, that a study of the number-systems of primitive peoples, and indeed of the civilized, yield a direct insight into the modes in which numbers are thought. The psychology of number-consciousness is, therefore, a direct key to our mathematical use of numbers.

But is there another and more efficient key, not perhaps explaining the nature of our consciousness of numbers, but explaining why they are found to be applicable to experience or even susceptible of metempirical developments? To this question the logisticians respond with a various affirmative, "various" because, while for some logistic is a purely nominalistic science (or, more correctly, purely symbolistic), for others it is the clue to a realism transcending the fictions which impair all empirically-originated speech.

It must be owned that there is a kind of experiential warrant for each of these views—the Uranian as well as the Pandemian. For if the latter can appeal to the universal conformity of number notions in process of formation, to our physical and mental structure and needs, the Uranian reason can retort with the universal and seemingly superhuman validity of mathematics. Mathematical demonstrations need only to be understood in order to be convincing, and if there be such a thing as infallibility there can be no test for it save this. From such infallibility the Uranian may infer, with a show of force, that number is not the product of our experience, but is imposed on us by the structure of the universe. Mathematical truth is, at all events, more universal than anything else we know.

But this is a doctrine, not of logic, but of epistemology. Uranians do not like the word,—it has psychological associations. They prefer to mark their own science as at once hyper-psychological, hyper-epistemological, hyperlogical—a science which can have no name, since every name is contaminated with the experiential (humanly experiential) references of language. They aim rather at a system of symbols which shall be untalkable, though catholic of the meanings of speech as well as of all other meanings;[31] they would introduce us into a sphere where human relations and merely human thinking are merged into the crystalline structure of the de-reified reality of a cosmos transcending speech.

"Extravagant realism" is the only historic caption that can fit this point of view, and extravagant realism is the philosophical creed which Russell at least is ready to make his own.[32] That some adherents of the movement balk at this is no matter of surprise; but surely it is with ill reason, for the philosophic alternative which is left them is a nominalism without even the consolations of speech. When symbols are refined to such an extent that they are but the symbols of systems of unutterable ideas, whose generality outgeneralizes nature, then surely their inventors are worse than dumb; they have become cousin-german to the apostles of the flux, and, with Cratylus, nothing is left them but to wag impotent digits.

When the rigorous following out of the mathematical reason leads to such extreme views, we may well bear in mind M. Milhaud's caution against a too naive confidence in the dogmatisms of our understanding. We may well ask by what right (since it is from no definable experience) transcendental realism justifies its *ex cathedra* affirmations; or, with Poincaré, what value is to be attached to a symbolism so ineffable that no testimony of familiar fact can sustain it. And we will surely be led to inquire if there be not some secure middle way, satisfying at once to our reason and our sense.

[31] I can imagine no more downright statement of the point of view than that of A. Padoa (*Bibliothèque du Congrès International de Philosophie*, 1901, Vol. III, pp. 317f.). Surely, when we are told that science is the peril of logic, that reasoning in order to be safe must be empty, we may well draw heretical breaths!

[32] *Monist*, October, 1914.

Now it would be presumption to affirm that the Kantian view—which we might term the "moderate realism" of the development—even as amended by Poincaré and Bergson is wholly satisfying. There are unquietable difficulties besetting every relativism, and these become accentuated when the relativity is between such extreme factors as reason and sensibility. It is far more comfortable to fashion a shapely abode of ideas of a single order and name it intellect than to be faithful to all the factors that enter into the cognizable world; nevertheless, it is only with this inclusive faithfulness at once to fact and to reason that temperaments of a certain kind can find their rest.

Herein is the merit of the neo-Kantian view. It sees the crudities of the old naive empiricism quite as clearly as do the logisticians; but for all that it is unwilling to abandon empirical leadings or to deny the centrality of our human experience, for mathematical as for all other meanings. Indeed, it asks, and asks fairly, of the logisticians by what right they assume that the numbers and measures that tell and mete the physical world are only illustrative cases to be subsumed under some cosmic Number, super-human and supra-mundane. Why, for example, is "the suite of *natural* numbers" so named, and why made the model for the conceptualization of all other series, if it be not due to some greater intimacy of nature which number has with this suite than with the others?

Referring to the arithmetical definition of continuity Poincaré says:[33] "This definition makes a ready disposal of the intuitive origin of the notion of continuity, and of all the riches which this notion conceals. It returns to the type of those definitions—so frequent in mathematics since the tendency to arithmetize this science—definitions mathematically sound, but philosophically unsatisfying. They replace the objects to be defined and the intuitive notion

[33] *Dernières pensées*, p. 65.

of this object by a construction made of simpler materials; one sees indeed that one can effectively make this construction with these materials, but one sees also that one can make many others. What is not to be seen is the deeper reason why one assembles these materials in just this, and not in another fashion." And again:[34] "Among all the constructions that one can make with the materials furnished by logic, a choice must be made; the true geometer makes this choice judiciously because he is guided by a sure instinct, or by some vague consciousness of I know not what geometry more profound and more hidden, which alone makes the value of the edifice built."

There is a sense, as we have said, in which the world *is* all possible worlds; but there is a commoner and more valuable sense according to which the world we call real is only one among many possible worlds. The problem at once of philosophy and of all rational life is to tell us just what this unique reality is, why the materials of creation have been assembled in just this, and not in another fashion.

Both Poincaré and Bergson recognize in mathematical reasoning a power or enterprise of the spirit which is in some sense prior to experience. It is in this that they are Kantians. This power, or intuition as they agree in calling it, gives to mathematical truths their sanctioning validity. But the validity of mathematics is not supposed, as with the logisticians, to derive from a firmament above the firmament; it holds only within the ranges of human insight, and indeed it is the definition of the utmost reach of this insight. "When I speak of all the whole numbers, I mean by that all the whole numbers that have been discovered and will one day be discovered....And it is just this possibility of discovery that is the infinite," says Poincaré. If I read Bergson aright, I judge his conception of

[34] *Science et méthode*, p. 158.

the unity of living time, within which number is generated in the perception of differences, to be not radically divergent from Poincaré's meaning; and certainly their common view squares with the kind of interpretation which language can give of number, and which the ordinarily thoughtful intelligence can accept.

Nor do I hesitate to add that its metaphysical implications are rich and profound. For a view of number which, while holding it within the leash of human experience makes of it the measure of our expectation of life, is surely sufficiently grandiose for any imagination, if it seem to make that expectation infinite. The intuition which gives the sanction becomes the testimony to a truth in number transcending the facts to which it is applied—that is, the little range of life here present—though not transcending the possibilities of real experience. Plato found in mathematical intuitions recollections from a previous life of the intelligence, Bergson and Poincaré treat them rather as prophecies of life to come; but these are only variations of a common doctrine.

HARTLEY BURR ALEXANDER.
UNIVERSITY OF NEBRASKA.

THE ULTIMATE CONSTITUENTS OF MATTER.*

I WISH to discuss in this article no less a question than the ancient metaphysical query, "What is matter?" The question, "What is matter?" in so far as it concerns philosophy, is, I think, already capable of an answer which in principle will be as complete as an answer can hope to be; that is to say, we can separate the problem into an essentially soluble and an essentially insoluble portion, and we can now see how to solve the essentially soluble portion, at least as regards its main outlines. It is these outlines which I wish to suggest in the present article. My main position, which is realistic, is, I hope and believe, not remote from that of Professor Alexander, by whose writings on this subject I have profited greatly.[1] It is also in close accord with that of Dr. Nunn.[2]

Common sense is accustomed to the division of the world into mind and matter. It is supposed by all who have never studied philosophy that the distinction between mind and matter is perfectly clear and easy, that the two do not at any point overlap, and that only a fool or a philosopher could be in doubt as to whether any given entity is mental or material. This simple faith survives in Descartes and in a somewhat modified form in Spinoza, but with Leibniz it begins to disappear, and from his day to our own almost every philosopher of note has criticized and rejected the dualism of common sense. It is my intention in this article to defend this dualism; but before defending

* An address delivered to the Philosophical Society of Manchester in February 1915.

[1] Cf. especially Samuel Alexander, "The Basis of Realism," *British Academy*, Vol. VI.

[2] "Are Secondary Qualities Independent of Perception?" *Proc. Arist. Soc.*, 1909-10, pp. 151-218.

it we must spend a few moments on the reasons which have prompted its rejection.

Our knowledge of the material world is obtained by means of the senses, of sight and touch and so on. At first it is supposed that things are just as they seem, but two opposite sophistications soon destroy this naive belief. On the one hand the physicists cut up matter into molecules, atoms, corpuscles, and as many more such subdivisions as their future needs may make them postulate, and the units at which they arrive are uncommonly different from the visible, tangible objects of daily life. A unit of matter tends more and more to be something like an electromagnetic field filling all space, though having its greatest intensity in a small region. Matter consisting of such elements is as remote from daily life as any metaphysical theory. It differs from the theories of metaphysicians only in the fact that its practical efficacy proves that it contains some measure of truth and induces business men to invest money on the strength of it; but in spite of its connection with the money market, it remains a metaphysical theory none the less.

The second kind of sophistication to which the world of common sense has been subjected is derived from the psychologists and physiologists. The physiologists point out that what we see depends upon the eye, that what we hear depends upon the ear, and that all our senses are liable to be affected by anything which affects the brain, like alcohol or hasheesh. Psychologists point out how much of what we think we see is supplied by association or unconscious inference, how much is mental interpretation, and how doubtful is the residuum which can be regarded as crude datum. From these facts it is argued by the psychologists that the notion of a datum passively received by the mind is a delusion, and it is argued by the physiologists that even if a pure datum of sense could be obtained by the analysis of experience, still this datum could not belong, as common sense supposes, to the outer world, since its whole nature is conditioned by our nerves and sense organs, changing as they change in ways which it is thought impossible to connect with any change in the matter supposed to be perceived. This physiologist's argument is exposed to the rejoinder, more specious than solid, that our knowledge of the existence of the sense organs and nerves is obtained by that very process which the physiologist has been engaged in discrediting, since the existence of the nerves and sense organs is only known through the evidence of the senses themselves. This argument may prove that some reinterpretation of the results of physiology is necessary before they can acquire metaphysical validity. But it does not upset the physiological argument in so far as this constitutes merely a *reductio ad absurdum* of naive realism.

These various lines of argument prove, I think, that some part of the beliefs of common sense must be abandoned. They prove that, if we take these beliefs as a whole, we are forced into conclusions which are in part self-contradictory; but such arguments cannot of themselves decide what portion of our common-sense beliefs is in need of correction. Common sense believes that what we see is physical, outside the mind, and continuing to exist if we shut our eyes or turn them in another direction. I believe that common sense is right in regarding what we see as physical and outside the mind, but is probably wrong in supposing that it continues to exist when we are no longer looking at it. It seems to me that the whole discussion of matter has been obscured by two errors which support each other. The first of these is the error that what we see, or perceive through any of our other senses, is subjective: the second is the belief that what is physical must be persistent. Whatever physics may regard as the ultimate constituents of matter, it always supposes these constituents to be indestructible. Since the immediate data of sense are not indestructible but in a state of perpetual flux, it is argued that these data themselves cannot be among the ultimate constituents of matter. I believe this to be a sheer mistake. The persistent particles of mathematical physics I regard as logical constructions, symbolic fictions enabling us to express compendiously very complicated assemblages of facts; and, on the other hand, I believe that the actual data in sensation, the immediate objects of sight or touch or hearing, are extra-mental, purely physical, and among the ultimate constituents of matter.

My meaning in regard to the impermanence of physical entities may perhaps be made clearer by the use of Bergson's favorite illustration of the cinematograph. When I first read Bergson's statement that the mathematician conceives the world after the analogy of a cinematograph, I had never seen a cinematograph, and my first visit to one was determined by the desire to verify Bergson's statement, which I found to be completely true, at least so far as I am concerned. When, in a picture palace, we see a man rolling down hill, or running away from the police, or falling into a river, or doing any of those other things to which men in such places are addicted, we know that there is not really only one man moving, but a succession of films, each with a different momentary man. The illusion of persistence arises only through the approach to continuity in the series of momentary men. Now what I wish to suggest is that in this respect the cinema is a better metaphysician than common sense, physics, or philosophy. The real man too, I believe, however the police may swear to his identity, is really a series of momentary men, each different one from the other, and bound together, not by a numerical identity, but by continuity and certain intrinsic causal laws. And what applies to men applies equally to tables and chairs, the sun, moon and stars. Each of these is to be regarded, not as one single persistent entity, but as a series of entities succeeding each other in time, each lasting for a very brief period, though probably not for a mere mathematical instant. In saying this I am only urging the same kind of division in time as we are accustomed to acknowledge in the case of space. A body which fills a cubic foot will be admitted to consist of many smaller bodies, each occupying only a very tiny volume; similarly a thing which persists for an hour is to be regarded as composed of many things of less duration. A true theory of matter requires a division of things into time-corpuscles as well as into space-corpuscles.

The world may be conceived as consisting of a multitude of entities arranged in a certain pattern. The entities which are arranged I shall call "particulars." The arrangement or pattern results from relations among particulars. Classes or series of particulars, collected together on account of some property which makes it convenient to be able to speak of them as wholes, are what I call logical constructions or symbolic fictions. The particulars are to be conceived, not on the analogy of bricks in a building, but rather on the analogy of notes in a symphony. The ultimate constituents of a symphony (apart from relations) are the notes, each of which lasts only for a very short time. We may collect together all the notes played by one instrument: these may be regarded as the analogues of the successive particulars which common sense would regard as successive states of one "thing." But the "thing" ought to be regarded as no more "real" or "substantial" than, for example, the rôle of the trombone. As soon as "things" are conceived in this manner it will be found that the difficulties in the way of regarding immediate objects of sense as physical have largely disappeared.

When people ask, "Is the object of sense mental or physical?" they seldom have any clear idea either what is meant by "mental" or "physical," or what criteria are to be applied for deciding whether a given entity belongs to one class or the other. I do not know how to give a sharp definition of the word "mental," but something may be done by enumerating occurrences which are indubitably mental: believing, doubting, wishing, willing, being pleased or pained, are certainly mental occurrences; so are what we may call experiences, seeing, hearing, smelling, perceiving generally. But it does not follow from this that what is seen, what is heard, what is smelt, what is perceived, must be mental. When I see a flash of lightning, my seeing of it is mental, but what I see, although it is not quite the same as what anybody else sees at the same moment, and although it seems very unlike what the physicist would describe as a flash of lightning, is not mental. I maintain, in fact, that if the physicist could describe truly and fully all that occurs in the physical world when there is a flash of lightning, it would contain as a constituent what I see, and also what is seen by anybody else who would commonly be said to see the same flash. What I mean may perhaps be made plainer by saying that if my body could remain in exactly the same state in which it is, although my mind had ceased to exist, precisely that object which I now see when I see the flash would exist, although of course I should not see it, since my seeing is mental. The principal reasons which have led people to reject this view have, I think, been two: first, that they did not adequately distinguish between my seeing and what I see; secondly, that the causal dependence of what I see upon my body has made people suppose that what I see cannot be "outside" me. The first of these reasons need not detain us, since the confusion only needs to be pointed out in order to be obviated; but the second requires some discussion, since it can only be answered by removing current misconceptions, on the one hand as to the nature of space, and on the other, as to the meaning of causal dependence.

When people ask whether colors, for example, or other secondary qualities are inside or outside the mind, they seem to suppose that their meaning must be clear, and that it ought to be possible to say yes or no without any further discussion of the terms involved. In fact, however, such terms as "inside" or "outside" are very ambiguous. What is meant by asking whether this or that is "in" the mind? The mind is not like a bag or a pie; it does not occupy a certain region in space, or, if it does, what is in that region is presumably part of the brain, which would not be said to be in the mind. When people say that sensible qualities are in the mind, they do not mean "spatially contained in" in the sense in which the blackbirds were in the pie. We might regard the mind as an assemblage of particulars, namely what would be called "states of mind," which would belong together in virtue of some specific common quality. The common quality of all states of mind would be the quality designated by the word "mental"; and besides this we should have to suppose that each separate person's states of mind have some common characteristic distinguishing them from the states of mind of other people. Ignoring this latter point, let us ask ourselves whether the quality designated by the word "mental" does, as a matter of observation, actually belong to objects of sense, such as colors or noises. I think any candid person must reply that, however difficult it may be to know what we mean by "mental," it is not difficult to see that colors and noises are not mental in the sense of having that intrinsic peculiarity which belongs to beliefs and wishes and volitions, but not to the physical world. Berkeley advances on this subject a plausible argument[3] which seems to me to rest upon

[3] First dialogue between Hylas and Philonous, *Works* (Fraser's edition), I, p. 266; *Three Dialogues* (published by Open Court Pub. Co.), p. 15.

an ambiguity in the word "pain." He argues that the realist supposes the heat which he feels in approaching a fire to be something outside his mind, but that as he approaches nearer and nearer to the fire the sensation of heat passes imperceptibly into pain, and that no one could regard pain as something outside the mind. In reply to this argument, it should be observed in the first place that the heat of which we are immediately aware is not in the fire but in our own body. It is only by inference that the fire is judged to be the cause of the heat which we feel in our body. In the second place (and this is the more important point), when we speak of pain we may mean one of two things: we may mean the object of the sensation or other experience which has the quality of being painful, or we may mean the quality of painfulness itself. When a man says he has a pain in his great toe, what he means is that he has a sensation associated with his great toe and having the quality of painfulness. The sensation itself, like every sensation, consists in experiencing a sensible object, and the experiencing has that quality of painfulness which only mental occurrences can have, but which may belong to thoughts or desires, as well as to sensations. But in common language we speak of the sensible object experienced in a painful sensation as a pain, and it is this way of speaking which causes the confusion upon which the plausibility of Berkeley's argument depends. It would be absurd to attribute the quality of painfulness to anything non-mental, and hence it comes to be thought that what we call a pain in the toe must be mental. In fact, however, it is not the sensible object in such a case which is painful, but the sensation, that is to say, the experience of the sensible object. As the heat which we experience from the fire grows greater, the experience passes gradually from being pleasant to being painful, but neither the pleasure nor the pain is a quality of the object experienced as opposed to the experience, and it is therefore a fallacy to argue that this object must be mental on the ground that painfulness can only be attributed to what is mental.

If, then, when we say that something is in the mind we mean that it has a certain recognizable intrinsic characteristic such as belongs to thoughts and desires, it must be maintained, on grounds of immediate inspection that objects of sense are not in any mind.

A different meaning of "in the mind" is however to be inferred from the arguments advanced by those who regard sensible objects as being in the mind. The arguments used are, in the main, such as would prove the causal dependence of objects of sense upon the percipient. Now the notion of causal dependence is very obscure and difficult, much more so in fact than is generally realized by philosophers. I shall return to this point in a moment. For the present however, accepting the notion of causal dependence without criticism, I wish to urge that the dependence in question is rather upon our bodies than upon our minds. The visual appearance of an object is altered if we shut one eye, or squint, or look previously at something dazzling; but all these are bodily acts, and the alterations which they effect are to be explained by physiology and optics, not by psychology.[4] They are in fact of exactly the same kind as the alterations effected by spectacles or a microscope. They belong therefore to the theory of the physical world, and can have no bearing upon the question whether what we see is causally dependent upon the mind. What they do tend to prove, and what I for my part have no wish to deny, is that what we see is causally dependent upon our body and is not, as crude common sense would suppose, something which would exist equally if our eyes and nerves and brain were absent, any more than the visual appearance presented by an object seen through a microscope would re-

[4] This point has been well urged by the American realists.

main if the microscope were removed. So long as it is supposed that the physical world is composed of stable and more or less permanent constituents, the fact that what we see is changed by changes in our body appears to afford reason for regarding what we see as not an ultimate constituent of matter. But if it is recognized that the ultimate constituents of matter are as circumscribed in duration as in spatial extent, the whole of this difficulty vanishes.

There remains however another difficulty, connected with space. When we look at the sun we wish to know something about the sun itself, which is ninety-three million miles away; but what we see is dependent upon our eyes, and it is difficult to suppose that our eyes can affect what happens at a distance of ninety-three million miles. Physics tells us that certain electromagnetic waves start from the sun, and reach our eyes after about eight minutes. They there produce disturbances in the rods and cones, thence in the optic nerve, thence in the brain. At the end of this purely physical series, by some odd miracle, comes the experience which we call "seeing the sun," and it is such experiences which form the whole and sole reason for our belief in the optic nerve, the rods and cones, the ninety-three million miles, the electromagnetic waves, and the sun itself. It is this curious oppositeness of direction between the order of causation as affirmed by physics, and the order of evidence as revealed by theory of knowledge, that causes the most serious perplexities in regard to the nature of physical reality. Anything that invalidates our seeing, as a source of knowledge concerning physical reality, invalidates also the whole of physics and physiology. And yet, starting from a common-sense acceptance of our seeing, physics has been led step by step to the construction of the causal chain in which our seeing is the last link, and the immediate object which we see cannot be regarded as that initial cause which we believe to be ninety-three million miles away, and which we are inclined to regard as the "real" sun.

I have stated this difficulty as forcibly as I can, because I believe that it can only be answered by a radical analysis and reconstruction of all the conceptions upon whose employment it depends.

Space, time, matter and cause, are the chief of these conceptions. Let us begin with the conception of cause.

Causal dependence, as I observed a moment ago, is a conception which it is very dangerous to accept at its face value. There exists a notion that in regard to any event there is something which may be called *the* cause of that event—some one definite occurrence, without which the event would have been impossible and with which it becomes necessary. An event is supposed to be dependent upon its cause in some way in which it is not dependent upon other things. Thus men will urge that the mind is dependent upon the brain, or, with equal plausibility, that the brain is dependent upon the mind. It seems not improbable that if we had sufficient knowledge we could infer the state of a man's mind from the state of his brain, or the state of his brain from the state of his mind. So long as the usual conception of causal dependence is retained, this state of affairs can be used by the materialist to urge that the state of our brain causes our thoughts, and by the idealist to urge that our thoughts cause the state of our brain. Either contention is equally valid or equally invalid. The fact seems to be that there are many correlations of the sort which may be called causal, and that, for example, either a physical or a mental event can be predicted, theoretically, either from a sufficient number of physical antecedents or from a sufficient number of mental antecedents. To speak of *the* cause of an event is therefore misleading. Any set of antecedents from which the event can theoretically be inferred by means of correlations might be called *a* cause of the event. But to speak of *the* cause is to imply a uniqueness which does not exist.

The relevance of this to the experience which we call "seeing the sun" is obvious. The fact that there exists a chain of antecedents which makes our seeing dependent upon the eyes and nerves and brain does not even tend to show that there is not another chain of antecedents in which the eyes and nerves and brain as physical things are ignored. If we are to escape from the dilemma which seemed to arise out of the physiological causation of what we see when we say we see the sun, we must find, at least in theory, a way of stating causal laws for the physical world, in which the units are not material things, such as the eyes and nerves and brain, but momentary particulars of the same sort as our momentary visual object when we look at the sun. The sun itself and the eyes and nerves and brain must be regarded as assemblages of momentary particulars. Instead of supposing, as we naturally do when we start from an uncritical acceptance of the apparent dicta of physics, that *matter* is what is "really real" in the physical world, and that the immediate objects of sense are mere phantasms, we must, instead, regard matter as a logical construction, of which the constituents will be just such evanescent particulars as may, when an observer happens to be present, become data of sense to that observer. What physics regards as the sun of eight minutes ago will be a whole assemblage of particulars, existing at different times, spreading out from a center with the velocity of light, and containing among their number all those visual data which are seen by people who are now looking at the sun. Thus the sun of eight minutes ago is a class of particulars, and what I see when I now look at the sun is one member of this class. The various particulars constituting this class will be correlated with each other by a certain continuity and certain intrinsic laws of variation as we pass outwards from the center, together with certain modifications correlated extrinsically with other particulars which are not members of this class. It is these extrinsic modifications which represent the sort of facts that, in our former account, appeared as the influence of the eyes and nerves in modifying the appearance of the sun.[5]

The *prima facie* difficulties in the way of this view are chiefly derived from an unduly conventional theory of space. It might seem at first sight as if we had packed the world much fuller than it could possibly hold. At every place between us and the sun, we said, there is to be a particular which is to be a member of the sun as it was a few minutes ago. There will also, of course, have to be a particular which is a member of any planet or fixed star that may happen to be visible from that place. At the place where I am, there will be particulars which will be members severally of all the "things" I am now said to be perceiving. Thus throughout the world, everywhere, there will be an enormous number of particulars coexisting in the same place. But these troubles result from contenting ourselves too readily with the merely three-dimensional space to which schoolmasters have accustomed us. The space of the real world is a space of six dimensions, and as soon as we realize this we see that there is plenty of room for all the particulars for which we want to find positions. In order to realize this we have only to return for a moment from the polished space of physics to the rough and untidy space of our immediate sensible experience. The space of one man's sensible objects is a three-dimensional space. It does not appear probable that two men ever both perceive at the same time any one sensible object; when they are said to see the same thing

[5] Cf. T. P. Nunn, "Are Secondary Qualities Independent of Perception?" *Proc. Aris. Soc.*, 1909-1910.

or hear the same noise, there will always be some difference, however slight, between the actual shapes seen or the actual sounds heard. If this is so, and if, as is generally assumed, position in space is purely relative, it follows that the space of one man's objects and the space of another man's objects have no place in common; that they are in fact different spaces, and not merely different parts of one space. I mean by this that such immediate spatial relations as are perceived to hold between the different parts of the sensible space perceived by one man, do not hold between parts of sensible spaces perceived by different men. There are therefore a multitude of three-dimensional spaces in the world: there are all those perceived by observers, and presumably also those which are not perceived, merely because no observer is suitable situated for perceiving them.

But although these spaces do not have to one another the same kind of spatial relations as obtain between the parts of one of them, it is nevertheless possible to arrange these spaces themselves in a three-dimensional order. This is done by means of the correlated particulars which we regard as members (or aspects) of one physical thing. When a number of people are said to see the same object, those who would be said to be near to the object see a particular occupying a larger part of their field of vision than is occupied by the corresponding particular seen by people who would be said to be farther from the thing. By means of such considerations it is possible, in ways which need not now be further specified, to arrange all the different spaces in a three-dimensional series. Since each of the spaces is itself three-dimensional, the whole world of particulars is thus arranged in a six-dimensional space, that is to say, six coordinates will be required to assign completely the position of any given particular, namely three to assign its position in its own space and three more to assign the position of its space among the other spaces.

There are two ways of classifying particulars: we may take together all those that belong to a given "perspective," or all those that are, as common sense would say, different "aspects" of the same "thing." For example, if I am (as is said) seeing the sun, what I see belongs to two assemblages: (1) the assemblage of all my present objects of sense, which is what I call a "perspective"; (2) the assemblage of all the different present particulars which would be called aspects of the sun—this assemblage is what I define as *being* the sun at the present time. Thus "perspectives" and "things" are merely two different ways of classifying particulars. It is to be observed that there is no *a priori* necessity for particulars to be susceptible of this double classification. There may be what might be called "wild" particulars, not having the usual relations by which the classification is effected; perhaps dreams and hallucinations are composed of particulars which are "wild" in this sense.

The exact definition of what is meant by a perspective is not quite easy. So long as we confine ourselves to visible objects or to objects of touch we might define the perspective of a given particular as "all particulars which have a simple (direct) spatial relation to the given particular." Between two patches of color which I see now, there is a direct spatial relation which I equally see. But between patches of color seen by different men there is only an indirect constructed spatial relation by means of the placing of "things" in physical space (which is the same as the space composed of perspectives). Those particulars which have direct spatial relations to a given particular will belong to the same perspective. But if, for example, the sounds which I hear are to belong to the same perspective with the patches of color which I see, there must be particulars which have no direct spatial relation and yet belong to the same perspective. We cannot define a perspective as all the data of one percipient at one time, because we wish to allow the possibility of perspectives which are not perceived by any one. There will be need, therefore, in defining a perspective, of some principle derived neither from psychology nor from space.

Such a principle may be obtained from the consideration of *time*. The one all-embracing time, like the one all-embracing space, is a construction; there is no *direct* time-relation between particulars belonging to my perspective and particulars belonging to another man's. On the other hand, any two particulars of which I am aware are either simultaneous or successive, and their simultaneity or successiveness is sometimes itself a datum to me. We may therefore define the perspective to which a given particular belongs as "all particulars simultaneous with the given particular," where "simultaneous" is to be understood as a direct simple relation, not the derivative constructed relation of physics. It may be observed that the introduction of "local time" suggested by the principle of relativity has effected, for purely scientific reasons, much the same multiplication of times as we have just been advocating.

The sum-total of all the particulars that are (directly) either simultaneous with or before or after a given particular may be defined as the "biography" to which that particular belongs. It will be observed that, just as a perspective need not be actually perceived by any one, so a biography need not be actually lived by any one. Those biographies that are lived by no one are called "official."

The definition of a "thing" is effected by means of continuity and of correlations which have a certain differential independence of other "things." That is to say, given a particular in one perspective, there will usually in a neighboring perspective be a very similar particular, differing from the given particular, to the first order of small quantities, according to a law involving only the difference of position of the two perspectives in perspective space, and not any of the other "things" in the universe. It is this continuity and differential independence in the law of change as we pass from one perspective to another that defines the class of particulars which is to be called "one thing."

Broadly speaking, we may say that the physicist finds it convenient to classify particulars into "things," while the psychologist finds it convenient to classify them into "perspectives" and "biographies," since one perspective *may* constitute the momentary data of one percipient, and one biography *may* constitute the whole of the data of one percipient throughout his life.

We may now sum up our discussion. Our object has been to discover as far as possible the nature of the ultimate constituents of the physical world. When I speak of the "physical world" I mean, to begin with, the world dealt with by physics. It is obvious that physics is an empirical science, giving us a certain amount of knowledge and based upon evidence obtained through the senses. But partly through the development of physics itself, partly through arguments derived from physiology, psychology or metaphysics, it has come to be thought that the immediate data of sense could not themselves form part of the ultimate constituents of the physical world, but were in some sense "mental," "in the mind," or "subjective." The grounds for this view, in so far as they depend upon physics, can only be adequately dealt with by rather elaborate constructions depending upon symbolic logic, showing that out of such materials as are provided by the senses it is possible to construct classes and series having the properties which physics assigns to matter. Since this argument is difficult and technical, I have not embarked upon it in this article. But in so far as the view that sense-data are "mental" rests upon physiology, psychology, or metaphysics, I have tried to show that it rests upon confusions and prejudices —prejudices in favor of permanence in the ultimate constituents of matter, and confusions derived from unduly simple notions as to space, from the causal correlation of sense-data with sense-organs, and from failure to distinguish between sense-data and sensations. If what we have said on these subjects is valid, the existence of sense-data is logically independent of the existence of mind, and is causally dependent upon the *body* of the percipient rather than upon his mind. The causal dependence upon the body of the percipient, we found, is a more complicated matter than it appears to be, and, like all causal dependence, is apt to give rise to erroneous beliefs through misconceptions as to the nature of causal correlation. If we have been right in our contentions, sense-data are merely those among the ultimate constituents of the physical world, of which we happen to be immediately aware; they themselves are purely physical, and all that is mental in connection with them is our awareness of them, which is irrelevant to their nature and to their place in physics.

Unduly simple notions as to space have been a great stumbling-block to realists. When two men look at the same table, it is supposed that what the one sees and what the other sees are in the same place. Since the shape and color are not quite the same for the two men, this raises a difficulty, hastily solved, or rather covered up, by declaring what each sees to be purely "subjective"—though it would puzzle those who use this glib word to say what they mean by it. The truth seems to be that space—and time also—is much more complicated than it would appear to be from the finished structure of physics, and that the one all-embracing three-dimensional space is a logical construction, obtained by means of correlations from a crude space of six dimensions. The particulars occupying this six-dimensional space, classified in one way, form "things," from which with certain further manipulations we can obtain what physics can regard as matter; classified in another way, they form "perspectives" and "biographies," which may, if a suitable percipient happens to exist, form respectively the sense-data of a momentary or of a total experience. It is only when physical "things" have been dissected into series of classes of particulars, as we have done, that the conflict between the point of view of physics and the point of view of psychology can be overcome. This conflict, if what has been said is not mistaken, flows from different methods of classification, and vanishes as soon as its source is discovered.

In favor of the theory which I have briefly outlined, I do not claim that it is *certainly* true. Apart from the likelihood of mistakes, much of it is avowedly hypothetical. What I do claim for the theory is that it *may* be true, and that this is more than can be said for any other theory except the closely analogous theory of Leibniz. The difficulties besetting realism, the confusions obstructing any philosophical account of physics, the dilemma resulting from discrediting sense-data, which yet remain the sole source of our knowledge of the outer world—all these are avoided by the theory which I advocate. This does not prove the theory to be true, since probably many other theories might be invented which would have the same merits. But it does prove that the theory has a better chance of being true than any of its present competitors, and it suggests that what can be known with certainty is likely to be discoverable by taking our theory as a starting-point, and gradually freeing it from all such assumptions as seem irrelevant, unnecessary, or unfounded. On these grounds, I recommend it to attention as a hypothesis and a basis for further work, though not as itself a finished or adequate solution of the problem with which it deals.

CAMBRIDGE, ENGLAND. BERTRAND RUSSELL.

NEWTON'S HYPOTHESES OF ETHER AND OF GRAVITATION FROM 1693 TO 1726.

AFTER his correspondence with Bentley and a letter of 1693 to Leibniz, referred to in §VI below, Newton does not seem to have made any more pronouncements about the ether or the nature of gravitation until the Latin edition of his *Opticks,* which was published in 1706. Discussions[1] on the cause of gravitation were greatly stimulated by the appearance of Newton's *Principia* in 1687, and continued — especially between Leibniz and Huygens — until 1694; but it would not be relevant to our present subject to consider these discussions further here.

We have seen that Newton himself did not regard gravitation as an essential property of matter, implanted in it by the Creator. In the *Principia,* he merely considered it as a starting-point for mathematical deductions; the discovery of its nature and cause was a physical and not a mathematical problem. From the letters of 1692 and 1693 to Bentley we learn that he did not pretend to know what the cause of gravity might be, but it seemed to him incomprehensible that matter should act on other matter without the intervention of a medium. Still he explicitly stated that he did not express any opinion as to "whether this agent be material or immaterial." In the first edition of the *Opticks* (1704) there was no mention in the "Queries" of the ether or gravitation.

[1] Rosenberger, *Isaac Newton und seine physikalischen Principien,* pp. 227-248.

I.

In the preface to Newton's *Opticks: or, a Treatise of the Reflexions, Refractions, Inflexions, and Colours of Light,* which was published at London in 1704, he mentioned that the work consisted of: (1) The optical memoir of 1675; (2) Additions made in 1687; (3) Stray papers collected after this date into the third Book and the last proposition of the second Book. The printing of the work was delayed so that controversy might be avoided,[2] and even then it was only the importunity of his friends that led him to print at all. Newton's optical memoir of 1672 is not mentioned, and it is just possible that Newton's words: "If any papers writ on this subject are got out of my hands, they are imperfect and were perhaps written before I had tried all the experiments here set down, and fully satisfied myself about the laws of colors," refer to these memoirs.

The *Opticks* of 1704[3] is only hypothetical—at least intentionally[4]—in the "Queries" at the end. Of these[5] the first English edition only contained the first seven, the first sentence of the eighth, the ninth, the first two-thirds of the tenth, the first third of the eleventh, the twelfth to the fifteenth inclusive, and part of the sixteenth. The first Latin edition of 1706[6] contained in addition the second part of the eighth, the last third of the tenth, the last two-thirds of the eleventh, and the twenty-fifth to the thirty-first inclusive. The second English edition of 1717[7] contained in

[2] Hooke died on March 3, 1703.

[3] German annotated translation by William Abendroth in Nos. 96 and 97 of *Ostwald's Klassiker* (Leipsic, 1898). An account of the contents of the *Opticks* is given by Rosenberger on pp. 294-301 of his book; the "Queries" were dealt with on pp. 301-327.

[4] See below, toward the end of the present section.

[5] Cf. Rosenberger, *op. cit.*, pp. 302-303.

[6] *Optice: sive de Reflexionibus, Refractionibus, Inflexionibus et Coloribus Lucis Libri Tres*; translated by Samuel Clarke, London, 1706. Other editions of this Latin translation were published in 1719, 1740, 1747, 1749, and 1773.

[7] *Opticks: or, a Treatise of the Reflections, Refractions, Inflections and Colours of Light.* The Second Edition, with Additions. London, 1717.

addition the last third of the eighth, the seventeenth to the twenty-fourth inclusive, and many additions to the thirty-first. Other editions (1718, 1721, 1730) published in Newton's lifetime or revised by Newton before his death contained various additions to and omissions from many of the queries, especially the last.[8]

Rosenberger[9] has remarked that "while in the *Opticks* of 1704 the observations and measurements are taken without any alteration, on account of their unsurpassed accuracy, from the great optical memoir of 1675, the theory, or rather the hypothesis which is its foundation, receives a completely new form. In the memoir of 1675, Newton still considered it likely that the rays of light excite vibrations in the ether contained in bodies when the rays meet this ether, and that these vibrations allow the transmission of light or cause its reflection according to the phase in which they meet the rays. In the *Opticks,* on the other hand, after he had had to let the ether drop, Newton considered rays of light without reference to any vibrations there may be in bodies and ascribed the alternating transmission and reflection of light which the colored rings indicate, merely to the internal nature of rays of light."

In fact, Newton began the book with the words: "My design in this book is not to explain the properties of light by hypotheses, but to propose and prove them by reason and experiments: in order to which I shall premise the following definitions and axioms."

In spite of this declaration, Newton was obliged, as Rosenberger[10] has pointed out, to attribute hypothetical properties to rays of light,—that the rays have "fits of easy transmission and reflection." But an addition (Query 17) to the second edition of 1717 explains these "fits" by

[8] This is practically what Rosenberger says; but the English edition of 1721 is unaltered from the second edition. The second edition is reprinted in Vol. IV of *Horsley.*

[9] *Op. cit.,* pp. 293-294.

[10] *Op. cit.,* p. 296.

the hypothesis of undulations which are excited in bodies by the rays of light.

With regard to Rosenberger's view that Newton was gradually forced to give up the assumption of an ether, this, as we shall see, is by no means likely if we consider Newton's own words without prejudice. Rosenberger, indeed, seems much too prone to attribute to Newton himself the views which some of his school held.

In the next section we will review those queries added to the edition of 1706 which have a bearing on our present subject. In the third section, we must consider the second edition (1713) of the *Principia*. In the fourth section we consider the relevant queries added to the edition of the *Opticks* published in 1717. In the fifth section reference is made to Newton's later (1716, 1725) remarks on Leibniz's criticism that he viewed gravitation as an "occult cause" and a "miracle"; and the sixth section deals with Newton's opinions on an ether and the nature of gravitation from the general point of view which has been reached.

II.

The twenty-seventh query is[11]

"Are not all hypotheses erroneous which have hitherto been invented for explaining the phenomena of light by new modifications of the rays? For those phenomena depend not upon new modifications, as has been supposed, but upon the original and unchangeable properties of the rays."

The long twenty-eighth query[12] begins:

"Are not all hypotheses erroneous in which light is supposed to consist in pression or motion propagated through a fluid medium? For in all these hypotheses the phenomena of light have been hitherto explained by supposing that

[11] *Horsley,* Vol. IV, pp. 231-232. Cf. Rosenberger, *op. cit.,* p. 315.

[12] *Horsley,* Vol. IV, pp. 232-238. Cf. Rosenberger, *op. cit.,* pp. 315-318.

they arise from new modifications of the rays, which is an erroneous supposition.

"If light consisted only in pression propagated without actual motion, it would not be able to agitate and heat the bodies which refract and reflect it. If it consisted in motion propagated to all distances in an instant, it would require an infinite force every moment in every shining particle to generate that motion. And if it consisted in pression or motion propagated either in an instant or in time, it would bend into the shadow. For pression or motion cannot be propagated in a fluid in right lines beyond an obstacle which stops part of the motion, but will bend and spread every way into the quiescent medium which lies beyond the obstacle.[13] Gravity tends downwards, but the pressure of water arising from gravity tends every way with as much force sideways as downwards and through crooked passages as through straight ones. The waves on the surface of stagnating water, passing by the sides of a broad obstacle which stops part of them, bend afterwards, and dilate themselves gradually into the quiet water behind the obstacle. The waves, pulses or vibrations of the air wherein sounds consist bend manifestly; though not so much as the waves of water. For a bell or a cannon may be heard beyond a hill which intercepts the sight of the sounding body, and sounds are propagated as readily through crooked pipes as through straight ones. But light is never known to follow crooked passages nor to bend into the shadow. For the fixed stars, by the interposition of any of the planets, cease to be seen. And so do the parts of the sun by the interposition of the moon, Mercury or Venus. The rays which pass very near to the edges of any body are bent a little by the action of the body, as we showed above; but this bending is not toward but from the shadow, and is performed only in the passage of the ray

[13] *Principia*, Book II, Prop. XLII.

by the body and at a very small distance from it. So soon as the ray is past the body it goes right on."

In the course of this query, Newton remarked:[14] "And against filling the heavens with fluid mediums, unless they be exceeding rare, a great objection arises from the regular and very lasting motions of the planets and comets in all manner of courses through the heavens. For thence it is manifest that the heavens are void of all sensible resistance and, by consequence, of all sensible matter."

Another part of the same query is:[15]

"And therefore to make way for the regular and lasting motions of the planets and comets it is necessary to empty the heavens of all matter, except perhaps some very thin vapors, steams or effluvia arising from the atmosphere of the earth, planets and comets, and of such an exceedingly rare ethereal medium as we described above. A dense fluid can be of no use for explaining the phenomena of nature, the motions of the planets and comets being better explained without it. It serves only to disturb and retard the motions of those great bodies and make the frame of nature languish. And in the pores of bodies it serves only to stop the vibrating motions of their parts wherein their heat and activity consists. And as it is of no use and hinders the operations of nature and makes her languish, so there is no evidence for its existence, and therefore it ought to be rejected. And if it be rejected, the hypotheses that light consists in pression or motion propagated through such a medium are rejected with it.

"And for rejecting such a medium we have the authority of the oldest and most celebrated philosophers of Greece and Phoenicia, who made a vacuum and atoms and the gravity of atoms the first principles of their philosophy, tacitly attributing gravity to some other cause than dense matter.

[14] *Horsley,* Vol. IV, p. 234.

[15] *Horsley,* Vol. IV, pp. 236-238, Rosenberger, *op. cit.,* pp. 343-344.

Later philosophers banish the consideration of such a cause out of natural philosophy, feigning hypotheses for explaining all things mechanically and referring other causes to metaphysics: whereas the main business of natural philosophy is to argue from phenomena without feigning hypotheses and to deduce causes from effects till we come to the very first cause, which certainly is not mechanical; and not only to unfold the mechanism of the world, but chiefly to resolve these and such like questions. What is there in places almost empty of matter and whence is it that the sun and planets gravitate toward one another without dense matter between them? Whence is it that nature does nothing in vain; and whence arises all that order and beauty which we see in the world? To what end are comets, and whence is it that planets move all one and the same way in concentric orbits, while comets move all manner of ways in orbits very eccentric, and what hinders the fixed stars from falling upon one another? Does it not appear from phenomena that there is a Being incorporeal, living, intelligent, omnipresent, who in infinite space, as it were in his sensory, sees the things themselves intimately?" and so on.

In the twenty-ninth query, Newton[16] proceeded to develop his own emission-theory of light. It begins:

"Are not the rays of light very small bodies emitted from shining substances? For such bodies will pass through uniform mediums in right lines without bending into the shadow, which is the nature of the rays of light. They will also be capable of several properties and be able to conserve their properties unchanged in passing through several mediums, which is another condition of the rays of light."

"It is remarkable," said Rosenberger,[17] "that the state-

[16] *Horsley*, Vol. IV, pp. 238-241. Cf. Rosenberger, *op. cit.*, pp. 319-321.
[17] *Op. cit.*, pp. 320-321.

ment [in this query] of the necessity of attractive forces and [in the preceding one] of the impossibility of an ether is followed by a reference intercalated in the edition of 1717, to the derivation of this attraction by means of this ether. This reference is: 'What I mean in this question by a *vacuum* and by the attraction of the rays of light towards glass or crystal may be understood by what was said in the 18th, 19th, and 20th questions.'[18] Apparently Newton wished to show, even in his queries, that his theories are reconcilable with all hypotheses...."

It is obviously incorrect to speak, as Rosenberger does, of Newton's "statement...of the impossibility of an ether." As a rule, we have no means of deciding, from the "Queries," what Newton's real opinions on an ether were; but the letters to Bentley throw a great deal of light on the subject. Indeed, the weight of evidence seems to tell against Rosenberger's[19] view and in favor of the view which has become traditional, that Newton believed in some sort—not the Cartesian—of ether on the ground that he could not imagine a propagation of force without a medium.[20]

The thirtieth query[21] begins: "Are not gross bodies and light convertible into one another; and may not bodies receive much of their activity from the particles of light which enter their composition?" We know that for long after this, the matter of light was considered as a possible part of the subject-matter of chemistry.

The thirty-first query[22] was greatly added to in later editions, but we will here collect all that is said in it in its final form about the subjects that interest us at present. It begins:

"Have not the small particles of bodies certain powers,

[18] *Horsley,* Vol. IV, p. 241. These queries are given in § IV below.
[19] Cf. also *op. cit.,* pp. 333-334.
[20] Cf. § VI below.
[21] *Horsley,* Vol. IV, pp. 241-242. Cf. Rosenberger, *op. cit.,* pp. 321-322.
[22] *Horsley,* Vol. IV, pp. 242-264. Cf. Rosenberger, *op. cit.,* pp. 322-327.

virtues or forces by which they act at a distance, not only upon the rays of light for reflecting, refracting and inflecting them, but also upon one another for producing a great part of the phenomena of nature? For it is well known that bodies act one upon another by the attractions of gravity, magnetism and electricity, and these instances show the tenor and course of nature and make it not improbable that there may be more attractive powers than these. For nature is very consonant and conformable to herself. How these attractions may be performed, I do not here consider. What I call attraction may be performed by impulse or by some other means unknown to me. I use that word here to signify only in general any force by which bodies tend toward one another, whatever be the cause. For we must learn from the phenomena of nature what bodies attract one another and what are the laws and properties of the attraction, before we inquire the cause by which the attraction is performed. The attractions of gravity, magnetism and electricity reach to very sensible distances and so have been observed by vulgar eyes, and there may be others which reach to so small distances as hitherto escape observation; and perhaps electrical attraction may reach to such small distances even without being excited by friction."

"All bodies," said Newton,[23] "seem to be composed of hard particles." And again:[24] ". . . .it seems probable to me that God in the beginning formed matter in solid, massy, hard, impenetrable, movable particles of such sizes and figures and with such other properties and in such proportion to space[25] as most conduced to the end for

[23] *Horsley*, Vol IV, p. 251. [24] *Ibid.*, pp 260-262.

[25] "*Eoque numero et quantitate pro ratione spatii in quo futurum erat ut moverentur.* Dr. Clarke's first Latin; and so the sentence stands in Dr. Clarke's second Latin edition, which in most places was so corrected as to agree exactly with the second English. And to make sense of the passage, something is evidently wanting here to answer to the words of the Latin, *in quo futurum erat ut moverentur.* For to speak of particles of matter as bearing proportion to space indefinitely were absurd."—Note by Horsley.

which he formed them, and that these primitive particles being solids, are incomparably harder than any porous bodies compounded of them; even so very hard as never to wear or break in pieces; no ordinary power being able to divide what God himself made one in the first creation. While the particles continue entire, they may compose bodies of one and the same nature and texture in all ages; but should they wear away or break in pieces, the nature of things depending on them would be changed. Water and earth composed of old worn particles and fragments of particles would not be of the same nature and texture now with water and earth composed of entire particles in the beginning. And therefore that nature may be lasting, the changes of corporeal things are to be placed only in the various separations and new associations and motions of these permanent particles; compound bodies being apt to break, not in the midst of solid particles but where those particles are laid together and only touch in a few points.

"It seems to me further that these particles have not only a *vis inertiae* accompanied with such passive laws of motion as naturally result from that force, but also that they are moved by certain active principles, such as is that of gravity and that which causes fermentation and the cohesion of bodies. These principles I consider not as occult qualities, supposed to result from the specific forms of things, but as general laws of nature by which the things themselves are formed: their truth appearing to us by phenomena, though their causes be not yet discovered. For these are manifest qualities, and their causes only are occult. And the Aristotelians gave the name of occult qualities not to manifest qualities but to such qualities only as they supposed to lie hid in bodies and to be the unknown causes of manifest effects: such as would be the causes of gravity and of magnetic and electric attractions and of fermentations, if we should suppose that these forces or actions arose from qualities unknown to us and incapable of being discovered and made manifest. Such occult qualities put a stop to the improvement of natural philosophy, and therefore of late years have been rejected. To tell us that every species of things is endowed with an occult specific quality by which it acts and produces manifest effects, is to tell us nothing: but to derive two or three general principles of motion from phenomena, and afterwards to tell us how the properties of motion follow from phenomena, and afterwards to tell us how the properties and actions of all corporeal things follow from those manifest principles, would be a very great step in philosophy, though the causes of those principles were not yet discovered. And therefore I scruple not to propose the principles of motion above mentioned, they being of very general extent, and leave their causes to be found out.

"Now by the help of these principles, all material things seem to have been composed of the hard and solid particles above mentioned, variously associated in the first creation by the counsel of an intelligent Agent. For it became Him who created them to set them in order. And if he did so, it is unphilosophical to seek for any other origin of the world or to pretend that it might arise out of a chaos by the mere laws of nature; though being once formed, it may continue by those laws for many ages. For while comets move in very eccentric orbits in all manner of positions, blind Fate could never make all the planets move one and the same way in orbits concentric, some inconsiderable irregularities excepted, which may have arisen from the mutual actions of comets and planets upon one another, and which will be apt to increase till this system wants a reformation. Such a wonderful uniformity in the planetary system must be allowed the effect of choice. And so must the uniformity in the bodies of animals."

III.

Between the publication of the Latin translation and the second edition of the *Opticks* came that of the second edition of the *Principia* in 1713, which was very carefully edited by Roger Cotes.[26] Frequent mention of this edition has been already made in these articles:[27] what is of the greatest interest to us in this connection is that Newton, while emphasizing his neutral attitude toward the question as to whether *gravitation* was an essential property of bodies or no, added the famous *regulae philosophandi*. In the third rule, extension, hardness, impenetrability, mobility *and inertia* are classed together as universal qualities of bodies which can neither be increased nor diminished. In the second place, Cotes's preface, which expressed the views of Newton's school rather than of Newton himself, is usually supposed, and somewhat incorrectly supposed, to contain a distinct enunciation of the view—which Newton repeatedly disclaimed[28]—that gravity is an essential property of bodies.

Newton's own changes relating to our present subject in this edition have already been dealt with in §§ III and IV of my article in the April number of this magazine, and chiefly emphasize Newton's aversion to being supposed to state that gravity was an essential property of bodies. We will now fix our attention on Cotes's preface. In it is the passage:[29]

"Since, then, all bodies, whether upon earth or in the heavens, are heavy, so far as we can make any experiments or observations concerning them, we must certainly allow

[26] See on this point, Edleston, *op. cit.*; Brewster, *op. cit.*, Vol. I, pp. 312-318; Vol. II, pp. 248-252, 254; Rouse Ball, *op. cit.*, pp. 124-135; Rosenberger, *op. cit.*, pp. 368-385.

[27] See *Monist* for October, 1914, § XV, and for April, 1915, § IV.

[28] It should be noticed that Newton expressly declined to see all of Cotes's preface lest he should be considered to be responsible for it (cf. Rosenberger, *op. cit.*, p. 373).

[29] Cf. Rosenberger, *op. cit.*, pp. 376-377.

that gravity is found in all bodies universally. And just as we ought not to suppose that any bodies can be otherwise than extended, movable or impenetrable; so we ought not to conceive that any bodies can be otherwise than heavy. The extension, mobility and impenetrability of bodies become known to us only by experiments; and in the very same manner their gravity becomes known to us. All bodies we can make any observations upon are extended, movable and impenetrable; and thence we conclude that all bodies, even those concerning which we have no observations, are extended and movable and impenetrable. So we find that all bodies on which we can make observations are heavy; and thence we conclude that all bodies, even those of which we have no observations, are heavy also. If any one should say that the bodies of the fixed stars are not heavy because their gravity is not yet observed, he may say for the same reason that they are neither extended nor movable nor impenetrable, because these affections of the fixed stars are not yet observed. In short, either gravity must have a place among the primary qualities of all bodies, or extension, mobility and impenetrability must not. And if the nature of things is not rightly explained by the gravity of bodies, it will not be rightly explained by their extension, mobility and impenetrability.

"Some I know disapprove this conclusion, and mutter something about occult qualities.[30] They continually are caviling with us that gravity is an occult property and occult causes are to be quite banished from philosophy. But to this the answer is easy, that those are indeed occult causes whose existence is occult and imagined but not proved, but not those whose real existence is clearly demonstrated by observations. Therefore gravity can by no

[30] Leibniz in 1710 had accused Newton of introducing occult qualities and miracles into philosophy. On the subsequent controversy between Leibniz, Clarke, and others, see Brewster, *op. cit.*, Vol. II, pp. 282-289; Rosenberger, *op. cit.*, pp. 512-519.

means be called an occult cause of the celestial motions; because it is plain from the phenomena that such a virtue does really exist. Those rather have recourse to occult causes who postulate imaginary vortices of a matter entirely fictitious and imperceptible by our senses to direct those motions. But shall gravity be therefore called an occult cause and thrown out of philosophy because the cause of gravity is occult and not yet discovered? Those who affirm this should be careful not to fall into an absurdity that may overturn the foundations of all philosophy. For causes are wont to proceed in a continuous chain from those that are more compounded to those that are more simple; and when we have arrived at the most simple cause, we can go no farther. Therefore no mechanical account or explanation of the most simple cause is to be expected or given; for if it could be given, the cause were not the most simple. These most simple causes will you then call occult and reject them? Then you must reject those that immediately depend upon them, and those which depend upon the last, till philosophy is quite cleared and disencumbered of all causes.

"Some there are who say that gravity is preternatural and call it a perpetual miracle. Therefore they would have it rejected because preternatural causes have no place in physics. It is hardly worth while to spend time in answering this ridiculous objection, which overturns all philosophy. For either they will deny gravity to be in bodies, which cannot be said, or else they will call it preternatural because it is not produced by the other affections of bodies and therefore not by mechanical causes. But certainly there are primary affections of bodies, and these, because they are primary, have no dependence on the others. Let them consider whether all these are not in like manner preternatural, and in like manner to be rejected, and then what kind of philosophy we are like to have."

With this passage it is important to compare the following letter written by Cotes to Samuel Clarke. It is all the more important as it does not seem to be sufficiently emphasized by Rosenberger.[31]

Cotes wrote to Samuel Clarke[32] on June 25, 1713:[33]

"I received your very kind letter. I return you my thanks for your corrections of the Preface, and particularly for your advice in relation to that place where I seemed to assert gravity to be essential to bodies. I am fully of your mind that it would have furnished matter for caviling, and therefore I struck it out immediately upon Dr. Cannon's mentioning your objection to me, and so it never was printed. The impression of the whole book was finished about a week ago.

"My design in that passage was not to assert gravity to be essential to matter, but rather to assert that we are ignorant of the essential properties of matter, and that, in respect of our knowledge, gravity might possibly lay as fair a claim to that title as the other properties which I mentioned. For I understand by essential properties such properties without which no others belonging to the same substance can exist: and I would not undertake to prove that it were impossible for any of the other properties of bodies to exist without even extension."

The second edition of the *Principia* seems to have been published at the beginning of July, 1713. Edleston[34] thus commented on the above letter:

"It appears from the above letter that a meaning has been given to expressions in Cotes's Preface which he did not intend them to convey. He has been understood to assert that gravity is an essential property of bodies: his words are: *'Inter primarias qualitates corporum universorum vel*

[31] *Op. cit.*, p. 374. But cf. pp. 381-382.

[32] On Clarke see Rosenberger, *op. cit.*, pp. 287-288.

[33] Edleston, *op. cit.*, pp. 158-159. [34] *Ibid.*, pp. 159-160.

Gravitas habebit locum; vel Extensio, Mobilitas et Impenetrabilitas non habebunt.'" This passage is translated above.

IV.

The first notable change in the second English edition of 1717 was a second "Advertisement" dated July 16, 1717:

"And, to show that I do not take gravity for an essential property of bodies, I have added one question concerning its cause, choosing to propose it by way of a question because I am not yet satisfied about it for want of experiments."[35]

Queries eighteen to twenty are as follows:[36]

"Qu. 18. If in two large tall inverted cylindrical vessels of glass two little thermometers be suspended so as not to touch the vessels, the air be drawn out of one of these vessels, and these vessels thus prepared be carried out of a cold place into a warm one; the thermometer *in vacuo* will grow warm as much and almost as soon as the thermometer which is not *in vacuo*. And when the vessel is carried back into the cold place, the thermometer *in vacuo* will grow cold almost as soon as the other thermometer. Is not the heat of the warm room conveyed through the vacuum by the vibrations of a much subtler medium than air, which, after the air was drawn out, remained in the vacuum? And is not this medium the same as that medium by which light is refracted or reflected, and by whose vibrations light communicates heat to bodies, and is put into fits of easy reflection and easy transmission? And do not the vibrations of this medium in hot bodies contribute to the intenseness and duration of their heat? And do not hot

[35] This declaration was probably drawn from Newton by the then recent controversy between Leibniz and Clarke. Cf. also *Macc. Corr.*, Vol. II, p.437. At the end of the preface to the second edition of the *Opticks* was added to the preface to the first edition the date: April 1, 1704. There is a similar peculiarity about the preface to the *Principia*; and Edleston (*op. cit.*, p. lxxi) remarked that the dispute with Leibniz about the invention of the calculus had probably taught Newton the importance of dates.

[36] *Horsley*, Vol. IV, pp. 223-224. Cf. Rosenberger, *op. cit.*, pp. 306-307.

bodies communicate their heat to contiguous cold ones by the vibrations of this medium propagated from them into the cold ones? And is not this medium exceedingly more rare and subtle than the air and exceedingly more elastic and active? And does it not readily pervade all bodies? And is it not (by its elastic force) expanded through all the heavens?

"Qu. 19. Does not the refraction of light proceed from the different density of this ethereal medium in different places, the light receding always from the denser parts of the mediums? And is not the density thereof greater in free and open spaces void of air and other grosser bodies than within the pores of water, glass, crystal, gems, and other compact bodies? For when light passes through glass or crystal, and, falling very obliquely upon the farther surface thereof, is totally reflected, the total reflection ought to proceed rather from the density and vigor of the medium without and beyond the glass than from the rarity and weakness thereof.

"Qu. 20. Does not this ethereal medium, in passing out of water, glass, crystal and other compact and dense bodies into empty spaces, grow denser and denser by degrees, and by that means refract the rays of light not in a point but by bending them gradually in curve lines? And does not the gradual condensation of this medium extend to some distance from the bodies, and thereby cause the inflections of the rays of light which pass by the edges of dense bodies at some distance from the bodies?"

The twenty-first query runs:[37]

"Qu. 21. Is not this medium much rarer within the dense bodies of the sun, stars, planets, and comets than in the empty celestial spaces between them? And in passing from them to great distances, does it not grow denser and

[37] *Opticks*, 1721, pp. 325-327; *Horsley*, Vol. IV, pp. 224-225. Cf. Rosenberger, *op. cit.*, pp. 307-308.

denser perpetually and thereby cause the gravity of those great bodies toward one another and of their parts toward the bodies, every body endeavoring to go from the denser parts of the medium toward the rarer? For if this medium be rarer within the sun's body than at its surface, and rarer there than at the hundredth part of an inch from its body, and rarer there than at the fiftieth part of an inch from its body, and rarer there than at the orb of Saturn; I see no reason why the increase of density should stop anywhere and not rather be continued through all distances from the Sun to Saturn and beyond. And though this increase of density may at great distances be exceeding slow, yet if the elastic force of this medium be exceeding great it may suffice to impel bodies from the denser parts of the medium towards the rarer with all that power which we call gravity. And that the elastic force of this medium is exceeding great may be gathered from the swiftness of its vibrations. Sounds move about 1140 English feet in a second of time, and in seven or eight minutes of time they move about one hundred English miles. Light moves from the sun to us in about seven or eight minutes of time, which distance is about 70,000,000 English miles, supposing the horizontal parallax of the sun to be about 12 seconds. And the vibrations of pulses of this medium, that they may cause the alternate fits of easy transmission and easy reflection, must be swifter than light, and by consequence above 700,000 times swifter than sounds. And therefore the elastic force of this medium in proportion to its density must be above 700,000 times 700,000 (that is, above 490,000,000,000) times greater than the elastic force of the air is in proportion to its density. For the velocities of the pulses of elastic mediums are in a subduplicate ratio of the elasticities and the rarities of the mediums taken together.

"As attraction is stronger in small magnets than in great ones in proportion to their bulk, and gravity is greater in the surfaces of small planets than in those of great ones in proportion to their bulk, and small bodies are agitated much more by electric attraction than great ones, so the smallness of the rays of light may contribute very much to the power of the agent by which they are refracted. And so if any one should suppose that ether (like our air) may contain particles which endeavor to recede from one another (for I do not know what this ether is) and that its particles are exceedingly smaller than those of air or even than those of light, the exceeding smallness of its particles may contribute to the greatness of the force by which those particles may recede from one another, and thereby make that medium exceedingly more rare and elastic than air and by consequence exceedingly less able to resist the motions of projectiles and exceedingly more able to press upon gross bodies by endeavoring to expand itself."

The twenty-second query is:[38]

"May not planets and comets and all gross bodies perform their motions more freely and with less resistance in this ethereal medium than in any fluid which fills all space adequately without leaving any pores, and by consequence is much denser than quicksilver or gold. And may not its resistance be so small as to be inconsiderable? For instance, if this ether (for so I call it) should be supposed 700,000 times more elastic than our air and above 700,000 times more rare, its resistance would be above 600,000,000 times less than that of water. And so small a resistance would scarce make any sensible alteration in the motions of the planets in ten thousand years. If any one would ask how a medium can be so rare, let him tell me how the air in the upper parts of the atmosphere can be above hundred thousand times rarer than gold. Let him also tell me how an electric body can by friction emit an exhalation so rare

[38] *Horsley*, Vol. IV, pp. 225-226; Rosenberger, *op. cit.*, pp. 308-309.

and subtle and yet so potent as by its emission to cause no sensible diminution of the weight of the electric body, and to be expanded through a sphere whose diameter is above two feet and yet to be able to agitate and carry up leaf-copper or leaf-gold at the distance of above a foot from the electric body? And how the effluvia of a magnet can be so rare and subtle as to pass through a plate of glass without any resistance or diminution of their force, and yet so potent as to turn a magnetic needle beyond the glass?"

To base on the eighteenth query to the twenty-second query an opinion that as time went on Newton inclined more and more to the undulatory theory of light with its necessary assumption of an ether, and here, in 1717, denied the doctrine of his school which asserted action at a distance is, according to Rosenberger,[39] incorrect. It seems true that Newton, for what were then good reasons, never abandoned the emission theory. It is also true that the hint as to the derivation of gravitation from different densities of the ether is merely vague. But this does not prove that Newton had not a decided leaning toward the notion that action was always propagated by a medium. But Rosenberger makes a very apposite remark when he states that the matter of these "Queries" is taken from the "Hypothesis" of 1675 and the letter to Boyle of 1679. It may be that these old speculations were again brought forward to show that Newton had studied theories of the ether as carefully as his opponents—Leibniz and the Cartesians.[40]

Finally, an addition to the twenty-ninth query is referred to in § II above.

V.

In a letter of February 26, 1716,[41] to the Abbé Conti,

[39] *Op. cit.*, pp. 309-311. [40] *Ibid.*, p. 311.

[41] *Horsley*, Vol. IV, p. 597; Brewster, *op. cit.*, Vol. II, pp. 288-289; Rosenberger, *op. cit.*, pp. 382-383.

Newton commented on Leibniz's use,[42] in 1710, of the terms "occult causes" and "miracles"; but Newton's remarks are not of much importance. This was[43] also dwelt upon in the unsigned preface to the edition of the *Commercium Epistolicum* published in 1725, and this preface is known[44] to have been written by Newton himself.

Finally, in the third edition of the *Principia*, which was edited by Henry Pemberton and published in 1726,[45] there is, as we saw in § IV of my article in *The Monist* for April, 1915, one addition emphasizing Newton's wish not to be understood as asserting that gravity was an essential property of bodies.

VI.

Rosenberger[46] says: "It results quite clearly from Newton's utterances that he held that a kinetic or even a physical explanation of gravity as an effect brought about by an intervening medium is impossible. In the *Principia* he decisively refuted the possibility of an explanation of gravity and the celestial motions by Descartes's vortices. But he also refuted the many attempts at the improvement of this doctrine which were given at that time by destroying their fundamental supposition—that there exists an ethereal matter which fills all space—by his researches on the resistance which this matter must present to the celestial motions. It might have been urged that by this the impossibility of an ether in general was not proved: only of one whose density could be measured by us. It might have been urged that Newton himself admitted a light-matter which is distributed everywhere like light and must thus just like the ether hinder the motions of the planets. But Newton explained that his corpuscles

[42] See above, § III.

[43] Brewster, *op. cit.*, Vol. II, p. 75.

[44] Cf. Brewster, *op. cit.*, Vol. II, pp. 378-384, 549-556; Rouse Ball, *op. cit.*, pp. 135-136.

[45] Rosenberger, *op. cit.*, pp. 383-384.

[46] *Op. cit.*, p. 409.

are much too thinly distributed in space for their resistance to be sensible, while the Cartesian ether, which completely fills space, must under all circumstances give rise to a very great resistance."

Newton's views on the subjects which concern us at present are thus summarized by Rosenberger.[47]

"All particles of matter accessible to our senses and all bodies move as if they attracted one another in the direct ratio of their masses and the inverse ratio of the squares of their distances from one another. This mutual action is not action at a distance but is brought about by some intermediary not yet certainly to be determined. Since, however, a matter suitable to play the part of this intermediary cannot be found, this agent is probably immaterial and in all likelihood God himself. It is doubtful whether God does this directly or indirectly, though probably the former. Hence follows that the mutual action in all matter is not an essential and necessary property of it like impenetrability and mobility, but a quality given to matter by the creator in perfect freedom and in the way which seemed proper to him."

It is not impossible that this was Newton's real view. But it seems impossible to doubt that Newton decidedly leaned toward the hypothesis of a very rare ether. Certainly he thought that he had refuted the Cartesian theory of a dense ether. And Newton himself has given some further indication of what his views were, and this indication seems, like the letters to Bentley, to support our conjecture. Leibniz had asked Newton what was his opinion of what Huygens had said in the appendix, *Discours de la Cause de la Pesanteur,* to his *Traité de la Lumière* of 1690. On October 26, 1693, Newton replied:[48]

"I cannot admit that a subtle matter fills the heavens,

[47] *Op. cit.*, p. 422.

[48] Mentioned in another connection by Rosenberger, *op. cit.*, pp. 461-462.

for the celestial motions are too regular to arise from vortices, and vortices would only disturb the motion. But if any one should explain gravity and all its laws by the action of some subtle mediums, and should show that the motions of the planets and comets were not disturbed by this matter, I should by no means oppose it."

It would seem that Newton felt just as strongly as did Descartes or Huygens or Leibniz or Faraday or Maxwell a need for a medium by which to transmit force. A weapon sometimes used against Cartesian doctrines by those whose interests or emotions led them to condemn what they fancied might be construed as a slight on the omnipotence of God, was that Descartes's world was so planned as to leave God out of account altogether. But something like this is the ideal of every scientific man. However pious a man of science may be—and some even eminent men of science have been models of unthinking devotion to certain religious sects—he will try to explain by natural causes phenomena which have hitherto appeared inexplicable except as miracles wrought by God. It is difficult to imagine that religious belief could ever interfere with this postulate of scientific investigation, and thus it can hardly be believed that Newton preferred to help himself out by supposing certain actions on the part of God, when there was a chance that gravitation might be explained by the hypothesis of a rarefied ether.

PHILIP E. B. JOURDAIN.

CAMBRIDGE, ENGLAND.

CRITICISMS AND DISCUSSIONS.

THE WORKS OF WILLIAM OUGHTRED.*

CLAVIS MATHEMATICAE.

William Oughtred (1574 (?)–1660), though by profession a clergyman, was one of the world's great teachers of mathematics and should still be honored as the inventor of that indispensable mechanical instrument, the slide-rule. It is noteworthy that he showed a marked disinclination to give his writings to the press. His first paper on sun-dials was written at the age of twenty-three, but we are not aware that more than one brief mathematical manuscript was printed before his fifty-seventh year. In every instance, publication in printed form seems to have been due to pressure exerted by one or more of his patrons, pupils or friends. Some of his manuscripts were lent out to his pupils who prepared copies for their own use. In some instances they urged upon him the desirability of publication and assisted in preparing copy for the printer. The earliest and best known book of Oughtred was his *Clavis mathematicae.* As he himself informs us, he was employed by the Earl of Arundel about 1628 to instruct the Earl's son, Lord William Howard (afterwards Viscount Stafford), in the mathematics. For the use of this young man Oughtred composed a treatise on algebra which was published in Latin in the year 1631 at the urgent request of a kinsman of the young man, Charles Cavendish, a patron of learning.

The *Clavis mathematicae,*[1] in its first edition of 1631, was a booklet of only 88 small pages. Yet it contained in very condensed form the essentials of arithmetic and algebra as known at that time.

Aside from the addition of four tracts, the 1631 edition underwent some changes in the editions of 1647 and 1648 which two are much alike. The twenty chapters of 1631 are reduced to nineteen in 1647 and in all the later editions. Numerous minute alterations

* For further details see the author's article on "The Life of Oughtred" in *The Open Court,* August, 1915, where fuller references are given to some of the books cited here.

[1] The full title of the *Clavis* of 1631 is as follows: *Arithmeticae in numeris et speciebvs institvtio: Quae tvm logisticae, tvm analyticae, atqve adeo totivs*

from the 1631 edition occur in all parts of the books of 1647 and 1648. The material of the last three chapters of the 1631 edition is re-arranged with some slight additions here and there. The 1648 edition has no preface. In the print of 1652 there are only slight alterations from the 1648 edition; after that the book underwent hardly any changes, except for the number of tracts appended, and brief explanatory notes added at the close of the chapters in the English edition of 1694 and 1702. The 1652 and 1667 editions were seen through the press by John Wallis; the 1698 impression contains on the title-page the words: *Ex Recognitione D. Johannis Wallis, S.T.D. Geometriae Professoris Saviliani.*

The cost of publishing may be a matter of some interest. When arranging for the printing of the 1667 edition of the *Clavis,* Wallis wrote Collins:[2] "I told you in my last what price she [Mrs. Lichfield] expects for it, as I have formerly understood from her, viz., 40 l. for the impression, which is about 9½d. a book."

mathematicae, quasi clavis est.—Ad nobilissimvm spectatissimumque invenem Dn. Guilelmvm Howard, Ordinis qui dicitur, Balnei Equitem, honoratissimi Dn. Thomae, Comitis Arvndeliae & Surriae, Comitis Mareschalli Angliae, &c filium—Londini, Apud Thomam Harpervm. M.DC.XXXI.

In all there appeared five Latin editions, the second in 1648 at London, the third in 1652 at Oxford, the fourth in 1667 at Oxford, the fifth in 1693 and 1698 at Oxford. There were two independent English editions: the first in 1647 at London, translated in greater part by Robert Wood of Lincoln College, Oxford, as is stated in the preface to the 1652 Latin edition; the second in 1694 and 1702 is a new translation, the preface being written and the book recommended by the astronomer Edmund Halley. The 1694 and 1702 impressions labored under the defect of many sense-disturbing errors due to careless reading of the proofs. All the editions of the *Clavis,* after the first edition, had one or more of the following tracts added on:

Eq. = *De Aequationum affectarum resolutione in numeris.*
Eu. = *Elementi decimi Euclidis declaratio.*
So. = *De Solidis regularibus tractatus.*
An. = *De Anatocismo, sive usura composita.*
Fa. = *Regula falsae positionis.*
Ar. = *Theorematum in libris Archimedis de Sphaera & cylindro declaratio.*
Ho. = *Horologia scioterica in plano; geometricè delineandi modus.*

[The abbreviated titles given here are, of course, our own. The lists of tracts added to the *Clavis mathematicae* of 1631 in its later editions, given in the order in which the tracts appear in each edition, are as follows: *Clavis* of 1647, *Eq., An., Fa., Ho.; Clavis* of 1648, *Eq., An., Fa., Eu., So.; Clavis* of 1652, *Eq., Eu., So., An., Fa., Ar., Ho.; Clavis* of 1667, *Eq., Eu., So., An., Fa., Ar., Ho.; Clavis* of 1693 and 1698, *Eq., Eu., So., An., Fa., Ar., Ho.; Clavis* of 1694 and 1702, *Eq.*.

The title-page of the *Clavis* was considerably modified after the first edition. Thus, the 1652 Latin edition has this title-page: *Guilelmi Oughtred Aetonensis, quondam Collegii Regalis in Cantabrigia Socii, Clavis mathematicae denvo limata, sive potius fabricata. Cum aliis quibusdam ejusdem commentationibus, quae in sequenti pagina recensentur. Editio tertia auctior & emendatior Oxoniae, Excudebat Leon. Lichfield, Veneunt apud Tho. Robinson. 1652.*

[2] Rigaud, *op. cit.,* Vol. II, p. 476.

As compared with other contemporary works on algebra, Oughtred's distinguishes itself for the amount of symbolism used, particularly in the treatment of geometric problems. Extraordinary emphasis was placed upon what he called in the *Clavis* the "analytical art."[3] By that term he did not mean our modern analysis or analytical geometry, but the art "in which by taking the thing sought as knowne, we finde out that we seeke."[4] He meant to express by it condensed processes of rigid, logical deduction expressed by appropriate symbols, as contrasted with mere description or elucidation by passages fraught with verbosity. In the preface to the first edition (1631) he says:

"In this little book I make known...the rules relating to fundamentals, collected together, just like a bundle, and adapted to the explanation of as many problems as possible."

As stated in this preface, one of his reasons for publishing the book, is "...that like Ariadne I might offer a thread to mathematical study by which the mysteries of this science might be revealed, and direction given to the best authors of antiquity, Euclid, Archimedes, the great geometrician Apollonius of Perga, and others, so as to be easily and thoroughly understood, their theorems being added, not only because to many they are the height and depth of mathematical science (I ignore the would-be mathematicians who occupy themselves only with the so-called practice, which is in reality mere juggler's tricks with instruments, the surface so to speak, pursued with a disregard of the great art, a contemptible picture), but also to show with what keenness they have penetrated, with what mass of equations, comparisons, reductions, conversions and disquisitions these heroes have ornamented, increased and invented this most beautiful science."

The *Clavis* opens with an explanation of the Hindu-Arabic notation of decimal fractions. Noteworthy is the absence of the words "million," "billion," etc. Although used on the continent by certain mathematical writers long before this, these words did not become current in English mathematical books until the eighteenth century. The author was a great admirer of decimal fractions, but failed to introduce the notation which in later centuries came to be

[3] See, for instance, the *Clavis mathematicae* of 1652, where he expresses himself thus (p. 11): "*Speciosa haec Arithmetica arti Analyticae (per quam ex sumptione quaesiti, tanquam noti, investigatur quaesitum) multo accommodatior est, quam illa numerosa.*"

[4] Oughtred, *The Key of the Mathematicks*, London, 1647, p. 4.

universally adopted. Oughtred wrote 0.56 in this manner 0|56; the point he used to designate ratio. Thus 3:4 was written by him 3·4. The decimal point (or comma) was first used by the inventor of logarithms, John Napier, as early as 1616 and 1617. Although Oughtred had mastered the theory of logarithms soon after their publication in 1614 and was a great admirer of Napier, he preferred to use the dot for the designation of *ratio.* This notation of ratio is used in all his mathematical books, except in two instances. The two dots (:) occur as symbols of ratio in some parts of Oughtred's posthumous work, *Opuscula mathematica hactenus inedita,* Oxford, 1677, but may have been due to the editors and not to Oughtred himself. Then again the two dots (:) are used to designate ratio on the last two pages of the tables of the Latin edition of Oughtred's *Trigonometria* of 1657. In all other parts of that book the dot (.) is used. Probably some one who supervised the printing of the tables introduced the (:) on the last two pages, following the logarithmic tables, where methods of interpolation are explained. The probability of this conjecture is the stronger, because in the English edition of the *Trigonometrie,* brought out the same year (1657) but *after* the Latin edition, the notation (:) at the end of the book is replaced by the usual (.), except that in some copies of the English edition the explanations at the end are omitted altogether.

Oughtred introduces an interesting, and at the same time new, feature of an abbreviated multiplication and an abbreviated division of decimal fractions. On this point he took a position far in advance of his time. The part on abbreviated multiplication was re-written in slightly enlarged form and with some unimportant alterations in the later editions of the Clavis. We give it as it occurs in the revision. Four cases are given. In finding the product of 246|914 and 35|27, "if you would have the Product without any Parts" (without any decimal part), "set the place of Unity of the lesser under the place of Unity in the greater: as in the Example," writing the figures of the lesser number in *inverse order.* From the example it will be seen that he begins by multiplying by 3, the right-hand digit of the multiplier. In the first edition of the *Clavis* he began with 7, the left digit. Observe also that he "carries" the nearest tens in the product of each lower digit and the upper digit one place to its

```
2 4 6|9 1 4
  7 2|5 3
-----------
7 4 0 7
1 2 3 5
    4 9
    1 7
-----------
8 7 0 8
```

right. For instance, he takes $7 \times 4 = 28$ and carries 3, then he finds $7 \times 2 + 3 = 17$ and writes down 17.

The second case supposes that "you would have the Product with some places of parts" (decimals), say 4; "Set the place of Unity of the lesser Number under the Fourth place of the Parts of the greater." The multiplication of 246|914 by 35|27 is now performed thus:

```
2 4 6|9 1 4
      7 2|5 3
-------------
7 4 0 7 4 2.0 0.
1 2 3 4 5 7 0 0
    4 9 3 8 2 8
    1.7 2 8 4 0
-------------
8 7 0 8|6 5 6 8
```

In the third and fourth cases are considered factors which appear as integers, but are in reality decimals; for instance, the sine of 54° is given in the tables as 80902 when in reality it is .80902.

Of interest as regards the use of the word "parabola" is the following (*Clavis*, 1694, p. 19 and the *Clavis* of 1631, p. 8): "The Number found by Division is called the *Quotient*, or also *Parabola*, because it arises out of the Application of a plain Number to a given Longitude, that a congruous Latitude may be found." This is in harmony with etymological dictionaries which speak of a parabola as the application of a given area to a given straight line. The dividend or product is the area; the divisor or factor is the line.

Oughtred gives two processes of long division. The first is identical with the modern process, except that the divisor is written below every remainder, each digit of the divisor being crossed out as soon as it has been used in the partial multiplication. The second method of long division is one of the several types of the old "scratch method." This antiquated process held its place by the side of the modern method in all editions of the *Clavis*. The author divides 467023 by 357|0926425, giving the following instructions: "Take as many of the first Figures of the Divisor as are necessary, for the first Divisor, and then in every following particular Division drop one of the Figures of the Divisor towards the Left Hand, till you have got a competent Quotient." He does not explain abbreviated division as thoroughly as abbreviated multiplication.

```
                          17
                         303
                        2803
                      109930
357 |0926425)  467023 · (1307·|80
                      357093
                      107127
                        2500
                         286
```

Oughtred does not examine the degree of reliability or accuracy of his processes of abbreviated multiplication and division. Here as in other places he gives in condensed statement the mode of procedure, without further discussion.

He does not attempt to establish the rules for the addition, subtraction, multiplication and division of positive and negative numbers. "If the Signs are both alike, the Product will be affirmative, if unlike, negative"; then he proceeds to applications. This attitude is superior to that of many writers of the eighteenth and nineteenth centuries, on pedagogical as well as logical grounds: Pedagogically, because the beginner in the study of algebra is not in a position to appreciate an abstract train of thought, as every teacher well knows, and derives better intellectual exercise from the applications of the rules to problems; logically, because the rule of signs in multiplication does not admit of rigorous proof, unless some other assumption is first made which is no less arbitrary than the rule itself. It is well known that the proofs of the rule of signs given by eighteenth-century writers are invalid. Somewhere they involve some surreptitious assumption. This criticism applies even to the proof given by Laplace, which tacitly assumes the distributive law in multiplication.

A word should be said on Oughtred's definition of + and –. He recognizes their double function in algebra by saying (*Clavis*, 1631, p. 2): "*Signum additionis, sive affirmationis, est + plus*" and "*Signum subductionis, sive negationis est – minus.*" They are symbols which indicate the *quality* of numbers in some instances and *operations* of addition or subtraction in other instances. In the 1694 edition of the *Clavis*, thirty-four years after the death of Oughtred, these symbols are defined as signifying operations only, but are actually used to signify the quality of numbers as well. In this respect the 1694 edition marks a recrudescence.

The characteristic in the *Clavis* that is most striking to a modern reader is the total absence of indices or exponents. There is much discussion in the leading treatises of the latter part of the sixteenth and the early part of the seventeenth centuries on the theory of indices, but modern exponential notation, a^n, is of later date. The modern notation, for positive integral exponents, first appears in Descartes's *Géométrie*, 1637; fractional and negative exponents were first used in the modern form by Sir Isaac Newton, in his announcement of the binomial formula, in a letter written in 1676. This total absence of our modern exponential notation in Oughtred's *Clavis* gives it a strange aspect. Like Vieta, Oughtred uses ordinarily the capital letters, A, B, C,... to designate given numbers; A^2 is written Aq, A^3 is written Ac; for A^4, A^5, A^6 he has, respectively, Aqq, Aqc, Acc. Only on rare occasions, usually when some parallelism in notation is aimed at, does he use small letters[5] to represent numbers or magnitudes. Powers of binomials or polynomials are marked by prefixing the capital letters Q (for square), C (for cube), QQ (for the fourth power), QC (for the fifth power), etc.

Oughtred does not express aggregation by ( ). Parentheses had been used by Girard, and by Clavius as early as 1609,[6] but did not come into general use in mathematical language until the time of Leibniz and by the Bernoullis. Oughtred indicates aggregation by writing a colon (:) at both ends. Thus, Q:A−E: means with his $(A-E)^2$. Similarly, $\sqrt{}$q:A+E: means $\sqrt{(A+E)}$. The two dots at the end are frequently omitted when the part affected includes all the terms of the polynomial to the end. Thus, C:A+B −E=.. means $(a+B-E)^3=..$ There are still further departures from this notation, but they occur so seldom that we incline to the interpretation that they are simply printer's errors. For proportion Oughtred uses the symbol (: :). The proportion $a:b=c:d$ appears in his notation $a\cdot b::c\cdot d$. Apparently, a proportion was not fully recognized in his day as being the expression of an equality of ratios. That probably explains why he did not use = here as in the notation of ordinary equations. Yet Oughtred must have been very close to the interpretation of a proportion as an equality; for he says in his *Elementi decimi Euclidis declaratio*, "*proportio, sive ratio aequalis* : :" That he introduced this extra symbol, when

[5] See, for instance, Oughtred's *Elementi decimi Euclidis declaratio*, 1652, p. 1, where he uses A and E, and also *a* and *e*.

[6] See *Christophori Clavii Bambergensis Operum mathematicorum, tomus secundus*, Moguntiae, M.DC.XI, Algebra, p. 39.

the one for equality was sufficient, is a misfortune. Simplicity demands that no unnecessary symbols be introduced. However, Oughtred's symbolism is certainly superior to those which preceded. Consider the notation of Clavius.[7] He wrote $20:60=4:x$, $x=12$, thus: "20.60.4? *fiunt* 12." The insufficiency of such a notation in the more involved expressions frequently arising in algebra is readily seen. Hence Oughtred's notation (: :) was early adopted by English mathematicians. It was used by John Wallis at Oxford, by Samuel Foster at Gresham College, by James Gregory of Edinburgh, by the translators into English of Rahn's algebra and by many other early writers. Oughtred has been credited generally with the introduction of St. Andrews's cross × as the symbol for multiplication in the *Clavis* of 1631. We have discovered that this symbol, or rather the letter x which closely resembles it, occurs as the sign of multiplication thirteen years earlier in an anonymous "Appendix to the Logarithmes, shewing the practise of the Calculation of Triangles etc." to Edward Wright's translation of John Napier's *Descriptio*, published in 1618. Later we shall give our reasons for believing that Oughtred is the author of that "Appendix." The × has survived as a symbol of multiplication.

Another symbol introduced by Oughtred and found in modern book is ∼, expressing difference; thus $C \sim D$ signifies the difference between C and D, even when D is the larger number.[8] This symbol was used by John Wallis in 1657.[9]

Oughtred represented in symbols also certain composite expressions, as for instance $A+E=Z$, $A-E=X$, where A is greater than E. He represented by a symbol also each of the following: A^2+E^2, A^3+E^3, A^2-E^2, A^3-E^3.

Oughtred practically translated the 10th book of Euclid from its ponderous rhetorical form into that of brief symbolism. An appeal to the eye was a passion with Oughtred. The present writer has collected the different mathematical symbols used by Oughtred and has found more than one hundred and fifty of them.

The differences between the seven different editions of the *Clavis* lie mainly in the special parts appended to some editions and dropped in the latest editions. The part which originally con-

[7] *Christophori Clavii operum mathematicorum Tomus Secundus*, Moguntiae, M.DC.XI., *Epitome arithmeticae*, p. 36.

[8] See *Elementi decimi Euclidis declaratio*, 1652, p. 2.

[9] See Johannis Wallisii *Operum mathematicorum pars prima*, Oxonii, 1657, p. 247.

stituted the *Clavis* was not materially altered, except in two or three of the original twenty chapters. These changes were made in the editions of 1647 and 1648. After the first edition, great stress was laid upon the theory of indices upon the very first page as also in passages further on. Of course, Oughtred did not have our modern notation of indices or exponents, but their theory had been a part of algebra and arithmetic for some time. Oughtred incorporated this theory in his brief exposition of the Hindu-Arabic notation and in his explanation of logarithms. As previously pointed out, the last three chapters of the 1631 edition were considerably rearranged in the later editions and combined into two chapters, so that the *Clavis* proper had nineteen chapters instead of twenty in the editions after the first. These chapters consisted of applications of algebra to geometry and were so framed as to constitute a severe test of the student's grip of the subject. The very last problem deals with the division of angles into equal parts. He derives the cubic equation upon which the trisection depends algebraically, also the equations of the fifth degree and seventh degree upon which the divisions of the angle into 5 and 7 equal parts depend, respectively. The exposition was severely brief, yet accurate. He did not believe in conducting the reader along level paths or along slight inclines. He was a guide for mountain climbers and woe unto him who lacked nerve.

Oughtred lays great stress upon expansions of powers of a binomial. He makes use of these expansions in the solution of numerical equations. To one who does not specialize in the history of mathematics such expansions may create surprise, for did not Newton invent the binomial theorem after the death of Oughtred? As a matter of fact, the expansions of positive integral powers of a binomial were known long before Newton, not only to seventeenth-century but even sixteenth-century mathematicians. Oughtred's *Clavis* of 1631 gave the binomial coefficients for all powers up to and including the tenth. What Newton really accomplished was the generalization of the binomial expansion which makes it applicable to negative and fractional exponents and converts it into an infinite series.

As a specimen of Oughtred's style of writing we quote his solution of quadratic equations, accompanied by a translation into English and into modern mathematical symbols.

As a preliminary step he lets[10]

[10] *Clavis* of 1631, Chap. XIX, sect. 5, p. 50.

$$Z = A + E \quad \text{and} \quad A > E;$$

he lets also $X = A - E$. From these relations he obtains identities which, in modern notation, are $\frac{1}{4}Z^2 - AE = \frac{1}{4}(\frac{1}{2}Z - E)^2 = \frac{1}{4}X^2$. Now, if we know Z and AE, we can find $\frac{1}{2}X$. Then $\frac{1}{2}(Z + X) = A$, and $\frac{1}{2}(Z - X) = E$, and

$$A = \tfrac{1}{2}Z + \sqrt{\tfrac{1}{4}Z^2 - AE.}$$

Having established these preliminaries, he then proceeds. (We translate the Latin passage, using the modern exponential notation and parentheses.)

"Given therefore an unequally divided line Z (10), and a rectangle beneath the segments AE (21) which is a gnomon. Half the difference of the segments $\frac{1}{2}X$ is given, and consequently the segment itself. For, if one of the two segments is placed equal to A, the other will be $Z - A$. Moreover, the rectangle is $ZA - A^2 = AE$. And because Z and AE are given, and there is $\frac{1}{4}Z^2 - AE = \frac{1}{4}X^2$, and by 5c.18, $\frac{1}{2}Z + \frac{1}{2}X = A$, and $\frac{1}{2}Z - \frac{1}{2}X = E$, the equation will be solved thus: $\frac{1}{2}Z \pm \sqrt{(\frac{1}{4}Z^2 - AE)} = A \begin{cases} \text{major segment} \\ \text{minor segment.} \end{cases}$

"And so an equation having been proposed in which three species (terms) are in equally ascending powers, the highest species, moreover, being negative, the given magnitude which constitutes the middle species is the line to be bisected. And the given absolute magnitude to which it is equal is the rectangle beneath the unequal segments, without gnomon. As $ZA - A^2 = AE$, or in numbers, $10x - x^2 = 21$. And A or x is one of the two unequal segments. It may be found thus:

"The half of the middle species is $Z^2/2$ (5). its square is $Z^2/4$ (25). From it subtract the absolute term AE (21), and $(Z^2/4) - A^2$ (4) will be the square of half the difference of the segments. The square root of this, $\sqrt{[(Z^2/2)^2 - AE]}$ (2) is half the difference. If you add it to half the coefficient $Z/2$ (5), the longer segment is obtained, if you subtract it, the smaller segment is obtained. I say:

$$(Z/2) + [\sqrt{(Z^2/4 - AE)}] = A \begin{cases} \text{major segment} \\ \text{minor segment.''} \end{cases}$$

The quadratic equation $Aq + ZA = AE$ receives similar treatment. This and the preceding equation, $ZA - Aq = AE$, constitute together a solution of the general quadratic equation, $x^2 + ax = b$, provided that E or Z are not restricted to positive values, but admit of being either positive or negative, a case not adequately treated by Oughtred. Imaginary numbers and imaginary roots receive no consideration whatever.

A notation suggested by Vieta and favored by Girard made vowels stand for unknowns and consonants for knowns. This conventionality was adopted by Oughtred in parts of his algebra, but not throughout. Near the beginning he used Q to designate the unknown, though usually this letter stood with him for the "square" of the expression after it.[11]

We quote the description of the *Clavis* that was given by Oughtred's greatest pupil, John Wallis. It contains additional information of interest to us. Wallis devotes Chapter XV of his *Treatise of Algebra*, London, 1685, pp. 67-69, to Mr. Oughtred and his *Clavis*, saying:

"Mr. William Oughtred (our Country-man) in his *Clavis Mathematicae*, (or Key of Mathematicks,) first published in the Year 1631, follows Vieta (as he did Diophantus) in the use of the Cossick Denominations; omitting (as he had done) the names of *Sursolids*, and contenting himself with those of *Square* and *Cube*, and the Compounds of these.

"But he doth abridge Vieta's Characters or Species, using only the letters q, c, &c. which in Vieta are expressed (at length) by *Quadrate, Cube*, &c. For though when Vieta first introduced this way of Specious Arithmetick, it was more necessary (the thing being new,) to express it in words at length: Yet when the thing was once received in practise, Mr. Oughtred (who affected brevity, and to deliver what he taught as briefly as might be, and reduce all to a short view,) contented himself with single Letters instead of Those words.

"Thus what Vieta would have written

$$\frac{\text{A } \textit{Quadrate}\text{, into B } \textit{Cube,}}{\text{C D E } \textit{Solid,}} \quad \textit{Equal to} \text{ F. G. } \textit{Plane,}$$

would with him be thus expressed

$$\frac{A_q\ B_c}{C\,D\,E} = FG.$$

"And the better to distinguish upon the first view, what quantities were Known, and what Unknown, he doth (usually) denote the Known by *Consonants*, and the Unknown by *Vowels*; as Vieta (for the same reason) had done before him.

[11] We have noticed the representation of known quantities by consonants and the unknown by vowels in Wingate's *Arithmetick made easie*, edited by

"He doth also (to very great advantage) make use of several Ligatures, or Compendious Notes, to signify *Summs, Differences,* and *Rectangles* of several Quantities. As for instance, Of two Quantities A (the Greater), and E (the Lesser), the Sum he calls Z, the Difference X, the Rectangle AE...."

"Which being of (almost) a constant signification with him throughout, do save a great circumlocution of words, (each Letter serving instead of a Definition;) and are also made use of (with very great advantage) to discover the true nature of divers intricate Operations, arising from the various compositions of such Parts, Sums, Differences, and Rectangles; (of which there is great plenty in his *Clavis,* Cap. 11, 16, 18, 19. and elsewhere,) which without such Ligatures, or CompendiousNotes, would not be easily discovered or apprehended..

"In know there are who find fault with his *Clavis,* as too obscure, because so short, but without cause; for his words be always full, but not Redundant, and need only a little attention in the Reader to weight the force of every word, and the Syntax of it;... And this, when once apprehended, is much more easily retained, than if it were expressed with the prolixity of some other Writers; where a Reader must first be at the pains to weed out a great deal of superfluous Language, that he may have a short prospect of what is material; which is here contracted for him in short Synopsis"...

"Mr. Oughtred in his *Clavis,* contents himself (for the most part) with the solution of Quadratick Equations, without proceeding (or very sparingly) to Cubick Equations, and those of Higher Powers; having designed that Work for an *Introduction* into *Algebra* so far, leaving the Discussion of Superior Equations for another work.... He contents himself likewise in Resolving Equations, to take notice of the *Affirmative* or *Positive Roots*; omitting the *Negative* or *Ablative* Roots, and such as are called *Imaginary* or *Impossible Roots.* And of those which he calls *Ambiguous* Equations, (as having more Affirmative Roots than one,) he doth not (that I remember) any where take notice of more than *Two* Affirmative Roots: (Because in Quadratick Equations, which are those he handleth, there are indeed no more.) Whereas yet in *Cubick* Equations, there may be *Three,* and in those of Higher Powers, yet more. Which Vieta was well aware of, and men-

John Kersey, London, 1650, algebra, p. 382; and in the second part, section 19, of Jonas Moore's *Arithmetick in two parts,* London, 1660, second part; Moore suggests as an alternative the use of z, y, x, etc. for the unknowns. The practice of representing unknowns by vowels did not spread widely in England.

tioneth in some of his Writings; and of which Mr. Oughtred could not be ignorant."

OUGHTRED'S CIRCLES OF PROPORTION AND TRIGONOMETRY.

Oughtred wrote and had published three important mathematical books, the *Clavis*, the *Circles of Proportion*[12] and a *Trigonometry*.[13] This last appeared in the year 1657 at London, in both Latin and English.

It is claimed that the trigonometry was "neither finished nor published by himself, but collected out of his scattered papers; and though he connived at the printing it, yet imperfectly done, as appears by his MSS.; and one of the printed Books, corrected by his own Hand."[14] Doubtless more accurate on this point is a letter of Richard Stokes who saw the book through the press:[15]

"I have procured your Trigonometry to be written over in a fair hand, which when finished I will send to you, to know if it be according to your mind; for I intend (since you were pleased to give your assent) to endeavour to print it with Mr. Briggs his Tables, and so soon as I can get the Prutenic Tables I will turn those of the sun and moon, and send them to you."

In the preface to the Latin edition Stokes writes:

"Since this trigonometry was written for private use without the intention of having it published, it pleased the Reverend Author, before allowing it to go to press, to expunge some things, to change

[12] There are two title-pages to the edition of 1632. The first title-page is as follows: *The Circles of Proportion and The Horizontall Instrument. Both invented, and the uses of both Written in Latine by Mr. W. O. Translated into English: and set forth for the publique benefit by William Forster. London. Printed for Elias Allen maker of these and all other mathematical Instruments, and are to be sold at his shop over against St. Clements church with out Temple-barr. 1632. T. Cecill Sculp.*

In 1633 there was added the following, with a separate title-page: *An addition unto the Use of the Instrument called the Circles of Proportion. London, 1633,* this being followed by Oughtred's *To the English Gentrie etc.* In the British Museum there is a copy of another impression, dated 1639, with the *Addition unto the use of the Instrument etc.,* bearing the original date, 1633, and with the epistle, *To the English Gentrie* etc., inserted immediately after Forster's dedication, instead of at the end of the volume.

[13] The complete title of the English edition is as follows: *Trigonometrie, or, The manner of calculating the Sides and Angles of Triangles, by the Mathematical Canon, demonstrated. By William Oughtred Etoneus. And published by Richard Stokes Fellow of Kings Colledge in Cambridge, and Arthur Haughton Gentleman. London, Printed by R. and W. Leybourn, for Thomas Johnson at the Golden Key in St. Paul's Church-yard.* M.DC.LXII.

[14] Jer. Collier, *The Great Historical, Geographical, Genealogical and Poetical Dictionary*, Vol. II, London, 1701, art. "Oughtred."

[15] Rigaud, *op. cit.*, Vol. I, p. 82.

other things and even to make some additions and insert more lucid methods of exposition."

This much is certain, the *Trigonometry* bears the impress characteristic of Oughtred. Like all his mathematical writings, the book was very condensed. Aside from the tables, the text covered only 36 pages. Plane and spherical triangles were taken up together. The treatise is known in the history of trigonometry as among the very earliest works to adopt a condensed symbolism so that equations involving trigonometric functions could be easily taken in by the eye. In the work of 1657 contractions are given as follows. *s* = sine, *t* = tangent, *se* = secant, *s co* = cosine (sine complement), *t co* = cotangent, *se co* = cosecant, *log* = logarithm, *Z cru* = sum of the sides of a rectangle or right angle, *X cru* = difference of these sides. It has been generally overlooked by historians that Oughtred used the abbreviations of trigonometric functions named above, a quarter of a century earlier, in his *Circles of Proportion,* 1632, 1633. Moreover, he used sometimes also the abbreviations which are current at the present time, namely sin = sine, tan = tangent, sec = secant. We know that the *Circles of Proportion* existed in manuscript many years before they were published. The symbol *sv* for *sinus versus* occurs in the *Clavis* of 1631. The great importance of well-chosen symbols needs no emphasis to readers of the present day. With reference to Oughtred's trigonometric symbols, Augustus De Morgan said:[16] "This is so very important a step, simple as it is, that Euler is justly held to have greatly advanced trigonometry by its introduction. Nobody that we know of has noticed that Oughtred was master of the improvement, and willing to have taught it, if people would have learnt." We find, however, that even Oughtred cannot be given the whole credit in this matter. As early as 1624, the contractions *sin* for sine and *tan* for tangent appear on the drawing representing Gunter's scale, but Gunter did not use them in his books, except in the drawing of his scale.[17] A closer competitor for the honor of first using these trigonometric abbreviations is Richard Norwood in his *Trigonometrie,* London, 1631, where *s* stands for sine, *t* for tangent, *sc* for sine complement (cosine), *tc* for tangent complement (cotangent), and *sec* for secant. Norwood was a teacher of mathematics in London and a well-known

[16] A. De Morgan, *Budget of Paradoxes,* London, 1872, p. 451; 2d edition, Chicago, 1915, Vol. II, p. 303.

[17] E. Gunter, *Description and Use of the Sector, the Crosse-staffe and other Instruments,* London, 1624. The second book, p. 31.

writer of books on navigation. Aside from the abbreviations just cited, Norwood did not use nearly as much symbolism in his mathematics as did Oughtred. The innovation of designating the sides and angles of a triangle by A, B, C and *a*, *b*, *c*, so that A was opposite *a*, B opposite *b*, and C opposite *c*, is attributed to Leonard Euler (1753), but was first used by Richard Rawlinson of Queen's College, Oxford, sometime after 1655 and before 1668. Oughtred did not use Rawlinson's notation.[18]

Mention should be made of trigonometric symbols used even earlier than any of the preceding, in "An Appendix to the Logarithmes, shewing the practise of the Calculation of Triangles, etc." printed in Edward Wright's edition of Napier's *A Description of the Admirable Table of Logarithmes*, London, 1618. We referred to this "Appendix" in tracing the origin of the sign ×. It contains, on page 4, the following passage: "For the Logarithme of an arch or an angle I set before (s), for the antilogarithme or compliment thereof (s*) and for the Differential (t)." In further explanation of this rather unsatisfactory passage, the author (Oughtred?) says, "As for example: sB+BC=CA. that is, the Logarithme of an angle B. at the Base of a plane right-angled triangle, increased by the addition of the Logarithm of BC, the hypothenuse thereof, is equall to the Logarithme of CA the cathetus."

Here "logarithme of an angle B" evidently means "log sin B," just as with Napier, "Logarithms of the arcs" signifies really "Logarithms of the sines of the angles." In Napier's table, the numbers in the column marked "Differentiae" signify log. sine minus log. cosine of an angle; that is, the logarithms of the tangents. This explains the contraction (t) in the "Appendix." The conclusion of all this is that as early as 1618 the signs *s*, *s**, *t* were used for *sine, cosine,* and *tangent,* respectively.

In trigonometry English writers of the first half of the seventeenth century used contractions more freely than their continental contemporaries, yea even more freely than English writers of a later period. Von Braunmühl, the great historian of trigonometry, gives Oughtred much praise for his trigonometry, and points out that half a century later the army of writers on trigonometry had hardly yet reached the standard set by Oughtred's[19] analysis. Oughtred must be credited also with the first complete proof that

[18] F. Cajori, "On the History of a Notation in Trigonometry" in *Nature*, Vol. 94, 1915, pp. 642, 643.

[19] A. v. Braunmühl, *Geschichte der Trigonometrie*, 2. Teil, Leipsic, 1903, pp. 42, 91.

was given to the first two of "Napier's analogies." His trigonometry contains seven-place tables of sines, tangents and secants, and six-place tables of logarithmic sines and tangents; also seven-place logarithmic tables of numbers. At the time of Oughtred there was some agitation in favor of a wider introduction of decimal systems. This movement is reflected in these tables which contain the centesimal division of the degree, a practice which is urged for general adoption in our own day, particularly by the French.

SOLUTION OF NUMERICAL EQUATIONS.

In the solution of numerical equations Oughtred does not mention the sources from which he drew, but the method is substantially that of the great French algebraist Vieta, as explained in a publication which appeared in 1600 in Paris under the title, *De numerosa potestatum purarum atque adfectarum ad exegesin resolutione tractatus.* In view of the fact that Vieta's process has been described inaccurately by leading modern historians including H. Hankel[20] and M. Cantor,[21] it may be worth while to go into some detail.[22] By them it is made to appear as identical with the procedure given later by Newton. The two are not the same. The difference lies in the divisor used. What is now called "Newton's method" is Newton's method as modified by Joseph Raphson.[23] The Newton-Raphson method of approximation to the roots of an equation $f(x)=0$ is usually given the form $a-[f(a)/f'(a)]$, where a is an approximate value of the required root. It will be seen that the divisor is $f'(a)$. Vieta's divisor is different; it is

$$|f(a+s_1)-f(a)|-s^n,$$

where $f(x)$ is the left of the equation $f(x)=k$, n is the degree of equation and s_1 is a unit of the denomination of the digit next to be found. Thus in $x^3+420000x=247651713$, it can be shown that 417 is approximately a root; suppose that a has been taken to be 400, then $s_1=10$; but if, at the next step of approximation, a is taken

[20] H. Hankel, *Geschichte der Mathematik im Alterthum und Mittelalter,* Leipsic, 1874, pp. 369, 370.

[21] M. Cantor, *Vorlesungen über die Geschichte der Mathematik,* II, 1900, pp. 640, 641.

[22] This matter has been discussed in a paper "A History of the Arithmetical Methods of Approximation etc." by F. Cajori, in the *Colorado College Publication,* General Series No. 51, 1910, pp. 182-184. Later this subject was again treated by G. Eneström in *Bibliotheca mathematica,* 3. Folge, Vol. 11, 1911, pp. 234, 235.

[23] See F. Cajori, *loc. cit.,* p. 193.

to be 410, then $s_1 = 1$. In this example, taking $a = 400$, Vieta's divisor would have been 9120000; Newton's divisor would have been 900000.

A comparison of Vieta's method with the Newton-Raphson method reveals the fact that Vieta's divisor is more reliable, but labors under the very great disadvantage of requiring a much larger amount of computation. The latter divisor is accurate enough and easier to compute. Altogether the Newton-Raphson process marks a decided advance over that of Vieta.

As already stated, it is the method of Vieta that Oughtred explains. The Englishman's exposition is an improvement on that of Vieta, printed forty years earlier. Nevertheless, Oughtred's explanation is far from easy to follow. The theory of equations was at that time still in its primitive stage of development. Algebraic notation was not sufficiently developed to enable the argument to be condensed into a form easily surveyed. So complicated does Vieta's process of approximation appear, that M. Cantor failed to recognize that Vieta possessed a uniform mode of procedure. But when one has in mind the general expression for Vieta's divisor which we gave above, one will recognize that there was marked uniformity in Vieta's approximations.

Oughtred allows himself twenty-eight sections in which to explain the process and at the close cannot forbear remarking that 28 is a "perfect" number (being equal to the sum of its divisors, 1, 2, 4, 7, 14).

The early part of his exposition shows how an equation may be transformed so as to make its roots 10, 100, 1000 or 10^m times smaller. This simplifies the task of "locating a root"; that is, of finding between what integers the root lies.

Taking one of Oughtred's equations, $x^4 - 72x^3 + 238600x = 8725815$, upon dividing $72x^3$ by 10, $238600x$ by 1000, and 8725815 by 10,000, we obtain $x^4 - 7\cdot2x^3 + 238\cdot6x = 872\cdot5$. Dividing both sides by x, we obtain $x^3 + 238\cdot6 - 7\cdot2x^2 = x)872\cdot5$. Letting $x = 4$, we have $64 + 238\cdot6 - 115\cdot2 = 187\cdot4$.

But $4)872\cdot5(218\cdot1$; 4 is too small. Next let $x = 5$, we have $125 + 238\cdot6 - 180 = 183\cdot6$.

But $5)872\cdot5(174\cdot5$; 5 is too large. We take the lesser value, $x = 4$, or in the original equation, $x = 40$. This method may be used to find the second digit in the root. Oughtred divides both sides of the equation by x^2, and obtains $x^2 + x)238600 - 72x = x^2)8725815$. He tries $x = 47$ and $x = 48$, and finds that $x = 47$.

He explains also how the last computation may be done by logarithms. Thereby he established for himself the record of being the first to use logarithms in the solution of affected equations.

"Exemplus II.

$$1 + 420000_l = 247651713$$

Hoc est, $L_c + C_q L = D_c$.

	247	651	713	(417
	42	000	0	C_q
	64			A_c
	168	000	0	C_q A
	232	000	0	Ablatit.
R	15	651	713	
	4	8		3 A_q
		12		3 A
	4	200	00	C_q
	9	120	00	Divisor.
	4	8		3 A_q E
		12		3 A E_q
		1		E_c
	4	200	00	C_q E
	9	121	00	Ablatit.
R	6	530	713	
		504	3	3 A_q
		1	23	3 A
		420	000	C_q
		925	530	Divisor.
	3	530	1	3 A_q E
		60	27	3 A E_q
			343	E_c
	2	940	000	C_q E
	6	530	713	Ablatit."

4	1	
16	8	
		1
16	8	1

As an illustration of Oughtred's method of approximation, after the root sought has been located, we choose for brevity a cubic in preference to a quartic. We select the equation $x^3 +$

$420000x = 247651713$. By the process explained above a root is found to lie between $x = 400$ and $x = 500$. From this point on, the approximation as given by Oughtred is as shown on previous page.

In further explanation of this process, observe that the given equation is of the form $L_c = C_qL = D_c$, where L is our x, $C_q = 420000$, $D_c = 247651713$. In the first step of approximation, let $L = A + E$, where $A = 400$ and E is, as yet, undetermined. We have $L_c = (A+E)^3 = A^3 + 3A^2E + 3AE^2 + E^3$
and $C_qL = 420000\,(A+E)$.
Subtract from 247651713 the sum of the known terms A^3 (his A_c) and 420000 A (his C_qA). This sum is 232000000; the remainder is 15651713.

Next, he evaluates the coefficients of E in $3A^2E$ and 420000 E, also 3A, the coefficient of E^2. He obtains $3A^2 = 480000$, $3A = 1200$, $C_q = 420000$. He interprets $3A^2$ and C_q as tens, 3A as hundreds. Accordingly, he obtains as their sum 9120000, which is the *Divisor* for finding the second digit in the approximation. Observe that this divisor is the value of $|f(a+s_1) - f(a)| - s_1^n$ in our general expression, where $a = 400$, $s_1 = 10$, $n = 3$, $f(x) = x^3 + 420000x$.

Dividing the remainder 15651713 by 9120000, he obtains the integer 1 in tens place; thus $E = 10$, approximately. He now computes the terms $3A^2E$, $3AE^2$ and E^3 to be respectively, 4800000, 120000, 1000. Their sum is 9121000. Subtracting it from the previous remainder 15651713, leaves the new remainder, 6530713.

From here on each step is a repetition of the preceding step. The new A is 410, the new E is to be determined. We have now in closer approximation, $L = A + E$. This time we do not subtract A^3 and C_qA, because this subtraction is already affected by the preceding work.

We find the second trial divisor by computing the sum of $3A^2$, 3A and C_q; that is, the sum of 504300, 1230, 420000, which is 925530. Again, this divisor can be computed by our general expression for divisors, by taking $a = 410$, $s_1 = 1$, $n = 3$.

Dividing 6530713 by 925530 yields the integer 7. Thus $E = 7$. Computing $3A^2E$, $3AE^2$, E^2 and subtracting their sum, the remainder is 0. Hence 417 is an exact root of the given equation.

Since the extraction of a cube root is merely the solution of a pure cubic equation, $x^3 = n$, the process given above may be utilized in finding cube roots. This is precisely what Oughtred does in Chapter XIV of his *Clavis*. If the above computation is modified by putting $C_q = 0$, the process will yield the approximate cube root of 247651713.

Oughtred solves 16 examples by the process of approximation here explained. Of these, 9 are cubics, 5 are quartics, and 2 are quintics. In all cases he finds only one or two real roots. Of the roots sought, five are irrational, the remaining are rational and are computed to their exact values. Three of the computed roots have 2 figures each, 9 roots have 3 figures each, 4 roots have 4 figures each. While no attempt is made to secure all the roots—methods of computing complex roots were invented much later—he computes roots of equations which involve large coefficients and some of them are of a degree as high as the fifth. In view of the fact that many editions of the *Clavis* were issued, one impression as late as 1702, it contributed probably more than any other book to the popularization of Vieta's method in England.

Before Oughtred, Thomas Harriot and William Milbourn are the only Englishmen known to have solved numerical equations of higher degrees. Milbourn published nothing. Harriot slightly modified Vieta's process by simplifying somewhat the formation of the trial divisor. This method of approximation was the best in existence until the publication by Wallis in 1685 of Newton's method of approximation.

LOGARITHMS.

Oughtred's treatment of logarithms is quite in accordance with the more recent practice.[24] He explains the finding of the *index* (our *characteristic*); he states that "the sum of two Logarithms is the Logarithm of the Product of their Valors; and their difference is the Logarithm of the Quotient," that "the Logarithm of the side [436] drawn upon the Index number [2] of dimensions of any Potestas is the logarithm of the same Potestas" [436^2], that "the logarithm of any Potestas [436^2] divided by the number of its dimensions [2] affordeth the Logarithm of its Root [436]." These statements of Oughtred occur for the first time in the *Key of the Mathematicks* of 1647; the *Clavis* of 1631 contains no treatment of logarithms.

If the characteristic of a logarithm is negative, Oughtred indicates this fact by placing the = *above* the characteristic. He separates the characteristic and mantissa by a *comma*, but still uses

[24] See William Oughtred's *Key of the Mathematicks*, London, 1494, pp. 173-175, tract, "Of the Resolution of the Affected Equations," or any edition of the *Clavis* after the first.

the sign L to indicate decimal fractions. He uses the contraction "log."

INVENTION OF THE SLIDE RULE; CONTROVERSY ON PRIORITY OF INVENTION.

Oughtred's most original line of scientific activity is the one least known to the present generation. Augustus De Morgan, in speaking of Oughtred who was sometimes called "Oughtred Aetonensis," remarks: "He is an animal of extinct race, an Eton mathematician. Few Eton men, even of the minority which knows what a sliding rule is, are aware that the inventor was of their own school and college."[25] The invention of the slide rule has, until recently,[26] been a matter of dispute; it has been erroneously ascribed to Edmund Gunter, Edmund Wingate, Seth Partridge and others. We have been able to establish that William Oughtred was the first inventor of slide rules, though not the first to publish thereon. We shall see that Oughtred invented slide rules about 1622, but the descriptions of his instruments were not put into print before 1632 and 1633. Meanwhile one of his own pupils, Richard Delamain, who probably invented the circular slide rule independently, published a description in 1630, at London, in a pamphlet of 32 pages entitled *Grammelogia; or the Mathematicall Ring.* In editions of this pamphlet which appeared during the following three or four years, various parts were added on, and some parts of the first and second editions eliminated. Thus Delamain antedates Oughtred two years in the publication of a description of a circular slide rule. But Oughtred had invented also a rectilinear slide rule, a description of which appeared in 1633. To the invention of this Oughtred has a clear title. A bitter controversy sprang up between Delamain on one hand, and Oughtred and some of his pupils on the other, on the priority and independence of invention of the circular slide rule. Few inventors and scientific men are so fortunate as to escape contests. The reader needs only to recall the disputes which have arisen, involving the researches of Sir Isaac Newton and Leibniz on the differential and integral calculus, of Thomas Harriot and René Descartes relating to the theory of equations, of Robert Mayer, Hermann v. Helmholtz and Joule on the principle of the conservation of energy, or of Robert Morse, Joseph Henry, Gauss and Weber, and others on the telegraph, to see that questions of

[25] A. De Morgan, *op. cit.*, p. 451; 2d ed., II, p. 303.

[26] See F. Cajori, *History of the Logarithmic Slide Rule*, New York, 1909, pp. 7-14, Addenda, p. ii.

priority and independence are not uncommon. The controversy between Oughtred and Delamain embittered Oughtred's life for many years. He refers to it in print on more than one occasion. We are preparing a separate article giving the details of this controversy and shall confine ourselves at present to the statement that it is by no means clear that Delamain stole the invention from Oughtred; Delamain was probably an independent inventor. Moreover, it is highly probable that the controversy would never have arisen, had not some of Oughtred's pupils urged and forced him into it. William Forster stated in the preface to the *Circles of Proportion* of 1632 that while he had been carefully preparing the manuscript for the press, "another to whom the Author [Oughtred] in a louing confidence discovered this intent, using more hast then good speed, went about to preocupate." It was this passage which started the conflagration. Another pupil, W. Robinson, wrote to Oughtred, when the latter was preparing his *Apologeticall Epistle* as a reply to Delamain's counter-charges:[27] "Good sir, let me be beholden to you for your Apology whensoever it comes forth, and (if I speak not too late) let me entreat you, whip ignorance well on the blind side, and we may turn him round, and see what part of him is free." As stated previously, Oughtred's circular slide rule was described by him in his *Circles of Proportion*, London, 1632, which was translated from Oughtred's Latin manuscript and then seen through the press by his pupil, William Forster. In 1633 appeared *An Addition unto the Use of the Instrument called the Circles of Proportion* which contained at the end "The Declaration of the two Rulers for Calculation," giving a description of Oughtred's rectilinear slide rule. This *Addition* was bound with the *Circles of Proportion* as one volume. About the same time Oughtred described a modified form of the rectilinear slide rule, to be used in London for gauging.[28]

MINOR WORKS.

Among the minor works of Oughtred must be ranked his booklet of forty pages to which reference has already been made, entitled, *The New Artificial Gauging Line or Rod*, London, 1633. His different designs of slide rules and his inventions of sun-dials as well as his exposition of the making of watches show that he displayed unusual interest and talent in the various mathematical

[27] Rigaud, *op. cit.*, Vol. I, p. 12.

[28] *The New Artificial Gauging Line or Rod: together with rules concerning the use thereof: Invented and written by William Oughtred.* London, 1633.

instruments. A short tract on watch-making was brought out in London as an appendix to the *Horological Dialogues* of a clock and watch maker who signed himself "J. S." (John Smith?). Oughtred's tract appeared with its own title-page, but with pagination continued from the preceding part, as *An Appendix wherein is contained a Method of Calculating all Numbers for Watches. Written originally by that famous Mathematician Mr. William Oughtred, and now made Publick. By J. S. of London, Clockmaker.* London, 1675.

"J. S." says in his preface:

"The method following was many years since Compiled by Mr. Oughtred for the use of some Ingenious Gentlemen his friends, who for recreation at the University, studied to find out the reason and Knowledge of Watch-work, which seemed also to be a thing with which Mr. Oughtred himself was much affected, as may in part appear by his putting out of his own Son to the same Trade, for whose use (as I am informed) he did compile a larger tract, but what became of it cannot be known."

Notwithstanding Oughtred's marked activity in the design of mathematical instruments, and his use of surveying instruments, he always spoke in depreciating terms of their importance and their educational value. In his epistle against Delamain he says:[29]

"The Instruments I doe not value or weigh one single penny. If I had been ambitious of praise, or had thought them (or better then they) worthy, at which to have taken my rise, out of my secure and quiet obscuritie, to mount up into glory, and the knowledge of men: I could have done it many yeares before...

"Long agoe, when I was a young student of the Mathematicall Sciences, I tryed many wayes and devices to fit my selve with some good Diall or Instrument portable for my pocket, to finde the houre, and try other conclusions by, and accordingly framed for that my purpose both Quadrants, and Rings, and Cylinders, and many other composures. Yet not to my full content and satisfaction; for either they performed but little, or els were patched up with a diversity of lines by an unnaturall and forced contexture. At last I....found what I had before with much studie and paines in vaine sought for."

Mention has been made on the previous pages of two of his papers on sun-dials, and prepared (as he says) when he was in his twenty-third year, and was first published in the *Clavis* of 1647. The second paper appeared in his *Circles of Proportion.*

[29] W. Oughtred, *Apologeticall Epistle*, p. 13

Both before and after the time of Oughtred much was written on sun-dials. Such instruments were set up against the walls of prominent buildings, much as the faces of clocks in our time. The inscriptions that were put upon sun-dials are often very clever: "I count only the hours of sunshine," "Alas, how fleeting." A sun-dial on the grounds of Merchiston Castle, in Edinburgh, where the inventor of logarithms, John Napier, lived for many years, bears the inscription, "Ere time be tint, tak tent of time" (Ere time be lost, take heed of time).

Portable sun-dials were sometimes carried in pockets, as we carry watches. Thus Shakespeare, in *As You Like It,* Act II, Sc. 7:

"And he drew a diall from his poke."

Watches were first made for carrying in the pocket about 1658.

Because of this literary, scientific and practical interest in methods of indicating time it is not surprising that Oughtred devoted himself to the mastery and the advancement of methods of time-measurement.

Besides the accounts previously noted, there came from his pen: *The Description and Use of the double Horizontall Dyall: Whereby not onely the hower of the day is shewne; but also the Meridian Line is found: And most Astronomical Questions, which may be done by the Globe, are resolved. Invented and written by W. O.*, London, 1636.

The "Horizontall Dyall" and "Horologicall Ring" appeared again as appendices to Oughtred's translation from the French of a book on mathematical recreations.

The fourth French edition of that work appeared in 1627 at Paris, under the title of *Recreations mathematiqve,* written by "Henry van Etten," a pseudonym for the French Jesuit Jean Leurechon (1591-1690). English editions appeared in 1633, 1653 and 1674. The full title of the 1653 edition conveys an idea of the contents of the text:

Mathematicall Recreations, or, A Collection of many Problemes, extracted out of the Ancient and Modern Philosophers, as Secrets and Experiments in Arithmetick, Geometry, Cosmographie, Musick, Opticks, Architecture, Statick, Mechanicks, Chemistry, Waterworks, Fire-works, &c. Not vulgarly manifest till now. Written first in Greek and Latin, lately compil'd in French, by Henry Van Etten, and now in English, with the Examinations and Augmenta-

tions of divers Modern Mathematicians. Whereunto is added the Description and Use of the Generall Horologicall Ring. And The Double Horizontall Diall: Invented and written by William Oughtred. London, Printed for William Leake, at the Signe of the Crown in Fleet-street, between the two Temple-Gates. MDCLIII.

The graphic solution of spherical triangles by the accurate drawing of the triangles on a sphere and the measurement of the unknown parts in the drawing, was explained by Oughtred in a short tract which was published by his son-in-law, Christopher Brookes, under the following title:

The Solution of all Sphaerical Triangles both right and oblique By the Planisphaere: Whereby two of the Sphaerical partes sought, are at one position most easily found out. Published with consent of the Author, By Christopher Brookes, Mathematique Instrument-maker, and Manciple of Wadham Colledge, in Oxford.

Brookes says in the preface: "I have oftentimes seen my Reverend friend Mr. W. O. in his resolution of all sphaericall triangles both right and oblique, to use a planisphaere, without the tedious labour of Trigonometry by the ordinary Canons: which planisphaere he had delineated with his own hands, and used in his calculations more than Forty years before."

Interesting as one of the sources from which Oughtred obtained his knowledge of the conic sections is his study of Mydorge. A tract which he wrote thereon was published by Jonas Moore, in his *Arithmetick in two books....* [containing also] *the two first books of Mydorgius his conical sections analyzed by that reverend devine Mr. W. Oughtred, Englished and completed with cuts.* London, 1660. Another edition bears the date 1688.

To be noted among the minor works of Oughtred are his posthumous papers. He left a considerable number of mathematical papers which his friend Sir Charles Scarborough had revised under his direction and published at Oxford in 1676 in one volume under the title, *Gulielmi Oughtredi, Etonensis, quondam Collegii Regalis in Cantabrigia Socii, Opuscula Mathematica hactenus inedita.* Its nine tracts are of little interest to a modern reader.

Here we wish to give our reasons for our belief that Oughtred is the author of an anonymous tract on the use of logarithms and on a method of logarithmic interpolation which, as previously noted, appeared as an "Appendix" to Edward Wright's translation into English of John Napier's *Descriptio,* under the title, *A Description of the Admirable Table of Logarithmes,* London, 1618.

The "Appendix" bears the title, "An Appendix to the Logarithmes, showing the practise of the Calculation of Triangles, and also a new and ready way for the exact finding out of such lines and Logarithmes as are not precisely to be found in the Canons." It is an able tract. A natural guess is that the editor of the book, Samuel Wright, a son of Edward Wright, composed this "Appendix." More probable is the conjecture which (Dr. J. W. L. Glaisher informs me) was made by Augustus De Morgan, attributing the authorship to Oughtred. Two reasons in support of this are advanced by Dr. Glaisher, the use of *x* in the "Appendix" as the sign of multiplication (to Oughtred is generally attributed the introduction of the cross × for multiplication in 1631), and the then unusual designation "cathetus" for the vertical leg of a right triangle, a term appearing in Oughtred's books. We are able to advance a third argument, namely the occurrence in the "Appendix" of (S*) as the notation for sine complement (cosine), while Seth Ward, an early pupil of Oughtred, in his *Idea trigonometriae demonstratae*, Oxford, 1654, used a similar notation (S'). It has been stated elsewhere that Oughtred claimed Seth Ward's exposition of trigonometry as virtually his own. Attention should be called also to the fact that, in his *Trigonometria*, page 2, Oughtred uses (') to designate 180°-angle.

COLORADO COLLEGE. FLORIAN CAJORI.

BERGSON'S THEORY OF INTUITION.

Probably the best example of Bergson's application of the intuitive method is to be found in his account of the ideal genesis of the intelligence in the third chapter of *Creative Evolution*. This gives us the gist of his whole philosophy, and serves to illustrate the difficulties of Bergson's view not only of the nature of intellect, but also of intuition itself. What Bergson proposes to do is "to engender intelligence, by setting out from the consciousness which envelopes it"; that is to say, he proposes that we should actually experience in our own selves the process by which duration, which is pure heterogeneity and pure activity, is degraded into the spatializing intellect and spatialized matter. The intellect left to itself, Bergson argues, naturally tends to the homogeneous and the extended and the static. That is to say, the impression we get of the intellect is as of something unmaking itself. "Extension appears only as a tension which is interrupted." But this suggests to us a reality of which the intellect is merely the degradation and suppression. "The vision we have of the material world is that of a weight which falls; no image drawn from matter, properly so called, will ever give us the idea of the weight rising." But in the case of life we see "an effort to mount the incline that matter descends." Living things "reveal to us the possibility, the necessity even, of a process the inverse of materiality, creative of matter by its interruption alone" (p. 259), a reality which is purely active, a cosmic impulse which makes itself incessantly.

Now if by means of a powerful effort of the mind we succeed in attaining to this reality, if, as Bergson expresses it, "we put back our being into our will, and our will itself into the impulsion it prolongs, we understand, we feel, that reality is a perpetual growth, a creation pursued without end" (p. 252). But if then we relax the tension which this effort demands, we shall ourselves see, or rather *be,* the reverse movement by which the cosmic impetus is degraded, by a kind of process of solidification or chilling or crystalization, into matter and intellect. Reality is pure creative activity, but apparently this creative activity is interrupted or diverted, and in this interruption of the creative current the material world and the spatializing intellect arise. But the creative current is not degraded utterly nor all at once. It still retains even in its degradation some of the force of the main cosmic stream from which it has been diverted. And so the material world and the materialized and materializing intellect, short apparently of pure mathematics and the mathematical intellect, always exhibit two contrary movements. Matter tends naturally toward homogeneous space and necessary determination, just as the intellect left to itself tends toward geometry. But nevertheless this movement is always counteracted by some form of life the function of which is always to convert determination into indetermination and liberty.

By means of this theory, Bergson thinks, it is possible to avoid the difficulty which confronts the Kantian philosophy as to how it has come about that the categories are adapted to work upon the manifold of sensibility at all. Kant had supposed "that there are three alternatives, and three only, among which to choose a theory of knowledge: either the mind is determined by things, or things are determined by the mind, or between mind and things we must suppose a mysterious agreement. But the truth is that there is a fourth alternative which consists first of all in regarding the intellect as a special function of the mind, essentially turned toward inert matter; then in saying that neither does matter determine the form of the intellect, nor does the intellect impose its form on matter, nor have matter and intellect been regulated in regard to one another by we know not what pre-established harmony, but that intellect and matter have progressively adapted themselves one to the other in order to attain at last a common form. *This adaptation has, moreover, been brought about quite naturally, because it is the same inversion of the same movement which creates at once the intellectuality of mind and the materiality of things*" (p. 217).

This theory seems to raise far more difficulties than it solves. In the first place it is difficult to understand how the cosmic impulse ever can become degraded at all. Is it because the cosmic impulse, which is God, unceasing life, action and freedom, becomes weary? If so, what becomes of the argument that the cosmic impulse is pure creative activity?—an argument which alone, according to Bergson, can save us from the difficulties and deadlocks of the intellect. The metaphor of the stream of life which becomes diverted by matter only to get a better grip on matter does not help in the least, because this theory was put forward as explaining the genesis of matter. Instead of pure duration explaining matter, matter has to be appealed to in order to explain duration.

Moreover there is a further difficulty in this account of the ideal genesis of matter in connection with Bergson's view of the nature and validity of mathematics. Matter is constituted by the reversal of the cosmic impetus, but this movement of matter toward externality and spatiality is never complete. "Matter is extended without being absolutely extended," because in every actual material system there is always a certain amount of interaction between the parts, whereas in a purely extended system every part would be utterly indifferent to every other part. But although the reversal of the cosmic impetus has originated at once "the intellectuality of mind and the materiality of things," yet the intellect outruns the spatiality of things, and so we get pure mathematics. If this is so then it is untrue to say, as Bergson does, that "intellect and matter have progressively adapted themselves one to another to attain at last a common form" (*Creative Evolution*, p. 217), and we have not bridged over the Kantian antithesis of matter and form.

"Our perception," Bergson says, "whose rôle it is to hold up a light to our actions, works a dividing up of matter that is always too sharply defined, always subordinate to practical needs, consequently always requiring revision. Our science, which aspires to the mathematical form, over-accentuates the spatiality of matter; its formulas are, in general, too precise, and ever need remaking" (p. 218). "Laws mathematical in form can never be applied completely to matter; for that matter would have to be pure space, and to separate itself from duration." "One cannot insist too much on the artificial element in the mathematical form of a physical law, and consequently in our scientific knowledge of things." "Physics comprehends its rôle when it pushes matter in the direction of spatiality." This becomes still more puzzling when we find that although mathematics pursues this process of further falsifying the false product of the intellect, yet at the finish mathematics gives us "a veritable means of contact" with the Absolute.

The whole argument seems to reduce to this: The practical life, which is, so to speak, a smaller stream diverted from the cosmic impulse in which reality consists, is occupied with the penetration and utilization of material things in order to overcome their determination. In order to help the practical life to realize this object the intellect misrepresents the nature of material things. Mathematics goes one better and carries out completely that process of falsifying reality for the sake of which the intellect was created by life, but in so doing mathematics succeeds in attaining to that reality of which not only material things, but even life itself, are mere degradations. And, further, this reality has degraded itself into intellect and matter in order to overcome the resistance of those falsities, with which it is the business of the intellect to provide life, in order to help life to overcome these falsities.

This is an argument which simply makes one giddy. And it is an argument which shows quite conclusively that Bergson can get meaning into his intuition only by appealing to intellect. Instead of intuition explaining intellect it is always intellect which is used to explain intuition. In answer to this it does not help at all to say, as Bergson does, that matter is always "ballasted with geometry." Matter is ballasted with geometry because our intellect tends naturally toward mathematics. But if our intellect tends towards mathematics, so much the worse, on Bergson's doctrine, for our intellect. Bergson has really repeated the performance of Kant. He has offered a justification of mathematics which is really the condemnation of mathematics. If the only reality is intuition then mathematics is false. And if, on the other hand, mathematics is true then the intellect and not intuition gives truth.

To sum up. All of Bergson's arguments for the incompetence

of the intellect break down. They either beg the question at once, in that intellect is defined in such a way as to mean something which cannot give truth, or they involve an appeal to the intellect the incompetence of which they are designed to demonstrate. On the other hand, Bergson's intuition, which is to give relief from the deadlocks which the intellect creates, will do nothing of the sort: Not only does it raise more difficulties than it solves, but it can only be expressed by reference to the intellect and the objects of the intellect.

The reason for this collapse of the Bergsonian philosophy is obvious. Bergson has only repeated the mistakes for which he reproaches Kant. In order to save the freedom of the will, God and immortality from all possible assaults of the intellect, Kant put these realities outside all possible knowledge. In much the same way, in order to have an answer to all possible difficulties which the intellect creates (and because he is apparently ignorant of the intellectual solution of certain classic difficulties), and in order to be able to say that what gives truth is not intellect, Bergson has to make intellect and intuition radically opposed to one another. But having so separated intellect and intuition, Bergson cannot justify either of them. He has not dealt fairly with intellect and has restricted it beforehand to that which is assumed not to be real. At the same time every attempt which Bergson makes to apply his doctrine of intuition, to show why intuition is necessary to supplement intellect, contradicts his own account of the nature of intuition.

E. H. STRANGE.

UNIVERSITY COLLEGE, CARDIFF, WALES.

ANYNESS AND PURE FORM.

On another page in this issue, Prof. E. H. Strange criticizes Bergson's theory of intuition and derives it from Bergson's opposition to Kant's idealism.

In this connection it is appropriate to state that Kant bases his philosophy on the consideration that the highest laws of nature are identical with the mathematical or purely formal theorems. The latter are verified and indeed created by pure reflection, which means they are mind-made; or, as Kant expresses himself, they are products of *a priori* thought, they are transcendental, they serve us as the forms with whose help we reduce sense-impressions to well regulated experiences.

Kant asks in his Prolegomena,[1] "How is the agreement between the highest laws of nature and the theorems of purely formal thought possible?" and he sees only two possibilities. Either, says Kant, we find these laws in nature by experience or the mind makes these laws, and his answer is that the human intellect is so constituted that it can see the world only as its own tools shape it. Kant declares that the world of material things surrounding us can be recognized by the mind only according to the mind's constitution, not as the things are in themselves. The mind imposes its own laws upon the objective world. The opposite view, that the mind has derived its laws from the objective world, is excluded because we know positively that mathematics are mind-made, they are *a priori*. We can construct all mathematics without appealing to any experience of the senses.

Crusius, a German contemporary of Kant, proposed the theory that some world intellect, the creator or God, has established a preconceived harmony between mind and the universe, equipping the mind of man with such a mentality as to enable him to build up the highest (the purely formal) laws of the world constitution out of his own mental resources—a proposition which is quite plausible before a tribunal of theologians, but scarcely acceptable to philosophers.

Now comes Bergson, and having gone through a study of Kant (according to Professor Strange) he finds himself nonplused by Kantian idealism, and he sees another, a fourth, way out of the dilemma. On the basis of a misconceived interpretation of evolution he proposes that "intellect and matter have progressively adapted themselves to one another to attain at last a common form" (*Creative Evolution*, p. 217). This fourth possibility as proposed by Bergson is probably the most unfortunate theory of all, for it presupposes the notion that neither the highest laws of nature nor the truths of mathematical propositions have been stable.

Bergson seems to assume that the highest laws of nature as well as mathematical theorems were loose rules in the beginning and have gradually hardened into definite norms. The intellect and the material world have been in contact and have influenced each other. Our observation of the stars has gradually impressed itself upon their movements so as to assume more and more a definite mathematical form. Finally Kepler succeeded in sum-

[1] This and the following quotations are from memory.

marizing their motions in definite mathematical formulas. Before the mind was in touch with them they may have had other uniformities, or lack of uniformity, of motion. On the other hand the mind was rambling at first and mathematical theorems varied; but gradually they assumed definite form, and now a thinking being can evolve them out of the resources of his own mind by *a priori* argument.

This kind of interpretation of the agreement between mind and nature by a mutual adaptation of the intellect on the one side and the objective world on the other, displays a lack of insight into the very nature of mathematics, and misconceives also the character of natural law.

Take for instance the simple *a priori* statement that $2 \times 2 = 4$. Can there ever have been a time in which this statement was not true? There was a time indeed when the mind could not think in figures at all, when an arithmetical equation or an algebraic formula or a geometrical theorem must have been unmeaning to a sentient being. Indeed formal thoughts are still void of meaning to animals and are above the comprehension of savages; nevertheless their truth is established, and the celestial bodies moved according to the laws of Kepler before mankind originated and mathematical theorems were ever constructed. Kepler discovered his three laws; he did not invent them. To think that the objective truth of the highest laws of nature originated through a process of evolution indicates a misunderstanding not only of the very nature of mathematics, but also of the theory of evolution, and finally also of science itself.

We believe that Kant raised the problem of problems in philosophy, and explained his reasoning in his *Prolegomena*, which therefore, in our opinion, is the most important book that came from his pen. Kant's significance and the prominent place he holds in philosophy are due to the fact that he put his finger on the critical question, though he did not succeed in answering it. He established beyond the shadow of a doubt the apriority of all the formal sciences, but he explained this truth wrongly and has thus given rise to a wrong idealism, deriving therefrom an agnosticism which he formulated in the doctrine that things in themselves are unknowable. His disciples have come to the conclusion that things in themselves do not exist, and we suggest that what he really meant were "forms in themselves" viz., the Platonic ideas or types of things and they are not unknowable.

In consideration of the significance of the Kantian problem, which was suggested to him by Hume's skepticism as to the universal validity of the law of causation, we have published a translation of Kant's *Prolegomena* with our own criticism, substituting for Kant's solution our own which is the basis of the philosophy of science.

We grant that all formal knowledge, including logic and mathematics, is *a priori,* but the conditions for a construction of mathematics after all presuppose experience and the basis of mathematics is the creation of an abstract realm of pure form. For a construction of the purely formal sciences we exclude everything particular and concrete, matter as well as energy, and retain only our own activity with a scope of pure motion which involves the possibility of constructing pure interrelations. In other words, the tools with which we operate are ultimately derived from experience. We retain our ability to operate, our activity, our mode of moving about, but we move in a field void of particularity, a field which therefore can be applied anywhere.

We insist that mathematics and all the other purely formal sciences are not constructed from nothingness; they are ultimately based on experience. But from this experience is excluded everything that pertains to sense-experience, and we produce in this way a domain in which we construct relations that do not contain particulars, but outline conditions which apply anywhere to any place and to any time, and we have called this field of pure thought "anyness." The very term anyness contains an explanation of why these propositions can be applied anywhere, and this application anywhere involves that *a priori* propositions are both (as Kant rightly declares) universal and necessary.

By understanding the full significance of anyness, we understand also that these laws of pure form must apply to any possible world, real or imaginary. Thus we can in pure thought deduce the inevitable results of conditions under any circumstances, and we can understand that if there is a world of concrete materiality, its motions, constructions, formations and results of any kind of actions are—so far as their forms, their relations, are concerned—predetermined by the laws of pure form, viz., by the laws of anyness.

Thus harmony must obtain between the purely formal laws as we have produced them by *a priori* construction and as they appear in the concrete world of reality, because the two are the same. Suppose two mathematicians construct a parabola with the same coordinates, would they not both come to the same conclusions as to the form of the parabola? And suppose that in reality a comet is determined by forces which possess a one-to-one correspondence with these same coordinates, would not the path of the comet possess a one-to-one correspondence to the figures of the parabolas of the two astronomers? The determinedness of all purely formal constructions is truly universal and applies anywhere in the domain of mathematics or pure thought and in any possible real world, also in this our world, i. e., the universe in which we live.

Considering the immanent necessity of the laws of form we can understand that this pre-established harmony has not been made by some supernatural being nor can it have originated gradually by a process of evolution, but it is intrinsically necessary. It is the immanent order which is the condition both of our natural laws and the intelligibility of existence. It is that same intrinsic regularity which can be observed everywhere in nature. This same regularity in the domain of form makes it possible that rational beings originate, that science can be established, that ideals can be proposed and lived up to, that a code of morality and a norm of right conduct can be formulated, and that the universe presents itself as a well-regulated and law-ordained cosmos.

A revision of almost all problems of philosophy from our standpoint will shed new light on their solutions, as will appear when we consider Prof. Hartley B. Alexander's article on "The Definition of Number." When enumerating the different conceptions of the interrelation between logical and mathematical views on the one side and philosophy on the other, he omits to mention the solution offered by the philosophy of form, which alone can be regarded as the philosophy of science.

Mr. Bertrand Russell sees the most essential feature of mathematics in its logical interrelations and goes so far as to claim that mathematics has nothing to do with space. Without objecting to definitions we prefer to regard at least geometry as the purely formal science of extension, which means space, not real space but pure or mathematical space. Mathematics presupposes logic and contains one additional element which is commonly called space, but like all purely formal sciences mathematics produces its objects of investigation by *a priori* construction. The elements with which we start are products of abstract thought in the realm of pure form created by thinking away everything that is particular, viz., all concrete objects that consist of matter and energy. Thus we retain the idea of pure motion and a possibility of establishing pure interrelations.

Pure motion means a change of place without implying energy, and a possibility of pure interrelations is a field of pure motion. We start with these two abstract notions; on the part of the subject an ability to move about, on the part of the object, (i. e.; the surrounding world), emptiness; and this emptiness offers a field of possible motion. With these conditions we construct whatever we may be pleased to build up, and observe the result.

In geometry we do something and note what will come of it. For instance, we move and note the trace of our motion. We call it a line. We move again and again, and let the traces of other lines enclose a space; we call the result a figure. Where two lines cross we have a point.

The system under construction may be Euclidean or non-Euclidean according to our start, whether or not we assume we are able to draw straight lines in the Euclidean space.[2] If in our plan of construction we exclude the straight line, we will have to move according to a definite principle in curves of a predetermined constant deviation, in which case our system will be different from the system of Euclid.

If two straight lines cross, the product of our construction is an angle, or rather four angles. The peculiarity of mathematics is to watch and observe the inevitable results of our own constructions, but the main characteristic of our constructions is this, that they are made in a field of anyness, i. e., they apply to any kind of construction made in the same way, not only in emptiness, but in any kind of a world filled with any kind of matter or any kind of energy.

The nature of matter and energy can only be discovered by experience through the senses, but the nature of pure interrelations can be determined by building up constructions in a field of anyness, as they must be under any conditions, which means under all conditions. Therefore the laws of pure form (in other words, the laws of anyness) will be valid for any kind of a world.

Thus we have an explanation why the theorems of pure mathematics are hyperphysical truths, and here we have a specimen of the nature of what theology has called the supernatural. There is only this difference between the old conception of the supernatural and this new conception of it which for the sake of distinction

[2] For an *a priori* construction of the plane, the straight line and the right angle see the author's *Foundations of Mathematics*.

we call the "hyperphysical," that the latter is as clear and self-evident as the former is mysterious, hazy, bewildering and mystifying.

The consequence of this conception of mathematics need not be traced here in all details, but we feel assured that in the long run it will solve all the modern problems of philosophy and dispose of the troubles which have been caused by pragmatism, Bergsonianism, by the advocates of the principle of relativity, and also by the logisticians. EDITOR.

LOUIS COUTURAT (1868-1914).

Besides the carnage in battleships and trenches, the great European war carries with it many accidental by-products of disaster not to be overlooked when casting up the grand total of losses the world is suffering. In the early days of last August when the first commotion in the commercial arteries to and from Paris was at its height, a heavy automobile at full speed chanced to run down the carriage in which Louis Couturat was traveling, and his immediate death was the result. Though only forty-six years old he held first rank in France among scientific workers in the philosophy of language, the philosophy of mathematics, and especially in the more modern aspect of logic—for which he agrees with English logicians in preferring the term "logistic," now that this word is but little known in its earlier significations listed in the dictionaries.

M. Couturat was singularly well informed on many questions, but the particular power and quality of his mind lay in a gift for deductive reasoning combined with the most punctilious intellectual honesty that would never countenance a compromise with the truths of reason. All his work is especially remarkable for the clearness of its representation. His style is never sullied by glittering and bizarre phrases intended to attract attention and admiration, but which often seem to cover a multitude of sins in the way of vague ideas and loose reasoning.

Couturat was first known by his painstaking and illuminating exposition of the mathematical infinite (*L'infini mathématique,* 1896) in which he discusses the idea of number and analyzes the concepts of continuity and the infinite, refuting practically all of Renouvier's arguments against the latter. His research in this line familiarized him with all the writings of Leibniz, and his next published work was an edition of more than two hundred fragments from Leibniz's unpublished manuscripts, some of which proved to be of the greatest philosophical interest. This was followed by a scholarly work on Leibnizian logic (*La logique de Leibniz*, 1901).

It was through their common interest in Leibniz that Couturat became acquainted with the Hon. Bertrand Russell in England, whose *Philosophy of Leibniz* appeared at this time, and their relation continued to be of the friendliest. Couturat added some notes to Cadenat's French translation of Russell's *Principles of Geometry* and introduced his *Principles of Mathematics* to the French public through a series of articles later collected into a book. Readers of *The Monist* will remember his answer to Poincaré's witty sallies against logistics in the issue of October, 1912. In an introduction to this article, M. Couturat's translator, Mr. Philip E. B. Jourdain, summed up the controversy between these two brilliant Frenchmen.

In the meantime, Couturat had published his *Algèbre de la logique*. In a small monograph of less than one hundred pages he presents a concise outline of the material contained in the first two volumes of Schröder's prolix three-volumed treatise. He follows Schröder in making the notion of inclusion the fundamental notion in his calculus in preference to the idea of equality, as the English logicians had done and as Schröder also had done in the beginning, though he made the change later under the influence of C. S. Peirce. Besides brevity Couturat's little work possesses the further advantage of clear-cut precision of argument which makes it practically the most easily intelligible presentation of the subject in any language. It is for this reason that the Open Court Publishing Company only last year issued an English edition of it.

Couturat believed thoroughly in the possibilities and desirability of an international artificial language, and he and Professor Ostwald are the two leading scientific men of whom the Esperanto and Ido movements can boast. In the light of M. Couturat's high character, talents and attainments it can only seem trite and trivial to say that the world has suffered an irreparable loss in his death. L. G. R.

CURRENT PERIODICALS.

The best produced scientific magazine in Great Britain is *Science Progress in the Twentieth Century: A Quarterly Journal of Scientific Work and Thought*, which is edited by the eminent pathologist Sir Ronald Ross. The first article in the number for April, 1915 is "Some Aspects of the Atomic Theory" by Frederick

Soddy. "Either matter must occupy space continuously or it must exist in the form of discrete particles. The historical origin of the atomic theory of matter is to be found in the choice between the two possible answers to these mutually exclusive alternatives......" However, "the true origin of the atomic theory is recognized universally to have been during the first decade of the last century in Dalton's discovery of the simple laws of chemical combination, though, even to the discoverer himself, the laws of gaseous behavior, upon which later the totally distinct but inextricably interwoven molecular theory was to be based, undoubtedly played a part in directing the interpretation he put upon these laws. Henceforth science was to deal no longer with atoms as the end results of a purely mental process of the subdivision of matter, a process which must of necessity have an end if matter does not occupy space continuously, but with atoms of definite mass determinable simply and exactly relatively, that is, the mass of any one kind of atom in terms of that of any other." The article, as we should expect, deals with the modern aspects. Francis Hyndman writes on "The Electrical Properties of Conductors at Very Low Temperatures," these properties indicating relations between widely different properties of matter. Arthur E. Everest writes on "The Anthocyan Pigments." The term "anthocyan" now denotes a large class of naturally occurring plant pigments, and the present article contains a very valuable account of the advances in this field of research from 1836 up to the present time. Richard Lydekker contributes a summary of "Vertebrate Palæontology in 1914." "The most important part of the year's work is undoubtedly that on the mammal-like reptiles and their structural resemblances and relationships." Charles Davison deals with "The Prevision of Earthquakes." "Between foreseeing and foretelling an unexpected event, there would seem to be little if any difference, beyond the fact that the one may be conducted in private while the other implies publication of some kind. But, to the corresponding words 'prevision' and 'prediction,' somewhat different meanings seem to be attributed, prevision being apparently considered as an approximate, and prediction as an accurate, form of forecast." This distinction is assumed in the present paper which contains a very good review of our knowledge on the subject. James Johnstone has an interesting discussion on "Is the Organism a Mechanism?" The concluding sentence of the article must be quoted here: "It may be, of course, that the activities of the organism are capable of reduction to chemical and physical processes, all of which are to be regarded as special cases of the second law—in that event biology is only a department of physical chemistry, and our conception of life must be a mechanistic one. But so long as physiology fails to provide physico-chemical explanations of vital processes, and so long as another physics and chemistry than that of the second law [of thermodynamics] is conceivable, then a real science of biology may be possible; and to insist on a mechanistic conception of the organism is only to dogmatize." Besides these articles, the number contains very interesting and long "Essay-Reviews" as well as shorter reviews of scientific books, and also correspondence.

* * *

In the number of "*Scientia*" (*Rivista di Scienza*) for March, 1915, the first article is by Fritz Frech on the saline seas of Anatolia and their importance for the problem of the origin of blocks of salt in the outer surface of the earth. Eugenio Rignano brings to a conclusion his series of articles on the higher forms of reasoning. In this third part, after a summary of his former two parts on the symbolism of mathematics, he compares mathematics with the new mathematical logic, and arrives at the conclusion that, from a psychological point of view, it would be quite a mistake to hope from the symbolism of mathematical logic the immense advantages that the introduction of symbolism has had in mathematics properly so-called. The inquiry upon the war still continues: this number contains an article written in Italian by Vilfredo Pareto of Lausanne, in which an attempt is made to treat the causes of the war from an entirely objective point of view; William J. Collins has an article in English discussing the deeper origins of the war; and Eduard Meyer writes in Garman on "England's War Against Germany and the Problems of the Future." These articles, except perhaps the last, have a refreshingly scientific air about them. Georges Chatterton-Hill contributes a critical note on Treitschke's *Ausgewählte Schriften*. There are reviews of books and periodicals, and a supplement containing French translations of the English, German and Italian articles.

In "*Scientia*" for April, 1915, the first article is by Aldo Mieli on the position of Lavoisier in the history of chemistry, in which it is brought out that Lavoisier ended a period instead of beginning one. J. W. Gregory writes on "The Reported Progressive Desiccation of the Earth," and finds no reason for believing that the earth is approaching a world-wide drought. The splendid scheme of "The Inquiry upon the War" continues: in this number we have articles by N. Kostyleff of Petrograd on the psychological factors of the war, by L. M. Hartmann of Vienna University on the causes of the war and by Lujo Brentano of Munch University on the deepest causes of the war. Of these three articles, the most interesting is undoubtedly the first very broad-minded study, writen from the laboratory of pathological psychology of the "Ecole pratique des Hautes Etudes" of Paris. There are the usual reviews of books and periodicals, a chronicle, and French translations of the Italian, English, and German articles. Φ

EDITORIAL COMMENT.

The opinion here expressed of the value of the *Scientia* contributions on the war represents the judgment of the English reviewer. We will only add that Eduard Meyer is a prominent historian who received the degree of doctor *honoris causa* from the University of Chicago. Writing from a German standpoint he naturally holds the English government responsible for the cause of the war. He enumerates his reasons in clear and terse language. In conclusion he predicts that unless the sea shall become equally free to all nations this war will be the beginning of further wars, and that an incidental but important result will be the unexpected growth of Japanese power and a gigantic struggle for supremacy in the Pacific and Indian oceans. Professor William J. Collins contrasts two world-conceptions, one is "science-ridden," "materialistic," in which "the state displaced the church," "matter and force are the masters," "disinterested virtue and sympathetic compassion are sacrificed to the will to power," "the will....heart, conscience, soul....[are] dismissed as so much metaphysical moonshine," "a brand new religion for Supermen." The nation that fits this description is not named but may easily be guessed if we bear in mind that the author is an Englishman who calls these curious comments "The Aetiology of the European Conflagration." This discussion of "the deeper origin of the war" has indeed "a refreshingly scientific air" about it. At any rate Professor Eduard Meyer will find this scientific conception of history refreshing. P. C.

VOL. XXV OCTOBER, 1915 NO. 4

THE MONIST

THE FUNDAMENTAL LAWS OF ARITHMETIC.[1]

[INTRODUCTORY NOTE.

Friedrich Ludwig Gottlob Frege was born on November 8, 1848, at Wismar, and since 1874 has taught at the University of Jena. It is well known that there has been in mathematics, especially during the last century, a constantly growing tendency toward more rigorous proofs and a more accurate determination of the limits of validity of mathematical propositions. For these purposes accurate definitions of mathematical concepts were needed; thus we obtained a much greater distinctness in definitions of a function, of the limits and continuity of a function, of the infinite, and of negative and irrational numbers. A natural continuation of this path of research led to the investigation of the question whether the concept of whole number is capable of definition, and whether the simplest laws which hold for integers are capable of proof. This we see in the work of Cantor, Dedekind, and Frege.[2] The object of a proof, as Frege has said, is not merely to raise the truth of a proposition above every doubt, but also to impart an insight into the dependence of truths on one another. The farther these investigations are continued, the fewer will be the fundamental truths to which everything can be reduced; and this simplification is in itself an end worthy to be striven for.

It was this desire for simplification, together with the philosophical questions as to the *a priori* or *a posteriori,* synthetic or analytic, nature of arithmetical truths, which moved Frege to his investigations. According to Frege, if in our proofs of mathematical truths we only meet the laws of logic and definitions we have an "analytic" truth, but if it is not possible to carry out the proof

[1] Translated, with the exception of the Introductory Note, from Professor Frege's *Grundgesetze der Arithmetik* by Johann Stachelroth and Philip E. B. Jourdain.

[2] It may be mentioned here that the Open Court Publishing Company of Chicago and London has issued translations of the most important work of Dedekind (*Essays on the Theory of Numbers*) and Cantor (*Contributions to the Founding of the Theory of Transfinite Numbers*) in this direction.

without using principles which are not, in general, of a logical nature, but refer to a special domain of knowledge, the theorem is "synthetic." This distinction of Frege's is not quite Kant's distinction, but it is an extension of Kant's more limited view that the sole source of analytic judgments is the principle of contradiction. "If," said Frege, "we call a theorem *a posteriori* or analytic, we do not judge about the psychological, physiological and physical conditions which made it possible to form the content of the theorem in our consciousness, nor about how another person has—perhaps in an erroneous manner—arrived at maintaining its truth, but about the ultimate foundation of the justification for the maintenance of its truth....A truth is *a posteriori* if its proof must depend on facts, that is to say, unprovable truths without generality that contain statements about definite objects. If, on the other hand, it is possible to carry out the proof wholly from general laws which themselves neither are capable of proof nor need it, the truth is *a priori*."[3] Of the four combinations, then, between analytic and synthetic on the one hand and *a priori* and *a posteriori* on the other, one only—analytic *a posteriori*—drops out.[4]

A still earlier account, written by Frege, is that he proposed to himself the question as to whether arithmetical judgments can be proved in a purely logical manner or must rest ultimately on facts of experience. Consequently he began by finding how far it was possible to go in arithmetic by inferences which depend merely on the laws of general logic. In order that nothing that is due to intuition should come in without being noticed, it was most important to preserve the unbrokenness of the chain of inferences; and ordinary language was found to be unequal to the accuracy required for this purpose.

Hence arose what Frege called his *Begriffsschrift*— a word that may be translated as "ideography"—which was described and shown in use in a small book published at Halle in 1879 under the title: *Begriffsschrift, eine der arithmetischen nachgebildete Formelsprache des reinen Denkens.* The fundamental idea of this book was the transference of the distinction of "variable" and "constant" from mathematical analysis to the wider domain of pure thought in general. In mathematics the distinction is not thoroughly carried out; but Frege's distinction was quite thorough.

[3] *Grundlagen der Arithmetik,* Breslau, 1884, pp. 3-4.

[4] *Ibid.,* p. 17.

He divided all the signs that he used into: (1) letters, "by which we can represent to ourselves different things," like those in the generally valid theorem in mathematics $(a+b)c=ac+bc$ and which serve principally to express *generality*; (2) signs which have quite a definite meaning, like +, —, 0, 1, or 2.

We have seen that arithmetic was the starting-point on the road that led Frege to his ideography. The aim of this ideography was not to provide a means of dealing systematically and rapidly with complicated logical questions, but to enable the question as to the empirical or purely logical basis of a branch of knowledge—in this case arithmetic—to be finally settled.

Frege began his *Begriffsschrift* by pointing out that, when we raise the question as to the foundation of a truth, the answer which —unlike that given by the recounting of the historical genesis and development of our knowledge of the truth in question—is connected with its inner being, consists in carrying out its proof purely logically, if that is possible, or, if it is not, in reducing it to the facts of experience on which the proof rests. The firmest proof is obviously a purely logical one, which, abstracting as it does from the special nature of things, is founded wholly on the laws on which all knowledge rests. Certainly a proposition may be capable of logical proof and yet could never, without sense-perception, enter into our consciousness. Indeed, this seems to be the case with *every* judgment, since no mental development without sense-perception appears possible. Thus it is not the psychological origin, but the completest manner of proof, that brings about the division of the class of all truths which need founding into (*a*) those which can be proved purely logically, and (*b*) those whose proofs rest on facts of experience.

And the very important ends for which Frege's ideography was designed were more or less overlooked by Venn, Schröder, and Peano, who criticized principally the cumbrousness of Frege's notation. This cumbrousness is a fact, but it may, as Bertrand Russell has shown, be avoided to a great extent. Far more important than the awkwardness of the form of many of the symbols, however, is the subtle and profound analysis of the ideas of logic, and the perfect avoidance of ambiguity and implicit assumptions. These are the most prominent characteristics of Frege's work.

In the following translation of part of Frege's mature exposition of 1893 and 1903, any notes or references which have been added by myself are put in square brackets. It is to be hoped that the present translation, for which Professor Frege has most kindly given me his permission, will help to make Frege's magnificent work better known. Frege's work is the first of that of the modern logicians. Mr. Bertrand Russell in his "Lowell Lectures" of 1914,[5] has given a notable example of the "logical-analytic" method in philosophy of which "the first complete example is to be found in the writings of Frege," and this method is now becoming almost as widely known as its importance deserves.—P. E. B. J.]

THE ideal of a strictly scientific method in mathematics, which I have tried to realize here and which perhaps might be named after Euclid, I would like to describe in the following way.

It cannot be expected that we should prove everything, because that is impossible; but we can demand that all propositions used without proof should be expressly mentioned as such, so that we can see distinctly upon what the whole construction is founded. We should, then, strive to diminish the number of these fundamental laws as much as possible by proving everything that can be proved. Furthermore I demand—and that is where I go beyond Euclid—that all the methods of inference used must be specified in advance. Otherwise it is impossible to satisfy the first demand.

At this ideal I believe I have arrived in essentials: only in a few points could one possibly be more exacting. In order to assure myself of more freedom and in order not to drop into excessive prolixity, I have taken the liberty of making tacit use of the interchangeability of the minor terms (conditions) and of the possibility of amalgamation of identical minor terms, and I have not reduced the modes of inference to their smallest number. Those who have read my *Begriffsschrift* will be able to gather from it that it

[5] *Our Knowledge of the External World as a Field for Scientific Method in Philosophy,* Chicago and London, 1914; cf. p. v.

would even in this respect be possible to satisfy the severest demand, but that it would at the same time involve a considerable increase in volume.

I believe that, apart from this, the only objections which could justly be raised to this book do not concern the rigor but only the choice of the course of the proofs and of the intermediate steps of the proofs. Often there are several modes of proof possible; I have not tried to adopt them all, and thus it is possible—even probable—that I have not always chosen the shortest. But let whoever has any fault to find with regard to this do better himself. There are other matters about which it is possible to dispute. Some might have preferred to increase the number of the modes of inference admitted and thereby to arrive at a greater mobility and brevity. But we have to stop somewhere if my ideal is approved of, and wherever we stop, people may say: "It would have been better to admit still more modes of inference."

By the uninterrupted connection of the chains of inference, each axiom, assumption, hypothesis, or whatever we like to call it, upon which a proof is founded, is brought to light, and so we gain a basis for judgment on the epistemological nature of the law proved. It has often been said that arithmetic is only a more highly developed logic; but that remains disputable as long as the proofs contain transitions from one proposition to another which are not performed according to acknowledged logical laws, but seem to be founded on intuitive kowledge. Only when these transitions are resolved into simple logical steps can we be sure that arithmetic is founded solely upon logic. I have gathered together everything that can facilitate the judgment as to whether the chains of inference are convincing and the buttresses firm. If any one perchance finds anything faulty, he must be able to indicate exactly where, to his thinking, the error lies—whether in the fundamental laws, in the definitions, in the rules, or in their application at a definite place. If we find everything correct, we know thus the exact bases upon which each single theorem is founded. A dispute can only, as far as I can see, arise because of my fundamental law of "ranges" (*Werthverläufe*),[6] which perhaps has not yet been specifically expressed by logicians, though it is in their minds when, for example, they speak of extensions (*Umfänge*) of concepts. I hold that it is purely logical. In any case the place is indicated where the decision has to be made.

My purpose requires many deviations from what is usual in mathematics. The requirements with regard to the rigor of proofs inevitably entail a great length of these proofs. Whoever does not think of this will often be surprised at the roundabout way in which a proposition is here proved, whereas he believes he can grasp the proof directly by a single act of understanding. This will surprise us especially if we compare the work of Dedekind, *Was sind und was sollen die Zahlen?*,[7] which is the most thorough work on the foundation of arithmetic that I have lately seen. In a much smaller compass it follows the laws of arithmetic much farther than I do here. This brevity is only arrived at, to be sure, by much not being really proved at all. Dedekind often says only that the proof follows from such-and-such theorems; he uses little dots which have the vague meaning of "and so on";[8] nowhere is there a statement of the logical or other laws on which he builds, and, even if there were, we could not possibly find out whether really no others were used,—for

[6] [This theorem is numbered V on pp. 36 and 240 of Vol. I (1893) of the *Grundgesetze*; and expresses that an equality of ranges both implies and is implied by the statement; thus an equation between functions holds quite generally. It first appeared on page 10 of Frege's lecture, *Funktion und Begriff* (Jena, 1891). Cf. p. 253 of Vol. II of the *Grundgesetze* (1903).]

[7] [English translation on pp. 29-115 of Dedekind's *Essays on the Theory of Numbers* (Chicago and London, 1901).]

[8] [Cf., for example, paragraph 8 on page 47 of the above translation.]

to do that the proof must be not merely indicated but completely carried out. Dedekind is also of the opinion that the theory of number is a part of logic; but his work hardly contributes to strengthen this opinion, because the expressions "system" and "a thing belongs to a thing" used by him are not usual in logic and are not reducible to accepted logical doctrine. I do not say this as a reproach, for his method may have been the most serviceable to him for his purpose; I only say it to make my intentions clear by putting them by the side of opposite intentions. The length of a proof is not to be measured by the yard. It is easy to make a proof appear short on paper by omitting many connecting links in the chain of inference and only indicating many things. Generally we are satisfied if every step in the proof is seen to be correct, and we may be so if we intend to arouse conviction of the truth of the theorem to be proved. If we wish to bring about an insight into the nature of this perception of the truth this method does not suffice, but we must put down all the intermediate stages of reasoning, in order that the full light of consciousness may fall upon them. As a rule mathematicians are only interested in the content of a theorem and in the fact that it is to be proved. The novelty of this book does not lie in the content of the theorems but in the development of the proofs and the foundations upon which they are based. That this altogether different point of view needs a quite different treatment ought not to appear strange. If we deduce one of our theorems in the usual way, it will be easy to overlook a proposition which does not appear necessary for the proof. If my proof is carefully thought out, the indispensability of this proposition will, I believe, be seen, unless an altogether different mode of procedure is adopted. Thus perhaps there are here and there in our theorems conditions which appear at first to be unnecessary but which after all prove to be necessary or at least to admit of removal only by a proposition to be specially proved.

With this book I accomplish an object which I had in view in my *Begriffsschrift* of 1879 and which I announced in my *Grundlagen der Arithmetik.*[9] I will here substantiate the opinion on the concept of number that I expressed in the book last mentioned. The fundamental part of my results is there expressed in § 46 in the words that the numerical datum contains an assertion about a concept; and upon this my present work is founded. If anybody is of another opinion let him try to construct a logical and usable exposition of his view by signs, and he will see that it is impossible. In language, it is true, the state of affairs is not so obvious, but if we look into the matter closely we find that here too a numerical datum always denotes a concept, not a group, an aggregate[10] or such-like things; and that if a group or aggregate is named, it is always determined by a concept, that is to say, by the properties an object must have in order to belong to the group, while that which makes the group a group or the system a system —the relations of members to each other—is altogether indifferent for the number.

The reason why the demonstration appears so long after the enunciation is to be found in part in essential changes of my ideography, which have forced me to discard a manuscript that was almost completed. These improvements may be mentioned here briefly. The fundamental signs employed in my *Begriffsschrift* have with one exception been used again here. Instead of the three parallel lines I have chosen the ordinary sign of equality because I convinced myself that it has exactly the same meaning in arithmetic that I wish to designate. I use the ex-

[9] Cf. the introduction and §§ 90 and 91 of my *Grundlagen der Arithmetik,* Breslau, 1884.

[10] [However, "aggregate" has become a technical term in mathematics for the translation of "*Menge*" or "*Begriffsumfang,*" and not "*Aggregat.*"]

pression "equal" in the same sense as "coinciding with" or "identical with," and this is just how the sign of equality is really used in arithmetic. The objection which might perhaps be raised against this rests on a defective distinction between sign and what is signified. It is true that in the equation $2^2 = 2 + 2$ the sign on the left is different from the one on the right, but both indicate or denote the same number.[11] To the old fundamental signs two more have been added: the "smooth breathing" (*spiritus lenis*) which serves for the designation of the "range" (*Werthverlauf*) of a function, and a sign which is meant to take the place of the definite article of ordinary language. The introduction of the ranges of functions is an important advance which makes possible a far greater flexibility. The former derived signs can now be replaced by other and simpler ones, though the definitions of one-to-one-ness, of a relation, of succession in a series, and of representation (*Abbildung*) are essentially the same as those which I have given partly in my *Begriffsschrift* and partly in my *Grundlagen der Arithmetik*. But the ranges have also a great fundamental importance; in fact I even define number itself as the extension of a concept, and extensions of concepts are, according to my definition, ranges. In consequence, we cannot do without them. The old fundamental signs, which reappear outwardly unchanged and whose algorithm has also hardly changed, have nevertheless been supplied with other explanations. The former "line of content" (*Inhaltsstrich*) reappears as a horizontal line (*Wagerechter*). There are consequences of an energetic development of my logical views. Formerly I distinguished in that proposition whose outer form is an assertion two things: (*a*) The recognition of the truth; (*b*) The content which is recognized as true. The content I called the "judicable content" (*beurtheil-*

[11] I also say: the meaning (*Sinn*) of the sign on the right is different from that of the one on the left but the denotation (*Bedeutung*) is the same (*Zeitschr. für Philos. und philos. Kritik*, Vol. C, 1892, pp. 25-50).

barer Inhalt). The latter has been divided into what I call "thought" (*Gedanken*) and "truth-value" (*Wahrheitswerth*). That is a consequence of the distinction between the meaning and denotation of a sign. In this case the meaning of a proposition is the thought and its denotation the truth-value. Besides this, we must grant that the truth-value is the true. I distinguish two truth-values: the true and the false. This distinction I have discussed more exhaustively and substantiated in my above mentioned essay on meaning and denotation. It may be mentioned here that incorrect speech can only thus be rightly understood. The thought which is otherwise the meaning of a proposition becomes, in incorrect speech, its denotation. How much more simple and distinct everything becomes by the introduction of truth-values can only be seen by an exhaustive examination of this book. These advantages alone put a great weight into the balance in favor of my view, which view perhaps may seem strange at first sight. Also the essence of the *function* in contradistinction from the *object* (*Gegenstand*) is more distinctly accentuated than in my *Begriffsschrift*. From this results further the distinction of function of the first and second "stage" (*Stufe*). As I have shown in my essay *Funktion und Begriff*, published at Jena in 1891, relations are functions in the meaning of the word which has been extended by me, and so we have to distinguish concepts of the first and second stage, relations of the same and of different stages.

From this it will be seen that the years have not passed in vain since the appearance of my *Begriffsschrift* and *Grundlagen*: they have brought my work to maturity. But just that which I recognize as an important advance stands, as I cannot help seeing, as a great obstacle in the way of the circulation and effectiveness of my book. And the strict completeness of the chain of conclusions, which seems to my way of thinking not its least value, will bring it, I am afraid, little thanks. I have got farther away from the traditional ideas and have by so doing given an appearance of paradox to my views. An expression which is encountered here and there on rapidly turning over these pages may easily appear strange and produce an unfavorable impression. I myself can judge somewhat with what opposition my innovations will be met because I have had to overcome something similar in myself. For not at random or because of the desire for innovation did I arrive at them, but I was forced by the matter itself.

With this I arrive at the second reason for my delay: the discouragement which at times came over me because of the cool reception, or rather the want of reception, by mathematicians,[12] of my works mentioned above and the opposing scientific currents against which my book would have to fight. Even the first impression must frighten people away: unknown signs, pages of nothing but strange-looking formulas. It is for that reason that I turned at times toward other subjects. But I could not keep the results of my thinking which seemed valuable to me myself locked up in my desk for any length of time; and the labor I had spent always required renewed labor that it might not be in vain. So the subject did not let go its hold upon me. In a case like the present one, when the value of a book cannot be recognized by a hasty perusal, criticism ought to be a help. But criticism is generally too badly paid. A critic can never hope to get paid in cash for the pains which the thorough study of this book will cost him. The only remaining hope is that somebody may have beforehand sufficient confidence in the matter to expect that the subjective gain will be sufficient recompense, and that

[12] In vain do we seek a notice of my *Grundlagen der Arithmetik* in the *Jahrbuch über die Fortschritte der Mathematik.* Investigators in the same domain, Dedekind, Otto Stolz, and von Helmholtz, do not seem to know my works. Nor does Kronecker mention them in his essay on the concept of number.

he will then publish the results of his searching examination. It is not as if only a laudatory review would satisfy me: quite the contrary. I would by far prefer an attack supported by a thorough acquaintance with the subject than to be praised in general terms which do not touch the root of the matter....

I must give up hope of securing as readers all those mathematicians who, when they come across logical expressions like "concept," "relation," "judgment," think: *Metaphysica sunt, non leguntur*; and those philosophers who at the sight of a formula call out: *Mathematica sunt, non leguntur*. Perhaps the number of these people is not very small. Perhaps also the number of mathematicians who trouble themselves about the foundation of their science is not great, and even those who do often seem in a great hurry to get past the foundations. And I hardly dare hope that my reasons for laborious rigor and consequent lengthiness will convince many of them. As we know, what is long established has great power over the minds of men. If I compare arithmetic with a tree which develops at the top into a multitude of methods and theorems while the root pushes downward, it seems to me that the pushing of the root is, at least in Germany, rather weak. Even in a work which might be classed among those dealing with foundations, the *Algebra der Logik* of E. Schröder, the top-growth soon predominates and, even before a great depth has been reached, causes a bending upward and a development into methods and theorems.

The widespread inclination to recognize only what can be perceived by the senses as existing is also unfavorable for my book. It is sought to deny, or at least to overlook, what cannot be thus perceived. Now the objects of arithmetic, that is to say numbers, are of a kind which cannot be thus perceived. How are we to deal with them? Very simply: the signs used for the numbers are explained to be the numbers themselves. Then in the signs there is something visible, and that is the chief thing. No doubt the signs have altogether different properties from the numbers themselves, but what does that matter? We simply ascribe to them the desired properties by means of what we call definitions. How on earth there can be a definition where there is no question about connections between sign and what is signified by it is a puzzle. We knead together sign and what is signified as far as possible without making any distinction between them, and, according to circumstances, we can assert the existence of the result with mention of its tangibility,[13] or we can bring into prominence the actual properties of numbers. Sometimes these number-signs are, it seems, regarded as chessmen and the so-called definitions as rules of the game. The sign then does not signify anything, but is the subject-matter itself. It is true that in this we overlook one little thing: that is, that we express a thought by $3^2 + 4^2 = 5^2$, while a position of chessmen does not express anything. Where people are satisfied with such superficialities, there is of course no basis for a deeper understanding.

Here it is of importance to make clear what defining is and what we can reach by it. It is, it seems, often credited with a creative power while really all there is to defining is that something is brought out, precisely limited and given a name. The geographer does not create a sea when he draws border lines and says: The part of the surface of the water surrounded by these lines, I am going to call the Yellow Sea; and no more can the mathematician really create anything by this process of definition. Nor can we by a mere definition magically give to a thing a property which it has not got. All we can do is to call

[13] Cf. E. Heine, "Die Elemente der Funktionslehre," Crelle's *Journal für Math.*, Vol. LXXIV, p. 173: "I place myself in my definition in a purely formal position and call certain tangible signs numbers so that in consequence the existence of these numbers is not in question.

this particular property by a new name. But that an oval drawn on paper with pen and ink should acquire by definition the property that when it is added to one one results, I can only regard as a scientific superstition. One might just as well make a lazy pupil diligent by a mere definition. Confusion easily arises here through lack of a distinction between concept (*Begriff*) and object (*Gegenstand*). If we say: "A square is a rectangle in which the adjacent sides are equal," we define the concept *square* by indicating what properties something must have in order to fall under this concept. I call these properties "characteristics" (*Merkmale*) of the concept. But it must be carefully noted that these characteristics are not the properties of the concept. The concept *square* is not a rectangle, only the objects which fall under this concept are rectangles, just as the concept *black cloth* is neither black nor a cloth. Whether or not such objects exist is not immediately known by means of their definitions. Now, for instance, suppose that we wish to define the number zero by saying: "It is something which when added to one gives one." With that we have defined a concept by stating what property an object must have to fall under this concept. But this property is not a property of the concept defined. It seems that we often imagine that we have created by our definition something which when added to one gives one. This is a delusion. Neither has the concept defined this property, nor is the definition a guarantee that the concept is satisfied. That requires first of all an investigation. Only when we have proved that there exists one object and one only with the required property are we in a position to give this object the proper name "zero." To create the zero is consequently impossible. I have already repeatedly explained this but, as it seems, without result.

JENA, GERMANY. GOTTLOB FREGE.

OUGHTRED'S IDEAS AND INFLUENCE ON THE TEACHING OF MATHEMATICS.*

GENERAL STATEMENT.

WILLIAM OUGHTRED has nowhere given a full and systematic exposition of his views on mathematical teaching. Nevertheless, he had very pronounced and clear cut ideas on the subject. That a man who was not a teacher by profession should have mature views on teaching is most interesting. We gather his ideas from the quality of the books he published, from his prefaces and from passages in his controversial writing against Delamain. As we proceed to give quotations unfolding Oughtred's views, we shall observe that three points receive special emphasis:

1. An appeal to the eye through suitable symbolism;
2. Emphasis upon rigorous thinking;
3. The postponement of the use of mathematical instruments until after the logical foundations of a subject have been thoroughly mastered.

The importance of these tenets is immensely reinforced by the conditions of the hour. This voice from the past speaks wisdom to specialists of to-day. Recent methods of determining educational values and the modern cult of utilitarianism have led some experts to extraordinary conclusions. Laboratory methods of testing, by the narrow-

* For details of William Oughtred's life we refer to *The Open Court* of August, 1915, and for a description of his works to *The Monist* of July, 1915.

ness of their range, often mislead. Thus far they have been inferior to the word of a man of experience, insight and conviction.

MATHEMATICS, "A SCIENCE OF THE EYE."

Oughtred was a great admirer of the Greek mathematicians—Euclid, Archimedes, Apollonius of Perga, Diophantus. But in reading their words he experienced keenly what many modern readers have felt, namely, that the almost total absence of mathematical symbols renders their writings unnecessarily difficult to read. Statements that can be compressed into a few well-chosen symbols which the eye is able to survey as a whole are expressed in long drawn out sentences. A striking illustration of the importance of symbolism is afforded by the history of the formula

$$ix = \log(\cos x + i \sin x).$$

It was given in Roger Cotes's *Harmonia mensurarum*, 1722, not in symbols, but expressed in rhetorical form, destitute of special aids to the eye. The result was that the theorem remained in the book undetected for 185 years and was meanwhile re-discovered by others. Owing to the prominence of Cotes as a mathematician it is very improbable that such a thing could have happened, had the theorem been thrust into view by the aid of mathematical symbols.

In studying the ancient authors Oughtred is reported to have written down on the margin of the printed page some of the theorems and their proofs, expressed in the symbolic language of algebra.

In the preface of his *Clavis* of 1631 and of 1647 he says:

"Wherefore, that I might more clearly behold the things themselves, I uncasing the Propositions and Demonstrations out of their covert of words, designed them in notes and species appearing to the very eye. After that by comparing the divers affections of Theorems, inequality, proportion, affinity, and dependence, I tryed to educe new out of them."

It was this motive which led him to introduce many abbreviations in algebra and trigonometry. The pedagogical experience of recent centuries has endorsed Oughtred's view, provided of course that the pupil is carefully taught the exact meaning of the symbols. There have been and there still are those who oppose the intensive use of symbolism. In our day the new symbolism for all mathematics, suggested by the school of Peano in Italy, can hardly be said to be received with enthusiasm. In Oughtred's day symbolism was not yet the fashion. To be convinced of this fact one need only open a book of Edmund Gunter, with whom Oughtred came in contact in his youth, or consult the *Principia* of Sir Isaac Newton who flourished after Oughtred. The mathematical works of Gunter and Newton, particularly the former, are surprisingly destitute of mathematical symbols. The philosopher Hobbes, in a controversy with John Wallis, criticized the latter for that "Scab of Symbols," whereupon Wallis replied, "I wonder how you durst touch M. Oughtred for fear of catching the Scab. For, doubtlesse, his book is as much covered over with the Scab of Symbols, as any of mine.... As for my Treatise of Conick Sections, you say, it is covered over with the Scab of Symbols, that you had not the patience to examine whether it is well or ill demonstrated."[1]

Oughtred maintained his view of the importance of symbols on many different occasions. Thus, in his *Circles of Proportion,* 1632, p. 20:

"This manner of setting downe Theoremes, whether

[1] *Due Correction for Mr. Hobbes. Or Schoole Discipline, for not saying his Lessons right. In answer to his Six Lessons, directed to the Professors of Mathematicks.* By the Professor of Geometry. Oxford, 1656, pp. 7, 47, 50.

they be Proportions, or Equations, by Symbols or notes of words, is most excellent, artificiall, and doctrinall. Wherefore I earnestly exhort every one, that desireth though but to looke into the noble Sciences Mathematicall, to accustome themselves unto it: and indeede it is easie, being most agreeable to reason, yea even to sense. And out of this working may many singular consectaries be drawne: which without this would, it may be, for ever lye hid."

RIGOROUS THINKING AND THE USE OF INSTRUMENTS.

The author's elevated concept of mathematical study as conducive to rigorous thinking shines through the following extract from his preface to the 1647 *Clavis*:

"...Which Treatise being not written in the usuall synthetical manner, nor with verbous expressions, but in the inventive way of Analitice, and with symboles or notes of things instead of words, seemed unto many very hard; though indeed it was but their owne diffidence, being scared by the newnesse of the delivery; and not any difficulty in the thing itselfe. For this specious and symbolicall manner, neither racketh the memory with multiplicity of words, nor chargeth the phantasie with comparing and laying things together; but plainly presenteth to the eye the whole course and processe of every operation and argumentation.

"Now my scope and intent in the first Edition of that my Key was, and in this New Filing, or rather forging of it, is, to reach out to the ingenious lovers of these Sciences, as it were Ariadnes thread, to guide them through the intricate Labyrinth of these studies, and to direct them for the more easie and full understanding of the best and antientest Authors;.... That they may not only learn their propositions, which is the highest point of Art that most Students aime at; but also may perceive with what solertiousnesse, by what engines of aequations, Interpretations, Comparations, Reductions, and Disquisitions, those antient Worthies have beautified, enlarged, and first found out this most excellent Science.... Lastly, by framing like questions problematically, and in a way of Analysis, as if they were already done, resolving them into their principles, I sought out reasons and means whereby they might be effected. And by this course of practice, not without long time, and much industry, I found out this way for the helpe and facilitation of Art."

Still greater emphasis upon rigorous thinking in mathematics is laid in the preface to the *Circles of Proportion* and in some parts of his *Apologeticall Epistle* against Delamain. In that preface William Forster quotes the reply of Oughtred to the question how he (Oughtred) had for so many years concealed his invention of the slide rules from himself (Forster) whom he had taught so many other things. The reply was:

"That the true way of Art is not by Instruments, but by Demonstration: and that it is a preposterous course of vulgar Teachers, to begin with Instruments, and not with the Sciences, and so instead of Artists, to make their Scholers only doers of tricks, and as it were Iuglers: to the despite of Art, losse of previous time, and betraying of willing and industrious wits, unto ignorance, and idlenesse. That the vse of Instruments is indeed excellent, if a man be an Artist: but contemptible, being set and opposed to Art. And lastly, that he meant to commend to me, the skill of Instruments, but first he would have me well instructed in the Sciences."

Delamain took a different view, arguing that instruments might very well be placed in the hands of pupils from the start. At the time of this controversy Delamain supported himself by teaching mathematics in London and he advertised his ability to give instruction in mathematics, including the use of instruments. Delamain brought the charge against Oughtred of unjustly calling "many of the [British] Nobility and Gentry doers of trickes and juglers." To this Oughtred replies:[2]

"As I did to Delamain and to some others, so I did to William Forster: I freely gave him my helpe and instruction in these faculties: only this was the difference, I had the very first moulding (as I may say) of this latter: But Delamain was already corrupted with doing upon Instruments, and quite lost from ever being made an Artist: I suffered not William Forster for some time so much as speake of any Instrument, except only the Globe it selfe; and to explicate, and worke the questions of the Sphaere, by the way of the Analemma: which also himselfe did describe for the present occasion. And this my restraint from such pleasing avocations, and holding him to the strictnesse of percept, brought forth this fruit, that in short time, even by his owne skill, he could not onely use any Instrument he should see, but also was able to delineate the like, and devise others."

As representing Delamain's views, we make the following selection from his *Grammelogia* (London, about 1633), the part near the end of the book and bearing the title, "In the behalfe of vulgar Teachers and others," where Delamain refers to Oughtred's charge that the scholars of "vulgar" teachers are "doers of tricks, as it were iuglers." Delamain says:

".... Which words are neither *cautelous,* nor *subterfugious,* but are as downe right in their *plainnesse,* as they are touching, and *pernitious,* by two much derogating from many, and glancing upon many noble *personages,* with too *grosse,* if not too *base* an attribute, in tearming them *doers of tricks, as it were to iuggle*: because they perhaps make use of a necessitie in the furnishing of themselves with such knowledge by *Practicall Instrumentall operation,*

[2] Oughtred, *Apologeticall Epistle,* p. 27.

when their more weighty *negotiations* will not permit them for *Theoreticall figurative demonstration*; those that are guilty of the aspertion, and are touched therewith may answer for themselves, and studie to be more *Theoreticall,* than *Practicall*: for the *Theory,* is as the *Mother* that produceth the *daughter,* the very sinewes and life of *Practise,* the excellencie and highest degree of true *Mathematicall Knowledge*: but for those that would make but a step as it were into that kind of *Learning,* whose onely desire is expedition, and facilitie, both which by the generall consent of all are best effected with Instrument rather than with tedious regular demonstrations, it was ill to checke them so grosly, not onely in what they have *Practised,* but abridging them also of their liberties with what they may *Practise,* which aspertion may not easily be slighted off by any *glosse* or *Apologie,* without an Ingenuous *confession,* or some mentall reservation: To which vilification, howsoever, in the behalfe of my selfe, and others, I answer; That *Instrumentall* operation is not only the Compendiating, and facilitating of *Art,* but even the glory of it, whole demonstration both of the making, and operation is soly in the *science,* and to an *Artist* or disputant proper to be knowne and so to all, who would truly know the cause of the *Mathematicall operations* in their originall; But, for none to know the use of a *Mathematicall Instrumen*[*t*], except he knowes the cause of its operation, is somewhat too strict, which would keepe many from affecting the *Art,* which of themselves are ready enough every where, to conceive more harshly of the difficultie, and impossibilitie of attayning any skill therein, than it deserves, because they see nothing but obscure propositions, and perplex and intricate demonstrations before their eyes, whose unsavoury tartnes, to an unexperienced palate like bitter pills is sweetned over, and made pleasant with an *Instrumentall compendious facilitie,* and made to goe downe the more readily, and yet to retaine the same vertue, and working; And me thinkes in this queasy age, all *helpes* may bee used to procure a *stomacke,* all *bates* and invitations to the declining studie of so noble a *Science,* rather than by rigid Method and generall *Lawes* to scarre men away. All are not of like disposition, neither all (as was sayd before) propose the same end, some resolve to *wade,* others to put a *finger* in onely, or wet a *hand*: now thus to tye them to an obscure and *Theoricall* forme of teaching, is to crop their hope, even in the very bud. . . . The beginning of a *man's knowledge* even in the use of an *Instrument,* is first founded on *doctrinal precepts,* and these precepts may be conceived all along in its use: and are so farre from being excluded, that they doe necessarily *concomitate* and are contained therein: the *practicke* being better understood by the *doctrinall part,* and this later explained by the *Instrumentall,* making precepts obvious unto sense, and the *Theory* going along with the *Instrument,* better informing and inlightning the understanding, etc. *vis vnita fortior,* so as if that in *Phylosophy* bee true, *Nihil est* [*in*] *intellectu quod non prius fuit in sensu.*"

The difference between Oughtred and Delamain as to the use of mathematical instruments raises an important question. Should the slide rule be placed in the hands of a boy before, or after, he has mastered the theory of logarithms? Should logarithmic tables be withheld from him until the theoretical foundation is laid in the mind of the pupil? Is it a good thing to let a boy use a surveying instrument unless he first learns trigonometry? Is it advisable to permit a boy to familiarize himself with the running of a dynamo before he has mastered the underlying principles of electricity? These and similar questions are even more vital to-day than they were in the seventeenth century. Does the use of instruments ordinarily discourage a boy from mastery of the theory? Or does such manipulation constitute a natural and pleasing approach to the abstract? On this particular point, who showed the profounder psychological insight, Oughtred or Delamain?

In July, 1914, there was held in Edinburgh a celebration of the three hundredth anniversary of the invention of logarithms. On that occasion there was collected at Edinburgh university one of the largest exhibits ever seen of modern instruments of calculation. The opinion was expressed by an experienced teacher that "weapons as those exhibited there are for men and not for boys, and such danger as there may be in them is of the same character as any form of too early specialization."

It is somewhat of a paradox that Oughtred who in his student days and during his active years felt himself impelled to invent sun-dials, planispheres and various types of slide rules—instruments which represent the most original contributions which he handed down to posterity—should discourage the use of such instruments in teaching mathematics to beginners. That without the aid of instruments he himself should have succeeded so well in attracting and inspiring young men constitutes the strongest evidence of his transcendent teaching ability. It may be argued that his pedagogic dogma, otherwise so excellent, here goes contrary to the course he himself followed instinctively in his self-education along mathematical lines. We read that Sir Isaac Newton, as a child, constructed sun-dials, wind-mills, kites, paper lanterns and a wooden clock. Should these activities have been suppressed? Ordinary children are simply Isaac Newtons on a smaller intellectual scale. Should their activities along these lines be encouraged or checked?

On the other hand it may be argued that the paradox alluded to above admits of explanation like all paradoxes, and that there is no inconsistency between Oughtred's pedagogic views and his own course of development. If he invented sun-dials, he must have had a comprehension of the cosmic motions involved; if he solved spherical triangles graphically by the aid of the planisphere, he must have understood the geometry of the sphere, so far as it relates to such triangles; if he invented slide rules, he had beforehand a thorough grasp of logarithms. The question at issue does not involve so much the invention of instruments, as the use by the pupil of instruments already constructed, before he fully understands the theory which is involved. Nor does Sir Isaac Newton's activity as a child establish Delamain's contention. Of course, a child should not be discouraged from manual activity along the line of producing interesting toys in imitation of structures and machines that he sees, but to introduce him to the realm of abstract thought by the aid of instruments is a different proposition, fraught with danger. A boy may learn to use a slide rule mechanically and, because of his ability to obtain practical results, feel justified in foregoing the mastery of underlying theory; or he may consider the ability of manipulating a surveying instrument quite sufficient, even though he be ignorant of geometry and trigonometry; or he may learn how to operate a dynamo and an electric switchboard, and be altogether satisfied, though having no grasp of electrical science. Thus instruments draw a youth aside from the path leading to real intellectual attainments and real efficiency; they allure him into lanes which are often blind alleys. Such were the views of Oughtred.

Who was right, Oughtred or Delamain? It may be claimed that there is a middle ground which more nearly represents the ideal procedure in teaching. Shall the slide rule be placed into the student's hands at the time when he is engaged in the mastery of principles? Shall there be an alternate study of the theory of logarithms and of the slide rule—on the idea of one hand washing the other—until a mastery of both the theory and the use of the instrument has been attained? Does this method not produce the best and most lasting results? Is not this Delamain's actual contention? We leave it to the reader to settle these matters from his own observation, knowledge and experience.

NEWTON'S COMMENTS ON OUGHTRED.

Oughtred is an author who has been found to be of increasing interest to modern historians of mathematics. But no modern writer has, to our knowledge, pointed out his importance in the history of the *teaching* of mathematics. Yet his importance as a teacher did receive recognition in the seventeenth century by no less distinguished a scientist than Sir Isaac Newton. On May 25, 1694, Sir Isaac Newton wrote a long letter in reply to a request for his recommendation on a proposed new course of study in mathematics at Christ's Hospital.[3] Toward the close of his letter, Newton says:

"And now I have told you my opinion in these things, I will give you Mr. Oughtred's, a Man whose judgment (if any man's) may be safely relyed upon. For he in his book of the circles of proposition, in the end of what he writes about Navigation (page 184) has this exhortation to Seamen. And if, sayth he, the Masters of Ships and Pilots will take the pains in the Journals of their Voyages diligently and faithfully to set down in severall columns, not onely the Rumb they goe on and the measure of the Ships way in degrees, and the observation of Latitude and variation of their compass; but alsoe their conjectures and reason of their correction they make of the aberrations they shall find, and the qualities and condition of their ship, and the diversities and seasons of the winds, and the secret motions or agitations of the Seas, when they begin, and how long they continue, how farr they extend and with

[3] J. Edleston, *Correspondence of Sir Isaac Newton and Professor Cotes*, London, 1850, pp. 279-292.

what inequality; and what else they shall observe at Sea worthy consideration, and will be pleased freely to communicate the same with Artists such as are indeed skilfull in the Mathematicks and lovers and enquirers of the truth: I doubt not but that there shall be in convenient time, brought to light many necessary precepts which may tend to the perfecting of Navigation, and the help and safety of such whose Vocations doe inforce them to commit their lives and estates in the vast Ocean to the providence of God. Thus farr that very good and judicious man Mr. Oughtred, I will add, that if instead of sending the Observations of Seamen to able Mathematicians at Land, the Land would send able Mathematicians to Sea, it would signify much more to the improvement of Navigation and safety of Mens lives and estates on that element."

May Oughtred prove as instructive to the modern reader as he did to Newton.

OUGHTRED AND HARRIOT.

Oughtred's *Clavis mathematicae* was the most influential mathematical publication in Great Britain which appeared in the interval between John Napier's *Mirifici logarithmorum canonis descriptio,* Edinburgh, 1614, and the time, forty years later, when John Wallis began to publish his important researches at Oxford. The year 1631 is of interest as the date of publication, not only of Oughtred's *Clavis,* but also of Thomas Harriot's *Artis analyticae praxis.* We have no evidence that these two mathematicians ever met. Through their writings they did not influence each other. Harriot died ten years before the appearance of his *magnum opus,* or ten years before Oughtred began to publish. Strangely, Oughtred who survived Harriot thirty-nine years, never mentions him. There is no doubt that, of the two, Harriot was the more original mind, more capable of penetrating into new fields of research. But he had the misfortune of having a strong competitor in René Descartes, in the development of Algebra, so that no single algebraic achievement stands out strongly and conspicuously as Harriot's own contribution to algebraic science. As a text to serve as an introduction to algebra, Harriot's *Artis analyticae praxis* was inferior to Oughtred's *Clavis*. The former was a much larger book, not as conveniently portable, compiled after the author's death by others and not prepared with the care in the development of the details, nor with the coherence and unity, and the profound pedagogic insight, which distinguish the work of Oughtred. Nor was Harriot's position in life such as to be surrounded by so wide a circle of pupils as was Oughtred. To be sure, Harriot had such followers as Torperley, William Lower and Protheroe in Wales, but this group is small as compared with Oughtred's.

OUGHTRED'S PUPILS.

There was a large number of distinguished men who, in their youth, either visited Oughtred's home and studied under his roof or else read his *Clavis* and sought his assistance by correspondence. We permit Aubrey to enumerate some of these pupils in his own gossipy style:[4]

"Seth Ward, M.A., a fellow of Sydney Colledge in Cambridge (now bishop of Sarum), came to him and lived with him halfe a yeare (and he would not take a farthing for his diet), and learned all his mathematiques of him. Sir Jonas More was with him a good while, and learn't; he was but an ordinary logist before. Sir Charles Scarborough was his scholar; so Dr. John Wallis was his scholar; so was Christopher Wren his scholar, so was Mr.... Smethwyck, Regiae Societatis Socius. One Mr. Austin (a most ingeniose man) was his scholar, and studyed so

[4] Aubrey, *op. cit.,* Vol. II, 1898, p. 108.

much that he became mad, fell a laughing, and so dyed, to the great griefe of the old gentleman. Mr.... Stokes, another scholar, fell mad, and dream't that the good old gentleman came to him, and gave him good advice, and so he recovered, and is still well. Mr. Thomas Henshawe, Regiae Societatis Socius, was his scholar (then a young gentleman). But he did not so much like any as those that tugged and tooke paines to worke out questions. He taught all free.

"He could not endure to see a scholar write an ill hand; he taught them all presently to mend their hands."

Had Oughtred been the means of guiding the mathematical studies of only John Wallis and Christopher Wren—one the greatest English mathematician between Napier and Newton, the other one of the greatest architects of England,—he would have earned profound gratitude. But the above list embraces nine men, most of them distinguished in their day. And yet Aubrey's list is very incomplete. It is easy to more than double it by adding the names of William Forster who translated from Latin into English Oughtred's *Circles of Proportion,* Arthur Haughton who brought out the 1660 Oxford edition of the *Circles of Proportion,* Robert Wood, an educator and politician who assisted Oughtred in the translation of the *Clavis* from Latin into English for the edition of 1647, W. Gascoigne, a man of promise who fell, 1644, at Marston Moor, John Twysden who was active as a publisher, William Sudell, N. Ewart, Richard Shuttleworth, William Robinson, and Henry Frederick Howard who was the son of the Earl of Arundel, for whose instruction Oughtred originally prepared the manuscript treatise that was published in 1631 as the *Clavis mathematicae.*

Nor must we overlook the names of Lawrence Rook (who "did admirably well read in Gresham Coll. on the sixth chapt. of the said book," the *Clavis,*), Christopher

Brooke (a maker of mathematical instruments who married a daughter of the famous mathematician), William Leech and William Brearly (who with Robert Wood "have been ready and helpfull incouragers of me [Oughtred] in this labour" of preparing the English *Clavis* of 1647) and Thomas Wharton who studied the *Clavis* and assisted in the editing of the *Clavis* of 1647.

The devotion of these pupils bears eloquent testimony not only of Oughtred's ability as a mathematician but also of his power of drawing young men to him—of his personal magnetism. Nor should we omit from the list Richard Delamain, a teacher of mathematics in London, who unfortunately had a bitter controversy with Oughtred on the priority and independence of the invention of the circular slide rule and a form of sun-dial. Delamain became later a tutor in mathematics to King Charles I, and perished in the civil war, before 1645.

OUGHTRED, THE "TODHUNTER OF THE SEVENTEENTH CENTURY."

To afford a clearer view of Oughtred as a teacher and mathematical expositor we quote some passages from various writers and from his correspondence. Anthony Wood[5] gives an interesting account of how Seth Ward and Charles Scarborough went from Cambridge University to the obscure home of the country mathematician, to be initiated into the mysteries of algebra:

"Mr. Cha. Scarborough, then an ingenious young student and fellow of Caius Coll. in the same university, was his [Seth Ward's] great acquaintance, and both being equally students in that faculty and desirous to perfect themselves, they took a journey to Mr. Will. Oughtred living then at Albury in Surrey, to be informed in many things in his *Clavis mathematica* which seemed at that

[5] Wood's *Athenae Oxonienses* (Ed. P. Bliss), Vol. IV, 1820, p. 247.

time very obscure to them. Mr. Oughtred treated them with great humanity, being very much pleased to see such ingenious young men apply themselves to these studies, and in short time he sent them away well satisfied in their desires. When they returned to Cambridge, they afterwards read the *Clav. Math.* to their pupils, which was the first time that that book was read in the said university. Mr. Laur. Rook, a disciple of Oughtred, I think, and Mr. Ward's friend, did admirably well in Gresham Coll. on the sixth chap. of the said book, which obtained him great repute from some and greater from Mr. Ward, who ever after had an especial favour for him."

Anthony Wood makes a similar statement about Thomas Henshaw:[6]

"While he remained in that coll. [University College, Oxford] which was five years....he made an excursion for about 9 months to the famous mathematician Will. Oughtred parson of Aldbury in Surrey, by whom he was initiated in the study of mathematics, and afterwards retiring to his coll. for a time, he at length went to London, was entered a student in the Middle Temple."

Extracts from letters of W. Gascoigne to Oughtred, of the years 1640 and 1641, throw some light upon mathematical teaching of the time:[7]

"Amongst the mathematical rarities these times have afforded, there are none of that small number I (a late intruder into these studies) have yet viewed, which so fully demonstrates their authors' great abilities as your Clavis, not richer in augmentations, than valuable for contraction;...."

"Your belief that there is in all inventions aliquid divinum, an infusion beyond human cogitations, I am confident will appear notably strengthened, if you please to afford this truth belief, that I entered upon these studies acciden-

[6] Wood, *op. cit.*, Vol. II, p. 445. [7] Rigaud, *op. cit.*, Vol. I, pp. 33, 35.

tally after I betook myself to the country, having never had so much aid as to be taught addition, nor the discourse of an artist (having left both Oxford and London before I knew what any proposition in geometry meant) to inform me what were the best authors."

The following extracts from two letters by W. Robinson, written before the appearance of the 1647 English edition of the *Clavis,* express the feeling of many readers of the *Clavis* on its extreme conciseness and brevity of explanation:[8]

"I shall long exceedingly till I see your *Clavis* turned into a pick-lock; and I beseech you enlarge it, and explain it what you can, for we shall not need to fear either tautology or superfluity; you are naturally concise, and your clear judgment makes you both methodical and pithy; and your analytical way is indeed the only way."....

"I will once again earnestly entreat you, that you be rather diffuse in the setting forth of your English mathematical *Clavis,* than concise, considering that the wisest of men noted of old, and said stultorum infinitus est numerus, these arts cannot be made too easy, they are so abstruse of themselves, and men either so lazy or dull, that their fastidious wits take a loathing at the very entrance of these studies, unless it be sweetened on with plainness and facility. Brevity may well argue a learned author that without any excess or redundance, either of matter or words, can give the very substance and essence of the thing treated of; but it seldom makes a learned scholar; and if one be capable, twenty are not; and if the master sum up in brief the pith of his own long labours and travails, it is not easy to imagine that scholars can with less labour than it cost their masters dive into the depths thereof."

Here is the judgment of another of Oughtred's friends:[9]

"... with the character I received from your and my

[8] Rigaud, *op. cit.,* Vol. I, pp. 16, 26. [9] Rigaud, *op. cit.,* Vol. I, p. 66.

noble friend Sir Charles Cavendish, then at Paris, of your second edition of the same piece, made me at my return into England speedily to get, and diligently peruse the same. Neither truly did I find my expectation deceived; having with admiration often considered how it was possible (even in the hardest things of geometry) to deliver so much matter in so few words, yet with such demonstrative clearness and perspicuity: and hath often put me in mind of learned Mersennus his judgment (since dead) of it, that there was more matter comprehended in that little book than in Diophantus, and all the ancients...."

Oughtred's own feeling was against diffuseness in textbook writing. In his revisions of his *Clavis* the original character of that book was not altered. In his reply to W. Robinson, Oughtred said:[10]

"... But my art for all such mathematical inventions I have set down in my Clavis Mathematica, which therefore in my title I say is tum logisticae cum analyticae adeoque totius mathematicae quasi clavis, which if any one of a mathematical genius will carefully study, (and indeed it must be carefully studied,) he will not admire others, but himself do wonders. But I (such is my tenuity) have enough fungi vice cotis, acutum reddere quae ferrum valet, exsors ipsa secundi, or like the touchstone, which being but a stone, base and little worth, can shew the excellence and riches of gold."

John Wallis held Oughtred's *Clavis* in high regard. When in correspondence with John Collins concerning plans for a new edition, Wallis wrote in 1666-67, six years after the death of Oughtred:[11]

"....But for the goodness of the book in itself, it is that (I confess) which I look upon as a very good book, and which doth in as little room deliver as much of the fundamental and useful part of geometry (as well as of

[10] *Ibid.*, p. 9. [11] *Ibid.*, p. 475.

arithmetic and algebra) as any book I know; and why it should not be now acceptable I do not see. It is true, that as in other things so in mathematics, fashions will daily alter, and that which Mr. Oughtred designed by great letters may be now by others be designed by small; but a mathematician will, with the same ease and advantage, understand A , and a^3 or *aaa*..... And the like I judge of Mr. Oughtred's Clavis, which I look upon (as those pieces of Vieta who first went in that way) as lasting books and classic authors in this kind; to which, notwithstanding, every day may make new additions.....

"But I confess, as to my own judgment, I am not for making the book bigger, because it is countrary to the design of it, being intended for a manual or contract; whereas comments, by enlarging it, do rather destroy it... But it was by him intended, in a small epitome, to give the substance of what is by others delivered in larger volumes...."

That there continued to be a group of students and teachers who desired a fuller exposition than is given by Oughtred is evident from the appearance, over fifty years after the first publication of the *Clavis*, of a booklet by Gilbert Clark, entitled *Oughtredus Explicatus,* London, 1682. A review of this appeared in the *Acta Eruditorum,* Leipsic, 1684, p. 168, wherein Oughtred is named "clarissimus Angliae mathematicus." John Collins wrote Wallis[12] in 1666-67 that Clark, "who lives with Sir Justinian Isham, within seven miles of Northampton," "intimates he wrote a comment on the *Clavis,* which lay long in the hands of a printer, by whom he was abused, meaning Leybourn."

We shall have occasion below to refer to Oughtred's inability to secure a copy of a noted Italian mathematical

[12] *Ibid.,* p. 471.

work published a few years before. In those days the condition of the book trade in England must have been somewhat extraordinary. Dr. J. W. L. Glaisher throws some light upon this subject.[13] He found in the Calendar of State Papers, Domestic Series, 1637, a petition to Archbishop Laud in which it is set forth that, when Hooganhuysen, a Dutchman, "heretofore complained of in the High Commission for importing books printed beyond the seas," had been bound "not to bring in any more," one Vlacq (the computer and publisher of logarithmic tables) "kept up the same agency and sold books in his stead."... "Vlacq is now preparing to go beyond the seas to avoid answering his late bringing over nine bales of books contrary to the decree of the Star Chamber." Judgment was passed that, "Considering the ill-consequence and scandal that would arise by strangers importing and venting in this kingdom books printed beyond the seas," certain importations be prohibited, and seized if brought over.

This want of easy intercommunication of results of scientific research in Oughtred's time is revealed in the following letter, written by Oughtred to Robert Keylway, in 1645:[14]

"I speak this the rather, and am induced to a better confidence of your performance, by reason of a geometric-analytical art of practice found out by one Cavalieri, an Italian, of which about three years since I received information by a letter from Paris, wherein was praelibated only a small taste thereof, yet so that I divine great enlargement of the bounds of the mathematical empire will ensue. I was then very desirous to see the author's own book while my spirits were more free and lightsome, but I could not get it in France. Since, being more stept into

[13] J. W. L. Glaisher, "On Early Logarithmic Tables, and their Calculators," *Philosophical Magazine*, 4th. Ser., Vol. XLV, 1873, pp. 378, 379.

[14] Rigaud, *op. cit.*, Vol. I, p. 65.

years, daunted and broken with the sufferings of these disastrous times, I must content myself to keep home, and not put out to any foreign discoveries."

It was in 1655, when Oughtred was about eighty years old, that John Wallis, the great forerunner of Newton in Great Britain, began to publish his great researches on the arithmetic of infinites. Oughtred rejoiced over the achievements of his former pupil. In 1655, Oughtred wrote John Wallis as follows:[15]

"I have with unspeakable delight, so far as my necessary business, the infirmness of my health, and the greatness of my age (approaching now to an end) would permit, perused your most learned papers, of several choice arguments, which you sent me: wherein I do first with thankfulness acknowledge to God, the Father of lights, the great light he hath given you; and next I congratulate you, even with admiration, the clearness and perspicacity of your understanding and genius, who have not only gone, but also opened a way into these profoundest mysteries of art, unknown and not thought of by the ancients. With which your mysterious inventions I am the more affected, because full twenty years ago, the learned patron of learning, Sir Charles Cavendish, shewed me a paper written, wherein were some few excellent new theorems, wrought by the way, as I suppose, of Cavalieri, which I wrought over again more agreeably to my way. The paper, wherein I wrought it, I shewed to many, whereof some took copies, but my own I cannot find. I mention it for this because I saw therein a light breaking out for the discovery of wonders to be revealed to mankind, in this last age of the world: which light I did salute as afar off, and now at a nearer distance embrace in your prosperous beginnings. Sir, that you are pleased to mention my name in your never dying papers, that is your noble favour to

[15] *Ibid.*, p. 87.

me, who can add nothing to your glory, but only my applause....."

The last sentence has reference to Wallis's appreciative and eulogistic reference to Oughtred in the preface. It is of interest to secure the opinion of later English writers who knew Oughtred only through his books. John Locke wrote in his journal under the date, June 24, 1681, "the best algebra yet extant is Outred's."[16] John Collins who is known in the history of mathematics chiefly through his very extensive correspondence with nearly all mathematicians of his day, was inclined to be more critical. He wrote Wallis[17] about 1667:

"It was not my intent to disparage the author, though I know many that did lightly esteem him when living, some whereof are at rest, as Mr. Foster and Mr. Gibson.....You grant the author is brief, and therefore obscure, and I say it is but a collection, which, if himself knew, he had done well to have quoted his authors, whereto the reader might have repaired. You do not like those words of Vieta in his theorems, ex adjunctione plano solidi, plus quadrato quadrati, etc., and think Mr. Oughtred the first that abridged those expressions by symbols; but I dissent, and tell you 'twas done before by Cataldus, Geysius, and Camillus Gloriosus,[18] who in his first decade of exercises, (not the first tract), printed at Naples in 1627, which was four years before the first edition of the Clavis, proposeth this equation just as I here give it you, viz. 1*ccc* + 16*qcc* + 41*qqc* — 2304*cc* — 1836*qc* — 133000*qq* — 54505*c* + 3728*q* + 8064 N *aequatur* 4608, finds N or a root of it to be 24, and composeth the whole out of it for proof, just in Mr. Oughtred's symbols and method. Catal-

[16] King's *Life of John Locke*, Vol. I, London, 1830, p. 227.

[17] Rigaud, *op. cit.*, Vol. I, pp. 477-480.

[18] *Exercitationum Mathematicarum Decas prima*, Naples, 1627, and probably Cataldus's *Transformatio Geometrica*, Bologna, 1612.

dus on Vieta came out fifteen years before, and I cannot quote that, as not having it by me."

". . . . And as for Mr. Oughtred's method of symbols, this I say of it; it may be proper for you as a commentator to follow it, but divers I know, men of inferior rank that have good skill in algebra, that neither use nor approve it. . . . Is not A^5 sooner wrote than A_{qc}? Let A be 2, the cube of 2 is 8, which squared is 64: one of the questions between Maghet Grisio and Gloriosus is whether $64 = A_{cc}$ or A_{qc}. The Cartesian method tells you it is A^6, and decides the doubt. . . ."

There is some ground for the criticisms passed by Collins. To be sure, the first edition of the *Clavis* is dated 1631—six years before Descartes suggested the exponential notation which came to be adopted as the symbolism in our modern algebra. But the second edition of the *Clavis,* 1647, appeared ten years after Descartes's innovation. Had Oughtred seen fit to adopt the new exponential notation in 1647, the step would have been epoch-making in the teaching of algebra in England. We have seen no indication that Oughtred was familiar with Descartes's *Géométrie* of 1637.

The year preceding Oughtred's death Mr. John Twysden expressed himself as follows in the Preface to his *Miscellanies*:[19]

"It remains that I should adde something touching the beginning, and use of these Sciences. . . . I shall only, to their honours, name some of our own Nation yet living, who have happily laboured upon both stages. That succeeding ages may understand that in this of ours, there yet remained some who were neither ignorant of these Arts, as if they had held them vain, nor condemn them as superfluous. Amongst them all let Mr. William Ought-

[19] *Miscellanies: or Mathematical Lucubrations, of Mr. Samuel Foster, Sometime publike Professor of Astronomie in Gresham Colledge in London,* by John Twysden, London, 1659.

red, of Aeton, be named in the first place, a Person of venerable grey haires, and exemplary piety, who indeed exceeds all praise we can bestow upon him. Who by an easie method, and admirable Key, hath unlocked the hidden things of geometry. Who by an accurate Trigonometry and furniture of Instruments, hath inriched, as well geometry, as Astronomy. Let D. John Wallis, and D. Seth Ward, succeed in the next place, both famous Persons, and Doctors in Divinity, the one of geometry, the other of astronomy, Savilian Professors in the University of Oxford."

The astronomer Edmund Halley, in his preface to the 1694 English edition of the *Clavis,* speaks of this book as one of "so established a reputation, that it were needless to say anything thereof," though "the concise Brevity of the author is such, as in many places to need Explication, to render it Intelligible to the less knowing in Mathematical matters."

In closing this part of our monograph, we quote the testimony of Robert Boyle, the experimental physicist, as given May 8, 1647, in a letter to Mr. Hartlib:[20]

"The Englishing of, and additions to Oughtred's *Clavis mathematica* does much content me, I having formerly spent much study on the original of that algebra, which I have long since esteemed a much more instructive way of logic, than that of Aristotle."

WAS DESCARTES INDEBTED TO OUGHTRED?

This question first arose in the seventeenth century, when John Wallis of Oxford, in his *Algebra* (the English edition of 1685, and more particularly the Latin edition of 1693) raised the issue of Descartes's indebtedness to the English scientists, Thomas Harriot and William Oughtred.

[20] *The Works of the Honourable Robert Boyle in five volumes to which is prefixed the Life of the Author,* Vol. I, London, 1744, p. 24.

In discussing matters of priority between Harriot and Descartes, relating to the theory of equations, Wallis is generally held to have shown marked partiality to Harriot. Less attention has been given by historians of mathematics to Descartes's indebtedness to Oughtred. Yet this question is of importance in tracing Oughtred's influence upon his time.

On January 8, 1688-89, Samuel Morland addressed a letter of inquiry to John Wallis, containing a passage which we translate from the Latin:[21]

"Some time ago I read in the elegant and truly precious book that you have written on *Algebra,* about Descartes, this philosopher so extolled above all for having arrived at a very perfect system by his own powers, without the aid of others, this Descartes, I say, who has received in geometry very great light from our Oughtred and our Harriot, and has followed their track though he carefully suppressed their names. I stated this in a conversation with a professor in Utrecht (where I reside at present). He requested me to indicate to him the page-numbers in the two authors which justified this accusation. I admitted that I could not do so. The *Géométrie* of Descartes is not sufficiently familiar to me, although with Oughtred I am fairly familiar. I pray you therefore that you will assume this burden. Give me at least those references to passages of the two authors from the comparison of which the plagiarism by Descartes is the most striking."

Following Morland's letter in the *De algebra tractatus,* is printed Wallis's reply, dated March 12, 1688 (" Stilo Angliae"), which is, in part, as follows:

"I nowhere give him the name of a plagiarist; I would not appear so impolite. However this I say, the major part of his algebra (if not all) is found before him in other authors (notably in our Harriot) whom he does not

[21] The letter is printed in John Wallis's *De Algebra Tractatus,* 1693, p. 206.

designate by name. That algebra may be applied to geometry, and that it is in fact so applied, is nothing new. Passing the ancients in silence, we state that this has been done by Vieta, Ghetaldi, Oughtred and others, before Descartes. They have resolved by algebra and specious arithmetic [literal arithmetic] many geometrical problems..... But the question is not as to application of algebra to geometry (a thing quite old), but of the Cartesian algebra considered by itself."

Wallis then indicates in the 1659 edition of Descartes's *Géométrie* where the subjects treated on the first six pages are found in the writings of earlier algebraists, particularly of Harriot and Oughtred. For example, what is found on the first page of Descartes, relating to addition, subtraction, multiplication, division and root extraction, is declared by Wallis to be drawn from Vieta, Ghetaldi and Oughtred.

It is true that Descartes makes no mention of modern writers, except once of Cardan. But it was not the purpose of Descartes to write a history of algebra. To be sure, references to such of his immediate predecessors as he had read would not have been out of place. Nevertheless Wallis fails to show that Descartes made illegitimate use of anything he may have seen in Harriot or Oughtred.

The first inquiry to be made is, did Descartes possess copies of the books of Harriot and Oughtred? It is only in recent time that this question has been answered as to Harriot. As to Oughtred it is still unanswered. It is now known that Descartes had seen Harriot's *Artis analyticae praxis* (1631). Descartes wrote a letter to Constantin Huygens in which he states that he is sending Harriot's book.[22]

An able discussion of the question, what effect, if any,

[22] See *La Correspondance de Descartes*, published by Charles Adam and Paul Tannery, Vol. II, Paris, 1898, pp. 456 and 457.

Oughtred's *Clavis mathematicae* of 1631 had upon Descartes's[23] *Géométrie* of 1637, is given by H. Bosmans in a recent article. According to Bosmans no evidence has been found that Descartes possessed a copy of Oughtred's book, or that he had examined it. Bosmans believes nevertheless that Descartes was influenced by the *Clavis,* either directly or indirectly. Says he:[24]

"If Descartes did not read it carefully, which is not proved, he was none the less well informed with regard to it. No one denies his intimate knowledge of the intellectual movement of his time. The *Clavis mathematica* enjoyed a rapid success. It is impossible that, at least indirectly, he did not know the more original ideas which it contained. Far from belittling Descartes, as I much desire to repeat, this rather makes him the greater."

We ourselves would hardly go as far as does Bosmans. Unless Descartes actually examined a copy of Oughtred it is not likely that he was influenced by Oughtred in appreciable degree. Book reviews were quite unknown in those days. No evidence has yet been adduced to show that Descartes obtained a knowledge of Oughtred by correspondence. A most striking feature about Oughtred's *Clavis* is its notation. No trace of the Englishman's symbolism has been pointed out in Descartes's *Géométrie* of 1637. Only six years intervened between the publication of the *Clavis* and the *Géométrie.* It took longer than this period for the *Clavis* to show evidence of its influence upon mathematical books published in *England*; it is not probable that *abroad* the contact was more immediate than at home. Our study of seventeenth century algebra has led us to the conviction that Oughtred deserves a higher place in the development of this science than is usually accorded·

[23] H. Bosmans, S. J., "La première édition de la *Clavis Mathematica* d'Oughtred. Son influence sur la Géométrie de Descartes," in *Annales de la société scientifique de Bruxelles,* 35th Year, 1910-1911, Part II, pp. 24-78.

[24] H. Bosmans, *loc. cit.,* p. 78.

to him; but that it took several decennia for his influence fully to develop.

THE SPREAD OF OUGHTRED'S NOTATIONS.

An idea of Oughtred's influence upon mathematical thought and teaching can be obtained from the spread of his symbolism. This study indicates that the adoption was not immediate. The earliest use that we have been able to find of Oughtred's notation for proportion, A.B:: C.D, occurs nineteen years after the *Clavis mathematica* of 1631. In 1650 John Kersey brought out in London an edition of Edmund Wingate's *Arithmetique made easie*, in which this notation is used. After this date publications employing it become frequent, some of them being the productions of pupils of Oughtred. We have seen it in Vincent Wing (1651),[25] Seth Ward (1653),[26] John Wallis (1655),[27] in "R. B.," a schoolmaster in Suffolk,[28] Samuel Foster (1659),[29] Jonas Moore (1660),[30] and Isaac Barrow (1657).[31] In the latter part of the seventeenth century Oughtred's notation, A.B:: C.D, became the prevalent, though not universal, notation in Great Britain. A tremendous impetus to their adoption was given by Seth Ward, Isaac Barrow, and particularly by John Wallis who was rising to international eminence as a mathematician.

In France we have noticed Oughtred's notation for proportion in Franciscus Dulaurens (1667),[32] J. Prestet

[25] Vincent Wing, *Harmonicon coeleste*, London, 1651, p. 5.

[26] Seth Ward, *In Ismaelis Bullialdi astronomiae philolaicae fundamenta inquisitio brevis*, Oxford, 1653, p. 7.

[27] John Wallis, *Elenchus geometriae Hobbianae*, Oxford, 1655, p. 48.

[28] *An Idea of Arithmetick, at first designed for the use of the Free Schoole at Thurlow in Suffolk....By R. B., Schoolmaster there*, London, 1655, p. 6.

[29] *The Miscellanies: or Mathematical Lucubrations, of Mr. Samuel Foster* ....by John Twysden, London, 1659, p. 1.

[30] *Moor's Arithmetick in two Books*, London, 1660, p. 89.

[31] Isaac Barrow, *Euclidis data*, Cambridge, 1657, p. 2.

[32] *Francisci Dulaurens Specima mathematica*, Paris, 1667, p. 1.

(1675),[33] R. P. Bernard Lamy (1684),[34] Ozanam (1691),[35] R. P. Petro Nicolas (1697).[36].

In the Netherlands we have noticed it in R. P. Bernard Lamy (1680),[37] and in an anonymous work of 1690.[38] In German and Italian works of the seventeenth century we have not seen Oughtred's notation for proportion.

In England a modified notation soon sprang up in which ratio was indicated by two dots instead of a single dot, thus A: B:: C: D. The reason for the change lies probably in the inclination to use the single dot to designate decimal fractions. W. W. Beman pointed out that this modified symbolism (:) for ratio is found as early as 1657 in the end of the trigonometric and logarithmic tables that were bound with Oughtred's *Trigonometria.*[39] It is not probable however that this notation was used by Oughtred himself. The *Trigonometria* proper has Oughtred's A.B :: C.D throughout. Moreover in the English edition of this trigonometry which appeared the same year, 1657, but subsequent to the Latin edition, the passages which contained the colon as the symbol for ratio, when not omitted, are recast, and the regular Oughtredian notation is introduced. In Oughtred's posthumous work, *Opuscula mathematica hactenus inedita,* 1677, the colon appears quite often but is most likely due to the editor of the book.

We have noticed that the notation A: B:: C: D antedates the year 1657. Vincent Wing, the astronomer, published in 1651 in London the *Harmonicon coeleste* in which is found not only Oughtred's notation A.B:: C.D but also

[33] *Elémens des mathématiques,* Paris, 1675, Preface signed "J. P."

[34] *Nouveaux élémens de géométrie,* Paris, 1692 (permission to print 1684).

[35] Ozanam, *Dictionnaire mathématique,* Paris, 1691, p. 12.

[36] Petro Nicolas, *De conchoidibus et cissoidibus exercitationes geometricae,* Toulouse, 1697, p. 17.

[37] R. P. Bernard Lamy, *Elémens des mathématiques,* Amsterdam, 1692 (permission to print 1680).

[38] *Nouveaux élémens de géométrie,* 2d. ed., The Hague, 1690, p. 304.

[39] W. W. Beman in *L'intermédiaire des mathématiciens,* Paris, Vol. IX, 1902, p. 229, question 2424.

the above modified form of it. The two are used interchangeably. His later works, the *Logistica astronomica* (1656), *Doctrina spherica* (1655) and *Doctrina theorica,* published in one volume in London, all use the symbols A: B:: C: D exclusively. The author of a book entitled, *An Idea of Arithmetick at first designed for the use of the Free Schoole at Thurlow in Suffolk...by R. B., Schoolmaster there,* London, 1655, writes A: *a*:: C: *c,* though part of the time he uses Oughtred's unmodified notation.

We can best indicate the trend in England by indicating the authors of the seventeenth century whom we have found using the notation A: B:: C: D and the authors of the eighteenth century whom we have found using A.B:: C.D. The former notation was the less common during the seventeenth but the more common during the eighteenth century. We have observed the symbols A: B :: C: D, (besides the authors already named) in John Collins (1659),[40] James Gregory (1663),[41] Christopher Wren (1668-69),[42] William Leybourn (1673),[43] William Sanders (1686),[44] John Hawkins (1684),[45] Joseph Raphson (1697),[46] E. Wells (1698)[47] and John Ward (1698).[48]

Of English eighteenth century authors the following still clung to the notation A.B:: C.D: John Harris's translation of F. Ignatius Gaston Pardies (1701),[49] George

[40] John Collins, *The Mariner's Plain Scale New Plain'd,* London, 1659, p. 25.

[41] James Gregory, *Optica promota,* London, 1663, pp. 19, 48.

[42] *Philosophical Transactions,* Vol. III, London, p. 868.

[43] William Leybourn, *The Line of Proportion,* London, 1673, p. 14.

[44] *Elementa geometriae....a Gulielmo Sanders,* Glasgow, 1686, p. 3.

[45] *Cocker's Decimal Arithmetick,*....perused by John Hawkins, London, 1695 (preface dated 1684), p. 41.

[46] Joseph Raphson, *Analysis Aequationum universalis,* London, 1697, p. 26.

[47] E. Wells, *Elementa arithmeticae numerosae et speciosae,* Oxford, 1698, p. 107.

[48] John Ward, *A Compendium of Algebra,* 2d ed., London, 1698, p. 62.

[49] *Plain Elements of Geometry and Plain Trigonometry,* London, 1701, p. 63.

Shelley (1704),[50] Sam Cobb (1709),[51] John Craig (1718),[52] Jo. Wilson (1724).[53] During the seventeenth century the notation A: B:: C: D acquired almost complete ascendancy in England.

In France Oughtred's unmodified notation A.B:: C.D, having been adopted later, was also discarded later than in England. An approximate idea of the situation appears from the following data. The notation A.B:: C.D was used by M. Carré (1700),[54] M. Guisnée (1705),[55] M. de Fontenelle (1727),[56] M. Varignon (1725),[57] M. Robillard (1753),[58] M. Sebastien le Clerc (1764),[59] Clairaut (1731),[60] M. L'Hopital (1781).[61]

In Italy Oughtred's modified notation $a:b::c:d$ found entrance the latter part of the eighteenth century. In Germany the symbolism $a: b = c: d$, suggested by Leibniz, found wider acceptance.[62]

It is evident from the data presented that Oughtred proposed his notation for ratio and proportion at a time

[50] George Shelley, *Wingate's Arithmetick*, London, 1704, p. 343.

[51] *A Synopsis of Algebra, Being a posthumous work of John Alexander of Bern, Swisserland....Done from the Latin* by Sam. Cobb, London, 1709, p. 16.

[52] John Craig, *De Calculo fluentium*, London, 1718, p. 35. The notation A: B:: C: D is given also.

[53] *Trigonometry*, 2d ed., Edinburgh, 1724, p. 11.

[54] *Méthode pour la mésure des surfaces, la dimension des solides..par M. Carré de l'académie r. des sciences*, 1700, p. 59.

[55] *Application de l'algèbre à la géométrie*...Paris, 1705.

[56] *Elémens de la géométrie de l'infini*, by M. de Fontenelle, Paris, 1727, p. 110.

[57] *Eclaircissemens sur l'analyse des infiniment petits*, by M. Varign, Paris, 1725, p. 87.

[58] *Application de la géométrie ordinaire et des calculs différentiel et intégral*, by M. Robillard, Paris, 1753.

[59] *Traité de géométrie théorique et pratique*, new ed., Paris, 1764, p. 15.

[60] *Recherches sur les courbes à double courbure*, Paris, 1731, p. 13.

[61] *Analyse des infiniment petits*, by the Marquis de L'Hopital. New ed. by M. Le Fèvre, Paris, 1781, p. 41. In this volume passages in fine print, probably supplied by the editor, contain the notation $a:b::c:d$; the parts in large type give Oughtred's original notation.

[62] The tendency during the eighteenth century is shown in part by the following data: *Jacobi Bernoulli Opera; Tomus primus*, Geneva, 1744, gives B.A :: D.C on page 368, the paper having been first published in 1688; on page 419 is given GE: AG = LA: ML, the paper having been first published in 1689. *Bernhardi Nieuwentiit analysis infinitorum*, Amsterdam, 1695, has on page 276,

when the need of a specific notation began to be generally felt, that his symbol for ratio $a.b$ was temporarily adopted in England and France but gave way in the eighteenth century to the symbol $a:b$, that Oughtred's symbol for proportion :: found almost universal adoption in England and France and was widely used in Italy, the Netherlands, the United States and to some extent in Germany; it has survived to the present time but is now being gradually displaced by the sign of equality $=$.

Oughtred's notation to express aggregation of terms has received little attention from historians but is nevertheless interesting. His books, as well as those of John Wallis, are full of parentheses but they are not used as symbols of aggregation in algebra; they are simply marks of punctuation for parenthetical clauses. We have seen that Oughtred writes $(a+b)^2$ and $\sqrt{a+b}$ thus, Q: $a + b$:, $\surd$: $a + b$:, or Q: $a + b$, $\surd$: $a + b$, using on rarer occasions a single dot in place of the colon. This notation did not originate with Oughtred but, in slightly modified form, occurs in writings from the Netherlands. In 1603 *C. Dibvadii in geometriam Evclidis demonstratio numeralis,* Leyden, contains many expressions of this sort,

$x:c-x::s:r$. Paul Halcken's *Deliciae mathematicae,* Hamburg, 1719, gives $a:b::c:d$. Johannis Baptistae Caraccioli, *Geometria algebraica universa,* Rome, 1759, p. 79 has $a.b::c.d$. *Delle corde ouverto fibre elastiche schediasmi fisico-matematici del conte Giordano Riccati,* Bologna, 1767, p. 65 gives $P:b::r:ds$. *"Produzioni mathematiche" del Conte Giulio Carlo di Fagnano,* Vol. I, Pesario, 1750, p. 193, has $a.b::c.d$. *Géométrie du compas,* by L. Mascheroni, translated by A. M. Carette, Paris, 1798, p. 188, gives $\surd 3:2::\surd 2:Lp$. Danielis Melandri and Paulli Frisi, *De theoria lunae commentarii,* Parma, 1769, p. 13, has $a:b::c:d$. *Institutiones analyticae,* Vicentio Riccato and Hieronymo Saladino, Vol. I, Bologna, 1765, p. 47, gives $x:a::m:n+m$. R. S. Boscovich, *Opera pertinentia ad opticam et astronomiam, Bassani,* 1785, p. 409, uses $a:b::c:d$. Jacob Bernoulli, *Ars Conjectandi,* Basel, 1713, has $n-r.n-1:c.d$. Pavlini Chelvicii, *Institutiones analyticae, editio post tertiam Romanum prima in Germania,* Vienna, 1761, p. 2, $a.b::c.d$. Christiani Wolfii, *Elementa matheseos universae,* Vol. III, Geneva, 1735, p. 63, has $AB:AE=1:q$. Johann Bernoulli, *Opera omnia,* Vol. I, Lausanne and Geneva, 1742, p. 43, has $a:b=c:d$. *Analyse des mesures des rapports et des angles,* by D. C. Walmesley, Paris, 1749, uses extensively $a.b::c.d$, later $a:b::c:d$. *Institutiones geometriae sublimoris,* by G. W. Krafft, Tübingen, 1753, p. 194, has $a:b=c:d$. J. H. Lambert, *Photometria,* 1760, p. 104, has $C:\pi=BC^2:MH^2$. *Meccanica sublime del Dott. Domenico Bartaloni,* Naples, 1765, has $a:b::c:d$. Occasionally ratio is not designated by $a.b$, nor by $a:b$, but by

$\sqrt{\cdot}\ 136 + \sqrt{2048}$, signifying $\sqrt{(136 + \sqrt{2048})}$. The dot is used to indicate that the root of the binomial (not of 136 alone) is called for. This notation is used extensively in *Ludolphi à Cevlen de circulo,* Leyden, 1619, and in *Willebrordi Snellii De circuli dimensione,* Leyden, 1621. In place of the single dot Oughtred used the colon (:), probably to avoid confusion with his notation for ratio. To avoid further possibility of uncertainty he usually placed the colon both before and after the algebraic expression under aggregation. This notation was adopted by John Wallis and Isaac Barrow. It is found in the writings of Descartes. Together with Vieta's horizontal bar, placed over two or more terms, it constituted the means used almost universally for denoting aggregation of terms in algebra. Before Oughtred the use of parentheses had been suggested by Clavius[63] and Girard.[64] The latter wrote for instance $\sqrt{(2 + \sqrt{3})}$. While parentheses never became popular in algebra before the time of Leibniz and the Bernoullis they were by no means lost sight of. We are able to point to the following authors who made use of them: I. Errard de Bar-le-Duc (1619),[65] Jacobo De Billy (1643),[66] one of whose books containing this notation was translated into English, and also the posthumous works of Samuel Foster.[67]

a, b, as for instance in A. de Moivre's *Doctrine of Chance,* London, 1756, p. 34, where he writes *a, b*: : 1, *q*. A further variation in the designation of ratio is found in James Atkinson's *Epitome of the Art of Navigation,* London, 1718, p. 24, namely, 3. .2: : 72. .48. Curious notations are given in Rich, Balam's *Algebra,* London, 1653.

[63] *Chr. Clavii Operum mathematicorum tomus secundus,* Mayence, 1611, algebra, p. 39.

[64] *Invention nouvelle en l'algèbre,* by Albert Girard, Amsterdam, 1629, p. 17.

[65] *La géométrie et pratique générale d'icelle, par I. Errard de Bar-le-Duc, Ingénieur ordinaire de sa Majesté.* 3d ed., revised by D. H. P. E. M., Paris, 1619, p. 216.

[66] *Novae geometriae clavis algebra, authore P. Jacobo de Billy,* Paris, 1643, p. 157; also an *Abridgement of the Precepts of Algebra. Written in French by James de Billy,* London, 1659, p. 346.

[67] *Miscellanies: or Mathematical Lucubrations, of Mr. Samuel Foster, sometime publike Professor of Astronomie in Gresham Colledge in London,* London, 1659, p. 7.

The symbol for the arithmetical difference between two numbers, ∽, is usually attributed to John Wallis but it occurs in Oughtred's *Clavis Mathematicae* of 1652, in the tract on *Elementi decimi Euclidis declaratio,* at an earlier date than in any of Wallis's books. As Wallis assisted in putting this edition through the press it is possible though not probable that the symbol was inserted by him. Were the symbol Wallis's, Oughtred would doubtless have referred to its origin in the preface. During the eighteenth century the symbol found its way into foreign texts even in far off Italy.[68] It is one of three symbols presumably invented by Oughtred and which are still used at the present time. The other two are × and : :

The curious and ill-chosen symbols, ⊏ for "greater than," and ⊐ for "less than," were certain to succumb in their struggle for existence against Harriot's admirably chosen > and <. Yet such was the reputation of Oughtred that his symbols were used in England quite extensively during the seventeenth and beginning of the eighteenth centuries. Considerable confusion has existed among algebraists and also among historians as to what Oughtred's symbols really were. Particularly is this true of the sign for "less than" which is frequently written ⊐· Oughtred's symbols, or these symbols turned about in some way, have been used by Seth Ward,[69] John Wallis,[70] Isaac Barrow,[71] John Kersey,[72] E. Wells,[73] John Hawkins,[74] Tho.

[68] Pietro Cossali, *Origine, trasporto in Italia primi progressi in essa dell' algebra, Vol. I, Parmense,* 1797, p. 52.

[69] *In. Is. Bullialdi astronomiae philolaicae fundamenta inquisitio brevis, Auctore Setho Wardo,* Oxford, 1653, p. 1.

[70] John Wallis, *Algebra,* London, 1685, p. 321, and in some of his other works. He makes greater use of Harriot's symbols.

[71] *Euclidis data,* 1657, p. 1; also *Euclidis elementorum libris XV,* London, 1659, p. 1.

[72] John Kersey, *Algebra,* London, 1673, p. 321.

[73] E. Wells, *Elementa arithmeticae numerosae et speciosae,* Oxford, 1698, p. 142.

[74] Cocker's *Decimal Arithmetick,* perused by John Hawkins, London, 1695 (preface dated 1684), p. 278.

Baker,[75] Richard Sault,[76] Richard Rawlinson,[77] Franciscus Dulaurens,[78] James Milnes,[79] George Cheyne,[80] John Craig[81] and Jo. Wilson.[82]

General acceptance has been accorded to Oughtred's symbol ×. The first printed appearance of this symbol for multiplication in 1618 in the form of the letter *x* hardly explains its real origin. The author of the "Appendix" (be he Oughtred or some one else) may not have used the letter *x* at all but may have written the cross ×, called the St. Andrews cross, while the printer, in the absence of any type accurately representing that cross, may have substituted the letter *x* in its place. The hypothesis that the symbol × of multiplication owes its origin to the old habit of using two directed bars to indicate that two numbers are to be combined, as for instance in the multiplication of 23 and 34, thus,

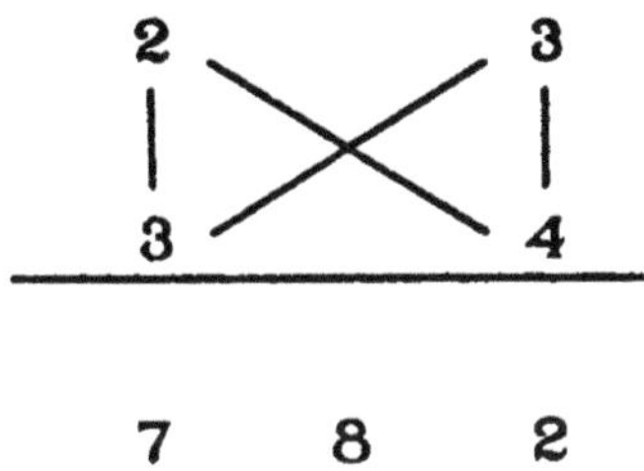

has been advanced by two writers, C. Le Paige[83] and Gravelaar.[84] Bosmans is more inclined to the belief that

[75] Th. Baker, *The geometrical Key,* London, 1684, p. 15.

[76] Richard Sault, *A New Treatise of Algebra,* London (no date).

[77] Richard Rawlinson in a pamphlet without date, issued sometime between 16555 and 1668, containing trigonometric formulas. There is a copy in the British Museum.

[78] F. Dulaurens, *Specma mathematca,* Pars, 1667, p. 1.

[79] J. Milnes, *Sectionum conicarum elementa,* Oxford, 1702, p. 42.

[80] Cheyne, *Philosophical Principles of Natural Religion,* London, 1705, p. 55.

[81] J. Craig, *De calculo fluentium,* London, 1718, p. 86.

[82] Jo. Wilson, *Trigonometry,* 2d ed., Edinburgh, 1724, p. v.

[83] C. Le Paige, "Sur l'origine de certains signes d'opération," in *Annales de la société scientifique de Bruxelles,* 16th year, 1891-1892, Part II, pp. 79-82.

[84] Gravelaar, "Over den oorsprong van ons maaltecken (×)," *Wiskundig Tijdschrift,* 6th year. We have not had access to this article.

Oughtred adopted the symbol somewhat arbitrarily, much as he did the numerous symbols in his *Elementi decimi Euclidis declaratio*.[85] In the absence of any further facts the mind is quite free to indulge in the sweets of unrestricted speculation as to the origin of this symbol.

FLORIAN CAJORI.

COLORADO COLLEGE.

[85] H. Bosmans, *loc. cit.*, p. 40.

MUTATION CONCEPTS IN RELATION TO ORGANIC STRUCTURE.

THE MUTATION CONCEPT.

SINCE 1900, the idea of discontinuity, perhaps better termed definiteness, in variation, has steadily grown in biological circles. The classical experiments of de Vries on the discontinuous origin of characters in the evening primroses, and of Bateson and the Mendelians on the discontinuous inheritance of characters, has brought much greater definiteness and precision into the thinking on this subject. As a result of the experimental method the different kinds of variation can now be classified, though as yet imperfectly. The type of variation called by de Vries "mutation" has now been studied in many organisms —plants and animals—from bacteria to mammals; and the results of these studies make possible an analysis of the nature of mutation as a natural process.

Of all organisms, the Oenotheras among plants and the pumice fly, Drosophila, among animals, have been most intensively studied from this point of view. In recent years the cytological investigation of the Oenotheras[1] has thrown much light upon the nature of the mutation process, and has been particularly useful in limiting the speculations on

[1] See Gates, "A Study of Reduction in *Oenothera rubrinervis*," *Bot. Gaz.*, XLVI, 1-34, 1908. "Tetraploid Mutants and Chromosome Mechanisms, *Biol. Centralbl.*, XXXIII, 92-99, 113-150, 1913.

Gates and Thomas, "A Cytological Study of *Oenothera* mut. *Lata* and *Oe.* mut. *semilata* in Relation to Mutation," *Quart. Journ. Micro. Sci.*, LIX, 523-571, 1914, etc.

this subject. These cell studies combined with breeding experiments have not only shown that mutation is a phenomenon of variation and not merely of inheritance or hybridization, but they have also thrown considerable light upon the nature of the various changes involved in the origin of different mutants.

These questions have been considered in detail elsewhere,[2] but we may mention here a few of the conclusions regarding the nature of mutations, and a selection of the facts on which these conclusions rest. *Oenothera lata*, one of the mutants from *O. Lamarckiana*, has very characteristic foliage and habit, and is more or less completely male-sterile. This mutant was discovered by de Vries in 1887 and is now known to have constantly 15 instead of 14 chromosomes in its nuclei. This condition arises through one germ cell, when formed, receiving in addition to its normal number (7), a chromosome which does not belong to it. This extra chromosome therefore appears in the fertilized egg and is passed on by mitosis or cell division to every cell in the organism. The mutation is therefore a cell change propagated by mitosis, and the peculiarities of *lata* result from the fact that every nucleus contains an extra chromosome. We shall see that in the same way all the other mutations of *Oenothera* result from different kinds of cell change.

In contrast with *lata*, which arises through an irregular distribution of chromosomes in mitosis, we find in *gigas* a doubling of the whole series of chromosomes, to give an organism having 28 chromosomes in all its cells. The precise manner in which this condition, known as tetraploidy, arises is not yet clear, but a long list of cases of a similar relationship between related species is now known in many genera of plants. Thus we find it among the

[2] *The Mutation Factor in Evolution.* London: Macmillan, 1915. See especially Chapters IX and X.

violets, lady's tresses and cinquefoils, to mention only a few. the tetraploid condition is usually accompanied by gigantism not only of the cells but of the whole plant.

A third and very different type of mutation is found in *O. rubricalyx*, which originated from my cultures of *rubrinervis* in 1907. This mutant differs from its parent only in pigmentation. It is a marked color variety, having deep red buds, with red pigment developed also to a much greater extent in every part of the plant.[3] The offspring of this mutant gave *rubricalyx* and *rubrinervis* in the Mendelian ratio 3: 1. The chromosome-number in *rubricalyx* is unchanged—14, as in *rubrinervis* from which it originated. The origin and hereditary behavior of this mutant may therefore both be explained if we assume that one chromosome of *rubrinervis* has undergone a permanent chemical change so that its presence in the cell leads to greatly increased pigment-production. There is every evidence that this mutation is also a cell change, propagated throughout the developing organism by mitosis, for cells in all parts of *rubricalyx* show an increased content in the anthocyanin pigment.

With these few facts in mind we may now examine briefly some of the points of view which arise.

1. In order to be inherited completely the variation must arise in the nucleus of some cell or cells in the germ track of the organism. Wherever in the life cycle the change originally occurs (and this is usually during the process of chromosome reduction), it will come in the next generation to date from the fertilized egg. As the fertilized egg divides, the variation will be passed on as a *cell-feature* to all parts of the organism.

2. These nuclear changes are, as already observed, of various kinds, some of them essentially morphological,

[3] See Gates, "Studies on the Variability and Heritability of Pigmentation in Oenothera," *Zeitschr. f. Abst. u. Vererbungslehre*, IV, 337-372, 1911.

others essentially chemical. This conclusion is of much importance for evolution, for if correct it means that abundant material is supplied for evolution to have taken place in many directions at once. In this way the divergent and multifarious character of evolution is emphasized.

The Mendelian experimentation with hybrids has crystallized into the presence-absence hypothesis, according to which it is supposed that a recessive character is negative, due to the loss of something from the germ plasm, and a dominant character positive, due to the addition of something. Bateson[4] and others, basing their views of evolution on this hypothesis, have finally narrowed down the evolutionary process to the loss of "factors" or "inhibitors" for factors. This assumes that a single type of germinal change, such as occurs in the origin of *O. rubricalyx,* is the only type of discontinuous variation known. But we have already seen that mutation is a composite process, and that the various kinds of departures from the parent form cannot all be explained on the basis of one idea.

A still more fundamental alteration of the presence-absence hypothesis will be required if the view here expressed be correct. For this view implies that the origin of any pair of Mendelian characters is due, not to the loss or "dropping out" of something from the germ plasm of the organism, giving the negative (recessive) character, but to the sudden modification of the positive (dominant) character to produce the negative, or (in some instances) of the negative character to produce the positive. Thus in the case above mentioned, *O. rubricalyx* has originated from *rubrinervis,* not through the loss of an "inhibitor" from the latter but through a chemical alteration in the germ plasm, or rather in a particular part of it, namely, one chromosome. In the same way we may consider the differ-

[4] Bateson, *Problems of Genetics.* London: Humphrey Milford, 258 pages, 1913.

ence between a round pea and a wrinkled pea to have arisen through an alteration in the chemical nature of one chromosome of the round-pea race, of such nature that, when replacing the unchanged chromosome in the cell, it leads to the production of a race in which the sugar fails to be transformed to starch and the peas are therefore wrinkled. According to this view each new Mendelian character is to be looked upon as the result, not of the loss of something from the cell, but of a *modification* of one part or organ of the cell, or rather of the nucleus.

The conception that each recessive character has resulted from the loss of something from the germ plasm, was very reasonably founded on such cases as that of two white races of sweet pea which when crossed produce in F_1 the purple Sicilian sweet pea, the ancestor of both. It was very reasonable to suppose in such a case that each white race had arisen through the loss of a different "factor" for the production of color, since putting the two together by crossing immediately gave the color. And indeed, so long as no further evidence is available this method of viewing the matter is entirely legitimate and satisfactory.

But if we view each negative character as due to the *modification* rather than the loss of something, at the same time a similar result follows which is more in accord with a sound evolutionary view. Thus in the case of *Oenothera lata* we know that a change which is certainly not a loss, has occurred, yet in the cross *lata* × *nanella,* for example, *Lamarckiana* (the parent of both), as well as *lata* and *nanella*, are produced in F_1. In this instance, since *O. nanella* is a dwarf, it is easiest to think of it as having originated through the loss, or at least the permanent inactivity, of something in the germ plasm. Yet there is probably an equally fundamental sense in which even *nanella* represents a germinal modification rather than a loss, while in *lata* the loss-conception is excluded. Hence, while the symbols of the presence-absence hypothesis are most useful in dealing with the inheritance of Mendelian characters, yet in order to be strictly accurate we need to modify this terminology when considering the *origin* of these character-differences.

3. We thus arrive at the position that not only is mutation a composite process involving various types of germinal change, but that Mendelian characters also originate in each case through the modification of a particular part of the germ cell. In the phylogeny of organisms we may therefore expect innumerable divergencies, with a number of lines sometimes radiating from the same point. The fact that parallel mutations, i. e., corresponding germinal changes in unrelated lines of phylogeny, frequently take place, increases this radiating tendency.

Aristotle, as is well known, arranged or attempted to arrange all organisms in a single linear series, and it is only in modern times, beginning with Lamarck, that the divergent and radiating nature of phylogenies have been recognized more and more. Herbert Spencer briefly traced the history of thought on this subject in his *Principles of Biology*. Since Spencer's time, as knowledge of the relationships of organisms has grown, this tendency has become still more pronounced, until now biologists recognize that probably never can three living species be arranged in linear series of descent, and paleontologists continually find that forms at first considered in the "direct line of descent" are rather on a longer or shorter "side line" of their own. All this is of course to be expected when we consider that particular elements of the germ plasm vary, each time, and not the germ plasm as a whole. The radiating tendencies must greatly outweigh any tendency to progress in a straight line. Mere divergence is of course to be expected on almost any hypothesis which assumes descent with modification, as was abundantly shown by Darwin in the theory of natural selection. But the mutation conception as I have stated it, in which particular elements of the germ plasm vary independently each time, makes it possible much more easily to account for the prolific radiating tendencies which, according to the consensus of opinion of naturalists, organisms display.

THE EVOLUTIONISM OF BERGSON.

It seems worth while to compare the views of variation and phylogeny resulting from these experimental studies of mutations, with certain views on these matters expressed by Bergson.[5] I am not competent to discuss the fundamentals of Bergson's philosophy, and indeed that is unnecessary, for they have been criticised with admirable lucidity and, as it appears to me, with justice, by Bertrand Russell in this journal.[6] The critic points out, for example, that Bergson's views of number are confused and inconsistent and that number does not necessarily imply space; while Bergson's theory of duration and time rests upon a confusion between "the present occurrence of a recollection and the past occurrence which is recollected," i. e., between the act of knowing and the object known.

Zeno's argument of the arrow Bergson meets by denying that the arrow is ever at any point of its course. He criticizes the mathematical view of change by the statement that it "implies the absurd proposition that movement is made of immobilities." But Russell points out that this absurdity vanishes when it is realized that motion really implies change of relations. Finally the critic considers that when the identification of subject and object which results from Bergson's theory of duration is rejected, his whole system collapses, including the theories of time and

[5] *Creative Evolution.* New York, 1911.
[6] "The Philosophy of Bergson," *Monist,* XXII, 321-347, 1912.

space, his belief in real contingency, and his views that the universe contains only actions and changes but not things.

There are nevertheless certain elements in Bergson's views of evolution in their biological aspects, which appear worthy of consideration. Thus he has clearly recognized and emphasized the nature of the phylogenetic divergence to which I have referred. Life, in his view, is a tendency whose essence is to split up in the course of its development, giving simultaneous divergent or sometimes parallel lines of progress in the form of a sheaf. Such a separation of tendencies led to the plant world which specialized in fixity, insensibility and the accumulation and storage of energy from the sun by means of the chlorophyllian function; and to the animal world with mobility, consciousness, nerve centers and the explosive expenditure of energy in locomotion. All this may be regarded as sufficiently orthodox biology. The questions arise concerning the nature and causes of the diverging tendencies.

Bergson is also doubtless correct in pointing out (p. 135) as a cardinal error of philosophers from Aristotle onward, the idea that vegetative, instinctive and rational life are three successive degrees of development of one tendency. They are rather "three divergent directions of an activity that has split up as it grew," so that the difference is not one of degree but of kind.

Bergson believes that not only have organisms traveled over many diverging roads as an expression of the original *élan vital,* but they have constructed or created the road itself as they traveled; or rather, their own evolution constitutes the road, so that of necessity the road leads to no fixed or predetermined goal such as is implied in a teleological view. We may agree that at the present time science can offer no adequate reason for supposing that the particular directions many phylogenies have taken have been directly determined or narrowly limited by the conditions on the earth's surface. The distinguishing features of, e. g., mosses, ferns, mammals, echinoderms and mollusks cannot be equated in terms of their different environments; indeed, each of the higher phyla of animals, such as reptiles and mammals, has tended to spread out and occupy all the main types of environment, aerial, terrestrial and aquatic. Nor can we formulate any adequate reason why the characteristic phyla of animals and plants should not, in another evolution under precisely the same earth-conditions, have worked out into quite different end-results. If this is the case, are we justified as biologists in taking the mechanistic attitude that all is given in the original protoplasm, and that the result of evolution has been in this sense a predetermined one? Bergson answers No, that the result has not been narrowly predetermined either in a mechanistic or a teleological sense; and I can see certain reasons for agreeing with him on this point, without at the same time becoming a vitalist. For it is not necessary to take the next step with Bergson, and assume that life is a force or impulse directed against matter and endeavoring to overcome its inertia. The biologist is perhaps more acustomed to think of life as a condition which appears when certain physical and chemical conditions of aggregation have been reached and disappears when the equilibrium of this system is sufficiently disturbed, — a mechanistic point of view.

And now to return to the reasons for agreeing with Bergson that evolution is to some extent, at any rate, indeterminate, so that the history of life on the earth under the conditions which have actually existed might have been different, as regards the characteristics of the various plant and animal phyla, from that which we have witnessed. This, I think, follows from the conclusion reached on a previous page—that particular elements of the germ plasm vary independently. For, this being the case, the *order* of the occurrence of these variations will be more or less a matter of chance, depending in part on environmental vicissitudes; and each variation, like a move on a chess board, will help to determine by limitation the succeeding variations. If millions of different games can be played with thirty-two chess pieces, no limitation need be placed on the number of organic worlds which might have evolved from the first protoplasm. Nevertheless, if evolution has any meaning we see progress in complexity, and simultaneous development in many phyla as though a number of games were being played through simultaneously to the end without altering the rules of any game during its progress. The irritability of protoplasm and the increase in the organism's control over its environment are, however, rather slender threads on which to hang a completely mechanistic explanation of progressive evolution.

Many biologists will probably agree with Bergson when he says (p. 102), "The truth is that adaptation explains the sinuosities of the movement of evolution, but not its general directions, still less the movement itself." Nor should I dissent from the further statement (p. 101), "Evolution will thus prove to be something entirely different from a series of adaptations to circumstances, as mechanism claims; entirely different also from the realization of a plan of the whole, as maintained by the doctrine of finality. . . . It is one thing to recognize that outer circumstances are forces evolution must reckon with, another to claim that they are the directing causes of evolution." But although we may agree with these statements, we cannot admit the further one that evolution creates, as it goes on, "not only the forms of life, but the ideas that will enable the intellect to understand it." This leads to Bergson's peculiar and complicated philosophic views of the relations between the mind and things—that intellect and matter have progressively adapted themselves to one another in the course of evolution (p. 204), a conception into which we need not enter.

Before leaving this aspect of the subject we may refer to Bergson's attitude toward the evolutionism of Spencer, which he criticizes as an attempt to reconstruct evolution from fragments of the evolved. His comparison of the Spencerian philosophy of evolution to the thought of a child which may put together the parts of a puzzle picture and in doing so imagine it is creating the design, is a telling argument for Bergson, who points out that the putting together of the fragments has nothing to do with the act of the original artist in producing the design.

We may, therefore, agree with Bergson that one of the great problems of evolution, so great that biologists have scarcely yet acquired the means of beginning a successful attack upon it, concerns the nature and causes of the general currents of animal and plant phylogeny. But his suggestion of an original impulse or *élan vital* impinging upon matter and spreading out into sheafs of organic movement, while a conception most stimulating to thought, is not of a sufficiently explanatory nature to be satisfying to the scientific mind.

VARIATION CONCEPTS IN RELATION TO ONTOGENY.

In his consideration of evolution Bergson naturally adopts attitudes, sometimes implied rather than definitely expressed, toward various questions of variation, heredity and ontogeny, which are worthy of discussion. Like many other writers he selects the eye as an example of a highly adapted organ, and asks how it can have arisen independently in mollusks and vertebrates through purely fortuitous circumstances. In stating the case, however, he is led to make certain assumptions which from our present point of view unnecessarily increase the admittedly great difficulties of any explanation. He says (p. 64): "If the variations are accidental, how can they ever agree to arise in every part of the organ at the same time, in such way that the organ will continue to perform its function? Darwin quite understood this; it is one of the reasons why he regarded variation as insensible."

But I think we may say that we now know that inherited variations do *not* usually arise independently and simultaneously in different parts of the organism. According to the views of inherited variation already expressed in this paper, the inherited difference is due to a change in the fertilized egg. That change is a *single* thing, although in ontogeny it may work out in variations which express themselves in different parts of the organism and so appear to be independent of each other. Moreover, each inherited change is really a cell change, transmitted as such in plants through all the cells of the organism, and in animals, at least through the cell generations of the germ track. This is therefore the basis of the well-known cases of correlated changes which Bergson aptly characterizes (p. 66) as solidary, for instance the imperfection of the teeth in hairless dogs.

He finds greater difficulties with *complementary* changes, for example in different parts of the eye to improve its function. But these correlations are much less mysterious since the discovery of hormones, which may be produced by one organ and help to regulate the activity of wholly different and structurally remote and independent organs. Still more illuminating in this connection is the manner in which during development one organ is known to influence and even to cause the development of another. Thus it has been shown by Warren Harmon Lewis[7] that when a portion of skin from any part of the tadpole of a frog is grafted over the region where the

[7] Lewis, W. H., "Experimental Studies on the Development of the Eye in Amphibia," *Journ. Exptl. Zoology*, 1905, II, 431-446, pls. 2. Also *Amer. Journ. Anat.*, Vols. III, VI, and VII.

optic vesicle from the brain is developing, the skin of this region will invaginate and form a lens. From these experiments it may be concluded that in normal development the formation of the lens from ectoderm is the result of a stimulus emanating from the optic vesicle. With such facts in mind it is not difficult to understand that many changes apparently complementary and independent are really so interrelated as to be the result of a single change in the germ. The number of ways in which such interrelations can occur, increases the probability of explaining each case of correlated variations as the result of a single original change. This difficulty of Bergson's therefore disappears.

Pursuing the subject further, Bergson asks (p. 65): "How could the same small variations, incalculable in number, have ever occurred in the same order on two independent lines of evolution, if they were purely accidental? And how could they have been preserved by selection and accumulated in both cases, the same in the same order, when each of them, taken separately, was of no use?" The first question we will come to later. With regard to the second the case is overstated, because owing to the correlations of variations mentioned in the last paragraph, a *relatively* short series of evolutionary stages requires to be postulated to account for the evolution of the eye, though it may be admitted that a mere shortening of the series does not remove any of the difficulties. The second question harbors a misapprehension in supposing that the various stages in the perfecting of an organ are in themselves of no service to the organism.

Darwin was at some pains to show that the contrary is really the case. He held that each stage in the evolution of a particular structure was of use to its possessor, although the function of the structure might change completely in the process of development. Thus in the *Origin of Species* (6th ed., I, 285-290), in answering an objection of Mivart, he suggests a comparison of the condition of the baleen in various whales with that of the palate in members of the duck family. He shows that in the ducks there is a series of stages in the development of the horny plates of the palate, yet each stage is serviceable to the species possessing it, though different species use the structure for different purposes. In conclusion Darwin remarks (p. 289): "Nor is there the least reason to doubt that each step in this scale might have been as serviceable to certain Cetaceans, with the functions of the parts slowly changing during the progress of development, as are the gradations in the beaks of the different existing members of the duck family." The important fact that apparently new organs are often a remoulding and readaptation of organs characteristic of members of a previous phylum or family, is frequently neglected. In such cases, as Darwin points out, the difficulty about the selection of undeveloped rudiments of an organ does not exist because the organ is functioning in every stage although the function changes gradually during the evolution. But the readaptation of organs can never account for their original appearance. This must have taken place in their simplest form, and it has generally been recognized that the fact of mutations or definite variations will help to bridge this difficulty.

Bergson turns next to the hypothesis of sudden variations, to see whether it will solve his problem. He says (p. 65): "It certainly lessens the difficulty on one point, but it makes it much worse on another. If the eye of the mollusk and that of the vertebrate have both been raised to their present form by a relatively small number of sudden leaps, I have less difficulty in understanding the resemblance of the two organs than if the resemblance were due to an incalculable number of infinitesimal resemblances acquired successively; in both cases it is chance that operates, but in the second case chance is not required to work the miracle it would have to perform in the first....But here there arises another problem, no less formidable, viz., how do all the parts of the visual apparatus, suddenly changed, remain so well coordinated that the eye continues to exercise its function? For the change of one part alone will make vision impossible....The parts must then all change at once, each consulting the others."

But we have already pointed out that the changes *must* be correlated and such as to make development and survival possible, for in order to be inherited they must have arisen in the egg, whence their influence radiates in ontogeny. Germinal changes leading to a less perfectly functional condition of the eye would immediately be eliminated by natural selection. Heredity maintains the species, while it "waits" for another germinal variation which will give the individual an advantage and so lead to the perpetuation of the change and its adoption by the species. The parts concerned do then "all change at once." This is not, however, because each consults the others but because all together are expressions of a germinal change which occurred in the egg. Nor is such a view teleological, because some changes will be advantageous, some innocuous, some bizarre, some harmful; but all unforeseeable even if we knew the nature of the change in the egg, for we at present know practically nothing of the relation between chemical composition and external form in organisms.

Bergson says truly (p. 67) that function is less narrowly bound to form in plants than in animals, a change in leaf-form for example producing no appreciable effect on the function of the leaf. In animals not only is there usually a closer relation between form and function, but there is also, as we have already observed, a greater interaction of organs upon one another through the blood circulation, particularly by means of internal secretions and hormones.

Having briefly considered the subject of accidental variations, and found that Bergson's objections to chance variations as material for evolution are not always well founded, let us return to the subject of parallel evolution, as in the case of the vertebrate and the molluscan eye.

Patten[8] has studied the eyes of Pecten and of other mollusks and arthropods with much care, and we may therefore first examine his results. Some members of nearly all the higher invertebrate groups have relatively highly developed eyes. Thus they are found in many annelid worms and mollusks, and in nearly all Arthropoda. These eyes show a great variety of structure, but may be mainly classed as of three types: (1) the vertebrate type, having a lens; (2) much more commonly, the so-called "compound eye," composed of ommatidia and characteristic of the Arthropoda; and (3) much simpler structures composed essentially of depressed pigment spots. Very often, more than one type of eye occurs in the same individual, and there is no doubt that, as Patten says, "Many complex eyes have originated independently in very limited groups of animals." The same thing is true of various other structures, such as the seed in plants, the seed-habit having developed independently in different plant phyla. We agree with Bergson that the production of such organs represents the expression of a tendency; indeed, this is a frequent scientific form of statement of the facts as observed in phylogenies. The problem which Bergson fully apprehends and seeks to solve is, then, why do we find parallel expressions of the same tendency in independent phyla?

The tendency to form eyes does not appear in all phyla. Thus, so far as I am aware, definite eye structures do not

[8] Patten, Wm., "Eyes of Molluscs and Arthropods," *Mittheilungen zu d. Zool. Station zu Neapel*, VI, 542-756, pls. 28-32, 1886.

occur in any of the Echinodermata. One may think of this fact as indirectly connected with their mode of life, which does not call for highly developed vision. Useless characters which may have appeared through a single fortuitous mutation are to be found in all groups, particularly among plants. But an elaborate mechanism like the eye will only be developed when of sufficient advantage to the organism to have been built up by selection continuing in one direction for many generations. If vision is of no particular advantage to a starfish in its conditions of existence, then there is no "incentive" for the selection of any variations which may occur leading to the formation of organs having increased light-sensibility. Of course the absence of eyes in echinoderms may be due to some other cause, such as the very rudimentary condition of the nervous system, but this is at any rate a possible reason.

One of the remarkable features of the eyes in many mollusks in their great number. Thus, according to Patten, Arca has 250 compound eyes, 800 or 900 invaginated eyes or pigmented pits like those of Patella, and about 200 minute and simple ocelli, making a total of about 1300 eyes. And in addition to these there are numerous small groups of ommatidia. Again, in Pecten there are from 60 to 100 eyes of the highly developed type, while Onchidium and Chiton each have several thousand. In Pecten the eyes on the left mantle are usually arranged in pairs and are larger than those of the right mantle, the latter being spaced at regular intervals on long stalks. This is connected with the fact that the animal rests on its right valve and will turn over if placed on its left. In the young Pecten the ophthalmic fold of the mantle is covered with small pigmented pits like the invaginated eyes of Arca. There are also pigmented papillae containing a few ommatidia, but these later degenerate and disappear. Patten interprets this to mean that the ancestors of Pecten possessed many invaginated eyes and isolated ommatidia, a condition nearly comparable with that of the present Arca.

The structure of the larger eyes of Pecten is remarkably similar to that of the vertebrate eye. Without going into detail it may be mentioned that there is not only a lens but a cornea and pupil surrounded by a pigmented iris. Focal adjustment of the lens is accomplished (1) by change in shape of the lens, (2) by bodily movement of the lens by means of contractile fibres. It can be shown that a perfect inverted image of any object is thrown by the lens on the rods of the retina, the retina being inverted or reversed in structure as in the vertebrate eye. In certain species of Pecten a number of the eyes have their pupils covered with pigment so they must be functionless, yet they are perfect in structure.

In development, however, as Bergson points out (p. 75), the eye of Pecten differs from the vertebrate eye, in that the whole structure, including both the retina and the lens, is differentiated from an outgrowth from the mantle. Hence the lens does not arise from a separate invagination, and the retina is derived directly from the ectoderm.

Notwithstanding the remarkable efficiency of these molluscan eyes as a mechanism for forming images on the retina, yet the nervous system is in a rudimentary condition and the stimuli are carried to ganglia which cannot properly be considered a brain. In the vertebrates we may (if we choose) think of the image on the retina being transmitted along the optic nerve in the form of differences in nervous stimuli, much as a telephone wire conducts its current. From these stimuli-differences the brain reconstructs the "image" in consciousness. But these eyes in Pecten are evidently developed as image-formers, far beyond the possibility of their use by its simple ganglia. So conspicuous is this over-development that Patten tries to avoid the difficulty by supposing that the primary function of the eyes in mollusks is to act as heliophags or absorbers of light-energy, while vision is a secondary function of the more highly developed eyes. But I know of no evidence for this view, and it does not seem to have been taken up later. Since the eyes are used in detecting shadows, to which the animal quickly responds, it is probable that this is sufficient to account for their high state of development. Bergson would probably say that the *élan vital* has impelled the organism to form eyes while leaving the nervous system rudimentary, but this is scarcely a causal explanation. On the other hand, one may suppose that natural selection was concerned in the development of these remarkable eyes, for each improvement in the eyes would render the organism better aware of its surroundings (even with an unimproved nervous system) and so aid in its preservation. For some unknown reason, favorable variations leading to great development of the nervous system have not occurred in Mollusca, and hence could not be selected. In the vertebrates on the other hand it is doubtless significant that the optic vesicle originates as a lateral outgrowth from the brain, which later controls the development of the lens. Hence in this case the evolution of the eye and the brain must have gone on together; for according to the view expressed in this paper, each successive germinal variation must have occurred so as to modify the rudiment from which develops both eye and brain. This being the case, as progressive variations successively appeared they would always be coordinated in the two structures, while retrogressive variations, being inefficient, would be eliminated.

Bergson stakes his whole case against mechanism on such instances as this of parallel evolution. Thus he says (p. 54): "Pure mechanism, then, would be refutable, and finality in the strict sense in which we understand it would be demonstrable in a certain aspect, if it could be proved that life may manufacture the like apparatus by unlike means on divergent lines of evolution." But it is noteworthy that the philosopher and the scientist proceed from opposite ends of the story in approaching a subject of this kind. In discussing, for example, parallel adaptations, the scientist selects a simple case, and having offered an explanation proceeds to apply it to the more difficult ones. But M. Bergson always selects the most difficult and inscrutable instances in making it appear that science cannot solve the problem involved. The simpler cases he passes over entirely.

Thus we know that wings in one form or another have been evolved a number of times independently, as adaptations to aerial flight. The adaptation of a limb for aerial locomotion is a simple change compared with the development of the eye to react efficiently to the extremely delicate wave-motion of light. Yet one cannot but feel, as Darwin felt, that any explanation which applies to the simpler case must also be applicable to the more remote ones. We can understand the modification of fore-limbs into wings through the selection of definite variations which occurred in many directions but were of advantage for flight only when they occurred in one or a few directions. But in the more abstruse case of the eye it is possible to make the facts appear more recondite than they really are. For example, Bergson says (p. 71) regarding the eye: "Certainly the photograph [pigment spot in simple organisms] has been gradually turned into a photographic apparatus [eye]; but could light alone, a physical force, ever have provoked this change, and converted an impression left by it into a machine capable of using it?" In the first place, that the pigment spot is a direct response of the cell to light is an assumption which will require a good deal of proof. But if we consider the simpler case of the wing in flight, it seems absurd to ask, How could the air convert a limb into a structure capable of using the air in flight? We can realize that the air has not been acting on the limb to produce a wing, and neither need we assume that light acted on a pigment spot to produce an eye. The method has been much more round-about. Conclusions such as this of Bergson's lead us to feel that the solid ground of plodding science is preferable because safer than the more spectacular methods of philosophy.

It appears therefore that although we have not reached a complete understanding of the many cases of parallel evolution, yet the scientific method of attack is the only safe one to follow, for the philosopher's rapid strides constantly lead him into pitfalls.

THE RELATION OF INSTINCTS TO STRUCTURE.

The subject of the variation and development of instinct and intelligence contains several features of interest in this connection. Bergson considers that instinct and intelligence had a common origin, from which they evolved as diverging tendencies, — unlike solutions of the same problem,—culminating on the one hand in the ants and bees and on the other hand in man; the Arthropoda having specialized in instinct while the Vertebrata specialized in intelligence. These two psychic activities or methods of reaction to environment are therefore in a sense complementary and not consecutive stages in any evolutionary series, the most evolved intelligence still retaining something of instinct, and the most advanced instincts something of intelligence.

As in his treatment of parallel evolution, Bergson again singles out a few of the most striking and complex instincts when he comes to consider their origin. He particularly considers (p. 146) the beetle Sitaris which lays its eggs so that the larva will come in contact with the male bee, Anthophora, whence it passes to the female and thence to one of her eggs where it undergoes a metamorphosis, feeding on the contents of the egg and afterwards on the honey in which the egg floats. The other instinct particularly considered (p. 172) is that of certain Hymenoptera (Ammophila, Scolia, Sphex) which sting their victims in the proper nerve centers to cause paralysis without death, and then store them up as food for the larvae when they hatch. Thus Sphex uses the cricket for this purpose, and stings each victim successively in its three ventral nerve ganglia so as to produce paralysis of movement.

It is, then, Bergson's aim to show that these instincts could not have been evolved by any of the methods proposed by science. He says (p. 169): "These instincts surely could not have attained all at once their present degree of complexity; they have probably evolved; but in a hypothesis like that of the neo-Darwinians the evolution of instinct could have come to pass only by the progressive addition of new pieces which in some way by happy accidents came to fit into the old. Now it is evident that in most cases instinct could not have perfected itself by simple accretion; each new piece really requires, if it is not to be spoiled, a complete recasting of the whole." And then he asks triumphantly, "How could mere chance work a recasting of the whole?"

But this all implies a mistaken conception of the relation of variation to ontogeny. The real variation, as we have already emphasized, in order to be inherited must arise in the germ cells, or the fertilized egg; and hence any variation, before it comes into expression, must have had an ontogenetic development which is a part of the ontogeny of the whole organism. Modification of an instinct, as of any other feature, through a variation, therefore means that *every ontogenetic stage is modified* and that the whole is necessarily to some extent recast. This reasoning applies most clearly to structural variations, but the same reasoning must be true in its application to variations in instincts. If such variations have a structural basis at all (and how else can we think of them?) they must result from the unfolding of variations which occurred in the egg. Hence it is reversing the course of events to think of successive variations as "new pieces" which by "happy accidents" come to fit into the old. No such happy accident is required or indeed possible, for every variation-stage of each structure or instinct must be not only compatible with development but also with survival and inheritance, until a new variation (which is subject to the same limitations) again modifies not only the end-stage but the whole series of stages of ontogeny.

It should be pointed out that the same reasoning applies when species are modified through inheritance of acquired characters. For in this conception also the germ cells are modified and the modification expresses itself in the variation of the adult offspring; the only difference being that the neo-Lamarckian doctrine postulates the variation of the germ as resulting from the reflection of environmental effects from the soma back into the germ cells. In either case the modification of the germ cells expresses itself in a modified ontogeny and adult stage; but in one case the variation originated in the egg or sperm from unknown causes, while in the other it originates in the soma from stress of the environment, and secondarily affects the germ cells. The cases of what is known as parallel induction, in which the organism is environmentally modified in its ontogeny by new conditions, and at the same time its germ cells are so altered as to produce the modified type even under ordinary conditions,[9] are in harmony with these views.

Bergson goes on to say (p. 169): "I agree that an acci-

[9] Cf. W. E. Agar, "Transmission of Environmental Effects from Parent to Offspring in *Simocephalus vetulus*," *Phil. Trans. Roy. Soc.*, B, 1913, CCIII, 319-350, Fig. 5.

dental modification of the germ may be passed on hereditarily, and may somehow wait for fresh accidental modifications to come and complicate it. I agree also that natural selection may eliminate all those of the more complicated forms of instinct that are not fit to survive. Still, in order that the life of the instinct may evolve, complications fit to survive have to be produced. Now they will be produced only if, in certain cases, the addition of a new element brings about the correlative change of all the old elements. *No one will maintain that chance could perform such a miracle* (my italics); in one form or another we shall appeal to intelligence."

But we have already seen that an inherited variation *must* cause just such correlative changes. They cannot be avoided. This we regard as the teaching both of embryology and cytology in plants and animals. And if this happens with regard to structure we cannot see any reason why it should not happen in the evolution of instincts. Bergson here again raises difficulties which are really non-existent; but in this he has followed many biologists who have held a similar view. But if the view I have expressed be correct (and it appears to be the inevitable conclusion of the more recent cytological work in embryology and mutation), then the problem of adaptation is vastly simplified. It is no longer necessary to call in intelligence, as Bergson does, to account for the fact that "the addition of a new element" brings about the correlative modification of all the old elements. That is the natural and essential way in which all variations, whether in structure or instinct, become incorporated into the species.

The comparative study of instincts makes it clear that modifications in instinct and in structure go together, and it seems reasonable to suppose that such correlated variations result from a change in the structure of the egg. If this is the case, the need for an "effort" on the part of the species, as Bergson suggests, to modify its instinct, is dispensed with. This idea of Bergson's is Lamarckism at its weakest.

It is no doubt a matter of great difficulty, if not impossibility, to conceive how certain instincts can be inherited, and therefore transmitted through the structure of the egg; e. g., the instincts already mentioned of the Hymenoptera which carefully sting their prey in the necessary spots to cause paralysis without death. But is the transmission of such an instinct through the structure of the egg any more difficult to conceive than the inheritance of intellectual differences in man, which we know to take place? If the instinct, like the structure, of the adult insect is implicit in the egg, then it is not necessary to invoke the inheritance of acquired characters, as does Bergson, to account for the origin and inheritance of instincts. The fact that instincts are variable does not militate against this view, for so are structures. May we not thus conceive of instincts developed stage by stage without stating them in terms of intelligence, though they are inherited, just as intelligence is inherited? This does not, however, help us to understand how instinct and intelligence are implicit in the structure of the egg.

R. Ruggles Gates.

University of London.

THE RELIGIOUS VIEWS OF EURIPIDES AS SHOWN IN THE "BACCHANALS."

THE "Bacchanals," apparently written by Euripides in his extreme old age and in Macedonia in an atmosphere wholly unlike that of Athens which he had left, contains religious views seemingly out of harmony with those expressed in his earlier dramas. And so, quite apart from the transcendent literary power of this magnificent play, "alone among extant Greek tragedies in picturesque splendor," so un-Greek in its enthusiastic proclaiming of man's affinity with nature, it has an importance in the development of religious thought in Greece. Its chief interest from this point of view is the long debated question whether it represents a recantation of earlier views of religion on the part of the aged poet.

At first glance the "Bacchanals" seems merely to record a phase of religious history—the victory of the late introduced cult of Dionysus into Greece. The wild and orgiastic rites of the primitive worship of the wine-god, though from the first exerting a powerful influence on the imagination of the people, could not have been accepted finally by the rational Greeks without great opposition. These exciting and secret rites, celebrated under cover of darkness and especially attracting the emotional natures of women, could never have gained their way in peace. The myth portrayed by Euripides, the persecution of the god in Thebes and his bloody revenge, seems to be but an echo of this prehistoric conflict. This older worship, as Hartung remarks, "represents a return to the primitive condition of nature and a renunciation of civilization, that is, a renunciation of rational life regulated by morality and law and a return to the innocency of the wilderness. Hence the Maenads took fawns to their breasts and clad themselves in fawn-skins, to transform themselves, as it were, into roes; hence they crowned themselves with twigs of oak and fir, and ate raw flesh."[1]

It represents, therefore, a period long prior to the historic epoch when this crude worship had become metamorphosed and spiritualized by the great reform of Orphism, which spread over Greece and South Italy in the sixth century B. C. Thereafter it was no longer the religion of primitive men, who, like the barbarous Thracians, had worshiped animals as gods and had actually torn and devoured beasts of the mountains during their orgies when under the spell of the god. Euripides, in his brilliant tragedy, knows nothing of this spirit of reform, but pictures the wilder scenes of the earlier worship.

A closer examination of the play shows there must have been a deeper motive than merely painting, though in such glorious colors, the story of the early history of the newly revealed faith. For the choral odes, among the most beautiful of Greek tragedy, are all deeply religious in tone and constantly denounce rationalism, τὸ σοφόν, i. e., the subtleties of the current philosophical speculations which were undermining traditional beliefs. In proportion as such knowledge is depreciated, is faith in the established religion inculcated. I will quote from the play a few of the more notable sentiments in illustration of this. Thus the chorus asserts the divine providence and moral government of the world in the two following

[1] *Bakchen*, p. 156 (translated by Beckwith in his edition of the play, p. 10, n. 1).

passages, which would be difficult to parallel elsewhere in the poet's works:

"Verily the gods dwelling in the ether still can view the affairs of men. Human wisdom is oft no wisdom, nor is the thinking upon things which are unfit for mortal minds."[2]

"Slowly but surely the strength divine is roused and punishes those of mortal men who honor folly's ends, and, urged on by madness, do not extol what belongs to the immortals. For cunningly the gods conceal the lazy foot of time and hunt out at last the impious man. For 'tis no profit to learn nor practise beyond the stablished customs."[3]

This same acceptance of old beliefs is again urged in these words:

"'Tis wise to keep both mind and heart from the lore of those who think themselves wise; whatever the common throng thinks and practises, that would I accept."[4]

Teiresias urges the same acceptance on Pentheus:

"Nor should we exalt mortal wisdom against that divine; our ancient traditions, which have existed from time immemorial, these no arguments shall overturn, nor the keenest subtleties of thought."[5]

The chorus praises the man who has renounced speculation, and who through the national faith has found knowledge of mysteries divine:

"Happy he who has 'scaped the storms of sea and reached his haven."[6]

"To preserve the mind in prudence and in a mood befitting mortals, brings a painless life to men who are ready to obey the behest of the gods."[7]

Human wisdom, however, is not to be neglected, but there are great mysteries beyond its ken:

"Wisdom I seek with diligence; but with joy I seek those other great things which direct our lives to what is good, both day and night teaching us to revere the gods and to throw aside all that violates the right."[8]

[2] 392 ff. The renderings are from my translation of the play published in *Records of the Past,* XI, Pt. 4, 1912.

[3] 882 ff. [4] 427 ff. [5] 200 ff. [6] 902 f. [7] 1002 ff. [8] 1005 ff.

From the consideration of such sentiments, we are almost persuaded into the belief that the play was written with the avowed intention of overthrowing the enemies of religion, and as an apotheosis of the popular faith. On this theory the play is merely what the Germans would call a *Tendenz-Drama,* and the moral is not hard to point. The inadequacy of human wisdom is shown in the character of Pentheus who, though well-intentioned, is a defender of τὸ σοφόν merely, and so is closed to all influences from that greater mysterious wisdom of the unknown whose glorification seems to be the chief purpose of the drama. His opposition, then, is but a signal example of rationalism failing to accept the supernatural, and he becomes but a type of the shallow free-thinker who, in accordance with his earth-born descent, has no insight into the mysteries of heaven, a type engendered by the sophistic teaching of Euripides's day, against which both the poet and Socrates strove. To quote Professor Moulton: "The plot of the play illustrates the unhappy fate of Pentheus, how those who oppose the worship of the vine are opposing a hidden omnipotence; if the votaries are imprisoned, an earthquake overturns the prison, chains drop off spontaneously, and a fire breaks out that men strive to quench in vain; or the Maenads themselves with supernatural might overturn trees and scatter the limbs of oxen with their hands."[9] It is just this contrast between the blindness of the Theban king, as seen in his scorn of the new superstition, and the hidden power of the god, which gives to the play its dramatic effect. His blindness drives him to madness and ultimately he rushes to his doom apparently with joy. Thus the whole intent of the drama appears to be didactic, that the acceptance of the national religion is the only true basis of human happiness and that the sceptical philosophy of the day is vicious and should be renounced.

[9] *Ancient Classical Drama,* p. 117.

Now in most of his other plays Euripides has nothing but contempt for the traditional theology.[10] This is most evident in the "Hippolytus," staged in 429 B. C., and in the equally powerful "Hercules Furens," which on grounds of style has been dated later, between 420 and 417 B. C. In the former the whole action of the plot is based upon a jealous feud between Aphrodite and Artemis. Because of a personal slight, the goddess of love inspires an ignoble passion in a mother for her step-son. Phaedra, who is one of the poet's noblest creations, Hippolytus and his father Theseus all become involved in an Olympian quarrel in which they are in no wise concerned. After the suicide of the mother and the destruction of the son, Euripides denounces the whole basis upon which the system of Olympus rests; for Artemis can not intercede for her favorite, though he has remained chaste, just because Aphrodite has willed it differently. Her own words are:

> "For Kypris willed that all this should befall
> To glut her spite, and this the Gods' wont is:—
> None doth presume to thwart the fixed design
> Willed by his fellow."[11]

In the "Hercules Furens" the poet also shows that the legendary imperfections of the gods evoked neither his faith nor praise. Here the plot turns on Hera's malicious persecution of her step-son and throughout the drama we are persuaded that she alone is to blame for the hero's madness and the consequent murder of his wife and children. When Hercules at last awakens from his frenzy and realizes his awful deed, he cries out in scorn:

> "To such a Goddess
> Who shall pray now?—who, for a woman's sake
> Jealous of *Zeus*, from Hellas cut off
> Her benefactors, guiltless though they were."[12]

[10] For his diatribe against the popular theology, see especially P. Decharme, *Euripide, et l'esprit de son théâtre* (Paris, 1893), Chap. 2; and cf. Verrall, *Euripides the Rationalist* (Cambridge, 1895), pp. 79-84.

[11] 1327 ff. (Way's translation).

[12] 1307 ff. (Way's translation).

Though the poet discloses the intriguing malevolence of the gods most clearly in these two plays, passages could be cited from all his other works in which they are held up to ridicule. Thus in the "Ion" Apollo is berated for lying and seduction;[13] in the "Andromache" the same god out of spite permits the murder of Neoptolemus, though the latter has come as a suppliant to his shrine.[14] In the "Electra"[15] and "Orestes,"[16] the murder of Clytemnestra, both its responsibility and consequences, is attributed to the Delphian god by Orestes, while in the "Iphigenia in Tauris"[17] the hero openly declares that Phoebus has deceived him. The injustice of the gods is a constant theme of the poet,[18] and the same iconoclastic spirit is seen in many of his dramas and fragments.[19] In fact only the "Alcestis" and "Suppliants" seem wholly free from such utterances, and Athena, Dionysus and Eros are about the only immortals who are left unscathed by the poet's profane hand. But it is unnecessary to quote further in evidence of his contempt of the received theology. In a word we can say that he never tries to soften the imperfections of the gods nor to bring out their higher natures as Æschylus and Sophocles did. They tried to "pour new wine into old bottles," to work over the old myths into harmony with their own sentiments by glossing over all that was objectionable. But Euripides, in view of his wide separation from traditional views, seemed to find such a reconciliation out of the question, and so, instead of trying to tone down their features, he brought out their grossness with perfect fidelity only that he might attack them the better. The famous fragment which runs

"If the gods do anything evil, then they are not gods,"[20]

[13] 436 ff. [14] 1111 ff. [15] 1190 ff. [16] 591 ff. [17] 711.

[18] E. g., "I. T.," 570 ff; "Troades," 469 f; "Herc. Fur.," 339 ff; "Cycl.," 355.

[19] E. g., "I. T.," 572 and 380 ff; "Hecuba," 488 ff; "Troades," 884 f; frags. 483, 793 etc.

[20] Frag. 294, 7. Cf. the sentiment in "I. T.," 391.

might be said to sum up all his objections to the traditional religion of his countrymen; in it we find the *Grundgedanke*—to quote Nestle[21]—of his whole polemic against Greek polytheism. And if we contrast this fragment with one of Sophocles, which asserts that "The gods never lead us into evil,"[22] we can gauge how essentially different was the point of view of these two contemporary poets. In one respect Greek drama was the gainer by Euripides's iconoclasm: the ideal which he failed to find in the gods he looked for in humanity. To him we are indebted for ideal types of mankind—such as Theseus for chivalry, Hippolytus for chastity, Alcestis for conjugal devotion, and many another. In many passages he even seems to take delight in contrasting the goodness of mortals with the capricious selfishness of the immortals.

If, then, we compare such iconoclastic sentiments as these with the perfervid religious ones of the "Bacchanals," the latter sound like a complete renunciation of speculative inquiry, like a retraction or "palinode" of earlier beliefs, or at least like an "eirenicon"—to use a phrase of James Adam[23]—or attempt of the poet to set himself right with public opinion before his death. The spirit of ethical contentment and speculative repose evident throughout the play seems to show that he was at last weary of his doubts and subtleties and that he had found peace in that same religion which he had denounced all his life. It would be a most striking example of poetic justice if this most skeptical of poets finally returned to the faith of his youth and met his end in conformity with Socrates's dictum "that a man should die in peace."[24] Accordingly, in spite of the fact that men of seventy and more do not so

[21] *Untersuchungen über d. philos. Quellen des Euripides*, 1902, p. 126; and cf. Gomperz, *Greek Thinkers*, II, p. 13.

[22] Frag. 226.

[23] *The Religious Teachers of Greece*, p. 312.

[24] Cf. "Phaedo," 117E.

easily change their lifelong opinions, this "recantation" explanation of the drama has been upheld by many able critics, e. g., Nägelsbach, Paley, Pohle, Wecklein, Bernhardy, K. O. Müller, Berlage, Pater and very recently Gomperz. Walter Pater has expressed it in these words: "Writing in old age, he is in that subdued mood,.... in which accustomed ideas, conformable to a sort of common sense regarding the unseen, oftentimes regain what they may have lost, in a man's allegiance. Euripides has said, or seemed to say, many things concerning Greek religion at variance with received opinion; and now, in the end of life, he desires to make his peace—what shall at any rate be peace with men. He is in a mood for acquiescence, or even for a palinode."[25]

However, this interpretation has had many equally strong opponents since Hartung first attacked it in 1844 in his *Euripides restitutus*, e. g., Roux, Patin, Bruhn, Nestle, Pfander, Tyrrel, Jebb, Decharme, Christ and Murray. The latter goes so far as to say that to look upon the play as "a reactionary manifesto in favor of orthodoxy is a view which hardly merits refutation."[26] In consequence, though many have been content merely to point out the vagueness and inconsistency of the poet,[27] others have offered very positive explanations of the purpose of the drama. The older view of Roux,[28] that the play is really a polemic against the popular faith, a thinly veiled criticism not only of the Dionysiac cult but of religion in general, has been revived in recent years.[29] Thus the scornful reply of Agave to Dionysus toward the end of the play,

[25] From his essay on the "Bacchanals," in *Greek Studies.*

[26] *Ancient Greek Literature,* p. 272.

[27] E. g., T. Rumpel, *De Euripidis atheismo,* Halle, 1839; J. Janske, *De philosophia Euripidis,* Breslau, 1857; and more recently Lewis Campbell, *Religion in Greek Literature,* London, 1898.

[28] E. Roux, *Du merveilleux dans la tragédie grecque,* Paris, 1846.

[29] E. g., by H. Patin, *Euripide,* Paris, 1894; E. Bruhn, in his edition of the *Bacchae,* Berlin, 1891.

"'Tis not meet that gods nurse their anger like men."[30]

has been taken as the starting-point for a reinterpretation of the piece on ironical grounds, on the theory that the poet spoke his own mind and meaning only in this one verse.[31] Similarly, the culminating motive of the play, Agave returning in triumph from her unwitting murder of her son, has been explained in an ironical light.[32] Still others[33] have discovered signs of malicious irony in the mystic legend of Dionysus contained in verses 286-297, though it has been pointed out often enough that the long speech of Teiresias in praise of the god as the giver of wine, inspirer of prophets and author of panics in armies (verses 266-327) could hardly have been interrupted by these verses which introduce a legend having nothing in common with the context. Consequently, most editors have rejected the passage,[34] and even if kept it should be looked upon merely as an account of the cult theology.[35] By a like process of reasoning the preceding speech of Pentheus (verses 242-7) has also been rejected. It is probable that the two passages in question were composed with reference to each other and added later. Other critics have found comic features in the character-drawing of Teiresias, especially in the passage in which the old seer describes Pentheus's madness (verses 200ff).[36]

[30] 1348.

[31] This is the view of Decharme, *op. cit.*; he is followed by H. Weil, *Etudes sur le drame antique*, Paris, 1897, and C. Lindskog, *Studien zum antiken Drama*, Lund, 1897.

[32] E. g., suggested by Campbell, *op. cit.*, pp. 309-310.

[33] E. g., G. Dalmeyda, *Ausgangspunkt der Bakchen*, Paris, 1908.

[34] It was kept, however, by both K. O. Müller, and Paley (*Eurip.*, Vol. II, p. 393). Dindorf rejected it because of its "*dictio inepta confusa omninoque non Euripidea*," and because it interrupts the context; he is followed by Tyrrel and others.

[35] As the following have done: Weil, *Etudes*, p. 113f; R. Hirzel, *Berichte der sächs. Gesell. der Wiss.*, XLVIII, 1896, p. 294; Christ, *Gesch. der griech. Litt.*, 6th ed, 1912, p. 374, n. 4.

[36] E. g., P. Girard, *Rev. des études grecques*, XVII, 1904, pp. 175f, in connection with a fantastic attempt to join the three plays which were brought out in the year after the death of Euripides (the "Iphigenia in Aulis," "Alcmaeon"

But is the real intention of the "Bacchanals" to be explained on either the "recantation" or "irony" theory? As for the latter, it may be said at once that with the exception of the line in question (1348) there is not a single other indication in the play of any of the blasphemous expressions which are so common in the poet's other works, and that instead of betraying any criticism of the wine-god or his cult, the entire drama extols his might with the utmost warmth and vigor. In fact it is extolled with such seriousness that Euripides cannot be said to give an unbiased account of the struggle between Pentheus and the hidden power of the god. For though his human sympathies are certainly with the unhappy upholder of "reason," just as they were with Hippolytus in the earlier play, still he seems to be wholly within the influence of the religious antagonism to reason, and to be writing as a subjective believer in the religious views expressed. Of course a good deal of this attitude can be explained by his desire to give a powerful and effective stage setting to the play.

On the other hand the advocates of the "palinode" theory are obliged to assume an essential change in the poet's attitude toward religion, and so to look upon the "Bacchanals" as a sort of death-bed confession of earlier heresies. But are we justified in assuming any such repentant relapse of the aged poet into the old epic orthodoxy which he had impugned all his life long? This was the view of Bernhardy[37] and Nägelsbach[38] long ago and has been recently revived by Gomperz,[39] who thinks that in this way the poet wished to atone for his "*Abfall vom Genius seines Volkes.*"

and "Bacchanals") in a *trilogie libre*. His "comic" theory has found adherents in Dalmeyda (*op. cit.*) and O. Schröder, *Zeitschr. für Gymnasialwesen*, LXIV, 1910, p. 193.

[37] *Griech. Litt.*, II, 2.

[38] *Nachhomerische Theologie*, Nürnberg, 1857, p. 463ff.

[39] *Griech. Denker*, II, 12.

Though the utterances of the chorus and the fate of Pentheus protest that speculative philosophy must be renounced, still it is perfectly clear that the poet's conception of Dionysus is rationalistic, and that he is pictured as in no sense a personal god. As Gilbert Murray has said: "If Dionysus is a personal god at all, he is a devil."[40] On any such theory the whole moral purpose of the play would be vitiated. But the god is nothing more than a personified principle, a rationalized idea, like the conception of Aphrodite in the "Hippolytus." Thus Teiresias, in his effort to convert Pentheus, says:

"But two things, oh youth, find worth among mankind; first our goddess Demeter; for she is earth, call her by what name thou wilt; 'tis she who nourishes men with food; but now Semele's offspring hath given us that liquid strength hidden in the grape, a boon to men, for it assuages the grief of wretched mortals so soon as they are filled with the sweetness of the vine; and it grants sleep, oblivious of daily toil, for forgetfulness is their only cure; and this gift of Bacchus is poured out in libation to the gods and through its means men are blessed."[41]

We should remember that the Theban seer always speaks with authority in Greek tragedy and is generally the mouthpiece of the dramatist, and so this rationalistic conception of Dionysus was doubtless Euripides's own. The sophist Prodicus had already conceived of Dionysus as the apotheosis of wine and Demeter of corn, and had identified Poseidon with water, Hephaestus with fire, etc. Cicero—who quotes his teaching in the *De natura deorum,* I, 118—looked upon this personification of the gods as natural objects as a complete denial of religion. So Euripides looked upon Dionysus merely as a principle—the embodiment of enthusiasm, not only the god of wine, but, in Adam's words, "a higher personification of passion in religion and joy in life,"—such a principle as that

[40] *Anc. Greek Lit.,* p. 272. [41] 274ff.

described by Plato in the "Phaedrus," where Socrates, in distinguishing good from evil madness, mentions four kinds of the former, the third of which he calls "poetic" madness. He says it takes "hold of a delicate and virgin soul, and there inspiring frenzy, awakens lyrical and all other numbers."[42] This poetic madness is best illustrated by the "Bacchanals," though there are indications in the play of the other varieties of madness as well. As Adam has observed, there is no other Greek poem in which the writer is so "possessed."[43]

Though Euripides was no consistent follower of Orphism, still he was interested in its mystic and ascetic phases, as we know from the fact that he devoted at least one play—the lost "Cretans"—to this subject. The two gods or "principles" of that sect, Dionysus and Eros, were always reverently treated in his plays. It may be that the early associations of his birthplace Phlye in Attica, where mysteries were celebrated in honor of Demeter and Core as well as Eros, the cosmic spirit of Orphism, influenced his attitude toward mysticism, just as Æschylus was influenced by the mysteries celebrated at his birthplace Eleusis. These gods, Dionysus and Eros, were nothing but "potencies" to the Orphics. As Miss Harrison has said:

"The religion of Orpheus is religious in the sense that it is the worship of the real mysteries of life, of potencies (δαίμονες) rather than personal gods (θεοί); it is the worship of life itself in its supreme mysteries of ecstacy and love.... In ancient Greek religion these (Bacchus and Eros) are the only real gods. Orpheus dimly divined the truth later to become explicit through Euripides....It is these real gods, this life itself, that the Greeks, like most men, were inwardly afraid to recognize and face, afraid even to worship....Now and again a philosopher or poet, in the very spirit of Orpheus, proclaims these true gods,

[42] 245 (Jowett).

[43] *Op. cit.*, p. 315.

and asks in wonder why to their shrines is brought no sacrifice."[44]

Since, then, Dionysus in the "Bacchanals" is conceived merely as the rationalized principle of enthusiasm, it is clear that the main problem of the play is not a question of skepticism against orthodoxy, but the relative value of "reason" and "enthusiasm" in life.[45] So the whole purport of the play is epitomized in such utterances as these which have already been quoted: "Human wisdom is oft no wisdom"; "Nor should we exalt mortal wisdom against that divine." Rationalism is denounced as insufficient; human knowledge, though valuable, is infinitesimally small in comparison with the great mysterious knowledge beyond, but yet it must not be neglected; "Wisdom I seek with diligence (τὸ σοφόν οὐ φθονῶ); but with joy I seek those other great things which direct our lives to what is good." We must bear in mind that the rationalism which the poet here condemns is only that of the sophists, the same which he had condemned long before in the "Hippolytus" and "Medea." There is something greater than this, and that is religious exaltation, which he offers as the true wisdom. As Gilbert Murray says: "Reason is great but it is not everything. There are in the world things not of reason, but both below and above it; causes of emotion, which we cannot express, which we tend to worship, which we feel perhaps to be the precious elements in life. These things are gods or forms of God; not fabulous immortal men, but 'Things which are,' things utterly non-human and non-moral, which bring man bliss or tear his life to shreds without a break in their own serenity."[46] He goes on to say that this is the kind of religion against which

[44] *Prolegomena to Greek Religion*, p. 658. In the "Symposium" of Plato, 189, Aristophanes says mankind has never understood the power of Eros, else they would have built him great shrines. In the "Hippolytus," the chorus sings a similar refrain, 538ff.

[45] Cf. Adam, *op. cit.*, p. 316, whom I follow in this connection.

[46] *Anc. Greek Lit.*, p. 272.

Tolstoy preached, which Bentham and Paley tried to abolish, and which Plato denounced and followed. And in a more recent work the same writer has given the rational basis of the Dionysiac worship in these words: "Dionysus was a fiction, the ritual of Dionysus a reality—the reality in fact out of which the fiction was developed or projected. It is the ritual of the spring, of the New Year, of *le renouveau*—the renewal after the dead winter of all the life of the world.... Further, if we would understand Dionysus-worship, we must realize that these vegetation-cults and all their grossness were bound up with the things that are the most beautiful in the world."[47] This true basis of the Dionysiac worship as the negation of rationality was felt by Euripides when writing this play, which pictures so passionately the sympathy of mankind with nature.

From this view-point of the rationalistic conception of the wine-god, the question as to whether the god or one of his priests played the chief rôle in the drama does not have the importance which many have thought. Doubtless the gap in the one manuscript preserving the play—ending with verse 1330, in which Dionysus continues his prophecy from the *theologeion*—would, if recovered, settle the question finally as to whether the Lydian stranger was Dionysus or a preacher of the new religion. However rationalistic Euripides's conception of Dionysus was, we should not forget that to an Athenian audience Dionysus was a personal god. Now he is portrayed as a human character throughout the action of the play; and to avoid the shearing and binding scene, which would have appeared repugnant in a theater whose representations were merely acts of homage to the god, we are justified in looking upon the comely stranger as a priest or an adept of the common type, inspired, if you like, to perform miracles which the ordinary stage-machinery of the day could have easily

[47] From *Greek and English Tragedy: A Contrast.*

represented. Nor are we obliged to explain features in the action of the play,—as, e. g., the destruction of the palace—on any theory of hypnotism of the audience as has been attempted recently.[48] Thus, it is more reasonable to assume that the god appeared only in the prologue and epilogue as is customary in the dramas of Euripides. But the loss of the passage in question is irreparable from a wholly different cause. We have lost almost the whole of Agave's speech, for it breaks off after the first verse (1329). The scene represented a frenzied mother who had unconsciously slain her son and transfixed his head on a spear; she slowly recovers her sanity and laments over the dead body. In so heart-rending a scene as this, the poet must have furnished a perfect example of Aristotle's idea of a "recognition."[49] If we compare the sentiment of this lost speech with that of Hecuba wailing over the body of Astyanax as preserved in the "Troades," we can imagine how effectively this most sympathetic of poets must have rendered so terrible a situation, perhaps the most moving he ever wrote, and we can thus form some idea of our loss.[50]

So if it was the intention of Euripides in the "Bacchanals" to portray Dionysus as a rational principle and thus to denounce the pretensions of a false philosophy as inadequate, the play is in no sense a reaction toward dogmatic orthodoxy. A study of his other dramas shows that though he was a disbeliever in the traditional theology, he had never actually denied the essential basis of religion. Though "by nature a destroyer of illusions,"[51] he probably

[48] As in G. Norwood's *Riddle of the Bacchae*, 1908.

[49] "Poetics," 1454a².

[50] Two passages in Apsines, a writer on rhetoric (*Rhet. Gr.*, IX, pp. 587 and 590, ed. Walz) gives us a faint idea of the purport of the speech. The author of *Christus Patiens*—wrongly ascribed to Gregory of Nazianzus—also probably had the missing portion before him. Hartung (*Euripides restitutus*) and Kirchhoff (*Philol.*, VIII, pp. 78-93) have reconstructed several lines of the lost passage of the "Bacchanals" from that drama.

[51] Croisèt (*Hist. de la littérature grecque*, I, p. 313) says of him: *"C'était par nature un destructeur d'illusions."*

never expressed disbelief in the idea of deity. It is true that his fellow Athenians looked upon him as a freethinker; Aristophanes has testified to their opinion in a famous passage in the "Thesmophoriazusae" in which a poor widow accuses the poet of depriving her of her livelihood—she was a weaver of sacrificial chaplets—by his teaching that there are no gods.[52] And the more famous fragment from the lost "Bellerophon," preserved to us by Justin Martyr,[53]

> "Doth any say there are Gods in heaven?
> Nay, there are none,"

has also been urged to prove the poet's disbelief in deity. But we have no idea of the context in which this fragment occurred; if the succeeding line were preserved, quite possibly its whole meaning would be different. We must be on our guard against accepting such fragments as conclusive evidence because of their disjointed nature and the fact that they are often tinged with Christian or Jewish interpolations.[54] It is always perplexity and doubt rather than positive disbelief which are the burden of many another passage. Thus in the "Helena" the chorus complains that no one can tell

> "What is God, or what is not God, or that which lies between."[55]

In the "Hercules Furens" the famous doubt is expressed:

> "Zeus, whoever Zeus is."[56]

And the same agnosticism meets us in this line of the "Orestes":

[52] 445ff.

[53] Frag. 288; see his "De Monarchia," ch. 5.

[54] Tyrrell (in his edition of the *Bacchae*, p. XXIII) cites frag. 256 (from the lost "Achelaus," which probably reflected a similar mental state as the "Bacchanals") as in itself evidencing the poet's dissatisfaction with the moral government of the world, a sentiment fortunately condemned in the preserved answer. He also notes that frag. 852 is of Jewish or Christian origin.

[55] 1327.

[56] 1263f, repeated in frag. 483. Adam (p. 444) remarks that "Greek writers not infrequently represent the Highest God as the inscrutable one whose name is not lightly to be spoken" and cites the "Troades," 885, and Plato's "Euthyphron," 12A, as examples.

"In thraldom to the Gods we live, whoever the Gods may be."[57]

He seemed to be constantly thwarted by the obscurity of everything connected with theology. Orestes's remark in the *Iphigenia in Tauris,*

"In things divine great confusion reigns,"[58]

might be quoted as a summary of his doubts. That there is no way, either by divination or otherwise, to learn the will of the gods whose purpose is ever invisible to man, is a common sentiment of the poet.[59] Iphigenia says:

"For all the acts of the gods move on invisibly and no one knows anything clearly."[60]

But such isolated passages—many of which are put into the mouths of actors only to be denounced—can only be interpreted in the light of his teaching as a whole. His polemic was aimed against the anthropomorphic ideas of the gods held by his countrymen, and so he came to be looked upon as an atheist. Whether he believed in ideal gods it is hard to determine, for here the evidence is again vacillating; sometimes he seems to believe and sometimes not. But that he had arrived at certain definite assumptions as to the true nature of the godhead, whose various names—Ether, Law, Necessity, Justice, Reason—are but attributes of the one all-embracing infinite substance, can be shown by adducing many passages in which the poet maintains that the gods must furnish a moral standard for men, that the notions of hegemony and clashing wills implied in polytheism are wrong and that the divine nature is self-sufficient.[61] Iphigenia cannot believe that Artemis really enjoys human sacrifices, but argues that the barbarous Taurians have attributed their own murderous customs to the goddess, and finally says:

[57] 418. [58] 572.

[59] E. g., "H. F.," 62; "Hel.," 744-5; "Alc.," 785f.

[60] "I. T.," 476-7; cf. Solon, frag. 16 (Hiller).

[61] E. g., "H. F.," 1307ff; and 1342ff; "I. T.," 385ff; "Ion," 442ff; frag. 1130, etc.

> "None of the gods I ween is evil or doeth wrong,"[62]

a sentiment which can be looked upon as the central idea in Euripides's constructive theology. That he believed that justice would finally guide all things to their goal is clear from the beautiful prayer which Hecuba makes to Zeus in the "Troades," ending:

> ". . . . for treading soundless paths
> In justice dost thou guide all mortal things."[63]

Thus Euripides did not reject the basic facts of religion but tried to interpret them in a way which would be in harmony with a belief in the benevolence of the divine nature.

Though the theology of the "Bacchanals," then, is conceived mainly in the same rational spirit which we see in his earlier works, still no one can read the play without being convinced that some great change has come over the religious attitude of the poet, who with such youthful fire and in such passionate language thus proclaims the power of this irresistible world-embracing divinity, which differs so essentially from the old Olympian gods. For this change[64] I think we should look almost wholly to the circumstances of the composition of the play in Macedonia, the home of the Dionysiac cult. In writing for a Macedonian audience it was but fitting that Euripides should have chosen for his subject the worship of their great god. Frequent allusions to the country clearly show his desire to compliment his friend and host Archelaus.[65] And the wholly un-Greek character of the play—only matched, perhaps, among his other works by the "Orestes"—was far better suited to the genius of this land of orgiastic worship

[62] "I. T.," 391; cf. the same thought in "Troades," 987ff.

[63] 887-8 (Way).

[64] Against the view of, e. g., Decharme, Weil, Tyrrell, Nestle (*Philol.*, 58, 1899, p. 362f) and most radically, Lindskog; the change is assumed by Christ and others.

[65] E. g., Pieria, 410 and 565; "Olympus," 561; the "Axius," 569, and "Lydias," 571.

and mystic ceremonies than to the more temperate states of Greece. The old poet, weary of his logical subtleties and lifelong doubts, has finally found peace in a form of mysticism—the mystic worship of Dionysus, whose real nature was first made clear to him here far from Athens, where he is now breathing an atmosphere of intellectual freedom. As Jebb has said: "The really striking thing in the 'Bacchae' is the spirit of contentment and of composure which it breathes,—as if the poet had ceased to be vexed by the seeming contradictions which had troubled him before."[66] The tendency toward mysticism,[67] long dormant in him, has at length asserted its power and now has full reign. He has finally, contrary to his custom, adopted the spirit of an enthusiastic convert; we are persuaded that he is convinced of all that he so passionately writes; the entire drama is pervaded with the exaltation of an overpowering vision.[68] Dominated by the new enthusiasm, he has returned to the peaceful worship of nature and no longer lets his feelings be restrained by any ethical or reflective doubts. James Adam has finely said: "No other ancient poem shows so rapturous a feeling of the kinship between man and nature. The very hills are thrilled with ecstacy in sympathy with the frenzied votaries of the god.[69] We feel that Dionysus has become a power pulsating throughout the whole of nature, both inorganic and organic, making the universe into a living, breathing whole; and we are stirred with a new sense of unification with the mystery

[66] *Encycl. Brit.* (11th ed.), art. "Euripides."

[67] Christ (*op. cit.*, p. 375) has found traces of this mystic tendency in his earlier dramas, e. g., in the "Ion," where the mystical renunciation of the world is glorified; in the character drawing of Eteocles in the "Phoenissae"; and in the "Cyclops," where rationalism is exposed. Recently Gomperz (II, p. 15) thinks he sees the same attitude of mind in the "Hippolytus."

[68] He is so much in sympathy with his subject that some have argued that he merely intended to terrorize his audience—whether Macedonian or Athenian—into a revival of the neglected worship of Dionysus; cf. Campbell, p. 309.

[69] In reference to the words of the messenger describing the revels on Cithaeron, 726ff: "And soon the whole mountain and the wild beasts were in a tumult, and all was in motion through their running hither and thither."

that surrounds us."[70] He likens this religion of the "Bacchanals" to the "added dimension of emotion," the "new reach of freedom" discussed by William James in his *Varieties of Religious Experience*.[71] It is this which makes the play a religious one. In a word it is "faith," which Professor Verrall says is the one thing new in the play, the thing which differentiates it not only from every other drama of Euripides, but from everything else in Greek literature, "the thing, the human phenomenon.... which is, in one word, faith or a faith—religion as we mostly now conceive it, exclusive in belief and universal in claim, enthusiastic, intolerant, and eager to conquer the world."[72] Though the phenomenon is common enough to us, it was apparently unknown to the Greece of the poet's time and was first revealed to him in his last days in Macedon.

It is this, then,—the praise of enthusiasm and inspiration in nature, the personification of exultation in life and emotion in religion—which forms the chief motive of this strange play. The victory of Dionysus over Pentheus, that is, the victory of enthusiasm over reason, the showing up of the defects of human wisdom in comparison with the greater knowledge of the mysterious unknown, all this teaches a lesson no less plain than that disclosed by the victory of Aphrodite in the "Hippolytus" written twenty-three years before. In these two companion plays, two great facts of nature, enthusiasm and love, are personified. These are two great necessities of our human natures, sources of happiness for weary mortals, and they cannot be reasoned away on any rational grounds, nor can they be disregarded without terrible effects, as is exemplified in the fate of both Pentheus and Hippolytus. Euripides

[70] *Op. cit.*, p. 317. His explanation of the play on the theory of Macedonian influence I have followed in the main.

[71] P. 48.

[72] *The Bacchanals of Euripides and Other Essays* (1910), p. 159.

constantly denounced every form of superstition; at the same time he was always opposed to a dogmatic rationalism; and so the "Bacchanals," written at the end of his life, is in a sense the summing up of his position.

Whether the new vision, which seems to have taken such complete hold of the poet, would have been lasting had he enjoyed a longer lease of life, is another question. Even in the play itself are indications of the old iconoclastic spirit reappearing; for example toward the end, in the brief colloquy between Dionysus and Agave,[73] the latter answers with disdain in the line already quoted,

> "'Tis not meet that gods nurse their anger like men."

And that after all the Greek gods are but the contemptible puppets of a vast and indefinable fate is attested by the final verses—which are also appended to several other plays[74]—and which doubtless contain the poet's true sentiments: "Many are the forms of things divine, and many things unhoped for the gods bring to pass. Both what was expected has not been fulfilled and of the unexpected God has found a solution. So hath it happened here."[75] In the "Hippolytus," Phaedra, father and son are all pictured as the puppets of divine caprice; here at the end of the "Bacchanals" Euripides goes a step further and makes not only Pentheus, Agave and the rest puppets of the gods, but the gods puppets of fate.

Thus the play, powerful though it is, contains just such conflicting views as his other works, and so is a true child of the poet. For Euripides, though his dramas were a tremendous factor in carrying on the protest against traditional views of religion which had been inaugurated the preceding century by Xenophanes and Heraclitus, made but little effort to construct a new theology. His mind

[73] 1345ff.

[74] I. e., the "Alcestis," "Medea," "Helena," "Andromache."

[75] 1388ff.

was essentially curious and impressionable to every influence; every thing—nature, society, humanity, religion, philosophy—appealed to him. A recent student of his philosophy has observed that there was scarcely a problem of his day, scarcely a theory in Greek thought before or during his lifetime, of which he did not take account.[76] But though he raised every question he gave a conclusive answer to none, and contented himself with throwing out a crowd of suggestions which at best seem only tentative gropings, and when taken together neither form a consistent whole nor are ruled by any one principle. As Croiset says: "*C'était une intelligence vive et pénétrante plutôt que forte.*"[77] It is quite possible that he had no definite views on religion; he was too great a thinker to yield to the temptation of any one solution, and so like many other great minds he took refuge in mysticism. His nature did not yearn for moral and intellectual anchorage, like that of Sophocles—evidence his shifting, almost kaleidoscopic views of the soul's future: sometimes he simply considers that the problem cannot be solved;[78] again he favors the view of Anaxagoras that is was a dreamless sleep, denying the survival of consciousness;[79] or he paints the usual epic gloomy region of never-ending night;[80] there are passages also in which he asserts that the spirits of the dead still feel with the living,[81] and in others he seems to maintain the Orphic conception, that life is death to the soul and that death is life.[82] This inconsistency in his views impresses us more than any other feature of his mind except his pessimism. As Gomperz puts it: "He delighted to suffer each shifting breath of opinion in turn to seize upon and move his soul."[83] In his defence

[76] Nestle, *op. cit.*, 560. [77] *Op. cit.*, p. 313. [78] "Hippol.," 192ff.

[79] Cf. "Troades," 631ff. [80] Cf. Frag. 536.

[81] Cf. "Electra," 677; "Orestes," 1237.

[82] Cf. Frag. 830 and 639. Cf. on the subject of his eschatological ideas, Adam, *op. cit.*, pp. 306ff.

[83] *Op. cit.*, II, p. 13.

we must remember his life was cast in a period of changing and conflicting thought; the old order of things was passing, but the new was not yet firmly established. It was his destiny to stimulâte, to interest, rather than to actually instruct; for his mind was not vigorous enough to embody a system of principles and to cling to them. He was a thinker but hardly a philosopher; and first and last he was a poet, and so in accordance with the Greek idea a teacher also. For Plato says in a beautiful passage that the poets "are to us in a manner the fathers and authors of wisdom."[84] And Aristophanes had already expressed a similar thought when he said that the poet "should conceal what is evil and neither bring it forward nor teach it. For just as children have teachers to direct them, so poets are teachers for grown people."[85] So the religious views of a Pindar, an Æschylus or Euripides, influenced the people deeply. In the "Bacchanals" there seems to be no trace of the great problem which constantly perplexed Euripides—the reconciliation of an imperfectly ruled world with the idea of a benevolent God. But its absence in this play is no guarantee that he had finally found its solution; more probably he never found any light to bring into harmony his intellectual doubts and his moral yearnings. Doubtless much of the pessimism which is evident in many of his plays—a pessimism which at times is synonymous with hopeless despair—is to be explained by this lack of unity.[86]

Walter Woodburn Hyde.

University of Pennsylvania.

[84] "Lysis," 214. [85] "Frogs," 1053ff.

[86] E. g., in the "Hercules Furens," "Hecuba," "Troades," "Andromache" and especially in frag. 452. Adam, p. 311, argues that this pessimism is not entirely due to the political and social changes of the poet's day, for Sophocles, his contemporary, was not affected by it; Gomperz, II, p. 10, ascribes it to the growth of reflection as well as to the unrest of the transition age in which Euripides lived.

THE FATHER OF MONISM.

IT will perhaps interest readers of *The Monist* to have before them the following attempt at an English version of the poem—or rather of the principal fragments of it that survive—in which the father[1] of monism embodied the passion, one might almost say the fury, of his conviction that What Is is One. The verses of Parmenides "On the Nature of Things" are remarkable for two reasons: they are the first thorough-going attempt to prove that reality is a unity, and they are the earliest expression of an idea which was to dominate philosophy with tremendous consequences for nearly two thousand years afterward. The conclusions of the Eleatic school as to the nature of reality were too fantastic to be widely accepted; but the theory stated by Parmenides, the first Eleatic, and never since more vigorously stated, that there is only one way of obtaining scientific knowledge about the world, established itself almost without question. That truths having the certainty of demonstration can only be reached by *a priori* reasoning and never by observation of phenomena, which therefore cannot be the objects of science,—this theory, once promulgated by Parmenides, was taken up into the main stream of Greek thought as a fundamental assumption. Plato and Aristotle shared it, and its validity, supported by the great fabric of the Aristotelian logic, was never seriously attacked until Galileo looked through his

[1] Parmenides was the father of monism rather than the first of monists. Xenophanes was "the first of those who went in for monizing" (Aristotle, *Met.*, A. 5. 986*b* 21), but he was primarily a poet and preacher and had little influence on systematic philosophy.

"optick glass." Even then it survived in part; for it is still true that we have no absolutely certain knowledge except such as can be deduced from general principles. But when science began to advance independently of Aristotle, the domain of the *a priori* was curtailed. We no longer think that no knowledge except the absolutely certain deserves to be called scientific; in investigating the laws of nature we are content with a high and ever-increasing degree of probability. The main interest of Parmenides's poem is that in it a tendency which was to defer that consummation for many centuries first becomes articulate.

It has the strangeness of all origins. No literary document of equal importance bristles with problems apparently so hopeless of solution. There are, to begin with, several difficulties connected with its structure. It has two parts: an exposition (with a proem) of the Way of Truth, and an exposition of the Way of Opinion, of which the first is preserved almost in its entirety, while perhaps one-tenth of the second survives.[2] In the opening lines the philosopher is whirled away in the chariot of the Sun to the abode of a Goddess, who expounds to him two doctrines, a true and a false, "the unshaken heart of well-rounded truth" and "the opinions of mortals." What is the nature of the journey, and who is the Goddess? Why, after she has declared the truth about the universe, should an account which is emphatically stated to be false then be put into her mouth? No certain answer seems possible to these questions. As to the journey, it looks at first sight as if Parmenides were conveyed in the chariot upwards from darkness to the "Gateway of the Paths of Night and Day," and that then he passes through the gateway into a realm of light where the Goddess makes her revelations. But it is just possible to interpret the text as a descent

[2] Hermann Diels, *Parmenides Lehrgedicht*, p. 26. Berlin, 1897.

to the nether world. On this view, which is that of Otto Gilbert,[3] the gate described so minutely in the proem (13-24)[4] is the door of Hades. We must conceive the philosopher as accompanying the Sun on its nightly journey to the under-world, and the Maidens who guide the car as persuading the Goddess to open the gate of Night and Day, which she guards, that they may pass through and the Sun resume his daily course. They then drive on and upwards, leaving Parmenides alone with the Goddess, who is no other than that "Justice" or "Necessity" mentioned in other parts of the poem. There is much to recommend this view, which is interesting as making Parmenides one of the illustrious company of poets, headed by Homer, Virgil and Dante, who have descended to the under-world; but the arguments for and against it cannot be discussed here. Whether the journey be heavenward or hellward, the identification of the Goddess with Justice and Necessity, and again with her who, in the cosmological part of the poem, is in the center of the "rings," "steers all things," and is the creator of the gods (187-192), has great plausibility. Mr. Cornford[5] has ingeniously connected her with the principle on which, in primitive religious systems, the universe is marked out by tabus. But on these points there is likely for some time to come to be more speculation than agreement among scholars.

As to the Way of Opinion, which forms the last part of the poem, and which seems to have contained a system of the world in which concentric spheres or rings of light and darkness played a part, and an account of the birth and decay of gods, of material objects, of animals and of the bodies and souls of men, the difficulty is to explain why Parmenides stated it in such detail. The few frag-

[3] "Der δαίμων des Parmenides," *Archiv für Geschichte der Philosophie*, Vol. XX, p. 25. Berlin, 1907.

[4] The figures in brackets in the text refer to the lines of my translation.

[5] Francis Cornford, *From Religion to Philosophy*, p. 217. London, 1912.

ments of it that we possess are not continuous, and I have therefore not translated them all. It appears from them that the cosmology of the Way of Opinion had an affinity to that of the Pythagoreans, and Professor Burnet has sought in this fact an explanation of our difficulty. Parmenides had been a Pythagorean, and was now, he suggests, founding a dissident school. It was therefore "necessary for him to instruct his disciples in the system they might be called on to oppose."[6] If we adopt this view, we may outline the trend of the argument as follows, disengaging it from the archaic language in which it is expressed.

Nothing can have any reality except What Is: for every thought must have an object—thought and its object in fact form an indivisible unity—and the object of a thought cannot be nothing (49, 61-64, 129-131). Further, reality must be eternal, i. e., without beginning and without end. It cannot come into being, because it cannot be produced by nothing, and nothing existed before the existence of that which is real (86-98). Again, no reason can be given why, if it began to be, it should begin at one time rather than another (92-94). And similarly it cannot come to an end (106-108). Thus it is a mistake to attribute any reality at all to the processes of change, growth and decay that we see going on round us (109-112, 135-140). And reality is absolutely single, simple and continuous. It cannot have parts, because, if there were parts, there would be empty gaps between them and thus more reality in some places than in others, which is absurd (113-117, 145-150) We must therefore conceive the substance of the universe as shaped like a sphere (since the spherical is the most unbroken and perfect of forms) with no vacuum anywhere, perfectly stable, with no differences, changes or motions (141-144). This sphere, though its

[6] J. Burnet, *Early Greek Philosophy*, p. 211. London, 1908.

existence is temporally endless, is limited in space; for if it were infinite there would always be "something lacking" to complete the sum-total of reality; but this is impossible (125-128). Thus the prejudices of common sense, which sees differences everywhere—differences of distance, for instance (49)—and thinks that things become and perish and that there is such a thing as change of sensible qualities (135-140), are all false, in spite of the difficulty we have in shaking them off, confirmed as they seem to be by constant experience (42). And not only so, the more refined views of philosophers are false too, particularly the views of Heraclitus of Ephesus, who holds that the only scientific truth attainable is that based on the endless flow of shifting sense-experience (69-76).[7] There is only one way of attaining truth, namely by following reason (45-48). There is, however, one account of the universe, that given by the Pythagoreans, which is so inherently plausible that it must be expounded at length; you must be versed in its details to be able to refute them (167, 168). It is based on a dualism—that of the "light" or "fiery" and "dark" or "heavy" elements — which of course cannot for a moment be accepted, as our argument proves conclusively that all things are One.

But when we have done the best we can with the journey and the Goddess and the Way of Opinion a stumbling-block still remains. It is not only modern readers to whom it seems strange that Parmenides wrote in verse; the fact disconcerted antiquity as well. It was felt that he was essentially prosaic. Why then did he drape his theory in the rich, stiff, hieratic dress of the hexameter, as the old sculptors clothed their idea of deity in stiffly falling lines of stone and bronze and wood? Why did this first

[7] It is generally agreed that the vituperation of these lines is directed against Heraclitus. For the opposition between Parmenides as the philosopher of pure reason and Heraclitus as the philosopher of experience see Emanuel Loew, "Parmenides und Herakleitos im Wechselkampfe," *Archiv für Geschichte der Philosophie,* Vol. XXIV, p. 343. Berlin, 1911.

founder of rationalism begin the custom, which has since had so long and so curious a history, of mixing argument with poetry? The essence of his gospel is "Cleave to the dry light of the intellect, whatever the richness of the facts that strike the senses," and one would think that, than such a gospel, nothing was less suitable to poetry, for which, besides, he evidently had but a meager gift. His technique is clumsy, his images artificial and insipid; his lines jolt and hobble, and he has no warmth of imagination, no glowing colors with which to enrich and soften the bald severity of his subject.

Perhaps it was partly out of opposition to Heraclitus, with his talent for hitting out a striking phrase in prose, that Parmenides chose verse. "Let this gross believer in the trustworthiness of sense-perception string his pedestrian sentences together; my doctrine of the perfect stability, the unbroken unity, of the real demands a form as stable and rounded as itself." Such may have been his feeling. And perhaps the influence of Hesiod went for something. Hesiod had written his account of "Works and Days," of the birth of gods and the ordering of the world, in hexameters, and there is more than one Hesiodic trait in Parmenides. Another influence may have been the Orphic poems current in the Pythagorean school from which Parmenides sprang. But whatever his motives, and whatever his defects as a poet (they have been exaggerated by some critics, minimized by others[8]), our verdict must on the whole be that he was justified. It is not so much that the introduction contains what Diels[9] calls "a powerful conception." That is a matter of opinion; many readers will find it unimpressive where it is vague (and it is nearly all vague), and pointless where it is precise, as in the

[8] Exaggerated by Proclus (*In Plat. Parm.*, I, 665, Paris, 1864), by Plutarch (*De Rat. Aud.*, 3, 45B, *Quomodo Adul.*, 2, 16C), by Philo (*De Prov.*, II, 39), by Cicero (*Ac.*, II, 74); minimized by Bergk, *Kleine Schriften*, II, 10). See Diels, *op. cit.*, pp. 4ff.

[9] *Ibid.*, p. 7.

description of the gate. Parmenides's real justification is the intensity of his passion for the truth.

All philosophers, no doubt, are impassioned for the truth, but not all philosophers are possessed of a passion for the compulsive force of argument. When a man has hit upon an abstract argument in which he can see no flaw and which leads to conclusions violently opposed both to common sense and to the views of other philosophers, his zeal is apt to take an almost religious tinge. Up to a point the love of reason seems, indeed, to be implanted in the human breast. The most irrational of men, those most impatient of logic, take an unconscious pleasure in the struggle to elicit conclusions from premises; the motions of their minds, sluggish though they may be, are always fumbling after some rudiments of a chain of inference. But let the beauties of logical connection once become the object of conscious admiration and be deliberately pursued for their own sake, and there are men who, having tasted blood, will stop nowhere. In them our natural, unconscious pleasure in ratiocination is heightened to the *n*th power; they exalt the value of consistency above everything in the world. It becomes a fixed idea; they give up everything for it; they embrace an abstraction with the abandonment with which the lover embraces his mistress, the devotee his god. The world, to them, is well lost for logic. Are the facts against them? So much the worse for the facts, they cry. They are the martyrs of reason; they are sublime. And they are more than sublime, they are right; for the progress of humanity depends in the long run on the love of reason.

Parmenides was such a man, and his verses are poetry because they are moulded by this passion. That is why they are least good in the half-mythological, half-allegorical preface with which, for reasons at which we can but dimly guess, he leads up to his belief that nothing Is except What Is, and best when he is in the thick of his argument, stumbling, stammering, repeating himself, and wrestling with the reluctance of the language of his day to express his ideas. In his desperate anxiety to make his point clear his verses become rough and harsh, and it is then that they take on a certain sublimity, as of igneous rocks compressed and thrown up by tremendous subterranean forces.

It will perhaps be objected that he could have made his point clear more easily in prose. To this an answer has been provided by a very different poet, Alexander Pope, who explains, in the introduction to the "Essay on Man," that he found he could actually express his philosophical ideas more concisely in verse than in prose. For the labor of throwing a theory into verse has at any rate this merit, that the philosopher who is diffuse is lost. The nature of the medium compels him to grind and sharpen his thoughts until, purged of all superfluities, they attain the utmost sparenesss and compactness of which they are capable. So true is this that far from blaming Parmenides we should wish that modern philosophers would imitate him and Lucretius and compose in verse; their arguments, if like Lucretius and Parmenides it is their arguments they are in earnest about, might be improved by the discipline. On the other hand if like Pope they care not a pin for the argument but greatly for the opportunities of verbal decoration, conceivably some entertaining poetry might be produced.

Passion, then, and conciseness—passion in spite of the lack of imaginative heat, conciseness in spite of clumsiness and repetition — are Parmenides's most striking qualities. That the quatrains into which I have transposed him preserve more than the dimmest reflection of these qualities it would be too much to hope. Hardly can the color and life of a phrase be conveyed from one living language to another, much less from an ancient to a living language. The only respect in which the translator can hope to be a faithful mirror is in giving, feature by feature, the connections of his author's thought; and, since in doing this he may be allowed to take the necessary liberties with his text, I have had no compunction in condensing here, amplifying there, and occasionally omitting a line or two altogether. Without trying to be always literal I have aimed at omitting no point of importance. The real difficulty was to find a vocabulary not too remote in spirit from the original. In the case of an early philosopher this difficulty is especially acute.

Parmenides was 65 years old when he came to Athens and talked with Socrates who was then a youth of 18 to 20 —a fact[10] which gives us 516-514, B. C., as the date of his birth—and at the time he taught the process of stretching the words and phrases of ordinary speech to fit philosophical ideas had scarcely begun. In the absence of a technical vocabulary thought both outruns language and is crippled by it, so that our more abstract colorless words which have a long philosophical evolution behind them seldom quite fit the early thinker's meaning. It is not that his ideas are vaguer than ours, but their vaguenss is of a different kind. Ours is a washed-out vagueness, theirs a dense, packed vagueness, pregnant with the germs of future growth. Thus the translator is in a dilemma. He cannot, since the thoughts he is to render are philosophical, altogether avoid words which, like "reason" or "infinite," have done philosophical duty for centuries; yet he knows that such words distort the spirit of the original, because their fifth-century Greek equivalents are only just beginning to have a specialized philosophical color. For this reason I have employed such words as sparingly as pos-

[10] Plato is the authority for this (*Parm.*, 127b). Diogenes's statement that Parmenides "flourished" 504-500 B. C. does not seem a sufficient ground for questioning Plato's accuracy.

sible. But then another danger arises. Modern technical phrases may strike a false note, but if we do not use them we risk blurring the outlines of the technical questions the author is struggling to state. Above all in Parmenides's poem the student is fascinated by the spectacle of later ideas stirring in embryo,—as where he announces in one place (62): "It must needs be that what can be thought and spoken of is," in another (129) that thought and "the goal of thought" (i. e., that for the sake of which the thought is, that to which it is directed, its *object,* as we say) are one and the same, and again (135, 158) that certain things, e. g., becoming and perishing, are mere names. Here we seem to catch logic and epistemology almost in the act of being born. What is meaning? What are propositions? Must not the object of every judgment be something real? Can an object of consciousness be conceived apart from a conscious subject? These vast questions are enfolded in the verses of Parmenides as the oak in the acorn. Another instance is the argument, on which he bases the oneness of What Is, that there cannot be more reality in one place than in another (51, 52, 113-116, 145-152). We may trace here the germ of Zeno's antinomy of the great and little,[11] which in its turn is the germ of that supposed self-contradictoriness of the infinite divisibility of space which has played so important a part in modern philosophy. Such problems hovered before the mind of Parmenides as in a glass darkly, and I shall be content if in my translation some faint image of them can still be discerned.

PARMENIDES ON THE NATURE OF THINGS.

I. The Journey.

And so, behind that team of sapient steeds,
On the illustrious road divine that leads
  The wise world-wanderer to his heart's desire,
The straining car that bears me onward speeds;

[11] Simplicius, *Ph.,* 141, 1, quoted by Diels, *op. cit.,* p. 83.

On, ever on, its forerunners a band
Of Maids. The axle-tree even as a brand
  Smouldered, and shrilled a music as of pipes
To the twin wheels that rac'd on either hand,

When, once again from the dim house of night
Hastening upwards to the realms of light,
  The Daughters of the Sun-God cast away
Their sable kerchiefs and their heads undight.

Here stands the portal where the paths divide
Of night and day; stony the threshold, wide
  The lintel; filled with mighty doors it is,
By which the great Avenger doth abide,—

Justice, who grasps the ever-changing key.
Her did the Maids pursuade with honey'd plea
  To slip the pin and smite the bolt away;
And the doors sprang asunder instantly,

As one by one the posts of knotted brass
Back on the hinges rolled their thick-wrought mass,
  Yawning to let the Maids and steeds and car
On through the gulph and up the highway pass.

And me the Goddess greeted, and with look
Benign my right hand in her right hand took,
  And "Hail!" she said "O Youth, for thou art sped
Divinely hither; hail!" and thus bespoke:

" 'Tis no ill doom hath led thee on this road
Far from the common track of mortals trod,
  But, tended by those deathless Charioteers,
Justice and Right bring thee to my abode.

"Thine be it now the steadfast heart to know
Of Truth well-rounded, and the ebb and flow
Of Semblance in men's minds; no sure belief
Is in it; thou must learn it even so,

"That, testing all things, so thou may'st declare
The Things that Seem, how men should judge they Are;
Yet must thou set a curb upon thy thought,
And ever of illusion's path beware,

"Lest, poring all too closely on that maze,
The force of use and wont distract thy gaze,
And, droning in thine ear an idle din,
Hurry thee babbling down deceitful ways.

"But hold to Reason when dispute is rife,
And thou shalt know there is not any strife
Can shake this much-tried argument of mine:
This is the proof, this is the Way of Life."

II. The Way of Truth.

"See how thought makes the far thing near! 'Tis plain
Thou canst not cleave the All that Is in twain;
'Tis not a thing of parcels that may be
Scattered abroad, nor yet heaped up again.

"Come, ponder deeply these two Ways of Thought
By which alone all knowledge must be sought,—
The Way of Truth and Suasion hand in hand,—
That What Is Is and Not to Be is Naught,—

"And then the Way of those who take for true
What neither tongue can tell nor thought pursue,—

That something Is Not and must needs Not Be:
That path as wholly blind thou shalt eschew.

"For how can what Is Not be ever known,
Since to be thought on and to be are one?
For everything may be, nay needs must be,
Which speech can name or the mind think upon;

"But what Is Not in Being hath no part.
Lay deeply, then, these precepts to thy heart,
That from the snare of false opinion's Way
Thy firm-set feet may evermore depart;

"Much more from that which witless mortals stray,
Double-faced fools who know not what they say,
But sightless, shiftless, lacking pilotage,
Palsied and deaf, they hither and thither sway;

"Dull herds, to whom the Thing that Is doth seem
The same as what Is Not; and then they deem
The same is not the same, and all the world
Whelm in an ever backward-flowing stream.

"Of this be sure, there is no argument
Shall prove What Is Not Is; be thou content
To curb thy wit from searching out that way,
On the one Way of Being wholly bent:

"Whereon is set full many a sign to tell
That All that Is is indestructible,
Nor ever was created; for complete,
And endless is it, and immovable.

"It never was nor will be; it Is now,
Whole, one, continuous. Its sources how

Wilt thou search out? Or whence draw its increase?
'From that which was before it,' sayest thou?

"But Nothing was before. From Nothing, then?
But this may not be utterèd of men,
Nay, nor conceived, that Nothing ever was.
And if from Nothing, what should choose the when,

"What fix the soon or late, by what decree,
When that which Is should start to grow and be?
Wherefore hold fast this Truth: the Thing which Is
Or all in all or not at all must be.

"Nor will the force of true belief allow
Out of what Is Not aught save Naught to grow;
Therefore things neither perish nor become;
Justice hath fettered them nor lets them go.

"Is it, or Is it Not? All must abide
That test. Let stern Necessity decide,
Who saith 'It Is' is true, and casts 'Is Not'
As nameless and unthinkable aside.

"How then could That which Is ever arise?
For if it was, it Is Not; and likewise
It can not be some day about to be;
Who saith 'It will be' that It Is denies.

"And thus becoming, like a flickering flame,
Is quite extinguished, and that other name,
Destruction, is an empty sound; What Is
Hath nor an end nor source from which it came.

"And how divide it where no difference is,
Nor more of it in that place than in this

To hold its unity apart? Thus all
Is full of it. What Is cleaves to What Is.

"And therefore, as in mighty bonds comprest,
Without beginning, in an endless rest
Is that Which Is, since we have spurned afar
Birth and destruction at the truth's behest.

"Ever the same and ever in one stay
(For strong Necessity hath every way
Fastened the limit round It) It abides,
And changes not, wrapt in Itself alway.

"And straitly bound in limits, as is fit,
The All that Is can not be infinite;
Else It would lack all things; but, lo, It lacks
Nothing; Naught can be added unto It.

"Thought and the goal of thought, these two are one.
For never shalt thou find beneath the sun
A thought exprest without the Thing that Is;
Since no things are, nor shall be, no not one,

"Save those which into the one perfect round
Of moveless being fate hath strictly bound.
Wherefore those names that mortals in their speech
Fix, and believe them true, are empty sound,

"Telling of birth and of destruction,
Of how things change their places and are gone,
How now they are, and now forsooth are not,
And how fair colors fade that brightly shone.

"But since What Is hath an extremest bound,
'Tis like a massy sphere's unbroken round,

Which, from the center poisèd equally,
Complete and equal every way is found.

"There is no Nothing anywhere to break
Its even unity, or greater make
Its plenitude in this place than in that;
It can not here be strong and there be weak;

"For not in any wise can That which Is
Be present more in that place than in this;
Out from the center to the utmost verge
All equal is and all inviolate is."

III. The Way of Opinion.

"Thus far the Truth with reasons sure and clear
Have I declar'd, and next what Shows appear
To mortal men must be in order told:
Do thou to my deceitful song give ear.

"Two Forms there are that mortals have in mind
To name, and naming one they wander blind;
They part the twain as opposite in shape,
And to each opposite are marks assigned.

"To one they give the Heaven's ethereal flame,
Gentle, exceeding light, ever the same,
Itself like to itself; contrariwise
To another Form they give another name,—

"The heavy body of darkness, solid night,
Set over against the influence of light.
(I tell thee all as all most likely seems,
That no man's subtlety may pass thee quite.)

"And then, their names being given to night and light
And to whate'er belongs to either's might,
Since neither in the other hath a share
All things are filled with equal light and night.

* * *

"The substance of the Heavens shalt thou know,
And all the high fixed signs that in them glow,
And those effulgent labors of the Sun—
Whence come his cleansing fires and whither go;

"The wandering Moon too, with her pale round face,
Her works and substance shall thy cunning trace;
And how the Heavens were born, by what dread law
They bind the world and hold the stars in place.

"And thou shalt know how Sun and Moon and Earth
And uttermost Olympus sprang to birth,
And all-embracing Ether, and the might
Of burning Stars, and the Heaven's milky girth.

* * *

"With unmixed fire are fill'd the inmost rings;
The next with darkness; and the appointed springs
Of flame gush in between; and in the midst
The Goddess is who sways and steers all Things,

"Urging all creatures on the sweets to prove
Of mating and the painful fruits thereof,
Male unto female, female unto male;
For of all Gods the first she fashioned Love."

Sydney Waterlow.

London, England.

CRITICISMS AND DISCUSSIONS.

"CHRISTIANITY OLD AND NEW."

This is the title of a course of lectures delivered by Prof. B. W. Bacon, D.D., of Yale Theological Seminary, at the University of California. In order to appreciate and understand the point of view of the lecturer it is necessary to recall the following facts: In the *Hibbert Journal* for January 1910 the present writer had an article entitled "The Collapse of Liberal Christianity"; and a year later another article on the same general theme under the caption, "Whitherward? A Question for the Higher Criticism," carrying the argument a little further. The purpose of both articles was to show that liberal Christianity had failed in its attempt to find a historical Jesus. The main proposition was that liberal Christianity began its course by repudiating the Christ of the church and by planting itself on a purely human Jesus who, of course, it took for granted was a historical person. It was pointed out that it had been engaged for over a hundred years in seeking for this historical Jesus, because he was necessary to the existence of the movement as a protest against orthodox Christianity. The writer admitted at the time and all along that the title of the article was ambiguous and was therefore liable to be misunderstood. But the meaning attached to the words was fully explained in the course of the article, which was not to assert that liberal Christianity or liberal thought had collapsed as a whole, but only that the attempt to find a historical Jesus had failed.

In the *Hibbert Journal* for July 1911 appeared an article by Professor Bacon, entitled "The Mythical Collapse of Historical Christianity," in which there was a misunderstanding of the above. A meaning was attached to the "collapse" never intended by the writer and a consequent wrong impression given to the readers of the Journal and the public generally. Professor Bacon called upon "those who were reading in a contrary sense such momentous signs of the times as the modernist movement, extension of the voluntary principle in church support, church federation, and the new impetus in religious education, not to be suddenly dismayed." That is to say, Professor Bacon represented the writer as asserting that modern thought had suddenly come to a standstill! What was meant by the title was one thing and one thing only, that the liberal search for a historical Jesus had proved a failure. In other respects the writer believed with Professor Bacon that liberal Christianity "so far from being in danger of collapse is advancing to-day by great strides towards the place of leadership and authority in modern religious life." And not only so, but he regards the effort of Professor Bacon and others to stop with a historical Jesus as a failure of liberal Christianity to be true to its principles. Liberal Christianity in the large sense of that phrase is, as Professor Bacon says, "but beginning its career, and rejoices as a strong man to run a race." And in pursuance of the course under the leadership of the Dutch school of criticism, of which Professor Bacon makes no mention either in his *Hibbert* articles or in this book, it is fulfilling its mission and carrying out its principles to their legitimate conclusion. Why should it come to a standstill with the historicists of Germany? Surely the doctrine that the central figure of the New Testament was a historical person is not a finality. The writer believes that those who refuse to stay with the historicists and who go on to interpret the New Testament in a more spiritual sense than is possible on that theory are *par excellence* liberal Christians. They are just now enduring what all must endure who venture to call in question the results of "established scholarship," and to affirm the symbolic character of the Gospel story.

In his new book, *Christianity Old and New,* Professor Bacon shows that he has come to see the mistake he made as regards the word "liberal." Not that he acknowledges it in words—that perhaps would be too much to expect—but it is implied in what he says. He contrasts the view the writer advocated in his articles with that of President Eliot of Harvard University in his essay entitled "The Religion of the Future." President Eliot has for a generation and more been the most distinguished Unitarian in America. He has been looked upon as the leader of Unitarians all that time, and his prognostication of what in his judgment Christianity is to be in the future has been universally accepted by Unitarians all over the world as embodying for them the truth. It is not necessary to say that Jesus is presented by President Eliot simply as a man, and that the "religion of the future" which he puts before the world is a Christianity denuded of all those elements which have made it the Christianity of the church. Not only does it lack the virgin birth and physical resurrection, but also those doctrines of incarnation and atonement which have ever been regarded as vital to Christianity. Professor Bacon's summing up of President Eliot's position as set forth in an article in the *Harvard Theological Review* (October, 1909) is worth quoting (p. 38): "President Eliot's reconstruction presents the distinctive type of what has claimed for itself, and has sometimes been accorded, the honorable name of 'liberal' Christianity. To him the mystical doctrines of personal religion, the doctrines of incarnation, atonement, immortality, represent mainly 'pagan' accretion. To restore to Christianity its true message for our times we must trace it back (thinks President Eliot) to its 'Hebrew purity' in the ethical teachings of Jesus. As for what are termed 'the consolations of religion' they will be mainly found in '....a universal good will, under the influence of which men will do their duty, and at the same time promote their own happiness. The devotees of a religion of service will always be asking what they can contribute to the common good....The work of the world must be done, and the great question is, shall it be done happily or unhappily?' Much of it is to-day done unhappily. The new religion will contribute powerfully toward the reduction of this mass of unnecessary misery, and will do so chiefly by promoting good will among men."

This, then, is "liberal Chritianity," at least it is the "liberal Christianity" which the writer had in view and which plants itself on a Jesus who was purely human. Such a Jesus is a necessity for it. Hence the efforts which the Liberals have been making for the last hundred years and over to discover a historical Jesus. Three things are worthy of attention at this point. The first is that this Christianity which President Eliot predicts is to be the "religion of the future" is a distinct break with the Christianity of the church of the past and of the church of the present. In all ages Christianity has been regarded as the religion of redemption; but redemption is eliminated from this conception of it. Professor Bacon recognizes this when he says that it "goes more than half way to meet the Reformed Synagogue and the liberal Ethical Society." None of the great theologians of the past would have recognized this as

Christianity. Professor Bacon asks, "Can this really be the 'Gospel' in which there is not one word of what Paul describes as 'the ministry of reconciliation, committed unto us' as ambassadors for God, 'how that in Christ God was reconciling the world unto himself, not imputing unto men their trespasses?'" And if Paul would have failed to see in this "religion of the future" his Gospel, so we may be sure would the great fathers and theologians of the church have failed. To one and all Christianity was a redemptive scheme, and they would not have understood a religion which had no incarnation or atonement, and which presented itself to men merely as a system of ethics.

It is safe to say that no church of the present would accept President Eliot's summation of Christianity. Neither the Roman Catholic nor the Greek church could do so. The Anglican church in all lands, the various branches of the Presbyterian church throughout the world, the numerous Methodist bodies, all with one accord would have to repudiate this version of Christianity as not Christianity at all. They would doubtless, as does Professor Bacon, recognize "the nobility of the ethical ideal" involved in it; they would say with him that it is "good as far as it goes, but it does not touch bottom"—and that because it does not meet man's deepest need which is for redemption rather than for ethics. Professor Bacon admits that "it may rightly claim to reflect in large measure the teaching of Jesus"; but it has always been held that the teaching of Jesus so called does not contain the distinctive Christian Gospel, because that consists of something which Jesus *did* rather than what he is reputed to have *said*. And hence the teachers of the church have gone to the Epistles of Paul instead of to the Sermon on the Mount for Christianity's distinctive message.

Some words of Professor Royce, a distinguished member of the faculty of Harvard University of which President Eliot was the head, are worthy of attention in elucidation of this point. In an essay on "What is Vital in Christianity" he tells us: "What is vital in Christianity depends upon regarding the mission and the life of Christ as an organic part of a divine plan for the redemption and salvation of man. While the doctrine of Christ, as his sayings record this doctrine, is indeed an essential part of this mission, one cannot rightly understand, above all apply, the teachings of Christ, one cannot live out the Christian interpretation of life, unless one learns first to view the person of Christ in its true relation to God, and the work of Christ as an entirely unique revelation and expression of God's will. The work of Christ culminated in his death. Hence, as the historical church has always maintained, it is the cross of Christ that is the symbol of whatever is most vital about Christianity."

Nowhere, perhaps, is the issue involved in this matter so clearly set forth as in the following words of Professor Royce in this same essay. "The question is simply this: Is the Gospel which Christ preached, that is, the teaching recorded in the authentic sayings and parables, intelligible, acceptable, vital, in case you take it by itself? Or does Christianity lose its vitality in case you cannot give a true sense to those doctrines of the incarnation and the atonement which the traditional Christian world so long held and so deeply loved? And furthermore, can you, in the light of modern insight, give any longer a reasonable sense to the traditional doctrines of the atonement and the incarnation? In other words: Is Christianity essentially a religion of redemption in the sense in which tradition defined redemption? Or is Christianity simply that religion of the love of God and the love of man which the sayings and the parables so richly illustrate?" Professor Royce maintains that "the whole authority, such as it is, of the needs and religious experience of the church of Christian history stands on the traditional view that the essence of Christianity consists first, in the doctrine of the superhuman person and the redemptive work of Christ, and secondly in the interpretive life that rests upon this doctrine. The church early found, or at least felt, that it could not live at all without thus interpreting the person and work of Christ."

The second point that needs to be carefully noticed is that Professor Bacon does not accept the historicity of the alleged events on which the doctrines of incarnation and atonement have rested in the past. This comes out both in his *Hibbert* article and in the book under review. New Testament criticism under his able hands gives us "Jesus as teacher and leader of humanity toward the ideal of the brotherhood of the race under the fatherhood of God."[1] On the preceding page he implies that the historical criticism of the New Testament of which he is such an ornament reveals Jesus as "truly human." He claims to be as free as any one to discard legendary elements in Gospel story, such as the virgin birth or physical resurrection. He declares that he has no "prejudice whatever against recognition of the mythological element in the New Testament." He sets all these aside just as much as does President

[1] *Hibbert Journal,* Vol. IX, No. 4, page 75.

Eliot, but he does not follow President Eliot in reducing Christianity to a mere ethical system. It is to be presumed that he would agree with Professor Royce in regarding the "reduction of what is vital in Christianity to the so-called pure Gospel of Christ, as he preached it and as it is recorded in the body of the presumably authentic sayings and parables as profoundly unsatisfactory"; but he no more accepts the historicity of those alleged facts on which the redemptive element in Christianity has all along rested than does President Eliot. The redemptive element comes from the "transcendentalized Messianism of Peter and the Hellenistic incarnation doctrine of Paul." These are the moulds, so to speak, into which the preachers of the new religion put their thought of Jesus. To use Professor Bacon's own words, "We cannot conceive any other vehicle of thought or speech than myth through which the preachers of the new religion could give utterance to their undisciplined sense of the teleological significance of what they themselves had witnessed." In his *Making of the New Testament* (page 52) he says that the mystery-religions of paganism formed "the only mould for Christology." That is to say, there was no basis in history itself for the Christology of the New Testament and the church, that basis is found in the apostolic interpretation of Peter and Paul which makes these apostles the real founders of Christianity and not Jesus. This agrees with what Professor Bacon says in the opening of his *Story of St. Paul*: "Christianity as we know it is St. Paul's Christianity." Now this comes as near as can be to the doctrine which Professor Bacon criticised in his *Mythical Collapse of Historical Christianity.* The Messianism of Peter and the Hellenistic incarnation of Paul were subjective experiences of these two apostles. This is divided by the thinnest of thin lines from the doctrine in the two first articles, and contains really all the writer contended for. What has been looked upon as Christianity from the beginning until now does not rest upon facts of history, but upon subjective experiences. Jesus was a man only, but Peter and Paul interpreted him as God. His influence upon them was so great that they could express what they felt about him only by taking advantage of what the devotees of the mystery-religions said of Adonis and Attis and Osiris. This he calls "the golden background of dogma, Pauline and later, against which the historical figure of Jesus has been seen projected by those who transmit the portrait to us." It is not the portrait itself. It is the "apostolic gospel about Jesus, the Petrine and Pauline interpretation of the significance of his person, his experience, his fate."

The difference between him and President Eliot is that the latter "has no use for it [the gospel about Jesus] but to cast it as rubbish to the void." Professor Bacon's gospel is *about* Jesus, not what Jesus was himself. The New Testament critic is more concerned with ideas than with facts. "When he discriminates concrete fact and event from the contemporary interpretation which they received, it is the thought rather than the thing which concerns him....In this field, it is true, historical facts are not unimportant, because when properly sifted they fail to be classified and interpreted in accordance with modern experience by modern standards. But contemporary judgments of the significance of facts, inferences, convictions, faiths, doctrines, are more important." Professor Bacon thus separates himself from the liberalism which makes its watchword the cry, "Back to Jesus." He follows the pragmatists in that it is the worth of Jesus to the apostles and not Jesus himself which is the important thing. He enters a much-needed protest against the liberal Christian of the President Eliot type who "has but one standard of value, historicity." To throw away the mythical and legendary element which he finds in the New Testament is for him to cast its most precious portion into the sea. He tells us that what would be left would be "an admirably simple summary of human duty," for its "morality would be the law of love," and its "emotion would be of two kinds: First, trust in a Heavenly Father,.... second, loyalty to the historic Jesus as a sublimely consistent and heroic leader of the world into its ideal and ultimate social order." To this reconstructed Christianity he would not deny the name Christian, just because it "places the historic Jesus in a position of permanent supremacy." But it would not be the Christianity of the New Testament or of the church, for that "historically is a gospel *about* Jesus, originating with the resurrection, which was not a historical fact, but a psychological experience of primitive believers under Greek influences."

The cry "Back to Jesus" which has been the watchword of liberal Christianity—"Christianity as Christ preached it"—has "overleaped itself and fallen on the other side." In the most emphatic way Professor Bacon declares that "the Christian religion did not originate with the earthly life of Jesus. That is an idea which arose after the period of the apostles in the age of the Evangelists such as Mark. Our religion began with the manifestation of the

Son of God which was not a physical but a psychical experience. It began with the cross and resurrection, the doctrine about Jesus." There is little profit in contending about names. But from all this it appears that Professor Bacon agrees with the statement that liberal Christianity has collapsed in the sense that it is not Christianity at all, not Christianity as the New Testament presents it, not Christianity as it has been understood in all the ages of its history. It appears, therefore, that Professor Bacon admits all that the writer's two *Hibbert* articles contended for. The difference is unimportant. Both say that the liberal Christianity represented by President Eliot in his "Religion of the Future" has "collapsed." The proposition of the writer is that it has "collapsed" because it has not been able to find a historical Jesus; Professor Bacon's is that the historical Jesus whom he thinks criticism has discovered does not give us Christianity, for that is "the doctrine *about* Jesus, the interpretation given by primitive believers to the work of God effected by the spirit of Jesus. His death, his resurrection, inwardly experienced by these men as 'the power of God unto salvation'—these are the most important data in all the psychology of religion." Much opprobrium has been cast upon Professor Drews for speaking of the "Christ-myth," but Professor Bacon cites with approval a declaration of "a great scholar of our time, describing the redemption doctrine of the Pauline missionary preaching: 'This whole point of view is a myth from beginning to end, and cannot be termed anything else.... It is the story of a God who had descended from heaven.'"

It has been assumed that Professor Drews denied the doctrine of redemption because he spoke of the "Christ-myth"; with how much injustice the following quotation will show: "To think of the world's activity as God's activity; of mankind's development, filled with struggles and sufferings, as the story of a divine struggle and passion; of the world-process as the process of a God, who in each individual creature fights, suffers, conquers and dies, so that he may overcome the limitations of the finite in the religious consciousness of man and anticipate his future triumph over all the sufferings of the world—that is the real Christian doctrine of redemption."[2] Professor Bacon tells us that Paul's interpretation of the career of Jesus was what it was required to be in order "to fit the capacity of a pre-philosophic age." It was not therefore the truth, but a symbolic representation of the truth adapted to minds incapable

[2] *The Christ-Myth,* page 298.

of apprehending the truth in its pure philosophic form, a concession to immaturity. What was the redemption which Paul tried to set forth by using the phraseology of the mystery-religions of paganism? Was it the inward work of God effected through the spirit of Jesus only in the minds of the primitive disciples, or was it the world-process of redemption of which Professor Drews speaks? Suppose that what the disciples experienced was a part of this world-process. Which, then, would be the most comprehensive idea of redemption? The historicity of Jesus cannot be necessary to the experience of redemption, for it is an experience which has been felt all over the world. The Roman poet Ovid, speaking of the god Æsculapius, sings:

"Hail, great physician of the world! All hail!
Hail, mighty infant! who in years to come
Shalt heal the nations and defraud the tomb.
Thy daring art shall animate the dead,
And draw the thunder on thy guilty head.
Then shalt thou die; but from thy dark abode
Shalt rise victorious, and be twice a god."

The rising of Adonis from the tomb was celebrated in words which have been versified as follows:

"Trust, ye saints, your God restored,
Trust ye in your risen Lord;
For the pains which he endured
Our salvation have procured."

This is the mould, according to Professor Bacon, into which Paul put his experience of Jesus, but is the experience which Paul and Peter and the rest had the only genuine experience? Suppose we say that both alike are symbolic representations to set forth the cosmic story of the divine struggle and passion, would we not have a grander idea of redemption than that which Professor Bacon stands for? He says in condemnation of President Eliot's repudiation of Peter's Messianism and Paul's doctrine of incarnation that "the very last thing the true critic and historian of religion will do with 'mythical' interpretations of genuine experience is to throw them away." May not the experience described by Ovid and in these lines about Adonis—words which might be sung in any Christian church to-day—express a genuine experience expressed as Paul did his experience in unphilosophic form? No one claims that Æsculapius or Adonis was a historical person, but that does not invalidate the experience any more than Paul's use of the mystery phraseology invalidated his experience. We are thus led to the crucial question of this whole discussion: Is the historicity of Jesus necessary to the genuineness of Paul's experience?

This is the third question that needs careful attention. I offer the following remarks: First, I find nowhere in this book or in any of Professor Bacon's writings any attempt even to prove the historicity of Jesus. He takes it for granted without an atom of proof. For example, on page 97 of this book he says that "Christianity prevailed because of its more solid basis of historic fact." How does he know that? The assumption is that what succeeds in our world must be based on historic fact. Now there is not a scrap of evidence for this proposition. It is pure assumption. The whole history of the world disproves it. Have we not all learned long ago that the world is led on from stage to stage of progress and knowledge "through illusion to the truth"? Suppose that we grant that Christianity would never have succeeded but for the belief in a historical Jesus, that does not prove that the historicity is a fact. It may, if we understand the times properly, prove the opposite. What if it were another case of concession to immaturity? Could Christianity have conquered the rude tribes that overran the fair fields of the old world, the Huns and Goths and Vandals from the North, had it been presented to them in the form that would satisfy Professor Bacon? Suppose that the story of a historic Jesus arose gradually as a higher type of religion declined, and prevailed just because it was a lower type. The question is, what was the earliest form of the faith? In the middle and latter part of the second century we have a creed setting forth the substance of the faith as a series of alleged historic facts, and we find great churchmen like Tertullian and Irenaeus planting themselves upon that creed and defending it against all comers. This was about the time when the canonical Gospels and Acts were taking shape and slowly gaining authority over the mind of the age. But there were other gospels and acts among the people. When we go back to the second century we do not find one church only, but the growing Catholic or central church in violent conflict with churches or communities which it looked upon as heretical. These heretical communities had their gospels and acts which were circulated among the people or members of these heretical communities. The Catholic or central church triumphed over these communities, and our canonical Gospels and Acts are the marks of the triumph. The

Romanist is right in his claim that the church gave the scriptures to the people in the sense that the canon of scripture was fixed by the church; that is to say, the question whether such and such books were to be admitted to, or excluded from, the canon was determined by the church. We should make a mistake if we came to the conclusion that it was always intrinsic merit that decided the question. To be convinced on this point one has only to read the reasons why there are only four Gospels given by Irenaeus himself in his work against "Heresies."

It is always foolish to find fault with the course of history, and no doubt the triumph of the Catholic or general church and the consequent triumph of the canonical scriptures served some good providential purpose. At the same time it is often the duty of after ages to go back and pick up something of value that has been left behind in the onward march of events. In the Gospels and Acts of these heretical communities we have an instance of this. Besides the four canonical Gospels of Matthew, Mark, Luke and John, there are the apocryphal Gospels according to the Egyptians, according to the Hebrews, according to Peter and others; and besides the canonical Acts there are the Acts of John, the Acts of Thomas, the Acts of Peter, the Acts of Paul, and others; and these are only parts that have come down to us of what was once a large literature.

The older view of the controversy of the second century is that it was over an elaborate attempt to alter the Christian faith as it had been handed down in the church from the beginning; that the Christian faith was from the first a body of historical facts such as we have in the Old Roman Symbol and the Apostles' Creed, just as it was the older view of Gnosticism that it was an outgrowth of Christianity, a heresy which gradually arose to trouble the church. It is just at this point that we are obliged to suspend our judgment, if not to reverse it altogether, and to regard the summarizing of the faith on the part of the general or Catholic church as the innovation upon an older form of the faith. The heretical Gospels and Acts, therefore, would have to be regarded as the oldest product of the Christian movement in the sense that they set forth the original form of the faith, and that the summary of alleged historical facts by Tertullian and Irenaeus, culminating in the Old Roman Symbol and finally in the Apostles' Creed, is a later heresy.

If we read the Old Roman Symbol and the Apostles' Creed in the light of these heretical Gospels and Acts, we shall discover the meaning of their various clauses, for we are walking over the grave of a buried controversy; every clause is directed against what was regarded as an innovating error, but was in reality the older view. It was the Old Roman Symbol and Apostles' Creed which were innovations; it was the view of the Gnostics represented by Marcion which was the conservative view. It has been the opinion of scholars up to recent times that the Old Roman Symbol "was already in use in Rome when he came there in 140 A. D., and joined the Catholic church";[3] but this scholar shows that all the passages which have been relied upon to bear out such an opinion are seen "not to bear the interpretation put upon them."[4] "There is no evidence in them nor is there evidence anywhere that Marcion knew and accepted the Old Roman Symbol." And one may add there is no evidence that this rule of faith was old and well known. It was a new thing, and was just coming into recognition. It had not existed from the beginning. The same scholar shows that neither Justin Martyr nor any of the other apologists of the day knew anything of the Old Roman Symbol as a rule of faith. There is evidence that the notion that the faith consists of certain historical facts is growing, but there is no evidence that it had reached the stage of a fixed creed such as it very soon became. There is mention in Justin of the birth, crucifixion, death, resurrection and ascension as historical facts. There is mention also of Pontius Pilate under whom the crucifixion took place. That is to say, the idea that Christianity consisted of a series of historical facts had evidently become fixed in the mind of the church by the time of Justin Martyr, but when we go back to Ignatius in the first quarter of the second century, while we find him setting forth a strictly historical interpretation of the Gospel, at the same time he does it as though he was stating something new, not what was old and well established. He "protests too much" for one who stands for the old truth. The Old Roman Symbol and the Apostles' Creed were evidently an expansion of an early baptismal formula which was simply "Into the name of the Lord Jesus," or "Into Jesus Christ." This was sufficient for the Jews as their God was the God of the Christians as well, which is evidence that the name "Jesus" was a name for a divine being, and not of a human historical person. When the heathen or Gentiles became Christians it was necessary to add the name "God," as their God was not the God of the Chris-

[3] McGiffert's *Apostles' Creed,* page 58.

[4] *Ibid.*, page 68.

tians, and the word "spirit" would naturally follow. The baptismal formula would thus be, "Into God and Jesus Christ and Holy Spirit."

If there is one thing that has been proved by recent scholarship it is that the Gnostics were the first Christians. The various clauses of the Old Roman Symbol and of the Apostles' Creed were added as the idea of an historical interpretation of the Gospel arose. They were not added to guard against the heresies of the day, but to defend an innovation. The Apostles' Creed alleges seven historical facts about Jesus Christ the son of the Creator, his birth, crucifixion, burial, resurrection, ascension, session at the right of God, and second coming, and all the seven emphasize the reality of the life of Jesus as against the older view. The truth is that the Old Roman Symbol and the Apostles' Creed are evidence that the church had lost the faculty of spiritual vision and had become a prey to the besetting sin of all ecclesiasticisms—the worship of the letter.

What confirms us in all this is the fact that when we go back to the first century we find that there were other communities or churches besides those which were organized around the tradition of a historical Jesus. The Epistles of Paul are evidences of this fact. It is impossible to believe that the churches or communities to whom Paul preached his view of a spiritual Christ or Messiah revealed to him by his own ecstatic experiences or visions were derived from the church of Jerusalem of which Peter and James and John were the founders and which was organized around the story of a historic Jesus. Paul was at variance with Peter and James and John whom he called "pillar apostles" not in a very complimentary way. In the letters of Paul we are introduced to communities or churches entirely different from those which took the synoptic Gospels as their inspiration and guides.

Paul does not follow the synoptic tradition at all; he follows a Christ of his own and speaks of his own gospel. To Paul the views of the "pillar apostles" seemed decidedly materialistic. It is indeed difficult to believe that there was any such record of the life and teaching of Jesus in existence as the synoptic Gospels contain in the possession of the church at Jerusalem; for with an authority such a record would imply, how could Paul have had any chance of successfully withstanding the "pillar apostles," or of persuading the communities or churches formed by them to leave them and follow him? The immense probability is that both "Jesus" and "Christ" were divine names before the Christian era, that both were equally unhistorical, and that they were brought together as denoting a single being by the movement that afterwards became historical Christianity. Whether this be so or not, Paul's Epistles bear witness to the existence of churches or communities which had been long in existence when Paul visited them. Paul's words and phrases are the same as those in use in these communities or churches; they knew what he was speaking about, so that he did not need to define his terms. Paul had no affinity with churches based upon the tradition of a historical Jesus such as we have in the synoptic Gospels; but he has a very close affinity with those other churches or communities whose members believed in a mystic Christ and whose technical terms were all borrowed from Gnosticism which recent research has proved to be pre-Christian.

Paul was not converted to belief in a historical Jesus. He was changed from being an official persecutor of the Messianic sects to a preacher of a mystic Christ or spiritual Messiah, the conception of which, he declares, he did not derive from man; that is to say, the Christ he preached was born of his own immediate experience and revelation. He got a chance of a hearing for his spiritual gospel because it was on a level with the belief in Jesus. If one had been historical and the other not, he would have been as one beating the air. What emerges clear as daylight is that the churches or communities he founded, as well as those he found already established when going on his missionary journeys, were not communities which believed in a historical Jesus; they were of a mystical nature resembling the Therapeutae of whom Philo tells us in his "On the Contemplative Life"—people devoted to the cultivation of the life of contemplation and of union with God. It is not an unlikely supposition that it was with some one of those communities that Paul spent his three years after his conversion, and that it was the light and inspiration he received from that source which emboldened him to be the apostle he afterwards became. It is here doubtless that we are to find the oldest form of the Christian faith. What we have in the synoptic Gospels is a teaching decidedly lower in spiritual insight and tone than that current in the mystical sects to which Paul ministered. They believed in a Saviour who was a heavenly being; belief in the Logos was a fundamental part of their creed; and if there was a historical Jesus at all, the great probability is that he was a member of one of the mystic sects of which the age was full. It is extremely unlikely that the historical Jesus shared the ignorant views of the people as the synoptic Gospels represent him as doing. The probability is that in these representations of the synoptic Gospels we have just that kind of misunderstanding which always takes place when a mystical teacher attempts to communicate truth to people on a lower level of life and experience. The supreme misunderstanding was the identification of the historical Jesus with the mystical Christ, the Logos. The real Saviour of men, as the real Jesus would doubtless have been the first to declare, is not a historical person, but a divine being who dwells in the soul as Paul teaches. This belief in a mystic Christ, in a heavenly being, in a divine Logos, long antedated the beginning of our era, both in Jewry and among the Greeks.

Now just as those mystic sects of the first century and before, represented by Paul, embodied a more spiritual conception of religion and of life than that embodied in the synoptic Gospels, so the communities or churches of the second century represented a phase of Christianity that was different from, and opposed to, that taught by the growing and triumphant Catholic church. And it is to be noticed further that this form of Christianity was the original one and that the Christianity of the Catholic church was a development of that. This original form of Christianity is known as Gnosticism. All the apocryphal Gospels and Acts are saturated with Gnosticism. Here is where recent investigations into the genesis and development of Gnosticism help us greatly to discover the first form of the Christian faith. Instead of Gnosticism being an outgrowth of Christianity as has long been supposed—a heresy which was persecuted and finally expelled out of existence—the various forms of Gnosticism, Jewish and Christian, of the early centuries, were only particular cases within a movement that included much more. The apocryphal Gospels and Acts tell us what Gnosticism was much better than the school dogmas of Basilides and Valentinus which we know only through the reports of their ecclesiastical enemies, because they formed the main means of Gnostic public propaganda. There was a very wide circulation of such Gospels and Acts in the second century. They are deeply spiritual in their meaning though the outward form was often fantastic and grotesque enough. But we must remember that it is only to the modern mind that they seem fantastic and grotesque. They were not so to the men of the second century; to every shade of mind of that age they were equally and entirely credible. And it was not the mythical and legendary element that offended the orthodox party of the day; it was the inner spiritual teaching, and that they assailed with misrepresentation, and tried to overwhelm with ridicule. It is just to say that we of this age would be repelled by the marvelous nature of the stories they relate. The apocryphal Gospels and Acts which embody the inner spiritual teachings of those Gnostics read to us like wild romances, but to them they symbolized actual occurrences of the inner life, facts of direct spiritual consciousness. The teaching is for those who knew the nature of the inner life by direct experience; for all others they were foolishness. We have the principle stated by Paul in his letter to the Corinthians: "The natural man perceiveth not the things of the spirit of God, for they are foolishness unto him; neither can he know them, for they are spiritually discerned."

It has always been a mystery how such wild imaginings and learned subtleties as the doctrines of the Gnostics seem to be (as represented by the orthodox Church Fathers) could make any deep impression on the minds of men of that age or indeed of any age. The mystery is explained when we turn our attention to the popular literature of the movement as embodied in the apocryphal Gospels and Acts of the second century; and when, especially, we are able to look below the surface and discern the inner spiritual meaning of the narratives. They were so popular in the second century that they could not be disposed of by ridicule simply, and the orthodox Church Fathers had to have recourse to other means to meet them. It is because of this fact that we have these apocryphal Gospels and Acts at all. The orthodox Church Fathers boldly adopted the most popular narratives from the heretical books, and after carefully eliminating what they deemed the "poison of false doctrine" replaced them in this purified form in the hands of the people. Fortunately for us this purification has not been complete, and some of the "poison" has been preserved. Many things of great beauty are found in these Gospels and Acts amid much that seems fantastic and grotesque. But, as I have said, they are so because we do not possess the key that will open up the meaning. This key is found in the man-mystery, the man-myth, or man-doctrine, which was central in all the mystery institutions of antiquity.

Briefly put, it is the story of the descent of man from his heavenly home and his return to that state of glory after having mastered the powers of the world. There is nothing so ancient as this doctrine; it is lost in the mists of antiquity, and in the centuries immediately preceding the beginning of our era it was a well-developed doctrine in the whole Graeco-Roman world. It was the jealously guarded secret of every mystery institution of antiquity. The whole ancient world was honeycombed with these mystery institutions. They were practically universal, being found in Chaldea, Phenicia, Palestine, Egypt, Phrygia and Greece; and in every one of them the central doctrine was this myth or mystery of man. In Plato, whose writings were the Bible of the Greeks, we have allegory upon allegory describing the soul of man in his heavenly home. The state of man in this world these Gnostics called a state of death. We have a hint of this in Paul's letter to the Colossians where he describes man as "dead" and his "life as hid with Christ in God" (Col. iii. 3). He means that the true life of man is buried in matter and awaits resurrection, which does not mean resuscitation of a dead body, but the awakening of the spirit of man into consciousness of its divine life. In the Epistle to the Ephesians the apostle quotes a part of a Gnostic hymn: "Awake thou that sleepest, and arise from the dead, and the Christ shall shine upon thee," and this does not mean a call upon dead bodies to come out of graves, which would be absurd, but a call upon the spirit to awaken out of its state of unconsciousness and realize its true life. With the Gnostics of the apocryphal Gospels and Acts the death of Jesus was the symbol of a profound experience which the individual spirit must pass through on its upward journey as a condition of its further advancement. The resurrection of Jesus they similarly looked upon as a symbol of the new birth of illumination of the spirit, its coming to life from its previous death state. The instruction given in the apocryphal Gospels and Acts, as well as in many Gnostic treatises, such as *Pistis Sophia,* is represented as having been given by Jesus to his disciples after his resurrection, which means that the truth taught is what the soul sees in its state of illuminated consciousness. The germ of the Christ life, the spark of divinity which the poet Browning says "disturbs our clod," the image of God all men bear, the light which every man brings with him into the world, must descend into matter; the "dead" with the Gnostic writers and with Paul are those in whom the consciousness of the divine has not been awakened. Resurrection is the awakening of this germ to life. This is the real resurrection of which the historicized rising from the dead of the body of Jesus the canonical Gospels speak of is a symbol. The story of the descent of the soul into matter, its gradual conquest of matter, its awakening to its true life, and its return to its former state having mastered the powers of the world is the myth of man found in all the ancient mysteries. It is the same story which the New Testament tells in the form of a symbolic life.

Now from a human point of view it was necessary that such a form of Christianity should not become the Christianity of the church. For very soon came the fall of the Western Empire and the inrush of the barbarians from the north. Very soon a wild sea of savage tribes surged and heaved where once the cultured fields of the Old World had been. It was impossible that the strong virile minds of Goth, Hun, and Vandal could comprehend the religion that satisfied these philosophers of the East. A cruder faith was needed and a cruder faith became the faith of the Catholic church. The purer faith became a heresy and was bitterly opposed by the dominant church. As the Catholic church grew in power it grew too in priestly claim and in arrogance. Even as early as the latter part of the second century it had become a visible hierarchy. We find Irenaeus uttering the famous dictum that where the church is —and even as early as his day the church was a visible organization with its clergy and sacraments—there is the spirit of God, and where the spirit of God is there is the church.

A proud, arrogant, ambitious church in the course of its history has been guilty of many crimes, but perhaps the blackest record its history can show is its persecution of these Gnostics. These people had a long ancestry. "The method of history," says Prof. G. P. Fisher of Yale, "is never magical. In proportion to the magnitude of the event are the length of time and the variety of agencies which are employed in producing it." Professor Fisher applies this remark to the Reformation of the sixteenth century, showing that "never was a historical criticism more elaborately prepared for, and this through a train of causes which reach back into the remote past." But the words apply specially to the advent of Christianity; for as a matter of fact Christianity was in the womb of the pagan world for centuries. As Gnosticism was the child of paganism, so Christianity was the child of Gnosticism. The words of St. Augustine are strictly true. "The very thing which now is called the Christian religion existed among the ancients, nor was it absent in the beginning of the human race before Christ came in the flesh, since when the true religion which already existed began to be called Christian." In the nicknames which the heresy hunters of the time hurled at the Gnostics we have a clue to the question whence they derived their teaching. The orthodox Church Fathers were neither sparing nor nice in the names they applied to the Gnostic heretics—devils, snakes, hounds, wolves, vipers, and first-born of Satan. These names of course do not give us much light except upon those who used them; but when less thoroughly aroused with theological passion, and consequently in less bitter mood, they said that the Gnostics derived their teaching from Pythagoras and Plato and Heraclitus and Cleanthes, and from the mystery institutions of Greece, Egypt and the East generally. This was the truth, but instead of being a reproach it was their glory. This meant that the teaching was the best in the religious teaching of the ancient world. Instead of coming into a world of universal darkness with its one divine light of truth, Christianity came from the same source as Gnosticism. In the Epistles of Paul we have echoes of what was taught in Egypt and Greece two or three hundred years before. There is nothing of which we are so sure as the existence of a well-developed and well-defined doctrine in the Hellenistic world of the first centuries before Christ, of the descent of man from the heavenly or archetypal man, and of his return to pristine glory with the experience he has gathered from his contact with, and conquest of, the world of matter and form. This Paul calls the "mystery" of Christ, the mystery hid from ages and generations, but now made manifest.

The story of a Christ who was the Saviour of the world, the divine man who was the representative of a great spiritual process, the mediator between God and men, the ideal man who was overcome in his struggles for human salvation but conquered in being overcome, is the story which the world has repeated to itself over and over again. It is not original with the New Testament, every feature of it was familiar to those who were initiated into the mysteries. This should be enough to show us that we are not in the presence of literal fact. There is no doubt that the crucifixion as Paul conceived it had cosmic significance—it is not merely the death of a martyr. The center and soul of the gnosis of the ancient world was the Cross. The technical phrase for it among the Gnostics is one used by Paul, the "cross the power of God." Wherever the gnosis had established itself the kernel was the cross. It is obvious that in these places it could not mean the death of Jesus for that was a local happening. It meant the great world-passion, the sacrifice of God in the creation, Deity laying down his life in the universe of matter and form. And to Paul the cross was the symbol of this heart-moving conception.

The interpretation of Paul's determination not to know anything among men save Jesus Christ and him crucified that makes him mean to refer to a series of historic facts eviscerates it of all real content. In the creation was the Calvary of Deity. The cross is thus the background plan of the universe. To know the cross from this higher standpoint is to know all there is to know; there is nothing beyond this. The cross was the symbol of a profound mystery which opened up the heart of Deity himself to the gaze of the world. The divine sufferer was God himself, who in creating the universe sacrificed himself for it. The cross, therefore, represents the greatest of all sacrifices, not something that happened once and once for all, but something that is eternal and timeless—the sacrifice of God in and for his own creation that could not be unless he poured his own life into it and restricted himself within the forms of matter. "Confessedly great is the mystery of godliness." Unthinkable in its magnitude is this sacrifice, for it means nothing less than the identification of the infinite with the finite in its lowest forms. Here is the profoundest mystery open to human contemplation to speak of which is possible only in forms of symbol and parable. The literal truth is too vast, too mysterious, too sublime, to be made known to human comprehension. It is the mystery before which angels, we are told, veil their faces; and to gain a single glimpse of it one may well surrender all other knowledge and determine, as Paul did, to know nothing else. Here is the oldest form of the Christian faith. The story of Jesus is the parable of this infinitely larger truth. It is the symbol of the Lamb slain from the foundation of the world, that is, prior to human history, the emblem of divine body and blood voluntarily sacrificed in outward physical nature and entombed in the lower consciousness of man. It was the claim of the second century Gnostics that Christianity was none other than the consummation of the inner doctrine of the mystery institutions of all the nations; and it is this interpretation of the Gospel story which is set forth in the apocryphal Gospels and Acts. The end of them all was the revelation of the mystery of man which is none other than the mystery of Christ.

DUNDEE, SCOTLAND. K. C. ANDERSON.

HAMILTON'S HODOGRAPH.

In Mach's *Mechanics* the space devoted to the hodograph of Sir William Rowan Hamilton is barely a page, half of which is taken up by the diagram; the diagram, too, is not drawn strictly according to the construction of Hamilton, but according to the usual manner of present-day text-books. This seems to me to be something of an injustice to an exceedingly brilliant piece of work; for from it and Hamilton's theorem of the isochronism of the circular hodograph can be deduced the more important properties of motion in orbits described to a center of force according to the Newtonian law, Lambert's theorem for the area of an elliptic sector in terms of the bounding *radii vectores* and the chord of the sector, and Euler's corresponding expression for the area of a parabolic sector. The proofs are exceedingly simple and demand very little knowledge of the properties of conics, and no calculus or coordinate geometry at all. For other interesting and elegant applications of the hodograph, reference should be made to Tait's *Quaternions* and papers in the *Proc. R. S. E.*, and to Tait and Steele's *Dynamics of a Particle*. But the matter which follows should, I think, be sufficient to corroborate the opinion expressed above.

I. The first use of the curve is ascribed to Bradley,[1] and it is probably his definition that is generally given in elementary text-books, where its only use is to obtain the acceleration towards the center of a particle moving in a circle with uniform speed.

Def. 1. If a point be in motion with any velocity in any orbit, and if at any instant a line be drawn from a fixed point representing on some chosen scale the velocity of the point at the instant in magnitude and direction, the locus of its end is the "hodograph" of the motion.

Not even in the particular case of motion in a circle does this, the usual definition, so readily demonstrate the connection between the hodograph and the orbit as the definition originally given by Hamilton in a paper communicated to the Royal Irish Academy in 1846,[2] which is as follows:

Def. 2. "If, in an orbit *round a center of force*, there be taken on the perpendicular from the center on the tangent at each point a length equal to the velocity at that point of the orbit, the extremities of these lengths will trace out the hodograph."

Note. The use of the word "equal" does not introduce any difficulty, unless we attempt to verify the formulas obtained by reference to the theory of dimensional units. It is to be noted that

[1] Sir Robert Ball, Article on "Gravitation," *Encyc. Brit.*

[2] *Proc. Roy. Ir. Acad.*, 1847.

the definition of Hamilton is more specialized than the other, referring only to central orbits.

II. Newton showed that for any central force the areas swept out by the radius vector are proportional to the times.[3] The following is a simple proof of this theorem.

If O is the center of force, and P, Q, R points on the orbit separated by *very small unit intervals* of time, and MQN, PM, RN are drawn perpendicular to OQ, MQ, QN respectively; then MQ, QN measure the velocities transverse to OQ, before and after the position Q.

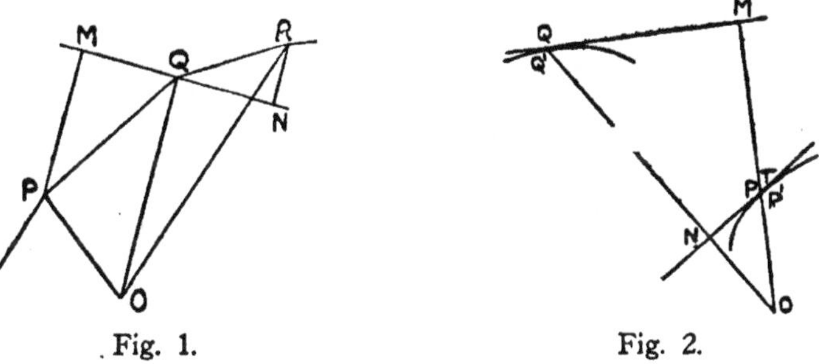

Fig. 1. Fig. 2.

Since the force is central, MQ = QN,

$$\therefore \triangle \mathrm{OPQ} = \triangle \mathrm{OQR};$$

and hence the proposition follows immediately.

It follows from Newton's theorem that, if the rate at which the area is swept out is denoted by $\frac{1}{2}h$, and the perpendicular from O on the tangent at P by p, then $pv = h$.

Hence, in Fig. 2, ON.OQ = h, and Q is the image of N in a circle whose radius is $\sqrt{h}$; also, if P′, Q′ are near points to P, Q, and the tangents at P, P′ meet in T, then Q, Q′ are the poles of two lines passing through T, and therefore QQ′ is the polar of T. That is, the tangent at Q is the polar of P.

The hodograph is therefore the polar reciprocal of the orbit.

It is also evident that OM = h/OP; or, in other words, the product of the length of the perpendicular from the center on the tangent to the hodograph and the length of the corresponding radius vector of the orbit is constant (= h).

Again, since the tangent at Q is the direction of the velocity of Q in the hodograph, this velocity is perpendicular to the radius

[3] Newton, *Principia*, Book I, Prop. 1.

vector. The hodograph given by the usual text-book definition is therefore identical with that given by Hamilton's definition, when turned through a right angle.

Further, since OQ, OQ′ represent the velocities at P, P′ turned through a right angle, it follows that QQ′ represents the change of velocity between P and P′ when turned through a right angle. Hence the radial acceleration of P is measured by the velocity of Q in the hodograph.

IV. The angle between the normals at QQ′ is equal to the angle between the radii OP, OP′.

Hence in Fig. 3 we have

$$QQ'/\rho = PN/r = 2\triangle OPP'/r^2;$$

and if the acceleration in the orbit is denoted by f, then

$$f/\rho = h/r^2.$$

This formula for the radius of curvature of the hodograph solves immediately the case

$$f \propto 1/r^2.$$

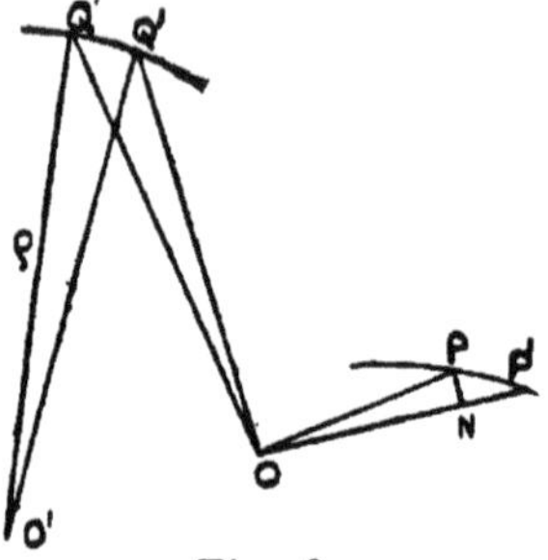

Fig. 3.

For, if $f \propto 1/r^2$, ρ is constant, and the hodograph is therefore a circle, and its polar reciprocal is a conic section with the pole as a focus; conversely, if the orbit is conic, with a center of force at a focus, the polar reciprocal is a circle, ρ is constant, and the law of force is $f \propto 1/r^2$.

The feet of the perpendiculars from the focus to the tangents to the orbit lie on the auxiliary circle (the tangent at the vertex in the case of the parabola). Hence the hodograph is an inverse of the auxiliary circle or the tangent at the vertex in the case of the parabola. It follows that the focus is within, on, or without the hodograph, according as the orbit is an ellipse, parabola, or hyperbola.

On account of the fact that the hodograph of an orbit described under the Newtonian law, $f \propto 1/r^2$, is a circle, Hamilton designated the law as the "Law of the Circular Hodograph."

V. If the law is $f = \mu/r^2$, the diameter of the hodograph is easily seen to be $2\mu/h$. Also, the diameter through O of the hodograph corresponds to the diameter aa' of the orbit and is similarly divided at O.

In Fig. 4, let A, B, A′, B′ correspond with the tangents at a, b, a', b', and therefore OA, OB, OA′, OB′ represent the velocities at the points a, b, a', b'.

Now, $aa' = Oa + Oa' = h(1/OA + 1/OA') = h.AA'/OA.OA'$.

If, then $aa' = 2a$, we have $a = h\rho/OB^2$; i. e., $OB^2 = h\rho/a = \mu/a$.

Therefore, the velocity at the end of the minor axis of the eclipse

$$= \sqrt{\mu/a}.$$

The velocity at any point of the orbit is now at once obtainable.

CASE I. When O is within the hodograph, as in Fig. 5.

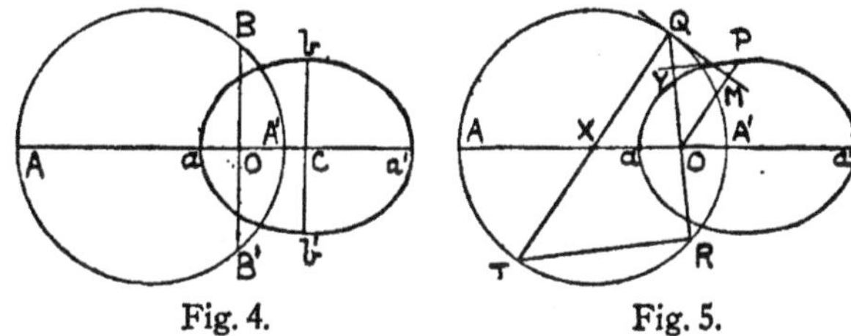

Fig. 4. Fig. 5.

If QO and QX meet the hodograph a second time in R and T, the triangles OQM, QTR are similar;

$$QT : OQ = QR : OM,$$

$$\therefore 2\rho . QM = OQ.QR = OQ^2 + QO.OR = OQ^2 + AO.OA';$$

$$\therefore OQ^2 = 2\rho h/r - \rho h/a \qquad \text{(from § IV)}$$

$$\text{i. e., } V^2 = \mu(2/r - 1/a).$$

CASE II. When O is on the hodograph, $V^2 = 2\mu/r$.

Case III. When O is without, $V^2 = \mu(2/r + 1/a)$.

VI. A most remarkable theorem connected with the hodograph was communicated to the Royal Irish Academy in March, 1847, without demonstration,[4] by Hamilton; he however furnished a proof by quaternions in 1853.[5] The following simple geometrical proof arises from hints given by Hamilton's proof.[6]

THEOREM. "If two circular hodographs, which have a common chord passing or tending through a common center of force, be both cut at right angles by a third circle, the times of hodographically describing the intercepted arcs will be equal."

[4] Cayley's report to the Brit. Assoc., 1862.

[5] Hamilton, *Lectures on Quaternions*, 1853.

[6] Professor Blyth, Article on "Hodograph" in *Encyc. Brit.*

If ρ is the radius of the hodographic circle in Fig. 6, and the law of force is $f=\mu/r^2$, then, by § IV, we have

$$\rho h = fr^2 = \mu \text{ (a constant)};$$

also, by § III, we have $r.\text{OM} = h$, and therefore

$$t = \text{PQ}/f = \mu.\text{PQ}/\rho^2.\text{OM}^2.$$

Now the angles PXQ, RVR′ are equal and small,
$\therefore \text{PQ} = \rho.\sin \text{RVR}' = \rho.\text{RR}'.\sin \text{VRR}'/\text{VR}' = \rho.\text{RR}'.\text{OM}/\text{OR.PR}$ ultimately; and, from the similar triangles, XPL, ROM,

$$\rho.\text{OM} = \text{OR.PL};$$

$$t = \mu.\text{RR}'/\text{OR}^2.\text{PL.PR} = \lambda/\text{PL}.$$

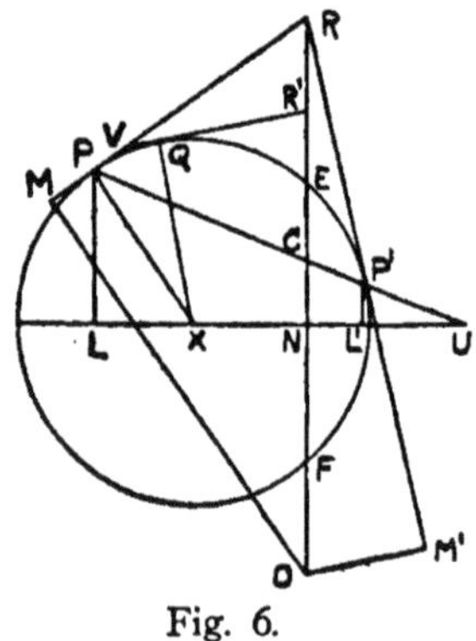

Fig. 6.

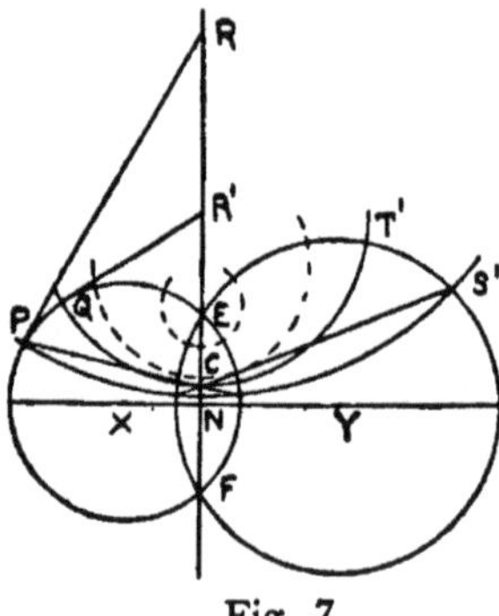

Fig. 7.

Similarly, for the description of the arc P′Q′, we have $t = \lambda/\text{P}'\text{Q}'$,

$$t + t' = \lambda(1/\text{PL} + 1/\text{P}'\text{L}') = 2\lambda/\text{CN}.$$

But any two circles, intersecting in EF, are cut orthogonally by a system of circles having their centers on EF produced in either direction. If we start with the orthogonal PSP′S′ in Fig. 7, C is the radical center of the three circles whose centers are R, X, Y; and hence, since the times of describing arc PQ + arc P′Q′ and arc ST + arc S′T′ are each equal to $2\lambda/\text{CN}$, these times are equal. Therefore, by "filling up" the arcs PP′, SS′ with a system of orthogonals, it follows that the times of description of the whole arcs PP′ and SS′ are equal.

VII. Let us consider the whole system of coaxal circles passing through E and F, and their corresponding orbits.

If the diameters of the hodographs passing through O are drawn, the products of the segments into which they are divided at O are respectively equal to μ/a_1, μ/a_2, μ/a_3, ..., where a_1, a_2, a_3, ...are the semi-major axes of the orbits, when O does not coincide with either E or F. Hence, since O is on the radical axis of the system, it follows that the major axes are all equal.

If O coincides with E or F, and $4a$ is the latus-rectum of one of the parabolic orbits, $2p.a=h$, or $a=h^2/2\mu$.

Again, any one of the hodographs can be completely traced out by a set of orthogonal circles whose centers traverse the whole of the radical axis except the part EF intercepted within the hodographs. Therefore, by Hamilton's theorem, the periodic times are all equal, for each separate position of the point O.

Further, if the orbits are supposed to have their major axes all in one straight line, so that O is the middle point of EF, one of the orbits is the circle of radius a, which also passes through the ends of the minor axes of all the orbits. The radius of its hodograph is equal to the velocity at the end of a minor axis of the general orbit of the system, and is equal to $\sqrt{\mu/a}$. Also, the velocity in this hodograph is equal to the acceleration in the circular orbit, i. e., is equal to μ/a^2. Therefore, we have

$$\text{Periodic Time} = T = 2\pi\sqrt{\mu/a} \div \mu/a^2 = 2\pi\sqrt{a^3/\mu},$$

for the whole system of orbits.

VIII. Hamilton pointed out that his theorem of isochronism was the same as Lambert's theorem. This is not generally taken to mean the detailed elliptic quadrature theorem as given in Williamson's *Calculus* and elsewhere, but the central force theorem thus enunciated:

In elliptic orbits of equal major axes, described in the same periodic time, under the action of a central force to a focus, the times of describing any sectors are the same, if the chords of the sectors and also the sum of the bounding radii vectores are the same.

A geometrical proof of the theorem in this form was given by H. R. Droop,[7] who pointed out that Hamilton had not, to his knowledge, previously published any demonstration of it; a short analytical proof of Hamilton's theorem is to be found in Tait and Steele's *Dynamics of a Particle,* with the remark, "It will readily be seen that this is in substance the same as Lambert's theorem." On the other hand, Cayley gave an analytical proof of Hamilton's theorem by assuming that of Lambert.[8]

[7] *Quart. Journ. Math.*, Vol. I, pp. 374-378.

[8] *Phil. Mag.*, 1857, pp. 427-430.

The following simple demonstration is practically the same as that of Droop, with the slight improvement that the connection, with lines in the hodograph, of the sum of the *radii vectores* and of the chord of the sector is plainly shown.

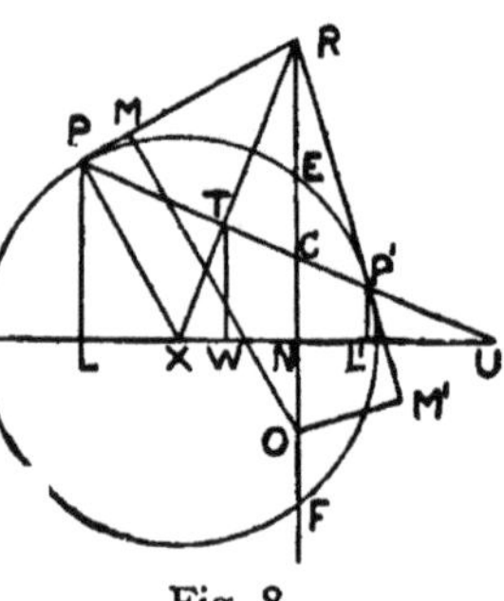

Fig. 8.

In Fig. 8, since the triangles XPL, ROM are similar, as are also XP′L′, ROM′,

$$\therefore r+r' = h/\mathrm{OM} + h/\mathrm{OM}',$$
$$= \rho h(1/\mathrm{PL} + 1/\mathrm{P'L'})/\mathrm{OR},$$
$$= 2\mu/\mathrm{OR.CN};$$

hence $r+r'$ is constant.

Again, if δ is the chord, p the perpendicular on it from the focus, and θ the angle between the radii in the orbit which is equal to the angle at the center of the hodograph, then, since R is the pole of the chord, $p.\mathrm{OR}=h$;

$$\therefore \delta = rr' \sin\theta/p = h\mathrm{OR}\sin\theta/\mathrm{OM.OM'} = \mu\rho\sin\theta/\mathrm{OR.PL.P'L'}.$$

$$\text{But } \mathrm{PL.P'L'} = \mathrm{TW.CN} = \mathrm{CN.NR.XT/XR},$$

$$\text{and } \rho\sin\theta = 2\mathrm{XT.PR/XR} = 2\mathrm{PR.XT/XR};$$

$$\therefore \delta = 2\mu.\mathrm{PR/CR.CN.NR} = \text{a constant}.$$

Note. $r+r' : \delta = \mathrm{NR} : \mathrm{PR}.$

IX. Although no loss of generality is introduced in the last part of § VII by the assumption that the axes of the orbits all lie in one straight line, there will be a loss of generality if we attempt to work out the time of description for a sector on the same assumption; for the inclusion of the circle whose center is O determines the value of $r+r'$ to be equal to $2a$. In this case the chord must be either parallel to the major axis of any orbit or a diameter of it; and the latter is excluded from consideration by Hamilton's theorem, since it is impossible for an orthogonal circle to cut a hodographic circle in points on opposite sides of the diameter perpendicular to the radical axis. When, however, O is not taken to be the middle point of EF, all positions of the *radii vectores* are included; and one of these positions is that in which the chord is parallel to the minor axis.

From Fig. 9, it is evident that area of $p\mathrm{C}q\mathrm{S} = \mathrm{CS}.p\mathrm{N}$, and area of $p\mathrm{C}q\mathrm{A} = a^2 \sin^{-1} y/b$;

$$\therefore \text{ area of PSQA} = ab\,(\sin^{-1} y/b - ey/b).$$

Similarly, in the case of the parabola, it is seen from Fig. 10 that, since area of segment PAQ = 4/3 area of ∝PAQ,

$$\therefore \text{ area of sector PSQA} = y(x+3a)/3.$$

X. From the results obtained in § IX, we can show in a very simple manner that not only does Hamilton's theorem contain that of Lambert in its detailed form, but also the corresponding theorem of Euler for a parabolic sector.

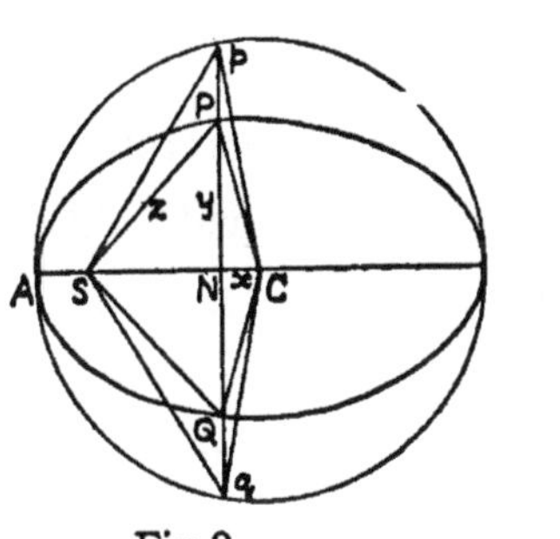

Fig. 9.

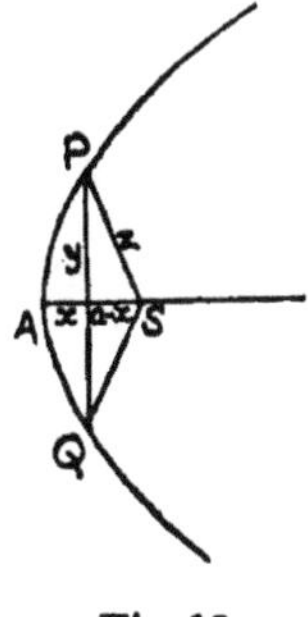

Fig. 10.

LAMBERT'S THEOREM:

Assume $\phi - \phi' = 2\sin^{-1} y/b$ and $\sin\phi = \sin\phi' = 2ey/b$;

then, since $\sin\frac{1}{2}(\phi-\phi') = y/b$, $\therefore \cos\frac{1}{2}(\phi-\phi') = x/a$;

also since $2\sin\frac{1}{2}(\phi-\phi')\cos\frac{1}{2}(\phi+\phi') = 2ey/b$,

$$\therefore \cos\tfrac{1}{2}(\phi+\phi') = e, \quad \therefore \sin\tfrac{1}{2}(\phi+\phi') = b/a;$$

$$\cos\phi' + \cos\phi = 2\cos\tfrac{1}{2}(\phi+\phi')\cos\tfrac{1}{2}(\phi-\phi') = 2ex/a,$$

$$\cos\phi' - \cos\phi = 2\sin\tfrac{1}{2}(\phi+\phi')\sin\tfrac{1}{2}(\phi-\phi') = 2y/a.$$

Now, referring to Fig. 9, if SP is equal to z, $a - ex = z$, and therefore $ex/a = 1 - z/a$; hence

$$\cos\phi = 1 - (z+y)/a, \text{ and } \cos\phi' = 1 - (z-y)/a;$$

and these expressions only contain z, y, a, which are equivalent to $\frac{1}{2}(r+r')$, $\frac{1}{2}\delta$, a; and these are invariable. The time of description being also invariable as well as the period for the whole orbit, we can say that in general,

Area of elliptic sector $= \frac{1}{2}ab\,[\phi - \phi' - (\sin\phi - \sin\phi')]$, where

$$4\sin^2\tfrac{1}{2}\phi=(r+r'+\delta)/a \text{ and } 4\sin^2\tfrac{1}{2}\phi=(r+r'-\delta)/a.$$

Euler's Theorem:

By VII, $h^2=2a\mu$; and the area described $=ht=\sqrt{2a\mu}t$; hence

$$t=y(x+3a)/3\sqrt{2a\mu}=2\sqrt{x}(x+3a)/3\sqrt{2\mu};$$

and, assuming $\lambda^2=z+y$, and $\mu^2=z-y$, we have

$$2(a+x)=2z=\lambda^2+\mu^2$$
$$2(a-x)=2\sqrt{(z^2-y^2)}=2\lambda\mu.$$

Therefore, $2\sqrt{x}=\lambda-\mu,\ x+3a=\lambda^2+\lambda\mu+\mu^2$

and $t=(\lambda^3-\mu^3)/3\sqrt{2\mu}$.

Now, t, z, or $\tfrac{1}{2}(r+r')$, y or $\tfrac{1}{2}\delta$, and therefore λ and μ, are all invariable; hence, in general, since area equals $\sqrt{2a\mu t}$, we have

$$\text{Area of parabolic sector}=\sqrt{a}(\lambda^3-\mu^3)/3,$$

where $2\lambda^2=r+r'+\delta$, and $2\mu^2=r+r'-\delta$.

Note. The sign of μ changes when PQ cuts AS produced.

J. M. Child.

Derby, England.

MONISM AND THE ANTINOMIES.

In the following sketch it is the purpose of the author to offer a few brief suggestions with a view to clearing up some of the long-mooted problems of philosophy and theology, particularly in regard to the so-called philosophical antinomies. Of these Kant has enumerated four, viz., (1) whether the universe is temporal and finite, or eternal and infinite; (2) whether composite substances are capable of resolution into irresolvable simple parts, or whether "naught that is simple exists"; (3) whether causality is the sole cause of phenomena or whether free will must be considered along with it; and (4) whether the world (i. e., the sum-totality of existence) possesses or does not possess some form of necessary existence. The contention of Kant is that these paradoxes do not exist, save in our own thought, and that it is due to the limitation of our mental powers that we seem to see such antinomies. With regard to the most important of these, namely, whether causality is the sole cause of existence, he has demonstrated absolutely, and with consummate skill, the perfect compatibility of inexorable necessity with free will; and while it would appear that he has not demonstrated conclusively the existence of free will in itself, yet he gives the latter a presumptive status so strong that we are practically obliged to admit that it is part and parcel of the scheme of things and must therefore be considered at length in all serious philosophical inquiry.

To these metaphysical antinomies of Kant there must be added the theological antinomies of Mansel, which we cannot better set forth than by quoting the following from Mansel, as given in Spencer's *First Principles* (p. 35):

"How....can Infinite Power be able to do all things, and yet Infinite Goodness be unable to do evil? How can Infinite Justice exact the utmost penalty for every sin, and yet Infinite Mercy pardon the sinner? How can Infinite Freedom be at liberty to do or to forbear? How is the existence of Evil compatible with that of an infinitely perfect Being; for if he wills it, he is not infinitely good; and if he wills it not, his will is thwarted, and his sphere of action limited?"

All of these, it will be seen at a glance, have to do directly with the antinomy of free will. Besides, their pragmatic interest is of highest importance; and, being apparently in direct paradox to the doctrine of monism, which maintains the essential oneness and unity of everything, they must receive more detailed consideration here.

The first two antinomies of Kant, relating to the infinitude of the universe and to its complexity, have little direct bearing on monism, as far as our purposes are concerned, since it is necessary that all parts of an entirety, whether finite or infinite, or whether capable of resolution into simple parts, or incapable of such analysis, must bear certain unalterable relations to one another, since that is what the concept of entirety implies.

His third antinomy offers greater difficulty. If causality were the sole cause of everything, it would be necessary that monism should obtain. On the other hand, if causality is not the sole cause, but free will must be considered along with it, then even if free will can only modify things spontaneously along the lines or within the bounds which necessity prescribes, a higher law must be shown to exist, or at least its possibility must be shown to be reasonable, as an intellectual conception, before we can include it (i. e., free will) alongside of causality in a complete body of monistic doctrine.

Here we will add, as giving an important side-light on this

question, that due regard must be paid to the general consensus of human kind, to the effect that there is an essential moral element in a certain class of actions (lying within the scope of ethics)—a conception which thousands of years of philosophical thought and dispute have failed to shake.

The notion of a spontaneous cause, infinite in its operation and in its scope of activity, is not difficult to form; and the presumptive evidence which militates so strongly in favor of the doctrine of free will in human agents, must carry with it, as a necessary corollary, the doctrine of a freedom, not finite as with man, but absolutely infinite.

That such an infinite freedom must be rational, goes without saying. For an infinite being, omnipotent and omniscient, to err, even in a moral sense, were an utter absurdity. We should, therefore, presumptively ascribe to this infinite freedom a higher law of freedom, transcending all concept of natural law, just as the concept of infinite freedom, on the other hand, transcends all our ideas of the limited freedom possessed by man. In addition, we must not think of natural law as a limitation upon the infinite, but as part and parcel—an integral portion so to speak— of its higher law of liberty. And this higher liberty of the infinite is to be considered, theologically, as the goal which the regenerated human soul ever strives to attain through an infinite series of spiritual progressions.

The difficulty in regard to the inabilty of the absolute, infinitely good, to do evil, must be regarded in the light of an inscrutable problem. Of course, it is only moral evil of which we here speak. To infer that since God created man, and man sins, God must be the author of evil, were well-nigh blasphemous. Man attains the privilege of grace only by the exercise of his divine prerogative of freedom, and whenever he abuses it *he* becomes the author of evil.

The reconciliation of infinite justice with infinite mercy should be an easy matter. It is not reasonable to suppose that the justified sinner escapes the natural penalty of his sins, but rather that he escapes the added penalty that would be inflicted for his continuance in the way of evil. Justification when used in a theological sense means exactly what that word naturally implies,—that the saved sinner is justified, because in the agony of his contrition and in the diminished possibilities of future happiness which he has already incurred, he has, at the moment of conversion, paid the full penalty for his sins. The exercise of the divine prerogative of mercy is thoroughly at one with the higher law of absolute freedom.

"How can Infinite Freedom be at liberty to do or to forbear?" Because it is *Infinite Freedom.*

And as to the existence of moral evil being a limitation of the freedom of the absolute, as some one has well said, "a self-imposed limitation is no limitation at all," and we might add that God, in sharing his prerogative of freedom with man, diminishes his own limitation not one whit, because what is infinite in the first instance is incapable of diminution.

The conclusion to be arrived at from a more detailed consideration of this theme is as follows: That the universe of material things and forces is a totality, but not the totality of all existence; that the freedom of man is consistent through and through with the universality of natural law; that the existence of an absolute being is in no way incompatible with the existence of other entities, of a finite character; and lastly, that the sum total of material things and forces, of man and his actions, of mind and its thoughts, of freedom and its prerogatives and privileges, each and every one of them, together with the absolute, are woven together, as it were, in conformity with a higher law transcending all natural law,—all in a comprehensive, necessary, consistent and perfect monistic scheme of existence.

Carl V. Poland.

Milwaukee, Wis.

KANT'S ANTINOMIES AND THEIR SOLUTION.

Kant's antinomies have proved a puzzle to thinkers. The great author of the *Critique of Pure Reason* believes that there are some statements concerning which the affirmative and the negative can be defended with equally valid proof and logically correct arguments. But these four double statements present each two contradictory affirmations of which only one side can be right; or if both are right they must be affirmed according to the sense which we attach to the words or as we interpret the meaning of the proposition. Antinomies are contradictory, and, according to Kant, they express a deeper truth than reason can fathom, the word being derived from *anti* (in the sense of "contrary") and *nomos* (law).

Reason, according to Kant, is not absolute. Reason is the order which dominates the world of reality, and this world of reality is conditioned. Why the world is thus conditioned is another question, but where the world touches its boundaries in time and space we are confronted with different conditions and reason is no longer our reliable guide. Here nature changes into metaphysics, and so it is to be expected that Kant's problem here touches the religious problems of philosophy.

Kant's four antinomies is the field of theology, but we must grant that they have not been taken seriously by naturalists, who, as a rule, have ignored them. In the hands of thinking theologians however they have become a welcome weapon in favor of an ultimate agnosticism and have proved the foundation for the acceptance, by rationalistic adherents of Kant, of church dogmas which otherwise would have proved objectionable.

The first antinomy concerns the problem of infinity, and here Kant takes infinity as an object, a thing that exists in a concrete bodily shape. Naturally he is puzzled, and, while knowing that infinity is a clear and undeniable thought in mathematics, he is unable to point it out in the world of reality. If Kant had investigated the nature of infinity he would have come to the conclusion that it is not a concrete object but a function. Infinity is a possibility, not a thing. All things are bodies of a definite mass, with definite limits, but infinity is unlimited; it is a process that can be carried on without end.

Therefore infinity is a feature of certain actions or processes, but it is never an actual event. For instance I can count to one thousand and farther; I can count to one million and farther; there is no limit. I can count to a billion, and still there is no end of counting. I can think a series of numbers amounting to infinitude, and even then I need not stop, for I can invent transfinite numbers, calling them $\infty+1$, $\infty+2$, $\infty+3$, etc. Infinitude is always a function, a possibility; and whenever I have a real concrete number it is not infinite. A real count of an actual distance, be it in space, as in miles, or in time, as in years, may be ever so great but it is always definite and finite.

Infinitude is not a problem too deep for reason, nor is it an unmeaning idea. Mathematics has made good use of it, and theology employs the term to express functions that will not, or should not, be limited or clearly defined—for we should have a liberal margin for possibilities which we cannot as yet understand. In this sense we call God infinite, to indicate that we can never grasp the full meaning of the God idea. But infinitude is not identical with divinity, for everything is infinite in its possibilities. The human soul is infinite and human progress is infinite; yea, every atom, every speck of actual existence is infinite. Every point in space is surrounded with infinitude, and the same may be said of every moment of time, the infinitude of time being called eternity. We can move in thought out into the world of space and reach Sirius, the nearest fixed star; we can go beyond and reach more distant stars; we can travel to the outskirts of the Milky Way and even then we have not reached the end of our journey. We can go farther and discover other stellar systems, on and on, leaving an infinitude behind and ever having an infinitude before us. And let us assume that at last we reach the outer limits of concrete existence but can still proceed into the surrounding void. This means that while the concrete immensity of the world must be definite and at a definite time, space itself, which is not a concrete thing but the possibility of existence or the scope of motion (as we have defined it elsewhere), is infinite.

And the same is true of time. We may go back to the moment when our solar system originated from the conflagration of the world-dust that was gathered in the mighty whirls of a collision of mighty comets. We might go further back to the time when these comets were worlds, as is now our solar system; and beyond to the time when they originated. We might go back still further, when the whole Milky Way differentiated into clusters of commotion in an ocean of indifferent ether. Here we must stop for we know nothing of ether, as we may call the primordial stuff which by contraction and differentiation is capable of forming matter in its successive stages as chemical elements. But suppose that, previous to the original contraction of the primordial ether, there has been a calm of non-activity, we can still further go back into emptiness. Just as we count now from the birth of Christ as *A.D.* and the time before Christ as *B.C.*, so we could speak of world-eons since the origin of the cosmos and of world-eons before the birth of the cosmos. Eternities stretch out before us as well as behind us. Time is infinite.

Besides this conception of infinitude and eternality there are the aspects of relations which are independent of time and space. Such are natural laws, or mathematical theorems, or universal principles of thought, or fundamental principles of right, of truth, of morality. They are also called eternal, but this eternality is different from the eternality of continued existence. This quality of being above time and space denotes the universality of certain relations; and these indicate their independence of localized and temporary realization and bear the stamp of intrinsic or absolute necessity.

When we understand the nature of infinitude we see at once that every concrete thing and every definite event, also the definite entirety of our solar system, yes even the immeasurable cosmos of the Milky Way with its uncounted stars, has a definite beginning and a definite end. Nothing concrete and particular is infinite. Infinitude is a process, a function, a thought or a plan or a possibility of unending continuance.

The laws of existence, those uniformities which condition the formation of all things, are independent of space and time; they are infinite and eternal in the sense that they are superspatial and supertemporal. They are intrinsically necessary and constitute that which is commonly called Deity or God. They are the formative factors of existence and in religion have been personified as Creator.

Such considerations throw light upon the nature of all the four antinomies of Kant. Here are the four antinomies stated in non-contradictory terms:

1. The actual and concrete universe is temporal and limited, but existence in its potentialities is infinite and the conditions of existence are eternal and infinite. The norms or laws, called God in religion, are superspatial and supertemporal.

2. As a mathematical line is divisible into infinitely small portions, so every atom is theoretically possessed of parts, of an upper and lower portion, a right and left side, an inside and an outside, etc. It is possible that our chemists cannot produce the conditions under which we shall be able to resolve the atoms, but that is not the question in Kant's antinomies. Theoretically every concrete body, even the smallest one, be it an atom or a molecule, is of a definite size and consists of definite parts. We may assume that every molecule has originated under definite conditions, by a law of formation still unknown to us, from a primitive homogeneous stuff, perhaps the ether, but we must assume that every one of the tiniest units of actual mass represents a definite amount of ether and that these minute portions themselves are also in turn theoretically infinitely divisible, as is the smallest geometrical line.

3. In connection with the third antinomy, I refer to my dis-

cussions of free will in previous expositions of the problem. The problem of free will is based upon a confusion of the words necessity and violence or compulsion. I act freely, that is, according to my free will, if my action is determined by my own character, if it expresses my own true will and if I act without compulsion. If I am compelled to act against my will I am not free but suffer violence.

In either case, whether I be free in my decision or compelled to act against my will, my action is strictly determined. If my free action were undetermined, free will would be haphazard and without moral significance. Thus causality is a universal law which dominates even the decisions of free will, and the theory of indeterminism is simply a confusion of thought.

4. Finally, the question of God, which Kant bears in mind when discussing the antinomy of an absolutely necessary being, resolves itself into the meaning of necessity. Certainly there is not an absolutely necessary being, but there is necessity. This necessity is not a being, not a creature, not an individual, not a person, not anything concrete, not a somebody who is in a definite space and is eternal in the sense of an enduring or continued temporal existence. Necessity is a factor, a norm, a regulative principle. It is supertemporal and superspatial. It possesses all the qualities which philosophical thought has attributed to God. It is the creator, for it is the formative principle of the world. It is the ruler and Lord of the universe, for it is the law, the totality of all natural laws, physical, psychical and moral. It is omnipresent; it is eternal; it is unfailing; it is the standard of both truth and error, right and wrong. This conception of God is not personal, but superpersonal; it is the condition under and through which, in the course of evolution, the rational, i. e., human personality is produced.

The antinomies of Kant have done their service. Religious people became convinced that the ideas of God, freedom and immortality had become untenable in the modern interpretation of dogmatic Christianity. And yet they felt that they contained great truths which could not be dispensed with. Thus the Kantian notion that they were *transcendent,* that they were profounder than human comprehension, was a welcome principle which found an apparently rational basis in the theory of the four antinomies.

From the standpoint of a rigid radicalism such as I advocate the contradictory form of the antinomies can be disregarded and their meaning stated in clear terms; or it can be preserved if its words are interpreted in two different senses. And antinomies contain a truth but no real contradiction.[1]

The truth underlying the antinomies is preserved by the higher conception of God, the doctrine of the Overgod, which I preach, and by clearness of thought as to the meaning of infinitude and an elucidation of the true nature of free will.

EDITOR.

PROFESSOR VON GARBE ON THE JEWS OF MALABAR.

In the April number of *The Monist* (p. 283) Mr. Wilfred H. Schoff asserts the probability of the tradition of the Jews of Malabar which claims that they had migrated to India in 68 A. D., to the number of 10,000, although he doubts whether there were so many of them. This tradition, however, is not "well attested" as Schoff says, but originated in the late Middle Ages. Also the "ancient" Cochin grant of Bhâskara Revivarman quoted by Fleet from the *Epigr. Ind.*, III, 66, is a late copper-plate grant in the Tamil language.

But to pass judgment on such things one must constantly bear in mind how important it is to regard all learned traditions (especially late ones) of the Orient with a critical eye.

Benjamin of Tudela only went as far as Persia in the second half of the twelfth century; and although it may seem quite probable from his report and that of Marco Polo (end of the thirteenth century) that there were Jews in India in *their* time, this proves nothing for a thousand years earlier. Without *trustworthy* sources for the antiquity of Judaism in Malabar no definite conclusion can be reached.

The *possibility* that Jews may have come to Malabar at quite an early date is not, to be sure, excluded; but if they did come, it was not in large numbers but singly. In Abyssinia also, where the native Jews are black and speak an Agau language, and in Yemen, certainly only comparatively few have spread Judaism among the natives, just as in the case of the Christians. But Malabar is pretty distant from the starting-point of Jewish migration, and the Jews have never been a sea-faring people except once, and that was in Solomon's time under the protection of the Phenicians who served

[1] The same subject has been discussed in my treatment of Kant's philosophy in connection with my translation of his *Prolegomena*.

as their guides. In order to judge the case in question, the analogy of the Thomas Christians is instructive. They were not baptized by an apostle as their own tradition recorded, but the sect originated at a much later time.

The literature on the white and black Jews in Malabar might be considerably multiplied, but without throwing any light on the historicity of the native tradition.

TÜBINGEN, GERMANY. R. GARBE.

MATHEMATICIANS AND PHILOSOPHERS.

Jonathan Swift, in the second chapter of that part of *Gulliver's Travels* which describes Gulliver's third voyage, made Gulliver say of the mathematicians of Laputa:

"They are very bad reasoners and vehemently given to opposition unless when they happen to be of the right opinion, which is seldom their case. Imagination, fancy and invention they are wholly strangers to, nor have they any words in their language by which those ideas can be expressed; the whole compass of their thoughts and mind being shut up within the two fore-mentioned sciences [mathematics and music].

"Most of them, and especially those who deal in the astronomical part, have great faith in judicial astrology although they are ashamed to own it publicly. But what I chiefly admired, and thought altogether unaccountable, was the strong disposition I observed in them towards news and politics, perpetually inquiring into public affairs, giving their judgments in matters of state, and passionately disputing every inch of a party opinion. I have indeed observed the same disposition among most of the mathematicians I have known in Europe, although I could never discover the least analogy between the two sciences."

Gulliver's Travels was published in 1726. In 1734 George Berkeley (1685-1753), the famous philosopher and Bishop of Cloyne in Ireland, published *The Analyst, or a Discourse to an Infidel Mathematician,*[1] the object of which was to show that the principles of the infinitesimal calculus are no clearer than, or perhaps not as clear as, the principles of Christianity. The "infidel mathe-

[1] Cf. on this book and the controversy to which it gave rise M. Cantor, *Vorlesungen über Geschichte der Mathematik,* Vol. III, 2d. ed., Leipsic, 1901, pp. 737-746; Cf. Vol. IV (Leipsic, 1908; article by G. Vivanti, pp. 644, 648, 649) for references to Berkeley on the subject of the theory of the compensation of errors with Lagrange and Lazare Carnot.

matician" referred to was Edmund Halley (1656-1742), the distinguished astronomer and friend of Isaac Newton, and of whom the story is told[2] that, when he indulged in jest concerning theological questions, he was curtly repulsed by Newton with the remark: "I have studied these things; you have not!"

The incident which led Berkeley to write his *Analyst* was this. A friend of Berkeley's refused the offer of spiritual consolation when he was on a bed of sickness because Halley, the skilled mathematician, had convinced him of the inconceivability of the doctrines of Christianity. Now Berkeley showed very skilfully that the principles of infinitesimal analysis—the method of fluxions, in Newton's terminology—were by no means clear. The *Analyst* provoked a great deal of controversy: Dr. James Jurin wrote under a pseudonym *Geometry No Friend to Infidelity*; a Dublin professor named Walton wrote a *Vindication of Sir Isaac Newton's Principles of Fluxions*; Berkeley replied with a *Defence of Freethinking in Mathematics*; Jurin wrote in 1735 *The Minute Mathematician, or the Freethinker no Just Thinker*;[3] Benjamin Robins and Pemberton entered the lists on behalf of Newton's method of fluxions and against Jurin's clumsy defence of it; and lastly, Berkeley's *Analyst* has the credit of inspiring Maclaurin to write his famous *Treatise of Fuxions* of 1742, in which a rigorous foundation of the method of fluxions was attempted.

"The *Analyst*," said De Morgan,* "was intentionally a publication involving the principle of Dr. Whately's argument against the existence of Buonaparte; and Berkeley was strictly to take what he found. The *Analyst* is a tract which could not have been written except by a person who knew how to answer it. But it is singular that Berkeley, though he makes his fictitious character nearly as clear as afterwards did Whately, has generally been treated as a real opponent of fluxions. Let us hope that the arch Archbishop [Whately] will fare better than the arch Bishop."

But Berkeley's tract had another merit. In it are given the foundations of the theory that the correct results of the infinitesimal calculus are obtained by a compensation of errors. This theory

[2] Mach, *Mechanics* (Chicago, 1907), pp. 448-449.

[3] The most comical mis-translation I have ever come across is of the title of a work of which this reminds me, I mean Berkeley's *Alciphron, or the Minute Philosopher* (1733)—a dialogue in which he critically examines the various forms of freethinking in the age. A "minute philosopher" is, of course, a philosopher who examines things minutely; but Montucla, in his *Histoire des Mathématiques*, translates it as "le petit philosophe"!

* *Phil. Mag.*, Nov., 1852.

was rediscovered, apparently independently of others and of each other, by Lagrange and Lazare Carnot in 1797.

In view of this merit, R. Adamson[4] seems rather too severe. Speaking of another work of Berkeley's he says that a "great part of the *Common Place Book* [containing Berkeley's thoughts on physics and philosophy from about 1703] is occupied with a vigorous and in many points exceedingly ignorant polemic against the fundamental conception of the fluxional and infinitesimal calculus, a polemic which Berkeley carried on to the end of his days." Also it is hardly correct to say, with Adamson: "....in his *Analyst* he attacked the higher mathematics, as leading to freethinking; this involved him in a hot controversy." Berkeley did not attack mathematics; only the vague ideas and expositions of some mathematicians.

If the fact that Berkeley's early mathematical work was bad is any excuse for depreciating his later mathematical work, then indeed the *Analyst* might excusably be condemned; for Berkeley's early mathematical work of 1707 was, according to Cantor,[5] insignificant. But the theory of the compensation of errors in the infinitesimal calculus is perfectly correct and was, apparently,[6] stated for the first time by Berkeley.

* * *

Most mathematicians, like the unphilosophical among men of science, are so occupied with the use of methods which, judged by the results of years of application to the problems of nature, are manifestly reliable, that they too often succumb to the temptation of taking d'Alembert's maxim for mathematicians—*Allez en avant, la foi vous viendra*—as a maxim for logicians and philosophers, and of treating with hasty contempt the criticisms of philosophers. In the case of Berkeley, the mathematicians missed the point as much as Dr. Johnson did when he refuted Berkeleyanism by kicking a stone. In the case of Hegel, the mathematicians appear to have been more in the right. The principal criticism to which Hegel's criticism is subject is that it is too uncritical: it accepts some mathematician's obscurities and concludes obscurity in mathematics. The mathematicians denied obscurity in mathematics, and they were right. But still the fundamental conceptions

[4] *Encycl. Brit.*, 9th ed., Vol. III, 1875, p. 590.

[5] *Op. cit.*, Vol. III, p. 737.

[6] Berkeley's opponents, apparently mistakenly, said that the idea of compensation was old (*ibid.*, pp. 743-744).

of the infinitesimal calculus had not been presented in a logically rigorous form when Hegel wrote.

The care for exactness in dealing with principles is of comparative late growth in mathematics. We shall not be far wrong if we put its birth after Kant published his great *Critique* in 1781. I cannot find any evidence for a direct influence of Kant on Lagrange, Gauss, Cauchy, or Weierstrass; it seems that criticism was "in the air." And so, in the settlement of the logical and philosophical difficulties of mathematics philosophers have not hitherto had a large share. "....Philosophy asks of Mathematics: What does it mean? Mathematics in the past was unable to answer, and Philosophy answered by introducing the totally irrelevant notion of mind. But now Mathematics is able to answer, so far at least as to reduce the whole of its propositions to certain fundamental notions of logic. At this point, the discussion must be resumed by Philosophy."[7]

* * *

There is another aspect of the distinction between mathematicians and logicians. In modern times, from the time of Leibniz up to the middle of the nineteenth century, the only mathematicians of eminence who were also eminent logicians were John Wallis (1616-1703) and perhaps Leonhard Euler (1707-1783). About the middle of the nineteenth century there began, of course, with Boole and De Morgan, a new era for logic, in which the symbolism and methods of algebra were used to give generality and precision to logical conclusions and to create new logical methods. "Every science," says De Morgan,[8] "that has *thriven* has thriven upon its own symbols: logic, the only science which is admitted to have made no improvements in century after century, is the only one which has *grown no symbols*." Again, De Morgan in his *Syllabus*,[9] says: "I end with a word on the new symbols which I have employed. Most writers on logic strongly object to all symbols except the venerable *Barbara, Celarent*, etc..... I should advise the reader not to make up his mind on this point until he has well weighed two facts which nobody disputes, both separately and in connection. Firstly, logic is the only science which has made no progress since the revival of letters; secondly, logic is the only science which has produced no growth of symbols."

[7] B. Russell, *The Principles of Mathematics*, Cambridge, 1903, p. 4; cf. pp. 129-130.

[8] *Trans. Camb. Phil. Soc.*, Vol. X, 1864, p. 184.

[9] *Syllabus of a Proposed System of Logic*, London, 1860, p. 72.

But De Morgan saw the advantages that would result from the use by logic of a symbolism analogous to the algebraical. In his third paper "On the Syllogism"[10] he says: "As joint attention to logic and mathematics increases, a logic will grow up among the mathematicians, distinguished from the logic of the logicians by having the mathematical elements properly subordinated to the rest. This 'mathematical logic'—so-called *quasi lucus a non nimis lucendo*—will commend itself to the educated world by showing an actual representation of their form of thought—a representation, the truth of which they recognize—instead of a mutilated and one-sided fragment, founded upon canons of which they neither feel the force nor see the utility."

* * *

At the present time the prejudice of logicians against the use of symbols that happen to have been used beforehand in mathematics has almost disappeared, thanks principally to the work of Dr. J. Venn.[11] The whole objection of the old-fashioned logicians really rested on no better grounds than this: The use of x and y, which are used in mathematics, ought not to be used instead of the logical X and Y, *because x and y have been used for something quantitative.*[12] As if the word "cabbage" had any rigid connection with the essence of the vegetable of which that word reminds us! In symbolic logic the arithmetical signs +, –, and × were used because certain logical operations have many analogies with arithmetical operations. There is no objection that can be urged against this—a fertile source of discoveries—*except* that when we write out mathematical theorems in symbolic logic there may be a confusion of terms. But we must be careful not to pursue the analogy too far. Logical addition, for example, and mathematical addition are not identical. There is a point where the analogy breaks down. And when we go deeply into the matter, the differences will begin to outweigh the identities in importance. Broadly speaking, we may say that *modern logic is symbolic but has got beyond the rather evident analogies it has with algebra,* and a man who seemed rather deep and abstract in his mathematics and logic fifty years ago now seems rather a superficial and *naïf* person. In one form or another, analogy probably is always guiding us in our researches, but, as we

[10] *Trans. Camb. Phil. Soc.,* Vol. X, 1864, note on page 176.

[11] *Symbolic Logic,* London, 1881, 2d ed. 1894.

[12] Cf. *ibid.,* p. ix (of either edition).

progress in subtlety, we become more and more convinced of the limitations of the more obvious analogies.

* * *

Let us now return to Swift. In his description of Gulliver's voyage to Laputa, he describes the mathematicians of that country as silly and useless dreamers, whose attention has to be awakened by flappers. Also, the mathematical tailor measures his height by a quadrant, and deduces his other dimensions by a rule and compasses, producing a suit of very illfitting clothes. On the other hand, the mathematicians of Laputa, by their marvelous invention of the magnetic island floating in the air, ruled the country and maintained their ascendency over their subjects. Dr. Whitehead[13] says: "Swift, indeed, lived at a time peculiarly unsuited for gibes at contemporary mathematicians. Newton's *Principia* had just been written, one of the great forces which have transformed the modern world. Swift might just as well have laughed at an earthquake." We cannot wholly subscribe to this, for it seems not unlikely that Swift, like everybody else, could not doubt the usefulness, importance, and correctnesss of the mathematician's work, but shared, with the philosopher, a doubt of the mathematician's being able to state his principles clearly and reasonably, just as we may doubt the existence of a knowledge of thermodynamics in a man who drives a railway engine.

CAMBRIDGE, ENGLAND. PHILIP E. B. JOURDAIN.

CURRENT PERIODICALS.

In the number of *Scientia* for August, 1915, Georges Bohn gives the second part of his article on new ideas on adaptation and evolution. It is interesting to notice that, according to the author, both Lamarck and Darwin were finalists. E. Carnevale contributes the second part of his study on democracy and penal justice. The articles concerned with questions raised by the war are by W. J. Ashley on "The Economic Conversion of England" and Charles Guignebert on the part played by the Roman Catholic Church— or what, according to him is the same thing, the Pope—in the European war. There is a short note by Federigo Enriques on the art of writing a treatise, prompted by his forthcoming book on the geometrical theory of equations and algebraic functions. There are reviews of books and periodicals, and French translations of the Italian and English articles.

[13] A. N. Whitehead, *An Introduction to Mathematics*, London, 1911, p. 10.

It is very pleasant to see the *Revue de Métaphysique et de Morale,* whose publication has been suspended since the beginning of the European war. The number for September, 1914, appeared in June, 1915, and the only mark of the war on it is the article by Gustave Belot on war and democracy, and a study by André Lalande of the work of Louis Couturat. Couturat was a victim of the war: though not a combatant, he was killed on the day (August 3, 1914) on which Germany declared war on France, by a heavy automobile which was carrying orders of mobilization. The article is followed by a bibliography of Couturat's works together with a list of some of the reviews and translations of them. Couturat's literary activity may broadly be characterized by the names of his principal publications: (1) *De l'infini mathématique* of 1896; (2) *La Logique de Leibniz* of 1901 and *Opuscules et fragments inédits de Leibniz* of 1903; (3) *L'Algèbre de la Logique* of 1905; (4) *Les Principes des Mathématiques* of 1905. Since 1901 Couturat has been more and more busied with the problem of an international language, and Ido in particular, and here we may remind our readers of his article in *The Monist* for 1905. The other articles in this number of the *Revue* are Emile Boutroux's presidential address (April, 1914) to the international congress of mathematical philosophy; C. Bouglé's remarks on "polytelism"—the multiplicity of ends that one and the same means allows us to reach—; Désiré Roustan's on science as a vital instrument, and Léon Cahen's publication of some hitherto unpublished fragments of Condorcet on instinct, the words "nature" and "natural," and so on.

* * *

Scientia (*Rivista di Scienza*) begins, with the first number (June and July, 1915) of the eighteenth volume, a second series, under the sole editorship of Eugenio Rignano. The reason for this is that in the future there will be, in addition to articles on scientific synthesis and organization, articles of international interest which carry a political responsibility that cannot be divided among a board of editors. The inquiry upon the causes of the war ends in this number, but there will be in future discussions of various problems raised by the war. The only purely scientific article in this number is one by Georges Bohn, pointing out that there are disharmonies in living beings, and that biologists, like metaphysicians, have hitherto had recourse to a theory of adaptation for special ends to explain what they took to be harmonies. The inquiry upon the war consists of a French article by Louis Havet, an English article by J. Holland Rose emphasizing the part played by nationality, and an Italian summary of the whole inquiry by Eugenio Rignano. Besides this there are reviews of books and other periodicals and French translations of the English and Italian articles.

* * *

The first article in *Science Progress* for July 1015 is by H. Spencer Jones, "On the Structure of the Universe." The many recent researches upon the distances and distribution of stars, upon the relative distances of stars of different types, upon the numbers of stars of different magnitudes, and upon allied topics, have all contributed in throwing some light on the problem of the structure and the evolution of the universe; and the author gives an account of these researches. The second article is an answer to Miss Stebbing's criticisms on Mercier's logic, by Charles A. Mercier. "Miss Stebbing's reply to my charges against logic," says the author, "does not seem to me successful, but as it does seem successful to some people, a rejoinder may be permitted." It is as impossible for a modern logician to deny the essential justice of Mercier's attack on the futile stuff taught as "logic" in the schools and the antiquated doctrine that the syllogism is the only principle of reasoning, as it is for any one with a sense of humor not to be amused by his writings. Maurice Copisarow gives a technical paper on "Carbon: Its Molecular Structure and Mode of Oxidation." None of the theories of Lang (1888), Baker (1888) and Dixon (1896, 1899), and Rhead and Wheeler (1910-1913) are absolutely wrong or a complete representation of the facts. The author starts from three fundamental assumptions as a basis. "i. A carbon molecule is polyatomic (This is suggested by its high volatilization-point and products of moist oxidation). ii. A carbon atom is potentially always tetravalent (Comberg's work on triphenylmethyl and Nef's on polymethylene compounds do not necessarily imply the non-tetravalency of a carbon atom). iii. Carbon exists in three allotropic modifications (Several new modifications suggested by Brodie, Berthelot, Luzi, and others have been proved by Moissan and Le Chatelier to be either compounds or solutions and mixtures of carbon with some other element)." There is an imaginative blank verse by George William Bettany on "A Bit of Rock." D. F. Harris and H. J. M. Creighton write on "The Role of Reductase in Tissue Respiration,"—also a technical paper. S. C. Bradford writes on "The History of Adrenalin." "The story of the discovery of the function of the suprarenal capsules, followed by the isolation of the active principle of their secretion, the determination of its structure, and its subsequent synthesis, forms one of the most fascinating chapters in the history of bio-chemistry." Of more general interest is the discussion by A. G. Thacker of "Some Eugenic Aspects of War." W. Lawrence Balls contributes an interesting account of "The Spinning Properties of Cotton." In a recent number of *Science Progress* he has indicated some of the ways by which purely scientific investigations were likely to yield results of economic value to the cotton trade. The present paper is to show how some unexpected light has since been thrown upon the causes on which the strength of yarn depends, thereby indicating the possibility of a substantial advance in the technique of spinning. Besides these articles, the number contains interesting essay-reviews and "Recent Advances in Science: Mathematics, Astronomy, Physics, Chemistry, Geology, Botany, Zoology, Anthropology." There are also notes and short reviews of various books. Φ

Lightning Source UK Ltd.
Milton Keynes UK
UKHW020621110119
335177UK00005B/193/P

9 780656 108329